THE

BLACK PHALANX

THE

BLACK PHALANX

AFRICAN AMERICAN SOLDIERS IN THE WAR OF INDEPENDENCE, THE WAR OF 1812, AND THE CIVIL WAR

BY

JOSEPH T. WILSON

LATE OF THE 2ND. REG'T. LA. NATIVE GUARD VOLS. 54TH MASS. VOLS.
AIDE-DE-CAMP TO THE COMMANDER-IN-CHIEF G. A. R.
AUTHOR OF
"EMANCIPATION," "VOICE OF A NEW RACE," "TWENTY-TWO YEARS OF FREEDOM," ETC., ETC.

New Foreword by
DUDLEY TAYLOR CORNISH

DA CAPO PRESS

Library of Congress Cataloging in Publication Data

Wilson, Joseph T. (Joseph Thomas), 1836–1891.
The Black phalanx: African American soldiers in the War of Independence, the War of 1812, and the Civil War / by Joseph T. Wilson; foreword by Dudley Taylor Cornish.—1st Da Capo Press ed.
p. cm.
Previously published: Hartford, Conn.: American Pub. Co., 1890.
Includes bibliographical references.
ISBN 0-306-80550-2
1. Afro-American soldiers—History. 2. United States—History—Civil War, 1861-1865—Participation, Afro-American. 3. United States—History—Revolution, 1775-1783—Participation, Afro-American. 4. United States—History—War of 1812—Participation, Afro-American. I. Cornish, Dudley Taylor. II. Title.
E185.63.W632 1994 93-40117
973.7—dc20 CIP

First Da Capo Press edition 1994

This Da Capo Press paperback edition of *The Black Phalanx* is an unabridged republication of the edition published in Hartford, Connecticut, in 1887. It is here supplemented with a new foreword by Dudley Taylor Cornish.

Published by Da Capo Press
A Member of the Perseus Books Group
http://www.dacapopress.com

Manufactured in the United States of America
10 9 8 7 6 5 4

FOREWORD TO THE DA CAPO EDITION

A 1967 critical bibliography of Civil War Books described *The Black Phalanx* as a "significant work by a former Negro soldier; full of official dispatches and lengthy essays; uneven and poorly documented, but valuable for a discussion of anti-Negro prejudice in the army." A year later, in the introduction to the Arno Press edition, the late great Sara Dunlap Jackson, writing from the heart of the National Archives, declared that the book "stands out as a monument to the memory of the author who, without academic training, accomplished so much. For students and scholars of American Negro history," she maintained, "this volume remains an indispensable storehouse of information." Careful rereading of Joseph Wilson's history persuades me that the Jackson judgment is far and away more valid and just.

This book, originally published by the well known American Publishing Company in 1887, is a spirited account of the roles African Americans played as soldiers of the Republic during the Great Rebellion. Wilson gives the American Revolution one chapter, with equal room for the War of 1812; his primary attention is fixed on the American Civil War—his war. His comrades in the Grand Army of the Republic (G. A. R.) selected him for the task at an 1882 reunion. They could hardly have made a better choice. Here was a veteran of their war, an authentic soldier who had served in two Union regiments, the Second Louisiana Native Guards and the famous 54th Massachusetts Infantry; he had been mustered out of the 54th with a medical discharge after a battlefield wound. Verily, he had seen the elephant.

Furthermore, after his discharge in Massachusetts, this veteran returned to his native Virginia to play an active part in Republican Reconstruction politics. Energetically involved in G. A. R. activities, Wilson climbed the organizational ladder to become Aide-de-Camp to the Commander in Chief, with the honorary rank of Colonel. As if those were not sufficient qualifications for writing the history of black Union troops, Wilson had already begun to compile a modest publishing record. In 1881 Hampton Normal School brought out his *Emancipation: Its Course from 1481 to 1875*; he followed it with a volume of poetry, *Voice of a New Race*, in 1882, and in that same year *Twenty-Two Years of Freedom*. It is significant that the poetry volume sold out its first printing (1,000 copies) in two months, the proceeds going to Wilson's G. A. R. post in Norfolk. In addition, he had edited several political newspapers, most notably *The American Sentinel* in 1880, supporting the Garfield-Arthur ticket.

How was a man so richly qualified in some ways to go about the gigantic, the really appalling work, of collecting adequate and reliable records of the more than 150 regiments of black soldiers who had served the Union in every theater of the war? Clearly, he could not depend on his own limited experience and recollections—and one needs to remember Sara Jackson's phrase, "without academic training." This, however, overlooks some small schooling in Massachusetts: Joseph Thomas Wilson had been born in Virginia in 1836—"later settling in New Bedford." How did he move from the Old Dominion to the Old Bay State? Garland Penn wrote in 1891 that Wilson had graduated from "the schools of New Bedford" in 1855. Only months after the conclusion of that undefined schooling, according to Penn, Joseph Wilson, like a true son of New Bedford, signed on for a three-year whaling voyage in the Pacific. In Valparaiso, Chile, in 1862 he learned of the outbreak of civil war and immediately took ship for home, going first to New York and then to New Orleans, reportedly to search for his father who had, much earlier, been "sold south."

Arriving in the Crescent City shortly after its fall to Union arms, while Major General Benjamin F. Butler commanded the Department of the Gulf, Wilson was caught up in the movement to augment Union strength by mustering into federal service three Louisiana regiments of "free men of color," not all of whom were free and not all of whom had belonged to Louisiana (Confederate) militia organizations. Be that as it may, Butler did effectively muster into federal service three regiments of Louisiana Native Guard Volunteers, in September, October, and November of 1862. Former whaler Wilson enlisted in the Second Louisiana Native Guard regiment (later the 74th United States Colored Troops) on September 30, scarcely a week after President Abraham Lincoln had issued his preliminary Emancipation Proclamation.

For nearly a year Wilson served in that Second Louisiana, participating in a grueling variety of military activities including impressively violent (as well as fatally heroic) action against Port Hudson, Confederate bastion on the Mississippi. Then and there, without realizing it, Wilson was beginning to collect material for the history he would begin to organize twenty years later.

Discharged from the Second Louisiana December 1, 1863, Wilson returned to his Massachusetts home and there enlisted, on December 13, in Company C, 54th Massachusetts Infantry, already the most famous black regiment in the Union Army (which it remains to this day). Wilson's tour of duty with the 54th was remarkably short: He was wounded in action in the Battle of Olustee, Florida, on February 20, 1864, a grim and bloody day in the regiment's history. Back north in Boston, he was discharged on May 8, 1864. Company C's roster tersely sums up his career in that "brave black regiment": "Wilson, Joseph T., 27, seaman, New Bedford, 18 December 63—May 8 64. wdd Olustee, Fla., 20 Feb 64. to Norfolk, Va."

His life after his return to Virginia must have been much like that of other ambitious veterans enjoying their new freedom and eagerly looking for the main chance. Wilson moved from a Secret Service post to handling government stores to the Internal Revenue Service, finally transferring to Customs. He was always, apparently, active in the internal struggles of the Republican Party in Reconstruction Virginia. His political activity as well as his enthusiastic membership in the G. A. R. (if the two can be practically separated) provided him with ample and recurring opportunities to develop his oratorical powers and especially to refine his ability as a raconteur. Indeed, his frequent story-telling at veterans' reunions was a primary factor in his selection to record their contributions to Union victory. He entered on this new career with enthusiasm, determination, and devotion.

Wilson was fortunate in his timing. Interest in the Civil War had grown in the years since Appomattox, and all manner of records, public and private, had been collected and many had appeared in print. Quick perusal of his bibliography (see page 517) will disclose a wide variety among its 34 items, from Horace Greeley and Adam Badeau to Thomas Wentworth Higginson and William Wells Brown, from general overviews to biographies, regimental histories, and reports from the Committee on the Conduct of the War. While the raw material for his projected history was plentiful, in libraries, state capitals, and the War Department, Wilson lacked a model unless it be Brown's *Negro in the Rebellion*, which that prolific writer had published in 1867. Reviewers had not been kind to Brown, scoring him for shallow research, lack of documentation, and his anecdotal style. As research and letters of inquiry brought more and more rich material to his desk, Wilson perforce put together his own outline and forged ahead.

He divided the work into three parts, devoting the first (only two chapters) to the Revolution and the War of 1812—hardly any real improvement over Brown. Part II, however, the heart of the book, he called "The War between the States," crowding in a dozen detailed and discursive chapters, from "Public Opinion" to "The Confederate Service." Part III he correctly labelled "Miscellany"—three brief chapters treating "The Phalanx at School," "Benevolence and Frugality," and one page of bibliography. Loath to put aside his pen, Wilson added an appendix including, *inter alia*, an eight-page history of the 29th Connecticut Negro Volunteers. One gets the impression that those items reached Wilson too late to be more appropriately presented.

Logically and chronologically, Wilson unfolded his history with a readable account of General David Hunter's pioneering efforts to recruit and organize the First South Carolina Colored Volunteer Infantry (afterward the 33rd United States Colored Troops). On the light side, Wilson included great detail on Hunter's sardonic correspondence with the Secretary of War—and especially its reception in Congress. On a more somber note, Wilson reproduced Jefferson Davis's declaration of Hunter and his officers as outlaws to be hanged upon capture. This led naturally to a laudatory discussion of the officers of black regiments, whom Wilson praised for their courage and self-sacrifice. Significantly, Wilson dedicated his work to "the brave men who commanded the Black Phalanx."

When Hunter began to organize black soldiers in South Carolina, the Union War Department choked off the experiment until late August; then orders came down directing Brigadier General Rufus Saxton to organize five thousand black troops! This abrupt change in policy came at the end of the disastrous Peninsular Campaign. Meanwhile, Butler in the Department of the Gulf began recruiting those Louisiana Native Guard regiments (for the most part, with black company officers), mustering all three that fall. Hunter's First South (Company A at any rate) was the very first unit of former slaves to be permitted to join the Union Army. Butler's three regiments (free men of color and former slaves) were the first officially mustered into Union ranks.

Beyond South Carolina and Louisiana, a third region of the Union, comfortably distant from Washington, played an early role in the revolutionary step to arm black men to kill their white masters. "Kansas," Wilson asserted with characteristic conviction, "has undoubtedly the honor of being the first State in the Union to *begin* the organization of negroes as soldiers for the Federal army." It should surprise no one to discover that he gave Kansas and her two black regiments comprehensive and laudatory treatment for their frontier service from August 1862 to the end of the war. It is instructive to note his research technique: His account of the career of the First Kansas Colored Volunteer Infantry (later the 79th U. S. C. T.) is firmly based on orders, correspondence, and reports of Colonel James Williams, regimental commander. His treatment of the Second Kansas Colored (later the 83rd U. S. C. T.) drew heavily from a lengthy 1885 letter from Colonel Samuel J. Crawford, its commander. In what he wrote about the Kansas regiments, Wilson was wonderfully detailed, especially on their long and punishing service in Arkansas as part of the ill-starred Camden Expedition.

One of the real strengths of his book lies in the fact that Wilson grasped the scope of the war, understood that there was more to it than the Virginia campaigns, and marching and counter-marching in Kentucky and Tennessee, not to forget Georgia and Florida. The Trans-Mississippi West was more than a geographical expression for him, and therefore black regiments raised and fielded by Arkansas, Iowa, Missouri, Kansas, and Louisiana, belong in his comprehensive Phalanx ranks. In his chapters on the Frontier, places like Cabin Creek, Poison Spring, and Honey Spring become real to the reader. East of the Mississippi Wilson marches with George H. Thomas to drive back John Bell Hood at Nashville, to get painfully pushed around at Olustee, and to fight a desperate rear-guard action at Brice's Cross Roads. In a word, Wilson's *The Black Phalanx* involves the entire Civil War, wherever black troops fought for the Union, and they fought in every theater of the war.

Critics have chided Wilson for what has been called tedious repetition, for his biting criticisms of Confederate policy toward Union blacks, and for over-praising those men. One comment rather backs into the subject with these words: "Despite the high praise which the work accords the military services, one feels that the praise was deserved, and that *The Black Phalanx* was in general rather temperately written." That critic concluded with "the volume was well received by the public, although it was very soon superceded by George Washington Williams' study on this subject."

After toiling in history's vineyards for nearly six years, Wilson, in late 1887, found a publisher, the prestigious American Publishing Company of Hartford. "By remarkable coincidence," as John Hope Franklin, Williams's biographer, put it, Harper and Brother published the Williams history at about the same time. Naturally the two books were frequently compared, occasionally in joint reviews. Most frequently quoted is this paragraph from the *Nation*'s review:

> Both of these books show honest intentions and a certain amount of praiseworthy diligence . . . but both show a want of method and an inability to command their own materials, so that they leave the reader with a renewed interest in the subject, but with a very imperfect sense of clear comprehension. Each gives some facts and documents which the other omits. Of the two, Mr. Williams's book is the more grandiloquent, while Mr. Wilson is grandiloquent once for all by yielding to the whim of calling the troops a phalanx.

Faint praise and sophisticated condescension. Fortunately, there were other more cordial and appreciative reviews. Garland Penn in 1891 voiced this almost unspoken praise: "This work needs no commendation here," and he continued with "Its sale surpasses that of any other work written by an Afro-American." It is impossible to verify that statement; one wishes it were true although Franklin maintains that "there is no proof . . . for a contemporary claim that the sale of the Wilson book 'Surpasses that of any other work written by an Afro-American.'" Competition between the rival claims of Williams and Wilson came to an abrupt end in 1891: Williams died in Blackpool, England, on August 2, and Wilson died only weeks later, on September 25, in Norfolk. He was fifty-five years old and presumably well off, thanks to steady sales of *The Black Phalanx*. Besides the original publication in Hartford in 1887, the work saw at least seven printings prior to the Arno edition of 1968. American Publishing Company, records show, besides 1887 and 1888, brought out printings in 1890, 1891, 1892, 1897, and 1900. It is reasonable to suppose that his political connections, his veterans activities and standing, and his personal popularity contributed to continuing sales.

It is reasonable to hope that the rampant racism and (at best) white condescension which greeted Wilson's book in 1887-88 are unwholesome, well nigh indigestible, gobbits of the American past. It is essential that readers opening this book realize that it was written in the 1880s, almost a decade before *Plessy v. Ferguson* gave the blessing of the U. S. Supreme Court to the doctrine of separate but equal. American history was in that time a Jim Crow history—which it continued to be until the post-World War II civil rights revolution brought about gradual and, one hopes, permanent change.

So what has Joseph Thomas Wilson, battle-scarred veteran of the American Civil War, to say to Americans in the last decade of the twentieth century? His is an authentic voice, remember; he speaks through the mouth and mind of a man born in slavery, whose father was "sold south," and who has seen his comrades killed in action, sometimes needlessly. His voice, by every rule of reason, has a right to be bitter. It comes close in the longest chapter of the book, "The Black Flag." We in our time can understand his sense of outrage at the treatment his comrades received at Fort Pillow and Poison Spring and in the Petersburg crater, to name a most obvious few. In a strictly scholastic sense, it comes down to this: Wilson's history, his facts and numbers and events, check out rather well. He carefully collected a wide assortment of material—wider than that collected by any predecessor or contemporary. While we may quarrel, somewhat, with his manner of presentation (no graduate school grooming for him, remember), we can hardly deny the fundamental accuracy of his case, the case after all, of the African Americans, 180,000 strong, who helped to save the Union and, in the process, carried freedom on their bayonets.

Dudley T. Cornish
September 1993

Dudley Taylor Cornish is Professor of History (Emeritus) at Pittsburg (Kansas) State University and the renowned author of The Sable Arm: Black Troops in the Union Army, 1861-1865.

INTRODUCTION.

By way of introduction to the American public, of the author and editor of this book, we beg to say that Mr. Wilson is not altogether unknown to the literary world, having already published several works relative to the Negro race.

His services during the war of the Rebellion secured for him a flattering recognition. He served in the 2nd Regiment Louisiana Native Guard Volunteers, also the 54th Massachusetts Volunteers,—the most famous of the Union negro regiments that engaged in the struggle, receiving several wounds. He was the first negro member ot the National Council of Administration of the Grand Army of the Republic, and a delegate to the National Encampment, and was appointed Colonel—A. D. C. to the Commander-in-Chief G. A. R. He was chosen by his comrades to be the historian of the negro soldiers, and has overcome many almost insurmountable difficulties in gathering the scattered facts, particularly those of the early wars of the United States, that were necessary to complete this work.

THE PUBLISHERS.

DEDICATION.

To the Brave Men Who Commanded the Black Phalanx.

SOLDIERS:—As a mark of esteem and respect for your patriotic devotion to the cause of human freedom, I desire to dedicate to you this record of the services of the negro soldiers, whom you led so often and successfully in the struggle for liberty and union during the great war of 1861–'65.

Your coming from the highest ranks of social life, undeterred by the prevailing spirit of caste prejudice, to take commands in the largest negro army ever enrolled beneath the flag of any civilized country, was in itself a brave act. The organization and disciplining of over two hundred thousand men, of a race that for more than two centuries had patiently borne the burdens of an unrequited bondage, for the maintenance of laws which had guaranteed to *them* neither rights nor protection, was indeed a magnificent undertaking.

You were outlawed by the decrees of Jefferson Davis, criticised by many friends at home, and contemptuously received by brother officers at headquarters, in the field, in the trenches, and at the mess table; yet, you did not waver in your fidelity to principle or in your heroic leadership of those whose valor was denied until it was proven in carnage and victory.

The record of the Black Phalanx invites the scrutiny of all who have been disposed to taunt you for associating with "armed barbarians." No massacre of vanquished foe stains the banners of those who followed you, giving quarter but receiving none. It was your teaching that served as a complete restraint against retaliation, though statesmen hinted that it would be just. Your training developed patriotism and courage, but not revenge. Ungrateful as Republics are said to be, ours has aimed to recognize merit and reward it, and those who at first hailed you with contumely, are now glad to greet you as heroes and saviors of a common country.

No true soldier desires to forget the price of his country's liberty, or that of his own; it is the recollection of the terrible bloody onset—the audacious charge—the enemy's repulse, which sweetens victory. And surely no soldiers can appreciate the final triumph with a keener sense of gladness than those who fought against such odds as did the Black Phalanx. Beating down prejudice and upholding the national cause at the same time, they have inscribed upon their banners every important battle from April, 1863, to April, 1865.

If what I have written here shall call to your minds, and present justly to the patriotic public, the indescribable hardships which you endured on the march, in the bivouac, and in the seething flames of the battle's front, my task will have served its purpose. In the name of and as a token of the gratitude of a freed race, this book is dedicated to you.

JOSEPH T. WILSON.

Navy Hill, Richmond, Va.

PREFACE.

It was a dark, stormy night in the winter of 1882, when less than a hundred men, all of whom had served their country in crushing the great Rebellion of 1861-'65, gathered around a camp-fire. The white and the colored American were there; so were the German, Frenchman, and Irishman,—all American citizens,—all veterans of the last war. The empty sleeve, the absent leg, the sabred face, the bullet-scarred body of the many, told the story of the service they had seen. It was the annual Encampment of the Department of Virginia, Grand Army of the Republic, and the comrades of Farragut Post had tastefully arranged their quarters for the occasion.

At midnight a sumptuous soldiers fare—baked beans, hot coffee and hard tack—was spread before the veterans, who ate and drank heartily as in the days when resting from the pursuit of the enemy. In the morning hour, when weary from the joy of song and toast, it was proposed that the history of the American negro soldier should be written, that posterity might have a fuller and more complete record of the deeds of the negro soldiers than had been given in the numerous already published histories of the conflicts in which they played so important a part.

The task of preparing the history fell to my lot, and it is in obedience to the duty laid upon me by my former comrades, with whom I shared the toils and joys of camp, march, battle and siege, that this volume, the result of my efforts, is launched upon the sea of war literature.

Whether or not there is any merit in the work, the reader must judge. His charity is asked, however, toward such defects as may be apparent, and which, perhaps, might be expected in the literary work of one whose life has been largely spent amid the darkness of the South American countries and the isolation of the South Sea Islands. It was not until May, 1862, while domiciled at the capitol of Chili, that I first learned of the war in the United States, when, hastening to this country, I fell into the ranks with the first negro soldiers that left the Touro Building at New Orleans, in November, 1862, and marched out on the Opelousas road, to serve in defence of the Union.

"With whatever foreboings of failure I entered upon the work of collecting the literature of the war, from which to cull and arrange much of the matter contained herein,—which has required years of incessant search and appeal,—I can but *feel* that it has been thoroughly done. The public libraries of the cities of Boston, Cincinnati, New Bedford, New York, the War Department at Washington, and the private libraries of several eminent citizens, have alike been made use of by me.

It seemed proper, also, that the memory of our forefathers should not be allowed to remain in longer obscurity; that it was fitting to recall *their* deeds of heroism, that all might know the sacrifices they made for the freedom their descendants were so long denied from enjoying. In gathering together the scattered facts relating to the negroe's participation in the wars of 1775 and 1812, difficulties well-nigh insurmountable have been over-come, and it has been only through patient and persistent effort that I have been able to prepare the chapters devoted to the early wars of the United States.

Descriptions of a number of the battles in which negro troops took part in the late war of the Rebellion, are given to call attention to the unsurpassed carnage which occurred, and to give them proper place in the war's history rather than to present a critical account of the battles. My aim has been to write in the spirit which impelled the soldiers to go forth to battle, and to reverse the accounts given in the popular histories which ascribe to the generals and colonels who commanded, instead of the soldiers who did the fighting, victory or defeat. "The troops who do what can neither be expected nor required, are the ones which are victorious. The men, who, tired and worn and hungry and exhausted, yet push into battle, are those who win. They who persist against odds, against obstacles, against hope, who proceed or hold out reasonably, are the conquerors," says Gen. Grant's historian. With no desire of detracting from the commanders—if I were able—the honor due them, my aim is to credit the soldiers with whatever heroism they may have displayed.

I acknowledge it has been a labor of love to fight many of the battles of the war of the rebellion over again, not because of a relish for blood and the destruction of human life, but for the memories of the past; of the bondage of a race and its struggle for freedom, awakening as they do the intense love of country and liberty, such as one who has been without either feels, when both have been secured by heroic effort.

To those who have responded to my appeal for information regarding the negro soldier, I have aimed to give full credit; if any are omitted it is not intentionally done. To no one am I more indebted for assisting in collecting data, than to Lt. J. M. Trotter, of the 55th Mass. Reg't. nor am I unmindful of the kindness of Hon. Robert Lincoln, late Secretary of War, nor that of Col. James D. Brady, member of Congress from Virginia, for copies of public records; to Col. H. C. Corbin, for the record of the 14th Regt.; and to Col. D. Torrance for that of the 29th Reg't. Conn. I am also indebted to Maj. Gen. Wm. Mahone for a map of the defences of Petersburg, showing the crater; to the librarian of the Young Men's Mercantile Library, of Cincinnati, for the use of Col. Albert's carved map of Fort Wagner, and to Col. G. M. Arnold and Hon. Joseph Jergenson for copies of historical papers; also to Hon. Libbey.

J. T. W.

CONTENTS.

PART I.

THE WARS FOR INDEPENDENCE.

CHAPTER I.—The War of 1775.

CHAPTER II.—The War of 1812.

Contents.

PART II.

THE WAR BETWEEN THE STATES.

CONTENTS.

ILLUSTRATIONS.

Illustrations.

PART I.

THE WARS FOR INDEPENDENCE

1775--1812.

A HISTORY OF THE

BLACK PHALANX.

CHAPTER I.

THE WAR OF 1775.

The history of the patriotic Negro Americans who swelled the ranks of the Colonial and Continental armies has never been written, nor was any attempt made by the historians of that day to record the deeds of those who dared to face death for the independence of the American Colonies. W. H. Day, in addressing a convention of negro men at Cleveland, O., in 1852, truly said: "Of the services and sufferings of the colored soldiers of the Revolution, no attempt has, to our knowledge, been made to preserve a record. Their history is not written; it lies upon the soil watered with their blood; who shall gather it? It rests with their bones in the charnel house; who shall exhume it?" Upon reading these lines, it occurred to me that somewhere among the archives of that period there must exist at least a clue to the record of the negro patriots of that war. If I cannot exclaim *Eureka*, after years of diligent search, I take pride in presenting what I *have* found scattered throughout the pages of the early histories and literature, and from the correspondence of men who in that period discussed the topics of the day—who led and fashioned public opinion, many of whom commanded in the field. Not a few biographers have contributed to my fund of knowledge. To avoid as much as possible the charge of plagiarism I have aimed to give credit to my informants for what shall follow regarding the colored patriots in the war of the Revolution. I have reason to believe that I have gathered much that has been obscure; that I have exhumed the bones of that noble Phalanx who, at Bunker Hill and Yorktown, in various military employments, served their country. It is true they were few in number when compared to the host that entered the service in the late Rebellion, but it must be remembered that their number was small at that time in the country, and that the seat of war was at the North, and not, as in the late war, at the South, where their numbers have always been large.

Of the three hundred thousand troops in the Revolutionary war, it has been estimated that five thousand were colored, and these came principally from the North, whose colored population at that time was about 50,000, while the Southern colonies contained about 300,000. The interest felt in the two sections for the success of the cause of independence, if referred to the army, can easily be seen. The Northern colonies furnished two hundred and forty-nine thousand, five hundred and three, and the Southern colonies one hundred and forty-seven thousand, nine hundred and forty soldiers, though the whole population of each section was within a few hundred of being equal.

The love of liberty was no less strong with the Southern than with the Northern colored man, as their efforts for liberty show. At the North he gained his freedom by entering the American army; at the South, only by entering the British army, which was joined by more than fifteen thousand colored men. Jefferson says 30,000 negroes from Virginia alone went to the British army. I make the digression simply to assert that had the colored men at the South possessed the same opportunity as those at the

North, of enlisting in the American army, a large force of colored men would have been in the field, fighting for America's independence. Of the services of the little band, scattered as they were throughout the army, two or three in a company composed of whites, a squad in a regiment, a few companies with an army, made it quite impossible for their record, beyond this, to be distinct from the organizations they were attached to. However, enough has been culled from the history of that conflict, to show that they bore a brave part in the struggle which wrested the colonies from the control of Great Britain, and won for themselves and offspring, freedom, which many of them never enjoyed. I have studiously avoided narrating the conduct of those who cast their fortune with the British, save those who went with Lord Dunmore, for reasons too obvious to make mention of.

The sentiments of a majority of the people of the colonies were in full accord with the declaration opposing slavery, and they sought to give it supremacy by their success in the conflict. Slavery, which barred the entrance to the army of the colored man at the South, had been denounced by the colonist before the adoption of the articles of confederation, and was maintained solely by local regulations. As early as 1774, all the colonies had agreed to, and their representatives to the congress had signed, the articles of the Continental Association, by which it was agreed, "that we will neither import nor purchase any slave imported after the first day of December next, (1774), after which we will wholly discontinue the slave trade, and will neither be concerned in it ourselves, nor will we hire our vessels, nor sell our commodities or manufactories to those who are concerned in it." Georgia not being represented in this Congress, consequently was not in the Association, but as soon as her Provincial Congress assembled in July, 1775, it passed the following resolutions:

"*I.—Resolved,* That this Congress will adopt and carry into execution all and singular the measures and recommendations of the late Continental Congress.

"*IV.—Resolved,* That we will neither import or purchase any slave imported from Africa or elsewhere after this day, (July, 6.")

The sincerity with which this agreement was entered into may be seen by the action of the colonists at Norfolk, Virginia, where, in March, 1775, a brig arrived from the coast of Guinea, via Jamaica, with a number of slaves on board consigned to a merchant of that town. To use a modern phrase the vessel was *boycotted* by the committee, who published the following:

"TO THE FREEMEN OF VIRGINIA.

COMMITTEE CHAMBER,
NORFOLK, March 6th, 1775.

"Trusting to your sure resentment against the enemies of your country, we, the committee, elected by ballot for the Borough of Norfolk, hold up for your just indignation Mr. John Brown, merchant, of this place.

"On Thursday, the 2nd of March, this committee were informed of the arrival of the brig Fanny, Capt. Watson, with a number of slaves for Mr. Brown; and, upon inquiry, it appeared they were shipped from Jamaica as his property, and on his account; that he had taken great pains to conceal their arrival from the knowledge of the committee; and that the shipper of the slaves, Mr. Brown's correspondent, and the captain of the vessel, were all fully apprised of the Continental prohibition against the article.

"From the whole of this transaction, therefore, we, the committee for Norfolk Borough, do give it as our unanimous opinion, that the said John Brown has wilfully and perversely violated the Continental Association, to which he had with his own hand subscribed obedience; and that, agreeable to the eleventh article, we are bound, forthwith, to publish the truth of the case, to the end that all such foes to the rights of British America may be publicly known and universally contemned as the enemies of American liberty, and that every person may henceforth break off all dealings with him."

This was the voice of a majority of the colonists, and those who dissented were regarded as Tories, and in favor of the crown as against the independence of the colonies, although there were many at the North and South who held slaves, and were yet loyal to the cause of the colonies; but the public sentiment was undoubtedly as strong against the institution as it was in 1864. But the Tories were numerous at the South, and by continually exciting the imagination of the whites by picturing massacre and insurrection on the part of the negros if they were armed, thwarted the effort of Col. Lauren's and of Congress to raise a "negro army" at the South. The leaders were favorable to it, but the colonists, for the reason cited, were distrustful of its practicability. Though a strong effort was made, as will be seen, the scare raised by the

Tories prevented its success. Notwithstanding, hundreds of colored men, slave and free, at the South, not only followed the army but in every engagement took an active part on the side of the colonist. They were not enrolled and mustered into the army, it is true, but they rendered important service to the cause.

The caste prejudice now so strong in the country was then in its infancy. A white man at that time lived with a colored woman without fear of incurring the ostracism of his neighbors, and with the same impunity he lived with an Indian Squaw. So common was this practice, that in order to correct it laws were passed forbidding it. The treatment of the slaves was not what it came to be after the war, nor had the spirit of resentment been stifled in them as it was subquently. Manifestations of their courage and manliness were not wanting when injustice was attempted to be practiced against them, consequently the spirit and courage with which they went into the conflict were quite equal to that of the whites, who were ever ready to applaud them for deeds of daring. It is only through this medium that we have discovered the meed of praise due the little Phalanx, which linked its fortune with the success of the American army, and of whom the following interesting facts can now be recorded.

It is well for the negro and for his decendants in America, cosmopolitan as it is, that his race retains its distinctive characteristicts, color and features, otherwise they would not have, as now, a history to hand down to posterity so gloriously patriotic and interesting. His amalgamation with other races is attributable to the relation which it bore to them, although inter-marriage was not allowed. By the common consent of his enslavers, he was allowed to live clandestinely with the women of his own color; sometimes from humane considerations, sometimes from a standpoint of gain, but always as a slave or a subject of the slave code. Reduced from his natural state of freedom by his misfortune in tribal war, to that of a slave, and then transported by the consent of his captors and enemies to these shores, and sold into an unrequited bondage, the fire of his courage,—like that of other races similarly situated, without hope of liberty; doomed to toil,—slackened into an apathetic state, and seeming willing servitude, which produced a resignation to fate from 1619 to 1770, more than a century and a half. At the latter date, for the first time in the history of what is now the United States, the negro, inspired with the love of liberty, aimed a blow at the authority that held him in bondage. In numerous instances, when the Indians attacked the white settlers, particularly in the Northern colonies, negroes were summoned and took part in the defense of the settlements.

As early as 1652, the militia law of Massachusetts required negroes, Scotchmen and Indians,—the indentured slaves of Cromwell, who encountered his army at the battle of Dunbar,—to train in the militia. Nor was it an uncommon occurrence for them to be manumitted for meritorious and courageous action in defending their masters' families, often in the absence of the master, when attacked by the red men of the woods. It was not infrequent to find the negro as a sentinel at the meeting-house door; or serving as a barricade for the master's mansion. The Indian was more of a terror to him than the boa-constrictor; though slaves, they knew that if captured by the Indians their fate would be the same as that of the white man; consequently they fought with a desperation equal to that of the whites, against the common enemy. So accustomed did they become to the use of arms, that one of the first acts of the settlers after the Indians were driven from the forest, was to disarm and forbid negroes keeping or handling fire-arms and weapons of every sort. This was done from a sense of self-preservation and fear that the negroes might (and many did) attempt to revenge themselves when cruelly treated, or rise in mutiny and massacre the whites.

But it was not until 1770, when the fervor of rebellion had influenced the people of the colonies, and Capt. Preston, with the King's soldiers, appeared in King Street, Boston, to enforce the decree of the British Parliament,

DEATH OF CRISPUS ATTUCKS,
While leading an attack against British troops in Boston.

that the people met the troops face to face. This lent force to the rebellious spirit against the Mother Country, which the people of the United Northern Colonies had felt called upon to manifest in public meetings and by written resolutions. The soldiers were regarded as invaders. And while the leading men of Boston were discussing and deliberating as to what steps should be taken to drive the British troops out of the town, Crispus Attucks, a negro runaway slave,* led a crowd against the soldiers, with brave words of encouragement. The soldiers fired upon them, killing the negro leader, Attucks, first, and then two white men, and mortally wounding two others. A writer says:

"The presence of the British soldiers in King Street, excited the patriotic indignation of the people. The whole community was stirred, and sage counsellors were deliberating and writing and talking about the public grievances. But it was not for the 'wise and prudant' to be first to *act* against the encroachments of arbitrary power. A motley rabble of saucy boys, negroes and mulattoes, Irish Jeazues, and outlandish Jack tars, (as John Adams described them in his plea in defence of the soldiers), could not restrain their emotion, or stop to enquire if what they *must* do was according to the letter of the law. Led by Crispus Attucks, the mulatto slave, and shouting, 'The way to get rid of these soldiers is to attack the main guard; strike at the root; this is the nest;' with more valor than discretion they rushed to King Street, and were fired upon by Capt. Preston's company. Crispus Attucks was the first to fall; he and Samuel Gray and Jonas Caldwell were killed on the spot. Samuel Maverick and Patrick Carr were mortally wounded. The excitement which followed was intense. The bells of the town were rung. An impromptu town-meeting was held, and an immense assembly was gathered. Three days after, on the 17th, a public funeral of the martyr took place. The shops in Boston were closed, and all the bells of Boston and the neighboring towns were rung. It is said that a greater number of persons assembled on this occasion, than ever before gathered on this continent for a similar purpose. The body of Crispus Attucks, the mulatto, had been placed in Fanueil Hall with that of Caldwell; both being strangers in the city. Maverick was buried from his mother's

*"Ran away from his master, William Brown, of Framingham, on the 30th of Sept. last, a Mullato Fellow, about 27 years of age, named *Crispus*, 6 feet 2 inches high, short, curl'd hair, his knees nearer together than commou; had on a light coloured Bearskin Coat, plain brown Fustain Jacket, or brown All Wool one, new Buck skin breeches, blue Yarn Stockings, and a checked woolen shirt. Whoever shall take up said Runaway, and convey him to his abovesaid master, shall have *ten pounds*, old Tenor Reward, and all necessary charges paid. And all Masters of Vessels and others, are hereby cautioned against concealing or carrying off said Servant on Penalty of the Law. Boston, October 2, 1750."—*Boston Gazette*,

house in Union Street, and Gray, from his brother's, in Royal Exchange Lane. The four hearses formed a junction in King Street, and then the procession marched in columns six deep, with a long file of coaches belonging to the most distinguished citizens, to the Middle Burying Ground, where the four victims were deposited in one grave; over which a stone was placed with the inscription:

'Long as in Freedom's cause the wise contend,
Dear to your country shall your fame extend;
While to the world the lettered stone shall tell
Where Caldwell, Attucks, Gray and Maverick fell.'

"The anniversary of this event was publicly commemorated in Boston by an oration and other exercises every year until our National Independence was achieved, when the Fourth of July was substituted for the Fifth of March, as the more proper day for a general celebration. Not only was the event commemorated, but the martyrs who then gave up their lives were remembered and honored."

Thus the first blood for liberty shed in the colonies was that of a real slave and a negro. As the news of the affray spread , the people became aroused throughout the land. Soon, in every town and village, meetings were held, and the colonists urged to resist the oppressive and aggresive measures which the British Parliament had passed, and for the enforcement of which troops had been stationed in Boston, and as we see, had shot down those who dared to oppose them. In all the colonies slavery was at this time tolerated, though the number of slaves was by no means large in the Northern Colonies, nor had there been a general ill treatment of them, as in after years in the Southern States. Their war-like courage, it is true, had been slackened, but their manhood had not been crushed.

Crispus Attucks was a fair representative of the colonial negro, as they evinced thereafter, during the prolonged struggle which resulted in the Independence of the United States. When the tocsin sounded "to arms, to arms, ye who would be free," the negro responded to the call, and side by side with the white patriots of the colonial militia, bled and died.

Mr. Bancroft in his history of the United States says:

"Nor should history forget to record, that as in the army at Cambridge, so also in this gallant band, the free negroes of the colony had their representatives. For the right of free negroes to bear arms in the public defense was, at that day, as little disputed in New England as other rights. They took their place, not in a seperate corps, but in the ranks with the white men; and their names may be seen on the pension-rolls of the country, side by side with those of other soldiers of the Revolution."

It was not the free only who took up arms in defence of America's independence; not alone those who, in preceding wars,—Indian and French,—had gained their liberty, that swelled the ranks of the colonial militia; but slaves, inspired by the hope of freedom, went to the front, as Attucks had done when he cut the Gordian knot that held the colonies to Great Britain. "From that moment we may date the severance of the British Empire," said Daniel Webster, in his Bunker Hill oration, referring to the massacre on the 5th of March, 1770. The thirst for freedom was universal among the people of New England. With them liberty was not circumscribed by condition and now, since the slave Attucks had struck the first blow for America's independence, thereby electrifying the colonies and putting quite a different phase upon their grievances, the people were called upon to witness a real slave struggling with his oppressors for his freedom. It touched the people of the colonies as they had never been touched before, and they arrayed themselves for true freedom.

Dr. Joseph Warren thus heralds the sentiment of the colonist, in his oration delivered at Boston, March 5th, 1775:

"That personal freedom is the natural right of every man, and that property, or an exclusive right to dispose of what he has honestly acquired by his own labor, necessarily arises therefrom, are truths which common sense has placed beyond the reach of contradiction. And no man, or body of men, can, without being guilty of flagrant injustice, claim a right to dispose of the persons or acquisitions of any other man or body of men, unless it can be proved that such a right has arisen from some compact between the parties, in which it has been explicitly and freely granted."

The year previous, John Hancock was the orator on the occasion of the 4th anniversary of the shedding of the first blood for the Independence of America, and he thus presents the case to a Boston audience yet smarting under the insult and sting given them by the British soldiery:

"But I forbear, and come reluctantly to the transactions of that dismal night, when in such quick succession, we felt the extremes of grief, astonishment and rage; when Heaven, in anger, for a dreadful moment suffered Hell to take the reins; when Satan with his chosen band opened the sluices of New England's blood, and sacrilegiously polluted our land with the dead bodies of her guiltless sons. Let this sad tale of death never be told without a tear; let the heaving bosom cause to burn with a manly indignation at the barbarous story, through the long tracts of future time; let every parent tell the shameful story to his listening children 'til tears of pity glisten in their eyes, and boiling passions shake their tender frames; and whilst the anniversary of that ill-fated night is kept a jubilee in the grim court of pandemonium, let all America join in one common prayer to Heaven, that the inhuman, unprovoked murders of the 5th of March, 1770, planned by Hillsborough and a knot of treacherous knaves in Boston, and executed by the cruel hand of Preston and his sanguinary coadjutors, may ever stand in history without a parallel. But what, my countrymen, withheld the ready arm of vengeance from executing instant justice on the vile assassins? Perhaps you feared promiscuous carnage might ensue, and that the innocent might share the fate of those who had performed the infernal deed. But were not all guilty? Were you not too tender of the lives of those who came to fix a yoke on your necks? But I must not too severely blame you for a fault which great souls only can commit. May that magnificence of spirit which scorns the low pursuit of malice; may that generous compassion which often preserves from ruin, even a guilty villain, forever actuate the noble bosoms of Americans! But let not the miscreant host vainly imagine that we feared their arms. No, those we despised; we dread nothing but slavery. Death is the creature of a poltroon's brains; 'tis immortality to sacrifice ourselves for the salvation of our country. We fear not death. That gloomy night, the pale-face moon, and the affrighted stars that hurried through the sky, can witness that we fear not death. Our hearts, which, at the recollection, glow with rage that four revolving years have scarcely taught us to restrain, can witness that we fear not death; and happy it is for those who dared to insult us, that their naked bones are not now piled up an everlasting monument of Massachusett's bravery. But they retired; they fled, and in that flight they found their only safety. We then expected that the hand of public justice would soon inflict that punishment upon the murderers, which, by the laws of God and man, they had incurred. But let the unbiassed pen of a Robertson, or perhaps of some equally famed American, conduct this trial before the great tribunal of succeeding generations. And though the murderers may escape the just resentment of an enraged people; though drowsy justice, intoxicated by the poisonous draft prepared for her cup, still nods upon her rotten seat, yet be assured, such complicated crimes will meet their due reward. Tell me, ye bloody butchers! ye villains high and low! ye wretches who contrived, as well as you who executed the inhuman deed! do you not feel the goads and stings of conscious guilt pierce through your savage bosoms? Though some of you may think yourselves exalted to a height that bids defiance to human justice, and others shroud yourselves beneath the mask of hypocrisy, and build your hopes of safety on the low arts of cunning, chicanery and falsehood; yet do you not sometimes feel the gnawings of that worm which never dies; do not the injured shades of Maverick, Gray, Cadwell, Attucks and Carr, attend you in your solitary walks; arrest you in the midst of your debaucheries and fill even your dreams with terror?"

The orators of New England poured out upon this once slave,—now hero and martyr,—their unstinted praise. We have but to recall the recollection of the earliest conflicts which the colonist had with the British, in order to see the negro occupying a place in the ranks of the patriot army. Their white fellow-citizens were only too glad to take ground to the left, in order that they could fall in on their colors. And they did good service whenever they fought, as the record shows.

The Committee of safety upon reviewing the situation and the army, before the first great battle of the Revolution had been fought, adopted the following resolution:

"*Resolved*, That it is the opinion of this committee, that as the contest now between Great Britain and the Colonies respects the liberties and privileges of the latter, which the Colonies are determined to maintain, that the admission of any persons, as soldiers, into the army now raising, but such as are Freeman, will be inconsistent with the principals that are supported, and reflect dishonor on this Colony; and that no Slaves be admitted into this army upon any consideration whatever."

The exception was well taken, and this act of the Committee, excluding slaves from the army, placed the rebels upon the basis of patriots, fighting for freedom. This, however, did not detract from those who had already distinguished themselves, by their bravery at Bunker Hill a few weeks previous, where Peter Salem, once a slave, fought side by side in the ranks with the white soldiers. When the British Major Pitcairn mounted the redoubt, upon that memorable occasion, shouting, "The day is ours!" Peter Salem poured the contents of his gun into that officer's body, killing him instantly, and checking, temporarily, the advance of the British. Swett, in his "Sketches of Bunker Hill Battle," says:

"Major Pitcairn caused the first effusion of blood at Lexington. In that battle, his horse was shot under him, while he was separated from his troops. With presence of mind he feigned himself slain; his pistols were taken from his hostlers, and he was left for dead, when he seized the opportunity and escaped. He appeared at Bunker Hill, and, says the historian, 'Among those who mounted the works was the gallant Major Pitcairn, who exultingly cried out, 'The day is ours!' when a black soldier, named Salem, shot him through and he fell. His agonized son received him in his arms, and tenderly bore him to the boats.' A contribution was made in the army for the colored soldier, and he was presented to Washington as having performed this feat."

Mr. Aaron White, of Thompson, Conn., in a letter to George Livermore, Esq., of the Massachusetts Historical Society, writes:

"With regard to the black Hero of Bunker Hill, I never knew him personally, nor did I ever hear from his lips the story of his achievements; but I have better authority. About the year 1809, I heard a soldier of the Revolution, who was present at the Bunker Hill Battle, relate to my father the story of the death of Major Pitcairn. He said the Major had passed the storm of fire without, and had mounted the redoubt, when, waving his sword, he commanded, in a loud voice, the 'rebels' to surrender. His sudden appearance, and his commanding air, at first startled the men immediately before him. They neither answered nor fired; probably not being exactly certain what was next to be done. At this critical moment, a negro soldier stepped forward, and, aiming his musket directly at the Major's bosom, blew him through. My informant declared that he was so near, that he distinctly saw the act. The story made quite an impression on my mind. I have frequently heard my farther relate the story, and have no doubt of its truth. My father on the day of the battle was a mere child, and witnessed the battle and burning of Charlestown from Roxbury Hill, sitting on the shoulders of the Rev. Mr. Jackson, who said to him as he placed him on the ground, 'Now, boy, do you remember this!' Consequently, after such an injunction, he would necessarily pay particular attention to anecdotes concerning the first and only battle he ever witnessed."

Salem was undoubtedly one of the chief heroes of that ever memorable battle. Orator, historian, poet, all give

BATTLE OF BUNKER HILL.
Peter Salem shooting the British Major Pitcairn.

this sable patriot credit for having been instrumental in checking the British advance and saving the day.

At the unveiling of the statue erected to the memory of Gen. Joseph Warren, who fell at Bunker Hill, the orator of the occasion, Hon. Edward Everett, said:

"It is the monument of the day of the event, of the battle of Bunker Hill; all of the brave men who shared its perils,—alike of Prescott and Putnam and Warren, the chiefs of the day, and the colored man, Salem, who, is reported to have shot the gallant Pitcairn, as he mounted the parapet. Cold as the clods on which it rests, still as the silent Heaven to which it soars, it is yet vocal, eloquent, in their individual praise."

The following is a copy of a petition now in the Archive Department of Massachusetts:

"TO THE HONORABLE GENERAL COURT OF THE MASSACHUSETTS' BAY.

"The subscribers beg leave to report to your Honorable House, (which we do in justice to the character of so brave a man), that under our own observation, we declare that a negro man named Salem Poor, of Col. Frye's regiment, Capt. Ame's company, in the late battle at Charleston, behaved like an experienced officer, as well as an excellent soldier. To set forth particulars of his conduct would be tedious. We only beg leave to say, in the person of this said negro, centers a brave and gallant soldier. The reward due to so great and distinguished a character, we submit to Congress.

"JONA. BREWER, Col.
THOMAS NIXON, Lt. Col.
WM. PRESCOTT, Col.
EPHM. COREY, Lieut.
JOSEPH BAKER, Lieut.
JOSHUA ROW, Lieut.
JONAS RICHARDSON, Capt.
ELIPHALET BODWELL, SG'T.
JOSIAH FOSTER, Lieut.
EBENR. VARNUM, 2nd Lieut.
WM. HUDSON BALLARD, Capt.
WM. SMITH, Cap.
JOHN MORTON, Sergt. (?)
Lieut. RICHARD WELSH.

CAMBRIDGE, Dec. 5, 1775.

"In Council Dec. 21, 1775.—Read, and sent down.

PEREZ MORTON, Dep'y Sec'y."

A biographical account of Peter Salem is given in the following newspaper extract:

"April, 1882, the town of Framingham voted to place a memorial stone over the grave of Peter Salem, alias Salem Middlesex, whose last resting place in the old burial ground an Framingham Centre has been unmarked for years. For this purpose $150 was appropriated by the town. The committee in charge of the matter has placed a neat granite memorial over his grave, and it bears the following inscription: "Peter Salem, a soldier of the revolution, Died Aug. 16, 1816. Concord, Bunker

Hill, Saratoga. Erected by the town, 1882." Peter Salem was the colored man who particularly distinguished himself in the revolutionary war by shooting down Major Pitcairn at the battle of Bunker Hill, as he was mounting a redoubt and shouting, "The day is ours!" this being the time when Pitcairn fell back into the arms of his son. Peter Salem served faithfully in the war for seven years in the companies of minute men under the command of Capt. John Nixon and Capt. Simon Edgell of Framingham, and came out of it unharmed. He was a slave, and was owned, originally, by Capt Jeremiah Belknap of Framingham, being sold by him to Major Lawson Buckminster of that town, he becoming a free man when he joined the army. Salem was born in Framingham, and, in 1783, married Katie Benson, a Granddaughter of Nero, living for a time near what is now the State muster field. He removed to Leicester after the close of the war, his last abode in that town being a cabin on the road leading from Leicester to Auburn. He was removed to Framingham, where he had gained a settlement in 1816 and there he died."

Salem was not the only negro at the battle of Bunker Hill. Says an authority:

"Col. Trumbull in his celebrated historic picture of this battle, introduces conspicuously the colored patriot. At the time of the battle, the artist, then acting as adjutant, was stationed with his regiment at Roxbury, and saw the action from this point. The picture was painted in 1786 when the event was fresh in his mind. It is a significant historical fact, pertinent to our present research, that, among the limited number of figures introduced on the canvas, more than one negro soldier can be distinctly seen."

Of the others who participated in the battle we have knowledge of Salem Poor, whose bravery won for him favorable comment.

Major Wm. Lawrence, who fought through the war for independence, from Concord, until the peace of 1783, participating in many of the severest battles of the war. Says a memoir:

"At Bunker Hill, where he was slightly wounded, his coat and hat were pierced with the balls of the enemy, and were preserved in the family for several years. At one time he commanded a company whose rank and file were all negroes, of whose courage, military discipline, and fidelity, he always spoke with respect. On one occasion, being out reconnoitering with his company, he got so far in advance of his command, that he was surrounded, and on the point of being made prisoner by the enemy. The men, soon discovering his peril, rushed to his rescue, and fought with the most determined bravery till that rescue was effectually secured. He never forgot this circumstance, and ever took special pains to show kindness and hospitality to any individual of the colored race, who came near his dwelling."

The Committee of Safety having excluded slaves from the army, many were thereafter manumitted, that they might enlist. There was no law regulating enlistment in the army at the time which required the color of a soldier's skin to be recorded or regarded. A prejudice existed in the legislature that prompted that body to begin a series of special enactments, regarding negroes, which did not exclude them altogether from the army, but looked to their organization into exclusive companies, batallions and regiments.

Notwithstanding the record made by the negroes who had swollen the ranks of the American army a few weeks after the battle of Bunker Hill, General Gates, then at Cambridge, issued the following order to the officers, then recruiting for the service:

"You are not to enlist any deserter from the Ministerial army, nor any stroller, negro, or vagabond, or persons suspected of being an enemy to the liberty of America, nor any under eighteen years of age. As the cause is the best that can engage men of courage and principle to take up arms, so it is expected that none but such will be accepted by the recruiting officer. The pay, provision, &c., being so ample, it is not doubted but that the officers sent upon this service will, without delay, complete their respective corps, and march the men forthwith to camp. You are not to enlist any person that is not an American born, unless such person has a wife and family, and is a settled resident in this country. The persons you enlist must be provided with good and complete arms."

This was in July, and on the 26th of the following September, Edward Rutledge, of South Carolina, moved in the Colonial Congress that all negroes be discharged that were in the army. As might be expected, his proposition was strongly supported by the Southern delegates, but the Northern delegates being so much stronger, voted it down. The negroes were crowding so rapidly into the army, and the Northern colonists finding their Southern comrades so strongly opposing this element of strength, submitted the question of their enlistment to a conference committee in October, composed of such men as Dr.

Franklin, Benjamin Harrison and Thomas Lynch, with the Deputy Governors of Connecticut and Rhode Island. This committee met at Cambridge, with a committee of the council of Massachusetts Bay. The object and duty of the meeting was to consider the condition of the army, and to devise means by which it could be improved.

General Washington was present at the meeting, and took part in the discussions. Among others, the following subject was considered and reported upon: "'Ought not negroes to be excluded from the new enlistment, especially those such as are slaves?' All were thought improper by the council of officers. '*Agreed*, That they may be rejected altogether.'"

In the organization of the new army, were many officers and men, who had served with negroes in the militia, and who had been re-enlisted in the colonial army. They protested against the exclusion of their old comrades, on account of color. So very strong were their protests that most of the rank and file of the Northern troops regarded the matter as of serious import to the colonies, and of danger to the wives and families of those in the field. There was quite a large number of free negroes in the Northern Colonies at this time, and the patriotism displayed by those who had the opportunity of serving in the militia during the early stages of the war, aroused a feeling which prompted a great many masters to offer to the commander of the army the services of their slaves, and to the slaves their freedom, if their services were accepted. So weighty were the arguments offered, and to soften the gloom which hung about the homes and the camps of the soldiers, Gen. Washington wrote to the President of Congress regarding the matter, from Cambridge, in December, 1775:

"It has been represented to me that the free negroes who have served in this army are very much dissatisfied at being discarded. As it is to be apprehended that they may seek employment in the Ministerial army, I have presumed to depart from the resolution respecting them, and have given license for their being enlisted. If this is disapproved by Congress, I will put a stop to it."*

* Mr. Sparks appends to this letter the following note: "At a meeting of the general officers, previously to the arrival of the committee from Congress in camp, it was unanimously resolved, that it was not expedient to enlist slaves in the new army; and,

The letter was submitted to Congress, and General Washington's action was sustained by the passage of the following resolution: "That the free negroes, who had served faithfully in the army at Cambridge, may be re-enlisted therein, but no others."

The question of color first entered the army by order of Washington's predecessor, Gen. Artemus Ward, who in his first general order required the "complexion" of the soldier to be entered upon the roll. In October, 1775, Gen. Thomas wrote the following letter to John Adams. The general was in every way competent to draw a true picture of the army, and had the opportunity of observation. He says:

"I am sorry to hear that any prejudices should take place in any Southern Colony, with respect to the troops raised in this. I am certain that the insinuations you mention are injurious, if we consider with what precipitation we are obliged to collect an army. In the regiments at Roxbury, the privates are equal to any that I served with in the last war; very few old men, and in the ranks very few boys. Our fifes are many of them boys. We have some negroes; but I look on them, in general, as equally servicable with other men for fatigue; and in action many of them have proved themselves brave. I would avoid all reflection, or anything that may tend to give umbrage; but there is in this army from the southward, a number called riflemen, who are the most indifferent men I ever served with. These privates are mutinous, and often deserting to the enemy; unwilling for duty of any kind; exceedingly vicious; and I think the army here would be as well off without them. But to do justice to their officers, they are, some of them, likely men."

Despite all prejudice, the negro, as in all conflicts since, sought every opportunity to show his patriotism, and his unquenchable thirst for liberty; and no matter in what capacity he entered the service, whether as body-servant, hostler or teamster, he always displayed the same characteristic courage. In November of the same year the Provincial Congress of South Carolina, by the passage of the following resolution, gave permission to her militia officers, to use slaves in the army for certain purposes:

by a large majority, negroes of every description were excluded from enlistment. When the subject was referred to the Committee in conference, the resolve was not adhered to, and probably for the reason here mentioned by Washington. Many black soldiers were in the service during all stages of the war."—Spark's Washington, Vol. III, pp. 218-219.

"On motion, *Resolved,* That the colonels of the several regiments of militia throughout the Colony have leave to enroll such a number of able male slaves, to be employed as pioneers and laborers, as public exegencies may require; and that a daily pay of seven shillings and sixpence be allowed for the service of each such slave while actually employed."

The foregoing resolution must not in any way be understood as sanctioning the employment of negroes as soldiers, notwithstanding some of the ablest men of the State advocated the enlistment of negroes in the army; the opposition was too strong to carry the measure through either Congress or the legislature. The feeling among the Northern colonists may be shown by citing the views of some of their leading men, and none perhaps was better calculated to give a clear expression of their views, than the Rev. Dr. Hopkins, of Newport, R. I., who wrote a "Dialogue Concerning the slavery of the Africans," published soon after the commencement of hostilities. Here is an extract from a note to the Dialogue:

"God is so ordering it in his providence, that it seems absolutely necessary something should speedily be done with respect to the slaves among us, in order to our safety, and to prevent their turning against us in our present struggle, in order to get their liberty. Our oppressors have planned to gain the blacks, and induce them to take up arms against us, by promising them liberty on this condition; and this plan they are prosecuting to the utmost of their power, by which means they have persuaded numbers to join them. And should we attempt to restrain them by force and severity, keeping a strict guard over them, and punishing them severely who shall be detected in attempting to join our oppressors, this will only be making bad worse, and serve to render our inconsistence, oppression, and cruelty more criminal, perspicuous, and shocking, and bring down the righteous vengeance of Heaven on our heads. The only way pointed out to prevent this threatening evil is to set the blacks at liberty ourselves by some public acts and laws, and then give them proper encouragement to labor, or take arms in the defence of the American cause, as they shall choose. This would at once be doing them some degree of justice, and defeating our enemies in the scheme that they are prosecuting."

Therefore it will be observed that public opinion regarding the arming of negroes in the North and South, was controlled by sectional interest in the one, and the love of liberty in the other. That both desired America's

Independence, no one will doubt, but that one section was more willing than the other to sacrifice slavery for freedom, I think is equally as plain. While the colonists were debating with much anxiety the subject of what to do with the negroes, the New England States were endeavoring to draw the Southern States or Colonies into the war by electing George Washington as Commander of the army at Cambridge, and accepting the mis-interpretations of the declarations of war. The Punic faith with which the Southern States entered the war for liberty humiliated the army, and wrung from its commander the letter written to Congress, and its approval of his course in re-enlisting free negroes. Meanwhile the British were actively engaged in recruiting and organizing negroes into their army and navy.

In November, 1775, Lord Dunmore visited Norfolk, Virginia,* and, as Governor, finding his authority as such not regarded by the whites, issued a proclamation offering freedom to the slaves who would join the British army. A full description of the State of affairs at that time, is thus given by an English historian:

"In letters which had been laid before the English Parliament, and published to the whole world, he (Lord Dunmore) had represented the planters as ambitious, selfish men, pursuing their own interest and advancement at the expense of their poorer countrymen, and as being ready to make every sacrifice of honesty and principle, and he had said more privately, that, since they were so anxious for liberty,—for more freedom than was consistent with the free institutions of the Mother Country and the charter of the Colony,—that since they were so eager to abolish a fanciful slavery in a dependence on Great Britain, he would try how they liked abolition of real slavery, by setting free all their negroes and indentured servants, who were, in fact, little better than *white* slaves. This to the Virginians was like passing a rasp over a gangrened place; it was probing a wound that was incurable, or one which had not yet been healed. Later in the year, when the battle of Bunker's Hill had been

* Dunmore after destroying Norfolk, sailed with his fleet of men-of-war and more than fifty transports, on board of which were many armed negroes and Royal troops, to the mouth of the Piankatank river, and took possession of Gwynn's Island, where he landed his troops and entrenched. Here he was attacked by Gen. Lewis' men from the opposite shore. One of Dunmore's ships was badly damaged by cannon balls, and he drew off and sailed up the Potomoc river, and occupied St. Georgia's Island, after having burned a mansion at the mouth of Aqua Creek. He was here attacked by a militia force and retired. Misfortune followed him; disease, shipwreck and want of provisions. He soon made sail, and with his negroes reached England, where he remained.

fought, when our forts on Lake Champlain had been taken from us, and when Montgomery and Arnold were pressing on our possessions in Canada, Lord Dunmore carried his threat into execution. Having established his headquarters at Norfolk, he proclaimed freedom to all the slaves who would repair to his standard and bear arms for the King. The summons was readily obeyed by the most of the negroes who had the means of escape to him. He, at the same time, issued a proclamation, declaring martial law throughout the colony of Virginia; and he collected a number of armed vessels, which cut off the coasting trade, made many prizes, and greatly distressed an important part of that Province. If he could have opened a road to slaves in the interior of the Province, his measures would have been very fatal to the planters. In order to stop the alarming desertion of the negroes, and to arrest his Lordship in his career, the provincial Assembly detached against him a strong force of more than a thousand men, who arrived in the neighborhood of Norfolk in the month of December. Having made a circuit, they came to a village called Great Bridge, where the river Elizabeth was traversed by a bridge; but before their arrival the bridge had been made impassable, and some works, defended chiefly by negroes, had been thrown up."

During the same month Edmund Pendleton wrote to Richard Henry Lee that many slaves had flocked to the British standard:

"The Governor, * * * * marched out with three hundred and fifty soldiers, Tories and *slaves*, to Kemp's Landing; and after setting up his standard, and issuing his proclamation, declaring all persons rebels who took up arms for the country, and inviting all slaves, servants and apprentices to come to him and receive arms, he proceded to intercept Hutchings and his party, upon whom he came by surprise, but received, it seems, so warm a fire, that the ragmuffins ran away. They were, however, rallied on discovering that two companies of our militia gave away; and left Hutchings and Dr. Reid with a volunteer company, who maintained their ground bravely till they were overcome by numbers, and took shelter in a swamp. The slaves were sent in pursuit of them; and one of Col. Hutching's, with another, found him. On their approach, he discharged his pistol at his slave, but missed him; and he was taken by them, after receiving a wound in the face with a sword. The number taken or killed on either side is not ascertained. It is said the Governor went to Dr. Reid's shop, and after taking the medicines and dressing necessary for his wounded men, broke all the others to pieces. Letters mention that slaves flock to him in abundance: but I hope it is magnified."

Five months after he issued the proclamation, Lord Dunmore thus writes, concerning his success:

[No. 1]

"*Lord Dunmore to the Secretary of State.*

SHIP 'DUNMORE,' IN ELIZABETH RIVER, VA.,
30th March, 1776.

"Your Lordship will observe by my letter, No. 34, that I have been endeavoring to raise two regiments here— one of white people, the other of black. The former goes on very slowly, but the latter very well, and would have been in great forwardness, had not a fever crept in amongst them, which carried off a great many very fine fellows."

[No. 3]

"SHIP 'DUNMORE,' IN GWIN'S ISLAND HARBOR, VA.,
June 26, 1776.

"I am extremely sorry to inform your Lordship, that that fever of which I informed you in my letter No. 1 has proved a very malignant one, and has carried off an incredible number of our people, especially the blacks. Had it not been for this horrid disorder, I am satisfied I should have had no doubt of penetrating into the heart of this colony."

The dread in which the colonists held the negro was equal to that with which they regarded the Indians. The incendiary torch, massacre, pillage, and revolt, was ever presenting a gloomy and disastrous picture to the colonists at the South. Their dreams at night; their thoughts by day; in the field and in the legislature hall, were how to keep the negro down. If one should be seen in a village with a gun, a half score of white men would rush and take it from him, while women in the street would take shelter in the nearest house. The wrongs which they continued to practice upon him was a terror to them through their conscience, though then, as in later years, many, and particularly the leaders, endeavored to impress others with their feigned belief of the natural inferiority of the negro to themselves. This doctrine served them, as the whistle did the boy in the woods; they talked in that way simply to keep their courage up, and their conscience down.

The commander of the American army regarded the action of Lord Dunmore as a serious blow to the national cause. To take the negroes out of the field from raising produce for the army, and place them in front of the patriots as opposing soldiers, he saw was a danger that should be averted. With this in view he wrote to Joseph Reed in December, saying:

"If the Virginians are wise, that arch-traitor to the rights of humanity, Lord Dunmore, should be instantly crushed, if it takes the whole army to do it; otherwise, like a snowball in rolling, his army will get size, some through fear, some through promises, and some through inclination, joining his standard; but that which renders the measure indispensable is the negroes; for, if he gets formidable, numbers of them will be tempted to join, who will be afraid to do it without."

Notwithstanding this, the Southern States still kept the negro out of the army. It was not until affairs became alarmingly dangerous, and a few weeks before the adoption of the Declaration of Independence, that the subject of arming the slaves came again before the people.

In May, 1777, the General Assembly of Connecticut postponed in one house and rejected in the other the report of a committee "that the effective negro and mulatto slaves be allowed to enlist with the Continental battallions now raising in this State." But under a law passed at the same session "white and black, bond and free, if 'able bodied,' went on the roll together, accepted as the representatives of their 'class,' or as substitutes for their employers." At the next session (October, 1777), the law was so amended as to authorize the selectmen of any town, on the application of the master.—after 'inquiry into the age, abilities, circumstances, and character' of the servant or slave, and being satisfied 'that it was likely to be consistent with his real advantage, and that he would be able to support himself,'—to grant liberty for his emancipation, and to discharge the master 'from any charge or cost which may be occasioned by maintaining or supporting the servant or slave made free as aforesaid.' Mr. J. H. Trumbull, of Connecticut, in giving the foregoing facts, adds:

"The slave (or servant for term of years) might receive his freedom; the master might receive exemption from draft, and a discharge from future liabilities, to which he must otherwise have been subjected. In point of fact, some hundreds of blacks,—slaves and freemen,—were enlisted, from time to time, in the regiments of State troops and of the Connecticut line."

The British were determined, it seems, to utilize all the available strength they could command, by enlisting negroes at the North as well as at the South. They conceived the idea of forming regiments of them at the North, as the letter of Gen. Greene to Gen. Washington will show:

"CAMP ON LONG ISLAND, July 21, 1776, two o'clock.

"SIR:—Colonel Hand reports seven large ships are coming up from the Hook to the Narrows.

"A negro belonging to one Strickler, at Gravesend, was taken prisoner (as he says) last Sunday at Coney Island. Yesterday he made his escape, and was taken prisoner by the rifle guard. He reports eight hundred negroes collected on Staten Island, this day to be formed into a regiment.

I am your Excellency's most obedient, humble servant,

N. GREENE.

"To His Excellency Gen. Washington, Headquarters, New York."

Occasionally the public would be startled by the daring and bravery of some negro in the American army, and then the true lovers of liberty, North and South, would again urge that negroes be admitted into the ranks of the army. When Lt.-Col. Barton planned for the capture of the British Maj.-Gen. Prescott, who commanded the British army at Newport R. I., and whose capture was necessary in order to effect the release of Gen. Lee, who was then in the hands of the British, and of the same rank as that of Gen. Prescott, Col. Barton's plan was made a success through the aid of Prince, a negro in Col. Barton's command. The daring of the exploit excited the highest patriotic commendations of the Americans, and revived the urgent appeals that had been made for a place in the armed ranks for all men, irrespective of color. The Pennsylvania Evening *Post* of Aug. 7th, 1777, gives the following account of the capture:

"They landed about five miles from Newport, and three quarters of a mile from the house, which they approached cautiously, avoiding the main guard, which was at some distance. *The Colonel went foremost, with a stout active negro close behind him, and another at a small distance; the rest followed so as to be near but not seen.*

"A single sentinel at the door saw and hailed the Colonel; he answered by exclaiming against and inquiring for, rebel prisoners, but kept slowly advancing. The sentinel again challenged him and required the countersign. He said he had not the countersign; but amused the sentry by talking about rebel prisoners, and still advancing till he came within reach of the bayonet, which, he presenting, the colonel struck aside, and seized him. He was immediately secured, and ordered to be silent, on pain of instant death. *Meanwhile, the rest of the men surrounding the house, the negro, with his head, at the second stroke, forced a passage into it, and then into the landlord's apartment. The landlord at first refused to give the necessary intelligence; but, on the prospect of present death, he pointed to the General's chamber, which being instantly opened by the negro's head, the Colonel, calling the General by name, told him he was a prisoner.*"

Congress voted Col. Barton a magnificent sword, but the real captor of Gen. Prescott, so far as known, received nothing. A surgeon in the American army, Dr. Thacher, writes, under date of Aug. 3d, 1777, at Albany:

"The pleasing information is received here that Lieut.-Col. Barton, of the Rhode Island Militia, planned a bold exploit for the purpose of surprising and taking Maj.-Gen. Prescott, the commanding officer of the Royal army at Newport. Taking with him, in the night, about forty men, in two boats, with oars muffled, he had the address to elude the vigilance of the ships-of-war and guard boats; and, having arrived undiscovered at the quarters of Gen. Prescott, they were taken for the sentinels; and the general was not alarmed till the captors were at the door of his lodging chamber, which was fast closed. *A negro man, named Prince, instantly thrust his beetle head through the panel door, and seized his victim while in bed.* This event is extremely honorable to the enterprising spirit of Col. Barton, and is considered an ample retaliation for the capture of Gen. Lee by Col. Harcourt. The event occasions great joy and exultation, as it puts in our possession an officer of equal rank with Gen. Lee, by which means an exchange may be obtained. Congress resolved that an elegant sword should be presented to Col. Barton, for his brave exploit."

To recite here every incident and circumstance illustrating the heroism and the particular services rendered the patriotic army by negroes, who served in regiments and companies with white soldiers, would fill this entire volume. Yet, with the desire of doing justice to the memory of all those negroes who aided in achieving the independence of America, I cannot forbear introducing notices, —gathered from various sources,—of some prominent examples.

Ebenezer Hill, a slave at Stonington, Conn., who served throughout the war, and who took part in the battles of Saratoga and Stillwater, and witnessed the surrender of Burgoyne.

Prince Whipple acted as bodyguard to General Whipple, one of Washington's aids. Prince is the negro seen on horseback in the engraving of Washington crossing the Delaware, and again pulling the stroke oar in the boat which Washington crossed in.

At the storming of Fort Griswold, Maj. Montgomery was lifted upon the walls of the fort by his soldiers, and called upon the Americans to surrender. John Freeman, a negro soldier, with his pike, pinned him dead to the earth. Among the American soldiers who were massacred by the British soldiers, after the surrender of the fort, were two negro soldiers, Lambo Latham and Jordan Freeman.

Quack Matrick, a negro, fought through the Revolutionary war, as a soldier, for which he was pensioned. Also Jonathan Overtin, who was at the battle of Yorktown. The grandfather of the historian Wm. Wells Brown, Simon Lee, was also a soldier "in the times which tried mens souls."

"Samuel Charlton was born in the State of New Jersey, a slave, in the familv of Mr. M., who owned, also, other members belonging to his family—all residing in the English neighborhood. During the progress of the war, he was placed by his master (as a substitnte for himself) in the army then in New Jersey, as a teamster in the baggage train. He was in active service at the battle of Monmouth, not only witnessing, but taking a part in, the great struggle of that day. He was also in several other engagements in different sections of that part of the State. He was a great admirer of General Washington, and was, at one time, attached to his baggage train, and received the General's commendation for his courage and devotion to the cause of liberty. Mr. Charlton was about fifteen or seventeen years of age when placed in the army, for which his master rewarded him with a silver dollar. At the expiration of his time, he returned to his master, to serve again in bondage, after having toiled, fought and bled for liberty, in common with the regular soldiery. Mr. M., at his death, by will, liberated his slaves, and provided a pension for Charlton, to be paid during his lifetime.

"James Easton, of Bridgewater, a colored man, participated in the erection of the fortifications on Dorchester Heights, under command of Washington, which the next morning so greatly surprised the British soldiers then encamped in Boston."

"Among the brave blacks who fought in the battles for American liberty was Major Jeffrey, a Tennesseean, who, during the campaign of Major-General Andrew Jackson in Mobile, filled the place of "regular" among the soldiers. In the charge made by General Stump against the enemy, the Americans were repulsed and thrown into disorder,—Major Stump being forced to retire, in a manner by no means desirable, under the circumstances. Major Jeffrey, who was but a common soldier, seeing the condition of his comrades, and comprehending the disastrous results about to befall them, rushed forward, mounted a horse, took command of the troops, and, by an heroic effort, rallied them to the charge,—completely routing the enemy, who left the Americans masters of the field. He at once received from the General the title of "Major," though he could not, according to the American policy, so commission him. To the day of his death, he was known by that title in Nashville, where he resided, and the circumstances which entitled him to it were constantly the subject of popular conversation.

Major Jeffrey was highly respected by the whites generally, and revered, in his own neighborhood, by all the colored people who knew him.

A few years ago receiving an indignity from a common ruffian, he was forced to strike him in self-defense; for which act, in accordance with the laws of slavery in that, as well as many other of the slave States, he was compelled to receive, on his naked person, *nine and thirty lashes with a raw hide!* This, at the age of seventy odd, after the distinguished services rendered his country,—probably when the white ruffian for whom he was tortured was unable to raise an arm in its defense,—was more than he could bear; *it broke his heart*, and he sank to rise no more, till summoned by the blast of the last trumpet to stand on the battle-field of the general resurrection."

Jeffrey was not an exception to this kind of treatment. Samuel Lee died on a tobacco plantation after the war.

The re-enslaving of the negroes who fought for American Independence became so general at the South, that the Legislature of Virginia in 1783, in compliance with her honor, passed an act directing the emancipation of certain slaves, who had served as soldiers of the State, and for the emancipation of the slave Aberdeen.

James Armistead during the war acted as a scout and spy for LaFayette during his campaign in Virginia, and at one time gave information of an intended surprise to be made upon the forces of the Marquis, thereby saving probably a rout of the army. Armistead, after the surrender of Cornwallis at Yorktown, was returned to his master three years after the close of the war. He was manumitted by especial act of the Virginia Legislature, whose attention was called to the worthiness of the service rendered by Armistead.

The opposition to the employment of negroes as soldiers, by the persistency of its advocates and the bravery of those who were then serving in white regiments, was finally overcome, so that their enlistment became general and regulated by law. Companies, battalions and regiments of negro troops soon entered the field and the struggle for independence and liberty, giving to the cause the reality of freedmen's fight. For three years the army had been fighting under the smart of defeats, with an occasional signal victory, but now the tide was about to be turned against the English. The colonists had witnessed the heroism of the negro in Virginia at Great Bridge, and at Norfolk; in Massachusetts at Boston and Bunker Hill, fighting, in the former, for freedom under the British flag, in the latter for liberty, under the banner of the colonies. The echoing shouts of the whites fell heavily upon the ears of the black people; they caught the strain as by martial instinct, and reverberated the appeal, "*Liberty and Independence.*"

The negro's ancestors were not slaves, so upon the alter of their hearts the fire of liberty was re-kindled by the utterances of the white colonists. They heard Patrick Henry and Samuel Adams, whose eloquence vehemently aroused their compatriots, and, like them, they too resolved to be free. They held no regular organized meetings; at the North they assembled with their white fellow-citizens; at the South each balmy gale that swept along the banks of the rivers were laden with the negro's ejaculations for freedom, and each breast was resolute and determined. The advocates and friends of the measure for arming all men for freedom, were on the alert, and now the condition of the army was such as to enable them to press the necessity of the measure upon the attention of the American people. Washington needed reinforcements; nay, more, the perilous situation of the army as it lay in camp at Valley Forge, at the conclusion of the campaign of 1777, was indeed distressing. The encampment consisted of huts, and there was danger of a famine. The soldiers were nearly destitute of comfortable clothing. "Many," says the historian, "for want of shoes, walked barefoot on the frozen ground; few, if any, had blankets for the night. Great numbers sickened; near three thousand at a time were incapable of bearing arms."

Within fifteen miles of them lay the city of Philadelphia and the British army. These gloomy circumstances overshadowed the recent victory at Bennington, and the surrender of Burgoyne. Under these circumstances, the difficulty of recruiting the patriot army may be easily imagined. A general enlistment bill had failed to pass the legislature in the spring, because, perhaps, the spirit of the patriots were up at the time; but now they were down, and the advocates of arming negroes sought the opportunity of carrying their plan. It was not attempted in Connecticut, but in the General Assembly of Rhode Island an act was passed for the purpose. Here are some of the principal provisions of this act:

"*It is Voted and Resolved,* That every able-bodied negro, mulatto, or Indian man slave in this State, may enlist into either of the said two battalions to serve during the continuance of the present war with Great Britain; that every slave so enlisted shall be entitled to receive all the bounties, wages, encouragements allowed by the Continentlal Congress to any soldier enlisted into their service.

"*It is further Voted and Resolved,* That every slave so enlisting shall, upon his passing muster before Col. Christopher Greene, be immediately discharged from the service of his master or mistress, and be absolutely free, as though he had never been encumbered with any kind of servitude or slavery. And in case such slave shall, by sickness or otherwise, be unable to maintain himself, he shall not be chargable to his master or mistress, but shall be supported at the expense of the State.

"And whereas slaves have been by the laws deemed the property of their owners; and therefore compensation ought to be made to the owners for the loss of their service,—

"*It is further Voted and Resolved,* That there be allowed, and paid by this State to the owners, for every such slave so enlisting, a sum according to his worth at a price not exceediug one hundred and twenty pounds for the most valuable slave, and in proportion for a slave of less value; *Provided* the owner of said slave shall deliver up to the officer who shall enlist him the clothes of said slave; or otherwise he shall not be entitled to said sum."

ON PICKET

To speak of the gallantry of the negro soldiers recalls the recollection of some of their daring deeds at Red Bank, where four hundred men met and repulsed, after a terrible, sanguinary struggle, fifteen hundred Hessian troops led by Count Donop.

"The glory of the defence of Red Bank, which has been pronounced one of the most heroic actions of the war, belongs in reality to black men; yet who now hears them spoken of in connection with it? Among the traits which distinguished the black regiment was devotion to their officers. In the attack made upon the American lines, near Croton river, on the 13th of May, 1781, Col. Greene, the commander of the regiment, was cut down and mortally wounded; but the sabres of the enemy only reached him through the bodies of his faithful blacks, who gathered around him to protect him, *and every one of whom was killed.*"

Now the negro began to take the field; not scattered here and there throughout the army, filling up the shattered ranks of white regiments, but in organizations composed entirely of men of their own race, officered, however, by white officers, men of high social and military character and standing. The success of the measure in Rhode Island, emboldened the effort in Massachusetts, where the advocates of separate negro organizations had been laboring zealously for its accomplishment. Officers of the army in the field, expressed their desire to be placed in command of negro troops, in separate and distinct organizations. Every effort, however, up to this time to induce Massachusetts to consent to the proposition had failed. Rhode Island alone sent her negro regiments to the field, whose gallantry during the war more than met the most sanguine expectations of their warmest friends, and fully merited the trust and confidence of the State and country. As the struggle proceeded, re-enforcements were more frequently in demand; but recruits were scarce, and the question of arming negroes became again prominent in the colonies and the army.

In April, 1778, Thomas Kench, then serving in an artillery regiment, addressed letters to the Massachusetts Legislature urging the enlistment of negroes. He wrote:

"A re-enforcement can quickly be raised of two or three hundred men. Will your honors grant the liberty, and give me the command of the party? And what I refer to is negroes. We have divers of them in our service, mixed with white men. But I think it would be more proper to raise a body by themselves, than to have them intermixed with the white men; and their ambition would entirely be to outdo the white men in every measure that the fortunes of war calls a soldier to endure. And I could rely with dependence upon them in the field of battle or to any post that I was sent to defend with them; and they would think themselves happy could they gain their freedom by bearing a part of subduing the enemy that is invading our land, and clear a peaceful inheritance for their masters, and posterity yet to come, that they are now slaves to."

The letter from which this extract was made was duly referred to a joint committee "to consider the same and report." Some days later "a resolution of the General Assembly of Rhode Island for enlisting negroes in the public service" was referred to the same committee. They duly reported the draft of a law, differing little from the Rhode Island Resolution. A separate organization of negro companies, by Kench, does not appear to have been deemed advisable at that time. The usage was continued of "taking," in the words of Kench, "negroes in our service, intermixed with the white men."

The negroes of Boston and their abolition friends, rather insisted upon the intermingling of the races in the army, believing that this course had a greater tendency to destroy slavery, and the inequality of rights among the blacks and whites; though it deprived the negroes, as we now see, of receiving due credit for their valor, save in a few individual cases. It was not in Massachusetts alone, but in many other States that the same idea prevailed; and now the facts connected with the services of the negroes are to be gathered only in fragments, from the histories of villages and towns, or among the archives of the State, in a disconnected and unsatisfactory form.

The legislature of New York, two months after the murder of Col. Greene and his faithful negro troops at Point's Bridge, in that State, by the British, passed an act (March, 1781) looking to the raising of two regiments. The sixth section of the act reads as follows:

"And it is further enacted by the authority aforesaid, that any person who shall deliver one or more of his able-bodied male slaves to any warrant officer, as aforesaid, to serve in either of the above regiments or independent corps, and produce a certificate thereof, signed by any person authorized to muster and receive the men to be raised by virtue of this act, and produce such certificate to the Surveyor-General, shall, for every male slave so entered and mustered as aforesaid, be entitled to the location and grant of one right, in manner as in and by this act is directed; and shall be, and hereby is discharged from any further maintainance of such slave, any law to the contrary notwithstanding. And such slave so entering as aforesaid, who shall serve for the term of three years or until regularly discharged, shall, immediately after such service or discharge, be, and is hereby declared to be, a free man of this State.

In 1821, in the convention which revised the constitution of New York, Mr. Clark, speaking in favor of allowing negroes to vote, said in the course of his remarks:

"My honorable colleague has told us, that, as the colored people are not required to contribute to the protection or defence of the State, they are not entitled to an equal participation in the privileges of its citizens. But, Sir, whose fault is this? Have they ever refused to do military duty when called upon? It is haughtily asked, Who will stand in the ranks shoulder to shoulder with a negro? I answer, No one, in time of peace; no one, when your musters and trainings are looked upon as mere pastimes; no one, when your militia will shoulder their muskets and march to their trainings with as much unconcern as they would go to a sumptuous entertainment or a splendid ball. But, Sir, when the hour of danger approaches, your white 'militia' are just as willing that the man of color should be set up as a mark to be shot at by the enemy, as to be set up themselves. In the War of the Revolution, these people helped to fight your battles by land and by sea. Some of your States were glad to turn out corps of colored men, and to stand 'shoulder to shoulder' with them.

"In your late war, they contributed largely towards some of your most splendid victories. On Lakes Erie and Champlain, where your fleets triumped over a foe superior in numbers and engines of death, they were manned, in a large proportion, with men of color. And, in this very house, in the fall of 1814, a bill passed, receiving the approbation of all the branches of your government, authorizing the Governor to accept the services of a corps of two thousand free people of color. Sir, these were times which tried men's souls. In these times it was no sporting matter to bear arms. These were times, when a man who shouldered his musket did not know but he barred his bosom to receive a death wound from the enemy ere he laid it aside; and in these times, these people were found as ready and as willing to volunteer in your service as any other. They were not compelled to go; they were not drafted. No, your pride had placed them beyond your compulsory power. But there was no necessity for its exercise; they were volunteers; yes, Sir, volunteers to defend that very country from the inroads and ravages of a ruthless and vindictive foe, which had treated them with insult, degradation and slavery.

"Volunteers are the best of soldiers. Give me the men, whatever be their complexion, that willingly volunteer, and not those who are compelled to turn out. Such men do not fight from necessity, nor from mercinary motives, but from principle."

Hon. Mr. Martindale, who represented a District of the State of New York, in Congress in 1828, thus speaks of the negro soldiers:

"Slaves, or negroes who have been slaves, were enlisted as soldiers in the War of the Revolution; and I myself saw a battalion of them, as fine martial-looking men as I ever saw, attached to the Northern army."

Up to this time the East had been the theatre of the war, with now and then a battle in some one of the Middle Colonies, but the British discovering that the people of the South acted indifferently in maintaining and recruiting the army, transferred their operations to that section. Maryland then stood as a middle State or Colony. Her statesmen, seeing the threatened danger of the invasion of Pennsylvania, endeavored to prepare to meet it, and taking council from her sister States at the East, accepted the negro as a soldier. In June, 1781, John Cadwater, writing from Annapolis, Md., to Gen. Washington, says:

"We have resolved to raise, immediately, seven hundred and fifty negroes, to be incorporated with the other troops; and a bill is now almost completed."

It does not appear that the negroes were formed into separate organizations in this State, but filled the depleted ranks of the Continental regiments, where their energy and daring was not less than that displayed by their white comrades, with whom they fought, shoulder to shoulder. The advocates of arming the negroes were not confined to the Eastern and Middle sections; some of the best men of the South favored and advocated the enlistment of free negroes, and made many, though for a long time unsuccessful, efforts to obtain legal sanction for such enlistment throughout the South. But their advice was not listened to, even in the face of certain invasion, and then the whites would not, and could not be induced to rally to the defence of their own particular section and homes.

For fear that I may be accused of too highly coloring the picture of the Southern laxity of fervor and patriotism, I quote from the valuable essay which accompanies the history of the American Loyalists:

"The whole number of regulars enlisted for the Continental service, from the beginning to the close of the struggle, was 231,959. Of these, I have once remarked, 67.907 were from Massachusetts; and I may now add, that every State south of Pennsylvania provided but 59;493, or 8,414 *less* than this single State."

The men of Massachusetts did not more firmly adhere to their policy of mixed troops as against separate organizations, based upon color, than did the men of the South to their peculiar institution, and against the arming of negroes, free or slave. The war having fairly set in upon Southern soil, and so urgent the necessity for recruiting the army, that Congress again took up the subject of enrolling negroes as soldiers. It was decided that the general Government had no control over the States in the matter, but a series of resolutions were adopted recommending to the States of Georgia and South Carolina, the arming of three thousand able-bodied negroes.

Now began an earnest battle for the carrying out of the policy, as recommended by Congress. Its friends were among the bravest and truest to the cause of freedom in the States. Hon. Henry Laurens lead in the effort. Even before the matter was brought to the attention of Congress, he wrote to Gen. Washington, as follows:

"Our affairs in the Southern department are more favorable than we had considered them a few days ago; nevertheless, the country is greatly distressed, and will be so unless further re-inforcements are sent to its relief. Had we arms for three thousand such black men as I could select in Carolina, I should have no doubt of success in driving the British out of Georgia, and subduing East Florida before the end of July."

Washington knew the temper of the Southerners. He was well aware that slaves could not be entrusted with arms within sight of the enemy's camp, and within hearing of his proclamation of freedom to all who would join his Majesty's standard, unless equal inducements were offered them by the colonists, and to this he knew the Southern colonist would not consent. In his reply to Mr. Laurens, he said:

"The policy of our arming slaves, is, in my opinion a moot point, unless the enemy set the example. For, should we begin to form battalions of them, I have not the smallest doubt, if the war is to be prosecuted, of their following us in it, and justifying the measure upon our own ground. The contest then must be, who can arm fastest. And where are our arms? Besides, I am not clear that a discrimination will not render slavery more irksome to those who remain in it. Most of the good and evil things in this life are judged of by comparison; and I fear a comparison in this case will be productive of much discontent in those who are held in servitude. But, as this is a subject that has never employed much of my thoughts, these are no more than the first crude ideas that have struck me upon the occasion."

Washington certainly had no doubts as to the value of the negro as a soldier, but for the reasons stated, did not give the weight of his influence, at this important juncture, to the policy of their enlistment, while so many of the leading men of the colonies were favorable to the action.

Among those who advocated the raising of negro troops was Col. John Laurens, a native of South Carolina and a brave patriot, who had acted as aide-de-camp to the commander-in-chief, and had seen service in Rhode Island and elsewhere. He was the son of Hon. Henry Laurens, at one time President of Congress, and was noted for his high qualities of character. A commission of lieutenant-colonel was granted to him by Congress, and he proceeded to South Carolina to use his personal influence to induce the Legislature to authorize the enlistment of negroes. His services in Rhode Island had given him an opportunity to witness the conduct and worth of the negro soldier.

Alexander Hamilton in the course of a long letter to John Jay, relating to the mission of Col. Laurens to South Carolina, says:

"I foresee that this project will have to combat much opposition from prejudice and self-interest. The contempt we have been taught to entertertain for the blacks makes us fancy many things that are founded neither in reason nor experience; and an unwillingness to part company with property of so valuable a kind wlll furnish a thousand arguments to show the impracticability or pernicious tendency of a scheme which requires such a sacrifice. But it should be considered, that, if we do not make use of them in this way, the enemy probably will; and that the best way to counteract the the temptations they will hold out will be to offer them ourselves. An essential part of the plan is to give them their freedom with their muskets. This will secure their fidelity, animate their courage, and, I believe, will have a good influence upon those who remain, by opening a door to their emancipation. This circumstance, I confess has no small weight in inducing me to wish the success of the project; for the dictates of humanity and true policy, equally interest me in favor of this unfortunate class of men."

The patriotic zeal of Col. Laurens for the accomplishment of his design was earnest and conscientious. He wrote to his friend Hamilton in these words:

"Ternant will relate to you how many violent struggles I have had between duty and inclination—how much my heart was with you, while I appeared to be most actively employed here. But it appears to me, that I should be inexcusable in the light of a citizen, if I did not continue my utmost efforts for carrying the plan of the black levies into execution, while there remains the smallest hope of success."

The condition of the colonies and the Continental army at that time was critical in the extreme. The campaign of 1779 had closed gloomily for the Americans. The British had not only been active in raiding in Virginia and destroying property, but in organizing negro troops. Lord Dunmore, as we have seen, as early as November, 1775, had issued a proclamation, inviting the negroes to join the Royal forces, to which a great many slaves responded, and were organized into companies. A regiment had been organized by the British on Long Island in 1776, and now, Sir Henry Clinton invited them by the following proclamation:

"By his Excellency Sir Henry Clinton, K. B., General and Commander-in-Chief of all his Majesty's Forces, within the Colonies lying on the Atlantic Ocean, from Nova Scotia to West Florida, inclusive, &c., &c.

PROCLAMATION.

"Whereas the enemy have adopted a practice of enrolling *Negroes* among their *Troops*, I do hereby give notice *That* all Negroes taken in arms, or upon any military *Duty*, shall be purchased for *the public service* at a stated *Price*; the money to be paid to the *Captors*.

"But I do most strictly forbid any *Person* to sell or claim *Right* over any Negro, the property of a Rebel, who may take refuge in any part of this *Army*: And I do promise to every negro who shall desert the *Rebel Standard*, full security to follow within these *Lines*, any Occupation which he shall think proper.

"Given under my Hand at Head-Quarters, Philipsburg, the 30th day of June, 1779. H. CLINTON.

"By his Excellency's command, John Smith, Secretary."

It is highly probable that many negroes made their way to the British camp. Col. Laurens wrote to General Washington, under date of February, 1780, six months after the issuing of Sir Henry Clinton's proclamation, as follows:

"Private accounts say that General Provost is left to command at Savannah; that his troops consist of Hessians and Loyalists that were there before, *re-inforced by a corps of blacks and a detachment of savages*. It is generally reported that Sir. Henry Clinton commands the present expedition."

Clinton left New York in the latter part of 1779, for the reduction of Charleston, which he completed in May, three months after the date of Col. Laurens' letter. Gen. Lincoln, who commanded the American forces at Charleston, joined in the effort to arm the negroes. In a letter to Gov. Rutledge, dated Charleston, March 13th, 1780, he says:

"Give me leave to add once more, that I think the measure of raising a black corps a necessary one; that I have great reason to believe, if permission is given for it, that many men would soon be obtained. I have repeatedly urged this matter, not only because Congress has recommended it, and because it thereby becomes my duty to attempt to have it executed, but because my own mind suggests the ulility and importance of the measure, as the safety of the town maks it necessary.

The project of raising negro troops gained some friends in all sections, and Statesmen, both South and North, as they talked about it, became more free to express their approbation of the measure. They had witnessed the militia from Virginia and North Carolina, at the battle of Camden, throw down their arms before the enemy;* they had seen black and white troops under com-

* At the first, onset, a large body of the Virginia militia, under a charge of the British infantry with fixed bayonets, threw down their arms and fled. A considerable part of the North Carolina militia followed their unworthy example. But the Conti-

mand of Gen. Provost occupy Savannah; the surrender of Charlestown had become necessary; and these evils were all brought about by the apathy of the white inhabitants.

Among those who spoke out in favor of Col. Laurens' and Gen. Lincoln's plan, was Hon. James Madison, who, on the 20th of November, 1780, wrote to Joseph Jones:

"I am glad to find the Legislature persisting in their resolution to recruit their line of the army for the war; though, without deciding on the expediency of the mode under their consideration, would it not be as well to liberate and make soldiers at once of the blacks themselves, as to make them instruments for enlisting white soldiers? It would certainly be more consonant with the principles of liberty: and, with white officers and a majority of white soldiers, no imaginable danger could be feared from themselves; as there certainly could be none from the effect of the example on those who should remain in bondage; experience having shown that a freedman immediately loses all attachment and sympathy with his former fellow slaves."

No circumstances under which the South was placed, could induce either their legislators or the people to adopt the recommendations of Congress or the advice of the patriots and statesmen of their section. The opposition to the arming of the negroes was much stronger than the love for independence. The British, however, adopted the plan, and left no stone unturned to augment the strength of their army. Thousands of negroes flocked to the Royal standard at every opportunity, just as in the war of the Rebellion in 1861-'65, they sought freedom under the national banner.

It has ever been the rule among American historians to omit giving credit to those negroes who sought to gain their freedom by joining the British. They have generally also failed to acknowledge the valor of those who swelled the ranks of the Continental army. Enough, however, can be gathered, mostly from private correspondence, to show that the hope of success for the Americans rested either in the docility of the negroes at the South, or in their loyalty to the cause of Independence. At all events, upon the action of the blacks more than upon the brav-

nentals evinced the most unyielding firmness, and pressed forward with unusual ardor. Never did men acquit themselves more honorably. They submitted only when forsaken by their brethren in arms, and when overpowered by numuers.

ery and valor of the American troops, depended the future status of the Colonies; hence the solicitude of officers and of the leading citizens; and it was not the love of universal freedom, which prompted their efforts for arming negroes; not at all, but their keen appreciation of the value of a neutral power, which could be utilized for the benefit of America's Independence. Nor do I attribute other than the same motive to the British, who did arm and did free a great many of the negroes, who joined their service, especially at the South, where they must have organized quite a large force,—not less than 5,000. Early in 1781, (Feb'y) Gen. Greene, then in command in North Carolina, writing to General Washington about the doings of the enemy in South Carolina, where he formally commanded, says:

"The enemy have ordered two regiments of negroes to be immediately embodied, and are drafting a great portion of the young men of that State [South Carolina], to serve during the war."

A few days after writing this letter, Gen. Greene met the British at Guilford Court House, and again witnessed the cowardice of the Southern militia,* whose conduct gave victory to the British, under Cornwallis.

The persistency of Col. Laurens in his effort to organize negro troops, was still noteworthy. Having returned from France, whither he went on important business, connected with the welfare of the States, he resumed his "favorite pursuit." Under date of May, 19, 1782, in a letter addressed to Washington, he says:

"The plan which brought me to this country was urged with all the zeal which the subject inspired, both in our Privy Council and Assembly; but the single voice of reason was drowned by the howling of a triple-headed monster, in which prejudice, avarice, and pusillanimity were united. It was some degree of consolation to me, however, to perceive that the truth and philosophy had gained some ground; the suffrages in favor of the measure being twice as numerous as on a former occasion. Some hopes have been lately given me from Georgia; but I fear, when

* The British loss, in this battle, exceeded five hundred in killed and wounded, among whom were several of the most distinguished officers. The American loss was about four hundred, in killed and wounded, of which more than three-fourths fell upon the Continentals. Though the numericial force of Gen. Greene nearly doubled that of Cornwallis, yet, when we consider the difference between these forces; the shameful conduct of the North Carolina militia, who fled at the first fire; the desertion of the second Maryland regiment, and that a body of reserve was not brought into action, it will appear that our numbers, actually engaged, but little exceeded that of the enemy."—*Grimshaw's U. S. History.*

the question is put, we shall be out-voted there with as much disparity as we have been in this country.

* * * * * *

"I earnestly desire to be where any active plans are likely to be executed, and to be near your Excellency on all occasions in which my services can be acceptable. The pursuit of an object which, I confess, is a favorite one with me, because I always regarded the interests of this country and those of the Union as intimately connected with it, has detached me more than once from your family, but those sentiments of veneration and attachments with which your Excellency has inspired me, keep me always near you, with the sincerest and most zealous wishes for a continuance of your happiness and glory."

Here ended the project of arming negroes in South Carolina, and before an earnest effort could be made in Georgia, the brave man laid his life upon the altar of American liberty.

But to show the state of public opinion at the South, as understood by the Commander-in-Chief of the American army, we have but to read Washington's reply to Col. Laurens' last letter, in which he speaks of "making a last effort" in Georgia. Gen. Washington uses this emphatic language:

"I must confess that I am not at all astonished at the failure of your plan. That spirit of freedom, which, at the commencement of this contest, would have gladly sacrificed everything to the attainment of its object, has long since subsided, and every selfish passion has taken its place. It is not the public but private interest which influences the generality of mankind; nor can the Americans any longer boast an exception. Under the circumstances, it would rather have been surprising if you had succeeded; nor will you, I fear, have better success in Georgia."

This letter settles forever any boast of the Southerners, that to them is due the credit of gaining the independence of the United States. It is true Cornwallis' surrender at Yorktown, Va., was the last of the series of battles fought for independence.* But we must remember that the

* The Burlington *Gazette*, in an issue of some time ago, gives the following account of an aged negro Revolutionary patriot: "The attention of many of our citizens has doubtless been arrested by the appearance of an old colored man, who might have been seen, sitting in front of his residence, in east Union street, respectfully raising his hat to those who might be passing by. His attenuated frame, his silvered head, his feeble movements, combine to prove that he is very aged: and yet, comparatively few are aware that he is among the survivors of the gallant army who fought for the liberties of our country.

"On Monday last, we stopped to speak to him, and asked how old he was. He asked the day of the month, and upon being told, that it was the 24th of May, replied, with trembling lips, 'I am very old—I am a hundred years old to-day.'

"His name is Oliver Cromwell, and he says that he was born at the Black Horse,

French were at Yorktown. It cannot be doubted but that from Charleston to Yorktown the Americans met negro troops more than once fighting under the Royal flag; while at the east, in every important engagement between the two enemies,—British and American,—the negro was found fighting with the Americans. This division of the negroes can easily be accounted for, since at the North and East the object of the war was acknowledged to be set forth in the Declaration of Independence; at the South only so much of the Declaration was accepted as demanded Independence from Great Britain. Therefore, though in separate and opposing armies, the object of the negro was the same—liberty. It is to be regretted that the historians of the Revolutionary period did not more particularly chronicle the part taken by negroes at the South, though enough is known to put their employment beyond doubt.

Johnson, the author of the life of Gen. Greene, speaking of Greene's recommendation to the Legislature of South Carolina to enroll negroes, says:

> "There is a sovereign, who, at this time, draws his soldiery from the same class of people; and finds a facility in forming and disciplining an army, which no other power enjoys. Nor does his immense military force, formed from that class of his subjects, excite the least apprehension; for the soldier's will is subdued to that of his officer, and his improved condition takes away the habit of identifying himself with the class from which he has been separated. Military men know what mere machines men become under discipline, and believe that any men, who may be obedient, may be made soldiers; and that increasing their numbers increases the means of their own subjection and government."

(now Columbus), in this county, in the family of John Hutchins. He enlisted in a company commanded by Capt. Lowry, attached to the Second New Jersey Regiment, under the command of Col. Israel Shreve. He was at the battles of Trenton, Brandywine, Princetown, Mommouth, and Yorktown, at which latter place, he told us, he saw the last man killed. Although his faculties are failing, yet he relates many interesting reminiscences of the Revolution. He was with the army at the retreat of the Delaware, on the memorable crossing of the 25th of December, 1776, and relates the story of the battle on the succeeding day, with enthusiasm. He gives the details of the march from Trenton to Princetown, and told us, with much humor, that they 'knocked the British around lively,' at the latter place. He was also at the battle of Springfield, and says that he saw the house burning in which Mrs. Caldwell was shot, at Connecticut Farms."

"I further learn, (says the author of the 'Colored Patriots of the Revolution'), that Cromwell was brought up a farmer, having served his time with Thomas Hutchins, Esq., his maternal uncle. He was, for six years and nine months under the immediate command of Washington, whom he loved affectionately."

"His discharge," says Dr. M'Cune Smith, "at the close of the war, was in Washington's own handwriting, of which he was very proud, often speaking of it. He received annually, ninety-six dollars pension. He lived a long and honorable life. Had he been of a little lighter complexion, (he was just half white), every newspaper in the land would have been eloquent in praise of his many virtues."

Cornwallis doubtless had gathered within his lines a large number of negroes, to whose energy and labor, the erection of his breastworks were mainly due. Lafayette feeling satisfied that the position of his army before Yorktown would confine the British, and make the escape of Cornwallis impossible without battle, wrote to Gen. Washington in September:

"I hope you will find we have taken the best precautions to lessen his Lordship's escape. I hardly believe he will make the attempt. If he does, he must give up ships, artillery, baggage, part of his horses, and all the negroes."

All this time in some of the Northern States an opposition as strong as at the South had existed against organizing negro troops, and in some instances even against employing them as soldiers. The effort for separate organizations had been going on, but with only the little success that has been already noticed. In a biographical sketch of Col. David Humphreys, in the "National Portrait Gallery of Distinguished Americans," is the following:

"In November, 1782, he was, by resolution of Congress, commissioned as a Lieutenant-Colonel, with order that his commission should bear date from the 23rd of June, 1780, when he received his appointment as aid-de-camp to the Commander-in-Chief. He had, when in active service, given the sanction of his name and influence in the establishment of a company of colored infantry, attached to Meigs', afterwards Butler's, regiment, in the Connecticut line. He continued to be the nominal captain of that company until the establishment of peace."

Though the Legislature of Connecticut had taken up the subject of arming negroes generally, as early as 1777, and a bill, as we have seen, was presented to that Legislature, for their enrollment, the advocates of the measure, in every attempt to pass it, had been beaten. Nevertheless, as appears by the record given above, Col. Humphrey took charge and organized a company, with which he served until the close of the war. But this company of fifty odd men were not all that did service in the army from Connecticut, for in many of her white regiments, negroes, bond and free, stood in the ranks with the whites. And, notwithstanding the unsuccessful attempts of Col. Laurens and the advocates of negro soldiery at the South, the negro was an attache of the Southern army, and rendered efficient aid during the struggle, in building breastworks, driving teams and piloting the army through dense woods, swamps, and across rivers. Not a few were spies and drummers. To select or point out a particular battle or seige, in which they rendered active service to the British, would not be a difficult task, though the information at hand is too limited for a detailed account of the part which they bore in these struggles. The true patriots of the Revolution were not slow in according to their black compatriots that meed of praise which was their due. In almost every locality, either North or South, after the war, there lived one or two privileged negroes, who, on great occasions,—days of muster, 4th of July, Washington's birthday, and the like,—were treated with more than ordinary courtesy by the other people. That a great and dastardly wrong was committed upon many, in like manner in which Simon Lee* was treated, is true. Many negroes at the South, who fought for American independence were re-enslaved, and this is so far beyond a doubt that no one denies it. The re-enslaving of these soldiers,—not by those who took part in the conflict, but the *stay-at-home's*,—was so flagrant an outrage that the Legislature of Virginia, in 1783, in order to give freedom to those who had been re-enslaved, and to rebuke the injustice of the treatment, passed the following act:

An Act directing the Emancipation of certain Slaves who had served as as Soldiers in this State, and for the Emancipation of the Slave, Aberdeen.

"I. Whereas, it hath been represented to the present General Assembly, that, during the course of the war, many persons in this State had caused their slaves to enlist in certain regiments or corps, raised within the same, having tendered such slaves to the officers appointed to recruit forces within the State, as substitutes for free persons whose lot or duty it was to serve in such regiments or corps, at the same time rep-

* Simon Lee, the grandfather of William Wells Brown, on his mother's side, was a slave in Virginia, and served in the war of the Revolution. Although honorably discharged, with the other Virginia troops, at the close of the war, he was sent back to his master, where he spent the remainder of his life toiling on a tobacco plantation.—*Patriotism of Colored Americans.*

resenting to such recruiting officers that the slaves, so enlisted by their direction and concurrence, were freemen; and it appearing further to this Assembly, that on the expiration of the term of enlistment of such slaves, that the former owners have attempted again to force them to return to a state of servitude, contrary to the principles of justice, and to their own solemn promise;

"II. And whereas it appears just and reasonable that all persons enlisted as aforesaid, who have faithfully served agreeable to the terms of their enlistment, and have hereby of course contributed towards the establishment of American liberty and independence, should enjoy the blessings of freedom as a reward for their toils and labors.

"*Be it therefore enacted*, That each and every slave, who, by the appointment and direction of his owner, hath enlisted in any regiment or corps raised within this State, either on Continental or State establishment, and hath been received as a substitute for any free person whose duty or lot it was to serve in such regiment or corps, and hath served faithfully during the term of such enlistment, or hath been discharged from such service by some officer duly authorized to grant such discharge, shall, from and after the passing of this act, be fully and completely emancipated, and shall be held and deemed free, in as full and ample a manner as if each and every one of them were specially named in this act; and the Attorney-general for the Commonwealth is hereby required to bring an action, *in forma pauperis*, in behalf of any of the persons above described who shall, after the passage of this act, be detained in servitude by any person whatsoever; and if, upon such prosecution, it shall appear that the pauper is entitled to his freedom in consequence of this act, a jury shall be empaneled to assess the damages for his detention.

"III. And whereas it has been represented to this General Assembly, that Aberdēen, a negro man slave, hath labored a number of years in the public service at the lead mines, and for his meritorious services is entitled to freedom;

"*Be it therefore enacted*, That the said slave Aberdeen, shall be, and he is hereby, emancipated and declared free in as full and ample a manner as if he had been born free."

In 1786 an act was passed to emancipate a negro slave who had acted as a spy for Lafayette. This practice was not perhaps wholly confined to the South. Although Massachusetts abolished slavery in 1783, her territory was, it seems, still subject to slave hunts, and her negro soldiers to the insult of an attempt to re-enslave them. But Gen. Washington, though himself a slave-holder, regarded the rights of those who fought for liberty and national independence, with too much sacredness and the honor of the country with too much esteem, to permit them to be set aside, merely to accommodate those who had rendered the nation's cause no help or assistance. Gen. Putnam received the following letter, which needs no explanation:

"HEADQUARTERS, Feb. 2, 1783.

"SIR:—Mr. Hobby having claimed as his property a negro man now serving in the Massachusetts Regiment, you will please to order a court of inquiry, consisting of five as respectable officers as can be found in your brigade, to examine the validity of the claim and the manner in which the person in question came into service. Having inquired into the matter, with all the attending circumstances, they will report to you their opinion thereon; which you will report to me as soon as conveniently may be.

"I am, Sir, with great respect, your most obedient servant,

"GEORGE WASHINGTON.

"P. S.—All concerned should be notified to attend.

"Brig.-Gen. Putnam."

Not only did some of the negro soldiers who fought in the American Army receive unjust treatment at the close of the war, but those who served under the Royal standard, also shared a fate quite different from what they supposed it would be when the proclamations of Lord Dunmore, Clinton and Cornwallis, were inviting them to cast their lot with the British.

The high character of Thomas Jefferson induces me to reproduce his letter to Dr. Gordon, or rather that portion of it which refers to the treatment of the negroes who went with the British army. Mr. Jefferson says:

"From an estimate I made at that time, on the best information I could collect, I supposed the State of Virginia lost, under Lord Cornwallis' hand, that year, about thirty thousand slaves; and that, of these, twenty-seven thousand died of the small-pox and camp fever; the rest were partly sent to the West Indies, and exchanged for rum, sugar, coffee and fruit; and partly sent to New York, from whence they went, at the peace, either to Nova Scotia or to England. From this last place, I believe they have lately been sent to Africa. History will never relate the horrors committed by the British army in the Southern States of America."

The heroism of the negro soldier has ever been eulogized by the true statesmen of our country, whenever the question of the American patriots was the theme. And I find no better eulogy to pronounce upon them than that Hon. Charles Pinckney, of South Carolina, delivered in the United States House of Representatives in 1820, and that of Hon Wm. Eustis, of Massachusetts, during the same debate. Mr. Pinckney said:

"It is a remarkable fact, that notwithstanding, in the course of the Revolution, the Southern States were continually overrun by the British, and that every negro in them had an opportunity of leaving their owners, few did; proving thereby not only a most remarkable attachment to their owners, but the mildness of the treatment, from whence their affection sprang. They then were, as they still are, as valuable a part of our population to the union as any other equal number of inhabitants. They were in numerous instances the pioneers, and in all the laborers, of your armies. To their hands were owing the erection of the greatest part of the fortifications raised for the protection of our country; some of which, particularly Fort Moultrie, gave, at the early period of the inexperience and untried valor of our citizens, immortality to American arms; and, in the Northern States, numerous bodies of them were enrolled into, and fought, by the side of the whites, the battles of the Revolution."—*Annals of Congress.*

And said Mr. Eustis:

"At the commmencement of the Revolutionary war, there were found in the Middle and Northern States, many blacks, and other people of color, capable of bearing arms; a part of them free, the greater part slaves. The freemen entered our ranks with the whites. The time of those who were slaves was purchased by the States; and they were induced to enter the service in eonsequence of a law by which, on condition of their serving in the ranks during the war, they were made freemen.

"The war over, and peace restored, these men returned to their respective States; and who could have said to them, on their return to civil life, after having shed their blood in common with the whites in the defence of the liberties of their country, 'You are not to participate in the liberty for which you have been fighting?' Certainly no white man in Massachusetts."

Such is the historic story of the negro in the American Revolution, and it is a sad one as regards any benefit to his own condition by his connection with either side. But it is one of the most memorable of all history on exhibition of the fidelity of a race to the cause of the freedom of all men.

CHAPTER II.

THE WAR OF 1812.

While there is no intention of entering into an examination of the causes of the war between the United States and Great Britain in 1812, yet in order to carry out the design of the author to show that in this war,—like all others in which the government of the United States has been engaged,—the negro, as a soldier, took part, it is deemed necessary to cite at least one of the incidents, perhaps *the* incident, which most fired the national heart of America, and hastened the beginning of hostilities.

The war between England and France gave to the American merchant marine interest an impetus that increased the number of vessels three-fold in a few years; it also gave command of the carrying trade of the West Indies, from which Napoleon's frigates debarred the English merchantmen. In consequence England sought and used every opportunity to cripple American commerce and shipping. One plan was to deprive American ships of the service of English seamen. Her war vessels claimed and exercised the right of searching for English seamen on board American vessels. During the year 1807, the English Admiral Berkeley, in command of the North American Station, issued instructions to commanders of vessels in his fleet to look out for the American frigate Chesapeake, and if they fell in with her at sea, to board her and search for deserters, as all English seamen in the American service were regarded by England. With the instructions, were the descriptions of four sailors, three negroes and one white man, who were missing.

The persons who deserted from the Melampus, then lying in Hampton Roads, were William Ware, Daniel Martin, John Strachan, John Little and Ambrose Watts. Within a month from their escape from the Melampus, the first three of these deserters offered themselves for enlistment, and were received on board the Chesapeake, then at Norfolk, Va, preparing for sea. The British consul at Norfolk, being apprized of the circumstance, wrote a letter to the American naval officer, requesting the men to be returned. With this request, the officer refused to comply, and the British lost no time in endeavoring to procure an order from the American government for their surrender. On receipt of the application, the Secretary of the Navy ordered an examination into the characters and claims of the men in question. The examination resulted in proof that the three negroes, Ware, Martin and Strachan were natives of America. The two former had "*protections*," or notarial certificates of their citizenship;* Strachan had no "*protection*," but asserted that he lost it previous to his escape. Such being the circumstances, the government refused to give the men up, insisting that they were American citizens, and though, they had served in the British navy, they were pressed into the service and had a right to desert it.

The Chesapeake was one of the finest of the frigates in the American Navy, and after receiving an outfit requiring six months to complete at the Gosport Navy Yard, at Norfolk, Va., started for the Mediterranean. The English frigate Leopard, which lay in the harbor at Norfolk when the Chesapeake sailed, followed her out to sea, hailed her and sent a letter to her commander, Commodore James Barron, demanding the surrender of the deserters. Barron sent a note refusing to comply with the demand, whereupon the Leopard fired several broadsides

* So indiscriminate were English officers in these outrages, that it sometimes happened that black men were seized as English seamen. At that time the public opinion of the world was such, that few statesmen troubled themselves much about the rights of negroes. But in another generation, when it proved convenient in the United States to argue that free negroes had never been citizens, it was remembered that the cabinets of Jefferson and Madison, in their diplomatic discussions with Great Britain, had been willing to argue that the impressment of a free negro was the seizure of an American citizen.—*Bryant's History of the United States.*

into the Chesapeake. Barron struck his colors without firing a shot, and permitted the officers of the Leopard to board his vessel and search her. The British captain refused to accept the surrender of the Chesapeake, but took from her crew the three men who had been demanded as deserters; also a fourth, John Wilson, a white man, claimed as a runaway from a merchant ship.

The white sailor, it was admitted by the American government, was a British subject, and his release was not demanded; he was executed for deserting the British Navy. Of the negroes, two only were returned by the British government, the other one having died in England. Says an American historian:

"An outrage like this, inflicted not by accident or the brutality of a separate commander, naturally excited the whole nation to the utmost. President Jefferson very soon interdicted American harbors and waters to all vessels of the English Navy, and forbade intercourse with them. He sent a vessel of war with a special minister to demand satisfaction. The English Admiral hanged the deserter, and dismissed the three black men with a reprimand, blaming them for *disturbing the peace of two nations.* That the outrage did not end in immediate war, was due partly to the fact that the Americans had no Navy to fight with."

Nearly four years elapsed before the final settlement of the Chesapeake affair, and then the English government insisted upon its right to, and issued orders for the search for British sailors to be continued; thus a cause for quarrel remained.

The principal grounds of war, set forth in a message of the President to Congress, June 1st, 1812, and further explained by the Committee on Foreign Relations, in their report on the subject of the message, were summarily:

"The impressment of American seamen by the British; the blockade of her enemy's ports, supported by no adequate force, in consequence of which the American commerce had been plundered in every sea, and the great staples of the country cut off from their legitimate markets; and the British orders in council."

On these grounds, the President urged the declaration of war. In unison with the recommendation of the President, the Committee on Foreign Relations concluded their reports as follows:

A NAVAL BATTLE.

"Your committee, believing that the freeborn sons of America are worthy to enjoy the liberty which their fathers purchased at the price of much blood and treasure, and seeing by the measures adopted by Great Britain, a course commenced and persisted in, which might lead to a loss of national character and independence, feel no hesitation in advising resistence by force, in which the Americans of the present day will prove to the enemy and the world, that we have not only inherited that liberty which our fathers gave us, but also the will and power to maintain it. Relying on the patriotism of the nation, and confidently trusting that the Lord of Hosts will go with us to battle in a righteous cause, and crown our efforts with success, your committee recommend an immediate appeal to *arms*."

War was declared by Congress on the 17th of June, and proclaimed by the President on the second day following.

The struggle was principally carried on upon the water, between the armed vessels of the two nations, consequently no great armies were called into active service upon the field. This was indeed fortunate for America, whose military establishments at the time were very defective. Congress called for twenty thousand men, but a very few enlisted. The President was authorized to raise fifty thousand volunteers and to call out one hundred thousand militia for the defence of the seacoast and frontiers; but officers could not be found to nominally command the few thousand that responded to the call; which state of affairs was no doubt largely due to the opposition to the war, which existed in the New England States.

Since the peace of 1783, a class of marine merchants at the North had vied with each other in the African slave-trade, in supplying the Southern planters. Consequently the increase in negro population was great; in 1800 it was 1,001,463, and in 1810, two years before war was declared, 1,377,810, an increase of 376,347. Of the 1,377,810, there were 1,181,362 slaves, and 186,448 free. Of course their increase was not due solely to the importation by the slave trade, but the aggregate increase was large, compared with the increase of the white pooulation for the same period.

The free negroes were mainly residents of the Northern States, where they enjoyed a nominal freedom. They entered the service with alacrity; excluded from the army, they enlisted in the navy, swelling the number of those who, upon the rivers, lakes, bays and oceans, manned the guns of the war vessels, in defense of Free Trade, Sailor's Rights and Independence on the seas as well as on the land. It is quite impossible to ascertain the exact number of negroes who stood beside the guns that won for America just recognition from the maritime powers of the world. Like the negro soldiers in the Revolutionary war who served with the whites, so the negro sailors in the war of 1812 served in the American Navy; in the mess, at the gun, on the yard-arm and in the gangway, together with others of various nationalities, they achieved many victories for the navy of our common country. The best evidence I can give in substantiation of what has been written, is the following letter from Surgeon Parsons to George Livermore, Esq., of the Massachusetts Historical Society:

"PROVIDENCE, October 18, 1862.

"MY DEAR SIR:—In reply to your inquiries about the employing of blacks in our navy in the war of 1812, and particularly in the battle of Lake Erie, I refer you to documents in Mackenzie's 'Life of Commodore Perry,' vol. i. pp. 166 and 187.

"In 1814, our fleet sailed to the Upper Lakes to co-operate with Colonel Croghan at Mackinac. About one in ten or twelve of the crews were black.

"In 1816, I was surgeon of the 'Java, under Commodore Perry. The white and colored seamen messed together. About one in six or eight were colored.

"In 1819, I was surgeon of the 'Guerriere,' under Commodore Macdonough; and the proportion of blacks was about the same in her crew. There seemed to be an entire absence of prejudice against the blacks as messmates among the crew. What I have said applies to the crews of the other ships that sailed in squadrons.

Yours very respectfully,

USHER PARSONS.

Dr. Parsons had reference to the following correspondence between Captain Perry and Commodore Chauncey, which took place in 1813, before the former's victory on Lake Erie. As will be seen, Perry expressed dissatisfaction as to the recruits sent him to man the squadron then on Lake Erie, and with which he gained a decisive victory over the British fleet, under command of Capt Barley:

"SIR,—I have this moment received, by express, the enclosed letter from General Harrison. If I had officers and men,—and I have no doubt you will send them,—I could fight the enemy, and proceed up the lake; but, having no one to command the 'Niagara,' and only one commissioned lieutenant and two acting lieutenants, whatever my wishes may be, going out is out of the question. The men that came by Mr Champlin are a motley set,—blacks, soldiers, and boys. I cannot think you saw them after they were selected. I am, however, pleased to see any thing in the shape of a man."—*Mackenzie's Life of Perry*, vol. i. pp. 165, 166.

Commodore Chauncey then rebuked him in his reply, and set forth the worth of the negro seaman:

"SIR,—I have been duly honored with your letters of the twenty-third and twenty-sixth ultimo, and notice your anxiety for men and officers. I am equally anxious to furnish you; and no time shall be lost in sending officers and men to you as soon as the public service will allow me to send them from this lake. I regret that you are not pleased with the men sent you by Messrs Champlin and Forest; for, to my knowledge, a part of them are not surpassed by any seamen we have in the fleet: and I have yet to learn that the color of the skin, or the cut and trimmings of the coat, can effect a man's qualifications or usefulness. I have nearly fifty blacks on board of this ship, and many of them are among my best men; and those people you call soldiers have been to sea from two to seventeen years; and I presume that you will find them as good and useful as any men on board of your vessel; at least if you can judge by comparison; for those which we have on board of this ship are attentive and obedient, and, as far as I can judge, many of them excellent seamen: at any rate, the men sent to Lake Erie have been selected with a view of sending a fair proportion of petty officers and seamen; and I presume, upon examination, it will be found that they are equal to those upon this lake."—*Mackenzie's Life of Perry*, vol. i. pp. 186, 187.

The battle of Lake Erie is the most memorable naval battle fought with the British; of it Rossiter Johnson, in his "History of the War of 1812," in the description of the engagement, says:

"As the question of the fighting qualities of the black man has since been considerably discussed, it is worth noting that in this bloody and brilliant battle a large number of Perry's men were negroes."

It was not left to Commodores Chauncey and Perry, solely, to applaud them; there was not an American war vessel, perhaps, whose crew, in part, was not made up of negroes, as the accounts of various sea fights prove. And they are entitled to no small share of the meed of praise given the American seamen, who fought and won victory over the British. Not only in the Navy, but on board the privateers,* the American negro did service, as the following extract will show:

"*Extract of a Letter from Nathaniel Shaler, Commander of the private-armed Schooner Gov. Tompkins, to his Agent in New York.*

AT SEA, Jan. 1, 1813.

"Before I could get our light sails on, and almost before I could turn round, I was under the guns, not of a transport, but of a large *frigate!* and not more than a quarter of a mile from her. * * Her first broadside killed two men and wounded six others * * My officers conducted themselves in a way that would have done honor to a more permanent service * * * The name of one of my poor fellows who was killed ought to be registered in the book of fame, and remembered with reverence as long as bravery is considered a virtue. He was a black man by the name of John Johnson. A twenty-four pound shot struck him in the hip, and took away all the lower part of his body. In this state, the poor brave fellow lay on the deck, and several times exclaimed to his shipmates, '*Fire away, my boy: no haul a color down*' The other was a black man, by the name of John Davis, and was struck in much the same way. He fell near me, and several times requested to be thrown overboard, saying he was only in the way of others.

"When America has such tars, she has little to fear from the tyrants of the ocean."—*Nile's Weekly Register, Saturday, Feb. 26, 1814.*

As in the late war of the rebellion, the negroes offered their services at the outset when volunteers were called for, and the true patriots at the North sought to have their services accepted; but the government being in the control of the opponents of universal freedom and the extention of the rights of citizenship to the negro, the effort to admit him into the ranks of the army, even in separate organizations, was futile. At the same time American whites would not enlist to any great extent, and but for the tide of immigration, which before the war had set in from Ireland, the fighting on shore would prob-

* "Hammond Golar, a colored man who lived in Lynn for many years, died a few years since at the age of 80 years. He was born a slave, was a privateer "powder boy" in the war of 1812, and was taken to Halifax as a prisoner. The English Government did not exchange colored prisoners because they would then be returned to slavery, and Golar remained a prisoner until the close of the war"

ably not have lasted six months; certainly the invasion of Canada would not have been attempted.

The reverses which met the American army in the first year of the war, slackened even the enlistment that was going on and imperiled the safety of the country, and the defences of the most important seaports and manufacturing states. Battle after battle had been lost, the invasion of Canada abandoned, and the British had turned their attention southward. The war in Europe had been brought to a close, and Napoleon was a captive. England was now at liberty to reinforce her fleet and army in America, and fears were entertained that other European powers might assist her in invading the United States. The negro soldier again loomed up, and as the British were preparing to attack New Orleans with a superior force to that of Gen. Jackson's, he sought to avail himself of every possible help within his reach. Accordingly he issued the following proclamation:

GENERAL JACKSON'S PROCLAMATION TO THE NEGROES.

HEADQUARTERS, SEVENTH MILITARY DISTRICT,
MOBILE, September 21, 1814.

To the Free Colored Inhabitants of Louisiana:

Through a mistaken policy, you have heretofore been deprived of a participation in the glorious struggle for national rights in which our country is engaged. This no longer shall exist.

As sons of freedom, you are now called upon to defend our most inestimable blessing. As Americans, your country looks with confidence to her adopted children for a valorous support, as a faithful return for the advantages enjoyed under her mild and equitable government. As fathers, husbands, and brothers, you are summoned to rally around the standard of the Eagle, to defend all which is dear in existence.

Your country, although calling for your exertions, does not wish you to engage in her cause without amply remunerating you for the services rendered. Your intelligent minds are not to be led away by false representations. Your love of honor would cause you to despise the man who should attempt to deceive you. In the sincerity of a soldier and the language of truth I address you.

To every noble-hearted, generous freeman of color volunteering to serve during the present contest with Great Britain, and no longer, there will be paid the same bounty, in money and lands, now received by the white soldiers of the United States, viz: one hundred and twenty-four dollars in money, and one hundred and sixty acres of land. The non-commissioned officers and privates will also be entitled to the same monthly pay, and daily rations, and clothes, furnished to any American soldier.

On enrolling yourselves in companies, the Major-General Commanding will select officers for your government from your white fellow-citizens. Your non-commissioned officers will be appointed from among yourselves.

Due regard will be paid to the feelings of freeman and soldiers. You will not, by being associated with white men in the same corps, be exposed to improper comparisons or unjust sarcasm. As a distinct, independent battalion or regiment, pursuing the path of glory, you will, undivided, receive the applause and gratitude of your countrymen.

To assure you of the sincerity of my intentions, and my anxiety to engage your invaluable services to our country, I have communicated my wishes to the Governor of Louisiana, who is fully informed as to the manner of enrollment, and will give you every necessary information on the subject of this address.

ANDREW JACKSON, *Major-General Commanding.*

[*Niles Register, vol. vii. p. 205.*]

When the news of Gen. Jackson arming the free negroes reached the North it created no little surprise, and greatly encouraged those, who, from the commencement of hostilities, had advocated it. The successes of the summer were being obliterated by the victories which the British were achieving. The national capitol was burned; Maine had virtually fallen into their hands; gloom and disappointment prevailed throughout the country. Enlistment was at a stand-still, and as the British were threatening with annihilation the few troops then in the field, it became evident that the States would have to look to their own defence. New York again turned her attention to her free negro population; a bill was prepared and introduced in the legislature looking to the arming of her negroes, and in October, a month after Gen. Jackson issued his appeal to the negroes of Louisiana, the Legislature passed a bill of which the following are the most important sections:

"*An Act to authorize the raising of Two Regiments of Men of Color; passed Oct. 24, 1814.*

"SECT. 1. Be it enacted by the people of the State of New York, represented in Senate and Assembly, That the Governor of the State be, and he is hereby authorized to raise, by voluntary enlistment, two regiments of free men of color, for the defence of the State for three years, unless sooner discharged.

"SECT. 2. And be it further enacted, That each of the said regiments shall consist of one thousand and eighty able-bodied men; and the said regiments shall be formed into a brigade, or be organized in such manner, and shall be employed in such service, as the Governor of the State of New York shall deem best adapted to defend the said State.

"SECT. 3. And be it further enacted, That all the commissioned officers of the said regiments and brigade shall be white men; and the Governor of the State of New York shall be, and he is hereby, authorized to commission, by brevet, all the officers of the said regiments and brigade, who shall hold their respective commissions until the council of appointment shall have appointed the officers of the said regiments and brigade, in pursuance of the Constitution and laws of the said State.

"SECT. 6. And be it further enacted, That it shall be lawful for any able-bodied slave, with the written assent of his master or mistress, to enlist into the said corps; and the master or mistress of such slave shall be entitled to the pay and bounty allowed him for his service: and, further, that the said slave, at the time of receiving his discharge, shall be deemed and adjudged to have been legally manumitted from that time, and his said master or mistress shall not thenceforward be liable for his maintenance.—*Laws of the State of New York, passed at the Thirty-eighth Session of the Legislature*, chap. xviii.

The organization of negro troops was now fairly begun; at the South enlistment was confined to the free negroes as set forth in Gen. Jackson's Proclamation. In New York, the slaves who should enlist with the consent of their owners were to be free at the expiration of their service, as provided in the Sixth section of the law quoted above.

Animated by that love of liberty and country which has ever prompted them, notwithstanding the disabilities under which they labored, to enter the ranks of their country's defenders whenever that country has been assailed by foes without or traitors within, the negroes responded to the call of General Jackson and to that of New York, with a zeal and energy characteristic only of a brave and patriotic people. Inspired by the hope of impartial liberty, they rallied to the support of that banner which Commodore Barron lowered when he failed to protect them from British aggression, but which Commodore Decatur gallantly and successfully defended.

The forcible capture and imprisonment of Ware, Martin and Strachan, the three negroes taken from the Chesapeake, and who were recognized by the United States authorities as citizens of the republic, was sounded as the key-note and rallying cry of the war; the outrage served greatly to arouse the people. The fact that the government sought to establish the liberty of the free negroes, and the further fact that she regarded them as citizens, heightened their indignation at the outrage committed by the British, and appealed to their keenest patriotic sensibilities. New York was not long in raising her two battalions, and sending it forward to the army, then at Sacket's Harbor.

On the 18th of December, 1814, following the issuing of his Proclamation, Gen. Jackson reviewed the troops under his command at New Orleans, amounting to about six thousand, and of this force about five hundred were negroes, organized into two battalions, commanded by Maj. Lacoste and Maj. Savory. These battalions, at the close of the review, says Parton, in his Life of Jackson, had read to them by Edward Livingston, a member of Jackson's staff, the following address, from the Commander of the American forces:

"TO THE EMBODIED MILITIA.—*Fellow Citizens and Soldiers:* The General commanding in chief would not do justice to the noble ardor that has animated you in the hour of danger, he would not do justice to his own feeling, if he suffered the example you have shown to pass without public notice. * * * * *

"Fellow-citizens, of every description, remember for what and against whom you contend. For all that can render life desirable—for a country blessed with every gift of nature—for property, for life—for those dearer than either, your wives and children—and for liberty, without which, country, life, property, are no longer worth possessing; as even the embraces of wives and children become a reproach to the wretch who could deprive them by his cowardice of those invaluable blessings.

* * * * *

"TO THE MEN OF COLOR.—Soldiers! From the shores of Mobile I collected you to arms,—I invited you to share in the perils and to divide the glory of your white countrymen. I expected much from you; for I was not uninformed of those qualities which must render you so formidable to an invading foe. I knew that you could endure hunger and thirst, and all the hardships of war. I knew that you loved the land of your nativity, and that, like ourselves, you had to defend all that is most dear to man. But you surpass my hopes. I have found in you, united to these qualities, that noble enthusiasm which impels to great deeds.

"Soldiers! The President of the United States shall be informed of your conduct on the present occasion; and the voice of the Representatives of the American nation shall applaud your valor, as your General now praises your ardor. The enemy is near. His sails cover the lakes. But the brave are united; and, if he finds us contending among ourselves, it will be for the prize of valor, and fame its noblest reward."—*Niles's Register*, vol. vii. pp. 345, 346.

Thus in line with the white troops on the soil of Louisiana, amid a large slave population, the negro soldiers were highly praised by the commanding General. The British had already made their appearance on the coast near the mouth of the Mississippi, and at the time of their landing, General Jackson went out to meet them with two thousand one hundred men; the British had two thousand four hundred. This was on the 23rd of December. The two armies met and fought to within a few miles of the city, where the British general, Pakenham, who had arrived with reinforcements, began on the 31st to lay seige. On Jan. 8th the short but terrible struggle took place which not only taxed the energies and displayed the great courage of both forces, but made the engagement one of historic interest. In the short space of twenty-five minutes seven hundred of the British were killed; fourteen hundred were wounded and four hundred were taken prisoners. The American army was so well protected that only four were killed and thirteen wounded. It was in this great battle that two battalions of negroes participated, and helped to save the city, the coveted prize, from the British. The two battalions numbered four hundred and thirty men, and were commanded by Maj. Lacoste and Maj. Savory. Great Britain also had her negro soldiers there,—a regiment imported from the West Indies which headed the attacking column against Jackson's right,—they led her van in the battle; their failure, with that of the Irish regiment which formed also a part of the advance column, lost the British the battle. The conduct of the negro soldiers in Gen. Jackson's army on that occasion has ever been applauded by the American people. Mr. Day, in Nell's "Colored Patriots of the American Revolution," says:

"From an authenticated chart, belonging to a soldier friend, I find that, in the battle of New Orleans, Major-General Andrew Jackson, Commander-in-Chief, and his staff, were just at the right of the advancing left column of the British, and that very near him were stationed the colored soldiers. He is numbered 6, and the position of the colored soldiers 8. The chart explanation of No. 8 reads thus:— '8. Captains Dominique and Bluche, two 24 pounders; Major Lacoste's battalion, formed of the men of color of New Orleans and, Major Daquin's battalion, formed of the men of color of St. Domingo, under Major Savary, second in command.'

"They occupied no mean place, and did no mean service.

"From other documents in my possession, I am able to state the number of the 'battalion of St. Domingo men of color' to have been one hundred and fifty; and of 'Major Lacoste's battalion of Louisiana men of color,' two hundred and eighty.

"Thus were over four hundred 'men of color' in that battle. When it is remembered that the whole number of soldiers claimed by Americans to have been in that battle reached only 3600, it will be seen that the 'men of color' were present in much larger proportion than their numbers in the country warranted.

"Neither was there colorphobia then. Major Planche's battalion of uniformed volunteer companies, and Major Lacoste's 'men of color,' fought together; so, also, did Major Daquin's 'men of color,' and the 44th, under Captain Baker."

Hon. Robert C. Winthrop, in his speech in Congress on the Imprisonment of Colored Seamen, September, 1850, bore this testimony to their gallant conduct:

"I have an impression, that, not, indeed, in these piping times of peace, but in the time of war, when quite a boy, I have seen black soldiers enlisted, who did faithful and excellent service. But, however it may have been in the Northern States, I can tell the Senator what happened in the Southern States at this period. I believe that I shall be borne out in saying, that no regiments did better service, at New Orleans, than did the black regiments, which were organized under the direction of General Jackson himself, after a most glorious appeal to the patriotism and honor of the people of color of that region; and which, after they came out of the war, received the thanks of General Jackson, in a proclamation which has been thought worthy of being inscribed on the pages of history."

Perhaps the most glowing account of the services of these black American soldiers, appeared in an article in the New Orleans *Picayune*:

"Not the least interesting, although the most novel feature of the procession yesterday, was the presence of ninety of the colored veterans who bore a conspicuous part in the dangers of the day they were now for the first time called to assist in celebrating, and who, by their good conduct in presence of the enemy, deserved and received the approbation of their illustrious commander-in-chief. During the thirty-six years that have passed away since they assisted to repel the invaders from our shores, these faithful men have never before participated in the annual rejoicings for the victory which their valor contributed to gain. Their good deeds have been consecrated only in their memories, or lived but to claim a passing notice on the page of the historian. Yet, who more than they deserve the thanks of the country, and the gratitude of succeeding generations? Who rallied with more alacrity in response to the summons of danger? Who endured more cheerfully the hardships of the camp, or faced with greater courage the perils of the fight? If, in that hazardous hour, when our homes were menanced with the horrors of war, we did not disdain to call upon the colored population to assist in repelling the invading horde, we should not, when the danger is passed, refuse to permit them to unite with us in celebrating the glorious event, which they helped to make so memorable an epoch in our history. We were not too exalted to mingle with them in the affray; they were not too humble to join in our rejoicings.

"Such, we think, is the universal opinion of our citizens. We conversed with many yesterday, and, without exception, they expressed approval of the invitation which had been extended to the colored veterans to take part in the ceremonies of the day, and gratification at seeing them in a conspicuous place in the procession.

"The respectability of their appearance, and the modesty of their demeanor, made an impression on every observer, and elicited unqualified approbation. Indeed, though in saying so we do not mean disrespect to any one else, we think that they constituted decidedly the most interesting portion of the pageant, as they certainly attracted the most attention."

It was during the rebellion of 1861-65 that the author saw one of the colored drummer boys of that column beating his drum at the head of a negro United States regiment marching through the streets of New Orleans in 1862.

The New York battalion was organized and marched to the reinforcement of the American army at Sacket's

Harbor, then threatened by the enemy. This battalion was said to be a fine looking body of men, well drilled and disciplined. In Congress Mr. Martindale, of New York, said, in a speech delivered on the 22nd January 1828, before that body:

> "Slaves or negroes who had been slaves were enlisted as soldiers in the war of the Revolution: and I myself saw a battalion of them,—as fine martial looking men as I ever saw attached to the Northern army in the last war (1812),—on its march from Plattsburg to Sacket's Harbor, where they did service for the country with credit to New York and honor to themselves."

As in the dark days of the Revolution, so now in another period of national danger, the negroes proved their courage and patriotism by service in the field. However, the lamentable treatment of Major Jeffrey* is evidence that these services were not regarded as a protection against outrage.

In the two wars in which the history of the negroes has been traced in these pages, there is nothing that mitigates against his manhood, though his condition, either bond or free, was lowly. But on the contrary the honor of the race has been maintained under every circumstance in which it has been placed.

* See page 50

PART II.

THE WAR BETWEEN THE STATES.

1861.

UNSHACKLED.

CHAPTER I.

PUBLIC OPINION.

It seems proper, before attempting to record the achievements of the negro soldiers in the war of the Rebellion, that we should consider the state of public opinion regarding the negroes at the outbreak of the war; also, in connection therewith, to note the rapid change that took place during the early part of the struggle.

For some cause, unexplained in a general sense, the white people in the Colonies and in the States, came to entertain against the colored races therein a prejudice, that showed itself in a hostility to the latter's enjoying equal civil and political rights with themselves. Various reasons are alleged for it, but the difficulty of really solving the problem lies in the fact that the early settlers in this country came without prejudice against color. The Negro, Egyptian, Arab, and other colored races known to them, lived in European countries, where no prejudice, on account of color existed. How very strange then, that a feeling antagonistic to the negroes should become a prominent feature in the character of the European emigrants to these shores and their descendants. It has been held by some writers that the American prejudice against the negroes was occasioned by their docility and unresenting spirit. Surely no one acquainted with the Indian will agree that he is docile or wanting in spirit, yet occasionally there is manifested a prejudice against him; the recruiting officers in Massachusetts refused to enlist Indians, as well as negroes, in regiments and companies made up of white citizens, though members of both races, could sometimes be found in white regiments. During the rebellion of 1861-5, some Western regiments had one or two negroes and Indians in them, but there was no general enlistment of either race in white regiments.* The objection was on account of color, or, as some writers claim, by the fact of the races—negro and Indian †—having been enslaved. Be the cause what it may, a prejudice, strong, unrelenting, barred the two races from enjoying with the white race equal civil and political rights in the United States. So very strong had that prejudice grown since the Revolution, enhanced it may be by slavery and docility, that when the rebellion of 1861 burst forth, a feeling stronger than law, like a Chinese wall only more impregnable, encircled the negro, and formed a barrier betwixt him and the army. Doubtless peace—a long peace—lent its aid materially to this state of affairs. Wealth, chiefly, was the dream of the American from 1815 to 1860, nearly half a century; a period in which the negro was friendless, save in a few strong-minded, iron-hearted men like John Brown in Kansas, Wendell Philips in New England, Charles Sumner in the United States Senate, Horace Greeley in New York and a few others, who dared, in the face of strong public sentiment, to plead his cause, even from a humane platform. In many places he could not ride in a street car that was not inscribed, "*Colored persons ride in this car.*" The deck of a steamboat, the box cars of the railroad, the pit of the theatre and the gallery of the church, were the locations accorded him. The church lent its influence to the rancor and bitterness of a prejudice as deadly as the sap of the Upas.

To describe public opinion respecting the negro a half a century ago, is no easy task. It was just budding into

* I arrived in New York in August, 1862, from Valparaiso, Chili, on the steamship "Bio-Bio," of Boston, and in company with two Spaniards, neither of whom could speak English, enlisted in a New York regiment. We were sent to the rendezvous on one of the islands in the harbor. The third day after we arrived at the barracks, I was sent with one of my companions to carry water to the cook, an aged negro, who immediately recognized me, and in such a way as to attract the attention of the corporal, who reported the matter to the commanding officer, and before I could give the cook the hint, he was examined by the officer of the day. At noon I was accompanied by a guard of honor to the launch, which landed me in New York. I was a negro, that was all; how it was accounted for on the rolls I cannot say. I was honorably discharged, however, without receiving a certificate to that effect.

† The Indians referred to are many of those civilized and living as citizens in the several States of the Union.

maturity when DeTocqueville visited the United States, and, as a result of that visit, he wrote, from observation, a pointed criticism upon the manners and customs, and the laws of the people of the United States. For fear that I might be thought over-doing—heightening—giving too much coloring to the strength, and extent and power of the prejudice against the negro I quote from that distinguished writer, as he clearly expressed himself under the heading, "*Present and Future condition of the three races inhabiting the United States.*" He said of the negro:

> I see that in a certain portion of the United States at the present day, the legal barrier which separates the two races is tending to fall away, but not that which exists in the manners of the country. Slavery recedes, but the prejudice to which it has given birth remains stationary. Whosoever has inhabited the United States, must have perceived, that in those parts of the United States, in which the negroes are no longer slaves, they have in nowise drawn nearer the whites; on the contrary, the prejudice of the race appears to be stronger in those States which have abolished slavery, than in those where it still exists. And, nowhere is it so intolerant as in the states where servitude has never been known. It is true, that in the North of the Union, marriages may be legally contracted between negroes and whites, but public opinion would stigmatize a man, who should content himself with a negress, as infamous. If oppressed, they may bring an action at law, but they will find none but whites among their judges, and although they may legally serve as jurors, prejudice repulses them for that office. In theatres gold cannot procure a seat for the servile race beside their former masters, in hospitals they lie apart. They *are* allowed to invoke the same divinity as the whites. The gates of heaven are not closed against those unhappy beings; but their inferiority is continued to the very confines of the other world. The negro is free, but he can share, neither the rights, nor the labor, nor the afflictions of him, whose equal he has been declared to be, and he cannot meet him upon fair terms in life or death."

DeTocqueville, as is seen, wrote with much bitterness and sarcasm, and, it is but fair to state, makes no allusion to any exceptions to the various conditions of affairs that he mentions. In all cases matters might not have been exactly as bad as he pictures them, but as far as the deep-seated prejudice against the negroes, and indifference to their rights and elevation are concerned, the facts will freely sustain the views so forcibly presented.

The negro had no remembrance of the country of his

ancestry, Africa, and he abjured their religion. In the South he had no family; women were merely the temporary sharer of his pleasures; his master's cabins were the homes of his children during their childhood. While the Indian perished in the struggle for the preservation of his home, his hunting grounds and his freedom, the negro entered into slavery as soon as he was born, in fact was often purchased in the womb, and was born to know, first, that he was a slave. If one became free, he found freedom harder to bear than slavery; half civilized, deprived of nearly all rights, in contact with his superiors in wealth and knowledge, exposed to the rigor of a tyrannical prejudice moulded into laws, he contented himself to be allowed to live.

The Negro race, however, it must be remembered, is the only race that has ever come in contact with the European race, and been able to withstand its atrocities and oppression; all others, like the Indian, whom they could not make subservient to their use, they have destroyed. The Negro race, like the Israelites, multiplied so rapidly in bondage, that the oppressor became alarmed, and began discussing methods of safety to himself. The only people able to cope with the Anglo-American or Saxon, with any show of success, must be of *patient fortitude, progressive intelligence, brave in resentment and earnest in endeavor.*

In spite of his surroundings and state of public opinion the African lived, and gave birth, largely through amalgamation with the representatives of the different races that inhabited the United States, to a new race,—the *American Negro.* Professor Sampson in his mixed races says:

"The Negro is a new race, and is not the direct descent of any people that have ever flourished. The glory of the negro race is yet to come."

As evidence of its capacity to acquire glory, the record made in the late struggle furnishes abundant proof. At the sound of the tocsin at the North, negro waiter, cook, barber, boot-black, groom, porter and laborer stood ready at the enlisting office; and though the recruiting officer refused to list his name, he waited like the "patient ox" for the partition—*prejudice*—to be removed. He waited

ROBERT SMALLS, (pilot).
WILLIAM MORRISON, (sailor). A. GRADINE, (Engineer).
JOHN SMALLS, (sailor).

Four of the crew who, while the white officers were ashore in Charleston, S. C., ran off with the Confederate war steamer, "Planter," passed Fort Sumter and delivered the vessel to the United States authorities. On account of the daring exploit a special act of Congress was passed ordering one-half the value of the captured vessel to be invested in U. S. bonds, and the interest thereof to be annually paid them or their heirs. Robert Smalls joined the Union army, and after the war became active and prominent in politics.

two years before even the door of the partition was opened; then he did not hesitate, but walked in, and with what effect the world knows.

The war cloud of 1860 still more aroused the bitter prejudice against the negro at both the North and South; but he was safer in South Carolina than in New York, in Richmond than in Boston.

It is a natural consequence, when war is waged between two nations, for those on either side to forget local feuds and unite against the common enemy, as was done in the Revolutionary war. How different was the situation now when the threatened war was not one between nations, but between states of the same nation. The feeling of hostility toward the negro was not put aside and forgotten as other troublesome matters were, but the bitterness became intensified and more marked.

The Confederate Government though organized for the perpetual enslavement of the negro, fostered the idea that the docility of the negroes would allow them to be used for any purpose, without their having the least idea of becoming freemen. Some idea may be formed of public opinion at the South at the beginning of the war by what Mr. Pollard, in his history, gives as the feeling at the South at the close of the second year of the struggle:

"Indeed, the war had shown the system of slavery in the South to the world in some new and striking aspects, and had removed much of that cloud of prejudice, defamation, falsehood, romance and perverse sentimentalism through which our peculiar institution had been formerly known to Europe. It had given a better vindication of our system of slavery than all the books that could be written in a generation. It had shown that slavery was an element of strength to us; that it had assisted us in our struggle; that no servile insurrections had taken place in the South, in spite of the allurements of our enemy; that the slave had tilled the soil while his master had fought; that in large districts, unprotected by our troops, and with a white population, consisting almost exclusively of women and children, the slave had continued his work, quiet, faithful, and cheerful; and that, as a conservative element in our social system, the institution of slavery had withstood the shocks of war, and been a faithful ally of our army, although instigated to revolution by every art of the enemy, and prompted to the work of assassination and pillage by the most brutal examples of the Yankee soldiers."

With this view, the whole slave population was brought to the assistance of the Confederate Government, and thereby caught the very first hope of freedom. An innate reasoning taught the negro that slaves could not be relied upon to fight for their own enslavement. To get to the breastworks was but to get a chance to run to the Yankees; and thousands of those whose elastic step kept time with the martial strains of the drum and fife, as they marched on through city and town, enroute to the front, were not elated with the hope of Southern success, but were buoyant with the prospects of reaching the North. The confederates found it no easy task to watch the negroes and the Yankees too; their attention could be given to but one at a time; as a slave expressed it, "when marsa watch the Yankee, nigger go; when marsa watch the nigger, Yankee come." But the Yankees did not always receive him kindly during the first year of the war.

In his first inaugural, Mr. Lincoln declared "that the property, peace and security of no section are to be in anywise endangered by the new incoming administration.." The Union generals, except Fremont and Phelps and a few subordinates, accepted this as public opinion, and as their guide in dealing with the slavery question. That opinion is better expressed in the doggerel, sung in after months by the negro troops as they marched along through Dixie:

"McClellan went to Richmond with two hundred thousand braves,
He said, '*keep back the niggers and the Union he would save.*"
Little Mac. he had his way, still the Union is in tears,
And they call for the help of the colored volunteers."

The first two lines expressed the sentiment at the time, not only of the Army of the Potomoc, but the army commanders everywhere, with the exceptions named. The administration winked at the enforcement of the fugitive slave bill by the soldiers engaged in capturing and returning the negroes coming into the Union lines.* Undoubtedly it was the idea of the Government to turn the course of the war from its rightful channel, or in other words,—in

* See Appendix, "A."

QUARTERS PROVIDED FOR CONTRABANDS.

the restoration of the Union,—to eliminate the anti-slavery sentiment, which demanded the freedom of the slaves.

Hon. Elisha R. Potter, of Rhode Island,—"who may," said Mr. Greeley, "be fairly styled the hereditary chief of the Democratic party of that State,"—made a speech on the war in the State Senate, on the 10th of August 1861, in which he remarked:

I have said that the war may assume another aspect, and be a short and bloody one. And to such a war—*an anti-slavery war*—it seems to me we are *inevitably* drifting. It seems to me hardly in the power of human wisdom to prevent it. We may commence the war without meaning to interfere with slavery; but let us have one or two battles, and get our blood excited, and we shall not only not restore any more slaves, but shall proclaim freedom wherever we go. And it seems to me almost judicial blindness on the part of the South that they do not see that this must be the inevitable result, if the contest is prolonged."

This sentiment became bolder daily as the thinking Union men viewed the army turning aside from its legitimate purposes, to catch runaway negroes, and return them. Party lines were also giving away; men in the army began to realize the worth of the negroes as they sallied up to the rebel breastworks that were often impregnable. They began to complain, finding the negro with his pick and spade, a greater hinderance to their progress than the cannon balls of the enemy; and more than one said to the confederates, when the pickets of the two armies picnicked together in the battle's lull, as frequently they did: "We can whip you, if you keep your negroes out of your army."

Quite a different course was pursued in the navy. Negroes were readily accepted all along the coast on board the war vessels, it being no departure from the regular and established practice in the service. The view with which the loyal friends of the Union began to look at the negro and the rebellion, was aptly illustrated in an article in the Montgomery (Ala.) *Advertiser* in 1861, which said:

"THE SLAVES AS A MILITARY ELEMENT IN THE SOUTH.—The total white population of the eleven States now comprising the Confederacy is 6,000,000, and, therefore, to fill up the ranks of the proposed army (600,000) about ten per cent of the entire white population will be required. In any other country than our own such a draft could not be met, but the Southern States can furnish that number of men, and still not leave the material interests of the country in a suffering condition. Those who are incapacitated for bearing arms can oversee the plantations, and the negroes can go on undisturbed in their usual labors. In the North the case is different; the men who join the army of subjugation are the laborers, the producers, and the factory operatives. Nearly every man from that section, especially those from the rural districts, leaves some branch of industry to suffer during his absence. The institution of slavery in the South alone enables her to place in the field a force much larger in proportion to her white population than the North, or indeed any country which is dependent entirely on free labor. The institution is a tower of strength to the South, particularly at the present crisis, and our enemies will be likely to find that the 'moral cancer' about which their orators are so fond of prating, is really one of the most effective weapons employed against the Union by the South. Whatever number of men may be needed for this war, we are confident our people stand ready to furnish. We are all enlisted for the war, and there must be no holding back until the independence of the South is fully acknowledged."

The facts already noted became apparent to the nation very soon, and then came a change of procedure, and the war began to be prosecuted upon quite a different policy. Gen. McClellan, whose loyalty to the new policy was doubted, was removed from the command of the Army of the Potomac, and slave catching ceased. The XXXVII Congress convened in Dec. 1861, in its second session, and passed the following additional article of war:

"All officers are prohibited from employing any of the forces under their respective commands for the purpose of returning fugitives from service or labor who may have escaped from any persons to whom such service or labor is claimed to be due. Any officer who shall be found guilty by court-martial of violating this article shall be dismissed from the service."

This was the initatory measure of the new policy, which progressed to its fulfillment rapidly. And then what Mr. Cameron, Secretary of War, had recommended in December. 1861, and to which the President objected, very soon developed, through a series of enactments, in the arming of the negro; in which the loyal people of the whole country acquiesced, save the border states people, who fiercely opposed it as is shown in the conduct of Mr.

DRIVING GOVT. CATTLE

Wickliffe, of Kentucky; Salisbury, of Delaware, and others in Congress.

Public opinion was now changed, Congress had prohibited the surrender of negroes to the rebels, the President issued his Emancipation Proclamation, and more than 150,000 negroes were fighting for the Union. The Republican party met in convention at Chicago, and nominated Mr. Lincoln for the second term as President of the United States; the course of his first administration was now to be approved or rejected by the people. In the resolutions adopted, the fifth one of them related to Emancipation and the negro soldiers. It was endorsed by a very large majority of the voters. A writer in one of the magazines, prior to the election, thus reviews the resolutions:

"The fifth resolution commits us to the approval of two measures that have aroused the most various and strenuous opposition, the Proclamation of Emancipation and the use of negro troops. In reference to the first, it is to be remembered that it is a war measure. The expresss language of it is: 'By virtue of the power in me vested as commander-in-chief of the army and navy of the United States in time of actual armed rebellion against the authority and Government of the United States, and as a *fit and necessary war measure for suppressing said rebellion.*' Considered thus, the Proclamation is not merely defensible, but it is more; it is a proper and efficient means of weakening the rebellion which every person desiring its speedy overthrow must zealously and perforce uphold. Whether it is of any legal effect beyond the actual limits of our military lines, is a question that need not agitate us. In due time the supreme tribunal of the nation will be called to determine that, and to its decision the country will yield with all respect and loyalty. But in the mean time let the Proclamation go wherever the army goes, let it go wherever the navy secures a foothold on the outer border of the rebel territory, and let it summon to our aid the negroes who are truer to the Union than their disloyal masters; and when they have come to us and put their lives in our keeping, let us protect and defend them with the whole power of the nation. Is there anything unconstitutional in that? Thank God, there is not. And he who is willing to give back to slavery a single person who has heard the summons and come within our lines to obtain his freedom, he who would give up a single man, woman, or child, once thus actually freed, is not worthy the name of American. He may call himself Confederate, if he will.

"Let it be remembered, also that the Proclamation has had a very important bearing upon our foreign relations. It evoked in behalf of our country that sympathy on the part of the people in Europe, whose is the only sympathy we can ever expect in our struggle to perpetuate free institutions. Possessing that sympathy, moreover, we have had an element in our favor which has kept the rulers of Europe in wholesome dread of interference. The Proclamation relieved us from the false position before attributed to us of fighting simply for national power. It placed us right in the eyes of the world, and transferred men's sympathies from a confederacy fighting for independence as a means of establishing slavery, to a nation whose institutions mean constitutional liberty, and, when fairly wrought out, must end in universal freedom."

The change of policy and of public opinion was so strongly endorsed that it affected the rebels, who shortly passed a Congressional measure for arming 200,000 negroes themselves. What a reversal of things; what a change of sentiment, in less than twenty-four months!* Mr. Lincoln, in justifying the change, is reported to have said to Judge Mills, of Wisconsin:

"The slightest knowledge of arithmetic will prove to any man that the rebel armies cannot be destroyed with Democratic strategy. It would sacrifice all the white men of the North to do it. There are now in the service of the United States near two hundred thousand able-bodied colored men, most of them under arms, defending and acquiring Union territory. The Democratic strategy demands that these forces be disbanded, and that the masters be conciliated by restoring them to slavery. The black men who now assist Union prisoners to escape, they are to be converted into our enemies in the vain hope of gaining the good will of their masters. We shall have to fight two nations instead of one. You cannot conciliate the South if you guarantee to them ultimate success; and the experience of the present war proves their success is inevitable if you fling the compulsory labor of millions of black men into their side of the scale. Will you give our enemies such military advantages as insure success, and then depend on coaxing, flattery, and concession to get them back into the Union? Abandon all the posts now garrisoned by black men; take two hundred thousand men from our side and put them in the battlefield or cornfield against us, and we would be compelled to abandon the war in three weeks. We have to hold territory in inclement and sickly places; where are the Demo-

* "Those who have declaimed loudest against the employment of negro troops have shown a lamentable amount of ignorance, and an equally lamentable lack of common sense. They know as little of the military history and martial qualities of the African race as they do of their own duties as commanders.

All distinguished generals of modern times who have had opportunity to use negro soldiers, have uniformily applauded their subordination, bravery, and powers of endurance. Washington solicited the military services of negroes in the revolution, and rewarded them. Jackson did the same in the war of 1812. Under both those great captains, the negro troops fought so well that they received unstinted praise."—*Charles Sumner.*

crats to do this? It was a free fight, and the field was open to the war Democrats to put down this rebellion by fighting against both master and slave, long before the present policy was inaugurated. There have been men base enough to propose to me to return to slavery the black warriers of Port Hudson and Olustee, and thus win the respect of the masters they fought. Should I do so, I should deserve to be dammed in time and eternity. Come what will, I will keep my faith with friend and foe. My enemies pretend I am now carrying on this war for the sole purpose of abolition. So long as I am President, it shall be carried on for the sole purpose of restoring the Union. But no human power can subdue this rebellion without the use of the emancipation policy, and every other policy calculated to weaken the moral and physical forces of the rebellion. Freedom has given us two hundred thousand men raised on southern soil. It will give us more yet. Just so much it has subtracted from the enemy; and instead of alienating the South, there are now evidences of a fraternal feeling growing up between our men and the rank and file of the rebel soldiers. Let my enemies prove to the country that the destruction of slavery is not necessary to the restoration of the Union. I will abide the issue."

But the change of policy did not change the opinion of the Southerners, who, notwithstanding the use which the Confederate Government was making of the negro, still regarded him, in the *United States* uniform, as a vicious brute, to be shot at sight. I prefer, in closing this chapter, to give the Southern opinion of the negro, in the words of a distinguished native of that section. Mr. George W. Cable, in his "Silent South," thus gives it:

"He was brought to our shores a naked, brutish, unclean, captive, pagan savage, to be and remain a kind of connecting link between man and the beasts of burden. The great changes to result from his contact with a superb race of masters were not taken into account. As a social factor he was intended to be as purely zero as the brute at the other end of his plow line. The occasional mingling of his blood with that of the white man worked no change in the sentiment; one, two, four, eight, multiplied upon or divided in to zero, still gave zero for the result. Generations of American nativity made no difference; his children and childrens' children were born in sight of our door, yet the old notion held fast. He increased to vast numbers, but it never wavered. He accepted our dress, language, religion, all the fundamentals of our civilization, and became forever expatriated from his own land; still he remained, to us, an alien. Our sentiment went blind. It did not see that gradually, here by force and there by choice, he was fulfilling a host of conditions that earned at least a solemn moral right to that naturalization which no one at first had dreamed of giving him. Frequently he even bought back the freedom of which he had been robbed, became a tax-payer, and at times an educator of his children at his own expense; but the old idea of alienism passed laws to banish him, his wife, and children by thousands from the State, and threw him into loathsome jails as a common felon for returning to his native land. It will be wise to remember that these were the acts of an enlightened, God fearing people."

SCENE IN AND NEAR A RECRUITING OFFICE.

CHAPTER II.

RECRUITING AND ORGANIZING.

The recruiting officer, in the first year of the enlistment of negroes, did not have a pleasant service to perform. At New Orleans there was no trouble in recruiting the regiments organized under Butler's command, for, beside the free negroes, the slave population for miles around were eager to enlist, believing that with the United States army uniform on, they would be safe in their escape from "ole master and the rebs." And then the action of the confederate authorities in arming the free negroes lent a stimulent and gave an ambition to the whole slave population to be soldiers. Could arms have been obtained, a half a dozen regiments could have been organized in sixty days just as rapidly as were three. Quite early in 1862, while the negroes in New Orleans were being enrolled in the Confederate service, under Gov. Moore's proclamation, in separate and distinct organizations from the whites, the Indians and negroes were enlisting in the Union service, on the frontier, in the same company and regiments, with white officers to command them. In the "Kansas Home Guard," comprising two regiments of Indians, were over 400 negroes, and these troops were under Custer, Blunt and Herron. They held Fort Gibson twenty months against the assaults of the enemy. Two thousand five hundred negroes served in the Federal army from the Indian Nations, and these, in all probability, are a part of 5,896 "not accounted for" on the Adjutant General's rolls.

Quite a different state of things existed in South Carolina; rumors were early afloat, when recruiting began, that the government officers were gathering up the negroes to ship away to Cuba, Africa and the West Indies. These reports for a long time hindered the enlistment very much. Then there was no large city for contrabands to congregate in; besides they had no way of traveling from island to island except on government vessels. Before the Proclamation of freedom was issued, the city of Washington, with Virginia and Maryland as additional territory to recruit from, afforded an officer a better field to operate in than any other point except New Orleans. The conduct of the Government in revoking Gen. Fremont's Proclamation, and of McClellan's with the Army of the Potomac, in catching and returning escaped slaves, also had a tendency for some time to keep back even the free negroes of Virginia and Maryland. But this class of people never enlisted to any great numbers, either before or after 1863, and there finally came to be a general want of spirit with them, while with the slave class there was a ready enthusiasm to enlist. Senator Wilson, of Massachusetts, was Chairman of the Committee of Military Affairs, and reported from that committee on the 8th of July 1862, a bill authorizing the arming of negroes as a part of the army. The bill finally passed both houses and received the approval of the President on the 17th of July, 1862. The battle for its success is as worthy of record as any fought by the Phalanx. The debate was characterized by eloquence and deep feeling on both sides. Says an account of the proceedings in Henry Wilson's "Anti-slavery Measures of Congress:

"Mr. Sherman (Rep.) of Ohio said, "The question arises, whether the people of the United States, struggling for national existence, should not employ these blacks for the maintenance of the Government. The policy heretofore pursued by the officers of the United States has been to repel this class of people from our lines, to refuse their services. They would have made the best spies; and yet they have been driven from our lines."—"I tell the President," said Mr. Fessenden (Rep.) of Maine, "from my place here as a senator, I tell the generals of our army, they must reverse their practices and their course of proceeding on this subject. * * I advise it here from my place,—treat your enemies as

TEAMSTER OF THE ARMY

enemies, as the worst of enemies, and avail yourselves like men of every power which God has placed in your hands to accomplish your purpose within the rules of civilized warfare." Mr. Rice, (war Dem.) of Minnesota, declared that "not many days can pass before the people of the United States North must decide upon one of two questions: we have either to acknowledge the Southern Confederacy as a free and independent nation, and that speedily; or we have as speedily to resolve to use all the means given us by the Almighty to prosecute this war to a successful termination. The necessity for action has arisen. To hesitate is worse than criminal. Mr. Wilson said, "The senator from Delaware, as he is accustomed to do, speaks boldly and decidedly against the proposition. He asks if American soldiers will fight if we organize colored men for military purposes. Did not American soldiers fight at Bunker Hill with negroes in the ranks, one of whom shot down Major Pitcairn as he mounted the works? Did not American soldiers fight at Red Bank with a black regiment from your own State, sir? (Mr. Anthony in the chair.) Did they not fight on the battle-field of Rhode Island with that black regiment, one of the best and bravest that ever trod the soil of this continent? Did not American soldiers fight at Fort Griswold with black men? Did they not fight with black men in almost every battle-field of the Revolution? Did not the men of Kentucky and Tennessee, standing on the lines of New Orleans, under the eye of Andrew Jackson, fight with colored battalions whom he had summoned to the field, and whom he thanked publicly for their gallantry in hurling back a British foe? It is all talk, idle talk, to say that the volunteers who are fighting the battles of this country are governed by any such narrow prejudice or bigotry. These prejudices are the results of the teachings of demagogues and politicians, who have for years undertaken to delude and deceive the American people, and to demean and degrade them."

Mr. Grimes had expressed his views a few weeks before, and desired a vote separately on each of these sections. Mr. Davis declared that he was utterly opposed, and should ever be opposed, to placing arms in the hands of negroes, and putting them into the army. Mr. Rice wished "to know if Gen. Washington did not put arms into the hands of negroes, and if Gen. Jackson did not, and if the senator has ever condemned either of those patriots for doing so." "I deny," replied Mr. Davis, "that, in the Revolutionary War, there ever was any considerable organization of negroes. I deny, that, in the war of 1812, there was ever any organization of negro slaves. * * * In my own State, I have no doubt that there are from eighty to a hundred thousand slaves that belong to disloyal men. You propose to place arms in the hands of the men and boys, or such of them as are able to handle arms, and to manumit the whole mass, men, women, and children, and leave them among us. Do you expect us to give our sanction and our approval to these things? No, no! We would regard their authors as our worst enemies; and there is no foreign despotism that could come to our rescue, that we would not joyously embrace, before we would submit to any such condition of things as that. But, before we had invoked this foreign despotism, we would arm every man and boy that we have in the land, and we would meet you in a death-struggle, to overthrow together such an oppression and our oppressors." Mr. Rice remarked in reply to Mr. Davis, "The rebels hesitate at nothing. There are no means that God or the Devil has given them that they do not use. The honorable senator said that the negroes might be useful in loading and swabbing and firing cannon. If that be the case, may not some of them be useful in loading, swabbing, and firing the musket?"

On the 10th of February, 1864, Mr. Stevens (Republican) of Pennsylvania, in the House of Representatives, moved an amendment to the Enrollment Act. Says the same authority before quoted:

The Enrollment Bill was referred to a Conference Committee, consisting of Mr. Wilson of Massachusetts, Mr. Nesmet of Oregon, and Mr. Grimes of Iowa, on the part of the Senate; and Mr. Schenck of Ohio, Mr. Deming of Connecticut, and Mr. Kernan of New York, on the part of the House. In the Conference Committee, Mr. Wilson stated that he never could assent to the amendment, unless the drafted slaves were made free on being mustered into the service of the United States. Mr. Grimes sustained that position; and the House committee assented to it. The House amendment was then modified so as to read, "That all able-bodied male colored persons between the ages of twenty and forty-five years, whether citizens or not, resident in the United States, shall be enrolled according to the provisions of this act, and of the act to which this is an amendment, and form part of the national forces; and, when a slave of a loyal master shall be drafted and mustered into the service of the United States, his master shall have a certificate thereof; and thereupon such slave shall be free; and the bounty of a hundred dollars, now payable by law for each drafted man, shall be paid to the person to whom such drafted person was owing service or labor at the time of his muster into the service of the United States. The Secretary of War shall appoint a commission in each of the slave States represented in Congress, charged to award, to each loyal person to whom a colored volunteer may owe service, a just compensation, not exceeding three hundred dollars, for each such colored volunteer, payable out of the fund derived from commutation; and every such colored volunteer, on being mustered into the service, shall be free."

The report of the Conference Committee was agreed to; and it was enacted that every slave, whether a drafted man or a volunteer, shall be free on being mustered into the military service of the United States, not by the act of the master, but by the authority of the Federal Government."

When Gen. Banks took command of the Gulf Department, Dec. 1862, he very soon after found the negro

HEADQUARTERS OF VINCENT COLLYER, SUPT. OF THE POOR AT NEWBERNE, N. C.
Distributing clothing, captured from the Confederates, to the free negroes.

troops an indispensable quantity to the success of his expeditions; consequently he laid aside his prejudice, and endeavored to out-Herod Gen. Lorenzo Thomas, Adjutant General of the Army,—who in March had been dispatched on a military inspection tour through the armies of the West and the Mississippi Valley, and also to organize a number of negro regiments*—by issuing in May the following order:

Corps d'Afrique.

GENERAL ORDERS } No. 40. }

HEADQUARTERS, DEPARTMENT OF THE GULF,
19TH ARMY CORPS,
Opelousas, May 1, 1863.

The Major General commanding the Department proposes the organization of a corps d'armee of colored troops, to be designated as the "Corps d'Afrique." It will consist ultimately of eighteen regiments, representing all arms—Infantry, Artillery, and Cavalry, organized in three Divisions of three Brigades each, with appropriate corps of Engineers and flying Hospitals for each Division. Appropriate uniforms, and the graduation of pay to correspond with value of services, will be hereafter awarded.

In the field, the efficiency of every corps depends upon the influence of its officers upon the troops engaged, and the practicable limits of one direct command is generally estimated at one thousand men. The most eminent military historians and commanders, among others Thiers and Chambray, express the opinion, upon a full review of the elements of military power, that the valor of the soldier is rather acquired than natural. Nations whose individual heroism is undisputed, have failed as soldiers in the field. The European and American continents exhibit instances of this character, and the military prowess of every nation may be estimated by the centuries it has devoted to military contest, or the traditional passion of its people for military glory. With a race unaccustomed to military service, much more depends on the immediate influence of officers upon individual members, than with those that have acquired more or less of warlike habits and spirit by centuries of contest. It is deemed best, therefore, in the organization of the Corps d'Afrique, to limit the regiments to the smallest number of men consistent with efficient service in the field, in order to secure the most thorough instruction and discipline, and the largest influence of the officers over the troops. At first they will be limited to five hundred men. The average of American regiments is less than that number.

The Commanding General desires to detail for temporary or permanent duty the best officers of the army, for the organization, instruction and discipline of this corps. With their aid, he is confident that the corps will render important service to the Government. It is not established upon any dogma of equality or other theory, but as a practical and sensible matter of business. The Government makes use of mules, horses, uneducated and educated white men, in the defense of its institutions. Why should not the negro contribute whatever is in his power for the cause in which he is as deeply interested as other men? We may properly demand from him whatever service he can render. The chief defect in organizations of this character has arisen from incorrect ideas of the officers in command. Their discipline has been lax, and in some cases the conduct of the regiments unsatisfactory and discreditable. Controversies unnecessary and injurious to the service have arisen between them and other troops. The organization proposed will reconcile and avoid many of these troubles.

Officers and soldiers will consider the exigencies of the service in this Department, and the absolute necessity of appropriating every element of power to the support of the Government. The prejudices or opinions of men are in nowise involved. The co-operation and active support of all officers and men, and the nomination of fit men from the ranks, and from the lists of non-commissioned and commissioned officers, are respectfully solicited from the Generals commanding the respective Divisions.

BY COMMAND OF MAJOR GENERAL BANKS:

RICHARD B. IRWIN,
Assistant Adjutant General.

WAR DEPARTMENT,
Washington City, March 25th, 1863.

* GENERAL:—The exigencies of the service require that an inspection should be made of the Armies, military posts and military operations in the West; you will therefore make arrangements immediately to perform that service. Without entering into any minute details, I beg to direct your attention to the following subjects of investigation:

First. On arriving at Cairo, you will make a careful examination of the military condition of that post, in the various branches of service, and report to this Department, the result of your investigation, suggesting whatever in your opinion, the service may require. You will observe particularly the condition of that class of population known as contrabands; the manner in which they are received, provided for and treated by the military authorities, and give such directions to the Commissary and Quartermaster Departments, and to the officers commanding, as shall, in your judge-

His plan of organization is here given, but it was never fully consummated:

Corps d'Afrique.

GENERAL ORDERS No. 47.

HEADQUARTERS DEPARTMENT OF THE GULF, 19TH ARMY CORPS, *Before Port Hudson*, June 6th, 1863.

I.—The regiments of infantry of the Corps d'Afrique, authorized by General Orders No. 44, current series, will consist of ten companies each, having the following minimum organization:

1 Captain, 1 First Lieutenant, 1 Second Lieutenant, 1 First Sergeant, 4 Sergeants, 4 Corporals, 2 Buglers, 40 Privates.

To the above may be added hereafter, at the discretion of the Commanding General, four corporals and forty-two privates; thus increasing the strength to the maximum fixed by law for a company of infantry.

The regimental organization will be that fixed by law for a regiment of infantry.

II.—The Commissary and Assistant Commissaries of Musters will muster the Second Lieutenant into service as soon as he is commissioned; the First Lieutenant when thirty men are enlisted; and the Captain when the minimum organization is completed.

III.—The First, Second, Third and Fourth Regiments of Louisiana Native Guards will hereafter be known as the First, Second, Third and Fourth Regiments of Infantry of the Corps d'Afrique.

IV.—The regiment of colored troops in process of organization in the district of Pensacola will be known as the Fifth Regiment of Infantry of the Corps d'Afrique.

V.—The regiments now being raised under the direction of Brigadier General Daniel Ullman, and at present known as the First, Second, Third, Fourth and Fifth Regiments of Ullman's Brigade, will be respectively designated as the Sixth, Seventh, Eighth, Ninth and Tenth Regiments of Infantry of the Corps d'Afrique.

VI.—The First Regiment of Louisiana Engineers, Colonel Justin Hodge, will hereafter be known as the First Regiment of Engineers of the Corps 'dAfrique.

BY COMMAND OF MAJOR GENERAL BANKS:

RICHARD B. IRWIN,
Assistant Adjutant General.

OFFICIAL:
NATHANIEL BURBANK, Acting Assistant Adjutant General.

General Banks' treatment of the negroes was so very different from that which they had received from Gen. Butler,—displacing the negro officers of the first three regiments organized,—that it rather checkmated recruiting, so much so that he found it necessary to resort to the

---

ment, be necessary to secure to them humane and proper treatment, in respect to food, clothing, compensation for their service, and whatever is necessary to enable them to support themselves, and to furnish useful service in any capacity to the Government.

Second. You will make similar observation at Columbus, Memphis and other posts in your progress to the Headquarters of General Grant's Army.

Third. The President desires that you should confer freely with Major General Grant, and the officers with whom you may have communication, and explain to them the importance attached by the Government to the use of the colored population emancipated by the President's Proclamation, and particularly for the organization of their labor and military strength. You will cause it to be understood that no officer in the United States service is regarded as in the discharge of his duties under the Acts of Congress, the President's Proclamation, and orders of this Department, who fails to employ to the utmost extent, the aid and co-operation of the loyal colored population in performing the labor incident to military operations, and also in performing the duties of soldiers under proper organization, and that any obstacle thrown in the way of these ends, is regarded by the President as a violation of the Acts of Congress, and the declared purposes of the Government in using every means to bring the war to an end.

Fourth. You will ascertain what military officers are willing to take command of colored troops; ascertain their qualifications for that purpose, and if troops can be raised and organized, you will, so far as can be done without prejudice to the service, relieve officers and privates from the service in which they are engaged, to receive commissions such as they may be qualified to exercise in the organization of brigades, regiments and companies of colored troops. You are authorized in this connection, to issue in the name of this department, letters of appointment for field and company officers, and to organize such troops for military service to the utmost extent to which they can be obtained in accordance with the rules and regulations of the service. You will see, more over, and expressly enjoin upon the various staff departments of the service, that such troops are to be provided with supplies upon the requisition of the proper officers, and in the same manner as other troops in the service.

* * * * *

Very Respectfully Your Obedient Servant,
EDWARD M. STANTON, *Sec. of War.*

BRIG. GEN. L. THOMAS,
Adjt. Gen'l. U. S. Army.

PROVOST GUARD SECURING CONSCRIPTS.
Compelling all able-bodied men to join the army.

provost guard to fill up regiments, as the following order indicates:

Commission of Enrollment.

GENERAL ORDERS No. 64. HEADQUARTERS, DEPARTMENT OF THE GULF, *New Orleans*, August 29, 1863.

I. Colonel JOHN S. CLARK, Major B. RUSH PLUMLY and Colonel GEORGE H. HANKS, are hereby appointed a Commission to regulate the Enrollment, Recruiting and Employment and Education of persons of color. All questions concerning the enlistment of troops for the Corps d'Afrique, the regulation of labor, or the government and education of negroes, will be referred to the decision of this commission, subject to the approval of the Commanding General of the Department.

II. No enlistments for the Corps d'Afrique will be authorized or permitted, except under regulations approved by this Commission.

III. *The Provost Marshal General will cause to be enrolled all able-bodied men of color in accordance with the Law of Conscription, and such number as may be required for the military defence of the Department, equally apportioned to the different parishes, will be enlisted for the military service under such regulations as the Commission may adopt. Certificates of exemption will be furnished to those not enlisted, protecting them from arrest or other interference, except for crime.*

IV. Soldiers of the Corps d'Afrique will not be allowed to leave their camps, or to wander through the parishes, except upon written permission, or in the company of their officers.

V. Unemployed persons of color, vagrants and camp loafers, will be arrested and employed upon the public works, by the Provost Marshal's Department, without other pay than their rations and clothing.

VI. Arrests of persons, and seizures of property, will not be made by colored soldiers, nor will they be charged with the custody of persons or property, except when under the command, and accompanied by duly authorized officers.

VII. Any injury or wrong done to the family of any soldier, on account of his being engaged in military service, will be summarily punished.

VIII. As far as practicable, the labor of persons not adapted to military service will be provided in substitution for that of enlisted men.

IX. All regulations hitherto established for the government of negroes, not inconsistent herewith, will be enforced by the Provost Marshals of the different parishes, under the direction of the Provost Marshal General.

BY COMMAND OF MAJOR GENERAL BANKS:

RICHARD B. IRWIN,
Assistant Adjutant General.

In the department the actual number of negroes enlisted was never known, from the fact that a practice prevailed of putting a live negro in a dead one's place. For instance, if a company on picket or scouting lost ten men, the officer would immediately put ten new men in their places and have them answer to the dead men's names. I learn from very reliable sources that this was done in Virginia, also in Missouri and Tennessee. If the exact number of men could be ascertained, instead of 180,000 it would doubtless be in the neighborhood of 220,000 who entered the ranks of the army. An order was issued which aimed to correct the habit and to prevent the drawing, by collusion, of the dead men's pay.

The date of the first organization of colored troops is a question of dispute, but it seems as if the question might be settled, either by the records of the War Department or the personal knowledge of those interested. Of course the muster of a regiment or company is the record of the War Department, but the muster by no means dates the organization of the troops.* For example, a colonel may have been commissioned July, 1862, and yet the muster of his regiment may be September 1862, and even later, by two months, as is the case in more than one instance. It is just as fair to take the date of a soldier's enlistment as the date of the organization of a regiment, as that of the date of the order detailing an officer to recruit as the date of the colonel's commission. The writer's discharge from the Second Reg't. Louisiana Native Guards credits him as enlisting on the 1st day of September, 1862; at this date the 1st Reg't. La. N. G. was in the field, in November the Second Regiment took the field, so that the date of the organization of the first regiment of colored troops was in September, 1862. Col. Higginson, says in his volume:

"Except the Louisiana soldiers mentioned,—of whom no detailed reports have, I think, been published,—my regiment was unquestionably the first mustered into the service of the United States; the first company mustered bearing date, November 7, 1862, and the others following in quick succession."

Save the regiments recruited in Kansas, South Carolina and New Orleans during the year 1862, nothing was done towards increasing the negro army, but in January 1863, when the policy of the Government was changed and the Emancipation Proclamation foreshadowed the employment of negroes in the armed service, an activity

* Col. Thomas Wentworth Higginson in an appendix to his "Army Life in a Black Regiment," gives some account of the organization of negro troops, from which is condensed the following:

"It is well known that the first systematic attempt to organize colored troops during the war of the rebellion was the so-called "Hunter Regiment." The officer originally detailed to recruit for this purpose was Sergeant C. T. Trowbridge, of the New York Volunteer Engineers (Col. Serrell.) His detail was dated May 7, 1862, S. O. 84, Dept. South.

"The second regiment in order of muster was the First Kansas Colored, dating from January 13, 1863. The first enlistment in the Kansas regiment goes back to August 6, 1862; while the earliest technical date of enlistment in my regiment was October 19, 1862, although, as was stated above, one company really dated its organization back to May, 1862. My muster as Colonel dates back to November 10, 1862, several months earlier than any other of which I am aware, among colored regiments, except that of Col. Stafford, (First Louisiana Native Guards,) Sept. 27, 1862. Colonel Williams, of the First Kansas Colored, was mustered as Lt. Colonel on Jan. 13, 1863; as Col., March 8, 1863. These dates I have (with the other facts relating to the regiment) from Col. R. J. Hinton, the first officer detailed to recruit it.

"The first detachment of the Second South Carolina Volunteers (Col. Montgomery) went into camp at Port Royal Island, February 23, 1863, numbering one hundred and twenty men. I do not know the date of his muster; it was somewhat delayed, but was probably dated back to about that time.

"Recruiting for the Fifty-Fourth Massachusetts (colored) began on February 9, 1863, and the first squad went into camp at Readville, Massachusetts, on February 21, 1863, numbering twenty-five men. Col. Shaw's commission—and probably his muster—was dated April 17, 1863. (Report of Adjutant General of Massachusetts for 1863, pp. 896-899.) These were the earliest colored regiments, so far as I know."

such as had not been witnessed since the beginning of the war became apparent. Many officers without commands, and some with, but who sought promotion, were eager to be allowed to organize a regiment, a battalion or a brigade of negro troops. Mr. Lincoln found it necessary in less than six months after issuing his Proclamation of Freedom, to put the whole matter of negro soldiers into the hands of a board.* Ambition, as ambition will, smothered many a white man's prejudice and caused more than one West Pointer to forget his political education. This order was issued:

ADJUTANT GENERAL'S OFFICE,
Washington, D. C., January 13th, 1863.

BRIGADIER GENERAL D. ULLMAN, Washington, D. C.

SIR:—By direction of the Secretary of War you are hereby authorized to raise a Brigade of (four regiments) of Louisiana Volunteer Infantry, to be recruited in that State to serve for three years or during the War.

Each regiment of said Brigade will be organized as prescribed in General orders No. 126, series of 1862, from this office.

The recruitment will be conducted in accordance with the rules of the service, and the orders of the War Department, and by the said department all appointments of officers will be made.

All musters will be made in strict conformity to Paragraph 86 Revised Mustering Regulations of 1862. I am, Very Respectfully Your Obedient Servant,
THOMAS M. VINCENT, *Asst. Adjt. Gen'l.*

---

* GENERAL ORDERS, No. 143. WAR DEPARTMENT, ADJUTANT GENERAL'S OFFICE, *Washington*, May 22, 1863.

I.—A Bureau is established in the Adjutant General's Office for the record of all matters relating to the organization of Colored Troops. An officer will be assigned to the charge of the Bureau, with such number of clerks as may be designated by the Adjutant General.

II.—Three or more field officers will be detailed as Inspectors to supervise the organization of colored troops at such points as may be indicated by the War Department in the Northern and Western States.

III.—Boards will be convened at such posts as may be decided upon by the War Department to examine applicants for commissions to command colored troops, who, on application to the Adjutant General, may receive authority to present themselves to the board for examination.

IV—No persons shall be allowed to recruit for colored troops except specially authorized by the War Department; and no such authority will be given to persons who have not been examined and passed by a board; nor will such authority be given any one person to raise more than one regiment.

V.—The reports of Boards will specify the grade of commission for which each candidate is fit, and authority to recruit will be given in accordance. Commissions will be issued from the Adjutant General's Office when the prescribed number of men is ready for muster into service.

VI.—Colored troops may be accepted by companies, to be afterwards consolidated in battalions and regiments by the Adjutant General. The regiments will be numbered *seriatim*, in the order in which they are raised, the numbers to be determined by the Adjutant General. They will be designated: "— Regiment of U. S. Colored Troops."

VII.—Recruiting stations and depots will be established by the Adjutant General as circumstances shall require, and officers will be detailed to muster and inspect the troops.

VIII.—The non-commissioned officers of colored troops may be selected and appointed from the best men of their number in the usual mode of appointing non-commissioned officers. Meritorious commissioned officers will be entitled to promotion to higher rank if they prove themselves equal to it.

IX.—All personal applications for appointments in colored regiments, or for information concerning them, must be made to the Chief of the Bureau; all written communications should be addressed to the Chief of the Bureau, to the care of the Adjutant General.

BY ORDER OF THE SECRETARY OF WAR:
E. D. TOWNSEND, *Asst. Adjt. General.*

ADJUTANT GENERAL'S OFFICE,
Washington, D. C., March 24, 1863.

BRIG. GENERAL ULLMAN, Washington, D. C.

GENERAL:—By direction of the Secretary of War, you are hereby authorized to raise a Battalion (six companies) of Louisiana Volunteer Infantry to be used for scouting purposes, to be recruited in that State, and to serve for three years or during the war.

The said force will be organized as prescribed in Paragraph 83, Mustering Regulations.

The recruitment will be conducted in accordance with the rules of the service, and the orders of the War Department, and by the said Department all appointments of officers will be made.

All musters will be made in accordance with the orders given in reference to the troops authorized by the instructions from this office of January 13, 1863.

I am, General Very Respectfully Your Obedient Servant,
THOMAS M. VINCENT, *Asst. Adjt. General.*

In furtherance of the order General Ullman proceeded to New Orleans and assumed command of seven thousand troops already organized. It was said that he had arranged to place 500 white officers in command of the troops in Louisiana.

In October thereafter General Banks issued the following order, which fully explains itself:

Recruiting for the Corps d'Afrique.

GENERAL ORDERS} HEADQUARTERS, DEPARTMENT OF THE GULF.
No. 77. } *New Orleans*, October 27, 1863.

I. All persons of Color coming within the lines of the army, or following the army when in the field, other than those employed in the Staff Department of the army, or as servants of officers entitled by the Regulations to have servants, or cooks, will be placed in charge of and provided for by the several Provost Marshals of the Parishes, or if the army be on the march, or in the field, by the Provost Marshal of the Army.

II. The several Provost Marshals of the Parishes and of the Army will promptly forward to the nearest recruiting depot all able bodied males for service in the Corps d'Afrique.

III. Recruits will be received for the Corps d'Afrique of all able bodied men from sections of the country not occupied by our forces, and beyond our lines, without regard to the enrollment provided for in General Orders No. 64 and 70, from these Headquarters.

IV. Instructions will be given by the President of the Commission of Enrollment to the Superintendent of Recruiting, to govern in all matters of detail relating to recruiting, and officers will be held to a strict accountability for the faithful observance of existing orders and such instructions; but no officer will be authorized to recruit beyond the lines without first having his order approved by the officer commanding the nearest post, or the officer commanding the Army in the Field, who will render such assistance as may be necessary to make the recruiting service effective.

BY COMMAND OF MAJOR GENERAL BANKS:
G. NORMAN LIEBER, *Act. Asst. Adjt. Gen'l.*

At the North where negroes had been refused admission to the army, the President's Proclamation was hailed with delight. Gov. Andrew, of Massachusetts, at once began the organization of the 54th Regiment of his State, composed entirely of negroes, and on the 28th of May the regiment being ready to take the field, embarked for South Carolina. Other Northern States followed. Pennsylvania established Camp Wm. Penn, from which several regiments took their departure, while Connecticut and Rhode Island both sent a regiment.

The taste with which the negro soldiers arranged their quarters often prompted officers of white regiments to

NEW RECRUITS TAKING CARS FOR CAMP.

borrow a detail to clean and beautify the quarters of their commands. An occurrence of this kind came very near causing trouble on Morris Island, S. C. The matter was brought to the commanding General's attention and he immediately issued this order:

DEPARTMENT OF THE SOUTH, HEADQUARTERS IN THE FIELD.
GENERAL ORDERS, No. 77. *Morris Island, S. C.*, Sept. 17th, 1863.

I. It has come to the knowledge of the Brig. Gen. Commanding that detachments of colored troops, detailed for fatigue duty, have been employed in one instance at least, to prepare camps and perform menial duty for white troops. Such use of these details is unauthorized and improper, and is hereafter expressly prohibited. Commanding Officers of colored regiments are directed to report promptly, to the Headquarters, any violations of this order which may come to their knowledge.

BY ORDER OF GEN. Q. A. GILLMORE,
OFFICIAL: ED. W. SMITH, *Asst. Adjt. Gen'l.*
ISRAEL Z. SEALEY, Capt. 47th N. Y. Vols., Act. Asst. Adjt. General.

The Southern troops generally made no objection to cleaning the quarters of their white allies, but when a detail from the 54th Mass. Reg't., on its way to the front, was re-detailed for that purpose, they refused to obey. The detail was placed under arrest. When this information reached the regiment it was only by releasing the prisoners that a turbulent spirit was quieted. There were about ten thousand negro troops in and about Morris Island at that time, and they quickly sneezed at the 54th's snuff. The negro barbers in this department had been refusing to shave and to cut the hair of negro soldiers in common with the whites. Corporal Kelley of the 54th Mass. Regiment, who had been refused a shave at a shop located near one of the brigade Headquarters, went there one evening accompanied by a number of the members of Company C. The men gathered around the barber's place of business, which rested upon posts a little up from the ground; the negro barbers were seated in their chairs resting from their labors and listening to the concert, which it was customary for a band to give each evening. As the last strains of music were being delivered, one side of the barber shop was lifted high and then suddenly dropped; it came down with a crash making a wreck of the building and its contents, except the barbers, who escaped unhurt, but who never made their appearance again. The episode resulted in the issuing of an order forbidding discrimination on account of color.

The Washington authorities established recruiting stations throughout the South. Of the difficulties under which recruiting officers labored some idea may be formed by reading the following, written by the historian of the 7th Regiment:

"The position of recruiting officer for colored troops was by no means a sinecure; on the contrary, it was attended with hardships, annoyances and difficulties without number. Moving about from place to place; often on scant rations, and always without transportation, save what could be pressed into service; sleeping in barns, out-houses, public buildings,—wherever shelter could be found, and meeting from the people everywhere opposition and dislike. To have been an officer of colored troops was of itself sufficient to ostracize, and when, in addition, one had to take from them their slaves, dislike became absolute hatred. There were, of course, exceptions, and doubtless every officer engaged on this disagreeable duty can bear testimony to receiving at times a hospitality as generous as it was unexpected, even from people whom duty compelled them to despoil. But this was always from "*union men*," for it must be confessed that a large proportion of the property-holders on both the eastern and western shores of the Chesapeake were as deeply in sympathy with the rebellion as their brethren over the Virginia border.

"Perhaps the most disagreeable feature of this recruiting duty was that Gen. Birney (Supt. of recruiting of negro troops in Maryland) seldom saw fit to give his subordinates anything but *verbal* instructions. Officers were ordered to open recruiting stations; to raid through the country, carrying off slaves from under the eyes of their masters; to press horses for their own use and that of their men, and teams and vehicles for purposes of transportation; to take forage when needed; to occupy buildings and appropriate fuel; in short, to do a hundred things they had really no legal right to do, and had they been called upon, as was likely to happen at any time, for the authority under which they were acting, they would have had nothing to show but their commissions; and if, in carrying out these verbal instructions from their chief, they had become involved in serious difficulty, they had little reason to suppose that they would be sustained by him.

"When it is remembered that slavery was at that time still a recognized institution, and that the duty of a recruiting officer often required him to literally strip a plantation of its field hands, and that, too, at a time of the year when the crops were being gathered, it is perhaps to be wondered that the bitter feelings of the slave-owners did not often find vent in open resistence and actual violence. That this delicate and disagreeable duty was performed in a manner to avoid serious difficulty certainly speaks well for the prudence and good judgment of the officers and men engaged in it.

"The usual method of proceeding was, upon reaching a designated point, to occupy the most desirable public building, dwelling-house, warehouse, or barn found vacant, and with this as a rendezvous, small parties were sent into the surrounding country, visiting each plantation within a raidus of twenty or thirty miles. The parties, sometimes under charge of an officer, usually consisted of a non-commissioned officer and ten or twelve men.

"In these journeys through the country the recruiting officer often met with strange experiences. Recruits were taken wherever found, and as their earthly possessions usually consisted of but what they wore upon their backs, they required no time to settle their affairs. The laborer in the field would throw down his hoe or quit his plow and march away with the guard, leaving his late owner looking after him in speechless amazement. On one occasion the writer met a planter on the road, followed by two of his slaves, each driving a loaded wagon. The usual questions were asked and the whilom slaves joined the recruiting party, leaving their teams and late master standing in the highway. At another time a negro was met with a horse and wagon. Having expressed his desire to "'list," he turned his horse's head toward home, and marched away in the opposite direction.

"On one occasion the writer visited a large plantation near Capeville, Va., and calling upon the proprietor asked him to call in his slaves. He complied without a word, and when they came and were asked if they wished to enlist, replied that they did, and fell into the ranks with the guard. As they started away the old man turned to me, and with tears in his eyes, said, "Will you take them all? Here I am, an old man; I cannot work; my crops are ungathered; my negroes have all enlisted or run away, and what am I to do? A hard question, truly. Another officer was called upon by a gentleman with this question, "You have taken all my able-bodied men for soldiers, the others have run away, and only the women and children are left;—what do you propose to do with them?" Another hard question.

"At another time, when the *Balloon* was lying at the mouth of the Pocomoke, accompanied by Lieut. Brown and with a boat's crew, we pulled up the river to the plantation of a Mrs. D., a noted rebel sympathizer. We were met, as we expected, with the most violent abuse from the fair proprietoress, which was redoubled when three of her best slaves, each of whom had probably been worth a couple of thousand dollars in *ante-bellum* days, took their bundles and marched off to the boat. We bade the lady farewell, and pushed off amid the shouts and screams of a score of negro women and children, and the tears and execrations of the widow.

"To illustrate the unreasonable orders Gen. Birney was sometimes in the habit of giving to officers engaged under him on recruiting service, the writer well remembers being placed by him, at Pungoteague, Va., in charge of some 200 recruits he had forcibly taken from an officer recruiting under Col. Nelson's orders, and receiving from him (Gen. Birney) the most positive orders under no circumstances to allow Col. Nelson to get possession of them,—Col. Nelson's steamer was hourly expected—and that I should be held personally responsible that they were put on board his own steamer, and this when I had neither men nor muskets to enforce the order. Fortunately (for myself) Gen. Birney's steamer arrived first and the men were safely put on board. Some days later, Lieut. Brown, who was then in charge of the same station, had a squad of recruits taken from him by Col. Nelson, in retaliation.

"Many a hap-hazard journey was undertaken in search of recruits and recruiting stations. On one occasion an officer was ordered by Gen. Birney to take station at a town (?) not many miles from Port Tobacco, on the Potomac. After two days' careful search he discovered that the town he was in search of had been a post-office twenty years before, but then consisted of one house, uninhabited and uninhabitable, with not another within the circuit of five miles."

When the Government decided to arm the negroes and ordered the organization of a hundred regiments, it was with great difficulty the equipment department met the requisitions. It necessitated a departure from the accustomed uniform material for volunteers, and helped to arouse the animosity of the white troops. Instead of the coarse material issued at first, the Phalanx was clothed in a fine blue-black dress coat for the infantry, and a superb dark blue jacket for the artillery and cavalry, all neatly trimmed with brass buttons and white, red and yellow cord, representing the arm of service; heavy sky blue pantaloons, and a flannel cap, or high crown black flelt hat or *chapeau* with a black feather looped upon the right side and fastened with a brass eagle. For the infantry and for the cavalry two swords crossed; for the artillery two cannons on the front of the *chapeau* crossed, with the letters of the company, and number of the regiment to which the soldier belonged. On the caps these insignias were worn on the top of the crown. The uniform of the Phalanx put the threadbare clothes of the white veterans in sad contrast, and was the cause of many a black soldier being badly treated by his white comrades.*

---

* I attempted to pass Jackson Square in New Orleans one day in my uniform, when I was met by two white soldiers of the 24th Conn. They halted me and then ordered me to undress. I refused, when they seized me and began to tear my coat off. I resisted, but to no good purpose; a half a dozen others came up and began to assist. I recognized a sergeant in the crowd, an old shipmate on board of a New Bedford, Mass., Whaler; he came to my rescue, my clothing was restored and I was let go. It was nothing strange to see a black soldier *a la Adam* come into the barracks out of the streets. This conduct led to the killing of a portion of a boat's crew of the U. S. Gunboat *Jackson*, at Ship Island, Miss., by members of a Phalanx regiment stationed there.

At the outbreak of the Rebellion, the pay of soldiers (volunteers) was the same as soldiers of the regular army, by law, $13 per month. The soldiers of the Phalanx enlisted under the same law and regulations as did the white volunteers, as to pay and term of service, but the Secretary of War, after a few regiments were in the field, decided, and so ordered, that negro troops should be paid ten dollars per month. The instructions given to General Saxton on the 25th day of August, 1862, had stated that the pay would be the same as that of the other troops:

"In view of the small force under your command, and the inability of the Government at the present time to increase it, in order to guard the plantations and settlements occupied by the United States, from invasion, and to protect the inhabitants thereof from captivity and murder by the enemy, you are also authorized to arm, uniform, equip, and receive into the service of the United States, such number of volunteers of African descent as you may deem expedient, not exceeding five thousand, and may detail officers to instruct them in military drill, discipline and duty, and to command them. *The persons so received into service, and their officers, to be entitled to, and receive, the same pay and rations as are allowed, by law, to volunteers in the service.*"

As to the white officers they were paid in full, but the privates and non-commissioned officers were allowed but $10 per month, three of which were deducted on account of clothing. In several instances the paymaster not having received special instructions to that effect, disregarded the general orders, and paid the negro soldiers in full, like other volunteers; but the order was generally recognized, though many of the regiments refused to receive the $7 per month, which was particularly the case of regiments from the Northern States. The order at one time in the Department of the Gulf, came very near causing a mutiny among the troops, because white troops, and conscripts at that, and those who had done provost duty about the cities, were paid $16 per month,—Congress having raised the pay,—while the Phalanx regiments in the field and fortifications were offered $7. The dissatisfaction was so strongly manifested as to cause twelve members of the Phalanx to lose their lives, which were not the only ones lost by the bad faith on the part of the Government. However, in no instance did the Phalanx refuse to do its duty when called upon, and at the sound of the long roll, though the black flag was raised against them, and many of their families were suffering at home, their patriotic ardor never abated in the least. At the North, provisions were made by the States to relieve the families of the brave men. Massachusetts sent paymasters to make good the promises of the Government, but the deficiency was rejected. Her regiments, although a year without pay, refused to accept, and demanded full pay from the Government. The loyal people of the country, at public meetings and the press,* severely criticised the

---

* The injustice done the Phalanx, in discriminating between the Northern and Southern negro, may be clearly seen by the following letters:

"NEW VICTORIES AND OLD WRONGS.—*To the Editors of the Evening Post:* On the 2d of July, at James Island, S. C., a battery was taken by three regiments, under the following circumstances:

"The regiments were the One Hundred and Third New York (white), the Thirty-Third United States (formerly First South Carolina Volunteers), and the Fifty-Fifth Massachusetts, the two last being colored. They marched at one A. M., by the flank, in the above order, hoping to surprise the battery. As usual the rebels were prepared for them, and opened upon them as they were deep in one of those almost impassable Southern marshes. The One Hundred and Third New York, which had previously been in twenty battles, was thrown into confusion; the Thirty-Third United States did better, being behind; the Fifty-Fifth Massachusetts being in the rear, did better still. All three formed in line, when Colonel Hartwell, commanding the brigade, gave the order to retreat. The officer commanding the Fifty-Fifth Massachusetts, either misunderstanding the order, or hearing it countermanded, ordered his regiment to charge. This order was at once repeated by Major Trowbridge, commanding the Thirty-Third United States, and by the commander of the One Hundred and Third New York, so that the three regiments reached the fort in reversed order. The color-bearers of the Thirty-Third United States and of the Fifty-Fifth Massachusetts had a race to be first in, the latter winning. The One Hundred and Third New York entered the battery immediately after.

"These colored regiments are two of the five which were enlisted in South Carolina and Massachusetts, under the written pledge of the War Department that they should have the same pay and allowances as white soldiers. That pledge has been deliberately broken by the War Department, or by Congress, or by both, except as to the short period, since last New Year's Day. Every one of those killed in this action from these two colored regiments—under a fire before which the veterans of twenty battles recoiled—*died defrauded by the Government of nearly one-half of his petty pay.*

"Mr. Fessenden, who defeated in the Senate the bill for the fulfillment of the contract with these soldiers, is now Secretary of the Treasury. Was the economy of saving six dollars per man worth to the Treasury the ignominy of the repudiation?

"Mr. Stevens, of Pennsylvania, on his triumphal return to his constituents, used to them this language: 'He had no doubt whatever as to the final result of the present contest between liberty and slavery. The only doubt he had was whether the nation had yet been satisfactorily chastised for their cruel oppression of a harmless and long-suffering race.' Inasmuch as it was Mr. Stevens himself who induced the House of Representatives, most unexpectedly to all, to defeat the Senate bill for the fulfilment of the national contract with these soldiers, I should think he had excellent reasons for the doubt. Very respectfully, T. W. HIGGINSON,

July 10, 1864. *Col. 1st S. C. Vols. (now 33d U. S.)*

"*To the Editor of the New York Tribune:* No one can possibly be so weary of reading of the wrongs done by Government toward the colored soldiers as I am of writing about them. This is my only excuse for intruding on your columns again.

By an order of the War Department, dated Aug 1, 1864, it is at length ruled that colored soldiers shall be paid the full pay of soldiers from date of enlistment, provided they were free on April 19, 1861,—not otherwise; and this distinction is to be noted on the pay-rolls. In other words, if one half of a company escaped from slavery on April 18, 1861, they are to be paid thirteen dollars per month and allowed three dollars and a half per month for clothing. If the other half were delayed two days, they receive seven dollars per month and are allowed three dollars per month for precisely the same

SCENE AT NEW BERNE, N. C.
Enthusiasm of the Blacks at the prospect of their being allowed to enlist as U. S. Soldiers.

Government, while the patriotic black men continued to pour out their blood and to give their lives for liberty and the Union.

The matter being one for Congress to adjust, Henry Wilson, of Massachusetts, on the 8th of Jan. 1864, introduced in the Senate of the United States, a bill to promote enlistments in the army, and in this measure justice to the black soldiers was proposed. After months of debate, it was finally passed; not only placing the Phalanx soldiers on a footing with all other troops, but made free, the mothers, wives and children of the noble black troops.

The fight of the Phalanx for equal pay and allowance with the white troops, was a long one. The friends of the black soldiers in Congress fought it, however, to the successful issue. Senator Wilson, of Massachusetts, took the lead in the matter in the Senate, as he did in the amend-

articles of clothing. If one of the former class is made first sergeant, his pay is put up to twenty-one dollars per month; but if he escaped two days later, his pay is still estimated at seven dollars.

"It had not occurred to me that anything could make the pay-rolls of these regiments more complicated than at present, or the men more rationally discontented. I had not the ingenuity to imagine such an order. Yet it is no doubt in accordance with the spirit, if not with the letter, of the final bill which was adopted by Congress under the lead of Mr. Thaddeus Stevens.

"The ground taken by Mr. Stevens apparently was that the country might honorably save a few dollars by docking the promised pay of those colored soldiers whom the war had made free. *But the Government should have thought of this before it made the contract with these men and received their services.* When the War Department instructed Brigadier-General Saxton, August 25, 1862, to raise five regiments of negroes in South Carolina, it was known very well that the men so enlisted had only recently gained their freedom. But the instructions said: 'The persons so received into service, and their officers, to be entitled to and receive the same pay and rations as are allowed by law to volunteers in the service.' Of this passage Mr. Solicitor Whiting wrote to me: 'I have no hesitation in saying that the faith of the Government was thereby pledged to every officer and soldier enlisted under that call.' Where is that faith of the Government now?

"The men who enlisted under the pledge were volunteers, every one; they did not get their freedom by enlisting; they had it already. They enlisted to serve the Government, trusting in its honor. Now the nation turns upon them and says: Your part of the contract is fulfilled; we have had your services. If you can show that you had previously been free for a certain length of time, we will fulfil the other side of the contract. If not, we repudiate it. Help yourselves, if you can.

"In other words, a freedman (since April 19, 1861) has no rights which a white man is bound to respect. He is incapable of making a contract. No man is bound by a contract made with him. Any employer, following the example of the United States Government, may make with him a written agreement, receive his services, and then withhold the wages. He has no motive to honest industry, or to honesty of any kind. He is virtually a slave, and nothing else, to the end of time.

"Under this order, the greater part of the Massachusetts colored regiments will get their pay at last, and be able to take their wives and children out of the almshouses, to which, as Governor Andrew informs us, the gracious charity of the nation has consigned so many. For so much I am grateful. But toward my regiment, which had been in service and under fire, months before a Northern colored soldier was recruited, the policy of repudiation has at last been officially adopted. There is no alternative for the officers of South Carolina regiments but to wait for another session of Congress, and meanwhile, if necessary, act as executioners for these soldiers who, like Sergeant Walker, refuse to fulfil their share of a contract where the Government has openly repudiated the other share. If a year's discussion, however, has at length secured the arrears of pay for the Northern colored regiments, possibly two years may secure it for the Southern.

T. W. HIGGINSON,
Col. 1st S. C. Vols. (now 33d U. S.)

August 12, 1864.

ing of the enrolling acts, and the act calling out the militia, whereby negroes were enrolled.

In the winter of '64 Gen. Butler began the organization of the Army of the James and the enlistment of negro troops. A camp was established near Fortress Monroe, where a great many men enlisted. The Secretary of War gave permission to the several Northern States to send agents South, and to enlist negroes to fill up their quotas of troops needed. Large bounties were then being paid and many a negro received as much as $500 to enlist; while many who went as substitutes received even more than that. The recruiting officers or rather agents from the different States established their headquarters largely within Gen. Butlers departments, where negro volunteers were frequently secured at a much less price than the regular bounty offered, the agent putting into his own pocket the difference, which often amounted to $200 or even $400 on a single recruit. To correct this wrong, Gen. Butler issued the following order:

HEADQUARTERS DEP'T. VIRGINIA & NORTH CAROLINA,
GENERAL ORDERS, No. 90. IN THE FIELD, VA., *August 4th, 1864.*

* * * * *

With all the guards which the utmost vigilance and care have thrown around the recruitment of white soldiers, it is a fact, as lamentable as true, that a large portion of the recruits have been swindled of part, if not all, of their bounties. Can it be hoped that the colored man will be better able to protect himself from the infinite ingenuity of fraud than the white?

Therefore, to provide for the families of the colored recruits enlisted in this Department—to relieve the United States, as far as may be, from the burden of supporting the families,—and to insure that at least a portion of the bounty paid to the negro shall be received for his use and that of his family;

It is ordered: I—That upon the enlistment of any negro recruit into the service of the United States for three (3) years, by any State agent or other person not enlisting recruits under the direct authority of the War Department, a sum of one hundred (100) dollars, or one-third (⅓) of the sum agreed to be paid as bounty, shall be paid if the amount exceeds three times that sum, into the hands of the Superintendent of Recruiting, or an officer to be designated by him, and in the same proportion for any less time; and no Mustering Officer will give any certificate or voucher for any negro recruit mustered into the service of the United States, so that he may be credited to the quota of any State, or as a substitute, until a certificate is filed with him that the amount called for by this order has been paid, to the satisfaction of the Superintendent of Recruiting of the district wherein the recruit was enlisted; but the mustering officer will, in default of such payment, certify upon the roll that the recruit is not to be credited to the quota of any State, or as a substitute.

II—The amount as paid to the Superintendent of Recruiting shall be turned over, on the last day of each month, to the Superintendent of Negro Affairs, to be expended in aid of the families of negro soldiers in this Department. The certificates filed with Commissary of Musters will be returned to said Superintendent of Negro Affairs, on the first day of every month, so that the Superintendent may vouch for the accounts of the Superintendent of Recruiting, for the amounts received by him.

And the Superintendent of Negro Affairs will account monthly to the Financial Agent of this Department for the amounts received and expended by him.

III—As there are unfilled colored Regiments in this Department sufficient to receive all the negro recruits therein, no negro male person above the age of sixteen (16) years, shall be taken out or attempted to be taken out of this Department, either as a recruit, as officer's servant, or otherwise, in any manner whatever, without a pass from these Head Quarters. Any officer, Master of Transportation, Provost Marshal, or person,

MUSTERING INTO SERVICE.

Phalanx soldiers taking the oath of allegiance to the United States.

who shall aid, assist or permit any male negro of the age of sixteen (16) years or upwards, to go out of this Department, in contravention of this order, will be punished, on conviction thereof before the Provost Court, by not less than six (6) months imprisonment at hard labor, under the Superintendent of Prison Labor, at Norfolk, and if this offence is committed by or with the connivance of any Master of Steamboat, Schooner, or other vessel, the steamboat or other vessel shall be seized and sold, and the proceeds be paid to the Superintendent of Negro Affairs, for the use of the destitute negroes supported by the Government.

* * * * *

By command of Major General B. F. BUTLER:

R. S. DAVIS, Major and Asst. Adjt. General.

OFFICIAL: H. T. SCHROEDER, Lt. & A. A. A. Gen'l.
OFFICIAL: WM. M. PRATT, Lt. & Aide-de-Camp.

The chief result of Butler's order was the establishment of the Freedmens' Savings Bank. At the close of the war, there were in the hands of the Superintendent of Negro Affairs, eight thousand dollars unclaimed bounties, belonging, the most of it without doubt, to *dead men*; it was placed in a bank at Norfolk, Va. This sum served as a nucleus for the Freedmens' Bank, which, after gathering large sums of the Freedmens' money, collapsed suddenly.

At Camp Hamilton several regiments were organized, including two of cavalry. The general enlistment ordered by the War Department was pushed most actively and with great results, till more than one hundred and seventy-eight thousand, by the records, were enlisted into the army.

The opposition to negro soldiers did not cease with many of the Union generals even after the Government at Washington issued its mandate for their enlistment and impressment, and notwithstanding that the many thousands in the service, with their display of gallantry, dash and courage, as exhibited at Port Hudson, Milliken's Bend, Wagner, and in a hundred other battles, had astonished and aroused the civilized world. In view of all this, and, even more strangely, in the face of the Fort Pillow butchery, General Sherman wrote to the Washington authorities, in September, 1864, protesting against negro troops being organized in his department. If Whitelaw Reid's "Ohio in the War," is to be relied upon, Sherman's treatment of the negroes in his march to the sea was a counterpart of the Fort Pillow massacre. His opposition was in keeping with that of the authorities of his state,* notwithstanding it has credited to its quota

* "It has been said that one negro regiment was raised in 1863. More ought to have been secured; let it never be said that it was the fault of the colored men them-

of troops during the war 5,092 negroes, but one regiment was raised in the State, out of a negro population of 36,673 by the canvas of 1860.

According to the statisticts on file in the Adjutant General's office, the States are accredited with the following number of negroes who served in the army during the Rebellion:

ALABAMA,	2,969	MISSISSIPPI,	17,869
LOUISIANA,	24,052	MAINE,	104
NEW HAMPSHIRE,	125	VERMONT,	120
MASSACHUSETTS,	3966	RHODE ISLAND,	1,837
CONNECTICUT,	1,764	NEW YORK,	4,125
NEW JERSEY,	1.185	PENNSYLVANIA,	8,612
DELAWARE,	954	MARYLAND,	8,718
DISTRICT OF COLUMBIA,	3,269	VIRGINIA,	5,723
NORTH CAROLINA,	5,035	WEST VIRGINIA,	196
SOUTH CAROLINA,	5,462	GEORGIA,	3,486
FLORIDA,	1,044	ARKANSAS,	5,526
TENNESSEE,	20,133	KENTUCKY,	23,703
MICHIGAN,	1,387	OHIO,	5,092
INDIANA,	1,537	ILLINOIS,	1,811
MISSOURI,	8,344	MINNESOTA,	104
IOWA,	440	WISCONSIN,	165
KANSAS,	2080	TEXAS,	47
COLORADO TERRITORY,	95	NOT ACCOUNTED FOR,	5,896

TOTAL, - - - 178,975.

The losses these troops sustained from sickness, wounds, killed in battle and other casualties incident to war, was 68,178.

The aggregate negro population in the U. S. in 1860 was 4,449,201, of which 3,950,531 were slaves.

selves that they were not.

"At the first call for troops in 1861, Governor Dennison was asked if he would accept negro volunteers. In deference to a sentiment then almost universal, not less than to the explicit regulations of the Government, he replied that he could not. When the Emancipation Proclamation changed the status of negroes so completely, and the Government began to accept their services, they resumed their applications to the State authorities. Governor Tod still discouraged them. He had previously committed himself, in repelling the opportunities of their leaders, to the theory that it would be contrary to our laws, and without warrant either in their spirit or letter, to accept them, even under calls for militia. He now did all he could to transfer such as wished to enlist to the Massachusetts regiments.

"The Adjutant-General, in his report for 1863, professed his inability to say why Massachusetts should be permitted to make Ohio a recruiting-ground for filling her quotas. If he had looked into the correspondence which the Governor gave to the public in connection with his message, he would have found out. As early as May 11th the Governor said, in a letter to Hon. Wm. Porter, of Millon, Ohio: 'I do not propose to raise any colored troops. Those now being recruited in this State are recruited by authority from Governor Andrew, of Massachusetts.'

"A few days later he wrote to Hon. John M. Langston: 'As it was uncertain what number of colored men could be promptly raised in Ohio. I have advised and still do advise, that those disposed to enter the service promptly join the Massachusetes regiments. * * * Having requested the Governor of Massachusetts to organize the colored men from Ohio into separate companies, so far as practicable, and also to keep me fully advised of the names, age, and place of residence of each, Ohio will have the full benefit of all enlistments from the State, and the reoruits themselves the benefit of the State Associations to the same extent nearly as if organized into a State regiment.' And to persons proposing to recruit said companies he wrote that all commissions would be issued by the Governor of Massachusetts. In this course he had the sanction if not the original suggestion of the Secretary of War. Afterward his applications for authority to raise an Ohio regiment were for sometime refused, but finally he secured it, and the One Hundred and Twenty-Seventh was the quick result. Unfortunately it was numbered the Fifth United States Colored. The result of all this was that Ohio received credit for little over a third of her colored citizens who volunteered for the war."—*Reid's Ohio in the War, Vol. I, p. 176.*

PHALANX SOLDIERS ORGANIZING AND DRILLING.

CHAPTER III.

RECRUITING AND ORGANIZING IN SOUTH CAROLINA.

"Private Miles O'Reilly" was the *nom de plume* of a talented literary gentleman of the city of New York, who wrote much in humorous prose and verse. His real name was Charles G. Halpine. After an honorable service in the war, rising to high rank, he was elected Register of New York, and died suddenly while in office, in 1868. The following sketches from his pen, published during the war, give an account of matters connected with the recruiting and organizing of negro troops in South Carolina, and are quoted here as interesting historical facts connected with the subject:

"Black troops are now an established success, and hereafter—while the race can furnish enough able-bodied males—the probability would seem that one-half the permanent naval and military forces of the United States will be drawn from this material, under the guidance and control of the white officers. To-day there is much competition among the field and staff officers of our white volunteers—more especially in those regiments about being disbanded—to obtain commission of like or even lower grades in the colored regiments of Uncle Sam. General Casey's board of examination cannot keep in session long enough, nor dismiss incompetent aspirants quick enough, to keep down the vast throngs of veterans, with and without shoulder-straps, who are now seeking various grades of command in the colored brigades of the Union. Over this result all intelligent men will rejoice,—the privilege of being either killed or wounded in battle, or stricken down by the disease, toil and privations incident to the life of a marching soldier, not belonging to that class of prerogative for the exclusive enjoyment of which men of sense, and with higher careers open to them, will long contend. Looking back, however, but a few years, to the organization of the first regiment of black troops in the departments of the South, what a change in public opinion are we compelled to recognize! In sober verity, war is not only the sternest, but the quickest, of all teachers; and contrasting the Then and Now of our negro regiments, as we propose to do in this sketch, the contrast will forcibly recall Galileo's obdurate assertion that 'the world still moves.'

"Be it known, then, that the first regiment of black troops raised in our recent war, was raised in the Spring of 1862 by the commanding general of the department of the South, of his own motion, and without any direct authority of law, order, or even sanction from the President, the Secretary of War, or our House of Congress. It was done by General Hunter as 'a military necessity' under very peculiar circumstances, to be detailed hereafter; and although repudiated at first by the Government as were so many other measures originated in the same quarter, it was finally adopted as the settled policy of the country and of our military system; as have likewise since been adopted, all the other original measures for which these officers, at the time of their first announcement, was made to suffer both official rebuke and the violently vituperative denunciation of more than one-half the Northern press.

"In the Spring of 1862, General Hunter, finding himself with less than eleven thousand men under his command, and charged with the duty of holding the whole tortuous and broken seacoast of Georgia, South Carolina and Florida, had applied often, and in vain, to the authorities at Washington for reinforcements. All the troops that could be gathered in the North were less than sufficient for the continuous drain of General McClellan's great operations against the enemy's capital; and the reiterated answer of the War Department was: 'You must get along as best you can. Not a man from the North can be spared.'

"On the mainland of three States nominally forming the Department of the South, the flag of the Union had no permanent foothold, save at Fernandina, St. Augustine, and some few unimportant points along the Florida coast. It was on the Sea-islands of Georgia and South Carolina that our troops were stationed, and continually engaged in fortifying,—the enemy being everywhere visible, and in force, across the narrow creeks dividing us from the mainland; and in various raids they came across to our islands, and we drove them back to the mainland, and up their creeks, with a few gunboats to help us—being the order of the day; yea, and yet oftener, of the night.

"No reinforcements to be had from the North; vast fatigue duties in throwing up earthworks imposed on our insufficient garrison; the enemy continually increasing both in insolence and numbers; our only success the capture of Fort Pulaski, sealing up of Savannah; and this victory offset, if not fully counter-balanced, by many minor gains of the enemy; this was about the condition of affairs as seen from the headquarters fronting Port Royal bay, when General Hunter one fine morning, with twirling glasses, puckered lips, and dilated nostrils, (he had just received another 'don't-bother-us-for-reinforcements' dispatch from Washington) announced his intention of 'forming a negro regiment, and compelling every able-bodied black man in the department to fight for the freedom which could not but be the issue of our war.'

This resolution being taken, was immediately acted upon with vigor, the General causing all the necessary orders to be issued, and taking upon himself, as his private burden, the responsibility for all the irregular issues of arms, clothing, equipments, and rations involved in collecting and organizing the first experimental negro regiment. The men he intended to pay, at first, by placing them as laborers on the pay-roll of the Chief Quartermaster; but it was his hope that the obvious necessity and wisdom of the measure he had thus presumed to adopt without authority, would secure for it the immediate approval of the higher authorities, and the necessary orders to cover the required pay and supply-issue of the force he had in contemplation. If his course should be endorsed by the War Department, well and good; if it were not so indorsed, why, he had enough property of his own to pay back to the Government all he was irregularly expending in this experiment.

"But now, on the very threshhold of this novel enterprise, came the first—and it was not a trivial—difficulty. Where could experienced officers be found for such an organization? 'What! command niggers?' was the reply—if possible more amazed than scornful—of nearly every competent young lieutenant or captain of volunteers to whom the suggestion of commanding this class of troops was made. 'Never mind,' said Hunter, when this trouble was brought to his notice; 'the fools or bigots who refuse are enough punished by their refusal. Before two years they will be competing eagerly for the commission they now reject.' Straightly there was issued a circular to all commanding officers in the department, directing them to announce to the non-commissioned officers and men of their respective commands that commissions in the 'South Carolina Regiment of Colored Infantry,' would be given to all deserving and reputable sergeants, corporals; and men who would appear at department headquarters, and prove able to pass an examination in the manual and tactics before a Band of Examiners, which was organized in a general order of current date. Capt. Arthur M. Kenzie, of Chicago, aid-de-camp,—now of Hancock's Veterans Reserve Corps—was detailed as Colonel of the regiment, giving place, subsequently, in consequence of injured health, to the present Brig.-Gen. James D. Fessenden, then a captain in the Berdan Sharpshooters, though detailed as acting aid-de-camp on Gen. Hunter's staff. Capt. Kenzie, we may add, was Gen. Hunter's nephew, and his appointment as Colonel was made partly to prove—so violent was then the prejudice against negro troops—that the Commanding General asks nothing of them which he was not willing that one of his own flesh and blood should be engaged in.

"The work was now fairly in progress, but the barriers of prejudice were not to be lightly overthrown. Non-commissioned officers and men of the right stamp, and able to pass the examination requisite, were scarce articles. Ten had the hardihood or moral courage to face the screaming, riotous ridicule of their late associates in the white regiments. We remember one very striking instance in point, which we shall give as a sample of the whole.

"Our friend Mr. Charles F. Briggs, of this city, so well known in literary circles, had a nephew enlisted in that excellent regiment the 48th New York, then garrisoning Fort Pulaski and the works of Tybee Island. This youngster had raised himself by gallantry and good conduct to be a non-commissioned officer; and Mr. Briggs was anxious that he should be commissioned, according to his capacities, in the colored troops then being raised. The lad was sent for, passed his examination with credit, and was immediately offered a first lieutenancy, with the promise of being made captain when his company should be filled up to the required standard,—probably within ten days.

"The inchoate first-lieutenant was in ecstasies; a gentleman by birth and education, he longed for the shoulder-straps. He appeared joyously grateful; and only wanted leave to run up to Fort Pulaski for the purpose of collecting his traps, taking leave of his former comrades, and procuring his discharge-papers from Col. Barton. Two days after that came a note to the department headquarters respectfully declining the commission! He had been laughed and jeered out of accepting a captaincy by his comrades; and this—though we remember it more accurately from our correspondence with Mr. Briggs—was but one of many scores of precisely similar cases.

"At length, however, officers were found; the ranks were filled; the men learned with uncommon quickness, having the imitativeness of so many monkeys apparently, and such excellent ears for music that all evolutions seemed to come to them by nature. At once, despite all hostile influence, the negro regiment became one of the lions of the South; and strangers visiting the department, crowded out eagerly to see its evening parades and Sunday-morning inspection. By a strange coincidence, its camp was pitched on the lawn and around the mansion of Gen. Drayton, who commanded the rebel works guarding Hilton Head, Port Royal and Beaufort, when the same were first captured by the joint naval and military operations under Admiral DuPont and General Timothy W. Sherman,—General Drayton's brother, Captain Drayton of our navy, having command of one of the best vessels in the attacking squadron; as he subsequently took part in the first iron-clad attack on Fort Sumpter.

"Meantime, however, the War Department gave no sign, and the oracles of the Adjutant-General's office were dumb as the statue of the Sphynx. Reports of the organization of the First South Carolina infantry were duly forwarded to army headquarters; but evoked no comment, either of approval or rebuke. Letters detailing what had been done, and the reason for doing it; asking instructions, and to have commissions duly issued to the officers selected; appeals that the department paymaster should be instructed to pay these negro troops like other soldiers; demands that the Government should either shoulder the respon-

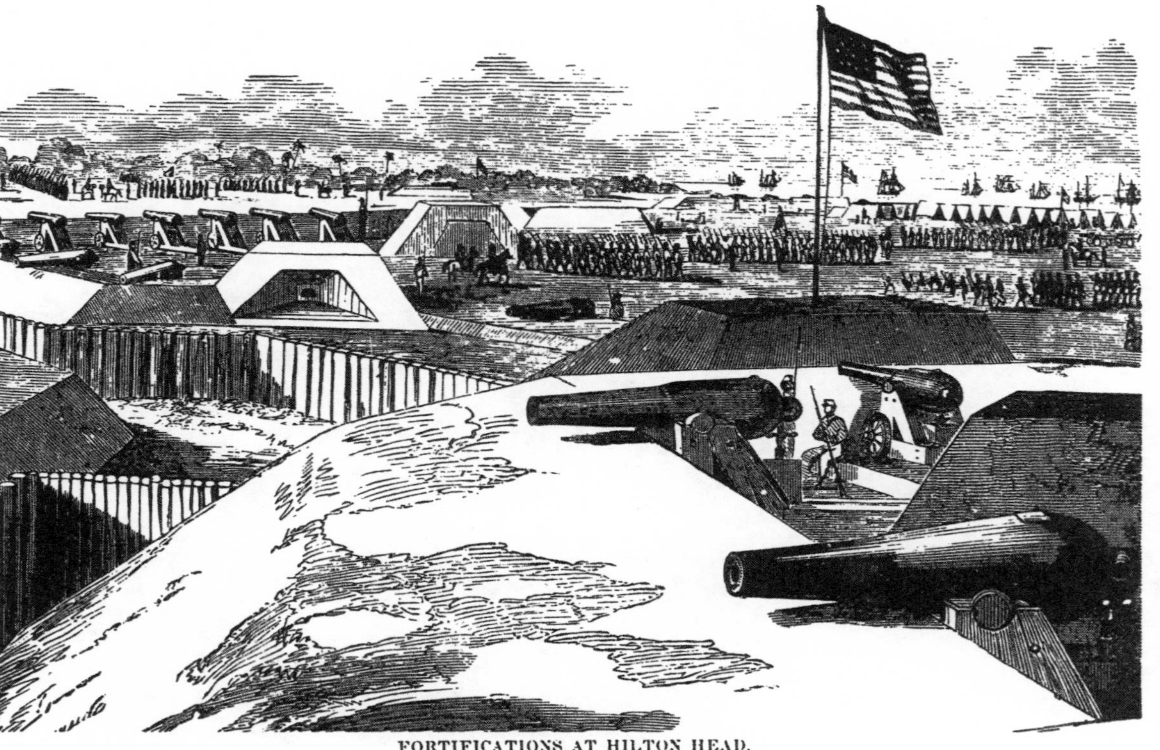

FORTIFICATIONS AT HILTON HEAD.
Gen'l. Hunter's black regiment in the distance.

sibility of sustaining the organization, or give such orders as would absolve Gen. Hunter from the responsibility of backing out from an experiment which he believed to be essential to the salvation of the country,—all these appeals to Washington proved in vain; for the oracles still remained profoundly silent, probably waiting to see how public opinion and the politicians would receive this daring innovation.

"At length one evening a special dispatch steamer plowed her way over the bar, and a perspiring messenger delivered into Gen. Hunter's hands a special despatch from the War Department, 'requiring immediate answer.' The General was just about mounting his horse for his evening ride along the picket-line, when this portentous missive was brought under his notice. Hastily opening it, he first looked grave, then began to smile, and finally burst into peals of irrepressible laughter, such as were rarely heard from 'Black David,' his old army name. Never was the General seen, before or since, in such good spirits; he literally was unable to speak from constant interruption of laughter; and all his Adjutant-General could gather from him was: 'That he would not part with the document in his hand for fifty thousand dollars.'

"At length he passed over the dispatch to his Chief of Staff, who on reading it, and re-reading it, could find in its texts but little apparent cause for merriment. It was a grave demand from the War Department for information in regard to our negro regiment—the demand being based on a certain resolution introduced by the Hon. Mr. Wickliffe, of Kentucky, asking for specific information on the point, in a tone clearly not friendly. These resolutions had been adopted by Congress; and as Hunter was without authority for any of his actions in this case, it seemed to his then not cheerful Adjutant-General that the documents in his hands were the reverse of hilarious.

"Still Hunter was in extravagant spirits as he rode along, his laughter startling the squirrels in the dense pine woods, and every attempt that he made to explain himself being again and again interrupted by renewed peals of inextinguishable mirth. 'The fools!' he at length managed to say; 'that old fool has just given me the very chance I was growing sick for! The War Department has refused to notice my black regiment; but now, in reply to this resolution, I can lay the matter before the country, and force the authorities either to adopt my negroes or to disband them.' He then rapidly sketched out the kind of reply he wished to have prepared; and, with the first ten words of his explanation, the full force of the cause he had for laughter became apparent. Never did a General and his Chief-of-Staff, in a more unseemly state of cachinnation, ride along a picket-line. At every new phase of the subject it presented new features of the ludicrous; and though the reply at this late date may have lost much of the drollery which then it wore, it is a serio-comic document of as much vital importance in the moral history of our late contest as any that can be found in the archives under the care of Gen. E. D. Townsend. It was received late Sunday evening, and was answered very late that night, in order to be in time for the steamer

Arago, which sailed at daylight next morning,—the dispatch-steamer which brought the request 'for immediate information' having sustained some injuries which prevented an immediate return. It was written after midnight, we may add, in a tornado of thunder and tempest such as has rarely been known even on that tornado-stricken coast; but loud as were the peals and vivid the flashes of heaven's artillery, there were at least two persons within the lines on Hilton Head who were laughing far too noisily themselves to pay any heed to external clamors. The reply thus concocted and sent, from an uncorrected manuscript copy now in our possession, ran as follows:

"HEADQUARTERS, DEPARTMENT OF THE SOUTH,
Hilton Head, S. C., June, 1862.

"To the HON. E. M. STANTON, Secretary of War, Washington, D. C.

"SIR:—I have the honor to acknowledge the receipt of a communication from the Adjutant-General of the Army, dated June 13, 1862, requesting me to furnish you with the information necessary to answer certain Resolutions introduced in the House of Representatives June 9, 1862, on motion of the Hon. Mr. Wickliffe, of Kentucky; their substance being to enquire:

"1st—Whether I had organized, or was organizing, a regiment of 'fugitive slaves' in this department.

"2d—Whether any authority had been given to me from the War Department for such an organization; and

"3rd—Whether I had been furnished, by order of the War Department, with clothing, uniforms, arms, equipments, and so forth, for such a force?

"Only having received the letter at a late hour this evening, I urge forward my answer in time for the steamer sailing to-morrow morning,—this haste preventing me from entering, as minutely as I could wish, upon many points of detail, such as the paramount importance of the subject would seem to call for. But, in view of the near termination of the present session of Congress, and the wide-spread interest which must have been awakened by Mr. Wickliffe's resolutions, I prefer sending even this imperfect answer to waiting the period necessary for the collection of fuller and more comprehensive data.

"To the first question, therefore, I reply: That no regiment of 'fugitive slaves' has been, or is being, organized in this department. There is, however, a fine regiment of loyal persons whose late masters are fugitive rebels—men who everywhere fly before the appearance of the national flag, leaving their loyal and unhappy servants behind them, to shift, as best they can, for themselves. So far, indeed, are the loyal persons composing the regiment from seeking to evade the presence of their late owners, that they are now, one and all, endeavoring with commendable zeal to acquire the drill and discipline requisite to place them in a position to go in full and effective pursuit of their fugacious and traitorous proprietors.

"To the second question, I have the honor to answer that the instructions given to Brig.-Gen. T. W. Sherman by the Hon. Simon Cameron, late Secretary of War, and turned over to me, by succession, for my guidance, do distinctly authorize me to employ 'all loyal persons offering their service in defence of the Union, and for the suppression of this rebellion,' in any manner I may see fit, or that circumstances may call for. There is no restriction as to the character or color of the persons to be employed, or the nature of the employment—whether civil or military—in which their services may be used. I conclude, therefore, that I have been authorized to enlist 'fugitive slaves' as soldiers, could any such fugitives be found in this department. No such characters, however, have yet appeared within view of our most advanced pickets,—the loyal negroes everywhere remaining on their plantations to welcome us, aid us, and supply us with food, labor and information. It is the masters who have in every instance been the 'fugitives,' running away from loyal slaves as well as loyal soldiers; and these, as yet, we have only partially been able to see—chiefly their heads over ramparts, or dodging behind trees, rifles in hand, in the extreme distance. In the absence of any 'fugitive master law,' the deserted slaves would be wholly without remedy had not the crime of treason given them right to pursue, capture and bring those persons of whose benignant protection they have been thus suddenly and cruelly bereft.

"To the third interrogatory, it is my painful duty to reply that I have never received any specific authority for issue of clothing, uniforms, arms, equipments and so forth, to the troops in question,—my general instructions from Mr. Cameron, to employ them in any manner I might find necessary, and the military exigencies of the department and the country, being my only, but I trust, sufficient justification. Neither have I had any specific authority for supplying these persons with shovels, spades, and pickaxes, when employing them as laborers; nor with boats and oars, when using them as lighter-men; but these are not points included in Mr. Wickliffe's resolution. To me it seemed that liberty to employ men in any particular capacity implied and carried with it liberty, also, to supply them with the necessary tools; and, acting upon this faith, I have clothed, equiped, and armed the only loyal regiment yet raised in South Carolina, Georgia or Florida.

"I must say, in vindication of my own conduct, that, had it not been for the many other diversified and imperative claims on my time and attention, a much more satisfactory result might to have been achieved; and that, in place of only one regiment, as at present, at least five or six well-drilled, and thoroughly acclimated regiments should, by this time, have been added to the loyal forces of the Union.

"The experiment of arming the blacks, so far as I have made it, has been a complete and even marvellous success. They are sober, docile, attentive, and enthusiastic; displaying great natural capacities in acquiring the duties of the soldier. They are now eager beyond all things to take the field and be led into action; and it is the unanimous opinion of the officers who have had charge of them that, in the peculiarities of this climate and country, they will prove invaluable auxiliaries, fully equal to the similar regiments so long and successfully used by the British authorities in the West India Islands.

"In conclusion, I would say, it is my hope—there appearing no possibility of other reinforcements, owing to the exigencies of the campaign in the Peninsula—to have organized by the end of next fall, and be able to present to the government, from forty-eight to fifty thousand of these hardy and devoted soldiers.

"Trusting that this letter may be made part of your answer to Mr. Wickliffe's resolutions, I have the honor to be,

Very respectfully your most obedient servant,

DAVID HUNTER, *Maj.-Gen. Commanding.*"

"This missive was duly sent, with many misgivings that it would not get through the routine of the War Department in time to be laid before Congress previous to the adjournment of that honorable body which was then imminent. There were fears; too, that the Secretary of War might think it not sufficiently respectful, or serious in its tone; but such apprehensions proved unfounded. The moment it was received and read in the War Department, it was hurried down to the House, and delivered, *ore retundo*, from the clerk's desk.

"Here its effects were magical. The clerk could scarcely read it with decorum; nor could half his words be heard amidst the universal peals of laughter in which both Democrats and Republicans appeared to vie as to which should be the more noisy. Mr. Wickliffe, who only entered durthe reading of the latter half of the document, rose to his feet in a frenzy of indignation, complaining that the reply, of which he had only heard some portion, was an insult to the dignity of the House, and should be severely noticed. The more he raved and gesticulated, the more irrepressibly did his colleagues, on both sides of the slavery question, scream and laugh; until finally, the merriment reached its climax on a motion made by some member—Schuyler Colfax, if we remember rightly —that 'as the document appeared to please the honorable gentleman from Kentucky so much, and as he had not heard the whole of it the Clerk be now requested to read the whole again'— a motion which was instantaneously carried amid such an uproar of universal merriment and applause as the frescoed walls of the chamber have seldom heard, either before or since. It was the great joke of the day, and coming at a moment of universal gloom in the public mind, was seized upon by the whole loyal press of the country as a kind of politico-military champaign cocktail.

"This set that question at rest forever; and not long after, the proper authorities saw fit to authorize the employment of 'fifty thousand able-bodied blacks for labor in the Quartermaster's Department,' and the arming and drilling as soldiers of five thousand of these, but for the sole purpose of 'protecting the women and children of their fellow-laborers who might be absent from home in the public service.'

"Here we have another instance of the reluctance with which the National Government took up this idea of employing negroes as soldiers; a resolution, we may add, to which they were only finally compelled by General Hunter's disbandment of his original regiment, and the storm of public indignation which followed that act.

"Nothing could have been happier in its effect upon the public mind than Gen. Hunter's reply to Mr. Wickliffe, of Kentucky, given in our last. It produced a general broad grin throughout the country, and the advocate who can set his jury laughing rarely loses his cause. It also strengthened the spinal column of the Government in a very marked degree; although not yet up to the point of fully endorsing and accepting this daring experiment.

"Meantime the civil authorities of course got wind of what was going on,—Mr. Henry J. Windsor, special correspondent of the New York *Times*, in the Department of the south, having devoted several very graphic and widely-copied letters to a picture of that new thing under the sun, 'Hunter's negro regiment.'

"Of course the chivalry of the rebellion were incensed beyond measure at this last Yankee outrage upon Southern rights. Their papers teemed with vindictive articles against the commanding general who had dared to initiate such a novelty. The Savannah *Republican*, in particular, denouncing Hunter as 'the cool-blooded abolition miscreant who, from his headquarters at Hilton Head, is engaged in executing the bloody and savage behest of the imperial gorilla who, from his throne of human bones at Washington, rules, reigns and riots over the destinies of the brutish and degraded North.'

"Mere newspaper abuse, however, by no means gave content to the outraged feeling of the chivalry. They therefore sent a formal demand

BUILDINC ROADS

to our Government for information as to whether Gen. Hunter, in organizing his regiment of emancipated slaves, had acted under the authority of our War Department, or whether the villany was of his own conception. If he had acted under orders, why then terrible measures of fierce retaliation against the whole Yankee nation were to be adopted; but if, *per contra*, the iniquity were of his own motion and without the sanction of our Government, then the foreshadowed retribution should be made to fall only on Hunter and his officers.

"To this demand, with its alternative of threats, President Lincoln was in no mood to make any definitive reply. In fact no reply at all was sent, for, as yet, the most far-seeing political augurs could not determine whether the bird seen in the sky of the Southern Department would prove an eagle or a buzzard. Public opinion was not formed upon the subject, though rapidly forming. There were millions who agreed with Hunter in believing that 'that the black man should be made to fight for the freedom which could not but be the issue of our war;' and then they were outraged at the prospect of allowing black men to be killed or maimed in company with our nobler whites.

"Failing to obtain any reply therefor, from the authorities at Washington, the Richmond people determined to pour out all their vengeance on the immediate perpetrators of this last Yankee atrocity; and forthwith there was issued from the rebel War Department a General Order number 60, we believe, of the series of 1862—reciting that 'as the government of the U. S. had refused to answer whether it authorized the raising of a black regiment by Gen. Hunter or not' said General, his staff, and all officers under his command who had directly or indirectly participated in the unclean thing, should hereafter be outlaws not covered by the laws of war; but to be executed as felons for the crimes of 'inciting negro insurrections wherever caught.'

"This order reached the ears of the parties mainly interested just as Gen. Hunter was called to Washington, ostensibly for consultation on public business; but really on the motion of certain prominent speculators in marine transportation, with those 'big things,' in Port Royal harbor,—and they were enormous—with which the General had seen fit to interfere. These frauds, however, will form a very fruitful and pregnant theme for some future chapters. At present our business is with the slow but certain growth in the public mind of this idea of allowing some black men to be killed in the late war, and not continuing to arrogate death and mutilation by projectiles and bayonets as an exclusive privilege for our own beloved white race.

"No sooner had Hunter been relieved from this special duty at Washington, than he was ordered back to the South, our Government still taking no notice of the order of outlawry against him issued by the rebel Secretary of War. He and his officers were thus sent back to engage, with extremely insufficient forces, in an enterprise of no common difficulty, and with an agreeable sentence of *sus. per col.*, if captured, hanging over their devoted heads!

"Why not suggest to Mr. Stanton, General, that he should either demand the special revocation of that order, or announce to the rebel War. Department that our Government has adopted your negro-regiment policy as its own—which would be the same thing.

"It was partly on this hint that Hunter-wrote the following letter to Jefferson Davis,—a letter subsequently suppressed and never sent, owing to influences which the writer of this article does not feel himself as yet at liberty to reveal,—further than to say that Mr. Stanton knew nothing of the matter. Davis and Hunter, we may add, had been very old and intimate friends, until divided, some years previous to our late war, by differences on the slavery question. Davis had for many years been adjutant of the 1st U. S. Dragoons, of which Hunter had been Captain Commanding; and a relationship of very close friendship had existed between their respective families. It was this thorough knowledge of his man, perhaps, which gave peculiar bitterness to Hunter's pen; and the letter is otherwise remarkable as a prophecy, or preordainment of that precise policy which Pres't. Johnson has so frequently announced, and reiterated since Mr. Lincoln's death. It ran—with some few omissions, no longer pertinent or of public interest—as follows:

"TO JEFFERSON DAVIS, TITULAR PRESIDENT OF THE SO-CALLED CONFEDERATE STATES.

"SIR:—While recently in command of the Department of the South, in accordance with the laws of the war and the dictates of common sense, I organized and caused to be drilled, armed and equipped, a regiment of enfranchised bondsmen, known as the 1st South Carolina Volunteers.

"For this action, as I have ascertained, the pretended government of which you are the chief officer, has issued against me and all of my officers who were engaged in organizing the regiment in question, a General Order of Outlawry, which announces that, if captured, we shall not even be allowed the usual miserable treatment extended to such captives as fall into your hands; but that we are to be regarded as felons, and to receive the death by hanging due to such, irrespective of the laws of war.

"Mr. Davis, we have been acquainted intimately in the past. We have campaigned together, and our social relations have been such as to make each understand the other thoroughly. That you mean, if it be ever in your power, to execute the full rigor of your threats, I am well assured; and you will believe my assertion, that I thank you for having raised in connection with me and my acts, this sharp and decisive issue. I shall proudly accept, if such be the chance of war, the martyrdom you menace; and hereby give you notice that unless your General Order against me and my officers be formally revoked, within thirty days from the date of the transmission of this letter, sent under a flag of truce, I shall take your action in the matter as finale; and will reciprocate it by hanging every rebel officer who now is, or may hereafter be taken, prisoner by the troops of the command to which I am about returning.

"Believe me that I rejoice at the aspect now being given to the war by the course you have adopted. In my judgment, if the undoubted felony of treason had been treated from the outset as it deserves to be—as the sum of all felonies and crimes—this rebellion would never have attained its present menacing proportions. The war you and your fellow conspirators have been waging against the United States must be regarded either as a war of justifiable defence, carried on for the integrity of the boundaries of a sovereign Confederation of States against foreign aggression, or as the most wicked, enormous, and deliberately planned conspiracy against human liberty and for the triumph of treason and slavery, of which the records of the world's history contain any note.

"If our Government should adopt the first view of the case, you and your fellow-rebels may justly claim to be considered a most unjustly treated body of disinterested patriots,—although, perhaps, a little mistaken in your connivance with the thefts by which your agent, John B. Floyd, succeeded in arming the South and partially disarming the North as a preparative to the commencement of the struggle.

"But if on the other hand—as is the theory of our Government—the war you have levied against the U. S. be a rebellion the most causeless, crafty and bloody ever known, —a conspiracy having the rule-or-ruin policy for its basis; the plunder of the black race and the reopening of the African slave trade for its object, the continued and further degredation of ninety per cent. of the white population of the South in favor of a slave driving ten per cent. aristocracy, and the exclusion of all foreign-born immigrants from participation in the generous and equal hospitality foreshadowed to them in the Declaration of Independence,—if this, as I believe, be a fair statement of the origin and motives of the rebellion of which you are the titular head, then it would have been better had our Government adhered to the constitutional view of treason from the start, and hung every man taken in arms against the U. S. from the first butchery in the streets of Baltimore, down to the last resultless battle fought in the vicinity of Sharpsburg. If treason, in other words, be any crime, it is the essence of all crimes; a vast machinery of guilt, multiplying assassinations into wholesale slaughter, and organizing plunder as the basis for supporting a system of National Brigandage. Your action, and that of those with whom you are in league, has its best comment in the sympathy extended to your cause by the despots and aristocracies of Europe. You have succeeded in throwing back civilization for many years; and have made of the country that was the freest, happiest, proudest, richest, and most progressive but two short years ago, a vast temple of mourning, doubt, anxiety and privation· our manufactories of all but war material nearly paralyzed; the inventive spirit which was forever developing new resources destroyed, and our flag, that carried respect everywhere, now mocked by enemies who think its glory tarnished, and that its power is soon to become a mere tradition of the past.

"For all these results, Mr. Davis, and for the three hundred thousand lives already sacrificed on both sides in the war—some pouring out their blood on the battle-field, and others fever stricken and wasting away to death in overcrowded hospitals—you and the fellow miscreants who have been your associates in this conspiracy are responsible. Of you and them it may, with truth be said, that if all the innocent blood which you have spilled could be collected in one pool, the whole government of your Confederacy might swim in it.

"I am aware that this is not the language in which the prevailing etiquette of our army is in the habit of considering your conspiracy. It has come to pass—through what instrumentalities you are best able to decide—that the greatest and worst crime ever attempted against the human family, has been treated in certain quarters as though it were a mere error of judgment on the part of some gifted friend; a thing to be regretted, of course, as causing more or less disturbance to the relation of amity and esteem heretofore existing between those charged with the repression of such eccentricities and the eccentric actors; in fact, as a slight political miscalculation or peccadillo, rather than as an outrage involving the desolation of a continent, and demanding the promptest and severest retribution within power of human law.

"For myself, I have never been able to take this view of the matter. During a lifetime of active service, I have seen the seeds of this conspiracy planted in the rank soil of slavery, and the upas-growth watered by just such tricklings of a courtesy alike false to justice, expediency, and our eternal future. Had we at an earlier day commenced to call things by their right names, and to look at the hideous features of slavery with our ordinary eyesight and common sense, instead of through the rose-colored glasses of supposed political expediency, there would be three hundred thousand more men alive to-day on American soil; and our country would never for a moment have forfeited her proud position as the highest exampler of the blessings—morals, intellectual and material—to be derived from a free form of government.

"Whether your intention of hanging me and those of my staff and other officers who were engaged in organizing the 1st S. C. Volunteers, in case we are taken prisoners in battle, will be likely to benefit your cause or not, is a matter mainly for your own consideration. For us, our profession makes the sacrifice of life a contingency ever present and always to be accepted; and although such a form of death as your order proposes, is not that to the contemplating of which soldiers have trained themselves, I feel well assured, both for myself and those included in my sentence, that we could die in no manner more damaging to your abominable rebellion and the abominable institution which is its origin.

"The South has already tried one hanging experiment, but not with a success—one would think—to encourage its repetition. John Brown, who was well known to me in Kansas, and who will be known in appreciative history through centuries which will only recall your name to load it with curses, once entered Virginia with seventeen men and an idea. The terror caused by the presence of his idea, and the dauntless courage which prompted the assertion of his faith, against all odds, I need not now recall. The history is too familiar and too painful. 'Old Ossawatomie' was caught and hung; his seventeen men were killed, captured or dispersed, and several of them shared his fate. Portions of his skin were tanned, I am told, and circulated as relics dear to the barbarity of the slave-holding heart. But more than a million of armed white men, Mr. Davis, are to-day marching South, in practical acknowledgement that they regard the hanging of three years ago as the murder of a martyr; and as they march to a battle which has the emancipation of all slaves as one of its most glorious results, his name is on their lips; to the music of his memory their marching feet keep time; and as they sling knapsacks each one becomes aware that he is an armed apostle of the faith preached by him,

"'Who has gone to be a soldier
In the army of the Lord!'

"I am content, if such be the will of Providence to ascend the scaffold made sacred by the blood of this martyr; and I rejoice at every prospect of making our struggle more earnest and inexorable on both sides; for the sharper the conflict the sooner ended; the more vigorous and remorseless the strife, the less blood must be shed in it eventually.

"In conclusion, let me assure you, that I rejoice with my whole heart that your order in my case, and that of my officers, if unrevoked, will untie our hands for the future; and that we shall be able to treat rebellion as it deserves, and give to the felony of treason a felon's death.

"Very obediently yours,
DAVID HUNTER, *Maj.-Gen.*"

"Not long after General Hunter's return to the Department of the South, the first step towards organizing and recognizing negro troops was taken by our Government, in a letter of instructions directing Brigadier-General Rufus Saxton—then Military Governor of South Carolina, Georgia and Florida, within the limits of Gen. Hunter's command—to forthwith raise and organize fifty thousand able-bodied blacks, for service as laborers in the quartermaster's department; of whom five thousand—only five thousand, mark you—might be armed and drilled as soldiers for the purpose of 'protecting the women and children of their fellow-laborers who might be absent from home in the public service.'

"Here was authority given to Gen. Saxton, over Hunter's head, to pursue some steps farther the experiment which Hunter—soon followed by General Phelps, also included in the rebel order of 'outlawry'—had been the first to initiate. The rebel order still remained in full force, and with no protest against it on the part of our Government; nor to our knowledge, was any demand from Washington ever made for its revocation during the existence of the Confederacy. If Hunter, therefore, or any of his officers, had been captured in any of the campaigns of the past two and a half years, they had the pleasant knowledge for their comfort that any rebel officers into whose hands they might fall, was

OFF FOR THE WAR.
Negro men marching aboard a steamer to join their regiments at Hilton Head, S. C.

strictly enjoined to—not 'shoot them on the spot,' as was the order of General Dix, but to hang them on the first tree; and hang them quickly.

"With the subsequent history of our black troops the public is already familiar. General Lorenzo Thomas, titular Adjutant-General of our army, not being regarded as a very efficient officer for that place, was permanently detailed on various services; now exchanging prisoners, now discussing points of military law, now organizing black brigades down the Mississippi and elsewhere. In fact, the main object seemed to be to keep this Gen. Thomas—who must not be confounded with Gen. George H. Thomas, one of the true heroes of our army,—away from the Adjutant-General's office at Washington, in order that Brigadier-General E. W. Townsend—only a Colonel until quite recently—might perform all the laborious and crushing duties of Adjutant-General of our army, while only signing himself and ranking as First Assistant Adjutant-General. If there be an officer who has done noble service in the late war while receiving no public credit for the same,—no newspaper puffs nor public ovation,—that man is Brigadier-General E. W. Townsend, who should long since have been made a major-general, to rank from the first day of the rebellion.

"And now let us only add, as practical proof that the rebels, even in their most rabid state, were not insensible to the force of proper "reasons," the following anecdote: Some officers of one of the black regiments —Colonel Higginson's, we believe—indiscreetly rode beyond our lines around St. Augustine in pursuit of game, but whether feathered or female this deponent sayeth not. Their guide proved to be a spy, who had given notice of the intended expedition to the enemy, and the whole party were soon surprised and captured. The next we heard of them, they were confined in the condemned cells of one of the Florida State prisons, and were to be "tried"—i. e., sentenced and executed—as 'having been engaged in inciting negro insurrection.'

"We had some wealthy young slave-holders belonging to the first families of South Carolina in the custody of Lieutenant-Colonel J. F. Hall—now Brigadier-General of this city, who was our Provost Marshal; and it was on this basis Gen. Hunter resolved to operate. 'Release my officers of black troops from your condemned cells at once, and notify me of the fact. Until so notified, your first family prisoners in my hands'—the names then given—'will receive precisely similar treatment. For each of my officers hung, I will hang three of my prisoners who are slave-holders.' This dose operated with instantaneous effect, and the next letter received from our captured officers set forth that they were at large on parole, and treated as well as they could wish to be in that miserable country.

"We cannot better conclude this sketch, perhaps, than by giving the brief but pregnant verses in which our ex-orderly, Private Miles O'Reilly, late of the Old Tenth Army Corps, gave his opinion on this subject. They were first published in connection with the banquet given in New York by Gen. T. F. Meagher and the officers of the Irish Brigade, to the returned veterans of that organization on the 13th of Jan. 1864, at Irving Hall. Of this song it may, perhaps, be said, in verity and without vanity, that, as Gen. Hunter's letter to Mr. Wickliffe had settled the negro soldiers' controversy in its official and Congressional form, so did the publication and immediate popular adoption of these verses conclude all argument upon this matter in the mind of the general public. Its common sense, with a dash of drollery, at once won over the Irish, who had been the bitterest opponents of the measure, to become its friends; and from that hour to this, the attacks upon the experiment of our negro soldiery have been so few and far between that, indeed, they may be said to have ceased altogether. It ran as follows, and appeared in the *Herald* the morning after the banquet as a portion of the report of the speeches and festivities:

"SAMBO'S RIGHT TO BE KIL'T.

(*Air—The Low-Backed Chair.*)

Some say it is a burnin' shame
To make the naygurs fight,
An' that the thrade o' being kilt
Belongs but to the white;
But as for me, upon me sowl,
So liberal are we here,
I'll let Sambo be murthered in place o' meself
On every day in the year.
On every day in the year, boys,
An' every hour in the day,
The right to be kil't I'll divide wid him,
An' divil a word I'll say.

In battle's wild commotion
I shouldn't at all object,
If Sambo's body should stop a ball
That was comin' for me direct;
An' the prod of a Southern bagnet,
So liberal are we here,
I'll resign and let Sambo take it,
On every day in the year.
On everv day in the year boys,
An' wid none o' your nasty pride,
All right in a Southern bagnet prod
Wid Sambo I'll divide.

The men who object to Sambo
Should take his place and fight;
An' it's betther to have a naygur's hue
Than a liver that's wake an' white;
Though Sambo's black as the ace o' spades
His finger a thrigger can pull,
An' his eye runs sthraight on the barrel sight
From under its thatch o' wool.
So hear me all, boys, darlins!
Don't think I'm tippen' you chaff,
The right to be kilt I'll divide wid him,
An' give him the largest half!

"In regard to Hunter's reply to Mr. Wickliffe, we shall only add this anecdote, told us one day by that brilliant gentleman and scholar, the Hon "Sunset" Cox, of Ohio (now of New York): 'I tell you, that letter from Hunter spoiled the prettiest speech I had ever thought of making. I had been delighted with Wickliffe's motion, and thought the reply to it would furnish us first-rate Democrat's thunder for the next election. I made up my mind to sail in against Hunter's answer—no matter what it was—the moment it came; and to be even more humorously successful in its delivery and reception than I was in my speech against War Horse Gurley, of Ohio, which you have just been complimenting. Well, you see, man proposes, but providence orders otherwise. When the Clerk announced the receipt of the answer, and that he was about to read it, I caught the Speaker's eye and was booked for the first speech against your negro experiment. The first sentence, being formal and official, was very well; but at the second the House began to grin, and at the third, not a man on the floor—except Father Wickliffe, of Kentucky, perhaps—who was not convulsed with laughter. Even my own risibles I found to be affected; and before the document was concluded, I motioned the Speaker that he might give the floor to whom he pleased, as my desire to distinguish myself in that particular tilt was over.'"

CHAPTER IV.

OFFICERS OF THE PHALANX.

The character, qualifications and proficiency of the men, who, as officers, commanded the negro troops, may be judged by the process which they had to undergo in order to obtain commissions. Unlike the officers of the white volunteers (with whom loyalty and dash were the essential qualifications) they were required to possess much more than an ordinary knowledge of military tactics. Major-General Hunter, by whose order the first negro regiment with white officers was organized, commencing May, 1862, had an eye single to the make up of the men who should be placed in command of the regiments. As a beginning, Gen. Saxton addressed the following letter to Capt. T. W. Higginson, of the 51st Reg't. Mass. Volunteers, Beaufort, S. C., Nov. 5th, 1862:

"MY DEAR SIR:—I am organizing the First Regiment of South Carolina Volunteers, with every prospect of success. Your name has been spoken of in connection with the command of this regiment, by some friends in whose judgment I have confidence. I take great pleasure in offering you the position of Col. in it, and hope that you may be induced to accept. I shall not fill the place until I hear from you, or sufficient time shall have passed for me to receive your reply. Should you accept I enclose a pass for Port Royal, of which I trust you will feel disposed to avail yourself at once. I am, with sincere regard,

Yours truly,

R. SAXTON,

Brig. Gen., Mil. Gov."

This was an excellent selection, and Captain Higginson's acceptance rather assured a fair trial for the men who should compose this regiment, as well as the quality of its officers.

MAJOR MARTIN R. DELANEY, U. S. A.

The first Kansas regiment which recruited in that State, commencing in August, 1862, was also fortunate in having Colonel R. J. Hinton.

General Butler, at New Orleans, was prevented by circumstances surrounding him at the time, from choosing among the friends of the negro race, as was the case in the before mentioned regiments, men to command the first and second regiments organized by him in the above named city, in August, 1862. He was only too glad to find white men of military capacity to take charge of the drilling and disciplining of the troops. As an experiment he was more than lucky in the appointment of Colonels Stafford and Daniels to the command of these regiments, seconded by Lieut. Cols. Bassett and Hall, and Finnegass of the 3rd Regiment. These officers proved themselves worthy of the trust reposed in them, and made these regiments, in drill and discipline, second to none in the Department of the Gulf. Notwithstanding the captains and subordinate officers of the first and second regiments were men, who like those in a large majority of the white regiments had never made arms a profession, and, who, through American prejudice, had but very limited opportunities for acquiring even the rudiments of a common English education. Several of them, however, being mulattoes, had had some training in the schools of the parishes, and some few in the higher schools of France, and in the Islands of the Carribean Sea. Maj. Dumas, of the 2nd Regiment, whose slaves composed nearly one whole company, was a gentleman of fine tact and ability, as were others.

Considering that they were all negroes, free and slave, their dash and manly courage, no less than their military aptitude, was equal, and in many instances superior, to those found in the regiments of Maine and New York. The 3rd Regiment was officered by soldiers of undoubted character and pluck, as they proved themselves to be, during the seige of Port Hudson, especially Capt. Quinn, who won distinction and promotion, as the record shows. The regiments raised thereafter were officered, more or less, by the non-commissioned officers of the white regiments, as a reward for gallantry and meritorious service upon the field, or on account of proficiency in drill. This rule of selection held good throughout all the departments in the organizing of negro troops. In May, 1863, President Lincoln, with a view of correcting an abuse that a certain commanding general had begun to practice in assigning inferior, though brave, men to the command of negro regiments; and in keeping with his new policy of arming the negroes, for which Gen. Lorenzo Thomas, Adjutant General of the Army, had gone into the Mississippi Valley region to raise twenty regiments, he appointed a Board for the examination of those applying for commands in negro regiments.

The "Record of the 7th Reg't. U.S. Colored Troops," in regard to the matter, says: "That the labors of this Board contributed very materially to the success of the experiment of raising this class of troops, no one cognizant with the facts can doubt. The operations of the Board can best be shown by quoting the following letter received from Gen. Casey in reply to some enquiries on the subject:

"BROOKLYN, Nov. 30th, 1875.

* * * "The Board for the Examination of candidates for officers in colored regiments, of which I was President, was appointed in May, 1863, and continued its duties about two years. This movement was, at first, very unpopular with a portion of the people of the country, as also with a large portion of the army. I, although doubting at first with regard to the expediency of operating in large bodies with this species of force, determined, that so far as I was concerned, it should have a fair trial.

"A system was adopted for the examination of candidates which did not allow influence, favor or affection to interfere with the enforcement of its provisions. The Board examined nearly three thousand candidates, seventeen hundred of whom they recommended for commissions in various grades, from colonel down.

"From my knowledge of the officers of white volunteers, gained in my duties connected with receiving and organizing, in the city of Washington, 300,000 of them, and also as commander of a division on the Peninsula, I have no hesitation in saying that the officers of the colored regiments, *who passed the Board*, as a body were superior to them, physically, mentally and morally.

"From the concurrent reports received from various sources, there is but little doubt that the success of the colored troops in the field was brought about in no small degree by the action of the Board.

"The following is the copy of a letter which I addressed to a gentleman of Philadelphia, and which you may find of interest:

'In conversation with you a few days since, I promised to elaborate somewhat the ideas which I expressed with regard to the appointment of officers of colored troops.

'Military men, whose opinion is worth having, will agree in this, that to have good and efficient troops it is indispensable that we should have good officers. The material for soldiers which the loyal States have furnished during this rebellion, I have no hesitation in saying, is the best that the world has ever seen. Such men deserve to have officers to command them who have been educated to the military profession. But few men are really fit to command men who have not had such an education. In default of this, as a sufficient number of such men cannot be found in the country, the number has to be made up from the best available material. In order to ascertain whether or not the aspirant possesses the proper knowledge and capacity for command, it is necessary that he be examined by a board of competent officers. The fact that the life and death of the men of the regiment is intimately connected with the competency of its officers, is not sufficiently appreciated by the community.

'The Board for the examination of officers of colored troops over which I preside, considers three things as indispensable before recommending a candidate, viz.: A good moral character, physical capacity, true loyalty to the country. A person possessing these indispensable qualifications is now submitted to an examination as to his knowledge of tactics and capacity for command.

'The following grades are entertained, viz.:

Colonel—	1st, 2d and 3d Class.	Lieut.-Colonel—	1st, 2d and 3d Class.
Major—	"	Captain—	"
1st Lieut.—	"	2d Lieut.—	"

and the recommendations for appointment made according to the applicant's merits.

'We have endeavored, to the best of our ability, to make this recommendation without partiality, favor or affection. We consider alone, in making our awards, the ability of the person to serve his country in the duties appertaining to the office. If, in the opinion of the Board, the person is not possessed of sufficient knowledge or capacity to fill either of the above named to the advantage of his country, he is rejected, notwithstanding any influence he may be able to bring to bear in the case. Let it be remembered that zeal alone is not sufficient; but what we require for a good officer is zeal combined with knowledge. No ordinary man can properly fill the office of colonel of a regiment. To acquire that knowledge of tactics as would fit him to command his regiment, as it ought to be in all situations, requires much study and practice, and is by no means easy. He should, besides, possess good administrative qualities, in order that affairs should run smoothly in his command, and the officers and privates be as contented and happy as circumstances admit.

Nor can too much trouble be taken properly to prepare persons to fill the responsible position of officers. Each State should have its military academy. In the meantime much good can be done by instituting a school for the instruction of persons (especially those who have had some experience in the service) who may have the requisite capacity and zeal to serve their country with advantage. Eschew all humbuggery and mere pretension, and let merit be the test of advancement.

'Let it be impressed deeply on the conscience of every man of influence and authority that when he places in command an incompetent officer he is guilty of manslaughter. The country has lost millions of treasure and thousands of lives by the incompetency of officers. We have many enemies on earth besides the Southern rebels. The fate of free institutions, not only in our own country, but in other lands, the destiny of millions unborn, depend upon our ability to maintain this contest to a successful issue against all our enemies, both foreign and domestic.

'The system of examination instituted by this Board, in my opinion, should be extended to the white as well as colored troops.

'Many of those who have been unsuccessful in the examination before the Board have, no doubt, in some cases, felt aggrieved, as also their friends.

'We have established a system of examination for officers, the good effects of which are already apparent in the colored organizations in the field. In the performance of this responsible, and not always agreeable duty, of presiding over this Board, I have always endeavored to be guided by conscientious regard for the good of the country, and I have every confidence that a just and intelligent people will award their approbation. SILAS CASEY,

Bvt. Major-General U. S. Army.'"

Of course this did not apply to regiments raised at the North, generally. They were officered by the *elite*, such as Col. R. G. Shaw, of the 54th Massachusetts, a former member of the 7th New York Regiment, and upon whose battle monument his name is carved. Cols. James C. Beecher, Wm. Birney and a host of others, whose names can now be found on the army rolls, with the prefix General, commanded these regiments, Of those who commanded Southern regiments this is equally true, especially of those who served in the 9th, 10th, 18th and 19th Corps. Col. Godfred Weitzel, who in March, 1865, had been promoted to Major General of Volunteers, commanded the 25th Corps of 30,000 negro soldiers. The select corps of officers intended to officer Gen. Ullman's brigade of four regiments to be raised at New Orleans by order of the War

CAPT. O. S. B. WALL, U. S. A.

Department, dated January 1863, as well as the battalion, which he was also ordered to raise for scouting purposes, the following March, included many men of rank. To command a negro regiment or company was at this date a coveted prize, for which men of wealth and education contended. The distinction which they were continually winning for their officers, frequently overcame the long-cherished prejudice of West Point, and the graduates of this caste institution now vied for commissions in negro regiments, in which many of them served during the Rebellion and since.

It was the idea of Gen. Banks when organizing the Corps d' Afrique to appoint even the non-commissioned officers from the ranks of white regiments, and he did so in several instances. His hostility to negro officers was the cause of his removing them from the regiments, which Major General Butler organized at New Orleans in 1862. In organizing the Corps d' Afrique, the order, No. 40, reads:

"The Commanding General desires to detail for temporary or permanent duty, the best officers of the army, for the organization, instruction, and discipline of this Corps. With them he is confident that the Corps will render important service to the Government. It is not established upon any dogma of equality or other theory, but as a practical and sensible matter of business. The Government makes use of mules, horses, uneducated white men in the defence of its institutions; why should not the negro contribute whatever is in his power, for the cause in which he is as deeply interested as other men? We may properly demand from him whatever service he can render."

At first it was proposed to pay the officers of negro troops less than was paid the officers of white soldiers, but this plan was abandoned. Toward the close of the war nearly all the chaplains appointed to negro regiments were negroes; non-commissioned officers were selected from the ranks, where they were found as well qualified as those taken from the ranks of white regiments. In the 10th and 18th Corps it was a common thing for the orderly sergeants to call their company's roll from memory, and the records of many companies and regiments are kept at the War Department in Washington, as mementoes of their efficiency.

Such were the men who commanded the Black Phalanx. The following are the names of the negro commissioned officers of the Butler Louisiana Regiments:

ROSTER OF NEGRO OFFICERS OF THE LOUISIANA NATIVE GUARD VOLUNTEER REGIMENTS.

FIRST REGIMENT.

Capts. Andrew Cailloux,	Louis A. Snaer,	John Depass
" Henry L. Rey,	Edward Carter,	Joseph Follin,
" James Lewis,	James H. Ingraham,	Aleide Lewis.
Lieuts. Lewis Petit,	Ernest Sougpre,	J. G. Parker,
" J. E. Moore,	Wm. Harding,	John Hardman,
" F. Kimball,	V. Lesner,	J. D. Paddock,
" Louis D. Lucien.		

SECOND REGIMENT.

Major F. E. Dumas,*		
Capts. E. A. Bertinnean,	Hannibal Carter,	E. P. Chase,,
" W. P. Barrett,	S. W. Ringgold,	P. B. S. Pinchback,
" William Bellez,	Monroe Menllim,	Joseph Villeverde,
" Samuel J. Wilkerson,	R. H. Isabella.	
Lieuts. Octave Rey,	J. P. Lewis,	Jasper Thompson,
" Ernest Murphy,	Calvin Glover,	J. Wellington,
" Louis Degray,	George T. Watson,	Joseph Jones,
" Alphonso Fluery,	Rufus Kinsley,	Ernest Hubian,
" Theo. A. Martin,	Soloman Hoys,	Alfred Arnis,
" Peter O. Depremont.		

THIRD REGIMENT.

Capts. Jacques Gla,	Peter A. Gardner,	Leon G. Forstall,
" Joseph C. Oliver,	Charles W. Gibbons,	Samuel Laurence,,
" John J. Holland		
Lieuts. Paul Paree,	Morris W. Morris,	Emile Detrege,
" Eugene Rapp,	E. T. Nash,	Alfred Bourgoan,
" E. Moss,	Chester W. Converse,	G. B. Miller,
" G. W. Talmon,	Octave Foy,	Chas. Butler.

NON-COMMISSIONED OFFICERS.

74TH U. S. C. T. Co. I, 2D LA. N. G.

Sergts. Joseph Boudraux,	Andrieu Vidal,	Joseph Bellevue,
" Louis Martin,	Jessy C. Wallace,	
Corpls. Paul Bonne,	Thos. William	Joseph Labeaud,
" Joseph Toolmer,	Louis Ford,	Peter Fleming,

As "muster in" rolls show.

74TH U. S. C. T. Co. D, 2ND N. G.

1st Sergts. Joseph Francois,	Adolph Augustin,	John Frick,
" Francois Remy,	Louis Duquenez.	
Corpls, Dorsin Sebatier,	Auguste Martin,	Lucien Boute "
" Adolphe Decoud,	Oscar Samuel,	Andre Gregoire,
" Joseph Armand,	Achilles Decoud.	

As "muster out" rolls show.

75TH U. S. C.T. Co. F, 3RD N. G.

Sergts. Hy. White,	Robert Williams,	Mathew Roden,
" Frank Nichols,		

---

*Capt. F. E. Dumas organized a company of his own slaves, and attached it to this regiment. He was promoted to the rank of Major, and commanded two companies at Pascagoula, Miss., during the fight. He was a free negro, wealthy, brave and loyal.

CAPT. P. B. S. PINCHBACK 2D LA VOLS.

SURGEON. A. T. AUGUSTA.

LT. JAMES M. TROTTER 55TH MASS. VOL.

LT. W. H. DUPREE 55TH MASS. VOLS.

Corpls. Alfred Kellie, Philip Craff, Julius Vick.
As mustered out.

73RD U. S. C. T. Co. A. 1ST LA. N. G.

Sergts. Joseph R, Forstall, Edmond Tomlinson, Edgar Thezan,
" Numa Brihou, Edward P. Ducloslange,
Corpls. John G. Seldon, Thelesphore J. Sauvinet, Alonzo Tocca,
" Joseph Francois Antonio Segura, Auguste Martin,
" Francois Remy, Ernest Brustic,

73RD U. S. C. T. Co. B. 1ST LA. N. G.

Sergts. Faustin Zenon Louis Francois, August Bartholenny,
" Joseph Alfred Wm. Armstrong,
Arthur Gaspard was a Sergeant at "muster in" of company; discharged for wounds Dec. 10th, 1863.
Corpls. Alphonse Barbe, Albert Victor, Wm. John Baptist
" Louis Gille.
These were non-commissioned officers of Co. B. at "muster out.'

73RD U. S. C. T. Co. H. 1ST LA. N. G.

Capt. Henry L. Rey. 1st Lieut. Eugene Rapp, 2nd Lieut. Louis Arthur Thibaut.
1st Sergt. Henry Mathieu, 2nd Sergt, Armand Daniel, 3rd Sergt. J. B. Dupre.
4th " Felix Mathieu, 5th " Lucien Dupre,
Corpls. Ernest Hewlett, Frank Delhomme, D. J. Marine,
" Felix Santini, Celestine Ferrand, Auguste Campbell,
" Narcis Hubert, Caliste Dupre.
As "muster in."

73RD U. S. C. T. Co. G, 1ST LA. N. G.

Sergts. Theodule Drinier, Peter Pascal, Peter Robin,
" Gustave St. Leger, Armand Le Blanc.
Corpls. Edward Louis, Cherry Fournette, Townsen Lee,
" John Thompson, Perrin Virgile, William Charity,
" John Marshall, Soloman Fisher.
The above were the non-commissioned officers at "muster out' of Company.
Corporal W. Heath, killed at Port Hudson.

74TH U. S. C. T. Co. G, 2ND LA. N. G.

Sergts. Thos. Martin, Etienne Duluc Arthur Frilot,
" Louis Martin, J. B. Lavigne,
Corpls. Martin Forstals, Emile Duval, Gustave Ducre,
" Joseph Naroce, Polin Paree,* Jerome Alugas,
" Ernest Butin, Pierre Jignac.
Deserted Oct. 5th, 1863.
The above were the non-commissioned officers at "muster in" of company, Oct. 1862.

OTHER REGIMENTS.

Surgeons U. S. Army.—Dr. W. P. Powell, Dr. A. T. Augusta.
Major, Martin R. Delaney. Capt., O. S. B. Wall.
Lieuts. 55th Regt.—James M. Trotter, Chas. L. Mitchell, W. H. Dupree,
" J. F. Shorter.

There were a number of negroes commissioned during the war whose record it has not been possible to obtain. Quite a number of mulattoes served in white regiments, some as officers; they were so light in complexion that their true race connection could not be told. This is true of one of the prominent Ohioans of to-day, who served on the staff of a Major General of volunteers. There were several among the Pennsylvania troops, and not a few in the New York and Massachusetts regiments. While lying on a battle-field wounded and exhausted, an officer of the brigade to which the writer belonged, rode up, passed me his canteen, and enquired if I knew him. A negative answer was given. "I am Tom Bunting," he replied. "You know me now, don't you? We used to play together in our boyhood days in Virginia; keep the canteen. I will let your people know about you." So saying he dashed away to his command; he belonged to a Massachusetts regiment. There was quite a large number of mulattoes who enlisted under Butler, at New Orleans, and served in white regiments; this is also true of the confederate army. The writer has an intimate acquaintance now living in Richmond, Va., who served in a New York Regiment, who, while marching along with his regiment through Broad street, after the capture of that city, was recognized by his mother, and by her was pulled from the ranks and embraced. A man who became United States Marshal of one of the Southern States after the war, was Captain in the 2nd Louisiana Native Guards Regiment. Numerous instances of this kind could be cited.

SERG'T. W. H. CARNEY.—Co. C. 54th Mass. Vols.
"The old flag never touched the ground, boys!"

CHAPTER V.

DEPARTMENT OF THE GULF.

When Admiral Farragut's fleet anchored at New Orleans, and Butler occupied the city, three regiments of confederate negro troops were under arms guarding the United States Mint building, with orders to destroy it before surrendering it to the Yankees. The brigade, however, was in command of a Creole mulatto, who, instead of carrying out the orders given him, and following the troops out of the city on their retreat, counter-marched his command and was cut off from the main body of the army by the Federal forces, to whom they quietly surrendered a few days after.

General Phelps commanded the Federal forces at Carrolton, about seven miles from New Orleans, the principal point in the cordon around the city. Here the slaves congregated in large numbers, seeking freedom and protection from their barbarous overseers and masters. Some of these poor creatures wore irons and chains; some came bleeding from gun-shot wounds. General Phelps was an old abolitionist, and had early conceived the idea that the proper thing to do was for the government to arm the negroes. Now came his opportunity to act. Hundreds of able-bodied men were in his camps, ready and willing to fight for their freedom and the preservation of the Union. The secessionists in that neighborhood complained to General Butler about their negroes leaving them and going into camp with the Yankees. So numerous were the complaints, that the General, acting under orders from Washington, and also foreseeing that

General Phelps intended allowing the slaves to gather at his post, issued the following order:

"NEW ORLEANS, May 23, 1862.

"GENERAL:—You will cause all unemployed persons, black and white, to be excluded from your lines.

"You will not permit either black or white persons to pass your lines, not officers and soldiers or belonging to the navy of the United States, without a pass from these head-quarters, except they are brought in under guard as captured persons, with information, and those to be examined and detained as prisoners of war, if they have been in arms against the United States, or dismissed and sent away at once, as the case may be. This does not apply to boats passing up the river without landing within the lines.

"Provision dealers and marketmen are to be allowed to pass in with provisions and their wares, but not to remain over night.

"Persons having had their permanent residence within your lines before the occupation of our troops, are not to be considered unemployed persons.

"Your officers have reported a large number of servants. Every officer so reported employing servants will have the allowance for servants deducted from his pay-roll.

Respectfully, your obedient servant,

B. F. BUTLER.

"Brig.-Gen. PHELPS, Commanding Camp Parapet."

This struck Gen. Phelps as an inhuman order, though he obeyed it and placed the slaves just outside of his camp lines. Here the solders, having drank in the spirit of their commander, cared for the fugitives from slavery. But they continued to come, according to divine appointment, and their increase prompted Gen. Phelps to write this patriotic, pathetic and eloquent appeal, knowing it must reach the President:

"CAMP PARAPET, NEAR CARROLLTON, LA., June 16, 1862.

"Capt. R. S. DAVIS, Acting Assistant Adjutant-General, New Orleans. La.:

"SIR: I enclose herewith, for the information of the major-general commanding the department, a report of Major Peck, officer of the day, concerning a large number of negroes, of both sexes and all ages, who are lying near our pickets, with bag and baggage, as if they had already commenced an exodus. Many of these negroes have been sent away from one of the neighboring sugar plantations by their owner, a Mr. Babilliard La Blanche, who tells them, I am informed, that 'the Yankees are king here now, and that they must go to their king for food and shelter.'

"They are of that four millions of our colored subjects who have no king or chief, nor in fact any government that can secure to them the simplest natural rights. They can not even be entered into treaty stipulations with and deported to the east, as our Indian tribes have been to the west. They have no right to the mediation of a justice of the peace or jury between them and chains and lashes. They have no right to wages for their labor; no right to the Sabbath; no right to the institution of marriage; no right to letters or to self-defense. A small class of owners, rendered unfeeling, and even unconscious and unreflecting by habit, and a large part of them ignorant and vicious, stand between them and their government, destroying its sovereignty. This government has not the power even to regulate the number of lashes that its subjects may receive. It can not say that they shall receive thirty-nine instead of forty. To a large and growing class of its subjects it can secure neither justice, moderation, nor the advantages of Christian religion; and if it can not protect *all* its subjects, it can protect none, either black or white.

"It is nearly a hundred years since our people first declared to the nations of the world that all men are born free; and still we have not made our declaration good. Highly revolutionary measures have since then been adopted by the admission of Missouri and the annexation of Texas in favor of slavery by the barest majorities of votes, while the highly conservative vote of two-thirds has at length been attained against slavery, and still slavery exists—even, moreover, although two-thirds of the blood in the veins of our slaves is fast becoming from our own race. If we wait for a larger vote, or until our slaves' blood becomes more consanguined still with our own, the danger of a violent revolution, over which we can have no control, must become more imminent every day. By a course of undecided action, determined by no policy but the vague will of a war-distracted people, we run the risk of precipitating that very revolutionary violence which we seem seeking to avoid.

"Let us regard for a moment the elements of such a revolution.

"Many of the slaves here have been sold away from the border States as a punishment, being too refractory to be dealt with there in the face of the civilization of the North. They come here with the knowledge of the Christian religion, with its germs planted and expanding, as it were, in the dark, rich soil of their African nature, with feel-

WASHING IN CAMP

ings of relationship with the families from which they came, and with a sense of unmerited banishment as culprits, all which tends to bring upon them a greater severity of treatment and a corresponding disinclination 'to receive punishment'. They are far superior beings to their ancestors, who were brought from Africa two generations ago, and who occasionally rebelled against comparatively less severe punishment than is inflicted now. While rising in the scale of Christian beings, their treatment is being rendered more severe than ever. The whip, the chains, the stocks, and imprisonment are no mere fancies here; they are used to any extent to which the imagination of civilized man may reach. Many of them are as intelligent as their masters, and far more moral, for while the slave appeals to the moral law as his vindication, clinging to it as to the very horns of the alter of his safety and his hope, the master seldom hesitates to wrest him from it with violence and contempt. The slave, it is true, bears no resentment; he asks for no punishment for his master; he simply claims justice for himself; and it is this feature of his condition that promises more terror to the retribution when it comes. Even now the whites stand accursed by their oppression of humanity, being subject to a degree of confusion, chaos, and enslavement to error and wrong, which northern society could not credit or comprehend.

"Added to the four millions of the colored race whose disaffection is increasing even more rapidly than their number, there are at least four millions more of the white race whose growing miseries will naturally seek companionship with those of the blacks. This latter portion of southern society has its representatives, who swing from the scaffold with the same desperate coolness, though from a directly different cause, as that which was manifested by John Brown. The trator Mumford, who swung the other day for trampling on the national flag, had been rendered placid and indifferent in his desperation by a government that either could not or would not secure to its subjects the blessings of liberty which that flag imports. The South cries for justice from the government as well as the North, though in a proud and resentful spirit; and in what manner is that justice to be obtained? Is it to be secured by that wretched resource of a set of profligate politicians, called 'reconstruction?' No, it is to be obtained by the abolition of slavery, and by no other course.

"It is vain to deny that the slave system of labor is giving shape to the government of the society where it exists, and that that government is not republican, either in form or spirit. It was through this system that the leading conspirators have sought to fasten upon the people an aristocracy or a despotism; and it is not sufficient that they should be merely defeated in their object, and the country be rid of their rebellion; for by our constitution we are imperatively obliged to sustain the State against the ambition of uprincipled leaders, and secure to them the republican form of government. We have positive duties to perform, and should hence adopt and pursue a positive, decided policy. We have services to render to certain states which they cannot perform for themselves. We are in an emergency which the framers of the constitution might easily have foreseen, and for which they have amply provided.

"It is clear that the public good requires slavery to be abolished; but in what manner is it to be done? The mere quiet operation of congressional law can not deal with slavery as in its former status before the war, because the spirit of law is right reason, and there is no reason in slavery. A system so unreasonable as slavery can not be regulated by reason. We can hardly expect the several states to adopt laws or measures against their own immediate interests. We have seen that they will rather find arguments for crime than seek measures for abolishing or modifying slavery. But there is one principle which is fully recognized as a necessity in conditions like ours, and that is that the public safety is the supreme law of the State, and that amid the clash of arms the laws of peace are silent. It is then for our president, the commander-in-chief of our armies, to declare the abolition of slavery, leaving it to the wisdom of congress to adopt measures to meet the consequences. This is the usual course pursued by a general or by a military power. That power gives orders affecting complicated interests and millions of property, leaving it to the other functions of government to adjust and regulate the effects produced. Let the president abolish slavery, and it would be an easy matter for congress, through a well-regulated system of apprenticeship, to adopt safe measures for effecting a gradual transition from slavery to freedom.

"The existing system of labor in Louisiana is unsuited to the age; and by the intrusion of the national forces it seems falling to pieces. It is a system of mutual jealousy and suspicion between the master and the man—a system of violence, immorality and vice. The fugitive negro tells us that our presence renders his condition worse with his master than it was before, and that we offer no alleviation in return. The system is impolitic, because it offers but one stimulent to labor and effort, viz.: the lash, when another, viz.: money, might be added with good effect. Fear, and the other low and bad qualities of the slave, are appealed to, but never the good. The relation, therefore, between capital and labor, which ought to be generous and confiding, is darkling, suspicious, unkindly, full of reproachful threats, and without concord or peace. This condition of things renders the interests of society a prey to politicians. Politics cease to be practical or useful.

"The questions that ought to have been discussed in the late extraordinary convention of Louisiana, are: *First*, What ought the State of Louisiana to do to adopt her ancient system of labor to the present advanced spirit of the age? And *Second*, How can the State be assisted by the general government in effecting the change? But instead of this, the only question before that body was how to vindicate slavery by flogging the Yankees!

"Compromises hereafter are not to be made with politicians, but with sturdy labor and the right to work. The interests of workingmen resent political trifling. Our political education, shaped almost entirely to the interest of slavery, has been false and vicious in the extreme, and it must be corrected with as much suddenness, almost, as that with which Salem witchcraft came to an end. The only question that remains to decide is how the change shall take place.

"We are not without examples and precedents in the history of the past. The enfranchisement of the people of Europe has been, and is still going on, through the instrumentality of military service; and by this means our slaves might be raised in the scale of civilization and prepared for freedom. Fifty regiments might be raised among them at once, which could be employed in this climate to preserve order, and thus prevent the necessity of retrenching our liberties, as we should do by a large army exclusively of whites. For it is evident that a considerable army of whites would give stringency to our government, while an army, partly of blacks, would naturally operate in favor of freedom and against those influences which at present most endanger our liberties. At the end of five years they could be sent to Africa, and their places filled with new enlistments.

"There is no practical evidence against the effects of immediate abolition, even if there is not in its favor. I have witnessed the sudden abolition of flogging at will in the army, and of legalized flogging in the navy, against the prejudice-warped judgments of both, and, from the beneficial effects there, I have nothing to fear from the immediate abolition of slavery. I fear, rather, the violent consequences from a continuance of the evil. But should such an act devastate the whole State of Louisiana, and render the whole soil here but the mere passage-way of the fruits of the enterprise and industry of the Northwest, it would be better for the country at large than it is now as the seat of disaffection and rebellion.

"When it is remembered that not a word is found in our constitution sanctioning the buying and selling of human beings, a shameless act which renders our country the disgrace of Christendom, and worse, in this respect, even than Africa herself, we should have less dread of seeing the degrading traffic stopped at once and forever. Half wages are already virtually paid for slave labor in the system of tasks which, in an unwilling spirit of compromise, most of the slave states have already been compelled to adopt. At the end of five years of apprenticeship, or of fifteen at farthest, full wages could be paid to the enfranchised negro race, to the double advantage of both master and man. This is just; for we now hold the slaves of Louisiana by the same tenure that the State can alone claim them, viz: by the original right of conquest. We have so far conquered them that a proclmation setting them free, coupled with offers of protection, would devastate every plantation in the State.

"In conclusion, I may state that Mr. La Blanche is, as I am informed, a descendant from one of the oldest families of Louisiana. He is wealthy and a man of standing, and his act in sending away his negroes to our lines, with their clothes and furniture, appears to indicate the convictions of his own mind as to the proper logical consequences and deductions that should follow from the present relative status of the two contending parties. He seems to be convinced that the proper result of the conflict is the manumission of the slave, and he may be safely regarded in this respect as a representative man of the State. I so regard him myself, and thus do I interpret his action, although my camp now contains some of the highest symbols of secessionism, which have been taken by a party of the Seventh Vermont volunteers from his residence.

"Meantime his slaves, old and young, little ones and all, are suffering from exposure and uncertainty as to their future condition. Driven away by their master, with threats of violence if they return, and with no decided welcome or reception from us, what is to be their lot? Considerations of humanity are pressing for an immediate solution of their difficulties; and they are but a small portion of their race who have sought, and are still seeking, our pickets and our military stations, declaring that they can not and will not any longer serve their masters, and that all they want is work and protection from us. In such a state of things, the question occurs as to my own action in the case. I cannot return them to their masters, who not unfrequently come in search of them, for I am, fortunately, prohibited by an article of war from doing that, even if my own nature did not revolt at it. I can not receive them, for I have neither work, shelter, nor the means or plan of transporting them to Hayti, or of making suitable arrangements with their masters until they can be provided for.

"It is evident that some plan, some policy, or some system is necessary on the part of the government, without which the agent can do nothing, and all his efforts are rendered useless and of no effect. This is no new condition in which I find myself; it is my experience during the some twenty-five years of my public life as a military officer of the government. The new article of war recently adopted by congress, rendering it criminal in an officer of the army to return fugitives from injustice, is the first support that I have ever felt from the government in contending against those slave influences which are opposed to its character and to its interests. But the mere refusal to return fugitives does not now meet the case. A public agent in the present emergency must be invested with wider and more positive powers than this, or his services will prove as valueless to the country as they are unsatisfactory to himself.

"Desiring this communication to be laid before the president, and leaving my commission at his disposal, I have the honor to remain, sir,

"Very respectfully, your obedient servant,

J. W. PHELPS, *Brigadier-General.*"

On the day on which he received this letter, Gen. Butler forwarded to Washington this dispatch:

"NEW ORLEANS, LA., June 18, 1862.

"HON. E. M. STANTON, Secretary of War:

"SIR:—Since my last dispatch was written, I have received the accompanying report from General Phelps.

"It is not my duty to enter into a discussion of the questions which it presents.

"I desire, however, to state the information of Mr. La Blanche, given me by his friends and neighbors, and also *Jack* La Blanche, his slave, who seems to be the leader of this party of negroes. Mr. La Blanche I have not seen. He, however, claims to be loyal, and to have taken no part in the war, but to have lived quietly on

COOKING IN CAMP

his plantation, some twelve miles above New Orleans, on the opposite side of the river. He has a son in the secession army, whose uniform and equipments, &c., are the symbols of secession of which General Phelps speaks. Mr. La Blanche's house was searched by the order of General Phelps, for arms and contraband of war, and his neighbors say that his negroes were told that they were free if they would come to the general's camp.

"That thereupon the negroes, under the lead of Jack, determined to leave, and for that purpose crowded into a small boat which, from overloading, was in danger of swamping.

"La Blanche then told his negroes that if they were determined to go, they would be drowned, and he would hire them a large boat to put them across the river, and that they might have their furniture if they would go and leave his plantation and crop to ruin.

"They decided to go, and La Blanche did all a man could to make that going safe.

"The account of General Phelps is the negro side of the story; that above given is the story of Mr. La Blanche's neighbors, some of whom I know to be loyal men.

"An order against negroes being allowed in camp is the reason they are outside.

"Mr. La Blanche is represented to be a humane man, and did not consent to the 'exodus' of his negroes.

"General Phelps, I believe, intends making this a test case for the policy of the government. I wish it might be so, for the difference of our action upon this subject is a source of trouble. I respect his honest sincerity of opinion, but I am a soldier, bound to carry out the wishes of my government so long as I hold its commission, and I understand that policy to be the one I am pursuing. I do not feel at liberty to pursue any other. If the policy of the government is nearly that I sketched in my report upon the subject and that which I have ordered in this department, then the services of General Phelps are worse than useless here. If the views set forth in his report are to obtain, then he is invaluable, for his whole soul is in it, and he is a good soldier of large experience, and no braver man lives. I beg to leave the whole question with the president, with perhaps the needless assurance that his wishes shall be loyally followed, were they not in accordance with my own, as I have now no right to have any upon the subject.

"I write in haste, as the steamer 'Mississippi' is awaiting this dispatch.

"Awaiting the earliest possible instructions, I have the honor to be,

"Your most obedient servant,

"B. F. BUTLER, *Major General Commanding.*"

Gen. Phelps waited about six weeks for a reply, but none came. Meanwhile the negroes continued to gather at his camp. He said, in regard to not receiving an answer, "I was left to the inference that silence gives consent, and proceeded therefore to take such decided measures as appeared best calculated, to me, to dispose of the difficulty." Accordingly he made the following requisition upon head-quarters:

"CAMP PARAPET, LA., July 30, 1862.

"Captain R. S. DAVIS, A. A. A. General, New Orleans, La.:

"SIR:—I enclose herewith requisitions for arms, accoutrements, clothing, camp and garrison equipage, &c., for three regiments of Africans, which I propose to raise for the defense of this point. The location is swampy and unhealthy, and our men are dying at the rate of two or three a day.

"The southern loyalists are willing, as I understand, to furnish their share of the tax for the support of the war; but they should also furnish their quota of men, which they have not thus far done. An opportunity now offers of supplying the deficiency; and it is not safe to neglect opportunities in war. I think that, with the proper facilities, I could raise the three regiments proposed in a short time. Without holding out any inducements, or offering any reward, I have now upward of three hundred Africans organized into five companies, who are all willing and ready to show their devotion to our cause in any way that it may be put to the test. They are willing to submit to anything rather than to slavery.

"Society in the South seems to be on the point of dissolution; and the best way of preventing the African from becoming instrumental in a general state of anarchy, is to enlist him in the cause of the Republic. If we reject his services, any petty military chieftain, by offering him freedom, can have them for the purpose of robbery and plunder. It is for the interests of the South, as well of the North, that the African should be permitted to offer his block for the temple of freedom. Sentiments unworthy of the man of the present day—worthy only of another Cain—could alone prevent such an offer from being accepted.

"I would recommend that the cadet graduates of the present year should be sent to South Carolina and this point to organize and discipline our African levies, and that the more promising non-commissioned officers and privates of the army be appointed as company officers to command them. Prompt and energetic efforts in this direction would probably accomplish more toward a speedy termination of the war, and an early restoration of peace and unity, than any other course which could be adopted.

"I have the honor to remain, sir, very respectfully, your obedient servant,

J. W. PHELPS, *Brigadier-General.*"

This reply was received:

NEW ORLEANS, July 31, 1862.

"GENERAL:—The general commanding wishes you to employ the contrabands in and about your camp in cutting down all the trees, &c., between your lines and the lake, and in forming abatis, according to the plan agreed upon between you and Lieutenant Weitzel when he visited you some time since. What wood is not needed by you is much needed in this city. For this purpose I have ordered the quartermaster to furnish you with axes, and tents for the contrabands to be quartered in.

"I am, sir, very respectfully, your obedient servant,

"By order of Major-General BUTLER.

"R. S. DAVIS, Capt. and A. A. A. G.

"To Brigadier-General J. W. PHELPS, Camp Parapet."

General Butler's effort to turn the attention of Gen. Phelps to the law of Congress recently passed was of no avail, that officer was determined in his policy of warring on the enemy; but finding General Butler as firm in his policy of leniency, and knowing of his strong pro-slavery sentiments prior to the war,—notwithstanding his "contraband" order at Fortress Monroe,—General Phelps felt as though he would be humiliated if he departed from his own policy and became what he regarded as a slave-driver, therefore he determined to resign. He replied to General Butler as follows:

"CAMP PARAPET, LA., July 31, 1862.

"Captain R. S. DAVIS, A. A. A. General, New Orleans, La.:

"SIR:—The communication from your office of this date, signed, 'By order of Major-General Butler,' directing me to employ the 'contrabands' in and about my camp in cutting down all the trees between my lines and the lake, etc., has just been received.

"In reply, I must state that while I am willing to prepare African regiments for the defense of the government against its assailants, I am not willing to become the mere slave-driver which you propose, having no qualifications in that way. I am, therefore, under the necessity of tendering the resignation of my commission as an officer of the army of the United States, and respectfully request a leave of absence until it is accepted, in accordance with paragraph 29, page 12, of the general regulations.

"While I am writing, at half-past eight o'clock P. M., a colored man is brought in by one of the pickets who has just been wounded in the side by a charge of shot, which he says was fired at him by one of a party of three slave-hunters or guerillas, a mile or more from our line of sentinels. As it is some distance from the camp to the lake, the party of wood-choppers which you have directed will probably need a considerable force to guard them against similar attacks.

"I have the honor to be, sir, very respectfully, your obedient servant,

"J. W. PHELPS, *Brigadier-General.*"

Phelps was one of Butler's most trusted commanders, and the latter endeavored, but in vain, to have him reconsider his resignation. General Butler wrote him:

NEW ORLEANS, August, 2, 1862.

"GENERAL:—I was somewhat surprised to receive your resignation for the reasons stated.

"When you were put in command at Camp Parapet, I sent Lieutenant Weitzel, my chief engineer, to make a reconnoissance of the lines of Carrollton, and I understand it was agreed between you and the engineer that a removal of the wood between Lake Pontchartrain and the right of your intrenchment was a necessary military precaution. The work could not be done at that time because of the stage of water and the want of men. But now both water and men concur. You have five hundred Africans organized into companies, you write me. This work they are fitted to do. It must either be done by them or my soldiers, now drilled and disciplined. You have said the location is unhealthy for the soldier; it is not to the negro; is it not best that these unemployed Africans should do this labor? My attention is specially called to this matter at the present time, because there are reports of demonstrations to be made on your lines by the rebels, and in my judgment it is a matter of necessary precaution thus to clear the right of your line, so that you can receive the proper aid from the gun-boats on the lake, besides preventing the enemy from having cover. To do this the negroes ought to be employed; and in so employing them I see no evidence of 'slave-driving' or employing you as a 'slave-driver.'

"The soldiers of the Army of the Potomac did this very thing last summer in front of Arlington Heights; are the negroes any better than they?

"Because of an order to do this necessary thing to protect your front, threatened by the enemy, you tender your resignation and ask immediate leave of absence. I assure you I did not expect this, either from your courage, your patriotism, or your good sense. To resign in the face of an enemy has not been the highest plaudit to a soldier, especially when the reason assigned is that he is ordered to do that which a recent act of congress has specially authorized a military commander to do, *i. e.*, employ the Africans to do the necessary work about a camp or upon a fortification.

"General, your resignation will not be accepted by me, leave of absence will not be granted, and you will see to it that my orders, thus necessary for the defense of the city, are faithfully and diligently executed, upon the responsibility that a soldier in the field owes to his superior. I will see that all proper requisitions for the food, shelter, and clothing of these negroes so at work are at once filled by the proper departments. You will also send out a proper guard to protect the laborers against the guerilla force, if any, that may be in the neighborhood.

"I am your obedient servant,

"BENJ. F. BUTLER, *Major-General Commanding.*

"Brigadier-General J. W. PHELPS, *Commanding at Camp Parapet.*"

On the same day, General Butler wrote again to General Phelps:

"NEW ORLEANS, August 2, 1862.

"GENERAL:—By the act of congress, as I understand it, the president of the United States alone has the authority to employ Africans in arms as a part of the military forces of the United States.

"Every law up to this time raising volunteer or militia forces has been opposed to their employment. The president has not as yet indicated his purpose to employ the Africans in arms.

"The arms, clothing, and camp equipage which I have here for the Louisiana volunteers, is, by the letter of the secretary of war, expressly limited to white soldiers, so that I have no authority to divert them, however much I may desire so to do.

"I do not think you are empowered to organize into companies negroes, and drill them as a military organization, as I am not surprised, but unexpectedly informed you have done. I cannot sanction this course of action as at present advised, specially when we have need of the services of the blacks, who are being sheltered upon the outskirts of your camp, as you will see by the orders for their employment sent you by the assistant adjutant-general.

"I will send your application to the president, but in the mean time you must desist from the formation of any negro military organization.

"I am your obedient servant,

"BENJ. F. BUTLER, *Major-General Commanding.*

"Brigadier-General PHELPS, *commanding forces at Camp Parapet.*"

General Phelps' resignation was accepted by the Government. He received notification of the fact on the 8th of September and immediately prepared to return to his farm in Vermont. In parting with his officers, who were, like his soldiers, much attached to him, he said: "And now, with earnest wishes for your welfare, and aspirations for the success of the great cause for which you are here, I bid you good-bye." Says Parton:

"When at length, the government had arrived at a negro policy, and was arming slaves, the president offered General Phelps a major-general's commission. He replied, it is said, that he would willingly accept the commission if it were dated back to the day of his resignation, so as to carry with it an approval of his course at Camp Parapet. This was declined, and General Phelps remains in retirement. I suppose the president felt that an indorsement of General Phelps' conduct would imply a censure of General Butler, whose conduct every candid person, I think, must admit, was just, forbearing, magnanimous."

General Butler was carrying out the policy of the Government at that time, but it was not long before he found it necessary to inaugurate a policy of his own for the safety of his command. On the 5th of August Breckenridge assaulted Baton Rouge, the capital of the State, which firmly convinced General Butler of the necessity of raising troops to defend New Orleans. He had somewhat realized his situation in July and appealed to the "home authorities" for reinforcements, but none could be sent. Still, the Secretary of War said to him, in reply to his application: "New Orleans must be held at all hazards."

With New Orleans threatened and no hope of reinforcement, General Butler, on the 22d day of August, before General Phelps had retired to private life, was obliged to accept the policy of arming negroes. He issued the following order:

"HEADQUARTERS DEPARTMENT OF THE GULF,
GENERAL ORDERS NO. 63. "NEW ORLEANS, August 22, 1862.

"Whereas on the 23d day of April, in the year eighteen hundred and sixty-one, at a public meeting of the free colored population of the city of New Orleans, a military organization, known as the "Native Guards"(colored,) had its existence, which military organization was duly and legally enrolled as a part of the militia of the State, its officers being commissioned by Thomas O. Moore, Governor and Commander-in-Chief of the militia of the State of Louisiana, in the form following, that is to say:

"'THE STATE OF LOUISIANA.
[Seal of the State.]

"'By Thomas Overton Moore, Governor of the State of Louisiana, and commander-in-chief of the militia thereof.

"'In the name and by the authority of the State of Louisiana: Know ye that ——— ———, having been duly and legally elected captain of the "Native Guards" (colored,) 1st division of the Militia of Louisiana, to serve for the term of the war,

"'I do hereby appoint and commission him captain as aforesaid, to take rank as such, from the 2d day of May, eighteen hundred and sixty-one.

"'He is, therefore, carefully and dilligently to discharge the duties of his office by doing and performing all manner of things thereto belonging. And I do strictly charge and require all officers, non-commissioned officers and privates under his command, to be obedient to his orders as captain; and he is to observe and follow such orders and directions, from time to time, as he shall receive from me, or the future Governor of the State of Louisiana, or other superior officers, according to the Rules and Articles of War, and in conformity to law.

"'In testimony whereof, I have caused these letters to be made patent, and the seal of the State to be hereunto annexed.

"'Given under my hand, at the city of Baton Rouge, on the second day of May, in the year of our Lord one thousand eight hundred and sixty-one.

[L.S.] [Signed,] THOS. O. MOORE.

"'By the Governor:

[Signed,] "'P. D. Hardy, Secretary of State.

[Endorsed.]

"'I, Maurice Grivot, Adjutant and Inspector General of the State of Louisiana, do hereby certify that ——— ———, named in the within commission, did, on the second day of May, in the year 1861, deposit in my office his written acceptance of the

office to which he is commissioned, and his oath of office taken according to law.
[Signed,] "'M. GRIVOT,
"'Adjutant and Inspector General, La.'

"And whereas, said military organization elicited praise and respect, and was complimented in General Orders for its patriotism and loyalty, and was ordered to continue during the war, in the words following:

"'HEADQUARTERS LOUISIANA MILITIA,
"'Order No. 426.] "'Adjutant General's Office, March 24, 1862.

"'I.—The Governor and Commander-in-Chief, relying implicitly upon the loyalty of the free colored population of the city and State for the protection of their homes, their property, and for Southern rights, from the pollution of a ruthless invader, and believing that the military organization which existed prior to the 15th of February, 1862, and elicited praise and respect for the patriotic motives which prompted it, should exist for and during the war, calls upon them to maintain their organization, and to hold themselves prepared for such orders as may be transmitted to them.

"'II.—The colonel commanding will report without delay to Major General Lewis, commanding State militia.

"'By order of THOS. O. MOORE, Governor.
[Signed,] "'M. GRIVOT, Adjutant General.'

"And whereas, said military organization, by the same order, was directed to report to Major-General Lewis for service, but did not leave the city of New Orleans when he did:

"Now, therefore, the Commanding General, believing that a large portion of this militia force of the State of Louisiana are willing to take service in the volunteer forces of the United States, and be enrolled and organized to 'defend their homes from 'ruthless invaders;' to protect their wives and children and kindred from wrong and outrage; to shield their property from being seized by bad men; and to defend the flag of their native country as their fathers did under Jackson at Chalmette against Packenham and his myrmidons, carrying the black flag of 'beauty and booty:'

"Appreciating their motives, relying upon their 'well-known loyalty and patriotism,' and with 'praise and respect' for these brave men—it is ordered that all the members of the 'Native Guards' aforesaid, and all other free colored citizens recognized by the first and late governor and authorities of the State of Louisiana as a portion of the militia of the State, who shall enlist in the volunteer service of the United States, shall be duly organized by the appointment of proper officers, and accepted, paid, equipped, armed and rationed as are other volunteer troops of the United States, subject to the approval of the President of the United States. All such persons are required at once to report themselves at the Touro Charity Building, Front Levee St., New Orleans, where proper officers will muster them into the service of the United States.

By command of Major General Butler:
R. S. DAVIS, *Capt. and A. A. A. G.*"

Notwithstanding the harsh treatment they had been receiving from Military-Governor Shepley and the Provost Guard, the rendezvous designated was the scene of a busy throng the next day. Thousands of men were enlisted during the first week, and in fourteen days a regiment was organized. The first regiment's line officers were colored, and the field officers were white. Those who made up this regiment were not all free negroes by more than half. Any negro who would swear that he was free, if physically good, was accepted, and of the many thousand slave fugitives in the city from distant plantations, hundreds found their way into Touro building and ultimately into the ranks of the three regiments formed at that building. The second, like the first, had all colored line officers; the third was officered regardless of color. This was going beyond the line laid down by General Phelps. He proposed that white men should take com-

10

mand of these troops exclusively. By November these three regiments were in the field, where in course of time they often met their former masters face to face and exchanged shots with them. The pro-slavery men of the North and their newspapers endeavored to make the soldiers in the field believe that the negroes would not fight; while not only the papers and the soldiers, but many officers, especially those from the West Point Academy, denounced General Butler for organizing the regiments. General Weitzel, to whose command these regiments were assigned in an expedition up the river, objected to them, and asked Butler to relieve him of the command of the expedition. Butler wrote him in reply:

"You say that in these organizations you have no confidence. As your reading must have made you aware, General Jackson entertained a different opinion upon that subject. It was arranged between the commanding general and yourself, that the colored regiments should be employed in guarding the railroad. You don't complain, in your report, that they either failed in this duty, or that they have acted otherwise than correctly and obediently to the commands of their officers, or that they have committed any outrage or pillage upon the inhabitants. The general was aware of your opinion, that colored men will not fight. You have failed to show, by the conduct of these free men, so far, anything to sustain that opinion. And the general cannot see why you should decline the command, especially as you express a willingness to go forward to meet the only organized enemy with your brigade alone, without farther support. The commanding general cannot see how the fact that they are guarding your line of communication by railroad, can weaken your defense. He must, therefore, look to the other reasons stated by you, for an explanation of your declining the command.

"You say that since the arrival of the negro regiment you have seen symptoms of a servile insurrection. But as the only regiment that arrived there got there as soon as your own command, of course the appearance of such symptoms is since their arrival.

"Have you not mistaken the cause? Is it the arrival of a negro regiment, or is it the arrival of United States troops, carrying by the act of congress freedom to this servile race? Did you expect to march into that country, drained, as you say it is, by conscription of all its able-bodied white men, without leaving the negroes free to show symptoms of servile insurrection? Does not this state of things arise from the very fact of war itself? You are in a country where now the negroes outnumber the whites ten to one, and these whites are in rebellion against the government, or in terror seeking its protection. Upon reflection, can you doubt that the same state of things would have arisen without the presence of a colored regiment? Did you not see symptoms of the same things upon the plantations here upon our arrival, although under much less favorable circumstances for revolt?

"You say that the prospect of such an insurrection is heart-rending, and that you cannot be responsible for it. The responsibility rests upon those who have begun and carried out this war, and who have stopped at no barbarity, at no act of outrage, upon the citizens and soldiers of the United States. You have forwarded me the records of a pretended court-martial, showing that seven men of one of your regiments, who enlisted here in the Eighth Vermont, who had surrendered themselves prisoners of war, were in cold blood murdered, and, as certain information shows me, required to dig their own graves! You are asked if this is not an occurrence as heart-rending as a prospective servile insurrection.

"The question is now to be met, whether, in a hostile, rebellious part of the state, where this very murder has been committed by the militia, you are to stop in the operations of the field to put down servile insurrection, because the men and women are terror-stricken? Whenever was it heard before that a victorious general, in an unsurrendered province, stopped in his course for the purpose of preventing the rebellious inhabitants of that province from destroying each other, or refuse to take command of a conquered province lest he should be made responsible for their self-destruction?

"As a military question, perhaps, the more terror-stricken the inhabitants are that are left in your rear, the more safe will be your lines of communication. You say there have appeared before your eyes the very facts, in terror-stricken women and children and men, which you had before contemplated in theory. Grant it. But is not the remedy to be found in the surrender of the neighbors, fathers, brothers, and sons of the terror-stricken women and children, who are now in arms against the government

POINT ISABEL, TEXAS.
Phalanx soldiers on duty, throwing up earthworks.

within twenty miles of you? And when that is done, and you have no longer to fear from these organized forces, and they have returned peaceably to their homes, you will be able to use the full power of your troops to insure your safety from the so much feared (by them, not by you) servile insurrection.

"If you desire, you can send a flag of truce to the commander of these forces, embracing these views, and placing upon him the responsibility which belongs to him. Even that course will not remove it from you, for upon you it has never rested. Say to them, that if all armed opposition to the authority of the United States shall cease in Louisiana, on the west bank of the river, you are authorized by the commanding general to say, that the same protection against negro or other violence will be afforded that part of Louisiana that has been in the part already in the possession of the United States. If that is refused, whatever may ensue is upon them, and not upon you or upon the United States. You will have done all that is required of a brave, humane man, to avert from these deluded people the horrible consequences of their insane war upon the government. * * *

"Consider this case. General Bragg is at liberty to ravage the houses of our brethren of Kentucky because the Union army of Louisiana are protecting his wife and his home against his negroes. Without that protection he would have to come back to take care of his wife, his home and his negroes. It is understood that Mrs. Bragg is one of the terrified women of whom you speak in your report.

"This subject is not for the first time under the consideration of the commanding general. When in command of the Department of Annapolis, in May, 1861, he was asked to protect a community against the consequences of a servile insurrection. He replied, that when that community laid down its arms, and called upon him for protection, he would give it, because from that moment between them and him war would cease. The same principle initiated there will govern his and your actions now; and you will afford such protection as soon as the community through its organized rulers shall ask it.

"* * * * In the mean time, these colored regiments of free men, raised by the authority of the president, and approved by him as the commander-in-chief of the army, must be commanded by the officers of the army of the United States, like any other regiment."

General Butler continued General Weitzel in command but placed the negroes under another officer. However, General Weitzel; like thousands of others, changed his mind in regard to the colored troops. "If he was not convinced by General Butler's reasoning," says Parton, "he must have been convinced by what he saw of the conduct of those very colored regiments at Port Hudson, where he himself gave such a glorious example of prudence and gallantry."

Notwithstanding these troops did good service, it did not soften or remove very much of the prejudice at the North against the negro soldiers, nor in the ranks of the army. Many incidents might be cited to show the feeling of bitterness against them.* However, General Butler's example was followed very soon by every officer in command, and by the time the President's Emancipation Proclamation was issued there were not less than 10,000 negroes armed and equipped along the Mississippi river. Of course the Government knew nothing of this.(?) Not

* In November, while the 2nd Regiment was guarding the Opelousas railway, about twenty miles from Algiers, La., their pickets were fired upon, and quite a skirmish and firing was kept up during the night. Next morning the cane field along the railroad was searched but no trace of the firing party was found. A company of the 8th Vermont (white) Regiment was encamped below that of the 2nd Regiment, but they broke camp that night and left. The supposition was that it was this company who fired upon and drove in the pickets of the Phalanx regiment.

only armed, but some of them had been in skirmishes with the enemy. That as a Phalanx they were invaluable in crushing the rebellion, let their acts of heroism tell. In the light of history and of their own deeds, it can be said that in courage, patriotism and dash, they were second to no troops, either in ancient or modern armies. They were enlisted after rigid scrutiny, and the examination of every man by competent surgeons. Their acquaintance with the country in which they marched, encamped and fought, made them in many instances superior to the white troops. Then to strengthen their valor and tenacity, each soldier of the Phalanx knew when he heard the long roll beat to arms, and the bugle sound the charge, that they were not to go forth to meet those who regarded them as opponents in arms, but who met them as a man in his last desperate effort for life would meet demons; they knew, also, that there was no reserve—no reinforcements behind to support them when they went to battle; their alternative was *life or death.* It was the consciousness of this fact that made the black phalanx a wall of adamant to the enemy.

The not unnatural willingness of the white soldiers to allow the negro troops to stop the bullets that they would otherwise have to receive was shown in General Bank's Red River Campaign. At Pleasant Grove, Dickey's black brigade prevented a slaughter of the Union troops. The black Phalanx were represented there by a brigade attached to the first division of the 19th Corps. When the confederates routed the army under Banks at Sabine Cross Roads, below Mansfield, they drove it for several hours toward Pleasant Grove, despite the ardor of the combined forces of Banks and Franklin. It became apparent that unless the confederates could be checked at this point, all was lost. General Emory prepared for the emergency on the western edge of a wood, with an open field sloping toward Mansfield. Here General Dwight formed a brigade of the black Phalanx across the road. Hardly was the line formed when out came the gallant foe driving 10,000 men before them.. Flushed with two days' victory, they came

THE RECRUITING OFFICE.

Negroes enlisting in the army, and being examined by surgeons.

charging at double quick time, but the Phalanx held its fire until the enemy was close upon them, and then poured a deadly volley into the ranks of the exultant foe, stopping them short and mowing them down like grass. The confederates recoiled, and now began a fight such as was always fought when the Southerners became aware that black soldiers were in front of them, and for an hour and a half they fought at close quarters, ceasing only at night. Every charge of the enemy was repulsed by the steady gallantry of General Emory's brigade and the black Phalanx, who saved the army from annihilation against a foe numbering three to one. During this memorable campaign the Phalanx more than once met the enemy and accepted the face of their black flag declarations. The confederates knew full well that every man of the Phalanx would fight to the last; they had learned that long before.

As early as June, 1863, General Grant was compelled, in order to show a bold front to Gens. Pemberton and Johnston at the same time, while besieging Vicksburg, to draw nearly all the troops from Milliken's Bend to his support, leaving three infantry regiments of the black Phalanx and a small force of white cavalry to hold this, to him an all-important post. Milliken's Bend was well fortified, and with a proper garrison was in condition to stand a siege. Brigadier-General Dennis was in command, and the troops consisted of the 9th and 11th Louisiana Regiments, the 1st Mississippi and a small detachment of white cavalry, in all about 1,400 men, raw recruits. General Dennis looking upon the place more as a station for organizing and drilling the Phalanx, had made no particular arrangements in anticipation of an attack. He was surprised, therefore, when a force of 3,000 men, under General Henry McCulloch, from the interior of Louisiana, attacked and drove his pickets and two companies of the 23d Iowa Cavalry, (white) up to the breastworks of the Bend. The movement was successful, however, and the confederates, holding the ground, rested for the night, with the expectation of marching into the fortifications in the morning, to begin a massacre, whether a resistance should be shown them or not. The knowledge this little garrison had of what the morrow would bring it, doubtless kept the soldiers awake, preparing to meet the enemy and their own fate. About 3 o'clock, in the early grey of the morning, the confederate line was formed just outside of the intrenchments; suddenly with fixed bayonets the men came rushing over the works, driving everything before them and shouting, "No quarter! No quarter to negroes or their officers!" In a moment the blacks formed and met them, and now the battle began in earnest, hand to hand. The gunboats "Choctaw" and "Lexington" also came up as the confederates were receiving the bayonets and the bullets of the Unionists, and lent material assistance. The attacking force had flanked the works and was pouring in a deadly, enfilading musketry fire. The defenders fell back out of the way of the gunboat's shells, but finally went forward again with what was left of their 150 white allies, and drove the enemy before them and out of the captured works. One division of the enemy's troops hesitated to leave a redoubt, when a company of brave black men dashed forward at double-quick time and engaged them. The enemy stood his ground, and soon the rattling bayonets rang out amid the thunders of the gunboats and the shouts of enraged men; but they were finally driven out, and their ranks thinned by the "Choctaw" as they went over the works. The news reached General Grant and he immediately dispatched General Mower's brigade with orders to re-enforce Dennis and drive the confederates beyond the Tensas river.

A battle can be best described by one who observed it. Captain Miller, who not only was an eye-witness, but participated in the Milliken's Bend fight, writes as follows:

"We were attacked here on June 7, about three o'clock in the morning, by a brigade of Texas troops, about two thousand five hundred in number. We had about six hundred men to withstand them, five hundred of them negroes. I commanded Company I, Ninth Louisiana. We went into the fight with thirty-three men. I had sixteen killed, eleven badly wounded, and four slightly. I was wounded slightly on the head, near the right eye, with a bayonet, and had a bayonet run through my right hand, near the forefinger; that will account for this miserable style of penmanship.

"Our regiments had about three hundred men in the fight. We had one colonel wounded, four captains wounded, two first and two second lieutenants killed, five lieutenants wounded, and three white orderlies killed, and one wounded in the hand, and two fingers taken off. The list of killed and wounded officers comprised nearly all the officers present with the regiment, a majority of the rest being absent recruiting.

"We had about fifty men killed in the regiment and eighty wounded; so you can judge of what part of the fight my company sustained. I never felt more grieved and

BATTLE OF
MILLIKEN'S BEND

sick at heart, than when I saw how my brave soldiers had been slaughtered,—one with six wounds, all the rest with two or three, none less than two wounds. Two of my colored sergeants were killed; both brave, noble men, always prompt, vigilant, and ready for the fray. I never more wish to hear the expression, 'The niggers wont fight.' Come with me, a hundred yards from where I sit, and I can show you the wounds that cover the bodies of sixteen as brave, loyal, and patriotic soldiers as ever drew bead on a rebel.

"The enemy charged us so close that we fought with our bayonets, hand to hand. I have six broken bayonets to show how bravely my men fought. The Twenty-third Iowa joined my company on the right; and I declare truthfully that they had all fled before our regiment fell back, as we were all compelled to do.

"Under command of Col. Page, I led the Ninth and Eleventh Louisiana when the rifle-pits were retaken and held by our troops, our two regiments doing the work.

"I narrowly escaped death once. A rebel took deliberate aim at me with both barrels of his gun; and the bullets passed so close to me that the powder that remained on them burnt my cheek. Three of my men, who saw him aim and fire, thought that he wounded me each fire; One of them was killed by my side, and he fell on me, covering my clothes with his blood; and, before the rebel could fire again, I blew his brains out with my gun.

"It was a horrible fight, the worst I was ever engaged in,—not even excepting Shiloh. The enemy cried, 'No quarter!' but some of them were very glad to take it when made prisoners.

"Col. Allen, of the Sixteenth Texas, was killed in front of our regiment, and Brig.-Gen. Walker was wounded. We killed about one hundred and eighty of the enemy. The gunboat "Choctaw" did good service shelling them. I stood on the breastworks after we took them, and gave the elevations and direction for the gunboat by pointing my sword; and they sent a shell right into their midst, which sent them in all directions. Three shells fell there, and sixty-two rebels lay there when the fight was over.

* * * * * *

"This battle satisfied the slave-masters of the South that their charm was gone; and that the negro as a slave, was lost forever. Yet there was one fact connected with the battle of Milliken's Bend which will descend to posterity, as testimony against the humanity of slave-holders; and that is, that no negro was ever found alive that was taken a prisoner by the rebels in this fight."

The Department of the Gulf contained a far greater proportion of the Phalanx than did any other Department, and there were very few, if any, important engagements fought in this Department in which the Phalanx did not take part.

It is unpleasant here, in view of the valuable services rendered by the Phalanx, to be obliged to record that the black soldiers were subjected to many indignities, and suffered much at the hands of their white fellow comrades in arms. Repeated assaults and outrages were committed upon black men wearing the United States' uniform, not only by volunteers but conscripts from the various States, and frequently by confederate prisoners who had been paroled by the United States; these outrages were allowed to take place, without interference by the commanding officers, who apparently did not observe what was going on.

At Ship Island, Miss., there were three companies of the 13th Maine, General Neal Dow's old regiment, and seven companies of the 2nd Regiment Phalanx, commanded by Colonel Daniels, which constituted the garrison at that point. Ship Island was the key to New Orleans. On the opposite shore was a railroad leading to Mobile by which re-enforcements were going forward to Charleston. Colonel Daniels conceived the idea of destroying the road to prevent the transportation of the confederate troops. Accordingly, with about two hundred men he landed at Pascagoula, on the morning of the 9th of April. Pickets were immediately posted on the outskirts of the town, while the main body marched up to the hotel. Before long some confederate cavalry, having been apprised of the movement, advanced, drove in the pickets, and commenced an attack on the force occupying the town. The cavalry made a bold dash upon the left of the negroes, which was the work of but a moment; the brave blacks met their charge manfully, and emptied the saddles of the front rank, which caused the rear ones first to halt and then retire. The blacks were outnumbered, however, five to one, and finally were forced to abandon the town; they went, taking with them the stars and stripes which they had hoisted upon the hotel when entering it. They fell back towards the river to give the gunboat "Jackson" a chance to shell their pursuers, but the movement resulted in an apparently revengeful act on the part of the crew of that vessel, they having previously had some of their number killed in the course of a difficulty with a black sentry at Ship Island.

The commanding officer of the land force, doubtless from prudential reasons, omitted to state in his report that the men fought their way through the town while being fired upon from house-tops and windows by boys and women. That the gunboat opened fire directly on them when they were engaged in a hand to hand conflict, which so completely cut off a number of the men from the main body of the troops that their capture appeared certain. Major Dumas, however, seeing the condition of things, put spurs to his horse and went to their succor, reaching them just as a company of the enemy's cavalry made a charge. The Major, placing himself at the head of the hard-pressed men, not only repulsed the cavalry and rescued the squad, but captured the enemy's stand-

UNLOADING GOVT. STORES

ard-bearer. The retreating force reached their transport with the loss of only one man; they brought with them some prisoners and captured flags. Colonel Daniels, in his report, speaks as follows of the heroism of the soldiers:

* * * * * *

"The expedition was a perfect success, accomplishing all that was intended; resulting in the repulse of the enemy in every engagement with great loss; whilst our casualty was only two killed and eight wounded. Great credit is due to the troops engaged, for their unflinching bravery and steadiness under this their first fire, exchanging volley after volley with the coolness of veterans; and for their determined tenacity in maintaining their position, and taking advantage of every success that their courage and valor gave them; and also to their officers, who were cool and determined throughout the action, fighting their commands against five times their numbers, and confident throughout of success,—all demonstrating to its fullest extent that the oppression which they have heretofore undergone from the hands of their foes, and the obloquy that had been showered upon them by those who should have been friends, had not extinguished their manhood, or suppressed their bravery, and that they had still a hand to wield the sword, and a heart to vitalize its blow.

"I would particularly call the attention of the Department to Major F. E. Dumas, Capt. Villeverd, and Lieuts. Jones and Martin, who were constantly in the thickest of the fight, and by their unflinching bravery, and admirable handling of their commands, contributed to the success of the attack, and reflected great honor upon the flag under and for which they so nobly struggled. Repeated instances of individual bravery among the troops might be mentioned; but it would be invidious where all fought so manfully and so well.

"I have the honor to be, most respectfully your obedient servant,

"N. U. DANIELS,

"*Col. Second Regiment La. N. G. Vols., Commanding Post.*

The 2nd Regiment, with the exception of the Colonel, Lieut.-Colonel and Adjutant, was officered by negroes, many of whom had worn the galling chains of slavery, while others were men of affluence and culture from New Orleans and vicinity.

The 2nd Regiment had its full share of prejudice to contend with, and perhaps suffered more from that cause than any other regiment of the Phalanx. Once while loading transports at Algiers, preparatory to embarking for Ship Island, they came in contact with a section of the famous Nim's battery, rated as one of the finest in the service. The arms of the 2nd Regiment were stacked and the men were busy in loading the vessel, save a few who were doing guard duty over the ammunition stored in a shed on the wharf. One of the battery-men attempted to enter the shed with a lighted pipe in his mouth, but was prevented by the guard. It was more than the Celt could stand to be ordered by a negro; watching for a chance when the guard about-faced, he with several others sprang upon him. The guard gave the Phalanx signal, and instantly hundreds of black men secured their arms and rushed to the relief of their comrade. The battery-men jumped to their guns, formed into line and drew their sabres. Lieut.-Colonel Hall, who was in command of the 2nd Regiment, stepped forward and demanded to know of the commander of the battery if his men wanted to take the men the guard had arrested. "Yes," was the officer's reply, "I want you to give them up." "Not until they are dealt with," said Colonel Hall. And then a shout and yell, such as the Phalanx only were able to give, rent the air, and the abortive menace was over. The gunners returned their sabres and resumed their work. Col. Hall, who always had perfect control of his men, ordered the guns stacked, put on a double guard, and the men of the 2nd Regiment resumed their labor of loading the transport. Of course this was early in the struggle, and before a general enlistment of the blacks.

The first, second and third regiments of the Phalanx were the nucleus of the one hundred and eighty that eventually did so much for the suppression of the rebellion and the abolition of slavery. The 1st and 3rd Regiments went up the Mississippi; the 2nd garrisoned Ship Island and Fort Pike, on Lake Pontchartrain, after protecting for several months the Opelousa railroad, so much coveted by the confederates.

A few weeks after the fight of the 2nd Regiment at Pascagoula, General Banks laid siege to Port Hudson, and gathered there all the available forces in his department. Among these were the 1st and 3rd Infantry Regiments of the Phalanx. On the 23rd of May the federal forces, having completely invested the enemy's works and made due preparation, were ordered to make a general assault along the whole line. The attack was intended to be simultaneous, but in this it failed. The Union batteries opened early in the morning, and after a vigorous bombardment Generals Weitzel, Grover and Paine, on the right, assaulted with vigor at 10 A. M., while Gen. Augur in the center, and General W. T. Sherman on the left, did not attack till 2 P. M.

Never was fighting more heroic than that of the federal army and especially that of the Phalanx regiments

If valor could have triumphed over such odds, the assaulting forces would have carried the works, but only abject cowardice or pitiable imbecility could have lost such a position under existing circumstances. The negro regiments on the north side of the works vied with the bravest, making three desperate charges on the confederate batteries, losing heavily, but maintaining their position in the advance all the while.

The column in moving to the attack went through the woods in their immediate front, and then upon a plane, on the farther side of which, half a mile distant, were the enemy's batteries. The field was covered with recently felled trees, through the interlaced branches of which the column moved, and for two or more hours struggled through the obstacles, stepping over their comrades who fell among the entangled brushwood pierced by bullets or torn by flying missiles, and braved the hurricane of shot and shell.

What did it avail to hurl a few thousand troops against those impregnable works? The men were not iron, and were they, it would have been impossible for them to have kept erect, where trees three feet in diameter were crashed down upon them by the enemy's shot; they would have been but as so many ten-pins set up before skillful players to be knocked down.

The troops entered an enfilading fire from a masked battery which opened upon them as they neared the fort, causing the column first to halt, then to waver and stagger; but it recovered and again pressed forward, closing up the ranks as fast as the enemy's shells thinned them. On the left the confederates had planted a six-gun battery upon an eminence, which enabled them to sweep the field over which the advancing column moved. In front was the large fort, while the right of the line was raked by a redoubt of six pieces of artillery. One after another of the works had been charged, but in vain. The Michigan, New York and Massachusetts troops—braver than whom none ever fought a battle—had been hurled back from the place, leaving the field strewn with their dead and wounded. The works must be taken. General Nelson was ordered by General Dwight to take the battery on the left. The 1st and 3rd Regiments went forward at double quick time, and they were soon within the line of the enemy's fire. Louder than the thunder of Heaven was the artillery rending the air shaking the earth itself; cannons, mortars and musketry alike opened a fiery storm upon the advancing regiments; an iron shower of grape and round shot, shells and rockets, with a perfect tempest of rifle bullets fell upon them. On they went and down, scores falling on right and left. "The flag, the flag!" shouted the black soldiers, as the standard-bearer's body was scattered by a shell. Two file-closers struggled for its possession; a ball decided the struggle. They fell faster and faster; shrieks, prayers and curses came up from the fallen and ascended to Heaven. The ranks closed up while the column turned obliquely toward the point of fire, seeming to forget they were but men. Then the cross-fire of grape shot swept through their ranks, causing the glittering bayonets to go down rapidly. "Steady men, steady," cried bold Cailloux; his sword uplifted, his face the color of the sulphureous smoke that enveloped him and his followers, as they felt the deadly hail which came apparently from all sides. Captain Cailloux* was killed with the col-

* Captain Andre Callioux fell, gallently leading his men (Co. E) in the attack. With many others of the charging column, his body lay between the lines of the Confederates and Federals, but nearer the works of the former, whose sharp-shooters guarded it night and day, and thus prevented his late comrades from removing it. Several attempts were made to obtain the body, but each attempt was met with a terrific storm of lead. It was not until after the surrender that his remains were recovered, and then taken to his native city, New Orleans. The writer of this volume, himself wounded, was in the city at the time, and witnessed the funeral pageant of the dead hero, the like of which was never before seen in that, nor, perhaps, in any other American city, in honor of a dead negro. The negro captains of the 2nd Regiment acted as pall-bearers, while a long procession of civic societies followed in the rear of detatchments of the Phalanx. A correspondent who witnessed the scene thus describes it:

"* * * * The arrival of the body developed to the white population here that the colored people had powerful organizations in the form of civic societies; as the Friends of the Order, of which Capt. Callioux was a prominent member, received the body, and had the coffin containing it, draped with the American flag, exposed in state in the commodious hall. Around the coffin, flowers were strewn in the greatest profusion, and candles were kept continually burning. All the rites of the Catholic Church were strictly complied with. The guard paced silently to and fro, and altogether it presented as solemn a scene as was ever witnessed.

"In due time, the band of the Forty-second Massachusetts Regiment made its appearance, and discoursed the customary solemn airs. The officiating priest, Father Le Maistre, of the Church of St. Rose of Lima, who has paid not the least attention to the excommunication and denunciations issued against him by the archbishop of this

PORT HUDSON.

Brilliant charge of the Phalanx upon the Confederate works.

ors in his hands; the column seemed to melt away like snow in sunshine, before the enemy's murderous fire; the pride, the flower of the Phalanx, had fallen. Then, with a daring that veterans only can exhibit, the blacks rushed forward and up to the brink and base of the fortified elevation, with a shout that rose above it. The defenders emptied their rifles, cannon and mortars upon the very heads of the brave assaulters, making of them a human hecatomb. Those who escaped found their way back to shelter as best they could.

The battery was not captured; the battle was lost to all except the black soldiers; they, with their terrible loss,

this diocese, then performed the Catholic service for the dead. After the regular services, he ascended to the president's chair, and delivered a glowing and eloquent eulogy on the virtues of the deceased. He called upon all present to offer themselves, as Callioux had done, martyrs to the cause of justice, freedom, and good government. It was a death the proudest might envy.

"Immense crowds of colored people had by this time gathered around the building, and the streets leading thereto were rendered almost impassable. Two companies of the Sixth Louisiana (colored) Regiment, from their camp on the Company Canal, were there to act as an escort; and Esplanade Street, for more than a mile, was lined with colored societies, both male and female, in open order, waiting for the hearse to pass through.

"After a short pause, a sudden silence fell upon the crowd, the band commenced playing a dirge; and the body was brought from the hall on the shoulders of eight soldiers, escorted by six members of the society, and six colored captains, who acted as pall-bearers. The corpse was conveyed to the hearse through a crowd composed of both white and black people, and in silence profound as death itself. Not a sound was heard save the mournful music of the band, and not a head in all that vast multitude but was uncovered.

"The procession then moved off in the following order: The hearse containing the body, with Capts. J. W. Ringgold, W. B. Barrett, S. J. Wilkinson, Eugene Mailleur, J. A Glea, and A. St. Leger, (all of whom, we believe, belong to the Second Louisiana Native Guards), and six members of The Friends of the Order, as pall-bearers; about a hundred convalescent sick and wounded colored soldiers; the two companies of the Sixth Regiment; a large number of colored officers of all native guard regiments; the carriages containing Capt. Callioux's family, and a number of army officers; followed by a large number of private individuals, and thirty-seven civic and religious societies.

"After moving through the principal down-town streets, the body was taken to the Beinville-street cemetery, and there interred with military honors due his rank." * *

The following lines were penned at the time:

ANDRE CAILLOUX.

He lay just where he fell,
Soddening in a fervid summer's sun,
Guarded by an enemy's hissing shell,
Rotting beneath the sound of rebels' gun
Forty consecutive days,
In sight of his own tent,
And the remnant of his regiment.

He lay just where he fell,
Nearest the rebel's redoubt and trench,
Under the very fire of hell,
A volunteer in a country's defence,
Forty consecutive days,
And not a murmur of discontent,
Went from the loyal black regiment.

A flag of truce couldn't save,
No, nor humanity could not give
This sable warrior a hallowed grave,
Nor army of the Gulf retrieve.
Forty consecutive days,
His lifeless body pierced and rent,
Leading in assault the black regiment.

But there came days at length,
When Hudson felt their blast,
Though less a thousand in strength,
For "our leader" vowed the last;
Forty consecutive days
They stormed, they charged, God sent
Victory to the loyal black regiment.

He lay just where he fell,
And now the ground was their's,
Around his mellowed corpse, heavens tell,
How his comrades for freedom swears.
Forty consecutive nights
The advance pass-word went,
Captain Cailloux of the black regiment.

had won and conquered a much greater and stronger battery than that upon the bluff. Nature seems to have selected the place and appointed the time for the negro to prove his manhood and to disarm the prejudice that at one time prompted the white troops to insult and assault the negro soldiers in New Orleans. It was all forgotten and they mingled together that day on terms of perfect equality. The whites were only too glad to take a drink from a negro soldier's canteen, for in that trying hour they found a brave and determined ally, ready to sacrifice all for liberty and country. If greater heroism could be shown than that of the regiments of the Phalanx already named, surely the 1st Regiment of Engineers displayed it during the siege at Port Hudson. This regiment, provided with picks and spades for the purpose of "mining" the enemy's works, often went forward to their labor without any armed support except the cover of heavy guns, or as other troops happened to advance, to throw up breastworks for their own protection. It takes men of more than ordinary courage to engage in such work, without even a revolver or a bayonet to defend themselves against the sallies of an enemy's troops. Nevertheless this Engineer Regiment of the black Phalanx performed the duty under such trying and perilous circumstances. Many times they went forward at a double-quick to do duty in the most dangerous place during an engagement, perhaps to build a redoubt or breastworks behind a brigade, or to blow up a bastion of the enemy's. "They but reminded the lookers on," said a correspondent of a Western newspaper, "of just so many cattle going to a slaughter-house."

A writer, speaking of the other regiments of the Phalanx, says:

> "They were also on trial that day, and justified the most sanguine expectations by their good conduct. Not that they fought better than our white veterans; they did not and could not."

But there had been so much incredulity avowed regarding the courage of the negroes; so much wit lavished on the idea of negroes fighting to any purpose, that General Banks was justified in according a special commendation to the 1st, 2nd and 3rd Regiments, and to the 1st Engineer Regiment, of the Phalanx, saying, "No troops could be more determined or daring." The 1st lost its Cailloux, the 2nd its Paine, but the Phalanx won honor for the race it represented. No higher encomium could be paid a regiment than that awarded the gallant 2nd by the poet Boker:

"THE BLACK REGIMENT, OR THE SECOND LOUISIANA AT THE STORMING OF PORT HUDSON.

Dark as the clouds of even,
Banked in the western heaven,
Waiting the breath that lifts
All the dread mass, and drifts
Tempest and falling brand,
Over a ruined land—
So still and orderly
Arm to arm, and knee to knee
Waiting the great event,
Stands the Black Regiment.

Down the long dusky line
Teeth gleam and eyeballs shine;
And the bright bayonet,
Bristling and firmly set,
Flashed with a purpose grand,
Long ere the sharp command
Of the fierce rolling drum
Told them their time had come—
Told them what work was sent
For the Black Regiment.

'Now,' the flag sergeant cried,
'Though death and hell betide,
Let the whole nation see
If we are fit to be,
Free in this land; or bound
Down like the whining hound—
Bound with red stripes of pain
In our old chains again!'
Oh! what a shout there went
From the Black Regiment.

'Charge!' trump and drum awoke;
Onward the bondmen broke
Bayonet and sabre stroke
Vainly opposed their rush
Through the wild battle's crush,
With but one thought aflush,
Driving their lords like chaff,
In the gun's mouth they laugh;
Or at the slippery brands
Leaping with open hands,
Down they tear, man and horse,
Down in their awful course;
Trampling with bloody heel
Over the crashing steel,
All their eyes forward bent,
Rushed the Black Regiment.

'Freedom!' their battle cry,
'Freedom!' or leave to die!'
Ah! and they meant the word,
Not as with us its heard,
Nor a mere party shout,
They gave their spirits out;
Trusted the end to God,
And on the gory sod
Rolled in triumphant blood,
Glad to strike one free blow,
Whether for weal or woe;
Glad to breathe one free breath,
Though on the lips of death
Praying—alas! in vain!
That they might fall again,
So they could once more see
That burst of liberty!
This was what 'Freedom' lent
To the Black Regiment.

Hundreds on hundreds fell;
But they are resting well;
Scourges and shackles strong
Never shall do them wrong.
Oh! to the living few,
Soldiers, be just and true!
Hail them as comrades tried;
Fight with them side by side;
Never in field or tent
Scorn the Black Regiment."

[See Appendix for further matter relating to the Department of the Gulf.]

CHAPTER VI.

THE ARMY OF THE FRONTIER.

At the Far West the fires of liberty and union burned no less brightly upon the altar of the negro's devotion than at the North, East and South. The blacks of Iowa responded with alacrity to the call of the governor to strengthen the Army of the Ohio. Though the negro population was sparce—numbering in 1860, only 1069—and thinly scattered over the territory, and were enjoying all the rights and privileges of American citizenship, nevertheless they gave up the luxuries of happy homes, threw down their implements of peaceful industry, broke from the loving embrace of wives and children, and with the generous patriotism which has always characterized the conduct of the race, they rushed to the aid of their yet oppressed countrymen, and the defense of the Union.

The Gibralters of the Mississippi, Vicksburg and Port Hudson, had fallen by the might of the Union armies; the Mississippi was open to the Gulf. The shattered ranks of the victorious troops, and the depleted ranks of the Phalanx, rent and torn by the enemy during the long siege of Port Hudson, lent an inspiring zeal to the negroes of the country, which manifested itself in the rapidity of the enlistment of volunteers to fill up the gaps.

In August, 1863, the authorities of the State of Iowa began the enlistment of negroes as a part of her quota. Keokuk was selected as the place of rendezvous. On the 11th of the following October nine full companies under the command of Colonel John G. Hudson, took the oath of allegiance to the United States, and became a part of

A PHALANX REGIMENT RECEIVING A GIFT OF COLORS.

the active military force of the National Government. The regiment was designated the 1st A. D. (African Descent) Regiment Iowa Volunteers, and was mustered for three years, or during the war. Leaving Keokuk Barracks, the regiment proceeded to St. Louis, Mo., and was quartered in Benton Barracks, as a part of the forces under command of Major-General J. M. Schofield. Here company G. joined the regiment, making ten full companies. A memorable and patriotic incident occurred here: Mrs. I. N. Triplet, in behalf of the ladies of the State of Iowa, and of the city of Muscatine, presented the regiment with a beautiful silk national flag, which was carried through the storms of battle, and returned at the close of the war to the State.

On the first day of January, 1864, the regiment was ordered to report to General Beaufort at Helena, Ark., becoming a part of the garrison of that place until the following March.

One Sergeant Phillips, with some others, agitated the propriety of refusing to accept the seven dollars per month offered them by the Government, and of refusing to do duty on account of it. Sergeant Barton, however, held it was better to serve without pay than to refuse duty, as the enforcement of the President's Emancipation Proclamation was essential to the freedom of the negro race. To this latter the regiment agreed, and passed concurrent resolutions, which quelled a discussion which otherwise might have led to mutiny.

While the regiment was at Helena it took part in several skirmishes and captured a number of prisoners. In July, Colonel W. S. Brooks, in command of the 56th, 60th, and a detachment of the 3rd Artillery Phalanx Regiment, with two field guns, sallied out of Helena and proceeded down the Mississppi River, to the mouth of White River, on a transport. Here the troops disembarked. The next morning, after marching all night, Brooks halted his command for breakfast; arms were stacked and the men became scattered over the fields. Suddenly, General Dobbins, at the head of a superior confederate force, made an attack upon them; the confederates at first formed no regular line of battle, but rushed pell-mell on the scattered federals, intending, doubtless, to annihilate them at once. The Union men soon recovered their arms, but before they got into line, their commander, Colonel Brooks, had been killed, and Captain Ransey of Co. C, 60th Regiment, assumed command. The men of the Phalanx, though they had had but a short time to rest from a long march, rallied with the ardor of veterans, and fought with that desperaation that men display when they realize that the struggle is either victory or death. It was not a question of numbers with them; it was one of existence, and the Phalanx resolved itself into a seeming column of iron to meet the foe as it rushed over the bodies of their dead and wounded with the rage of madmen.

The two field guns, skillfully handled by black artillery-men, did good work, plowing huge furrows through the assailants and throwing them into confusion at every charge. Still the confederates, having finally organized into line of battle, continued to charge after each repulse, pouring a terrific fire upon the United States force at each advance. It seemed as if the Phalanx must surrender; they were outnumbered two to one, and every line officer was dead or wounded. Sergeant Triplet was directing the fire of Company C; the artillery sergeant was in command of the field guns, and worked them well for two long hours. The enemy's sharp-shooters stationed in the trees no longer selected their victims, for one man of the Phalanx was as conspicuous as another.

Yet another assault was made; firm stood the little band of iron men, not flinching, not moving, though the dead lay thick before them. The cannon belched out their grape shot, the musketry rattled, and once more the enemy fled back to the woods with ranks disordered. Thus from six o'clock till noonday did the weary soldiers hold their foes back. The situation became critical with the Phalanx. Their ammunition was nearly exhausted; a few more rounds and their bayonets would be their only protection against a massacre; this fact however, did not cool their determination.

In front and on their flanks the enemy began massing for a final onset. For five hours the Phalanx had fought like tigers, against a ruthless foe, and though no black flag warned them, they were not unmindful of the fate of their comrades at Fort Pillow. General Dobbins was evidently preparing to sweep the field. Several times already had he sent his men to annihilate the blacks, and as many times had they been repulsed. There was no time for the Phalanx soldiers to manœuvre; they were in the closing jaws of death, and though they felt the day was lost, their courage did not forsake them; it was indeed a dreadful moment. The enemy was about to move upon them, when suddenly a shout,—not the yell of a foe, was heard in the enemy's rear, and the next moment a detachment of the 15th Illinois Cavalry, under command of Major Carminchæl, broke through the confederate ranks and rushed to the support of the Phalanx, aligning themselves with the black soldiers, amid the cheers of the latter. Gathering up their dead and wounded, the federal force now began a retreat, stubbornly yielding, inch by inch, each foot of ground, until night threw her mantle of darkness over the scene and the confederates ceased their firing. The Phalanx loss was 50, while that of the enemy was 150. At the beginning couriers were dispatched to Helena for re-enforcements, and Colonel Hudson, with the remainder of the Phalanx troops, reached them at night too late to be of any assistance, as the confederates did not follow the retreating column.

Two days later, Colonel Hudson, with all the available men of the two Phalanx regiments,—60th, 56th and a detachment of the 3rd Phalanx artillery, with two cannons,—went down the Mississippi and up the White river, disembarked and made a three days march across the country, where the enemy was found entrenched. The Phalanx, after a spirited contest, drove them out of their works, burned their store, captured a few Texas rangers and returned to Helena. In March, 1865, the 60th Regiment was ordered to join Brig.-Gen. Reynolds' command at Little Rock, where the regiment was brigaded with the

57th, 59th and 83rd Phalanx regiments. The brigade was ordered to Texas overland, but the surrender of General Lee to Grant obviated this march. The gallant 60th was mustered out at Davenport, Iowa, on the 2nd of November, 1865, "where," says Sergeant Burton, the regimental historian, "they were greeted by the authorities and the loyal thousands of Iowa."

Kansas has undoubtedly the honor of being the first State in the Union to *begin* the organization of negroes as soldiers for the Federal army. The State was admitted into the Union January 29, 1861, after a long reign of hostilities within her borders, carried on by the same character of men and strictly for the same purpose which brought on the war of the Great Rebellion. In fact, it was but a transfer of hostilities from Missouri and Kansas to South Carolina and Virginia. Missouri and the South had been whipped out of Kansas and the territory admitted into the Union as a free State. This single fact was accepted by the South as a precursor of the policy of the incoming Republican administration, and three Southern senators resigned or left the United States Senate before the vote was taken for the admission of Kansas. The act of admitting Kansas as a free State, was the torch that inflamed the South, and led to the firing upon Fort Sumter the following April. The men of Kansas had long been inured to field service, and used to practice with Sharps' rifles. The men of Kansas, more than in any other State of the Union, had a right to rush to the defence of the Federal government, and they themselves felt so.

On the 9th of February, eleven days after the admission of the State into the Union, Governor Robinson took the oath of office, and on the 15th of April President Lincoln called for seventy-five thousand volunteers. The first regiment responded to the call by the close of May; others speedily followed, until Kansas had in the field 20,000 soldiers. Of the regiments and companies which represented this State in the Federal army, several were composed of negroes, with a slight mixture of Indians.

It has been no easy task to learn about these regiments, but, after a long search, the writer has been enabled, through the patriotic efforts of Governor Crawford, of Kansas, who is also ex-Colonel of the 2nd Kansas Regiment, to find Mr. J. B. McAfee, late chaplain of the same regiment and Adjutant-General of Kansas, now engaged in business in Topeka. With the finding of Mr. McAfee came another difficulty; the report of the Adjutant-General, containing an account of the regiments in the war, had been accidentaly burned before leaving the printing office. This difficulty was overcome, however, by the consideration ever shown the negro by Mr. McAfee, who kindly loaned his only volume of the "Military History of Kansas."

The service rendered by the Phalanx soldiery of Kansas stands second to none upon the records of that State. Their patriotism was nothing less than a fitting return for the love of liberty shown by the Free State men in rescuing Kansas from the clutches of the slave power. The discussions at the national capitol pointed Kansas out to the negro as a place where he might enjoy freedom in common with all other American citizens. He regarded it then as he does now,* the *acme* of Republican States. Those negroes who enjoyed and appreciated the sentiment that made her so, were determined as far as they were able, to stand by the men who had thus enlarged the area of freedom.

Without comment upon the bravery of these troops, the report is submitted of their conduct in camp, field, on the march and in battle, as made by those who commanded them on various occasions.

"On the 4th day of August, 1862, Captain James M. Williams, Co. F, 5th Kansas Cavalry, was appointed by Hon. James H. Lane, Recruiting Commissioner for that portion of Kansas lying north of the Kansas River, for the purpose of recruiting and organizing a regiment of infantry for the United States service, to be composed of men of African descent. He immediately commenced the work of recruiting by securing the muster-in of recruiting officers with the rank of 2nd Lieutenant, and by procuring supplies from the Ordance Quartermaster and Commissary

* Not less than 70,000 negroes—5,000 at least of which fought for the Union,—have been driven by persecution into Kansas from the Southern States, and the exodus still continues.

departments, and by establishing in the vicinity of Leavenworth a camp of rendezvous and instruction.

"Capt. H. C. Seaman was about the same time commissioned with like authority for that portion of Kansas lying south of the Kansas river. The work of recruiting went forward with rapidity, the intelligent portion of the colored people entering into the work heartily, and evincing by their actions a willing readiness to link their future and share the perils with their white brethren in the war of the rebellion, which then waged with such violence as to seriously threaten the nationality and life of the Republic.

"Within sixty days five hundred men were recruited and placed in camp, and a request made that a battallion be mustered into the United States service. This request was not complied with, and the reasons assigned were wholly unsatisfactory, yet accompanied with assurances of such a nature as to warrant the belief that but a short time would elapse ere the request would be complied with.

"In the meantime complications with the civil authorities in the Northern District had arisen, which at one time threatened serious results. These complications originated from the following causes, each affecting different classes:

"1st.—An active sympathy with the rebellion.

"2nd.—An intolerant prejudice against the colored race, which would deny them the honorable position in society which every soldier is entitled to, even though he gained that position at the risk of his life in the cause of the nation, which could ill afford to refuse genuine sympathy and support from any quarter.

"3rd.—On the part of a few genuine loyalists who believed that this attempt to enlist colored men would not be approved by the War Department, and that the true interests of the colored man demanded that their time should not be vainly spent in the effort.

"4th.—A large class who believed that the negro did not possess the necessary qualifications to make efficient soldiers, and that consequently the experiment would result in defeat, disaster and disgrace.

"Col. Williams, acting under the orders of his military superiors felt that it was no part of his duty to take council of any or all of these classes. He saw no course for him to pursue but to follow his instructions to the letter. Consequently, when the civil authorities placed themselves in direct opposition to those of the military, by arresting and confining the men of the command on the most frivolous charges, and indicting their commanders for crime, such as unlawfully restraining persons of their liberty, &c., by enforcing proper military discipline, he ignored the right of the civil authorities to interfere with his military actions in a military capacity and under proper authority.

"On the 28th of October, 1862, a command consisting of detachments from Captain Seaman's and Captain William's recruits, were moved and camped near Butler. This command—about two hundred and twenty-five men, under Captain Seaman,—was attacked by a con-

PHALANX SOLDIERS REPELLING AN ATTACK.

federate force of about five hundred, commanded by Colonel Cockrell, but after a severe engagement the enemy was defeated with considerable loss. The negro loss was ten killed and twelve wounded, including Captain A. J. Crew, a gallant young officer, being among the first mentioned. The next morning the command was re-enforced by a few recruits under command of Captain J. M. Williams, when the enemy was pursued a considerable distance but without further fighting. This is supposed to have been the first engagement in the war in which colored troops were actually engaged. The work of recruiting, drilling and disciplining the regiment was continued under the adverse circumstances until the 13th of January, 1863, when a battallion of six companies, formed by the consolidation of Colonel Williams' recruits with those of Captain Seaman, was mustered into the U. S. service by Lieutenant Sabin, of the regular army. Between January 13th and May 2nd, 1863. the other four companies were organized, when the regimental organization was completed, appears by the roster of the regiment.

"Immediately after its organization, the regiment was ordered to Baxter Springs, where it arrived in May, 1863, and the work of drilling the regiment was vigorously prosecuted.

"Parts of two companies of the regiment, and a detachment of cavalry, and one piece of artillery, made a diversion on Shawnee, Mo. attacked and dispersed a small opposing force and captured five prisoners.

"While encamped here, on the 18th of May, a foraging party, consisting of twenty-five men from the Phalanx regiment and twenty men of the 2nd Kansas Battery, Major R. G. Ward commanding, was sent into Jasper County, Mo. This party was surprised and attacked by a force of three hundred confederates commanded by Major Livingston, and defeated, with a loss of sixteen killed and five prisoners, three of which belonged to the 2nd Kansas Battery and two of the black regiment. The men of the 2nd Kansas Battery were afterwards exchanged under a flag of truce for a like number of prisoners captured by the negro regiment. Livingston refused to exchange the black prisoners in his possession, and gave as his excuse that he should hold them subject to the orders of the confederate War Department. Shortly after this Col. Williams received information that one of the prisoners held by Livingston had been murdered by the enemy. He immediately sent a flag of truce to Livingston demanding the body of the person who committed the barbarous act. Receiving an evasive and unsatisfactory reply, Col. Williams determined to convince the Major that was a game at which two could play, and directed that one of the prisoners in his possession be shot, and within thirty minutes the order was executed. He immediately informed Major Livingston of his action, sending the information by the same party that brought the despatch to him. Suffice it to say that this ended the barbarous practice of murdering prisoners of war, so far as Livingston's command was concerned.

Colonel Williams says:

'I visited the scene of this engagement the morning after its occurrence, and for the first time beheld the horrible evidences of the demoniac spirit of these rebel fiends in their treatment of our dead and wounded. Men were found with their brains beaten out with clubs, and the bloody weapons left by their sides and their bodies most horribly mutilated.'

"It was afterwards ascertained that the force who attacked this foraging party consisted partially of citizens of the neighborhood, who, while enjoying the protection of our armies, had collected together to assist the rebel forces in this attack. Colonel Williams directed that the region of country within a radius of five miles from the scene of conflict should be devastated, and is of opinion that this effectually prevented a like occurrence in the same neighborhood.

"Subsequently, while on this expedition, the command captured a prisoner in arms who had upon his person the evidence of having been paroled by the commanding officer at Fort Scott, Kansas, he was shot on the spot.

"The regiment remained in camp at Baxter Springs until the 27th of June, 1863, when it struck tents and marched for Fort Gibson in connection with a large supply train from Fort Scott *en route* to the former place.

Colonel Williams had received information that satisfied him that the train would be attacked in the neighborhood of Cabin Creek, Cherokee Nation. He communicated this information to Lieutenant-Colonel Dodd, of the 2nd Colorado Infantry, who was in command of the escort, and volunteered to move his regiment in such manner as would be serviceable in case the expected attack should be made. The escort proper to the train consisted of six companies of the 2nd Colorado Infantry, a detachment of three companies of cavalry from the 6th and 9th Kansas, and one section of the 2nd Kansas Battery. This force was joined, on the 28th of June, by three hundred men from the Indian Brigade, commanded by Major Foreman, making altogether a force of about eight hundred effective men.

"On arriving at Cabin Creek, July 1st, 1863, the rebels were met in force—under command of Gen. Cooper. Some skirmishing occurred on that day, when it was ascertained that the enemy occupied a strong position on the south bank of the creek, and upon trial it was found that the stream was not fordable for infantry, on account of a recent shower; but it was supposed that the swollen current would have sufficiently subsided by the next morning to allow the infantry to cross. The regiment then took a strong position on the north side of the stream and camped for the night. After a consultation of officers, it was agreed that the train should be parked in the open prairie and guarded by three companies of the 2nd Colorado and a detachment of one hundred men of the 1st Colorado, and that the balance of the troops, Col. Williams commanding, should engage the enemy and drive him from his position.

"Accordingly, the next morning, July 2nd, 1863, the command moved, which consisted of the 1st Kansas Volunteer Colored Infantry, three companies of the 2nd Colorado Infantry, commanded by the gallant Major Smith, of that regiment, the detachments of cavalry and Indian troops before mentioned and four pieces of artillery, making altogether a force of about twelve hundred men. With this force, after an engagement of two hours duration, the enemy was dislodged and driven from his position in great disorder, with a loss of one hundred killed and wounded and eight prisoners. The loss on our side was eight killed and twenty-five wounded, including Major Foreman, who was shot from his horse while attempting to lead his men across the creek under the fire of the enemy, and Captain Ethan Earl, of the 1st Colored, who was wounded at the head of his company. This was the first battle in which the whole regiment had been engaged, and here they evinced a coolness and true soldiery spirit which inspired the officers in command with that confidence which subsequent battle scenes satisfactorily proved was not unfounded.

"The road being now open, the entire command proceeded to Fort Gibson, where it arrived on the evening of the 5th of July, 1863. On the 16th of July the entire force at Fort Gibson, under command of Gen. Blunt, moved upon the enemy, about six thousand strong, commanded by Gen. Cooper, and encamped at Honey Springs, twenty miles south of Fort Gibson. Our forces came upon the enemy on the morning of the 17th of July, aud after a sharp and bloody engagement of two hours' duration, the enemy was totally defeated, with a loss of four hundred killed and wounded, and one hundred prisoners. At the height of the engagement, Gen. Blunt ordered Colonel Williams to move his regiment against that portion of the enemy's line held by the 29th and 30th Texas regiments and a rebel battery, with directions to charge them if he thought he could carry and hold the position. The regiment was moved at a shoulder arms, pieces loaded and bayonets fixed, under a sharp fire, to within forty paces of the rebel lines, without firing a shot. The regiment then halted and poured into their ranks a well directed volley of 'buck and ball' from the entire line, such as to throw them into perfect confusion, from which they could not immediately recover. Col. Williams' intention was, after the delivery of this volley, to charge their line and capture their battery, which the effect of this volley had doubtless rendered it possible for him to accomplish. But he was at that instant rendered insensible from gunshot wounds, and the next officer in rank, Lieutenant-Colonel Bowles, not being aware of his intentions, the project was not fully carried out. Had the movement been made as contemplated, the entire rebel line must have been captured. As it was, most of the enemy escaped, receiving a lesson, however, which taught them not to despise on the battle field the race they had long tyrannized over as having 'no rights which a white man was bound to respect.'

'Colonel Williams says:

'I had long been of the opinion that this race had a right to kill rebels, and this day proved their capacity for the work. Forty prisoners and one battle flag fell into the hands of my regiment on this field.'

"The loss to the regiment in this engagement was five killed and thirty-two wounded. After this, the regiment returned to Fort Gibson and went into camp, where it remained until the month of September, when it again moved with the Division against the confederate force under General Cooper, who fled at our approach.

"After a pursuit of one hundred miles, and across the Canadian river to Perryville, in the Choctaw Nation, all hopes of bringing them to an engagement was abandoned, and the command returned to camp on the site of the confederate Fort Davis, situated on the south side of the Arkansas river, near its junction with Grand river.

"The regiment remained in this camp, doing but little duty, until October, when orders were received to proceed to Fort Smith, where it arrived during the same month. At this point it remained until December 1st, making a march to Waldron and returning via Roseville, Arkansas, and in the same month went into winter quarters at the latter place, situated fifty miles east of Fort Smith, on the Arkansas river. The regiment remained at Roseville until March, 1864, when the command moved to join the forces of Gen. Steele, then about starting on what was known as the Camden Expedition. Joining Gen. Steele's command at the Little Missouri river, distant twenty-two miles northeast of Washington, Arkansas, the entire command moved upon the enemy, posted on the west side of Prairie de Anne, and within fifteen miles of Washington. The enemy fled, and our forces occupied their works without an engagement.

"The pursuit of the enemy in this direction was abandoned. The command arrived at Camden on the 16th of April, 1864, and occupied the place with its strong fortifications without opposition. On the day following, Colonel Williams started with five hundred men of the 1st Colorado, two hundred Cavalry, detailed from the 2nd, 6th and 14th, Kansas regiments, and one section of the 2nd Indian Battery, with a train to load forage and provisions at a point twenty miles west of Camden, on the Washington road. On the 17th he reached the place and succeeded in loading about two-thirds of the train, which consisted of two hundred wagons. At dawn the command moved towards Camden, and loaded the balance of the wagons from plantations by the wayside. At a point fourteen miles west of Camden the advance encountered a small force of the enemy, who, after a slight skirmishing, retreated down the road in such a manner as to lead Col. Williams to suspect that this movement was a feint intended to cover other movements or to draw the command into an ambuscade.

"Just previous to this he had been re-enforced by a detachment of three hundred men of the 18th Iowa Infantry, and one hundred additional cavalry, commanded by Capt. Duncan, of the 18th Iowa.

"In order to prevent any surprise, all detached foraging parties were called in, and the original command placed in the advance, leaving the rear in charge of Captain Duncan's command, with orders to keep flankers well out and to guard cautiously against a surprise. Colonel Williams at the front, with skirmishers and flankers well out, advanced cautiously to a point about one and a half miles distant, sometimes called Cross Roads, but more generally known as Poison Springs, where he came upon a skirmish line of the enemy, which tended to confirm his previous suspicion of the character and purpose of the enemy. He therefore closed up the train as well as possible in this thickly timbered region, and made the necessary preparations for fighting. He directed the cavalry, under Lieutenant Henderson, of the 6th, and Mitchell, of the 2nd, to charge and penetrate the the rebel line of skirmishers, in order to develop their strength and intentions. The movement succeeded most admirably in its purposes, and the development was such that it convinced Colonel Williams that he had before him a struggle of no ordinary magnitude.

"The cavalry, after penetrating the skirmish line, came upon a strong force of the enemy, who repulsed and forced them back to their original line, not, however, without hard fighting and severe loss on our part in killed and wounded, including in the latter the gallant Lieutenant Henderson, who afterwards fell into the hands of the enemy.

"The enemy now opened on our lines with ten pieces of artillery—six in front and four on the right flank. From a prisoner Colonel Williams learned that the force of the enemy was from eight to ten thousand, commanded by Generals Price and Maxey. These developments and this information convinced him that he could not hope to defeat the enemy; but as there was no way to escape with the train except through their lines, and as the train and its contents were indispensable to the very existence of our forces at Camden, who were then out of provisions, he deemed it to be his duty to defend the train to the last extremity, hoping that our forces at Camden, on learning of the engagement, would attack the enemy in his rear, thus relieving his command and saving the train.

With this determination, he fought the enemy's entire force from 10 A. M. until 2 P. M., repulsing three successive assaults and inflicting upon the enemy severe loss.

"In his report Colonel Williams says:

'The conflict during these four hours was the most terrific and deadly in its character of any that has ever fallen under my observation.'

"At 2 P. M. nearly one-half of our force engaged had been placed *hors de combat*, and the remainder were out of ammunition. No supplies arriving, the Colonel was reluctantly compelled to abandon the train to the enemy and save as much of the command as possible by taking to the swamps and canebrakes and making for Camden by a circuitous route, thereby preventing pursuit by cavalry. In this manner most of the command that was not disabled in the field reached Camden during the night of the 18th. For a more specific and statistical report of this action, in which the loss to the 1st Colored alone was 187 men and officers, the official report of Colonel J. M. Williams is herewith submitted:

'CAMDEN, ARKANSAS, April 24, 1867.

'CAPTAIN:—I have the honor to submit the following report of a foraging expedition under my command:

'In obedience to verbal orders received from Brigadier-General Thayer, I left Camden, Arkansas on the 11th instant with 695 men and two guns, with a forage train of 198 wagons.

'I proceeded westerly on the Washington road a distance of eighteen miles, where I halted the train and dispatched part of it in different directions to load; one hundred wagons with a large part of the command, under Major Ward, being sent six miles beyond the camp. These wagons returned to camp at midnight, nearly all loaded with corn.

'At sunrise on the 18th, the command started on the return, loading the balance of the train as it proceeded, there being but a few wagon loads of corn to be found at any one place. I was obliged to detail portions of the command in different directions to load the wagons, until nearly all of my available force was so employed.

'At a point known as Cross Roads, four miles west of my camping ground, I was met by a re-enforcement of three hundred and seventy-five men of the 18th Iowa Infantry, commanded by Capt. Duncan, twenty-five men of the 6th Kansas, Lieut. Phillips commanding, forty-five men of the 2nd Kansas Cavalry, Lieut. Ross commanding, twenty men of the 14th Kansas Cavalry, Lieut. Smith commanding, and two mountain howitzers from the 6th Kansas Cavalry, Lieut. Walker commanding,—in all, 465 men and two mountain howitzers. These, added to my former command, made my entire force consist of eight hundred and seventy-five, two hundred and eighty-five cavalry, and four guns. But the excessive fatigue of the preceeding day, coming as it did at the close of a toilsome march of twenty-four hours without halting, had so affected the infantry that fully one hundred of the 1st Kansas Colored were rendered unfit for duty. Many of the cavalry had, in violation of orders, straggled from their command, so that at this time my effective force did not exceed one thousand men.

'At a point one mile east of this, my advance came upon a picket of the enemy, which was driven back one mile, when a line of the enemy's skirmishers presented itself. Here I halted the train, formed a line of the small force I then had in advance, and ordered that portion of the 1st Kansas Colored which had previously been guarding the rear of the train to the front, and gave orders for the train to be packed as closely as the nature of the ground would permit. I also opened a fire upon the enemy's line from the section of the 2nd Indiana Battery, for the double purpose of ascertaining if possible if the enemy had artillery in position in front, and also to draw in some foraging parties which had previously been dispatched upon either flank of the train. No response was elicited save a brisk fire from the enemy's skirmishers.

'Meanwhile, the remainder of the first Kansas Colored had come to the front, as also three detachments, which formed part of the original escort, which I formed in line facing to the front, with a detachment of the 14th Kansas Cavalry, on my right, and detachments of the 2nd and 6th Kansas Cavalry on the left flank. I also sent orders to Capt. Duncan, commanding the 18th Iowa Infantry, to so dispose of his regiment and the cavalry and howitzers which came out with him as to protect the rear of the train, and to keep a sharp lookout for a movement upon his rear and right flank.

'Meanwhile a movement of the enemy's infantry toward my right flank had been observed through the thick brush which covered the face of the country in that direction. Seeing this, I ordered forward the cavalry on my right, under Lieuts. Mitchell and Henderson, with orders to press the enemy's line, force it if possible, and at all events to ascertain his position and strength, fearing as I did that the silence of the enemy in front was but for the purpose of drawing me on to the open ground which lay in my front. At this juncture, a rebel rode into my lines and inquired for Col. DeMorse. From him I learned that General Price was in command of the rebel force, and that Col. DeMorse was in command of the force on my right.

'The cavalry had advanced but four hundred yards, when a brisk fire of musketry was opened upon them from the brush, which they returned with true gallantry, but were forced to fall back. In this skirmish many of the cavalry were unhorsed, and Lieut. Henderson, of the 6th Kansas Cavalry, fell, wounded in the abdomen, while bravely and gallantly urging his command forward.

'In the meantime I formed five companies of the 1st Kansas Colored, with one piece of artillery, on my right flank, and ordered up to their assistance four companies of the 18th Iowa Infantry. Soon my orderly returned from the rear with a message from Captain Duncan, stating that he was so closely pressed in the rear by the enemy's infantry and artillery that the men could not be spared.

'At this moment the enemy opened on me with two batteries,—one of six pieces, in front, and one, of three pieces, on my right flank,—pouring in an incessant and well directed cross-fire of shot and shell. At the same time he advanced his infantry both in front and on my right flank.

'From the force of the enemy—now the first time made visible—I saw that I could not hope to defeat him, but still resolved to defend the train to the last, hoping that re-enforcements would come up from Camden.

'I suffered them to approach within one hundred yards of my line, when I opened upon them with musketry charged with buck and ball, and after a contest of fifteen minutes duration compelled them them to fall back. Two fresh regiments coming up, they again rallied and advanced upon my line, this time with colors flying and continuous cheering, so loud as to drown even the roar of the musketry. Again I suffered them to approach even nearer than before, and opened upon them with buck and ball, their artillery still pouring in a crossfire of shot and shell over the heads of their infantry, and mine replying with vigor and effect. And thus, for another quarter of an hour, the battle was waged with desperate fury. The noise and din of this almost hand to hand conflict was the loudest and most terrific it has ever been my lot to listen

PHALANX CAVALRY BRINGING IN CONFEDERATE PRISONERS.

to. Again were they forced to fall back, and twice during this conflict were their colors brought to the ground, but as often raised.

'During these engagements fully one-half of my infantry engaged were either killed or wounded. Three companies were left without any officers, and seeing the enemy again re-enforced with fresh troops, it became evident that I could hold my line but little longer. I now directed Maj. Ward to hold the line until I could ride back and form the 18th Iowa in proper shape to support the retreat of the advanced line.

'Meanwhile, so many of the gunners had been shot from around their pieces that there were not enough to serve the guns, so I ordered them to retire to the rear of the train, and report to the cavalry officer there. Just as I was starting for the line of the 18th Iowa, my horse was shot, which delayed me until another could be procured, when I rode to the rear and formed a line of battle facing in the direction the enemy was advancing.

'Again did the enemy hurl his columns against the remnant of men that formed my front and right flank, and again were they met as gallantly as before. But my decimated ranks were unable to resist the overpowering force hurled against them, and after their advance had been checked, seeing that our lines were completely flanked on both sides, Major Ward gave the order to retire, which was done in good order, forming and charging the enemy twice before reaching the rear of the train.

'With the assistance of Major Ward and other officers, I succeeded in forming a portion of the 1st Kansas Colored in the rear of the 18th Iowa, and when the enemy approached this line, they gallantly advanced to the line of the 18th, and with them poured in their fire. The 18th maintained their line manfully, and stoutly contested the ground until nearly surrounded, when they retired, and forming again, checked the advancing foe, and still held their ground until again nearly surrounded, when they again retired across a ravine which was impassable for artillery, and I gave orders for the piece to be spiked and abandoned.

'After crossing the ravine I succeeded in forming a portion of the cavalry, which I kept in order to give the infantry time to cross the swamp which lay in our front, which they succeeded in doing. By this means nearly all, except the badly wounded, were enabled to reach the camp. Many wounded men belonging to the 1st Kansas Colored fell into the hands of the enemy, and I have the most positive assurance from eye-witnesses that they were murdered on the spot. I was forced to abandon everything to the enemy, and they thereby became possessed of the large train.

'With two six pounder guns and two twelve pounder mountain howitzers, together with what force could be collected, I made my way to this post, where I arrived at 11 P. M. of the same day.

'At no time during the engagement, such was the nature of the ground and size of the train, was I obliged to employ more than five hundred men and two guns to repel the assaults of the enemy, whose force, from the statement of prisoners, I estimate at ten thousand men and twelve guns. The columns of assault which were again thrown against my front and right flank consisted of five regiments of infantry and one of cavalry, supported by a strong force which operated against my left flank and rear. My loss, in killed, wounded and missing during this engagement was as follows: Killed—ninety-two, wounded—ninety-seven, missing—one hundred and six.

'Many of those reported missing are supposed to have been killed, others are supposed to have been wounded and taken prisoners. The loss of the enemy is not known, but in my opinion it will exceed our own. The conduct of all the troops under my command, officers and men, were characterized by true soldiery bearing, and in no case was a line broken, except when assaulted by an overwhelming force, and then falling back only when so ordered. The officers and men all evinced the most heroic spirit, and those that fell died the death of the true soldier. The action commenced at 10 A. M., and terminated at 2 P. M. I have named this engagement the action of Poison Springs, from a spring of that name in the vicinity.

'Very respectfully yours,

'J. M. WILLIAMS,

'*Colonel 1st Kansas Colored Vol. Infantry, Commanding Expedition.*

'Capt. WM. S. WHITTEN, *Assistant Adjutant General.*'

"On the 26th day of April following, Gen. Steele's command evacuated Camden and marched for Little Rock. At Saline Crossing, on the 30th of April, the rear of Gen. Steele's command was attacked by the entire force of the enemy, commanded by Gen. Kirby Smith. The engagement which followed resulted in the complete defeat of the enemy, with great loss on his part. In this engagement the 1st Kansas Colored was not an active participant, being at the moment of the attack in the advance, distant five miles from the rear and scene of the engagement. The regiment was ordered back to participate in the battle, but did not arrive on the line until after the repulse of the enemy and his retirement from the field.

"On the day following, May 1st, 1864, Colonel Williams was ordered to take command of the 2nd Brigade, composed of the following Phalanx regiments: 1st Regiment, commanded by Major Ward; 2nd Regiment, commanded by Colonel S. J. Crawford; 11th Regiment, commanded by Lieut.-Col. James M. Steele; 54th Regiment, Lieut.-Col. Chas. Fair;of the Frontier Division 7th Army Corps.

"Colonel Williams never afterwards resumed direct command of his regiment. It constituted for most of the time, however, a part of the Brigade, which he commanded until he was mustered out of service with the regiment.

"The regiment remained with the Division at Little Rock until some time during the month of May, when it Marched for Fort Smith,—then threatened by the enemy,—at which point it arrived during the same month. This campaign was one of great fatigue and privation, and accomplished only with great loss of life and material, with no adequate recompense or advantage gained.

"The regiment remained on duty at Fort Smith until January 16th, 1865, doing heavy escort and fatigue duty. On the 16th of September, 1864, a detachment of forty-two men of Co. K, commanded by Lieut. D. M. Sutherland, while guarding a hay-making party near Fort Gibson, were surprised and attacked by a large force of rebels under Gen. Gano, and defeated after a gallant resistence, with a loss of twenty-two killed and ten prisoners—among the latter the Lieutenant commanding. On the 16th of January, 1865, the regiment moved to Little Rock, where it arrived on the 31st of the same month, here it remained on duty until July 1865, when it was ordered to Pine Bluffs, Ark. Here it remained, doing garrison and escort duty, until October 1st, 1865, when it was mustered out of service and ordered to Fort Leavenworth for final payment and discharge. The regiment received its final payment and was discharged at Fort Leavenworth on the 30th day of October, 1865."

The heroism of the negro people of Kansas was not all centered in this one regiment. Elated with the success of their brethren already in the field, there was a general desire to emulate their heroic deeds. In June, 1863, the second regiment was organized at Fort Scott. The regimental organization was completed at Fort Smith, Ark., by the mustering in of the field and staff officers.

The regiment went into camp on the Poteau River, about two miles south of Fort Smith. Here the work of drill and discipline was the daily routine of duty until the regiment maintained a degree of proficiency second to none in the Army of the Frontier.

On the 24th of March, 1864, the regiment left Fort Smith and started on what was known as the Camden Expedition, forming a part of Colonel Williams' Brigade of General Thayer's Division. Major-General Steele's forces left Little Rock about the same time that General Thayer's Division left Fort Smith, the latter uniting with the former on the Little Missouri river, all destined for active operations in the direction of Red River.

Colonel Crawford, in reply to the writer's circular letter asking for information respecting the 2nd Regiment's service on the frontier, thus pungently details the operations of the army of which his regiment was a part:

"WASHINGTON, D. C., Dec. 31st., 1885.

"JOSEPH T. WILSON, Esq., Richmond, Va.

"MY DEAR SIR: * * * * * *

"The Second Kansas, afterwards designated as the 83rd United States Colored Troops, was organized at Fort Scott, Kansas, on the 3rd day of October, 1863. Most of the companies were organized and mustered into service during the spring and summer preceeding. The regiment, when organized, was full to the maximum, or nearly so, and composed of active, able-bodied young men. Immediately upon assuming command of the regiment, I moved to the front through Missouri, to Fort Smith, in Arkansas, where the regiment was stationed during the winter 1863-4, and when not on other duty or in the field, spent the time in company and regimental drill.

"On the 24th day of March, 1864, with the Kansas Division of the Frontier Army under the command of General Thayer, I moved south and joined the 7th Army Corps under the command of Major-General Fred. Steele, in an expedition against the rebel armies under-Generals Price, Kirby Smith and Dick Taylor, then encamped in the vicinity of Shreveport, La.

"While Steele was advancing from the North, General Banks was at the same time moving up the Red river from the East. Price, Smith and Taylor, seeing the two armies of Steele and Banks, closing in upon them, concentrated their forces, first upon Banks, and after defeating and routing his forces, turned upon Steele, who was then near Red river, in south-western Arkansas.

Steele hearing of the Banks disaster, changed his course and moved eastward, to Camden, a strongly fortified town on the Washita river. From the point at which he turned eastward, to Camden, a distance of about sixty miles, the march was almost continuous, except when it became necessary to skirmish with the enemy's cavalry, which hovered unpleasantly close during the greater part of the distance.

"In each of the light engagements which took place on this march from Red river to Camden, the 2nd Regiment participated, and behaved in a manner creditable to itself and the army.

"After remaining at Camden about three days (so as to give the victorious rebel armies full time to concentrate upon him) General Steele crossed the Washita to the North and commenced a disgraceful retreat or run back toward Little Rock.

"The enemy, under Price and Kirby Smith, followed in close pursuit, and within a few hours were again upon our flank and rear. The march or retreat was continuons, night and day, until the village of Princeton was reached, where Steele's army encamped one night, and received a full ration of fresh beef and New Orleans sugar, the latter of which had been captured, or rather found in Camden. Early on the following morning the army resumed its onward march, towards the North Pole as the apparent objective point.

"Now mind you this was an army (the 7th Army Corps) about thirty thousand strong; mostly Western troops, and splendidly armed and equipped. Better soldiers never wore spurs or carried muskets. Yet under the command of a tenor singing dog fancier, that magnificent army was thus retreating before an army in every way its inferior save, and except, the Commanding General.

"Thus things went, disgracefully, until the afternoon of the day on which we left Princeton, April 29, 1864. Then, for the first time after turning our backs to the enemy, in the vicinity of Red river, there seemed to be a bare possibility of escape,—not from the enemy, but from absolute disgrace and humiliation.

"At no time during that disgraceful retreat, was there a moment when the whole army corps, except the Commanding General, would not have welcomed a battle, with one universal shout.

"About 4 o'clock in the afternoon of the day mentioned, the rebel Cavalry appeared in force and commenced skirmishing with our forces in the rear, which continued, more or less, until darkness set in. Meantime our distinguished leader, the Major-General Commanding, had arrived at the crossing of the Saline river, thrown a pontoon bridge over that swollen stream, and made good his escape to the north side, taking with him the whole army, except one section of artillery and two brigades of infantry of which the 2nd Kansas colored formed a part.

"These two brigades—six regiments in all—stood in line of battle all night long, while the rain poured in torrents most of the time.

"During the night the enemy's infantry moved up and formed in our immediate front; in fact made every necessary preparation for battle, while the dog fancier, who was unfortunately at the head of our army across the river, was either sleeping or devising the ways and means by which he could most easily elude the enemy.

"But when daylight came the six regiments were there in line, every man ready, willing and determined to return, volley for volley, and if necessary force the fighting, so as to bring on a general engagement.

"There were but six regiments of us south of the river, with two pieces of artillery. But we were there to stay until a battle was fought.

"General Rice of Iowa, formed his brigade in the center; the 12th Kansas Infantry, commanded by Col. Hayes was on his left, and the 2nd Kansas Colored Infantry, commanded by myself, was on the right.

"As soon as it was fairly light, the battle began; both lines moving slightly forward until within close range. From the beginning, the crash of musketry was terrific. Our men stood firm against the advanced Division of the enemy's infantry, and used their Springfield and Enfield rifles with deadly effect.

"The enemy seeing our weakness in numbers, pressed heavily in the center and upon both flanks, with the evident design of breaking our line before re-enforcements could reach us.

"But in this they were disappointed. We held our position until re-enforcements arrived.

"At one time my regiment was under a heavy fire from the front and also from the flank, but not a man wavered. In fact it seemed to inspire them with additional courage. The re-enforcements as they arrived, passed to the rear and formed on the left, leaving me to hold the right. After about three hours hard fighting, the enemy having failed to dislodge my regiment from its position, which was regarded as the key to the situation, brought into position a battery of artillery, planted it immediately in front of my regiment and opened with canister.

"As soon as this was done I gave the order to cease firing and fix bayonets, and followed that immediately with the order to charge the battery.

"These orders were executed with a courage and daring seldom equaled by even older troops, and never excelled by a volunteer regiment.

"In less than two minutes from the time the charge was ordered, the rebel battery was in our possession, and out of thirty-six horses used in the battery, but two were left standing when we passed the guns.

"Most of the artillery-men lay dead and wounded around the battery while the line of infantry support in the rear of battery, fell back in disorder before our bayonets; not, however, until many of them had for the first time felt the effects of cold steel.

"The charge, though bloody on both sides, was pre-eminently successful, and my regiment, "the 2nd Iron Clads," as it was called, brought away the battery so captured.

"In the charge, the regiment lost in killed and wounded, some forty odd men and officers. All of our horses, field and staff, were shot and most of them killed. The color bearer Harrison Young, a hero among men, was wounded and fell, raised to his feet and was again twice wounded. A comrade then took the flag and was wounded, and a third man brought it off the field.

"A wounded lieutenant of the battery was brought to me, as a prisoner;* but in view of the massacre of colored troops by the rebels at Fort Pillow and other places, I sent the Lieutenant immediately back through the lines, pointing him to the regiment that had made the charge, and telling him that since the rebel authorities had concluded to take no prisoners, belonging to colored regiments, it would hardly be proper for me to hold him as a prisoner; that they had established the precedent, and that in so far as I was concerned, they could 'lay on MacDuff.' The Lieutenant rejoined his command a sadder if not a wiser man.

"After the charge I moved with my regiment to the centre, where the battle was then raging hottest. Here it remained in the thickest of the fight until an advance was

* "Colonel Crawford ordered the prisoners to be taken to the rear without insult or injury, which conduct on his part is in striking contrast to the treatment bestowed upon our colored troops at Poison Springs. He also told a rebel lieutenant and other prisoners to inform their commanding General that colored troops had captured them, and that he must from necessity leave some of his wounded men in hospitals by the way, and that he should expect the same kind treatment shown to them that he showed to those falling into his hands; but that just such treatment as his wounded men received at their hands, whether kindness or death, should from this time forward, be meted out to all rebel falling into his hands. That if they wished to treat as prisoners of war our colored soldiers, to be exchanged for theirs, the decision was their own; but if they could afford to murder our colored prisoners to gratify their fiendish dispositions and passions, the responsibity of commensurate retaliation, to bring them to a sense of justice, was also their own. But, notwithstanding the kindness shown to their prisoners, so soon as our command left, a Texas soldier, in the presence of one of their officers, killed, in the hospital, nine of the wounded men belonging to the 2nd Kansas Colored Infantry."—*McAfee's Military History of Kansas.*

PHALANX SOLDIERS BRINGING IN A CAPTURED BATTERY

ordered all along the line, which was made, the enemy falling back slowly before our troops, and finally retired from the field, leaving us in full possession, with a complete victory.

"Only infantry was engaged on either side except the rebel battery, which my regiment captured.

"Our cavalry, some five thousand strong, and artillery, about forty pieces, as already stated, were on the North side of the river, and could not be brought into action, to advantage, on account of the dense forest and swampy nature of the ground. We had about fifteen thousand men engaged, while the enemy had the armies of Price and Kirby Smith, from which our *gallant* commander, Steele, had for many days been fleeing, as from the wrath to come. During the entire battle Steele remained on the north side of the river, beyond the reach of the enemy's guns, and at a point from which he could continue his flight with safety in case of defeat. But the victory was ours, so the march from Saline river to Little Rock was made in peace.

"During this battle my regiment lost in killed and wounded about eighty men, but we were richly rewarded by the achievements of the day. We, perhaps, had as much to do with bringing on the battle as any other one regiment. I went into action in the morning without orders. In fact I disobeyed an order to cross the river at daylight, and instead, I formed my regiment and faced the enemy. The regiment charged the battery by my orders, and against an order from a superior officer, to hold back and wait for orders.

"My regiment, though among the first in action, and having suffered a greater loss than that of any other, was the last to leave the field.

"From this time forward until the close of the war, in so far as the Western army was concerned, we heard no more of the question, 'Will they fight?'

"The reputation of at least one colored regiment was established, and it stands today, in the estimation of men who served in the Western army, as the equal of any other volunteer regiment.

"After the Saline river battle the regiment moved back to Little Rock and thence to Fort Smith, in western Arkansas.

"In July 1864, with the 2nd and other troops, I conducted an expedition through the Choctaw Nation in the Indian Territory, against, or rather in pursuit of a brigade of rebel forces, driving them out of that country. During this campaign several light engagements were fought, in each of which the 2nd took a prominent part, and in each of which the 2nd was invariably successful.

* "In the fall of 1864, I resigned my position as Colonel to assume other duties.

"What took place from then until the regiment was mustered out of service, I only know from heresay, but it is safe to say that the regiment maintained its reputation as one of the best infantry regiments in the 7th Army Corps.

"A short time before I left the regiment, General Marcy, then Inspector General of the U. S. Army, inspected the Kansas Division, to which my regiment belonged, and his report, which is now on file in the War Department, if I am not mistaken, shows that the 2nd Colored in point of drill, discipline and military appearance, stood first of all the regiments in that Division.

*   *   *   *   *   *   *

Yours truly,
SAMUEL J. CRAWFORD.

Lieutenant-Colonel Gilpatrick, promoted from Major, took command of the regiment succeeding Colonel Crawford, and in December made a forced march to Hudson's crossing on the Neosho river, by way of Fort Gibson, a distance of one hundred and fifty miles, on quarter rations, and returned as escort to a large supply train. It was then, with all the Phalanx regiments at Fort Smith, ordered to Little Rock, where it arrived with a very large train of refugees under charge, on the 4th of February, after a march of seventeen days.

Colonel Gilpatrick says:

"The men suffered severely on the march by exposure to wet and

* About the middle of October, Colonel Crawford received information of his nomination for the office of Governor, and came from Fort Smith to Kansas, arriving about the 20th instant, just in time to be an active participant in the expulsion of General Price and his army from the border of the State.

cold and for the want of proper and sufficient food, clothing and shelter. Many of them were barefooted, almost naked, and without blankets."

The regiment remained at Little Rock until the spring of 1865, when it formed part of an expedition which proceeded some distance south of Little Rock, and operated against a band of guerillas on the Saline river, which they succeeded in driving out and partly capturing. On the 25th of July the regiment broke camp and proceeded to Camden, Arkansas, and was mustered out of the United States service, and proceeding by way of Pine Bluff, Ark., Memphis, Tenn., and St. Louis, Mo., reached Leavenworth, Kansas, where the men were finally paid and discharged on the 27th of November, 1865. These brave men immediately returned to their homes to enjoy the blessings of a free government.

THE WOODEN HORSE.
A mode of punishment for slight offences.

CHAPTER VII.

DEPARTMENT OF THE SOUTH.

The appearance of the negro in the Union army altered the state of affairs very much. The policy of the general Government was changed, and the one question which Mr. Lincoln had tried to avoid became *the* question of the war. General Butler, first at Fortress Monroe and then at New Orleans, had defined the status of the slave, "contraband" and then "soldiers," in advance of the Emancipation Proclamation. General Hunter, in command at the South, as stated in a previous chapter, had taken an early opportunity to strike the rebellion in its most vital part, by arming negroes in his Department, after declaring them free.

Notwithstanding the President revoked Hunter's order, a considerable force was organized and equipped as early as December, 1862; in fact a regiment of blacks was under arms when the President issued the Emancipation Proclamation. This regiment, the 1st South Carolina, was in commond of Colonel T. W. Higginson, who with a portion of his command ascended the St. Mary's river on transports, visited Florida and Georgia, and had several engagements with the enemy. After an absence of ten or more days, the expedition returned to South Carolina without the loss of a man.

Had there been but one army in the field, and the fighting confined to one locality, the Phalanx would have been mobilized, but as there were several armies it was distributed among the several forces, and its conduct in battle, camp, march and bivouac, was spoken of by the commanders of the various armies in terms which any class of soldiers, of any race, might well be proud of.

General Grant, on the 24th of July, following the capture of Vicksburg, wrote to the Adjutant-General:

> "The negro troops are easier to preserve discipline among than are our white troops, and I doubt not will prove equally good for garrison duty. All that have been tried have fought bravely."

This was six days after the unsurpassed bravery of the 54th Regiment Massachusetts Volunteers—representing the North in the black Phalanx—had planted its blood-stained banner on the ramparts of Fort Wagner. It was the Southern negroes, who, up to this time, had reddened the waters of the Mississippi. It was the freedman's blood that had moistened the soil, and if ignorance could be so intrepid still greater daring might be expected on the part of the more intelligent men of the race.

The assault on Fort Wagner, July 18, 1863, was one of the most heroic of the whole four years' war. A very graphic account of the entire movement is given in the following article:

> "At daylight, on the morning of the 12th of July a strong column of our troops advanced swiftly to the attack of Fort Wagner. The rebels were well prepared, and swept with their guns every foot of the approach to the fort, but our soldiers pressed on, and gained a foothold on the parapet; but, not being supported by other troops, nor aided by the guns of the fleet, which quietly looked on, they were forced to retreat, leaving many of their comrades in the hands of the enemy.
>
> "It is the opinion of many that if the fleet had moved up at the same time, and raked the fort with their guns, our troops would have succeeded in taking it; but the naval captains said in their defence that they knew nothing of the movement, and would have gladly assisted in the attack had they been notified
>
> "This, unfortunately, was not the only instance of a want of harmony or co-operation between the land and naval forces operating against Charleston. Had they been under the control of one mind, the sacrifice of life in the siege of Forts Wagner and Sumter would have been far less. We will not assume to say which side was at fault, but by far the greater majority lay the blame upon the naval officers. Warfare kindles up the latent germs of jealousy in the human breast, and the late rebellion furnished many cruel examples of its effects, both among the rebels and among the patriots. We have had the misfortune to witness

them in more than one campaign, and upon more than one bloody and disastrous field.

"By the failure of this attack, it was evident that the guns of Wagner must be silenced before a successful assault with infantry could be made; and, in order to accomplish this, a siege of greater or less duration was required. Therefore earthworks were immediately thrown up at the distance of about a thousand yards from the fort, and the guns and mortars from Folly Island brought over to be placed in position.

"This Morris Island is nothing but a narrow bed of sand, about three miles in length, with a breadth variable from a few hundred yards to a few feet. Along the central portion of the lower end a ridge of white sand hills appear, washed on one side by the tidal waves, and sloping on the other into broad marshes, more than two miles in width, and intersected by numerous deep creeks. Upon the extreme northern end, Battery Gregg, which the rebels used in reducing Fort Sumter in 1861, had been strengthened, and mounted with five heavy guns, which threw their shot more than half way down the island. A few hundred yards farther down the island, and at its narrowest portion, a strong fort had been erected, and armed with seventeen guns and mortars. This was the famous Fort Wagner; and, as its cannon prevented any farther progress up the island, it was necessary to reduce it before our forces could approach nearer to Fort Sumter.

"It was thought by our engineers that a continuous bombardment of a few days by our siege batteries and the fleet might dismount the rebel cannon, and demoralize the garrison, so that our brave boys, by a sudden rush, might gain possession of the works. Accordingly our seige train was brought over from Folly Island, and a parallel commenced about a thousand yards from Wagner. Our men worked with such energy that nearly thirty cannon and mortars were in position on the 17th of July. On the 18th of July the bombardment commenced. The land batteries poured a tempest of shot into the south side of Wagner, while the fleet moved up to within short range, and battered the east side with their great guns. In the mean time the rebels were not silent, but gallantly stood to their guns, returning shot for shot with great precision. But, after a few hours, their fire slackened; gun after gun became silent, as the men were disabled, and, when the clock struck four in the afternoon, Wagner no longer responded to the furious cannonade the Federal forces. Even the men had taken shelter beneath the bombproofs, and no sign of life was visible about the grim and battered fortress.

"Many of our officers were now so elated with the apparent result of demolition, that they urged General Gillmore to allow them to assault the fort as soon as it became dark. General Gillmore yielded to the solicitations of the officers, but very reluctantly, for he was not convinced that the proper time had arrived; but the order was finally given for the attack to take place just after dark. Fatal error as to time, for our troops in the daytime would have been successful, since they would not have collided with each other; they could have seen their foes, and the arena of combat, and the fleet could have assisted them with their guns, and prevented the landing of the re-enforcements from Charleston.

"It was a beautiful and calm evening when the troops who were to form the assaulting column moved out on to the broad and smooth beach left by the receding tide.

"The last rays of the setting sun illumined the grim walls and shattered mounds of Wagner with a flood of crimson light, too soon, alas! to be deeper dyed with the red blood of struggling men.

"Our men halted, and formed their ranks upon the beach, a mile and more away from the deadly breach. Quietly they stood leaning upon their guns, and awaiting the signal of attack. There stood, side by side, the hunter of the far West, the farmer of the North, the stout lumberman from the forests of Maine, and the black Phalanx Massachusetts had armed and sent to the field.

"In this hour of peril there was no jealousy, no contention. The black Phalanx were to lead the forlorn hope. And they were proud of their position, and conscious of its danger. Although we had seen many of the famous regiments of the English, French, and Austrian armies, we were never more impressed with the fury and majesty of war than when we looked upon the solid mass of the thousand black men, as they stood, like giant statues of marble, upon the snow-white sands of the beach, waiting the order to advance. And little did we think, as we gazed with admiration upon that splendid column of four thousand brave men, that ere an hour had passed, half of them would be swept away, maimed or crushed in the gathering whirlwind of death! Time passed quickly, and twilight was fast deepening into the darkness of night, when the signal was given. Onward moved the chosen and ill-fated band, making the earth tremble under the heavy and monotonous tread of the dense mass of thousands of men. Wagner lay black and grim in the distance, and silent. Not a glimmer of light was seen. Not a gun replied to the bombs which our mortars still constantly hurled into the fort. Not a shot was returned to the terrific volleys of the giant frigate Ironsides, whose shells, ever and anon, plunged into the earthworks, illuminating their recesses for an instant in the glare of their explosion, but revealing no signs of life.

"Were the rebels all dead? Had they fled from the pitiless storm which our batteries had poured down upon them for so many hours? Where were they?

"Down deep beneath the sand heaps were excavated great caverns, whose floors were level with the tide, and whose roofs were formed of huge trunks of trees laid in double rows. Still above these massive beams sand was heaped so deeply that even our enormous shells could not penetrate the roofs, though they fell from the skies above. In these dark subterranean retreats two thousand men lay hid, like panthers in a swamp, waiting to leap forth in fury upon their prey.

"The signal given, our forces advanced rapidly towards the fort,

AT FORT WAGNER.

Desperate charge of the 54th Mass. Vols. in the assault on Fort Wagner, July 18, 1863.

while our mortars in the rear tossed their bombs over their heads. The Fifty-fourth Massachusetts [Phalanx Regiment] led the attack, supported by the 6th Conn., 48th N. Y., 3rd N. H., 76th Penn. and the 9th Maine Regiments. Onward swept the immense mass of men, swiftly and silently, in the dark shadows of night. Not a flash of light was seen in the distance! No sentinel hoarsely challenged the approaching foe! All was still save the footsteps of the soldiers, which sounded like the roar of the distant surf, as it beats upon the rock-bound coast.

"Ah, what is this! The silent and shattered walls of Wagner all at once burst forth into a blinding sheet of vivid light, as though they had suddenly been transformed by some magic power into the living, seething crater of a volcano! Down came the whirlwind of destruction along the beach with the swiftness of lightning! How fearfully the hissing shot, the shrieking bombs, the whistling bars of iron, and the whispering bullet struck and crushed through the dense masses of our brave men! I never shall forget the terrible sound of that awful blast of death, which swept down, shattered or dead, a thousand of our men. Not a shot had missed its aim. Every bolt of steel, every globe of iron and lead, tasted of human blood.

"'Forward!' shouted the undaunted Putnam, as the column wavered and staggered like a giant stricken with death.

"'Steady, my boys!' murmured the brave leader, General Strong, as a cannon-shot dashed him, maimed and bleeding, into the sand.

"In a moment the column recovered itself, like a gallant ship at sea when buried for an instant under an immense wave.

"The ditch is reached; a thousand men leap into it, clamber up the shattered ramparts, and grapple with the foe, which yields and falls back to the rear of the fort. Our men swarm over the walls, bayoneting the desperate rebel cannoneers. Hurrah! the fort is ours!

"But now came another blinding blast from concealed guns in the rear of the fort, and our men went down by scores. Now the rebels rally, and, re-enforced by thousands of the chivalry, who have landed on the beach under cover of darkness, unmolested by the guns of the fleet. They hurl themselves with fury upon the remnant of our brave band. The struggle is terrific. Our supports hurry up to the aid of their comrades, but as they reach the ramparts they fire a volley which strikes down many of our men. Fatal mistake! Our men rally once more; but, in spite of an heroic resistance, they are forced back again to the edge of the ditch. Here the brave Shaw, with scores of his black warriers, went down, fighting desperately. Here Putnam met his death wound, while cheering and urging on the overpowered Phalanx men.

"What fighting, and what fearful carnage! Hand to hand, breast to breast! Here, on this little strip of land, scarce bigger than the human hand, dense masses of men struggled with fury in the darkness; and so fierce was the contest that the sands were reddened and soaked with human gore.

"But resistance was vain. The assailants were forced back again to the beach, and the rebels trained their recovered cannon anew upon the retreating survivors.

"What a fearful night was that, as we gathered up our wounded heroes, and bore them to a place of shelter! And what a mournful morning, as the sun rose with his clear beams, and revealed our terrible losses! What a rich harvest Death had gathered to himself during the short struggle! Nearly two thousand of our men had fallen. More than six hundred of our brave boys lay dead on the ramparts of the fatal fort, in its broad ditch, and along the beach at its base. A flag of truce party went out to bury our dead, but General Beauregard they found had already buried them, where they fell, in broad, deep trenches."

Colonel Shaw, the young and gallant commander of the 54th Regiment, was formerly a member of the famous 7th N. Y. Regiment. He was of high, social and influential standing, and in his death won destinction. The confederates added to his fame and glory, though unintentionally, by burying him with his soldiers, or as a confederate Major expressed the information, when a request for the Colonel's body was made, "we have buried him with his niggers!"

A poet has immortalized the occurrence and the gallant Shaw thus:

'They buried him with his niggers!'
Together they fought and died.
There was room for them all where they laid him,
(The grave was deep and wide),
For his beauty and youth and valor,
Their patience and love and pain;
And at the last together
They shall be found again.

'They buried him with his niggers!'
Earth holds no prouder grave;
There is not a mausoleum
In the world beyond the wave,
That a nobler tale has hallowed,
Or a purer glory crowned,
Than the nameless trench where they buried
The brave so faithful found.

'They buried him with his niggers!'
A wide grave should it be;
They buried more in that shallow trench
Than human eye could see.
Aye, all the shames and sorrows
Of more than a hundred years
Lie under the weight of that Southern soil
Despite those cruel sneers.

'They buried him with his niggers!'
But the glorious souls set free
Are leading the van of the army
That fights for liberty.
Brothers in death, in glory
The same palm branches bear;
And the crown is as bright o'er the sable brows
As over the golden hair.

Buried with a band of brothers
Who for him would fain have died;
Buried with the gallant fellows
Who fell fighting by his side;

Buried with the men God gave him,
Those whom he was sent to save;
Buried with the martyr heroes,
He has found an honored grave.

Buried where his dust so precious
Makes the soil a hallowed spot;
Buried where by Christian patriot,
He shall never be forgot.

Buried in the ground accursed,
Which man's fettered feet have trod;
Buried where his voice still speaketh,
Appealing for the slave to God;

Fare thee well, thou noble warrior,
Who in youthful beauty went
On a high and holy mission,
By the God of battles sent.

Chosen of him, 'elect and precious,'
Well didst thou fulfil thy part;
When thy country 'counts her jewels,'
She shall wear thee on her heart."

The heroic courage displayed by the gallant Phalanx at the assault upon Fort Wagner was not surpassed by the Old Guard at Moscow. Major-General Taliaferro gives this confederate account of the fight, which is especially interesting as it shows the condition of affairs inside the fort:

"On the night of the 14th the monster iron-plated frigate New Ironsides, crossed the bar and added her formidable and ponderous battery to those destined for the great effort of reducing the sullen earthwork which barred the Federal advance. There were now five monitors, the Ironsides and a fleet of gunboats and monster hulks grouped together and only waiting the signal to unite with the land batteries when the engineers should pronounce them ready to form a cordon of flame around the devoted work. The Confederates were prepared for the ordeal. For for fear that communications with the city and the mainland, which was had by steamboat at night to Cummings' Point should be interrupted, rations and ordnance stores had been accumulated, but there was trouble about water. Some was sent from Charleston and wells had been dug in the sand inside and outside the fort, but it was not good. Sand bags had been provided and trenching tools supplied sufficient for any supposed requirement.

"The excitement of the enemy in front after the 10th was manifest to the Confederates and announced an 'impending crisis.' It became evident that some extraordinary movement was at hand. The Federal forces on James Island had been attacked on the morning of the 16th by General Hagood and caused to retire, Hagood occupying the abandoned positions, and on the 17th the enemy's troops were transferred to Little Folly and Morris Islands. It has been stated that the key to the signals employed by the Federals was in possession of General Taliaferro at this time, and he was thus made acquainted with the intended movement and put upon his guard. That is a mistake. He had no such direct information, although it is true that afterwards the key was discovered and the signals interpreted with as much ease as by the Federals themselves. The 18th of July was the day determined upon by the Federal commanders for the grand attempt which, if successful, would level the arrogant fortress and confuse it by the mighty power of their giant artillery with the general mass of surrounding sand hills, annihilate its garrison or drive them into the relentless ocean, or else consign them to the misery of hostile prisons.

"The day broke beautifully, a gentle breeze slightly agitated the balmy atmosphere, and with rippling dimples beautified the bosom of the placid sea. All nature was serene and the profoundest peace held dominion over all the elements. The sun, rising with the early splendors of his midsummer glory, burnished with golden tints the awakening ocean, and flashed his reflected light back from the spires of the beleaguered city into the eyes of those who stood pausing to gather strength to spring upon her, and of those who stood at bay to battle for her safety. Yet the profound repose was undisturbed; the early hours of that fair morning hoisted a flag of truce between the combatants which was respected by both. But the tempest of fire which was destined to break the charm of nature, with human thunders then unsurpassed in war, was gathering in the south. At about half-past 7 o'clock the ships of war moved from their moorings, the iron leviathan the Ironsides, an Agamemnon among ships, leading and directing their movements, then monitor after monitor, and then wooden flagships. Steadily and majestically they marched; marched as columns of men would march, obedient to commands, independent of waves and winds, mobilized by steam and science to turn on a pivot and manœuvre as the directing mind required them; they halted in front of the fort; they did not anchor as Sir Peter Parker's ships had done near a hundred years before in front of Moultrie, which was hard by and frowning still at her ancient enemies of the ocean. They halted and waited for word of command to belch their consuming lightnings out upon the foe. On the land, engineering skill was satisfied and the deadly exposure for details for labor was ended; the time for retaliation had arrived when the defiant shots of the rebel batteries would be answered; the batteries were unmasked; the cordon of fire was complete by land and by sea; the doomed fort was encircled by guns.

"The Confederates watched from the ramparts the approach of the fleet and the unmasking of the guns, and they knew that the moment had arrived in which the problem of the capacity of the resistant power of earth and sand to the forces to which science so far developed in war could subject them was to be solved and that Battery Wagner was to be that day the subject of the crucial test. The small armament of the fort was really inappreciable in the contest about to be inaugurated. There was but one gun which could be expected to be of much avail against the formidable naval power which would assail it and on the land side few which could reach the enemy's batteries. When these guns were knocked to pieces and silenced there was nothing left but passive resistance, but the Confederates, from the preliminary tests which had been applied, had considerable faith in the capacity of sand and earth for passive resistance.

"The fort was in good condition, having been materially strengthened since the former assault by the indefatigable exertions of Colonel David Harris, chief engineer, and his valuable assistant, Captain Barnwell. Colonel Harris was a Virginian, ex-officer of the army of the United States and a graduate of West Point, who had some years before retired from the service to prosecute the profession of civil engineering. Under a tempest of shells he landed during the fiercest period of the bombardment at Cummings' Point, and made his way through the field of fire to the beleaguered fort to inspect its condition and to inspire the garrison by his heroic courage and his confidence in its strength. Escaping all the dangers of war, he fell a victim to yellow fever in Charleston, beloved and honored by all who had ever known him. The heavy work imposed upon the garrison in repairs and construction, as well as the strain upon the system by constant exposure to the enemy's fire, had induced General Beauregard to adopt the plan of relieving the garrison every few days by fresh troops. The objection to this was that the new men had to be instructed and familiarized with their duties; but still it was wise and necessary, for the same set of officers and men, if retained any length of time, would have been broken down by the arduous service required of them. The relief was sent by regiments and detachments, so there was never an entirely new body of men in the works.

"The garrison was estimated at one thousand seven hundred aggregate. The staff of General Taliaferro consisted of Captain Twiggs, Quartermaster General; Captain W. T. Taliaferro, Adjutant General; Lieutenants H. C. Cunningham and Magyck, Ordnance Officers; Lieutenants Meade and Stoney, Aides-de-Camp; Major Holcombe; Captain Burke, Quartermaster, and Habersham, Surgeon-in-Chief; Private Stockman, of McEnery's Louisiana Battalion, who had been detailed as clerk because of his incapacity for other duty, from most honorable wounds, acted also in capacity of aid.

"The Charleston Battalion was assigned to that part of the work which extended from the Sally port or Lighthouse Inlet creek around to the left until it occupied part of the face to the south, including the western bastion; the Fifty-first North Carolina connected with these troops on the left and extended to the southeast bastion; the rest of the work was to be occupied by the Thirty-first North Carolina Regiment, and a small force from that regiment was detailed as a reserve, and two campanies of the Charleston Battalion were to occupy outside of the fort the covered way spoken of and some sand-hills by the seashore; the artillery was distributed among the several gun-chambers and the light pieces posted on a traverse outside so as to sweep to sea face and the right approach. The positions to be occupied were well known to every officer and man and had been verified repeatedly by day and night, so there was no fear of confusion, mistake or delay in the event of an assault. The troops of course were not ordered to these positions when at 6 o'clock it was evident a furious bombardment was impending, but, on the contrary, to the shelter of the bomb-proofs, sand-hills and parapet; a few sentinels or videttes were detailed and the gun detachments only ordered to their pieces.

"The Charleston Battálion preferred the freer air of the open work to the stifling atmosphere of the bomb-proofs and were permitted to shelter themselves under the parapet and traverses. Not one of that heroic band entered the opening of a bomb-proof during that frightful day. The immense superority of the enemy's artillery was well understood and appreciated by the Confederate commander, and it was clear to him that his policy was to husband his resources and preserve them as best he could for the assault, which it was reasonable to expect would occur during the day. He recognized the fact that his guns were only defensive and he had little or no offensive power with which to contend with his adversaries. Acting on this conviction he had the light guns dismounted and covered with sand bags, and the same precaution was adopted to preserve some of the shell guns or fixed carriages. The propriety of this determination was abundantly demonstrated in the end.

"About a quarter past 8 o'clock the storm broke, ship after ship and battery after battery, and then apparently all together, vomited forth their horrid flames and the atmosphere was filled with deadly missiles. It is impossible for any pen to describe or for anyone who was not an eye-witness to conceive the frightful grandeur of the spectacle. The writer has never had the fortune to read any official Federal report or any other account of the operations of this day except an extract from the graphic and eloquent address of the Rev. Mr. Dennison, a chaplain of one of the Northern regiments, delivered on its nineteenth anniversary at Providence, R. I. He says: 'Words cannot depict the thunder, the smoke, the lifted sand and the general havoc which characterized that hot summer day. What a storm of iron fell on that island; the roar of the guns was incessant; how the shots ploughed the sand banks and the marshes; how the splinters flew from the Beacon House; how the whole island smoked like a furnace and trembled as from an earthquake.'

"If that was true outside of Wagner it is easy to conceive how intensified the situation was within its narrow limits towards which every hostile gun was pointed. The sand came down in avalanches; huge vertical shells and those rolled over by the ricochet shots from the ships, buried themselves and then exploded, rending the earth and forming great craters, out of which the sand and iron fragments flew high in the air. It was a fierce sirocco freighted with iron as well as sand. The sand flew over from the seashore, from the glacis, from the exterior slope, from the parapet, as it was ploughed up and lifted and driven by resistless force now in spray and now almost in waves over into the work, the men sometimes half buried by the moving mass. The chief anxiety was about the magazines. The profile of the fort might be destroyed, the ditch filled up, the traverses and bomb-proof barracks knocked out of shape, but the protecting banks of sand would still afford their shelter; but if the coverings of the magazines were blown away and they became exposed, the explosion that would ensue would lift fort and garrison into the air and annihilate all in general chaos. They were carefully watched and reports of their condition required to be made at short intervals during the day.

"Wagner replied to the enemy, her 10-inch columbiad alone to the ships, deliberately at intervals of fifteen minutes, the other guns to the land batteries whenever in range, as long as they were serviceable. The 32-pounder rifled gun was soon rendered useless by bursting and within two hours many other guns had been dismounted and their carriages destroyed. Sumter, Colonel Alfred Rhett in command, and Gregg, under charge of Captain Sesesne, with the Sullivan and James Island batteries at long range, threw all the power of their available metal at the assailants and added their thunders to the universal din; the harbor of Charleston was a volcano. The want of water was felt, but now again unconsciously the enemy came to the assistance of the garrison, for water was actually scooped from the craters made in the sand by the exploded shells. The city of Charleston was alive and aflame with excitement; the bay, the wharves, the steeples and streets filled with anxious spectators looking across the water at their defenders, whom they could not succor.

"At 2 o'clock the flag halliards were cut by a shot and the Confederate garrison flag was blown over into the fort; there was an instant race for its recovery through the storm of missiles, over the broken earth and shells and splinters which lined the parade. Major Ramsey, Sergeant Shelton and private Flinn, of the Charleston Battalion, and Lieutenant Riddick, of the Sixty-third Georgia, first reached it and bore it back in triumph to the flagstaff, and at the same moment Captain Barnwell, of the engineers, seized a battle-flag, and leaping on the ramparts, drove the staff into the sand. This flag was again shot away, but was again replaced by Private Gaillard, of the Charleston Battalion. These intrepid actions, emulating in a higher degree the conduct of Sergeant Jasper at Moultrie during the Revolution, were cheered by the command and inspired them with renewed courage.

"The day wore on; thousands upon thousands of shells and round shot, shells loaded with balls, shells of guns and shells of mortars, percussion shells, exploding upon impact, shells with graded fuses—every kind apparently known to the arsenals of war leaped into and around the doomed fort, yet there was no cessation; the sun seemed to stand still and the long midsummer day to know no night. Some men were dead and no scratch appeared on their bodies; the concussion had forced the breath from their lungs and collapsed them into corpses. Captain Twiggs, of the staff, in executing some orders was found apparently dead. He was untouched, but lifeless, and only strong restoratives brought him back to animation, and the commanding officer was buried knee-deep in sand and had to be rescued by spades from his imprisonment. The day wore on, hours followed hours of anxiety and grim endurance, but no respite ensued. At last night came; not however, to herald a cessation of the strife, but to usher in a conflict still more terrible. More than eleven hours had passed. The fort was torn and mutilated; to the outside observer it was apparently powerless, knocked to pieces and pounded out of shape, the outline changed, the exterior slope full of gaping wounds, the ditch half filled up, but the interior still preserved its form and its integrity; scarred and defaced it was yet a citadel which, although not offensive, was defiant.

It was nearly eight o'clock at night, but still twilight, when a calm came and the blazing circle ceased to glow with flame. The ominous pause was understood; it required no signals to be read by those to whom they were not directed to inform them that the supreme moment to test the value of the day's achievements was now at hand. It meant nothing but assault. Dr. Dennison says the assault was intended to be a surprise. He over-estimates the equanimity of the Confederate commander if he supposes that that bombardment, which would have waked the dead, had lulled him into security and repose. The buried cannon were at once exhumed, the guns remounted and the garrison ordered to their appointed posts. The Charleston Battalion were already formed and in position; they had nestled under the parapet and stood ready in their places. The other troops with the exception of part of one regiment, responded to the summons with extraordinary celerity, and the echoes of the Federal guns had hardly died away before more than three-fourths of the ramparts were lined with troops; one gap remained unfilled; the demoralized men who should have filled it clung to the bomb-proofs and stayed there. The gallant Colonel Simpkins called his men to the gun-chambers wherever guns existed. De Pass, with his light artillery on the traverse to the left, his guns remounted and untouched, stood ready, and Colonel Harris moved a howitzer outside the fort to the right to deliver an enfilade fire upon the assailants.

"The dark masses of the enemies columns, brigade after brigade, were seen in the fading twilight to approach; line after line was formed and then came the rush. A small creek made in on the right of the fort and intercepted the enemy's left attack; they did not know it, or did not estimate it. Orders were given to Gaillard to hold his fire and deliver no direct shot. It was believed the obstacle presented by the creek would confuse the assailants, cause them to incline to the right and mingle their masses at the head of the obstacle and thus their movements would be obstructed. It seemed to have the anticipated effect and the assaulting columns apparently jumbled together at this point were met by the withering volleys of McKethan's direct and Gaillard's cross-fire and by the direct discharge of the shell guns, supplemented by the frightful enfilading discharges of the lighter guns upon the right and left. It was terrible, but with an unsurpassed gallantry the Federal soldiers breasted the storm and rushed onward to the glacis.

"The Confederates, not fourteen hundred strong, with the tenacity of bull dogs and a fierce courage which was roused to madness by the frightful inaction to which they had been subjected, poured from the ramparts and embrasures sheets of flame and a tempest of lead and iron, yet their intrepid assailants rushed on like the waves of the sea by whose shore they fought. They fell by hundreds, but they pushed on, reeling under the frightful blasts that almost blew them to pieces, some up to the Confederate bayonets. The southeast bastion was weakly defended, and into it a considerable body of the enemy made their way but they were caught in a trap, for they could not leave it. The fight continued; but it was impossible to stem the torrent of deadly missiles which poured out from the fort, the reflux of that terrible tide which had poured in all day, and the Federals retreated, leaving near a thousand dead around the fort.

"There was no cessation of the Confederate fire. Sumter and Gregg threw their shells along with those of Wagner upon the retiring foe; nor was the conflict over in the fort itself. The party which had gained access by the salient next the sea could not escape. It was certain death to attempt to pass the line of concentrated fire which swept the faces of the work, and they did not attempt it; but they would not surrender, and in desperation kept up a constant fire upon the main body of the fort. The Confederates called for volunteers to dislodge them—a summons which was promptly responded to by Major McDonald, of the Fifty-first North Carolina, and by Captain Rion, of the Charleston Battalion, with the requisite number of men. Rion's company was selected, and the gallant Irishman, at the head of his company, dashed at the reckless and insane men, who seemed to insist upon immolation. The tables were now singularly turned; the assailants had become the assailed and they held a fort within the fort, and were protected by the traverses and gun chambers, behind which they fought. Rion rushed at them, but he fell, shot outright, with several of his men, and the rest recoiled. At this time General Hagood reported to General Taliaferro with Colonel Harrison's splendid regiment, the Thirty-second Georgia, sent over by Beauregard to his assistance as soon as a landing could be effected at Cummings' Point. These troops were ordered to move along on the traverses and bomb-proofs, and to plunge their concentrated fire over the stronghold. Still, for a time, the enemy held out, but at last they cried out and surrendered.

"The carnage was frightful. It is believed the Federals lost more men on that eventful night than twice the entire strength of the Confederate garrison. The Confederates lost eight killed and twenty wounded by the bombardment and about fifty killed and one hundred and fifty wounded altogether from the bombardment and assault. Among the killed were those gallant officers, Lieutenant Colonel Simkins and Major Ramsey and among the wounded Captains DePass and Twiggs, of the staff, and Lieutenants Storey (Aide-de-Camp), Power and Watties. According to the statement of Chaplain Dennison the assaulting columns in two brigades, commanded by General Strong and Colonel Putnam (the division under General Seymour), consisted of the Fifty-fourth Massachusetts, Third and Seventh New Hampshire, Sixth Connecticut and One Hundredth New York, with a reserve brigade commanded by General Stephenson. One of the assaulting regiments was composed of negroes (the Fifty-fourth Massachusetts) and to it was assigned the honor of leading the white columns to the charge. It was a dearly purchased compliment. Their Colonel (Shaw) was killed upon the parapet and the regiment almost annihilated, although the Confederates in the darkness could not tell the color of their assailants. Both the brigade commanders were killed as well as Colonel Chatfield.

"The same account says: 'We lost 55 officers and 585 men, a total of 640, one of the choicest martyr rolls of the war.' By 'lost,' 'killed' is supposed to be meant, but still that number greatly falls short of the number reported by the Confederates to have been buried on the 19th by them and by their own friends under a flag of truce. These reports show that 800 were buried, and as a number were taken prisoners, and it is fair to estimate that three were wounded to one killed, the total loss of the Federals exceeded 3,000. The writer's official report estimates the Federal loss at not less than 2,000; General Beauregard's at 3,000. The Federal official reports have not been seen.

"The limits prescribed for this paper would be exceeded if any account of the remaining forty-eight days of the heroic strife on Morris Island were attempted. It closes with the repulse of the second assault, and it is a fit conclusion to render the homage due to the gallantry of the contestants by quoting and adopting the language of Dr. Dennison's address: 'The truest courage and determination was manifested on both sides on that crimson day at that great slaughter-house, Wagner.'"

It was no longer a question of doubt as to the valor of Northern negroes. The assault on Fort Wagner completely removed any prejudice that had been exhibited toward negro troops in the Department of the South. General Gillmore immediately issued an order forbidding any distinction to be made among troops in his command. So that while the black Phalanx had lost hundreds of its members, it nevertheless won equality in all things save the pay. The Government refused to place them on a footing even with their Southern brothers, who received $7 per month and the white troops $13. However, they were not fighting for pay, as "Stonewall" of Company C argued, but for the "*freedom of our kin.*" Nobly did they do this, not only at Wagner, as we have seen, but in the battles on James Island, Honey Hill, Olustee and at Boykin's Mill.

In the winter of 1864, the troops in the Department of the South lay encamped on the islands in and about Charleston harbor, resting from their endeavors to drive the confederates from their strongholds. The city was five miles away in the distance. Sumter, grim, hoary and in ruins, yet defying the National authority, was silent. General Gillmore was in command of the veteran legions of the 10th Army Corps, aided by a powerful fleet of ironclads and other war vessels. There laid the city of Charleston, for the time having a respite. General Gillmore was giving rest to his troops, before he began again to throw Greek fire into the city and batter the walls of its defences. The shattered ranks of the Phalanx soldiers rested in the midst of thousands of their white comrades-in-arms, to whom they nightly repeated the story of the late terrible struggle. The solemn sentry pacing the ramparts of Fort Wagner night and day, his bayonet glittering in the rays of the sun or in the moonlight, seemed to be guarding the sepulchre of Col. Shaw and those who fell beside him within the walls of that gory fort, and who were buried where they fell. Only those who have lived in such a camp can appreciate the stories of hair-breadth escapes from hand-to-hand fights.

The repose lasted until January, when an important movement took place for the permanent occupation of Florida. The following account, written by the author of this book, was published in "The Journal," of Toledo, O.:

"The twentieth day of February, 1864, was one of the most disastrous to the Federal arms, and to the administration of President Lincoln, in the annals of the war for the union. Through private advice Mr. Lincoln had received information which led him to believe that the people in the State of Florida, a large number of them, at least, were ready and anxious to identify the State with the cause of the Union, and he readily approved of the Federal forces occupying the State, then almost deserted by the rebels. Gen. Gillmore, commanding the Department of the South had a large force before Charleston, S. C., which had been engaged in the capture of Fort Wagner and the bombardment of the city of Charleston, and the reduction of Sumter.

"These objects being accomplished, the army having rested several months, Gen. Gillmore asked for leave to undertake such expeditions within his Department as he might think proper. About the middle of December, 1863, the War Department granted him his request, and immediately he began making preparations for an expedition, collecting transports, commissary stores, drilling troops, etc., etc.

"About the 1st of January, 1864, General Gillmore wrote to the General-in-Chief, Halleck, that he was about to occupy the west bank of St. Johns river, with the view (1st) to open an outlet to cotton, lumber, etc., (2d) to destroy one of the enemy's sources of supplies, (3d) to give the negroes opportunity of enlisting in the army, (4th) to inaugurate measures for the speedy restoration of Florida to the Union.

"In accordance with instructions from President Lincoln received through the assistant Adjutant General, Major J. H. Hay, who would accompany the expedition, on the 5th of February the troops began to embark under the immediate command of General Truman Seymour, on board of twenty steamers and eight schooners, consisting of the following regiments, numbering in all six thousand troops, and under convoy of the gunboat Norwich:

"40th Massachusetts Mounted Infantry, Col. Guy V. Henry.

"7th Connecticut, Col. J. R. Hawley.

"7th New Hampshire, Col. Abbott.

"47th, 48th and 115th New York, Col. Barton's command.

"The Phalanx regiments were: 8th Pennsylvania, Col. Fribley; 1st North Carolina, Lt.-Col. Reed; 54th Massachusetts, Col. Hallowell; 2d South Carolina, Col. Beecher; 55th Massachusetts, Col. Hartwell, with three batteries of white troops, Hamilton's, Elder's and Langdon's. Excepting the two last named regiments, this force landed at Jacksonville on the 7th of February, and pushed on, following the 40th Massachusetts Mounted Infantry, which captured by a bold dash Camp Finnigan, about seven miles from Jacksonville, with its equipage, eight pieces of artillery, and a number of prisoners. On the 10th, the whole force had reached Baldwin. a railroad station twenty miles west of Jacksonville. There the army encamped, except Col. Henry's force, which continued its advance towards Tallahassee, driving a small force of Gen. Finnegan's command before him. This was at the time all the rebel force in east Florida. On the 18th Gen. Seymour, induced by the successful advance of Col. Henry, lead his troops from Baldwin with ten days' rations in their haversacks, and started for the Suwanee river, about a hundred and thirty miles from Baldwin station, leaving the 2d South Carolina and the 55th Massachusetts Phalanx regiments to follow. After a fatiguing march the column, numbering about six thousand, reached Barbour's Station, on the Florida Central Railroad, twenty miles from Baldwin. Here the command halted and bivouaced, the night of the 19th, in the woods bordering upon a wooded ravine running off towards the river from the railroad track.

"It is now nineteen years ago, and I write from memory of a night long to be remembered. Around many a Grand Army Camp-fire in the last fifteen years this bivouac has been made the topic of an evening's talk. It was attended with no particular hardship. The weather was such as is met with in these latitudes, not cold, not hot, and though a thick vapory cloud hid the full round moon from early eventide until the last regiment filed into the woods, yet there was a halo of light that brightened the white, sandy earth and gave to the moss-laden limbs of the huge pines which stood sentry-like on the roadside the appearance of a New England grove on a frosty night, with a shelled road leading through it.

"It was well in the night when the two Phalanx regiments filed out of the road into the woods, bringing up the rear of the army, and took shelter under the trees from the falling dew. Amid the appalling stillness that reigned throughout the encampment, except the tramp of feet and an occasional whickering of a battery horse, no sound broke the deep silence. Commands were given in an undertone and whispered along the long lines of weary troops that lay among the trees and the underbrush of the pine forest. Each soldier lay with his musket beside him, ready to spring to his feet and in line for battle, for none knew the moment the enemy, like a tiger, would pounce upon them. It was a night of intense anxiety, shrouded in mystery as to what to-morrow would bring. The white and black soldier in one common bed lay in battle panoply, dreaming their common dreams of home and loved ones.

"Here lay the heroic 54th picturing to themselves the memorable nights of July 17 and 18, their bivouac on the beach and their capture of Fort Wagner and the terrible fate of their comrades. They were all veteran troops save the 8th Pennsylvania, which upon many hard-fought fields had covered themselves with gallant honor in defense of their country's cause, from Malvern Hill to Morris Island.

It was in the gray of the next morning that Gen. Seymour's order aroused the command. The men partook of a hastily prepared cup of coffee and meat and hard-tack from their haversacks. At sunrise the troops took up the line of march, following the railroad for Lake City. Col. Henry, with the 40th Massachusetts Mounted Infantry and Major Stevens' independent battalion of Massachusetts cavalry, led the column. About half-past one o'clock they reached a point where the country road crossed the railroad, about two miles east of Olustee, and six miles west of Sanderson, a station through which the troops passed about half-bast eleven o'clock. As the head of the column reached the crossing the rebel pickets fired and fell back upon a line of skirmishers, pursued by Col. Henry's command. The enemy's main force was supposed to be some miles distant from this place, consequently General Seymour had not taken the precaution to protect his flanks, though marching through an enemy's country. Consequently he found his troops flanked on either side.

"Col. Henry drove the skirmishers back upon their main forces, which were strongly posted between two swamps. The position was admirably chosen; their right rested upon a low, slight earthwork, protected by rifle-pits, their center was defended by an impassable swamp, and on their left was a cavalry force drawn up on a small elevation behind the shelter of a grove of pines. Their camp was intersected by the railroad, on which was placed a battery capable of operating against the center and left of the advancing column, while a rifie gun, mounted on a railroad flat, pointed down the road in front.

"Gen. Seymour, in order to attack this strongly fortified position, had necessarily to place his troops between the two swamps, one in his front, the other in the rear. The Federal cavalry, following up the skirmishers, had attacked the rebel right and were driven back, but were met by the 7th New Hampshire, 7th Connecticut, a regiment of the black Phalanx (8th Pennsylvania), and Elder's battery of four and Hamilton's of six pieces. This force was hurled against the rebel right with such impetuosity that the batteries were within one hundred yards of the rebel line of battle before they knew it. However, they took position, and supported by the Phalanx regiment, opened a vigorous fire upon the rebel earthworks. The Phalanx regiment advanced within twenty or thirty yards of the enemy's rifle-pits, and poured a volley of minie balls into the very faces of those who did not fly on their approach.

"The 7th Connecticut and the 7th New Hampshire, the latter with their seven-shooters, Spencer repeaters, Col. Hawley, commanding, had taken a stand further to the right of the battery, and were hotly engaging the rebels. The Phalanx regiment (8th), after dealing out two rounds from its advanced position, finding the enemy's force in the center preparing to charge upon them, fell back under cover of Hamilton's battery, which was firing vigorously and effectively into the rebel column. The 7th Connecticut and New Hampshire about this time ran short of ammunition, and Col. Hawley, finding the rebels outnumbered his force three to one, was about ordering Col. Abbott to fall back and out of the concentrated fire of the enemy pouring upon his men, when he observed the rebels coming in for a down upon his column.

"Here they come like tigers; the Federal column wavers a little; it staggers and breaks, falling back in considerable disorder! Col. Hawley now ordered Col. Fribley to take his Phalanx Regiment, the 8th, to the right of the battery and check the advancing rebel force. No time was to be lost, the enemy's sharpshooters had already silenced two of Hamilton's guns, dead and dying men and horses lay in a heap about them, while at the remaining four guns a few brave artillerists were loading and fixing their pieces, retarding the enemy in his onward movement.

"Deficient in artillery, they had not been able to check the Federal cavalry in its dash, but the concentrated fire from right to center demoralized, and sent them galloping over the field wildly. Col. Fribley gave the order by the right flank, double quick! and the next moment the 8th Phalanx swept away to the extreme right in support of the 7th New Hampshire and the 7th Connecticut. The low, direct aim of the enemy in the rifle-pits, his Indian sharp-shooters up in the trees, had ere now so thinned the ranks of Col. Hawley's command that his line was gone, and the 8th Phalanx met the remnant of his brigade as it was going to the rear in complete disorder. The rebels ceased firing and halted as the Phalanx took position between them and their fleeing comrades. They halted not perforce, but apparently for deliberation, when with one fell swoop in the next moment they swept the field in their front.

"The Phalanx did not, however, quit the field in a panic-stricken manner but fell hastily back to the battery, only to find two of the guns silent and their brave workers and horses nearly all of them dead upon the field. With a courage undaunted, surpassed by no veteran troops on any battle-field, the Phalanx attempted to save the silent guns. In this effort Col. Fribley was killed, in the torrent of rebel bullets which fell upon the regiment. It held the two guns, despite two desperate charges made by the enemy to capture them, but the stubbornness of the Phalanx was no match for the ponderous weight of their enemy's column, their sharpshooters and artillery mowing down ranks of their comrades at every volley. A grander spectacle was never witnessed than that which this regiment gave of gallant courage. They left their guns only when their line officers and three hundred and fifty of their valient soldiers were dead upon the field, the work of an hour and a half. The battery lost forty of its horses and four of its brave men. The Phalanx saved the colors of the battery with its own. Col. Barton's brigade, the 47th, 48th and 115th New York, during the fight on the right had held the enemy in the front and center at bay, covering Elder's battery, and nobly did they do their duty, bravely maintaining the reputation they had won before Charleston, but like the other troops, the contest was too unequal. The rebels outnumbered them five to one, and they likewise gave way, leaving about a fourth of their number upon the field, dead and wounded.

"Col. Montgomery's brigade, comprising two Phalanx regiments, 54th Massachusetts and 1st North Carolina, which had been held in reserve about a mile down the road, now came up at double-quick. They were under heavy marching orders, with ten days' rations in their knapsacks, besides their cartridge boxes they carried ten rounds in their overcoat pockets. The road was sandy, and the men often found their feet beneath the sand, but with their wonted alacrity they speed on up the road, the 54th leading in almost a locked running step, followed closely by the 1st North Carolina. As they reached the road intersected by the railroad they halted in the rear of what remained of Hamilton's battery, loading a parting shot. The band of the 54th took position on the side of the road, and while the regiments were unstringing knapsacks as coolly as if about to bivouac, the music of the band burst out on the sulphureous air, amid the roar of artillery, the rattle of musketry and the shouts of commands, mingling its soul-stirring strains with the deafening yells of the charging columns, right, left, and from the rebel center. Thus on the very edge of the battle, nay, in the battle, the Phalanx band poured out in heroic measures 'The Star Spangled Banner.' Its thrilling notes, souring above the battles' gales, aroused to new life and renewed energy the panting, routed troops, flying in broken and disordered ranks from the field. Many of them halted, the New York troops particularly, and gathered at the battery again, pouring a deadly volley into the enemy's works and ranks. The 54th had but a moment to prepare for the task. General Seymour rode up and appealed to the Phalanx to check the enemy and save the army from complete and total annihilation. Col. Montgomery gave Col. Hallowell the order 'Forward,' pointing to the left, and away went the 54th Phalanx regiment through the woods, down into the swamp, wading up to their knees—in places where the water reached their hips; yet on they went till they reached terra firma. Soon the regiment stood in line of battle, ready to meet the enemy's advancing cavalry, emerging from the extreme left.

"'Hold your fire!' the order ran down the line. Indeed, it was trying. The cavalry had halted but the enemy, in their rifle-pits in the center of their line, poured volley after volley into the ranks of the Phalanx, which it stood like a wall of granite, holding at bay the rebel cavalry hanging on the edge of a pine grove. The 1st Phalanx regiment entered the field in front, charged the rebels in the centre of the line, driving them into their rifle-pits, and then for half an hour the carnage became frightful. They had followed the rebels into the very jaws of death, and now Col. Reid found his regiment in the enemy's enfilading fire, and they swept his line. Men fell like snowflakes. Driven by this terrific fire, they fell back. The 54th had taken ground to the right, lending whatever of assistance they could to their retiring comrades, who were about on a line with them, for although retreating, it was in the most cool and deliberate manner, and the two regiments began a firing at will against which the rebels, though outnumbering them, could not face. Thus they held them till long after sunset, and firing ceased.

"The slaughter was terrible; the Phalanx lost about 800 men, the white troops about 600. It was Braddock's defeat after the lapse of a century."

The rout was complete; the army was not only defeated but beaten and demoralized. The enemy had succeeded in drawing it into a trap for the purpose of annihilating it. Seymour had advanced, contrary to the orders given him by General Gillmore, from Baldwin's Station, where he was instructed to intrench and await orders. Whether or not he sought to retrieve the misfortunes that had attended him in South Carolina, in assaulting the enemy's works, is a question which need not be discussed here. It is only necessary to show the miserable mismanagement of the advance into the enemy's country. The troops were marched into an ambuscade, where they were slaughtered by the enemy at will. Even after finding his troops ambuscaded, and within two hundred yards of the confederate fortifications, General Seymour did not attempt to fall back and form a line of battle, though he had sufficient artillery, but rushed brigade after brigade up to the enemy's guns, only to be mowed down by the withering storm of shot. Each brigade in turn went in as spirited as any troops ever entered a fight, but stampeded out of it maimed, mangled and routed. At sunset the road, foot-paths and woods leading back to Saunders' Station, was full of brave soldiers hastening from the massacre of their comrades, in their endeavor to escape capture. At about nine o'clock that night, what remained of the left column, Colonel Montgomery's brigade, consisting of the 54th and 35th Phalanx Regiments, and a bat-

CHARGE OF THE PHALANX.

tery, arrived at the Station, and reported the confederates in hot pursuit. Instantly the shattered, scattered troops fled to the roads leading to Barber's, ten miles away, with no one to command. Each man took his own route for Barber's, leaving behind whatever would encumber him,—arms, ammunition, knapsacks and cartridge boxes; many of the latter containing forty rounds of cartridges. It was long past midnight when Barber's was reached, and full day before the frightened mob arrived at the Station. At sunrise on the morning of the 21st, the scene presented at Barber's was sickening and sad. The wounded lay everywhere, upon the ground, huddled around the embers of fagot fires, groaning and uttering cries of distress. The surgeons were busy relieving, as best they could, the more dangerously wounded. The foot-sore and hungry soldiers sought out their bleeding and injured comrades and placed them upon railroad flats, standing upon the tracks, and when these were loaded, ropes and strong vines were procured and fastened to the flats. Putting themselves in the place of a locomotive,—several of which stood upon the track at Jacksonville,—the mangled and mutilated forms of about three hundred soldiers were dragged forward mile after mile. Just in the rear, the confederates kept up a fire of musketry, as though to hasten on the stampede. It was well into the night when the train reached Baldwin's, where it was thought the routed force would occupy the extensive work encircling the station, but they did not stop; their race was continued to Jacksonville. At Baldwin's an agent of the Christian Commission gave the wounded each two crackers, without water. This over with, the train started for Jacksonville, ten miles further. The camp of Colonel Beecher's command, 2nd Phalanx Regiment, was reached, and here coffee was furnished. At daylight the train reached Jacksonville, where the wounded were carried to the churches and cared for. The battle and the retreat had destroyed every vestige of distinction based upon color. The troops during the battle had fought together, as during the stampede they had endured its horrors together.

The news of the battle and defeat reached Beaufort the night of the 23rd of February. It was so surprising that it was doubted, but when a boat load of wounded men arrived, all doubts were dispelled.

Colonel T. W. Higginson, who was at Beaufort at the time with his regiment, (1st S. C.), thus notes the reception of the news in his diary, which we quote with a few comments from his admirable book, "Army Life in a Black Regiment":

"'FEBRUARY, 19TH.

"'Not a bit of it! This morning the General has ridden up radiant, has seen General Gillmore, who has decided not to order us to Florida at all, nor withdraw any of this garrison. Moreover, he says that all which is intended in Florida is done—that there will be no advance to Tallahassee, and General Seymour will establish a camp of instruction in Jacksonville. Well, if that is all, it is a lucky escape.'

"We little dreamed that on that very day the march toward Olustee was beginning. The battle took place next day, and I add one more extract to show how the news reached Beaufort.

"'FEBRUARY 23, 1864.

"'There was a sound of revelry by night at a ball in Beaufort last night, in a new large building beautifully decorated. All the collected flags of the garrison hung round and over us, as if the stars and stripes were devised for an ornament alone. The array of uniforms was such, that a civilian became a distinguished object, much more a lady. All would have gone according to the proverbial marriage bell, I suppose, had there not been a slight palpable shadow over all of us from hearing vague stories of a lost battle in Florida, and from the thought that perhaps the very ambulances in which we rode to the ball were ours only until the wounded or the dead might tenant them.

"'General Gillmore only came, I supposed, to put a good face upon the matter. He went away soon, and General Saxton went; then came a rumor that the Cosmopolitan had actually arrived with wounded, but still the dance went on. There was nothing unfeeling about it—one gets used to things,—when suddenly, in the midst of the 'Lancers,' there came a perfect hush, the music ceasing, a few surgeons went hastily to and fro, as if conscience stricken (I should think they might have been),—and then there 'waved a mighty shadow in,' as in Uhland's 'Black Knight,' and as we all stood wondering we were aware of General Saxton who strode hastily down the hall, his pale face very resolute, and looking almost sick with anxiety. He had just been on board the steamer; there were two hundred and fifty wounded men just arrived, and the ball must end. Not that there was anything for us to do, but the revel was mis-timed, and must be ended; it was wicked to be dancing with such a scene of suffering near by.

PHALANX RIVER PICKETS DEFENDING THEMSELVES.

Federal picket boat near Fernandina, Fla., attacked by Confederate sharpshooters stationed in the trees on the banks.

"'Of course the ball was instantly broken up, though with some murmurings and some longings of appetite, on the part of some, toward the wasted supper.

"'Later, I went on board the boat. Among the long lines of wounded, black and white intermingled, there was the wonderful quiet which usually prevails on such occasions. Not a sob nor a groan, except from those undergoing removal. It is not self-control, but chiefly the shock to the system produced by severe wounds, especially gunshot wounds, and which usually keeps the patient stiller at first than at any later time.

"'A company from my regiment waited on the wharf, in their accustomed dusky silence, and I longed to ask them what they thought of our Florida disappointment now? In view of what they saw, did they still wish we had been there? I confess that in presence of all that human suffering, I could not wish it. But I would not have suggested any such thought to them.

"'I found our kind-hearted ladies, Mrs. Chamberlin and Mrs. Dewhurst, on board the steamer, but there was nothing f r them to do, and we walked back to camp in the radiant moonlight; Mrs. Chamberlin more than ever strengthened in her blushing woman's philosophy, 'I don't care who wins the laurels, provided we don't!'

"'FEBRUARY 29TH.

"'But for a few trivial cases of varioloid, we should certainly have been in that disastrous fight. We were confidently expected for several days at Jacksonville, and the commanding general told Hallowell that we, being the oldest colored regiment, would have the right of the line. This was certainly to miss danger and glory very closely.'"

At daybreak on the 8th of March, 1864, the 7th Regiment, having left Camp Stanton, Maryland, on the 4th and proceeded to Portsmouth, Va., embarked on board the steamer "Webster" for the Department of the South. Arriving at Hilton Head, the regiment went into camp for a few days, then it embarked for Jacksonville, Fla., at which place it remained for some time, taking part in several movements into the surrounding country and participating in a number of quite lively skirmishes. On the 27th of June a considerable portion of the Regiment was ordered to Hilton Head, where it arrived on July 1st; it went from there to James Island, where with other troops a short engagement with the confederates was had. Afterwards the regiment returned to Jacksonville, Fla., remaining in that vicinity engaged in raiding the adjacent territory until the 4th of August, when the regiment was ordered to Virginia, to report to the Army of the Potomoc, where it arrived on Aug. 8th. The 55th Massachusetts Regiment was also ordered to the Department of the South. It left Boston July 21st, 1863, on the steamer "Cahawba," and arrived at Newbern on the 25th. After a few days of rest, to recover from the effects of the voyage, the regiment was put into active service, and performed a large amount of marching and of the arduous duties required of a soldier. Many skirmishes and actions of more or less importance were participated in. February 13th, 1864, the regiment took a steamer for Jacksonville, Fla, and spent considerable time in that section and at various points on the St. Johns river. In June the regiment was ordered to the vicinity of Charleston, and took part in several of the engagements which occurred in that neighborhood, always sustaining and adding to the reputation they were acquiring for bravery and good soldierly conduct. The regiment passed its entire time of active service in the department to which it was first sent, and returned to Boston, Mass., where it was mustered out, amid great rejoicing, on the 23rd of September, 1865.

The battles in which the 54th Regiment were engaged were some of the most sanguinary of the war. The last fight of the regiment, which, like the battle of New Orleans, took place after peace was declared, is thus described by the Drummer Boy of Company C, Henry A. Monroe, of New Bedford, Mass.:

BOYKIN'S MILL.

"One wailing bugle note,—
Then at the break of day,
With Martial step and gay,
The army takes its way
From Camden town.

There lay along the path,
Defending native land;
A daring, desperate band
Entrenched on either hand
In ambuscade.

A low and dark ravine
Beneath a rugged hill,
Where stood the Boykin Mill
Spanning the creek, whose rill
Flows dark and deep.

Only a narrow bank
Where one can scarcely tread;
Thick branches meet o'erhead;
Across the mill-pond's bed
A bridge up-torn.

* NOTE.—Boykin's Mill, a few miles from Camden, S. C., was the scene of one of the bloodiest skirmishes that the 54th Regt. ever participated in. We had literally fought every step of the way from Georgetown to Camden, and the enemy made a last desperate stand at this place. No better position could be found for a defense, as the only approach to it, was by a narrow embankment about 200 yards long, where only one could walk at a time. The planks of the bridge over the mill-race were torn up, compelling the troops to cross on the timbers and cross-ties, under a galling fire which swept the bridge and embankment, rendering it a fearful 'way of death.' The heroes of Wagner and Olustee did not shrink from the trial, but actually charged in single file. The first to step upon the fatal path, went down like grass before the scythe, but over their prostrate bodies came their comrades, until the enemy, panic-stricken by such determined daring, abandoned their position and fled.

One single sharp report!
A hundred muskets peal,—
A wild triumphant yell,
As back the army fell
Stunned, bleeding, faint.

As when some mighty rock
Obstructs the torrent's course,
After the moment's pause
Twill rush with greater force
Resistless on.

A moment's pause and then,
Our leader from his post,
Viewing the stricken host,
Cried 'Comrades, all is lost
If we now fail!'

Forming in single file,
They gaze with bated breath,
Around—before—beneath—
On every hand, stern Death
His visage showed.

'Forward!' They quickly spring
With leveled bayonet;
Each eye is firmly set
Upon that pathway wet
With crimson gore.

That 'Balaklava' dash!
Right through the leaden hail,
O'er dyke and timbers frail,
With hearts that never fail
They boldly charge.

Facing the scathing fire
Without a halt or break;
Save when with moan or shriek,
In the blood-mingled creek
The wounded fall.

What could resist that charge?
Above the battle's roar,
There swells a deafening cheer
Telling to far and near,
The Mill is won!

The slaughter was terrible, and among the killed was young Lieutenant Stevenson, a graduate of Harvard. The affair was an unnecessary sacrifice of human life, for the war was over, peace had been declared, and President Lincoln had been assassinated; but in the interior of the Carolinas, the news did not reach until it was too late to prevent this final bloodshed of the war. Perhaps it may be regarded as a fitting seal of the negro to his new covenant with freedom and his country.

The very large number of negro troops which General Gillmore had under his command in the Department of the South, afforded him a better opportunity to test their fitness for and quality as soldiers, than any other commander had. In fact the artillery operations in Charleston harbor, conducted throughout with remarkable engineering skill, perseverence and bravery, won for General Gillmore and his troops the attention and admiration of the civilized world, and an exceptional place in the annals of military siege. Such fame is sufficient to prompt an inquiry into the capacity of the men who performed the labor of planting the "Swamp Angel," which threw three hundred pound shot into the heart of Charleston, more than four miles away, and also mounted the six 200-pound cannons which demolished the forts in the harbor two miles distant. The work of mounting these immense guns in swamp and mud could only be done by men who feared neither fatigue, suffering nor death. After the accomplishment of these worlds, wonders, and the subjugation of "arrogant" Wagner, the following circular was addressed to the subordinate engineers for information regarding the negro troops, which drew forth explicit and interesting answers:

"COLORED TROOPS FOR WORK.—CIRCULAR.

"HEADQUARTERS DEPARTMENT OF THE SOUTH,
"ENGINEER'S OFFICE, MORRIS' ISLAND, S. C., Sept. 10th, 1863.

"As the important experiment which will test the fitness of the American negro for the duties of a soldier is now being tried, it is desirable that facts bearing on the question be carefully observed and recorded.

"It is probable that in no military operations of the war have negro troops done so large a proportion, and so important and hazardous, fatigue duty, as in the siege operations on this island.

"As you have directed the operations of working parties of both white and black troops here, I respectfully ask, for the object above stated, an impartial and carefully prepared answer to the following inquiries, together with such statements as you choose to make bearing on this question:

"I. Courage as indicated by their behavior under fire.

"II. Skill and appreciation of their duties, referring to the quality of the work performed.

"III. Industry and perseverence, with reference, to the quantity of the work performed.

"IV. If a certain work were to be accomplished in the least possible time, *i. e.*, when enthusiasm and direct personal interest is necessary to attain the end, would whites or blacks answer best?

"V. What is the difference, considering the above points between colored troops recruited from the free States and those from the slave States?

Very respectfully your obedient servant,
"T. B. BROOKS,
Major, Aide-de-Camp and Ass't Engineer."

Six replies to these enquiries were received from engineer officers who had been engaged in the siege, the substance of which is embraced in the following summary, following which two replies are given in full,

"1. To the first question all answer that the black is more timorous than the white, but is in a corresponding degree more docile and obedient, hence more completely under the control of his commander, and much more infiuenced by his example.

"2. All agree that the black is less skillful than the white soldier, but still enough so for most kinds of siege work.

"3. The statements unanimously agree that the black will do a greater amount of work than the white soldier because he labors more constantly.

"4. The whites are decidedly superior in enthusiasm. The blacks cannot be easily hurried in their work, no matter what the emergency.

"5. All agree that the colored troops recruited from free States are superior to those recruited from slave States.

"It may with propriety be repeated here, that the average percentage of sick among the negro troops during the siege was 13.9, while that of the white infantry was 20.1 per cent.

"The percentage of tours of duty performed by the blacks as compared with the white infantry, was as 56 to 41. But the grand guard duty, which was considered much more wearing than fatigue, was all done by the whites.

"The efficiency and health of a battalion depenas so much upon its officers, that, in order to institute a fair comparison, when so small a number of troops are considered, this element should be eliminated. This has not, however, been attempted in this paper."

[*Reply in Full No. 1.*]

"MORRIS ISLAND, S. C., Sept. 11th, 1863.

"MAJOR:—In answer to your several queries as per circular of September 10, 1863, requesting my opinion as to the relative merits of white and black troops, for work in the trenches, I have the honor to make the the following replies:

"I. 'Their courage as indicated by their behavior under fire.' I will say, in my opinion, their courage is rather of the passive than the active kind. They will stay, endure, resist, and follow, but they have not the restless, aggressive spirit. I do not believe they will desert their officers in trying moments, in so great numbers as the whites; they have not the will, audacity or fertility of excuse of the straggling white, and at the same time they have not the heroic, nervous energy, or vivid perception of the white, who stands firm or presses forward.

"I do not remember a single instance, in my labors in the trenches, where the black man has skulked away from his duty, and I know that instances of that kind have occurred among the whites; still I think that the superior energy and intelligence of those remaining, considering that the whites were the lesser number by the greater desertion, would more than compensate.

"II. 'Skill and appreciation of their duties referring to the quality of the work.'

"They have a fair share of both; enough to make them very useful and efficient, but they have not apparently that superior intelligence and skill that may be found largely among the non-commissioned officers and privates of the white regiments.

"III. 'Industry and perseverence with reference to the quantity of the work done.'

"I think they will do more than the whites; they do not have so many complaints and excuses, but stick to their work patiently, doggedly, obediently, and accomplish a great deal, though I have never known them to work with any marked spirit or energy. I should liken the white man to the horse (often untractable and balky), the black man to the ox.

"IV. 'If a certain work were to be accomplished in the least possible time, *i. e.*, when enthusiasm and direct personal interest is necessary to attain the end, would whites or blacks answer best?'

"I cannot make up my mind that it is impossible to arouse the enthusiasm of the blacks, for I have seen enough of them to know that they are very emotional creatures; still though they might have more dash than I have seen and think possible, it is unquestionable to my mind that were the enthusiasm and personal interest of both aroused, the white would far surpass the black.

"It seems to me that there is a hard nervous organization at the bottom of the character of the white, and a soft susceptible one at the bottom of the character of the black.

"V. 'What is the difference, considering the above points, between colored troops recruited from the free States and those from the slave States?'

"I should say that the free State men were the best; they have more of the self-reliance, and approximate nearer to the qualities of the white man in respect to dash and energy, than those from the slave States.

"*Summary.*—To me they compare favorably with the whites; they are easily handled, true and obedient; there is less viciousness among them; they are more patient; they have great constancy. The character of the white, as you know, runs to extremes; one has bull-dog courage, another is a pitiful cur; one is excessively vicious, another pure and noble. The phases of the character of the white touches the stars and descends to the lowest depths. The blacks character occupies the inner circle. Their status is mediocrity, and this mediocrity and uniformity, for military fatigue duty, I think, answers best.

"I am respectfully your obedient servant,

"JOSEPH WALKER.

"*Captain New York Voluneeer Engineers.*

"Major T. B. BROOKS,

" *Aide-de-Camp and Ass't. Eng. Dept. of the South.*"

[*Reply in Full No. 2.*]

"MORRIS ISLAND, Sept. 16th, 1863.

"Major T. B. BROOKS, *Ass't. Engineer Dept. of the South.*

"SIR: I have the honor to state that I received from you a circular of inquiry respecting the comparative merits of white and black soldiers for fatigue duty, requesting my opinion as derived from observation and actual intercourse with them, on several specified points, which I subjoin with the respective answers.

"I. 'Courage as indicated by conduct under fire.'

"I have found that the black troops manifest more timidity under fire than the white troops, but they are at the same time more obedient to orders, and more under control of their officers, in dangerous situations, than white soldiers.

"II. 'Skill and appreciation of their duties with reference to the quality of the work performed.'

"White soldiers are more intelligent and experienced and of course more skillful than the black ones, but they have not generally a corresponding appreciation of their duties. As a consequence I have found in most cases the work as well done by black as by white soldiers.

"III. 'Industry and perseverence with reference to the amount of work performed.'

"White soldiers work with more energy while they do work than the black ones, but do not work as constantly. Black soldiers seldom intermit their labors except by orders or permission. The result, as far as my observations extends, is that a greater amount of work is usually accomplished with black than with white soldiers.

"IV. 'If a certain work were to be accomplished in the least possible time, when enthusiasm and direct personal interest is necessary to the attainment of the end, would whites or blacks answer best?'

"Whites. Because though requiring more effort to control, they possess a greater energy of character and susceptibility of enthusiasm than the black race, which can be called into action by an emergency or by a sufficient effort on the part of their officers.

"V. 'What is the difference, considering the above points, between colored troops recruited from the free States and those from the slave States?'

"I have observed a decided difference in favor of those recruited from the free States.

"The problem involved in the foregoing investigation is more difficult of a solution than appears at first sight, owing to the fact that the degree of efficiency peculiar to any company of troops depends so much on the character of their officers, an element that must eliminate from the question in order to ascertain the quality of the material of which the troops are composed.

"I have the honor to be your obedient servant,

"H. FARRAND,

"*1st Lieut. New York Volunteer Engineers.*"

In his report to Major-General Gillmore, dated "Morris Island, Sept. 27th, 1863," Major Brooks, his Assistant Engineer, says: "Of the numerous infantry regiments which furnished fatigue details, the Fourth New Hampshire Volunteers did the most and best work. Next follow the blacks, the Fifty-fourth Massachusetts Volunteers, and Third United States Colored Troops."

Annexed to these reports is also a statement of the labor days of the troops.

"WORKING PARTIES AND HEALTH OF TROOPS.

'The total number of days' work, of six hours each, expended in Major Brooks' operations was, by engineers, 4.500, and by infantry 19,000, total 23,500; of the 19,000 days' work by infantry, one-half was performed by colored troops. In addition to the above, 9,500 days' work was expended in preparing siege materials for Major Brooks' oper ations. The infantry soldiers' days' work is about one-fifth what a citizen laborer would do on civil works. Of my work, over eight-twentieths was against Wagner, about seven-twentieths on the defensive lines, and nearly five-twentieths on the batteries against Sumter.

"The approximate amount of labor actually expended on the more important works is as follows: One emplacement for a siege piece, 40 days; one emplacement for a heavy breaching gun, 100 days; one bomb-proof magazine, 250 days; construction and repairs of each yard of approach having splinter-proof parapet, 2 days; a lineal yard of narrow splinter-proof shelter, 4 days; a lineal yard of wide splinter-proof shelter, 8 days; to make and set one yard of inclined palisading, 2 days.

"At least three-fourths of the manual labor was simply shoveling sand; one-half of the remainder was carrying engineer material. The balance was employed in various kinds of work.

"About three-fourths of this work was executed in the night-time, and at least nine-tenths of it under a fire of artillery or sharpshooters, or both. The sharp-shooters seldom fired during the night. The artillery fire was most severe during the day. Thrity-five projectiles fired by the enemy at our works per hour was called "heavy firing," although sometimes more than double that number were thrown.

"In the order of their number the projectiles were from smooth-bore guns, mortars, and rifled guns.

"The James Island batteries were from two thousand to four thousand yards from our works; Fort Sumter and Battery Gregg were respectively about three thousand five hundred and two thousand one hundred; Fort Wagner was from thirteen hundred to one hundred yards.

"The total number of casualties in the working parties and the guard of the advanced trenches, (not including the main guard of the trenches), during the siege, was about one hundred and fifty. When it is considered that on an average over two hundred men were constantly engaged in these duties, being under fire for fifty days, the number of casualties is astonishingly small.

"The camp at which the fatigue parties were quartered and fed were, in order to be beyond the reach of the enemy's fires, two miles from the centre of the works; hence the distance of four miles had to be marched each tour of duty, which required nearly two hours, and added greatly to the labor of the siege.

"This siege has been conducted through the hottest part of the season,—July, August and September,—yet the troops have suffered but little from excess in heat, on account of the large proportion of night work, and the almost continual sea-breeze, which was always cool and refreshing.

"The amount of sickness was great, the large amount of duty being the probable cause. On the 7th of August the percentage was the smallest observed during the siege, being 18.6. At this date the aggregate garrison of Morris Island was 9,353, of which 1,741 were sick. On the 17th of August 22.9 per cent. of the whole garrison were on the sick list. This was the most unhealthy period of the siege.

"The average strength of the command on Morris Island during the siege was, of all arms, 10,678 men, of which the average percentage sick was 19.88. The number of black troops varied from 1,127 to 1947.

"Average percentage of sick in Artillery, 6.2; ditto, in Engineers, 11.9; ditto, in Black Infantry, 13.9; ditto, in White Infantry, (excluding one brigade), 20.1.

"This brigade consisted of the Ninety-seventh Pennsylvania, Twenty-fourth Massachusetts and Tenth Connecticut Volunteers. It averaged thirty per cent sick. This was due to the fact that these three regiments had been stationed, before moving to Morris Island, on Seabrook Island, which proved very unhealthy. The engineers and black infantry were employed exclusively on fatigue duty. The white infantry served as guard of the trenches, as well as for work in the same.

"Details from the troops on Folly Island took part in the operations on Morris Island.

"It was found by experience that men under these circumstances could not work more than one-fourth the time. A greater amount at once increased the sick list. Eight hours in thirty-two, or eight hours on and twenty-four off, was found to be the best arrangement, as it made a daily change in the hours of duty for those regiments permanently detailed for work.

"The organization found most advantageous in working a command permanently detailed for fatigue duty, was to divide its effective force into four equal detachments, on duty eight hours each, relieving each other at 4 A. M., 12 M. and 8 P. M. The large number of extra troops employed in the trenches each night were usually changed daily.

"The engineer officers in charge of the works were divided into corresponding groups, four in each, relieving each other at 8 A. M., 4 P. M., and 12 midnight, four hours different from the time of relieving the troops. This difference enabled the engineer officers to carry the work through the period of relieving the fatigue details.

"One engineer officer, having from two to four different kinds or jobs of work to superintend, was found to work advantageously in the night, with the help of non-commissioned officers of engineers, from one hundred to two hundred men.

"The working parties of engineers and black infantry seldom carried their arms into the trenches, while the white infantry fatigue parties usually did."

CHAPTER VIII.

THE ARMY OF THE CUMBERLAND.

Important services were rendered by the Phalanx in the West. The operations in Missouri, Tennessee and Kentucky, afforded an excellent opportunity to the commanders of the Union forces to raise negro troops in such portions of the territory as they held; but in consequence of the bitterness against such action by the semi-Unionists and Copperheads in the Department of the Ohio and Cumberland, it was not until the fall of 1863 that the organizing of such troops in these Departments fairly began. The Mississippi was well-nigh guarded by Phalanx regiments enlisted along that river, numbering about fifty thousand men. They garrisoned the fortifications, and occupied the captured towns. Later on, however, when the confederate General Bragg began preparations for the recovery of the Tennessee Valley, organization of the Phalanx commenced in earnest, and proceeded with a rapidity that astounded even those who were favorable to the policy. St. Louis became a depot and Benton Barracks a recruiting station, from whence, in the fall of 1863, went many a regiment of brave black men, whose chivalrous deeds will ever live in the annals of the nation. It was not long after this time that the noble Army of the Cumberland began to receive a portion of the black troops, whose shouts rang through the mountain fastnesses. The record made by the 60th Regiment is the boast of the State of Iowa, to which it was accredited: but of those which went to the assistance of General Thomas' army none won greater distinction and honor than the gallant brigade com-

CHANGED CONDITIONS.
The Confederate Generals Edward Johnson and G. H. Stewart, as prisoners, under guard of Phalanx Soldiers, May 12th, 1864.

manded by Colonel T. J. Morgan, afterwards raised to Brigadier-General. The gallant 14th Infantry was one of its regiments, the field officers of which were Colonel, Thomas J. Morgan, who had been promoted through various grades, from a 1st Lieutenancy in the 70th Indiana Volunteer Infantry; Lieutenant-Colonel, H. C. Corbin, who had risen from a 1st Lieutenancy of the 79th O. V. I., and Major N. J. Vail, who had served as an enlisted man in the 19th Illinois Volunteers. All the officers passed a rigid examination before the board of examiners appointed by the War Department for that purpose.

General Morgan, by request furnishes the following highly interesting and historical statement of his services with the Phalanx Brigade:

"The American Civil War of 1861-5 marks an epoch not only in the history of the United States, but in that of democracy, and of civilization. Its issue has vitally affected the course of human progress. To the student of history it ranks along with the conquests of Alexander; the incursions of the Barbarians; the Crusades; the discovery of America and the American Revolution. It settled the question of our National unity with all the consequences attaching thereto. It exhibited in a very striking manner the power of a free people to preserve their form of government against its most dangerous foe, Civil War. It not only enfranchised four millions of American slaves of African descent, but made slavery forever impossible in the great Republic, and gave a new impulse to the cause of human freedom. Its influence upon American slaves was immediate and startlingly revolutionary, lifting them from the condition of despised chattels, bought and sold like sheep in the market, with no rights which the white man was bound to respect,—to the exalted plane of American citizenship; made them free men, the peers in every civil and political right, of their late masters. Within about a decade after the close of the war, negroes, lately slaves, were legislators, state officers, members of Congress, and for a brief time one presided over the Senate of the United States, where only a few years before, Toombs had boasted that he would yet call the roll of his slaves in the shade of Bunker Hill.

"To-day slavery finds no advocate, and the colored race in America is making steady progress in all the elements of civilization. The conduct of the American slave during, and since the war, has wrought an extraordinary change in public sentiment, regarding the capabilities of the race.

"The manly qualities of the negro soldiers, evinced in camp, on the march and in battle, won for them golden opinions, made their freedom a necessity and their citizenship a certainty.

"Those of us who assisted in organizing, disciplining and leading negro troops in battle, may, perhaps, be pardoned for feeling a good degree of pride in our share of the thrilling events of the great war.

"When Sumter was fired upon, April, 1861, I was 21; a member of the Senior Class in Franklin College, Indiana. I enlisted in the 7th Indiana Volunteer infantry and served as a private soldier for three months in West Virginia, under Gen. McClellan,—'the young Napoleon,' as he was even then known. I participated in the battle of Carricks Ford, where Gen. Garnett was killed and his army defeated. In August 1862, I re-enlisted as a First Lieutenant in the 70th Indiana, (Col. Benjamin Harrison) and saw service in Kentucky and Tennessee.

"In January 1863, Abraham Lincoln issued the Proclamation of Emancipation, and incorporated in it the policy of arming the negro for special service in the Union army. Thus the question was fairly up, and I entered into its discussion with the deepest interest, as I saw that upon its settlement hung great issues.

"On the one hand the opponents of the policy maintained that to make soldiers of the negroes would be to put them on the same level with white soldiers, and so be an insult to every man who wore the blue. It was contended, too, that the negro was not fit for a soldier because he belonged to a degraded, inferior race, wanting in soldierly qualities; that his long bondage had crushed out whatever of manliness he might natuarally possess; that he was too grossly ignorant to perform, intelligently, the duties of the soldier; that his provocation had been so great as a slave, that when once armed, and conscious of his power as a soldier, he would abuse it by acts of revenge and wanton cruelty.

"It was urged, on the other hand, that in its fearful struggle for existence, the Republic needed the help of the able-bodied negroes; that with their natural instincts of self-preservation, desire for liberty, habit of obedience, power of imitation, love of pomp and parade, acquaintance with the southern country and adaptation to its climate, they had elements which peculiarly fitted them for soldiers. It was further urged that the negro had more at stake than the white man, and that he should have a chance to strike a blow for himself. It was particularly insisted upon that he needed just the opportunity which army service afforded to develop and exhibit whatever of manliness he possessed. As the war progressed, and each great battle-field was piled with heaps of the killed and wounded of our best citizens, men looked at each other seriously, and asked if a black man would not stop a bullet as well as a white man? Miles O'Reilly at length voiced a popular sentiment when he said,

"'The right to be killed I'll divide with the nayger,
And give him the largest half.'

"With the strong conviction that the negro was a man worthy of freedom, and possessed of all the essential qualities of a good soldier, I early advocated the organization of colored regiments,—not for fatigue or garrison duty, but for field service.

"In October, 1863, having applied for a position as an officer in the colored service, I was ordered before the Board of Examiners at Nashville, Tennessee, where I spent five rather anxious hours. When I entered the army I knew absolutely nothing of the details of army life; had never even drilled with a fire company. During the first three months I gathered little except a somewhat rough miscellaneous experience. As a lieutenant and staff officer I learned something, but as I had never had at any time systematic instruction from any one, I appeared before the Board with little else than vigorous health, a college education, a little experience as a soldier, a good reputation as an officer, a fair amount of common sense and a good supply of zeal. The Board averaged me, and recommended me for a Major.

"A few days after the examination, I received an order to report to Major George L. Stearns, who had charge of the organization of colored troops in that Department. He assigned me to duty temporarily in a camp in Nashville. Major Stearns was a merchant in Boston, who had been for years an ardent abolitionist, and who, among other good deeds, had befriended John Brown. He was a large-hearted, broad-minded genial gentleman. When the policy of organizing colored troops was adopted, he offered his services to the Government, received an appointment as Assistant Adjutant General, and was ordered to Nashville to organize colored regiments. He acted directly under the Secretary of War, and independently of the Department Commander. To his zeal, good judgment and efficient labor, was due, very largely, the success of the work in the West.

"November 1st, 1863, by order of Major Stearns, I went to Gallatin, Tennessee, to organize the 14th United States Colored Infantry. General E. A. Paine was then in command of the post at Gallatin, having under him a small detachment of white troops. There were at that time several hundred negro men in camp, in charge of, I think, a lieutenant. They were a motley crowd,—old, young, middle aged. Some wore the United States uniform, but most of them had on the clothes in which they had left the plantations, or had worn during periods of hard service as laborers in the army. Gallatin at that time was threatened with an attack by the guerilla bands then prowling over that part of the State. General Paine had issued a hundred old muskets and rifles to the negroes in camp. They had not passed a medical examination, had no company organization and had had no drill. Almost immediately upon my arrival, as an attack was imminent, I was ordered to distribute another hundred muskets, and to 'prepare every available man for fight.' I did the best I could under the circumstances, but am free to say that I regard it as a fortunate circumstance that we had no fighting to do at that time. But the men raw, and, untutored as they were, did guard and picket duty, went foraging, guarded wagon trains, scouted after guerillas, and so learned to soldier—by soldiering.

"As soon and as fast as practicable, I set about organizing the regiment. I was a complete novice in that kind of work, and all the young officers who reported to me for duty, had been promoted from the ranks and were without experience, except as soldiers. The colored men knew nothing of the duties of a soldier, except a little they had picked up as camp-followers.

"Fortunately there was one man, Mr. A. H. Dunlap, who had had some clerical experience with Col. Birney, in Baltimore, in organizing the 3rd U. S. Colored Infantry. He was an intelligent, methodical gentleman, and rendered me invaluable service. I had no Quartermaster; no Surgeon; no Adjutant. We had no tents, and the men were sheltered in an old filthy tobacco warehouse, where they fiddled, danced, sang, swore or prayed, according to their mood.

"How to meet the daily demands made upon us for military duty, and at the same time to evoke order out of this chaos, was no easy problem. The first thing to be done was to examine the men. A room was prepared, and I and my clerk took our stations at a table. One by one the recruits came before us *a la Eden*, *sans* the fig leaves, and were subjected to a careful medical examination, those who were in any way physically disqualified being rejected. Many bore the wounds and bruises of the slave-driver's lash, and many were unfit for duty by reason of some form of disease to which human flesh is heir. In the course of a few weeks, however, we had a thousand able-bodied, stalwart men.

"I was quite as solicitous about their mental condition as about their physical status, so I plied them with questions as to their history, their experience with the army, their motives for becoming soldiers, their ideas of army life, their hopes for the future, &c., &c. I found that a considerable number of them had been teamsters, cooks, officers' servants, &c., and had thus seen a good deal of hard service in both armies, in camp, on the march and in battle, and so knew pretty well what to expect. In this respect they had the advantage of most raw recruits from the North, who were wholly 'unusued to wars' alarms.' Some of them had very noble ideas of manliness. I remember picturing to one bright-eyed fellow some of the hardships of camp life and campaigning, and receiving from him the cheerful reply, 'I know all about that.' I then said, 'you may be killed in battle.' He instantly answered, 'many a better man than me has been killed in this war.' When I told another one who wanted to 'fight for freedom,' that he might lose his life, he replied, 'but my people will be free.'

"The result of this careful examination convinced me that these men, though black in skin, had men's hearts, and only needed right handling to develope into magnificent soldiers. Among them were the same varieties of physique, temperament, mental and moral endowments and experiences, as would be found among the same number of white men. Some of them were finely formed and powerful; some were almost white; a large number had in their veins white blood of the F. F. V. quality; some were men of intelligence, and many of them deeply religious.

"Acting upon my clerk's suggestion, I assigned them to companies according to their height, putting men of nearly the same height together. When the regiment was full, the four center companies were all composed of tall men, the flanking companies of men of medium height, while the little men were sandwiched between. The effect was excellent in every way, and made the regiment quite unique. It was not uncommon to have strangers who saw it parade for the first time, declare that the men were all of one size.

"In six weeks three companies were filled, uniformed, armed, and had been taught many soldierly ways. They had been drilled in the facings, in the manual of arms, and in some company movements.

"November 20th, Gen. G. H. Thomas commanding the Department of the Cumberland, ordered six companies to Bridgeport, Alabama, under command of Major H. C. Corbin. I was left at Gallatin to complete the organization of the other four companies. When the six companies were full, I was mustered in as Lieutenant-Colonel. The complete organization of the regiment occupied about two months, being finished by Jan. 1st, 1864. The field, staff and company officers were all white men. All the non-commissioned officers,—Hospital Steward, Quartermaster, Sergeant, Sergeant-Major, Orderlies, Sergeants and Corporals were colored. They proved very efficient, and had the war continued two years longer, many of them would have been competent as commissioned officers.

"When General Paine left Gallatin, I was senior officer and had command of the post and garrison, which included a few white soldiers besides my own troops. Colored soldiers acted as pickets, and no citizen was allowed to pass our lines either into the village or out, without a proper permit. Those presenting themselves without a pass were sent to headquarters under guard. Thus many proud Southern slave-holders found themselves marched through the street, guarded by those who three months before had been slaves. The negroes often laughed over these changed relations as they sat around their camp fires, or chatted together while off duty, but it was very rare that any Southerner had reason to complain of any unkind or uncivil treatment from a colored soldier.

"About the first of January occurred a few days of extreme cold weather, which tried the men sorely. One morning after one of the most severe nights, the officers coming in from picket, marched the men to headquarters, and called attention to their condition: their feet were frosted and their hands frozen. In some instances the skin on their fingers had broken from the effects of the cold, and it was sad to see their sufferings. Some of them never recovered from the effects of that night, yet they bore it patiently and uncomplainingly.

"An incident occurred while I was still an officer in a white regiment, that illustrates the curious transition through which the negroes were passing. I had charge of a company detailed to guard a wagon train out foraging. Early one morning, just as we were about to resume our march, a Kentucky lieutenant rode up to me, saluted, and said he had some runaway negroes whom he had arrested to send back to their masters, but as he was ordered away, he would turn them over to me. (At that time a reward could be claimed for returning fugitive slaves. I took charge of them, and assuming a stern look and manner, enquired, 'Where are you going?' 'Going to the Yankee army.' 'What for?' 'We wants to be free, sir.' 'All right, you are free, go where you wish.' The satisfaction that came to me from their heartfelt 'thank'ee, thank'ee sir,' gave me some faint insight into the sublime joy that the great emancipator must have felt when he penned the immortal proclamation that set free four millions of human beings.

"These men afterward enlisted in my regiment, and did good service. One day, as we were on the march, they—through their lieutenant—reminded me of the circumstance, which they seemed to remember with lively gratitude.

"The six companies at Bridgeport were kept very busily at work, and had but little opportunity for drill. Notwithstanding these difficulties, however, considerable progress was made in both drill and discipline. I made earnest efforts to get the regiment united and relieved from so much labor, in order that they might be prepared for efficient field service as soldiers.

"In January I had a personal interview with General Thomas, and secured an order uniting the regiment at Chattanooga. We entered camp there under the shadow of Lookout Mountain, and in full view of Mission Ridge, in February, 1864. During the same month Adjutant General Lorenzo Thomas, from Washington, then on a tour of inspection, visited my regiment, and authorized me to substitute the eagle for the silver leaf.

"Chattanooga was at that time the headquarters of the Army of the Cumberland. Gen Thomas and staff, and a considerable part of the army were there. Our camp was laid out with great regularity; our quarters were substantial, comfortable and well kept. The regiment numbered a thousand men, with a full compliment of field, staff, line and non-commissioned officers. We had a good drum corps, and a band provided with a set of expensive silver instruments. We were also fully equipped; the men were armed with rifled muskets, and well clothed. They were well drilled in the manual of arms, and took great pride in appearing on parade with arms burnished, belts polished, shoes blacked, clothes brushed, in full regulation uniform, including white gloves. On every pleasant day our parades were witnessed by officers, soldiers and citizens from the North, and it was not uncommon to have two thousand spectators. Some came to make sport, some from curiosity, some because it was the fashion, and others from a genuine desire to see for themselves what sort of looking soldiers negroes would make.

"At the time that the work of organizing colored troops began in the West, there was a great deal of bitter prejudice against the movement, and white troops threatened to desert, if the plan should be really carried out. Those who entered the service were stigmatized as 'nigger officers,' and negro soldiers were hooted at and mal-treated by white ones.

"Apropos of the prejudice against so called nigger officers, I may mention the following incident: While an officer in the 70th Indiana, I had met, and formed a passing acquaintance with Lieut.-Colonel —, of the — Ohio Regiment. On New Years Day, 1864, I chanced to meet him at a social gathering at General Ward's headquarters in Nashville. I spoke to him as usual, at the same time offering my hand, which apparently he did not see. Receiving only a cool bow from him, I at once turned away. As I did so he remarked to those standing near him that he 'did not recognize these nigger officers.' In some way, I do not know how, a report of the occurrence came to the ears of Lorenzo Thomas, the Adjutant-General of the Army, then in Nashville, who investigated the case, and promptly dismissed Colonel — from the United States service.

"Very few West Point officers had any faith in the success of the enterprise, and most Northern people perhaps, regarded it as at best a dubious experiment. A college classmate of mine, a young man of intelligence and earnestly loyal, although a Kentuckian, and a slave-holder, plead with me to abandon my plan of entering this service, saying, 'I shudder to think of the remorse you may suffer, from deeds done by barbarians under your command.'

"General George H. Thomas, though a Southerner, and a West Point graduate, was a singularly fair-minded, candid man. He asked me one day soon after my regiment was organized, if I thought my men would fight. I replied that they would. He said he thought 'they might behind breastworks.' I said they would fight in the open field. He thought not. 'Give me a chance General,' I replied, 'and I will prove it.'

"Our evening parades converted thousands to a belief in colored troops. It was almost a daily experience to hear the remark from visitors, 'Men who can handle their arms as these do, will fight.' General Thomas paid the regiment the compliment of saying that he 'never saw a regiment go through the manual as well as this one.' We remained in 'Camp Whipple' from February, 1864, till August, 1865, a period of eighteen months, and during a large part of that time the regiment was an object lesson to the army, and helped to revolutionize public opinion on the subject of colored soldiers.

"My Lieutenant-Colonel and I rode over one evening to call on General Joe Hooker, commanding the 20th Army Corps. He occupied a small log hut in the Wauhatchie Valley, near Lookout Mountain and not far from the Tennessee river. He received us with great courtesy, and when he learned that we were officers in a colored regiment, congratulated us on our good fortune, saying that he 'believed they would make the best troops in the world.' He predicted that after the rebellion was subdued, it would be necessary for the United States to send an army into Mexico. This army would be composed largely of colored men, and those of us now holding high command, would have a chance to win great renown. He lamented that he had made a great mistake in not accepting a military command, and going to Nicaragua with General Walker. 'Why,' said he, 'young gentlemen, I might have founded an empire.'

"While at Chattanooga, I organized two other regiments, the 42nd and the 44th United States Colored Infantry. In addition to the ordinary instruction in the duties required of the soldier, we established in every company a regular school, teaching men to read and write, and taking great pains to cultivate in them self-respect and all manly qualities. Our success in this respect was ample compensation for our labor. The men who went on picket or guard duty, took their books as quite as indispensable as their coffee pots.

"It must not be supposed that we had only plain sailing. Soon after reaching Chattanooga, heavy details began to be made upon us for men to work upon the fortifications then in process of construction around the town. This almost incessant labor, interfered sadly with our drill, and at one time all drill was suspended, by orders from headquarters. There seemed little prospect of our being ordered to the field, and as time wore on and arrangements began in earnest for the new campaign against Atlanta, we grew impatient for work, and anxious for opportunity for drill and preparations for field service.

"I used every means to bring about a change, for I believed that the ultimate status of the negro was to be determined by his conduct on the battle-field. No one doubted that he would work, while many did doubt that he had courage to stand up and fight like a man. If he could take his place side by side with the white soldier; endure the same hardships on the campaign, face the same enemy, storm the same works, resist the same assaults, evince the same soldierly qualities, he would compel that respect which the world has always accorded to heroism, and win for himself the same laurels which brave soldiers have always won.

"Personally, I shrink from danger, and most decidedly prefer a safe corner at my own fireside, to an exposed place in the face of an enemy on the battle-field, but so strongly was I impressed with the importance of giving colored troops a fair field and full opportunity to show of what mettle they were made, that I lost no chance of insisting upon our *right* to be ordered into the field. At one time I was threatened with dismissal from the service for my persistency, but that did not deter me, for though I had no yearning for martyrdom, I was determined if possible to put my regiment into battle, at whatever cost to myself. As I look back upon the matter after twenty-one years, I see no reason to regret my action, unless it be that I was not even more persistent in claiming for these men the rights of soldiers.

"I was grievously disappointed when the first of May, 1864, came, and the army was to start south, leaving us behind to hold the forts we had helped to build.

"I asked General Thomas to allow *me*, at least, to go along. He readily consented, and directed me to report to General O. O. Howard, commanding the 4th Army Corps, as Volunteer Aide. I did so, and remained with him thirty days, participating in the battles of Buzzard's

Roost, Resaca, Adairsville and Dallas. At the end of that time, having gained invaluable experience, and feeling that my place was with my regiment, I returned to Chattanooga, determined to again make every possible effort to get it into active service.

"A few days after I had taken my place on General Howard's staff, an incident occurred showing how narrowly one may escape death. General Stanley and a staff officer and General Howard and myself were making a little reconnoissance at Buzzards Roost. We stopped to observe the movements of the enemy, Stanley standing on the right, Howard next on his left, and I next. The fourth officer, Captain Flint, stood immediately in the rear of General Howard. A sharpshooter paid us a compliment in the shape of a rifle ball, which struck the ground in front of General Howard, ricocheted, passed through the skirt of his coat, through Captain Flint's cap, and buried itself in a tree behind.

"At Adairsville a group of about a dozen mounted officers were in an open field, when the enemy exploded a shell just in front and over us, wounding two officers and five horses. A piece of the shell passed through the right fore leg of my horse, a kind, docile, fearless animal, that I was greatly attached to. I lost a friend and faithful servant.

"On asking leave to return to my command, I was delighted to receive from General Howard the following note:

"'HEADQUARTERS 4TH ARMY CORPS,
"'ON ACKWORTH AND DALLAS ROAD, 8 MILES FROM DALLAS, GA., May 31st 1864.

"'COLONEL:—This is to express my thanks for your services upon my staff during the past month, since starting upon this campaign. You have given me always full satisfaction, and more, by your assiduous devotion to duty.

"'You have been active and untiring on the march, and fearless in battle. Believe me, Your friend, O. O. HOWARD.
"'*Major-General Commanding 4th Army Corps.*
"'To Col. T. J. Morgan, *Commanding 14th U. S. C. I.*'

"General James B. Steadman, who won such imperishable renown at Chickamauga, was then in command of the District of Etowah, with headquarters at Chattanooga. I laid my case before him; he listened with interest to my plea, and assured me that if there was any fighting to be done in his district, we should have a hand in it.

"DALTON, GA.—August 15th, 1864, we had our first fight, at Dalton, Georgia. General Wheeler, with a considerable force of confederate cavalry, attacked Dalton, which was occupied by a small detachment of Union troops belonging to the 2nd Missouri, under command of Colonel Laibold. General Steadman went to Laibold's aid, and forming line of battle, attacked and routed the Southern force. My regiment formed on the left of the 51st Indiana Infantry, under command of Col. A. D. Streight. The fight was short, and not at all severe. The regiment was all exposed to fire. One private was killed, one lost a leg, and one was wounded in the right hand. Company B, on the skirmish line killed five of the enemy, and wounded others. To us it was a great battle, and a glorious victory. The regiment had been recognized as soldiers; it had taken its place side by side with a white regiment; it had been under fire. The men had behaved gallantly. A colored soldier had died for liberty. Others had shed their blood in the great cause. Two or three incidents will indicate the significance of the day. Just before going into the fight, Lieutenant Keinborts said to his men: 'Boys, some of you may be killed, but remember you are fighting for liberty.' Henry Prince replied, 'I am ready to die for liberty.' In fifteen minutes he lay dead,—a rifle ball through his heart,—a willing martyr.

"During the engagement General Steadman asked his Aide, Captain Davis, to look especially after the 14th colored. Captain Davis rode up just as I was quietly rectifying my line, which in a charge had been disarranged. Putting spurs to his horse, he dashed back to the General and reassured him by reporting that 'the regiment was holding dress parade over there under fire.' After the fight, as we marched into town through a pouring rain, a white regiment standing at rest, swung their hats and gave three rousing cheers for the 14th Colored. Col. Streight's command was so pleased with the gallantry of our men that many of its members on being asked, 'What regiment?' frequentlyreplied, '51st Colored.'

"During the month of August we had some very hard marching, in a vain effort to have another brush with Wheeler's cavalry.

"The corn in East Tennessee was in good plight for roasting, and our men showed great facility in cooking, and marvelous capacity in devouring it. Ten large ears were not too much for many of them. On resuming our march one day, after the noon halt, one of the soldiers said he was unable to walk, and asked permission to ride in an ambulance. His comrades declared that, having already eaten twelve ears of corn, and finding himself unable to finish the thirteenth, he concluded that he must be sick, and unfit for duty.

"PULASKI, TENN.—September 27th, 1864, I reported to Major-General Rousseau, commanding a force of cavalry at Pulaski, Tenn. As we approached the town by rail from Nashville, we heard artillery, then musketry, and as we left the cars we saw the smoke of guns. Forest, with a large body of cavalry, had been steadily driving Rousseau before him all day, and was destroying the railroad. Finding the General, I said: 'I am ordered to report to you, sir.' 'What have you?' 'Two regiments of colored troops.' Rousseau was a Kentuckian, and had not much faith in negro soldiers. By his direction I threw out a strong line of skirmishers, and posted the regiments on a ridge, in good supporting distance. Rousseau's men retired behind my line, and Forest's men pressed forward until they met our fire, and recognizing the sound of the minie ball, stopped to reflect.

"The massacre of colored troops at Fort Pillow was well known to us, and had been fully discussed by our men. It was rumored, and thoroughly credited by them, that General Forest had offered a thousand dollars for the head of any commander of a 'nigger regiment.' Here, then, was just such an opportunity as those spoiling for a fight might desire. Negro troops stood face to face with Forest's veteran cavalry. The fire was growing hotter, and balls were uncomfortably thick. At length, the enemy in strong force, with banners flying, bore down toward us in full sight, apparently bent on mischief. Pointing to the advancing column, I said, as I passed along the line, 'Boys, it looks very much like fight; keep cool, do your duty.' They seemed full of glee, and replied with great enthusiasm: 'Colonel, dey can't whip us, dey nebber get de ole 14th out of heah, nebber.' 'Nebber, drives us away widout a mighty lot of dead men,' &c., &c.

"When Forest learned that Rousseau was re-enforced by infantry, he did not stop to ask the color of the skin, but after testing our line, and finding it unyielding, turned to the east, and struck over toward Murfreesboro.

"An incident occurred here, illustrating the humor of the colored soldier. A spent ball struck one of the men on the side of the head, passed under the scalp, and making nearly a circuit of the skull, came out on the other side. His comrades merrily declared that when the ball struck him, it sang out 'too thick' and passed on.

"As I was walking with my adjutant down toward the picket line, a ball struck the ground immediately in front of us, about four feet away, but it was so far spent as to be harmless. We picked it up and carried it along.

"Our casualties consisted of a few men slightly wounded. We had not had a battle, but it was for us a victory, for our troops had stood face to face with a triumphant force of Southern cavalry, and stopped their progress. They saw that they had done what Rousseau's veterans could not do. Having traveled 462 miles, we returned to Chattanooga, feeling that we had gained valuable experience, and we eagerly awaited the next opportunity for battle, which was not long delayed.

"DECATUR, ALA.—Our next active service was at Decatur, Alabama. Hood, with his veteran army that had fought Sherman so gallantly from Chattanooga to Atlanta, finding that his great antagonest had started southward and seaward, struck out boldly himself for Nashville. Oct. 27th I reported to General R. S. Granger, commanding at Decatur. His little force was closely besieged by Hood's army, whose right rested on the Tennessee river below the town, and whose left extended far beyond our lines, on the other side of the town. Two companies of my regiment were stationed on the opposite side of the river from Hood's right, and kept up an annoying musketry fire. Lieutenant Gillett, of Company G, was mortally wounded by a cannon ball, and some of the enlisted men were hurt. One private soldier in Company B, who had taken position in a tree as sharpshooter, had his right arm broken by a ball. Captain Romeyn said to him, 'You would better come down from there, go to the rear, and find the surgeon.' 'Oh no, Captain!' he replied, 'I can fire with my left arm,' and so he did.

"Another soldier of Company B, was walking along the road, when hearing an approaching cannon ball, he dropped flat upon the ground, and was almost instantly well nigh covered with the dirt plowed up by it, as it struck the ground near by. Captain Romeyn, who witnessed the incident, and who was greatly amused by the fellow's trepidation, asked him if he was frightened? His reply was, 'Fore God, Captain, I thought I was a dead man, sure!'

"Friday, Oct. 28th, 1864, at twelve o'clock, at the head of 355 men, in obedience to orders from General Granger, I charged and took a battery, with a loss of sixty officers and men killed and wounded. After capturing the battery, and spiking the guns, which we were unable to remove, we retired to our former place in the line of defense. The conduct of the men on this occasion was most admirable, and drew forth high praise from Generals Granger and Thomas.

"Hood, having decided to push on to Nashville without assaulting Decatur, withdrew. As soon as I missed his troops from my front, I notified the General commanding, and was ordered to pursue, with the view of finding where he was. About ten o'clock the next morning, my skirmishers came up with his rear guard, which opened upon us a brisk infantry fire. Lieutenant Woodworth, standing at my side, fell dead, pierced through the face. General Granger ordered me to retire inside of the works, and the regiment, although exposed to a sharp fire, came off in splendid order. As we marched inside the works, the white soldiers, who had watched the manœuvre, gave us three rousing cheers. I have heard the Pope's famous choir at St. Peters, and the great organ at Freibourg, but the music was not so sweet as the hearty plaudits of our brave comrades.

"As indicating the change in public sentiment relative to colored soldiers, it may be mentioned that the Lieutenant-Colonel commanding the 68th Indiana Volunteer Infantry, requested me as a personal favor to ask for the assignment of his regiment to my command, giving as a reason that his men would rather fight along side of the 14th Colored than with any white regiment. He was ordered to report to me.

"After Hood had gone, and after our journey of 244 miles, we returned to Chattanooga, but not to remain.

"NASHVILLE, TENN.—November 29, 1864, in command of the 14th, 16th and 44th Regiments U. S. C. I., I embarked on a railroad train at Chattanooga for Nashville. On December 1st, with the 16th and most of the 14th, I reached my destination, and was assigned to a place on the extreme left of General Thomas' army then concentrating for the defence of Nashville against Hood's threatened attack.

"The train that contained the 44th colored regiment, and two companies of the 14th, under command of Colonel Johnson, was delayed near Murfreesboro until Dec. 2nd, when it started for Nashville. But when crossing a bridge not far from the city, its progress was suddenly checked by a cross-fire of cannon belonging to Forest's command. I had become very anxious over the delay in the arrival of these troops, and when I heard the roar of cannon thought it must be aimed at them. I never shall forget the intensity of my suffering, as hour after hour passed by bringing me no tidings. Were they all captured? Had they been massacred? Who could answer? No one. What was to be done? Nothing. I could only wait and suffer.

"The next day Colonel Johnson reached Nashville, reporting that when stopped, he and his men were forced, under heavy fire, to abandon the train, clamber down from the bridge, and run to a blockhouse near by, which had been erected for the defence of the bridge, and was still in possession of the Union soldiers. After maintaining a stubborn fight until far into the night, he withdrew his troops, and making a detour to the east came into our lines, having lost in killed, wounded and missing, two officers and eighty men of the 44th, and twenty-five men of the 14th.

"Just as Captain C. W. Baker, the senior officer of the 14th, was leaving the car, a piece of shell carried off the top of his cap, thus adding immensely to its value—as a souvenir. Some of the soldiers who escaped lost everything except the clothes they had on, including knapsacks, blankets and arms. In some cases they lay in the water hiding for hours, until they could escape their pursuers.

"Soon after taking our position in line at Nashville, we were closely beseiged by Hood's army; and thus we lay facing each other for two weeks. Hood had suffered so terribly by his defeat under Schofield, at Franklin, that he was in no mood to assault us in our works, and Thomas needed more time to concentrate and reorganize his army, before he could safely take the offensive. That fortnight interval was memorable indeed. Hood's army was desperate. It had been thwarted by Sherman, and thus far baffled by Thomas, and Hood felt that he must strike a bold blow to compensate for the dreadful loss of prestige occasioned by Sherman's march to the sea. His men were scantily clothed and poorly fed; if he could gain Nashville, our great depot of supplies, he could furnish his troops with abundance of food, clothing and war material; encourage the confederacy, terrify the people of the North, regain a vast territory taken from the South at such great cost to us, recruit his army from Kentucky, and perhaps invade the North.

" Thomas well knew the gravity of the situation, and was unwilling to hazard all by a premature battle. I think that neither he nor any of his army ever doubted the issue of the battle when it should come, whichever force should take the initiative.

"The authorities at Washington grew restive, and the people at the North nervous. Thomas was ordered to fight, Logan was dispatched to relieve him if he did not, and Grant himself started West to take command. Thomas was too good a soldier to be forced to offer battle, until he was sure of victory. He knew that time was his best ally, every day adding to his strength and weakening his enemy. In the meantime the weather became intensely cold, and a heavy sleet covered the ground, rendering it almost impossible for either army to move at all. For a few days our sufferings were quite severe. We had only shelter tents for the men, with very little fuel, and many of those who had lost their blankets keenly felt their need.

"On December 5th, before the storm, by order of General Steadman, I made a little reconnoissance, capturing, with slight loss, Lieutenant Gardner and six men, from the 5th Mississippi Regiment. December 7th we made another, in which Colonel Johnson and three or four men were wounded. On one of these occasions, while my men were advancing in face of a sharp fire, a rabbit started up in front of them. With shouts of laughter, several of them gave chase, showing that even battle could not obliterate the negro's love of sport.

"But the great day drew near. The weather grew warmer; the ice gave way. Thomas was ready, and calling together his chiefs, laid before them his plan of battle.

"About nine o'clock at night December 14th, 1864, I was summoned to General Steadman's headquarters. He told me what the plan of battle was, and said he wished me to open the fight by making a vigorous assault upon Hood's right flank. This, he explained, was to be a feint, intended to betray Hood into the belief that it was the real attack, and to lead him to support his right by weakening his left, where Thomas intended assaulting him in very deed. The General gave me the 14th United States Colored Infantry, under Colonel H. C. Corbin; the 17th U. S. C. I., under the gallant Colonel W. R. Shafter; a detachment of the 18th U. S. C. I., under Major L. D. Joy; the 44th U. S. C. I., under Colonel L. Johnson; a provisional brigade of white troops under Colonel C. H. Grosvenor, and a section of Artillery, under Captain Osburn, of the 20th Indiana Battery.

"The largest force I had ever handled was two regiments, and as I rather wanted to open the battle in proper style, I asked General Steadman what suggestion he had to make. He replied: 'Colonel, to-morrow morning at daylight I want you to open the battle.' 'All right, General, do you not think it would be a good plan for me to —', and I outlined a little plan of attack. With a twinkle in his kindly eye, he replied: 'To-morrow morning, Colonel, just as soon as you can see how to put your troops in motion, I wish you to begin the fight.' 'All right, General, good night.' With these explicit instructions, I left his headquarters, returned to camp, and gave the requisite orders for the soldiers to have an early breakfast, and be ready for serious work at daybreak. Then taking Adjutant Clelland I reconnoitered the enemy's position, tracing the line of his camp fires, and decided on my plan of assault.

"The morning dawned with a dense fog, which held us in check for some time after we were ready to march. During our stay in Nashville, I was the guest of Major W. B. Lewis, through whose yard ran our line. He had been a warm personal friend of Andrew Jackson, occupying a place in the Treasury Department during his administration. He gave me the room formerly occupied by the hero of New Orleans, and entertained me with many anecdotes of him. I remember in particular one which I especially appreciated, because of the scarcity of fuel in our own camp. At one time General Jackson ordered certain troops to rendezvous for a few days at Nashville. Major Lewis, acting as Quartermaster, laid in a supply of several hundred cords of wood, which he supposed would be ample to last during their entire stay in the city. The troops arrived on a 'raw and gusty day,' and being accustomed to comfortable fires at home, they burned up every stick the first night, to the quartermaster's great consternation.

"To return: On the morning of December 15th, Major Lewis said he would have a servant bring me my breakfast, which was not ready, however, when I started. The boy, with an eye to safety, followed me afar off, *so* far that he only reached me, I think, about two o'clock in the afternoon. But I really believe the delay, improved the flavor of the breakfast.

"As soon as the fog lifted, the battle began in good earnest. Hood mistook my assault for an attack in force upon his right flank, and weakening his left in order to meet it, gave the coveted opportunity to Thomas, who improved it by assailing Hood's left flank, doubling it up, and capturing a large number of prisoners.

"Thus the first day's fight wore away. It had been for us a severe but glorious day. Over three hundred of my command had fallen, but everywhere our army was successful. Victory perched upon our banners. Hood had stubbornly resisted, but had been gallantly driven back with severe loss. The left had done its duty. General Steadman congratulated us, saying his only fear had been that we might fight too hard. We had done all he desired, and more. Colored soldiers had again fought side by side with white troops; they had mingled together in the charge; they had supported each other; they had assisted each other from the field when wounded, and they lay side by side in death. The survivors rejoiced together over a hard fought field, won by a common valor. All who witnessed their conduct, gave them equal praise. The day that we had longed to see had come and gone, and the sun went down upon a record of coolness, bravery, manliness, never to be unmade. A new chapter in the history of liberty had been written. It had been shown that, marching under a flag of freedom, animated by a love of liberty, even the slave becomes a man and a hero.

"At one time during the day, while the battle was in progress, I sat in an exposed place on a piece of ground sloping down toward the enemy, and being the only horseman on that part of the field, soon became a target for the balls that whistled and sang their threatening songs as they hurried by. At length a shot aimed at me struck my horse in the face, just above the nostril, and passing up under the skin emerged near the eye, doing the horse only temporary harm, and letting me off scot-free, much to my satisfaction, as may be supposed. Captain Baker, lying on the ground near by, heard the thud of the ball as it struck the horse, and seeing me suddenly dismount, cried out, 'the Colonel is shot,' and sprang to my side, glad enough to find that the poor horse's face had been a shield to save my life. I was sorry that the animal could not appreciate the gratitude I felt to it for my deliverance.

"During that night Hood withdrew his army some two miles, and took up a new line along the crest of some low hills, which he strongly fortified with some improvised breast works and abatis. Soon after our early breakfast, we moved forward over the intervening space. My posi tion was still on the extreme left of our line, and I was especially charged to look well to our flank, to avoid surprise.

"The 2nd Colored Brigade, under Colonel Thompson, of the 12th U. S. C. I., was on my right, and participated in the first days' charge upon Overton's Hill, which was repulsed. I stood where the whole movement was in full view. It was a grand and terrible sight to see those men climb that hill over rocks and fallen trees, in the face of a murderous fire of cannon and musketry, only to be driven back. White and black mingled together in the charge, and on the retreat.

"When the 2nd Colored Brigade retired behind my lines to re-form, one of the regimental color-bearers stopped in the open space between the two armies, where, although exposed to a dangerous fire, he planted his flag firmly in the ground, and began deliberately and coolly to return the enemy's fire, and, greatly to our amusement, kept up for some little time his independent warfare.

"When the second and final assault was made, the right of my line took part. It was with breathless interest I watched that noble army climb the hill with a steady resolve which nothing but death itself could check. When at length the assaulting column sprang upon the earthworks, and the enemy seeing that further resistance was madness, gave way and began a precipitous retreat, our hearts swelled as only the hearts of soldiers can, and scarcely stopping to cheer or to await orders, we pushed forward and joined in the pursuit, until the darkness and the rain forced a halt.

"The battle of Nashville did not compare in numbers engaged, in severity of fighting, or in the losses sustained, with some other Western battles. But in the issues at stake, the magnificent generalship of Thomas, the completeness of our triumph, and the immediate and far-reaching consequences, it was unique, and deservedly ranks along with Gettysburg, as one of the decisive battles of the war.

"When General Thomas rode over the battle-field and saw the bodies of colored men side by side with the foremost, on the very works of the enemy, he turned to his staff, saying: 'Gentlemen, the question is settled; negroes will fight.' He did me the honor to recommend me for promotion, and told me that he intended to give me the best brigade that he could form. This he afterward did.

"After the great victory, we joined in the chase after the fleeing foe. Hood's army was whipped, demoralized, and pretty badly scattered. A good many stragglers were picked up. A story circulated to this effect: Some of our boys on making a sharp turn in the road, came upon a forlorn Southern soldier, who had lost his arms, thrown away his accoutrements, and was sitting on a log by the roadside, waiting to give himself up. He was saluted with, 'Well, Johnny, how goes it?' 'Well, Yank, I'll tell ye; I confess I'm horribly whipped, and badly demoralized, but blamed if I'm *scattered!*'

"After we had passed along through Franklin, we had orders to turn about and return to that city. I was riding at the head of the column, followed by my own regiment. The men were swinging along 'arms at will,' when they spied General Thomas and staff approaching. Without orders they brought their arms to 'right shoulder shift,' took the step, and striking up their favorite tune of 'John Brown,' whistled it with admirable effect while passing the General, greatly to his amusement.

"We had a very memorable march from Franklin to Murfreesboro, over miserable dirt roads. About December 19th or 20th, we were on the march at an early hour, but the rain was there before us, and stuck by us closer than a brother. We were drenched through and through, and few had a dry thread. We waded streams of water nearly waist deep; we pulled through mud that seemed to have no bottom, and where many a soldier left his shoes seeking for it. The open woods pasture where we went into camp that night, was surrounded with a high fence made of cedar rails. That fence was left standing, and was not touched —until—well, I do believe that the owners bitterness at his loss was fully balanced by the comfort and good cheer which those magnificent rail fires afforded us that December night. They did seem providentially provided for us.

"During the night the weather turned cold, and when we resumed our march the ground was frozen and the roads were simply dreadful, especially for those of our men who had lost their shoes the day before and were now compelled to walk barefoot, tracking their way with blood. Such experiences take away something of the romance sometimes suggested to the inexperienced by the phase, 'soldiering in the Sunny South,' but then a touch of it is worth having for the light it throws over such historical scenes as those at Valley Forge.

"We continued in the pursuit of Hood, as far as Huntsville, Ala., when he disappeared to return no more, and we were allowed to go back to Chattanooga, glad of an opportunity to rest. Distance travelled, 420 miles.

"We had no more fighting. There were many interesting experiences, which, however, I will not take time to relate. In August, 1865, being in command of the Post at Knoxville, Tenn., grateful to have escaped without imprisonment, wounds, or even a day of severe illness, I resigned my commission, after forty months of service, to resume my studies.

"I cannot close this paper without expressing the conviction that history has not yet done justice to the share borne by colored soldiers in the war for the Union. Their conduct during that eventful period, has been a silent, but most potent factor in influencing public sentiment, shaping legislation, and fixing the status of colored people in America. If the records of their achievements could be put into such shape that they could be accessible to the thousands of colored youth in the South, they would kindle in their young minds an enthusiastic devotion to manhood and liberty."

CHAPTER IX.

THE PHALANX AT MARION, TENN.

In the winter of 1864, while Sherman was marching his army toward the sea, raiding parties and expeditions were sent out from the several departments to intercept rebel communications, destroy telegraph lines, railroads and stores; in nearly all of which Phalanx troops actively participated, and shared the perils and honors of the achievements.

From Vicksburg, Miss., Brevet Brigadier-General E. D. Osband, with the Third Phalanx Regiment, on the 27th of November captured and destroyed the Mississippi Central Railroad bridge over the Big Black River, near Canton, also thirty miles of the railroad, with two locomotives and a large amount of stores.

In the meantime, General Breckenridge, with a large confederate force, attacked the Federals under General Gillem, near Morristown, Tenn., captured the artillery, with several hundred men, and drove the remainder of Gillem's troops into Knoxville. Breckenridge soon retired, however, pursued by General Ammen's forces. On the 12th of December, General Stoneman having concentrated the commands of Generals Burbridge and Gillem, near Bean Station, Tenn., started in pursuit of Breckenridge intending to drive him into Virginia and to destroy the railroad and Salt Works at Saltville, West Virginia. General Burbridge's command was principally composed of Kentucky troops, three brigades, numbering about five thousand men, all mounted. The 6th Phalanx Cavalry

SERVING REFRESHMENTS TO UNION TROOPS.

was attached to the 3rd brigade, which Colonel Jas. F. Wade, of the 6th, commanded. Gillem's defeat rather inspired the men in the new column, and they dashed forward with a determination to annihilate the enemy. Four days after leaving Bean Station, the confederates were overtaken at Marion, General Vaughn being in command, and were routed, the Federals capturing all their guns, trains and a number of prisoners. Vaughn fell back to Wytheville, pursued by the Federals, who captured and destroyed the town, with its stores and supplies and the extensive lead mines.

Having accomplished their mission, the Federals about faced for Marion, where they met with a large force of confederates under Breckenridge, including the garrison of Saltville. Now came the decisive struggle for the Salt Works between the two forces. The Federals had been enjoying their signal victory, which they now attempted to enhance by pressing the enemy, who had crossed a bridge and there taken up a position. During the night an advance regiment succeeded in crossing the bridge, after re-laying the planks which the confederates had torn up, but they were driven back , and there remained till the next morning. The 6th Phalanx was assigned its usual position, and was held in reserve. The battle opened in the morning, and continued with varying success during the day. Late in the afternoon General Stoneman found his troops badly beaten, and unable to extricate themselves from the confederate coil; they were not the "Old Guard," and the question with them was not "victory or death," but surrender or death. Nor was this long a question. General Stoneman ordered up the 6th Phalanx, dividing them into three columns, placing himself at the head of one, and giving one each to Colonel Wade, (their valiant colonel), and his chief of staff, General Brisbin. The regiment dashed into the fight for the rescue of the pro-slavery Kentuckians and haughty Tennesseeians, who were now nearly annihilated. The historian of this campaign, General Brisbin, who but a day or two previous to this battle had attempted to shoot one of the brave black boys of the 6th for retaliating for the murder of one of his comrades by shooting a confederate prisoner, thus writes, twenty-two years afterwards, about the battle and the conduct of the 6th:

"Early in the day General Stoneman had sent General Gillem off to the right with orders to get in Breckenridge's rear and if possible cut him off from the salt works. It was believed the Kentucky troops could handle Breckenridge until Gillem could strike in the rear, but the action in front about noon became terrific and Gillem was recalled to aid Burbridge. Our right flank had been driven back and our extreme left was almost at right angles with the original position held early in the morning. To add to our misfortunes, a party of Confederate cavalry had got in our rear and captured some of our pack train. The packers had at one time become demoralized and fell back almost into the hands of the Confederates operating in our rear. General Burbridge saw the movement, and drawing his revolver placed himself in front of the leading packs and ordered them back, but the crazy men kept on until the General wounded the man who was leading them off, and with the aid of some officers who used their sabres freely, the packs were forced back into the timber close to our lines and compelled to stay there. Thus over five hundred packs and animals were saved to the army by the prompt action of the General and his aids.

"At 3:30 o'clock the situation was critical in the extreme. Colonel Boyle had been killed in leading a charge and his regiment repulsed. The Twelfth Ohio Cavalry had promptly come to Boyle's support and checked the confederates, who were coming into our centre. The hospital in our rear, where our sick were, had been charged, and for a short time was in the hands of the enemy. Burbridge and Stoneman had their headquarters on a little knoll near the centre of our line, where they could see the fighting. The Confederate right, in swinging around, had covered this hill and it was no longer tenable. A lieutenant, in reporting to General Burbridge on this knoll, had been shot by a Confederate rifleman through the head and fell dead at the General's feet. Orderlies, horses and men were being shot down, and I begged General Burbridge to retire. He asked me if there were no more troops we could bring up and put into action. I told him all we had left was the Sixth United States Colored Cavalry and the horse-holders. He said:

"'Well, go and bring up the negroes and tell everybody to tie the horses as well as they can. We might as well lose them as to be whipped, when we will lose them anyway.'

"I made haste to bring up the Sixth Colored and all the horse-holders I could get. The Sixth Colored was a fine regiment, but few had faith in the fighting qualities of the negroes. General Burbridge divided them into three columns, and taking one himself gave the other two to General Wade and myself. Wade had the right, Burbridge the left and I was in the centre. Wade got off first and sailed in in gallant style.

Burbridge piled his overcoat on the ground, and drawing his sword led his column forward. The men were all on foot and most of the officers. But few were mounted. It was unpleasant riding under fire where so many were on foot. Wade's horse was soon shot, but he kept on with his men, leading on foot. Looking to the left I saw Burbridge surrounded by a black crowd of men, his form towering above them and his sword pointing to the enemy. Wade was first to strike the Confederate line. They fired and fired, but the darkies kept straight on, closing for a hand-to-hand fight. Then the cry was raised along the Confederate lines that the negroes were killing the wounded. Wade went through the Confederate line like an iron wedge, and it broke and fled. Burbridge hit hard, but the resistence was less stubborn than in Wade's front. Of my own part in the action I prefer not to write. Suffice it to say that never did soldiers do better on any battle-field than the black men I led that day.

"When their guns were empty they clubbed them, and I saw one negro fighting with a gun barrel, swinging it about his head like a club, and going straight for the enemy. He did not hit anybody for nobody waited to be hit, but some of the Confederates jumped fully fifteen feet down the opposite side of that hill to get out of the way of the negroes, and I would have jumped too, probably, if I had been on their side, for I never yet saw anything in battle so terrible as an infuriated negro.

"Gillem returned just as night was putting an end to the fighting and in the approaching darkness we mistook his column for a new column of the enemy coming in on our right and rear. Burbridge hurried back wlth his victorious negroes and was about to advance with the Twelfth Ohio Cavalry and Eleventh Michigan, when the glad news came that the supposed Confederates were Gillem's column returning to our support.

"During the night Breckenridge retreated in the direction of the salt works, but Colonel Buckley, returning from the direction of the lead mines with his brigade, and having got in Breckenridge's rear at Seven Mile Ford, charged his advance, capturing ten prisoners. Breckenridge, no doubt thinking he had been outflanked and was about to be enclosed between two columns, abandoned all idea of going to the salt works and put back in confusion to Marion, where he took the North Carolina road and fled over the mountains. Colonel, Bentley, with his Twelfth Ohio, was sent up with Breckenridge's rear. The Confederates felled trees across the road to retard Bentley's advance, but he cleared them out and he and his gallant regiment hammered Breckenridge's rear all the way into North Carolina."

The road to the Salt Works was thus opened and their destruction accomplished by the bravery and matchless valor of the gallent Sixth. Many of the regiment forfeited their lives in rescuing the force from defeat, and securing a victory; those who survived the terrible struggle no longer had opprobrious epithets hurled at them, but modestly received the just encomiums that were showered upon them by the white troops, who, amid the huzzas of victory, greeted them with loud shouts of "Comrades!"

General Brisbin, continuing, says:

"There were many instances of personal bravery, but I shall only mention one. A negro soldier had got a stump quite close to the Confederate line, and despite all efforts to dislodge him, there he stuck, picking off their men. The Confederates charged the stump, but the Federal line observing it concentrated their fire on the advancing men and drove them back. Then there were long and loud cheers for the brave darkey, who stuck to his stump and fired away with a regularity that was wonderful. His stump was riddled with bullets, but he stuck to it, although he was at times nearer the Confederate lines than our own."

SCOUTS

CHAPTER X.

THE BLACK FLAG.

FORT PILLOW—EXCHANGE OF PRISONERS, ETC.

It was not long after each army received its quota of Phalanx soldiers, before the white troops began regarding them much as Napoleon's troops did the Imperial Guard, their main support. When a regiment of the Phalanx went into a fight, every white soldier knew what was meant, for the black troops took no ordinary part in a battle. Where the conflict was hottest; where danger was most imminent, there the Phalanx went; and when victory poised, as it often did, between the contending sides, the weight of the Phalanx was frequently thrown into the balancing scales; if some strong work or dangerous battery had to be taken, whether with the bayonet alone or hand grenade or sabre, the Phalanx was likely to be in the charging column, or formed a part of the storming brigade.

The confederates were no cowards; braver men never bit cartridge or fired a gun, and when they were to meet "their slaves," as they believed, in revolt, why, of course, honor forbade them to ask or give quarter. This fact was known to all, for, as yet, though hundreds had been captured, none had been found on parole, or among the exchanged prisoners. General Grant's attention was called to this immediately after the fight at Milliken's Bend, where the officers of the Phalanx, as well as soldiers, had been captured and hung. Grant wrote Gen. Taylor, commanding the confederate forces in Louisiana, as follows:

"I feel no inclination to retaliate for offences of irresponsible persons, but, if it is the policy of any general intrusted with the command of troops, to show no quarter, or to punish with death, prisoners taken in battle, *I will accept the issue.* It may be you propose a different line of policy to black troops, and officers commanding them, to that practiced toward white troops. If so, I can assure you that these colored troops are regularly mustered into the service of the United States. The government, and all officers under the government, are bound to give the same protection to these troops that they do to any other troops."

General Taylor replied that he would punish all such acts, "disgraceful alike to humanity and the reputation of soldiers," but declared that officers of the "Confederate Army" were required to turn over to the civil authorities, to be dealt with according to the laws of the State wherein such were captured, all negroes taken in arms.

As early as December, 1862, incensed by General Butler's administration at New Orleans in the arming of negroes, Jefferson Davis, President of the Confederate Government, issued the following proclamation:

"FIRST.—That all commissioned officers in the command of said Benjamin F. Butler be declared not entitled to be considered as soldiers engaged in honorable warfare, but as robbers and criminals, deserving death; and that they, and each of them, be, whenever captured, reserved for execution.

"SECOND.—That the private soldiers and non-commissioned officers in the army of said Benj. F. Butler, be considered as only instruments used for the commission of crimes, perpetrated by his orders, and not as free agents; that they, therefore, be treated when captured as prisoners of war, with kindness and humanity, and be sent home on the usual parole; that they will in no manner aid or serve the United States in any capacity during the continuance of war, unless duly exchanged.

"THIRD.—That all negro slaves captured in arms be at once delivered over to the executive authorities, of the respective States to which they belong, and to be dealt with according to the laws of said States.

"FOURTH.—That the like orders be executed in all cases with respect to all commissioned officers of the United States when found serving in company with said slaves in insurrection against the authorities of the different States of this Confederacy.

Signed and sealed at Richmond, Dec. 23, 1862.

JEFFERSON DAVIS."

This Proclamation was the hoisting of the black flag against the Phalanx, by which Mr. Davis expected to bring about a war of extermination against the negro soldiers.*

In his third annual message to the Confederate Congress, Mr. Davis said:

"We may well leave it to the instincts of that common humanity which a beneficient creator has implanted in the breasts of our fellow

* Among the captured rebel flags now in the War Department, Washington, D. C., are several Black Flags. No. 205 was captured near North Mountain, Md., Aug. 1st, 1864. Another Captured from General Pillow's men at Fort Donelson, is also among the rebel archives in that Department. Several of them were destroyed by the troops capturing them, as at Pascagoula, Miss., and near Grand Gulf on the Mississippi.

men of all countries to pass judgment on a measure by which several millions of human beings of an inferior race—peaceful and contented laborers in their sphere—are doomed to extermination, while at the same time they are encouraged to a general assassination of their masters by the insiduous recommendation to abstain from violence unless in necessary defence. Our own detestation of those who have attempted the most execrable measures recorded in the history of guilty man is tempered by profound contempt for the impotent rage which it discloses. So far as regards the action of this government on such criminals as may attempt its execution, I confine myself to informing you that I shall—unless in your wisdom you deem some other course expedient—deliver to the several State authorities all commissioned officers of the United States that may hereafter be captured by our forces in any of the States embraced in the Proclamation, that they may be dealt with in accordance with the laws of those States providing for the punishment of criminals engaged in exciting servile insurrection. The enlisted soldiers I shall continue to treat as unwilling instruments in the commission of these crimes, and shall direct their discharge and return to their homes on the proper and usual parole."

The confederate Congress soon took up the subject, and after a protracted consideration passed the following:

"*Resolved*, By the Congress of the Confederate States of America, in response to the message of the President, transmitted to Congress at the commencement of the present session. That, in the opinion of Congress, the commissioned officers of the enemy *ought* not to be delivered to the authorities of the respective States, as suggested in the said message, but all captives taken by the confederate forces, ought to be dealt with and disposed of by the Confederate Government.

"SEC. 2.—That in the judgment of Congress, the Proclamations of the President of the United States, dated respectively September 22nd, 1862, and January 1st, 1863, and other measures of the Government of the United States, and of its authorities, commanders and forces, designed or intended to emancipate slaves in the Confederate States, or to abduct such slaves, or to incite them to insurrection, or to employ negroes in war against the Confederate States, or to overthrow the institution of African slavery and bring on a servile war in these States, would, if successful, produce atrocious consequences, and they are inconsistent with the spirit of those usages which, in modern warfare, prevail among the civilized nations; they may therefore be lawfully suppressed by retaliation.

"SEC. 3.—That in every case wherein, during the war, any violation of the laws and usages of war among civilized nations shall be, or has been done and perpetrated by those acting under the authority of the United States, on the persons or property of citizens of the Confederate States, or of those under the protection or in the land or naval service of the Confederate States, or of any State of the Confederacy, the President of the Confederate States is hereby authorized to cause full and and ample retaliation to be made for every such violation, in such manner and to such extent as he may think proper.

"SEC. 4.—That every white person, being a commissioned officer, or acting as such, who during the present war shall command negroes or mulattoes in arms against the Confederate States, or who shall arm, train, organize or prepare negroes or mulattoes for military service against the Confederate States, or who shall voluntarily use negroes or mulattoes in any military enterprise, attack or conflict, in such service, shall be deemed as inciting servile insurrection, and shall, if captured, be put to death, or to be otherwise punished at the discretion of the court.

"SEC. 5.—Every person, being a commissioned officer, or acting as such in the service of the enemy, who shall during the present war, excite, attempt to excite, or cause to be excited a servile insurrection, or who shall incite, or cause to be incited a slave to rebel, shall, if captured, be put to death, or otherwise punished at the discretion of the court.

"SEC. 6.—Every person charged with an offence punishable under the preceeding resolutions shall, during the present war, be tried before the military court, attached to the army or corps by the troops of which he shall have been captured, or by such other military court as the President may direct, and in such manner and under such regulations as the President shall prescribe; and after conviction, the President may commute the punishment in such manner and on such terms as he may deem proper.

SEC. 7.—All negroes and mulattoes who shall be engaged in war, or be taken in arms against the Confederate States, or shall give aid or comfort to the enemies of the Confederate States, shall, where captured in the Confederate States, be delivered to authorities of the State or States in which they shall be captured, to be dealt with according to such present or future laws of such State or States."

In March, 1863, this same Confederate Congress enacted the following order to regulate the impressment of negroes for army purposes:

"SEC. 9.—Where slaves are impressed by the Confederate Government, to labor on fortifications, or other public works, the impressment shall be made by said Government according to the rules and regulations provided in the laws of the States wherein they are impressed; and, in the absence of such law, in accordance with such rules and regulations not inconsistent with the provisions of this act, as the Secretary of War shall from time to time prescribe; *Provided*, That no impressment of slaves shall be made, when they can be hired or procured by the owner or agent.

"SEC. 10.—That, previous to the 1st day of December next, no slave laboring on a farm or plantation, exclusively devoted to the production of grain and provisions, shall be taken for the public use, without the consent of the owner, except in case of urgent necessity."

Thus it is apparent that while the Confederate Government was holding aloft the black flag, even against the Northern Phalanx regiments composed of men who were never slaves, it was at the same time engaged in enrolling and conscripting slaves to work on fortifications and in trenches, in support of their rebellion against the United States, and at a period when negro troops were not accepted in the army of the United States.

Soon after the admission of negroes into the Union army, it was reported to Secretary Stanton that three negro soldiers, captured with the gunboat "Isaac Smith," on Stone river, were placed in close confinement, whereupon he ordered three confederate prisoners belonging to South Carolina to be placed in close confinement, and informed the Confederate Government of the action. The Richmond *Examiner* becoming cognizant of this said:

"It is not merely the pretension of a regular Government affecting to deal with 'rebels,' but it is a deadly stab which they are aiming at our institutions themselves; because they know that, if we were insane enough to yield this point, to treat black men as the equals of white, and insurgent slaves as equivalent to our brave white soldiers, the very foundation of slavery would be fatally wounded."

Several black soldiers were captured in an engagement before Charleston, and when it came to an exchange of prisoners, though an immediate exchange of all captured in the engagement had been agreed upon, the confederates would not exchange the negro troops. To this the President's attention was called, whereupon he issued the following order:

"EXECUTIVE MANSION, WASHINGTON, July 30th, 1863.

"It is the duty of every government to give protection to its citizens, of whatever color, class, or condition, and especially to those who are duly organized as soldiers in the public service. The law of nations and the usages and customs of war, as carried on by civilized powers, permit no distinction as to color in the treatment of prisoners of war, as public enemies. To sell or enslave any captured person, on account of his color, and for no offense against the laws of war, is a relapse into barbarism, and a crime against the civilization of the age. The government of the United States will give the same protection to all its soldiers; and if the enemy shall enslave or sell any one because of his color, the offense shall be punished by retaliation upon the enemy's prisoners in our possession. It is therefore ordered that for every soldier of the United States killed in violation of the laws of war, a rebel soldier shall be executed, and for every one enslaved by the enemy or sold into slavery, a rebel soldier shall be placed at hard labor on public works, and continued at such labor until the other shall be released and receive the treatment due to a prisoner of war.

"ABRAHAM LINCOLN,

"By order of the Secretary of War.

"E. D. TOWNSEND, Ass't. Adjt.-General."

However, this order did not prevent the carrying out of the intentions of the confederate President and Congress.

The saddest and blackest chapter of the history of the war of the Rebellion, is that which relates to the treatment of Union prisoners in the rebel prison pens, at Macon, Ga., Belle Island, Castle Thunder, Pemberton, Libbey, at and near Richmond and Danville, Va., Cahawba, Ala., Salisbury, N. C., Tyler, Texas, Florida, Columbia, S. C., Millen and Andersonville, Ga. It is not the purpose to attempt a general description of these modern charnel houses, or to enter into a detailed statement of the treatment of the Union soldiers who were unfortunate enough to escape death upon the battle-field and then fall captive to the confederates. When we consider the fact that the white men who were engaged in the war upon both sides, belonged to one nation, and were Americans, many of whom had been educated at the same schools, and many—very many—of them members of the same religious denominations, and church; not a few springing from the same stock and loins, the atrocities committed by the confederates against the Union soldiers, while in their custody as prisoners of war, makes their deeds more shocking and inhuman than if the contestants had been of a different nationality.

The English soldiers who lashed the Sepoys to the mouths of their cannon, and then fired the pieces, thus cruelly murdering the captured rebels, offered the plea, in mitigation of their crime, and as an excuse for violating the rules of war, that their subjects were not of a civilized nation, and did not themselves adhere to the laws govern-

TERRIBLE FIGHT WITH BLOODHOUNDS.

The 1st South Carolina Regiment was attacked by the Confederates with bloodhounds, at Pocatalago Bridge, Oct. 23rd, 1862. The hounds rushed fiercely upon the troops, who quickly shot or bayoneted them and exultingly held aloft the beasts that had been so long a terror to the negro race.

ing civilized nations at war with each other. But no such plea can be entered in the case of the confederates, who starved, shot and murdered 80,000 of their brethren in prison pens, white prisoners of war. If such treatment was meted to those of their own color and race, as is related by an investigating committee of Senators, what must have been the treatment of those of another race,—whom they had held in slavery, and whom they regarded the same as sheep and horses, to be bought and sold at will,—when captured in battle, fighting against them for the Union and their own freedom?

The report of the Congressional Committee furnishes ample proof of the barbarities:

38TH CONGRESS, *1st Session.* | REP. COM. *No. 68.*

"IN THE SENATE OF THE UNITED STATES.

"*Report of the Joint Committee on the Conduct and Expenditures of the War.*

"On the 4th inst., your committee received a communication of that date from the Secretary of War, enclosing the report of Colonel Hoffman, commissary general of prisoners, dated May 3, calling the attention of the committee to the condition of returned Union prisoners, with the request that the committee would immediately proceed to Annapolis and examine with their own eyes the condition of those who have been returned from rebel captivity. The committee resolved that they would comply with the request of the Secretary of War on the first opportunity. The 5th of May was devoted by the committee to concluding their labors upon the investigation of the Fort Pillow massacre. On the 6th of May, however, the committee proceeded to Annapolis and Baltimore, and examined the condition of our returned soldiers, and took the testimony of several of them, together with the testimony of surgeons and other persons in attendance upon the hospitals. That testimony, with the communication of the Secretary of War, and the report of Colonel Hoffman, is herewith transmitted.

"The evidence proves, beyond all manner of doubt, a determination on the part of the rebel authorities, deliberately and persistently practiced for a long time past, to subject those of our soldiers who have been so unfortunate as to fall in their hands to a system of treatment which has resulted in reducing many of those who have survived and been permitted to return to us in a condition, both physically and mentally, which no language we can use can adequately describe. Though nearly all the patients now in the Naval Academy hospital at Annapolis, and in the West hospital, in Baltimore, have been under the kindest and most intelligent treatment for about three weeks past, and many of them for a greater length of time, still they present literally the appearance of living skeletons, many of them being nothing but skin and bone; some of them are maimed for life, having been frozen while exposed to the inclemency of the winter season on Belle Isle, being compelled to lie on the bare ground, without tents or blankets, some of them without overcoats or even coats, with but little fire to mitigate the severity of the winds and storms to which they were exposed.

"The testimony shows that the general practice of their captors was to rob them, as soon as they were taken prisoners, of all their money, valuables, blankets, and good clothing, for which they received nothing in exchange except, perhaps, some old worn-out rebel clothing hardly better than none at all. Upon their arrival at Richmond they have been confined, without blankets or other covering, in buildings without fire, or upon Belle Isle with, in many cases, no shelter, and in others with nothing but old discarded army tents, so injured by rents and holes as to present but little barrier to the wind and storms; on several occasions, the witnesses say, they have arisen in the morning from their resting-places upon the bare earth, and found several of their comrades frozen to death during the night, and that many others would have met the same fate had they not walked rapidly back and forth, during the hours which should have been devoted to sleep, for the purpose of retaining sufficient warmth to preserve life.

"In respect to the food furnished to our men by the rebel authorities, the testimony proves that the ration of each man was totally insufficient in quantity to preserve the health of a child, even had it been of proper quality, which it was not. It consisted usually, at the most, of two small pieces of corn-bread, made in many instances, as the witnesses state, of corn and cobs ground together, and badly prepared and cooked, of, at times, about two ounces of meat, usually of poor quality, and unfit to be eaten, and occasionally a few black worm-eaten beans, or something of that kind. Many of your men were compelled to sell to their guards, and others, for what price they could get, such clothing and blankets as they were permitted to receive of that forwarded for their use by our government, in order to obtain additional food sufficient to sustain life; thus, by endeavoring to avoid one privation reducing themselves to the same destitute condition in respect to clothing and covering that they were in before they received any from our government. When they became sick and diseased in consequence of this exposure and privation, and were admitted into the hospitals, their treatment was little if any, improved as to food, though they, doubtless, suffered less from exposure to cold than before. Their food still remained insufficient in quantity and altogether unfit in quality. Their diseases and wounds did not receive the treatment which the commonest dictates of humanity would have prompted. One witness, whom your committee examined, who had lost all the toes of one foot from being frozen while on

Belle Isle, states that for days at a time his wounds were not dressed, and they had not been dressed for four days when he was taken from the hospital and carried on the flag-of-truce boat for Fortress Monroe.

"In reference to the condition to which our men were reduced by cold and hunger, your committee would call attention to the following extracts from the testimony. One witness testifies:

"'I had no blankets until our Government sent us some.

"'Question.—How did you sleep before you received those blankets?

"'Answer.—We used to get together just as close as we could, and sleep spoon-fashion, so that when one turned over we all had to turn over.'

"Another witness testifies:

"'Question.—Were you hungry all the time?

"'Answer.—Hungry! I could eat anything that came before us; some of the boys would get boxes from the North with meat of different kinds in them; and, after they had picked the meat off, they would throw the bones away into the spit-boxes, and we would pick the bones out of the spit-boxes and gnaw them over again.'

"In addition to this insufficient supply of food, clothing and shelter, our soldiers, while prisoners, have been subjected to the most cruel treatment from those placed over them. They have been abused and shamefully treated on almost every opportunity. Many have been mercilessly shot and killed when they failed to comply with all the demands of their jailors, sometimes for violating rules of which they had not been informed. Crowded in great numbers in buildings, they have been fired at and killed by the sentinels outside when they appeared at the windows for the purpose of obtaining a little fresh air. One man, whose comrade in the service, in battle and in captivity, had been so fortunate as to be among those released from further torments, was shot dead as he was waving with his hand a last adieu to his friend; and other instances of equally unprovoked murder are disclosed by the testimony.

"The condition of our returned soldiers as regards personal cleanliness, has been filthy almost beyond description. Their clothes have been so dirty and so covered with vermin, that those who received them have been compelled to destroy their clothing and re-clothe them with new and clean raiment. Their bodies and heads have been so infested with vermin that, in some instances, repeated washings have failed to remove them; and those who have received them in charge have been compelled to cut all the hair from their heads, and make applications to destroy the vermin. Some have been received with no clothing but shirts and drawers and a piece of blanket or other outside covering, entirely destitute of coats, hats, shoes or stockings; and the bodies of those better supplied with clothing have been equally dirty and filthy with the others, many who have been sick and in the hospital having had no opportunity to wash their bodies for weeks and months before they were released from captivity.

"Your committee are unable to convey any adequate idea of the sad and deplorable condition of the men they saw in the hospitals they visited; and the testimony they have taken cannot convey to the reader the impressions which your committee there received. The persons we saw, as we were assured by those in charge of them, have greatly improved since they have been received in the hospitals. Yet they are now dying daily, one of them being in the very throes of death as your committee stood by his bed-side and witnessed the sad spectacle there presented. All those whom your committee examined stated that they have been thus reduced and emaciated entirely in consequence of the merciless treatment they received while prisoners from their enemies; and the physicians in charge of them, the men best fitted by their profession and experience to express an opinion upon the subject, all say that they have no doubt that the statements of their patients are entirely correct.

"It will be observed from the testimony, that all the witnesses who testify upon that point state that the treatment they received while confined at Columbia, South Carolina, Dalton, Georgia, and other places, was far more humane than that they received at Richmond, where the authorities of the so-called confederacy were congregated, and where the power existed, had the inclination not been wanting, to reform those abuses and secure to the prisoners they held some treatment that would bear a public comparison to that accorded by our authorities to the prisoners in our custody. Your committee, therefore, are constrained to say that they can hardly avoid the conclusion, expressed by so many of our released soldiers, that the inhuman practices herein referred to are the result of a determination on the part of the rebel authorities to reduce our soldiers in their power, by privation of food and clothing, and by exposure, to such a condition that those who may survive shall never recover so as to be able to render any effective service in the field. And your committee accordingly ask that this report, with the accompanying testimony be printed with the report and testimony [which was accordingly done] in relation to the massacre of Fort Pillow, the one being, in their opinion, no less than the other, the result of a predetermined policy. As regards the assertions of some of the rebel newspapers, that our prisoners have received at their hands the same treatment that their own soldiers in the field have received, they are evidently but the most glaring and unblushing falsehoods. No one can for a moment be deceived by such statements, who will reflect that our soldiers, who, when taken prisoners, have been stout, healthy men, in the prime and vigor of life, yet have died by hundreds under the treatment they have received, although required to perform no duties of the camp or the march; while the rebel soldiers are able to make long and rapid marches, and to offer a stubborn resistance in the field.

"Your committee, finding it impossible to describe in words the deplorable condition of these returned prisoners, have caused photographs to be taken of a number of them, and a fair sample to be lithographed and appended to their report, that their exact condition may be known by all who examine it. Some of them have since died.

"There is one feature connected with this investigation, to which your committee can refer with pride and satisfaction; and that is the uncomplaining fortitude, the undiminished patriotism exhibited by our brave men under all their privations, even in the hour of death.

"Your committee will close their report by quoting the tribute paid these men by the chaplin of the hospital at Annapolis, who has ministered to so many of them in their last moments; who has smoothed their passage to the grave by his kindness and attention, and who has performed the last sad offices over their lifeless remains. He says:

"'There is another thing I would wish to state. All the men, without any exception among the thousands that have come to this hospital, have never in a single instance expressed a regret (notwithstanding the privations and sufferings they have endured) that they entered their country's service. They have been the most loyal, devoted and earnest men. Even on the last days of their lives they have said that all they hoped for was just to live and enter the ranks again and meet their foes. It is a most glorious record in reference to the devotion of our men to their country. I do not think their patriotism has ever been equalled in the history of the world.'

"All of which is respectfully submitted.

B. F. WADE, *Chairman.*"

Also the following:

"OFFICE OF COMMISSARY-GENERAL OF PRISONERS,
WASHINGTON, D. C., May 3, 1864.

"SIR:—I have the honor to report that, pursuant to your instructions of the 2nd instant, I proceeded, yesterday morning, to Annapolis, with a view to see that the paroled prisoners about to arrive there from Richmond were properly received and cared for.

"The flag-of-truce boat 'New York,' under the charge of Major Mulford, with thirty-two officers, three hundred and sixty-three enlisted men, and one citizen on board, reached the wharf at the Naval School hospital about ten o'clock. On going on board, I found the officers generally in good health, and much cheered by their happy release from the rebel prisons, and by the prospect of again being with their friends.

"The enlisted men who had endured so many privations at Belle Isle and other places were, with few exceptions, in a very sad plight, mentally and physically, having for months been exposed to all the changes of the weather, with no other protection than a very insufficient supply of worthless tents, and with an allowance of food scarcely sufficient to prevent starvation, even if of wholesome quality; but as it was made of coarsely-ground corn, including the husks, and probably at times the cobs, if it did not kill by starvation, it was sure to do it by the disease it created. Some of these poor fellows were wasted to mere skeletons, and had scarcely life enough remaining to appreciate that they were now in the hands of their friends, and among them all there were few who had not become too much broken down and dispirited by their many privations to be able to realize the happy prospect of relief from their sufferings which was before them. With rare exception, every face was sad with care and hunger; there was no brightening of the countenance or lighting up of the eye, to indicate a thought of anything beyond a painful sense of prostration of mind and body. Many faces showed that there was scarcely a ray of intelligence left.

"Every preparation had been made for their reception in anticipation of the arrival of the steamer, and immediately upon her being made fast to the wharf the paroled men were landed and taken immediately to the hospital, where, after receiving a warm bath, they were furnished with a suitable supply of new clothing, and received all those other attentions which their sad condition demanded. Of the whole number, there are perhaps fifty to one hundred who, in a week or ten days, will be in a convalescent state, but the others will very slowly regain their lost health.

"That our soldiers, when in the hands of the rebels, are starved to death, cannot be denied. Every return of the flag-of-truce boat from City Point brings us too many living and dying witnesses to admit of a doubt of this terrible fact. I am informed that the authorities at Richmond admit the fact, but excuse it on the plea that they give the prisoners the same rations they give their own men. But can this be so? Can an army keep the field, and be active and efficient, on the same fare that kills prisoners of war at a frightful percentage? I think not; no man can believe it; and while a practice so shocking to humanity is persisted in by the rebel authorities, I would very respectfully urge that retaliatory measures be at once instituted by subjecting the officers we now hold as prisoners of war to a similar treatment.

"I took advantage of the opportunity which this visit to Annapolis gave me to make a hasty inspection of Camp Parole, and I am happy to report that I found it in every branch in a most commendable condition. The men all seemed to be cheerful and in fine health, and the police inside and out was excellent. Colonel Root, the commanding officer, deserves much credit for the very satisfactory condition to which he has brought his command.

"I have the honor to be, very respectfully, your obedient servant,

W. HOFFMAN,

"Colonel 3rd Infantry, Commissary General of Prisoners.

"Hon. E. M. STANTON, *Secretary of War, Washington, D. C.*"

This report does not refer to the treatment of the soldiers of the *Phalanx* who were taken by the confederates in battle,* after the surrender of Fort Pillow, Lawrence

---

* General Brisbin, in his account of the expedition which, in the Winter of 1864, left Bean Station, Tenn., under command of General Stoneman, for the purpose of destroying the confederate Salt Works in West Virginia, says the confederates after capturing some of the soldiers of the Sixth Phalanx Cavalry Regiment, butchered them. His statement is as follows:

"For the last two days a force of Confederate cavalry, under Witcher, had been following our command picking up stragglers and worn-out horses in our rear. Part of our troops were composed of negroes and these the Confederates killed as fast as they

and Plymouth, and at several other places. It is inserted to enable the reader to form an opinion as to what the negro soldier's treatment must have been. The same committee also published as a part of their report, the testimony of a number,—mostly black, soldiers, who escaped death at Fort Pillow; a few of their statements are given:

38TH CONGRESS, 1st Session. } { REP. COM. No. 63 & 68.

IN THE SENATE OF THE UNITED STATES.

Report of the Joint Committee on the Conduct and Expenditures of the War to whom was Referred the Resolution of Congress Instructing them to Investigate the late Massacre at Fort Pillow.

"*Deposition of John Nelson in relation to the capture of Fort Pillow.*

"John Nelson, being duly sworn, deposeth and saith:

"'At the time of the attack on and capture of Fort Pillow, April 12, 1864, I kept a hotel within the lines at Fort Pillow, and a short distance from the works. Soon after the alarm was given that an attack on the fort was imminent, I entered the works and tendered my services to Major Booth, commanding. The attack began in the morning at about 5½ o'clock, and about 1 o'clock P. M. a flag of truce approached. During

caught them, laying the dead bodies by the roadside with pieces of paper pinned to their clothing, on which were written such warnings as the following: 'This is the way we treat all nigger soldiers,' and, 'This is the fate of nigger soldiers who fight against the South.' We did not know what had been going on in our rear until we turned about to go back from Wytheville, when we found the dead colored soldiers along the road as above described. General Burbridge was very angry and wanted to shoot a Confederate prisoner for every one of his colored soldiers he found murdered, and would undoubtedly have done so had he not been restrained. As it was, the whole corps was terribly excited by the atrocious murders committed by Witcher's men, and if Witcher had been caught he would have been shot."

This gallant soldier,(?) twenty years after the close of the war, writes about the incidents and happenings during the march of the army to Saltville, and says:

"Before we reached Marion we encountered Breckenridge's advance and charged it vigorously driving it back in confusion along the Marion and Saltville road for several miles. In one of these charges (for there were several of them and a sort of running fight for several miles) one of Witcher's men was captured and brought in. He was reported to me and I asked him what his name was and to what command he belonged. He gave me his name and said 'Witcher's command.' Hardly were the words out of his mouth before a negro soldier standing near raised his carbine and aimed at the Confederate soldier's breast. I called out and sprang forward, but was too late to catch the gun. The negro fired and the poor soldier fell badly wounded. Instantly the negro was knocked down by our white soldiers, disarmed and tied. I drew my revolver to blow his brains out for his terrible crime, but the black man never flinched. All he said was, pointing to the Confederate soldier, 'He killed my comrades; I have killed him.' The negro was taken away and put among the prisoners. The Provost Marshal had foolishly changed the white guard over the prisoners and placed them under some colored troops. An officer came galloping furiously to the front and said the negroes were shooting the prisoners. General Burbridge told me to go back quickly and do whatever I pleased in his name to restore order. It was a lively ride, as the prisoners were more than four miles back, being forced along the road as rapidly as possible toward Marion. All the prisoners, except a few wounded men, were on foot, and of course they could not keep up with the cavalry. I soon reached them and never shall I forget that sight while I live. Men with sabres were driving the poor creatures along the road like beasts. I halted the motley crew and scolded the officer for his inhumanity. He said he had orders to keep the prisoners up with the column and he was simply trying to obey his orders. As I was General Burbridge's chief of staff and all orders were supposed to emanate from my office, I thought I had better not continue the conversation. As it was, I said such orders were at an end and I would myself take charge of the prisoners."

the parley which ensued, and while the firing ceased on both sides, the rebels kept crowding up to the works on the side near Cold Creek, and also approached nearer on the south side, thereby gaining advantages pending the conference under the flag of truce. As soon as the flag of truce was withdrawn the attack began, and about five minutes after it began the rebels entered the fort. Our troops were soon overpowered, and broke and fled. A large number of the soldiers, black and white, and also a few citizens, myself among the number, rushed down the bluff toward the river. I concealed myself as well as I could in a position where I could distinctly see all that passed below the bluff, for a considerable distance up and down the river.

"'A large number, at least one hundred, were hemmed in near the river bank by bodies of the rebels coming from both north and south. Most all of those thus hemmed in were without arms. I saw many soldiers, both white and black, throw up their arms in token of surrender, and call out that they had surrendered. The rebels would reply, 'G—d d—n you, why didn't you surrender before?' and shot them down like dogs.

"'The rebels commenced an indiscriminate slaughter. Many colored soldiers sprang into the river and tried to escape by swimming, but these were invariably shot dead.

"'A short distance from me, and within view, a number of our wounded had been placed, and near where Major Booth's body lay; and a small red flag indicated that at that place our wounded were placed. The rebels however, as they passed these wounded men, fired right into them and struck them with the butts of their muskets. The cries for mercy and groans which arose from the poor fellows were heartrending.

"'Thinking that if I should be discovered, I would be killed, I emerged from my hiding place, and, approaching the nearest rebel, I told him I was a citizen. He said, 'You are in bad company, G—d d—n you; out with your greenbacks, or I'll shoot you.' I gave him all the money I had, and under his convoy I went up into the fort again.

"'When I re-entered the fort there was still some shooting going on. I heard a rebel officer tell a soldier not to kill any more of those negroes. He said that they would all be killed, any way, when they were tried.

"'After I entered the fort, and after the United States flag had been taken down, the rebels held it up in their hands in the presence of their officers, and thus gave the rebels outside a chance to still continue their slaughter, and I did not notice that any rebel officer forbade the holding of it up. I also further state, to the best of my knowledge and information, that there were not less than three hundred and sixty negroes killed and two hundred whites. This I give to the best of my knowledge and belief. JOHN NELSON.

"Subscribed and sworn to before me this 2nd day of May, A. D. 1864.

"J. D. LLOYD,

"Capt. 11th Inf., Mo. Vols., and Ass't. Provost Mar., Dist. of Memphis."

"Henry Christian, (colored), private, company B, 6th United States heavy artillery, sworn and examined. By Mr. Gooch:

'Question. Where were you raised? 'Answer. In East Tennessee.

'Question. Have you been a slave? 'Answer. Yes, sir.

'Question. Where did you enlist? 'Answer. At Corinth, Mississippi.

'Question. Were you in the fight at Fort Pillow? 'Answer. Yes, sir.

'Question. When were you wounded? 'Answer. A little before we surrendered.

'Question. What happened to you afterwards? 'Answer. Nothing; I got but one shot, and dug right out over the hill to the river, and never was bothered any more.

'Did you see any men shot after the place was taken? 'Answer. Yes, sir.

'Question. Where? 'Answer. Down to the river.

'Question. How many? 'Answer. A good many; I dont know how many.

'Question. By whom were they shot? 'Answer. By secesh soldiers; secesh officers shot some up on the hill.

'Question. Did you see those on the hill shot by the officers? 'Answer. I saw two of them shot.

'Question. What officers were they? 'Answer. I don't know whether he was a lieutenant or captain.

'Question. Did the men who were shot after they had surrendered have arms in their hands? 'Answer. No, sir; they threw down their arms.

'Question. Did you see any shot the next morning? 'Answer. I saw two shot; one was shot by an officer—he was standing, holding the officer's horse, and when the officer came and got his horse he shot him dead. The officer was setting fire to the houses.

'Question. Do you say the man was holding the officer's horse, and when the officer came and took his horse he shot the man down? 'Answer. Yes, sir; I saw that with my own eyes; and then I made away into the river, right off.

'Question. Did you see any buried? 'Answer. Yes, sir; a great many, black and white.

'Question. Did you see any buried alive? 'Answer. I did not see any buried alive.

"Jacob Thompson, (colored), sworn and examined. By Mr. Gooch:

'Question. Were you a soldier at Fort Pillow? 'Answer. No, sir, I was not a soldier; but I went up in the fort and fought with the rest. I was shot in the hand and the head.

'Question. When were you shot? 'Answer. After I surrendered.

'Question. How many times were you shot? 'Answer. I was shot but once; but I threw my hand up, and the shot went through my hand and my head.

'Question. Who shot you? 'Answer. A private.

'Question. What did he say? 'Answer. He said, 'G—d d—n you,

I will shoot you, old friend.'

'Question. Did you see anybody else shot? 'Answer. Yes, sir; they just called them out like dogs, and shot them down. I reckon they shot about fifty, white and black, right there. They nailed some black sergeants to the logs, and set the logs on fire.

'Question. When did you see that? 'Answer. When I went there in the morning I saw them; they were burning all together.

'Question. Did they kill them before they burned them? 'Answer. No, sir, they nailed them to the logs; drove the nails right through their hands.

'Question. How many did you see in that condition? 'Answer. Some four or five; I saw two white men burned.

'Question. Was there any one else there who saw that? Answer. I reckon there was; I could not tell who.

'Question. When was it that you saw them? 'Answer. I saw them in the morning after the fight; some of them were burned almost in two. I could tell they were white men, because they were whiter than the colored men.

'Question. Did you notice how they were nailed? 'Answer. I saw one nailed to the side of a house; he looked like he was nailed right through his wrist. I was trying then to get to the boat when I saw it.

'Question. Did you see them kill any white men? 'Answer. They killed some eight or nine there. I reckon they killed more than twenty after it was all over; called them out from under the hill, and shot them down. They would call out a white man and shoot him down, and call out a colored man and shoot him down; do it just as fast as they could make their guns go off.

'Question. Did you see any rebel officers about there when this was going on? 'Answer. Yes, sir; old Forrest was one.

'Question. Did you know Forrest? 'Answer. Yes, sir; he was a little bit of a man. I had seen him before at Jackson.

'Question. Are you sure he was there when this was going on? 'Answer. Yes, sir.

'Question. Did you see any other officers that you knew? 'Answer. I did not know any other but him. There were some two or three more officers came up there.

'Question did you see any buried there? 'Answer. Yes, sir; they buried right smart of them. They buried a great many secesh, and a great many of our folks. I think they buried more secesh than our folks.

'Question. How did they bury them? 'Answer. They buried the secesh over back of the fort, all except those on Fort hill; them they buried up on top of the hill where the gunboats shelled them.

'Question. Did they bury any alive? 'Answer. I heard the gunboat men say they dug two out who were alive.

'Question. You did not see them? 'Answer. No, sir.

'What company did you fight with? 'Answer. I went right into the fort and fought there.

'Question. Were you a slave or a free man? 'Answer. I was a slave.

'Question. Where were you raised? 'Answer. In old Virginia.

'Question. Who was your master? 'Answer. Colonel Hardgrove.

'Question. Where did you live? 'Answer. I lived three miles the other side of Brown's mills.

'Question. How long since you lived with him? 'Answer. I went home once and staid with him a while, but he got to cutting up and I came away again.

'Question. What did you do before you went into the fight? 'Answer. I was cooking for Co. K, of Illinois cavalry; I cooked for that company nearly two years.

'Question. What white officers did you know in our army? 'Answer. I knew Captain Meltop and Colonel Ransom; and I cooked at the hotel at Fort Pillow, and Mr. Nelson kept it. I and Johnny were cooking together. After they shot me through the hand and head, they beat up all this part of my head (the side of his head) with the breach of their guns.

"Ransome Anderson, (colored), Co. B, 6th United States heavy artillery, sworn and examined. By Mr. Gooch:

'Question. Where were you raised? 'Answer. In Mississippi.

'Question. Were you a slave? 'Answer. Yes, sir.

'Question. Where did you enlist? 'Answer. At Corinth.

'Question. Were you in the fight at Fort Pillow? 'Answer. Yes, sir.

'Question. Describe what you saw done there. 'Answer. Most all the men that were killed on our side were killed after the fight was over. They called them out and shot them down. Then they put some in the houses and shut them up, and then burned the houses.

'Question. Did you see them burn? 'Answer. Yes, sir.

'Question. Were any of them alive? 'Answer. Yes, sir; they were wounded, and could not walk. They put them in the houses, and then burned the houses down.

'Question. Do you know they were in there? 'Answer. Yes, sir; I went and looked in there.

'Question. Do you know they were in there when the house was burned? 'Answer. Yes, sir; I heard them hallooing there when the houses were burning.

'Question. Are you sure they were wounded men, and not dead, when they were put in there? 'Answer. Yes, sir; they told them they were going to have the doctor see them, and then put them in there and shut them up, and burned them.

'Question. Who set the house on fire? 'Answer. I saw a rebel soldier take some grass and lay it by the door, and set it on fire. The door was pine plank, and it caught easy.

'Question. Was the door fastened up? 'Answer. Yes, sir; it was barred with one of those wide bolts.

"James Walls, sworn and examined. By Mr. Gooch:

'Question. To what company did you belong? 'Answer. Company E, 13th Tennessee cavalry.

'Question. Under what officers did you serve? 'Answer. I was under Major Bradford and Captain Potter.

'Question. Were you in the fight at Fort Pillow? 'Answer. Yes, sir.

'Question. State what you saw there of the fight, and what was done after the place was captured. 'Answer. We fought them for some six or eight hours in the fort, and when they charged, our men scattered and ran under the hill; some turned back and surrendered, and were shot. After the flag of truce came in I went down to get some water. As I was coming back I turned sick, and laid down behind a log. The secesh charged, and after they came over I saw one go a good ways ahead of the others. One of our men made to him and threw down his arms. The bullets were flying so thick there I thought I could not live there, so I threw down my arms and surrendered. He did not shoot me then, but as I turned around he or some other one shot me in the back.

'Question. Did they say anything while they were shooting? 'Answer. All I heard was, 'Shoot him, shoot him!' 'Yonder goes one!' 'Kill him, kill him!' That is about all I heard.

'Question. How many do you suppose you saw shot after they surrendered? 'Answer. I did not see but two or three shot around me. One of the boys of our company, named Taylor, ran up there, and I saw him shot and fall. Then another was shot just before me, like—shot down after he threw down his arms.

'Question. Those were white men? 'Answer. Yes, sir. I saw them make lots of niggers stand up, and then they shot them down like hogs. The next morning I was lying around there waiting for the boat to come up. The secesh would be prying around there, and would come to a nigger and say, 'You ain't dead are you?' They would not say anything, and then the secesh would get down off their horses, prick them in their sides, and say, 'D——n you, you aint dead; get up.' Then they would make them get up on their knees, when they would shoot them down like hogs.

'Question. Do you know of their burning any buildings? 'Answer. I could hear them tell them to stick torches all around, and they fired all the buildings.

'Question. Do you know whether any of our men were in the buildings when they were burned? 'Answer. Some of our men said some were burned; I did not see it, or know it to be so myself.

'Question. How did they bury them—white and black together? 'Answer. I don't know about the burying; I did not see any buried.

'Question. How many negroes do you suppose were killed after the surrender? 'Answer. There were hardly any killed before the surrender. I reckon as many as 200 were killed after the surrender, out of about 300 that were there.

Question. Did you see any rebel officers about while this shooting was going on? 'Answer. I do not know as I saw any officers about when they were shooting the negroes. A captain came to me a few minutes after I was shot; he was close by me when I was shot.

'Question. Did he try to stop the shooting? 'Answer. I did not hear a word of their trying to stop it. After they were shot down, he told them not to shoot them any more. I begged him not to let them shoot me again, and he said they would not. One man, after he was shot down, was shot again. After I was shot down, the man I surrendered to went around the tree I was against and shot a man, and then came around to me again and wanted my pocket-book. I handed it up to him, and he saw my watch-chain and made a grasp at it, and got the watch and about half the chain. He took an old Barlow knife I had in my pocket. It was not worth five cents; was of no account at all, only to cut tobacco with."

"Nathan G. Fulks, sworn and examined. By Mr. Gooch:

'Question. To what company and regiment do you belong? 'Answer. To Company D, 13th Tennessee cavalry.

"Question. Where are you from? 'Answer. About twenty miles from Columbus, Tennessee.

'Question. How long have you been in the service? 'Answer. Five months, the 1st of May.

'Question. Were you at Fort Pillow at the time of the fight there? Answer.. Yes, sir.

'Question. Will you state what happened to you there? 'Answer. I was at the corner of the fort when they fetched in a flag for a surrender. Some of them said the major stood a while, and then said he would not surrender. They continued to fight a while; and after a time the major started and told us to take care of ourselves, and I and twenty more men broke for the hollow. They ordered us to halt, and some of them said, 'God d—n 'em, kill 'em!' I said, 'I have surrendered.' I had thrown my gun away then. I took off my cartridge-box and gave it to one of them, and said, 'Don't shoot me;' but they did shoot me, and hit just about where the shoe comes up on my leg. I begged them not to shoot me, and he said, 'God d—n you, you fight with the niggers, and we will kill the last one of you!' Then they shot me in the thick of the thigh, and I fell; and one set out to shoot me again, when another one said, 'Don't shoot the white fellows any more.'

'Question. Did you see any person shot besides yourself? 'Answer. I didn't see them shot. I saw one of our fellows dead by me.

'Question. Did you see any buildings burned? 'Answer. Yes, sir. While I was in the major's headquarters they commenced burning the buildings, and I begged one of them to take me out and not let us burn there; and he said, 'I am hunting up a piece of yellow flag for you.' I think we would have whipped them if the flag of truce had not come in. We would have whipped them if we had not let them get the dead-wood on us. I was told that they made their movement while the flag of truce was in. I did not see it myself, because I had sat down, as I had been working so hard.

'Question. How do you know they made their movement while the flag of truce was in? 'Answer. The men that were above said so. The rebs are bound to take every advantage of us. I saw two more white men close to where I was lying. That makes three dead ones, and myself wounded."

Later on during the war the policy of massacring was somewhat abated, that is it was not done on the battlefield. The humanity of the confederates in Virginia permitted them to take their black prisoners to the rear. About a hundred soldiers belonging to the 7th Phalanx Regiment, with several of their white officers, were captured at Fort Gilmer on the James River, Va., and taken to Richmond in September, 1864. The following account is given of their treatment in the record of the Regiment:

"The following interesting sketches of prison-life, as experienced by two officers of the regiment, captured at Fort Gilmer, have been kindly furnished. *The details of the sufferings of the enlisted men captured with them we shall never know, for few of them ever returned to tell the sad story.*

"'An escort was soon formed to conduct the prisoners to Richmond, some seven or eight miles distant, and the kinder behavior of that part of the guard which had participated in the action was suggestive of the free-masonry that exists between brave fellows to whatever side belonging. On the road the prisoners were subjected by every passer-by, to petty insults, the point in every case, more or less obscene, being the color of their skin. The solitary exception, curiously enough, being a *nymph du pave* in the suburbs of the town.*

"'About dusk the prisoners reached the notorious Libby, where the officers took leave of their enlisted comrades—from most of them forever. The officers were then searched and put collectively in a dark hole, whose purpose undoubtedly was similar to that of the 'Ear of Dionysius.' In the morning, after being again searched, they were placed among the rest of the confined officers, among whom was Capt. Cook, of the Ninth, taken a few weeks previously at Strawberry Plains. Some time before, the confederates had made a great haul on the Weldon Railroad, and the prison was getting uncomfortably full of prisoners and—vermin. After a few days sojourn in Libby, the authorities prescribed a change of air, and the prisoners were packed into box and stock cars and rolled to Salisbury, N. C. The comforts of this two day's ride are

* "When the successful attempt was made, by tunneling, to escape from Libby Prison in 1862, many of the fugitives were honorably harbored by this unfortunate class till a more quiet opportunity occurred for leaving the city. This I have from one of the escaped officers."

remembered as strikingly similar to those of Mr. Hog from the West to the Eastern market before the invention of the S. F. P. C. T. A.

"'At Salisbury the prisoners were stored in the third story of an abandoned tobacco factory, occupied on the lower floors by political prisoners, deserters, thieves and spies, who during the night made an attempt on the property of the new-comers, but were repulsed after a pitched battle. In the morning the Post-Commandant ordered the prisoners to some unusued negro quarters in another part of the grounds, separated from the latter by a line of sentries. During the week train-loads of prisoners—enlisted men—arrived and were corralled in the open grounds. The subsequent sufferings of these men are known to the country, a parallel to those of Andersonville, as the eternal infamy of Wirtz is shared by his *confrere* at Salisbury—McGee.

"'The weakness, and still more, the appalling ferocity of the guards, stimulated the desire to escape; but when this had become a plan it was discovered, and the commissioned prisoners were at once hurried off to Danville, Va., and there assigned the two upper floors of an abandoned tobacco warehouse, which formed one side of an open square. Here an organization into messes was effected, from ten to eighteen in each—to facilitate the issue of rations. The latter consisted of corn-bread and boiled beef, but gradually the issues of meat became like angels' visits, and then for several months ceased altogether. It was the art of feeding as practised by the Hibernian on his horse—only their exchange deprived the prisoners of testing the one straw per day.

"Among the democracy of hungry bellies there were a few aristocrats, with a Division General of the Fifth Corps as Grand Mogul, whose Masonic or family connections in the South procured them special privileges. On the upper floor these envied few erected a cooking stove, around which they might be found at all hours of the day, preparing savory dishes, while encircled by a triple and quadruple row of jealous noses, eagerly inhailing the escaping vapors, so conducive to day-dreams of future banquets. The social equilibrium was, however, bi-diurnally restored by a common pursuit—a general warfare under the black flag against a common enemy, as insignificant individually as he was collectively formidable—an insect, in short, whose domesticity on the human body is, according to some naturalists, one of the differences between our species and the rest of creation. This operation, technically, 'skirmishing,' happened twice a day, according as the sun illumined the east or west sides of the apartments, along which the line was deployed in its beams.

"Eating, sleeping, smelling and skirmishing formed the routine of prison-life, broken once in a while by a walk, under escort, to the Dan river, some eighty yards distant, for a water supply. Generally, some ten or twelve prisoners with buckets were allowed to go at once, and this circumstance, together with the fact that the guard for all the prisons in town were mounted in the open square in front, excited the first idea of escape. According to high diplomatic authority, empty stomachs are conducive to ingenuity, so the idea soon became a plan and a conspiracy. While the new guard had stacked arms in the open square preparatory to mounting, some ten or twelve officers, under the lead of Col. Ralston, the powerful head of some New York regiment, were to ask for exit under pretense of getting water, and then to overpower the opposing sentries, while the balance of the prisoners, previously drawn up in line at the head of the short staircase leading direct to the exit door, were to rush down into the square, seize the stacked arms and march through the Confederacy to the Union lines—perhaps!

"'Among the ten or twelve psuedo-water-carriers—the forlorn hope—were Col. Ralston, Capt. Cook, of the Ninth, and one or two of the Seventh—Capt. Weiss and Lieut. Spinney. On the guard opening the door for egress, Col. Ralston and one of the Seventh threw themselves on the first man, a powerful six-footer, and floored him. At the same moment, however, another guard with great presence of mind, slammed the door and turned the key, and that before five officers could descend the short staircase. The attempt was now a failure. One of the guards on the outside of the building took deliberate aim through the open window at Col. Ralston, who was still engaged with the struggling fellow, and shot him through the bowels. Col. Ralston died a lingering and painful death after two or three days. Less true bravery than his has been highly sung in verse.

"'This attempt could not but sharpen the discipline of the prison, but soon the natural humanity of the commandant, Col. Smith, now believed to be Chief Engineer of the Baltimore Bridge Company, asserted itself, and things went on as before. Two incidents may, however, be mentioned in this connection, whose asperities time has removed, leaving nothing but their salient grotesque features.

"'Immediately after the occurrence, an unlimited supply of dry-salted codfish was introduced. This being the first animal food for weeks, was greedily devoured in large quantities, mostly raw—producing a raging thirst. The water supply was now curtailed to a few bucketsful, but even these few drops of the precious fluid were mostly wasted in the *melee* for their possession. The majority of the contestants retired disappointed to muse on the comforts of the Sahara Desert, and as the stories about tapping camels recurred to them, suggestive glances were cast at the more fortunate rivals. After a few days, conspicuous for the sparing enjoyment of salt cod, the water supply was ordered unlimited. An immediate 'corner' in the Newfoundland staple took place, the stock being actively absorbed by *bona fide* investors, who found that it bore watering with impunity.

* * * * *

"'At the beginning of February, 1865, thirty boxes of provisions, etc., from friends in the North arrived for the prisoners. The list of owners was anxiously scanned and the lucky possessor would not have exchanged for the capital prize in the Havana lottery. The poor fellows of the Seventh were among the fortunate, and from that day none knew hunger more.

"'With the advent of the boxes came the dawn of a brighter day. Cartels of exchange were talked about, and by the middle of February the captives found themselves on the rail for Richmond. The old Libby appeared much less gloomy than on first acquaintance, the rays of hope throwing a halo about everywhere. Many asked and obtained the liberty of the town to lay in a supply of those fine brands of tobacco for which Richmond is famous. In a few days the preliminaries to exchange were completed, and on the 22d of February—Washington's birthday—the captives also stepped into a new life under the old flag."

"Captain Sherman, of Co. C., gives the following account:

"'Further resistence being useless, and having expressed our willingness to surrender, we were invited into the fort. As I stepped down from the parapet I was immediately accosted by one of the so-called F. F. V.'s, whose smiling countenance and extended hand led me to think I was recognized as an acquaintance. My mind was soon disabused of that idea, however, for the next instant he had pulled my watch from its pocket, with the remark, 'what have you there?' Quick as thought, and before he could realize the fact, I had seized and recovered the watch, while he held only a fragment of the chain, and placing it in an inside pocket, buttoned my coat and replied, 'that is my watch and you cannot have it.'

"'Just then I discovered Lieut. Ferguson was receiving a good deal of attention—a crowd having gathered about him—and the next moment saw his fine new hat had been appropriated by one of the rebel soldiers, and he stood hatless. Seeing one of the rebel officers with a Masonic badge on his coat, Lieut. F. made himself known as a brother Mason, and appealed to him for redress. The officer quickly responded and caused the hat to be returned to its owner, only to be again stolen, and the thief made to give it up as before.

"'In a little while we (seven officers and eighty-five enlisted men) were formed in four ranks, and surrounded by a guard, continued the march 'on to Richmond,' but under very different circumstances from what we had flattered ourselves would be the case, when only two or three hours before our brigade-commander had remarked, as he rode by the regiment, that we would certainly be in Richmond that night. We met a great many civilians, old and young, on their way to the front, as a general alarm had been sounded in the city, and all who could carry arms had been ordered to report for duty in the intrenchments. After a few miles march we halted for a rest, but were not allowed to sit down, as I presume the guards thought we could as well stand as they. Here a squad of the Richmond Grays, the *elite* of the city, came up and accosted us with all manner of vile epithets. One of the most drunken and boisterous approached within five or six feet of me, and with the muzzle of his rifle within two feet of my face swore he would shoot me. Fearless of consequences, and feeling that immediate death even could not be worse than slow torture by starvation, to which I knew that so many of our soldiers had been subjected, and remembering that the Confederate Congress had declared officers of colored troops outlaws, I replied, as my eyes met his, 'shoot if you dare.' Instead of carrying out his threat he withdrew his aim and staggered on. Here Lieut. Ferguson lost his hat, which had been already twice stolen and recovered. One of the rebs came up behind him and taking the hat from his head replaced it with his own and ran off. The lieutenant consoled himself with the reflection that at last he had a hat no one would steal.

"'At about 7 P. M. we arrived at Libby Prison *and were separated from the enlisted men, who, we afterward learned, suffered untold hardships, to which many of them succumbed. Some were claimed as slaves by men who had never known them; others denied fuel and shelter through the winter, and sometimes water with which to quench their thirst; the sick and dying neglected or maltreated and even murdered by incompetent and fiendish surgeons; without rations for days together; shot at without the slightest reason or only to gratify the caprice of the guards,—all of which harrowing details were fully corroborated by the few emaciated wrecks that survived.*

"'We were marched inside the prison, searched, and what money we had taken from us. I was allowed to retain pocket-book, knife and watch. Our names were recorded and we were told to follow the sergeant. Now, I thought, the question will be decided whether we are to go up stairs where we knew the officers were quartered, or be confined in the cells below. As we neared the corner of the large room and I saw the sergeant directing his steps to the stairs leading down, I thought it had been better had we fallen on the battle-field. He led the way down to a cell, and as we passed in barred and locked the door and left us in darkness. Here, without rations, the bare stone floor for a bed, the dampness trickling down the walls on either side, seven of us were confined in a close room about seven feet by nine. It was a long night, but finally morning dawned and as a ray of light shone through the little barred window above our heads we thanked God we were not in total darkness. About 9 A. M. rations, consisting of bread and meat, were handed in, and being divided into seven parts, were drawn for by lot. About noon we were taken from the cell and put in with the other officers. Here we met Capt. Cook, of the Ninth Regiment, who had been captured about a month previous while reconnoitering the enemy's line.

"'We were now in a large room, perhaps forty by ninety feet, with large windows, entirely destitute of glass. No blankets nor anything to sit or lie upon except the floor, and at night when we lay down the floor was literally covered.

"'About the middle of the second night we were all hurriedly marched out and packed in filthy box-cars—like sardines, for there was not room for all to sit down—for an unknown destination. After a slow and tedious ride we arrived at Salisbury, N. C. When we arrived there were but few prisoners, and for two or three days we received fair rations of brea., bean soup and a little meat. This did not last long, for as the number of prisoners increased our rations were diminished. There were four old log houses within the stockade and into these the officers were moved the next day, while a thousand or more prisoners, brought on from Petersburg, were turned into the pen without shelter of any kind. From these we were separated by a line of sentinels, who had orders to shoot any who approached within six paces of their beat on either side. This was called the 'dead-line,' which also extended around the enclosure about six paces from the stockade.

"'The second Sunday after our arrival, just as we were assembling to hear preaching, an officer who had thoughtlessly stepped to a tree on the dead-line was shot and killed by the sentry, who was on an elevated platform outside the fence, and only about two rods distant. For this fiendish act the murderer was granted a sixty days furlough.

"'Prisoners were being brought in almost daily, and at this time there were probably six thousand within the enclosure. A pretence of shelter was furnished by the issue of a few Sibley tents, but not more than a third of the prisoners were sheltered. Many of them built mud hovels or burrowed in the ground; some crawled under the hospital building. Very few had blankets and all were thinly clad, and the rations were barely sufficient to sustain life. What wonder that men lost their strength, spirits, and sometimes reason. The story of exposure, sickness and death is the same and rivals that of Andersonville.

"'The guard was strengthened, a portion of the fence taken down and a piece of artillery stationed at the corners to sweep down the crowd, should an outbreak occur. This we had thought of for some time, and a plan of action was decided upon. At a given signal all within the enclosure were to make a break for that part of the fence nearest them, and then scatter, each one for himself. Of course, some would probably be killed, but it was hoped most would escape before the guards could load and fire a second time. This plot, which was to have been carried out at midnight, was discovered the previous afternoon. The inside guard, separating the enlisted-men from the officers, had become more vigilant, and the only means of communication was to attach a note to a stone and throw it across. This an officer attempted. The note fell short; the sentry picked it up, called the corporal of the guard, who took it to the officer of the guard, and in less than five minutes the whole arrangement was known. Two hours afterward we were formed in line and learned that we were to change our quarters. We had then been in Salisbury twenty days. Before we left one of our mess found and brought away a bound copy of *Harper's Magazine.* It proved a boon to us, as it served for a pillow for one of us at night, and was being read by some one from dawn until night, until we had all read it through, when we traded it off for a volume of the *Portland Transcript.*

"'We were packed in box cars and started North. The next morning we arrived at Danville and were confined in a tobacco warehouse, built of brick and about eighty feet long, forty wide, and three stories high. When we first entered the prison the ration was fair in quantity. We had from twelve to sixteen ounces of corn-bread, and from two to four ounces of beef or a cup of pea-soup, but never beef and soup the same day. True, the soup would have an abundance of worms floating about in it, but these we would skim off, and trying to forget we had seen them, eat with a relish. Hunger will drive one to eat almost anything, as we learned from bitter experience. About the 1st of November the soup and beef ration began to decrease, and from the middle of the month to the 20th of February, when I was paroled, not a ration of meat or soup was issued. Nothing but corn-bread, made from unbolted meal, and water, and that growing less and less. Sometimes I would divide my ration into three parts and resolve to make it last all day, but invariably it would be gone before noon. Generally I would eat the whole ration at once, but that did not satisfy my hunger, and I had to go without a crumb for the next twenty-four hours. To illustrate how inadequate the ration was, I can say that I have seen officers picking potato-peelings from the large spittoons, where they were soaking in tobacco spittle, wash them off and eat them.

"'We had an abundance of good, pure water, which was a great blessing. Pails were furnished, and when five or six men were ready, the sentry would call the corporal of the guard, who would send a guard of from four to six with us to the river, about two hundred yards distant. Twice a day an officer would come in and call the roll; that is form us into four ranks and count the files. If any had escaped, it was essential that the number should be kept good for some days, to enable them to get a good start, and for this purpose various means were used. Sometimes one of the rear rank, after being counted, would glide along unseen to the left of the line and be recounted. A hole was cut in the upper floor, and while the officer was going upstairs, some would climb through the hole and be counted with those on the third floor. This created some confusion, as the number would occasionally overrun.

"As the season advanced we suffered more and more from the cold, for being captured in September our clothing was not sufficient for December and January. Very few had blankets, and the rebel authorities never issued either blankets or clothing of any kind. The windows of the lower rooms were without glass, and only the lower half of each boarded up; the wind would whistle through the large openings, and drawing up through the open floor, upon which we had to lie at night, would almost freeze us. I finally succeeded in trading my watch with one of the guard for an old bed-quilt and twenty dollars Confederate money. The money came in very good time, for I then had the scurvy so badly that my tongue, lips and gums were so swollen that by evening I could scarcely speak. In the morning the swelling would not be quite so bad, and by soaking the corn-bread in water, could manage to swallow a little. The surgeon, who visited the prison every day, cauterized my mouth, but it continued to grow worse, until at last I could not eat the coarse bread. Sometimes I would have a chance to sell it for from

ESCAPING PRISONERS FED BY NEGROES IN THEIR MASTER'S BARN.

one to two dollars, which, with the twenty, saved me from starvation. I bought rice of the guard for two dollars the half-pint, and good-sized potatoes for a dollar each. These were cooked usually over a little fire in the yard with wood or chips picked up while going for water. Sometimes, by waiting patiently for an hour or more, I could get near enough to the stove to put my cup on. The heating apparatus was a poor apology for a cylinder coal-stove, and the coal the poorest I ever saw, and gave so little heat that one could stand all day by it and shiver.

"'The bed-quilt was quite narrow, but very much better than none.

"'Capt. Weiss and I would spread our flannel coats on the floor, use our shoes for pillows, spread the quilt over us, and with barely space to turn over, would, if the night was not too cold, go to sleep; usually to dream of home and loved ones; of Christmas festivities and banquets; of trains of army wagons so overloaded with pies and cakes that they were rolling into the road; of a general exchange; a thirty day's leave of absence, and a thousand things altogether unlike that which we were experiencing; and would wake only to find ourselves cold and hungry.

"'Our mess had the volume of *Harper's Magazine*, found at Salisbury, and we each could have it an hour or more daily. A few games of checkers or cribbage, played sitting on the floor, tailor-fashion, were always in order. All who were accustomed to smoking would manage to secure a supply of tobacco at least sufficient for one smoke per day, and, if they could not obtain it in any other way, would sell half their scanty ration, and perhaps get enough to last a week. It was a good place to learn how to economize. I have known some to refuse a light from the pipe, for fear of losing a grain of the precious weed. Evenings we would be in darkness, and as we could not move about without frequent collisions, would gather in little groups and talk of home, friends, and the good time coming, when we would have one good, square meal; arrange the bill of fare, comprising all the delicacies that heart could wish, or a morbid mind prompted by a starving stomach could conceive; lay plans for escape and discuss the route to be followed; sing a few hymns and the national airs, and wind up with 'We'll Hang Jeff Davis on a Sour Apple Tree.'

"'There were with us two officers who, when we arrived at Salisbury, had been in solitary confinement and whom the rebels were holding as hostages for two guerillas whom Gen. Burnside had condemned to be shot. When the removal of the officers to Danville occurred, these two were released from close confinement and sent on with us, and it was thought they were no longer considered as hostages. They had planned an escape and well nigh succeeded. They had dug a hole through the brick wall, and passing into an adjoining unoccupied building, cut through the floor, dug under the stone foundation and were just coming through on the outside, when some one in passing stepped on the thin crust and fell in. Whether he or the men digging were the most frightened it would be hard to tell. The next morning these two who had worked so hard to regain their liberty were taken out and probably placed in close confinement again.

"'After this attempt to escape, the rebel authorities made an effort to rob us of everything, particularly pocket-knives, watches, or anything that could aid us to escape. In this they were foiled. They made us all go to one end of the room and placing a guard through the middle, searched us one by one and passed us to the other side. If one had a knife, watch or money, he had only to toss it over to some one already searched, and when his turn came would have nothing to show.

"'The guards would not allow us to stand by the windows, and on one occasion, without warning, fired through a second-story window and badly wounded an officer on the third floor.

"'My shoes were nearly worn out when I was captured, and soon became so worn that I could only keep *sole* and *body* together by cutting strings from the edge of the uppers and lacing them together. These strings would wear but a little while, and frequent cuttings had made the shoes very low.

"'Toward the last of January, Capt. Cook received intelligence that a special exchange had been effected in his case and he was to start at once for the North. Here was an opportunity to communicate with our comrades and friends, for up to this time we did not know whether any of our letters had been received. Capt. Cook had a pair of good stout brogans. These shoes he urged me to take in exchange for my dilapidated ones. At first, I felt reluctant to do so, but finally made the exchange and he left us with a light heart, but his anticipations were not realized, for instead of going directly North he was detained in Libby Prison until just before the rest of us arrived, and when we reached Annapolis he was still there awaiting his leave, and had been obliged to wear my old shoes until two days previous.

"'Rumors of a general exchange began to circulate, and a few boxes of provisions and clothing, sent by Northern friends, were delivered. Among the rest, was a well-filled box from the officers of our regiment, and twelve hundred dollars Confederate money (being the equivalent of sixty dollars greenbacks) which they had kindly contributed. Could we have received the box and money in November, instead of just before our release, we could have subsisted quite comfortably all winter. As it was, we lived sumptuously as long as the contents of the box lasted, and when about a week later we started for Richmond to be paroled, we had drawn considerably upon the twelve hundred dollars.

"'February 17th, we left Danville for Richmond and were again quartered in Libby. On the 19th, we signed the parole papers.

"'The second morning after signing the rolls, one of the clerks came in and said that for want of transportation, only a hundred would be sent down the river that day, and the rest would follow soon; that those whose names were called would fall in on the lower floor, ready to start. As he proceeded to call the roll there was a death-like stillness, and each listened anxiously to hear his own name. Of our mess only one name was called. As he stopped reading and folded his rolls and turned to leave, I thought, what if our army should commence active operations and put an end to the exchange, and resolved to go with the party that day, if possible. I had noticed that the clerk had not called the names in their order nor checked them, and knew he could not tell who had been called. I therefore hurried down to the lower floor and fell in with the rest, thinking all the time of the possibility of detection and the consequent solitary confinement, and although my conscience was easy so far as the papers I had signed were concerned—for I had only agreed not to take up arms until duly exchanged—I did not breath freely until I had disembarked from the boat and was under the Stars and Stripes. Fortunately, the rest of the party came down on the boat the next day.

"'One other incident and I am done: Sergt. Henry Jordan, of Company C, was wounded and captured with the rest of us, but on account of his wounds was unable to be sent South with the other enlisted-men. After his recovery he was kept as a servant about the office of Major Turner, the commandant of the prison, and when, on the 2d of April, 1865, the rebels evacuated Richmond and paroled the prisoners, he remained until our forces came in and took possession of the city. When, a few days later, Maj. Turner was captured by our troops and confined in the same cell we had occupied, Sergt. Jordan was detailed to carry him his rations, and although he was not of a vindictive or revengeful disposition, I will venture to say that the rations allowed Turner were not much better than had been given the sergeant through the winter. Had Turner been guarded by such men as Henry Jordan, or even by the poorest soldiers of the regiment, he would not have escaped within three days of his capture, as was the case.'"

Very few of the black soldiers were exchanged, though the confederate government pretended to recognize them and treat them as they did the whites. General Taylor's reply to General Grant, was the general policy applied to them when convenient. In the latter days of the war, when —in June, 1864, at Guntown, Miss.,—the confederate Gen. Forrest attacked and routed the Union forces, under Sturgis, through the stupidity of the latter, (alluded to more at length a few pages further on,) a number of black soldiers were captured, Sturgis having had several Phalanx regiments in his command. The confederates fought with desperation, and with their usual "no quarter," because, as Forrest alleges, the Phalanx regiments meant to retaliate for his previous massacre of the blacks at Fort Pillow. Seeking to justify the inhuman treatment of his black prisoners, he wrote as follows to General Washburn, commanding the District of West Tennessee:

"It has been reported to me that all of your colored troops stationed in Memphis took, on their knees, in the presence of Major General Hurlburt and other officers of your army, an oath to avenge Fort Pillow, and that they would show my toops no quarter. Again I have it from indisputable authority that the troops under Brigadier General Sturgis on their recent march from Memphis, publicly, and in many places, proclaimed that no quarter would be shown my men. As they were moved into action on the 10th they were exhorted by their officers to remember Fort Pillow. The prisoners we have captured from that command, or a large majority of them, have voluntarily stated that they expected us to murder them, otherwise they would have surrendered in a body rather than have taken to the bushes after being run down and exhausted."

The massacre at Fort Pillow had a very different effect upon the black soldiers than it was doubtless expected to have. Instead of weakening their courage it stimulated them to a desire of retaliation; not in the strict sense of that term, but to fight with a determination to subdue and bring to possible punishment, the men guilty of such atrocious conduct. Had General Sturgis been competent of commanding, Forrest would have found himself and his command no match for the Phalanx at Guntown and Brice's Cross Roads. Doubtless Forrest was startled by the reply of General Washburn, who justly recognized the true impulse of the Phalanx. He replied to Forrest, June 19, 1864, as follows:

"You say in your letter that it has been reported to you that all the negro troops stationed in Memphis took an oath, on their knees, in the presence of Major General Hurlburt and other officers of our army, to avenge Fort Pillow and that they would show your troops no quarter. I believe it is true that the colored troops did take such an oath, but not in the presence of General Hurlburt. From what I can learn this act of theirs was not influenced by any white officer, but was the result of their own sense of what was due to themselves and their fellows who had been mercilessly slaughtered."

The chief of Forrest's artillery writes in the Philadelphia *Times*, in September, 1883:

"Col. Arthur T. Reeve, who commanded the Fifty-fifth Colored Infantry in this fight, tells me that no oath was taken by his troops that ever he heard of, but the impression prevailed that the black flag was raised, and on his side was raised to all intents and purposes. He himself fully expected to be killed if captured. Impressed with this notion a double effect was produced. It made the Federals afraid to surrender and greatly exasperated our men, and in the break-up the affair became more like a hunt for wild game than a battle between civilized men."

In his description of the battle at Brice's Cross Roads, he says:

"The entire Confederate force was brought into action at once. We kept no reserves; every movement was quickly planned and executed with the greatest celerity. A potent factor which made the battle far bloodier than it would have been, was it being reported, and with some degree of truth, that the negroes had been sworn on their knees in line before leaving Memphis to show 'no quarter to Forrest's men,' and badges were worn upon which were inscribed, 'Remember Fort Pillow.' General Washburn, commanding the district of West Tennessee, distinctly admits that the negro troops with Sturgis had gone into this fight with the declared intention to give no quarter to Forrest's men."

The fate of the black soldiers taken in these fights is unknown, which is even worse than of those who are known to have been massacred.

The details of the massacre at Fort Pillow have been reserved for this portion of the present chapter in order to state them more at length, and in connection with important movements which soon after took place against the same confederate force.

The most atrocious of all inhuman acts perpetrated upon a brave soldiery, took place at Fort Pillow, Kentucky, on the 13th of April, 1864. No cause can be assigned for the shocking crime of wanton, indiscriminate murder of some three hundred soldiers, other than that they were "niggers," and "fighting with niggers."

On the 12th, General Forrest suddenly appeared before Fort Pillow with a large force, and demanded its surrender. The fort was garrisoned by 557 men in command of Major L. F. Booth, consisting of the 13th Tennessee Cavalry, Major Bradford, and the 6th Phalanx Battery of heavy artillery, numbering 262 men, and six guns. At sunrise on the 13th, General Forrest's forces advanced and attacked the fort. The garrison maintained a steady brisk fire, and kept the enemy at bay from an outer line of intrenchments. About 9 A. M. Major Booth was killed, and Major Bradford taking command, drew the troops back into the Fort, situated on a high, steep and partially timbered bluff on the Mississippi river, with a ravine on either hand. A federal gunboat, the "New Era," assisted in the defence, but the height of the bluff prevented her giving material support to the garrison. In the afternoon both sides ceased firing, to cool and clean their guns. During this time, Forrest, under a flag of truce, summoned the federals to surrender within a half hour. Major Bradford refused to comply with the demand. Meantime the confederates taking advantage of the truce to secret themselves down in a ravine, from whence they could rush upon the Fort at a given signal. No sooner was Bradford's refusal to surrender received, than the confederates rushed simultaneously into the Fort. In a moment almost the place was in their possession. The garrison, throwing away their arms fled down the steep banks, endeavoring to hide from the promised "no quarter," which Forrest had embodied in his demand for surrender: "*If I have to storm your works, you may expect no quarter.*" The confederates followed, "butchering black and white soldiers and non-combatants, men, women and children. Disabled men were made to stand up and be shot; others were burned within the tents wherein they had been nailed to the floor." This carnival of murder continued until dark, and was even renewed the next morning. Major Bradford was not murdered until he had been carried as a prisoner several miles on the retreat.

It is best that the evidence in this matter, as given in previous pages of this chapter, should be read. It is unimpeachable, though Forrest, S. D. Lee and Chalmers have attempted to deny the infernal work. The last named, under whose command these barbarous acts were committed, offered on the floor of the United States Congress, fifteen years afterward, an apologetic denial of what appears from the evidence of those who escaped, —taken by the Congressional Committee,—and also contradictory to the confederate General S. D. Lee's report, in which he fails to convince himself even of the inaccuracy of the reports of brutality, as made by the few who escaped being murdered. Lee says:

THE MASSACRE AT FORT PILLOW.—April 12th, 1864.

"The garrison was summoned in the usual manner, and its commanding officer assumed the responsibility of refusing to surrender after having been informed by General Forrest of his ability to take the Fort, and of his fears of what the result would be in case the demand was not complied with. The assault was made under a heavy fire, and with considerable loss to the attacking party. Your colors were never lowered, and your garrison never surrendered, but retreated under cover of a gunboat, with arms in their hands and constantly using them. This was true particularly of your colored troops, who had been firmly convinced by your teaching of the certainty of slaughter, in case of capture. Even under these circumstances, many of your men, white and black, were taken prisoners."

Continuing, he says:

"The case under consideration is almost an extreme one. You had a servile race armed against us. I assert that our officers with all the circumstances against them endeavored to prevent the effusion of blood."

This is an admission that the massacre of the garrison actually occurred, and because Phalanx troops were a part of the garrison. That the black soldiers had been taught that no quarter would be shown them if captured, or if they surrendered, is doubtless true. It is also too true that the teaching was the *truth*. One has but to read the summons for the surrender to be satisfied of the fact, and then recollect that the President of the Confederate States, in declaring General Butler an outlaw, also decreed that negroes captured with arms in their hands, their officers as well, should be turned over to the State authorities wherein they were captured, to be dealt with according to the laws of that State and the Confederacy.

The sentiment of the chief confederate commander regarding the employment of negroes in the Union army, notwithstanding the Confederate Government was the first to arm and muster them into service, as shown in previous and later chapters, is manifested by the following dispatch, though at the time of writing it, that General had hundreds of blacks under his command at Charleston building fortifications.

"CHARLESTON, S. C., Oct. 13th, 1862.

"HON. WM. P. MILES, RICHMOND, VA.

"Has the bill for the execution of abolition prisoners, after January next, been passed? Do it, and England will be stirred into action. It is high time to proclaim the black flag after that period; let the execution be with the garrote. G. T. BEAUREGARD."

The confederate thirst for "nigger" blood seemed to have been no stronger in Kentucky than in other Departments, but it does appear, for some reason, that Kentucky and northern Mississippi were selected by the confederate generals, Pillow and Forrest, as appropriate sections in which to particularly vent their spite. The success of Forrest at Fort Pillow rather strengthened General Beauford's inhumanity. He commanded a portion of Pillow's forces which appeared before Columbus the day after the Fort Pillow massacre, and in the following summons demanded its surrender:

"*To the Commander of the United States Forces, Columbus, Ky.:*

"Fully capable of taking Columbus and its garrison, I desire to avoid shedding blood. I therefore demand the unconditional surrender of the forces under your command. Should you surrender, the negroes in arms will be returned to their masters. Should I be compelled to take the place by force, *no quarter will be shown negro troops whatever;* white troops will be treated as prisoners of war.

"I am, sir, yours,

A. BEAUFORD, Brig. Gen."

Colonel Lawrence, of the 34th New Jersey, declined to surrender, and drove the enemy off, who next appeared in Paducah, but retired without making an assault upon the garrison.

These occurrences, with the mysterious surrender of Union City to Forrest, on the 16th of March, so incensed the commander of the Department that a strong force was organized, and in command of General S. D. Sturgis, started, on the 30th of April, in pursuit of Forrest and his men, but did not succeed in overtaking him. A few weeks later, General Sturgis, with a portion of his former force, combined with that of General Smith's,—just returning from the Red River (Banks) *fiasco*,—again went in pursuit of General Forrest. At Guntown, on the 10th of June, Sturgis' cavalry, under General Grierson, came up with the enemy, charged upon them, and drove them back upon their infantry posted near Brice's Cross Roads. General Grierson, needing support, sent back for the infantry, which was several miles in his rear. The day was intensely hot, and the roads, from constant rains, in very bad condition. However, Sturgis marched the troops up at double-quick to the position where General Grierson was holding the confederates in check. The infantry had become so exhausted when they reached the scene of action, that they were unable to fight as they otherwise would have done. Sturgis, either ignorant of what was going on or incapacitated for the work, heightened the disorder at the front by permitting his train of over two hundred wagons to be pushed up close to the troops, thus blocking their rear, and obstructing their manœuvring; finally the wagons were parked a short distance from the lines and in sight of the foe. The troops exhausted by the rapid march, without proper formation or commanders, had been brought up to the support of the cavalry, who were hotly engaged with the enemy, whose desperation was increased at the sight of the Phalanx regiments. General Beauford had joined Forrest, augmenting his force 4,000. Sturgis' force numbered about 12,000, in cavalry, artillery and infantry. Forrest was well provided with artillery, which was up early and took a position in an open field enfilading the Federal line, which fought with a determination worthy of a better fate than that which befel it.

A confederate writer says:

"At early dawn on the 10th Lyon took the advance, with Morton's artillery close behind, Rucker and Johnson following. Meanwhile, Bell, as we have stated, at Rienzi, eight miles further north, was ordered to move up at a trot. The roads, soaked with water from recent continuous heavy rains and so much cut up by the previous passage of cavalry and trains, greatly retarded the progress of the artillery, so that Rucker and Johnson soon passed us. On reaching old Carrollville, five miles northeast of Brice's Cross Roads, heavy firing could be heard just on ahead. Forrest, as was his custom, had passed to the front of the entire column with his escort.

"He had, however, ordered Lieutenant R. J. Black, a dashing young officer, temporarily attached to his staff, to take a detachment of men from the Seventh Tennessee Cavalry and move forward and develop the enemy. Black soon reported that he had met the advance of the Federal cavalry one and a half miles from Brice's Cross Roads and there was skirmishing with them. General Forrest ordered Lyon to press forward with his brigade. A courier hastening back to the artillery said: 'General Forrest says, 'Tell Captain Morton to fetch up the artillery at a gallop.' Lyon in the meantime had reached the enemy's outposts, dismounted his brigade and thrown it into line and had warmly opposed a strong line of infantry or dismounted cavalry, which, after stubborn resistance, had been driven back to within half a mile of Brice's Cross Roads."

The columns of the Federals could not do more than retreat, and if they had been able to do this in any order, and recover from their exhaustion, they would have been ready to drive the foe, but they were hotly pursued by the confederates, who were continually receiving re-enforcements. It was soon evident that the confederates intended to gain the rear and capture the whole of the Union troops. The Federals, therefore, began to retire leisurely.

Says the confederate account:

"General Forrest directed General Buford to open vigorously when he heard Bell on the left, and, taking with him his escort and Bell's Brigade, moved rapidly around southeastward to the Guntown-Ripley road. He formed Wilson's and Russel's Regiments on the right of the road, extending to Rucker's left, and placed Newsom's Regiment on the left of the road; Duff's Regiment, of Rucker's Brigade, was placed on the left of Newsom; Captain H. A. Tyler, commanding Company A, Twelfth Kentucky, was ordered by Lyon and subsequently by Forrest to take his company, with Company C, Seventh Kentucky, and keep mounted on the extreme left of the line. The escort, under Captain Jackson, moved around the extreme left of the line, and on striking the Baldwyn and Pontotoc road about two miles south of the cross roads had a sharp skirmish and pressed the enemy's cavalry back to where Tishamingo creek crosses that road; here it was joined by Captain Gartrell's Georgia company and a Kentucky company. By mutual agreement Captain Jackson, of the escort, was placed in command of the three companies and Lieutenant Geroge L. Cowan in command of the escort. Meanwhile General Buford had ordered Barteau's Second Tennessee Cavalry to move across the country and gain the Federal rear, and if possible destroy their trains and then strike them in flank."

The gallant conduct of the Federal cavalry inspired the other troops. They made a stand, and for awhile advanced, driving the confederate line before them on the right, doubling it up and gaining the rear.

The same writer says:

"It was at this critical moment an officer of Bell's staff dashed up to General Forrest, very much excited, and said: 'General Forrest, the enemy flanked us and are now in our rear. What shall be done?' Forrest, turning in his saddle, very coolly replied: 'We'll whip these in our front and then turn around, and wont we be in their rear? And then we'll whip them fellows!' pointing in the direction of the force said to be in his rear. Jackson and Tyler, charging on the extreme left, drove back two colored regiments of infantry upon their main line at the cross roads. In this charge the gallant Captain Tyler was severely wounded.

"Meanwhile the Federals, with desperation, hurled a double line of battle, with the four guns at Brice's house concentrated upon Rucker and Bell, which for a moment seemed to stagger and make them waver. In this terrible onslaught the accomplished Adjutant, Lieutenant W. S. Pope, of the Seventh Tennessee, was killed, and a third of his regiment was killed and wounded. Soon another charge was sounded. Lieutenant Tully Brown was ordered, with his section of three-inch rifles, close on the front at the Porter house, from which position he hurled a thousand pounds of cold iron into their stubborn lines. A section of twelve-pounder howitzers, under Lieutenant B. F. Haller, pressed still further to the front and within a stone's throw almost of the enemy's line. Mayson's section of three-inch rifles were quickly placed in line with Haller's. Just then, General Buford, riding up and seeing no support to the artillery, called General Forrest's attention to the fact, when Forrest remarked: 'Support, h—l; let it support itself; all the d——n Yankees in the country can't take it."'

The lines were now closing upon each other, and the confederates began to feel the effect of the Union fire. The dash of the Phalanx, charging the enemy's flank, gave renewed courage to the troops, now pouring deadly volleys into the confederate's faces, and their guns had gained a position, from which they began to sweep the enemy's lines.

Says the same account:

"Now rose the regular incessant volleys of musketry and artillery. The lines in many places were not over thirty paces apart and pistols were freely used. The smoke of battle almost hid the combatants. The underbrush and dense black-jack thickets impeded the advance of the dismounted cavalry as the awful musketry fire blazed and gushed in the face of these gallant men. Every tree and brush was barked or cut to the ground by this hail of deadly missiles. It was here the accomplished and gallant William H. Porter, brother of Major Thomas K. and Governor James D. Porter, fell mortally wounded. This promising young officer had not attained his manhood. He was a cadet in the regular Confederate States army and had been ordered to report to General Bell, who assigned him to duty as A. D. C. Captain J. L. Bell, General Bell's Assistant Inspector-General, had just been killed from his horse, and almost at the same moment young Porter lost his own horse and just mounted Captain Bell's when he received the fatal shot. Lieutenant Isaac Bell, aide-de-camp of Bell's staff, was severely wounded.

The loss in officers right here was very heavy; sixteen were killed and sixty-one wounded. Captain Ab Hust, a mere boy, who commanded Bell's escort, rendered most efficient service at this critical juncture, and Major Tom Allison, the fighting Quartermaster of Bell's Brigade, was constantly by the side of his fearless commander, and in this terrible loss in staff officers his presence was most opportune.

"Like a prairie on fire the battle raged and the volleying thunder can be likened in my mind to nothing else than the fire of Cleburne's Division at Chickamauga, on that terrible Saturday at dusk. At length the enemy's lines wavered, Haller and Mayson pressed their guns by hand to within a short distance of Brice's house, firing as they advanced. Bell, Lyon and Rucker now closed in on the cross roads and the Federals gave way in disorder, abandoning three guns near Brice's house. General Sturgis, in his official report of the fight, says: 'We had four pieces of artillery at the cross roads. * * * Finding our troops were being hotly pressed, I ordered one section to open on the enemy's reserves. The enemy's artillery soon replied, and with great accuracy, every shell bursting over and in the immediate vicinity of our guns.' A shell from one of the Confederate guns struck the table in Brice's porch, was used by General Sturgis, stunning that officer."

The terrible struggle which now ensued was not surpassed, according to an eye-witness, by the fighting of any troops. The Phalanx were determined, if courage could do it, to whip the men who had so dastardly massacred the garrison of Fort Pillow. This fact was known to Forrest, Buford and their troops, who fought like men realizing that anything short of victory was death, and well may they have thus thought, for every charge the Phalanx made meant annihilation. They, too, accepted the portentous fiat, victory or death.

Though more than twenty years have passed since this bloody fight, yet the chief of the confederate artillery portrays the situation in these words:

"Is was soon evident that another strong line had formed behind the fence by the skirt of woods just westward of Phillips' branch. General Forrest riding up, dismounted and approached our guns, which were now plying shell and solid shot. With his field glasses he took in the situation. The enemy's shot were coming thick and fast; leaden balls were seen to flatten as they would strike the axles and tires of our gun carriages; trees were barked and the air was ladened with the familiar but unpleasant sound of these death messengers.

Realizing General Forrest's exposure, we involuntarily ventured the suggestion that, 'You had better get lower down the hill, General.' Instantly we apologized, as we expected the General to intimate that it was none of our business where he went. He, however, stepped down the hill out of danger and seating himself behind a tree, seemed for a few moments in deep study, but soon the head of our cavalry column arriving, he turned to me and said: 'Captain, as soon as you hear me open on the right and flank of the enemy over yonder,' pointing to the enemy's position, 'charge with your artillery down that lane and cross the branch.' The genial and gallant Captain Rice coming up at this time and hearing the order, turned to me and said: 'By G–d! whoever heard of artillery charging?' Captain Brice's Battery had been stationed at Columbus, Miss., and other points on local duty, and only a few months previous had been ordered and assigned to our command. He accepted his initiation into the ways and methods of horse artillery with much spirit and good grace.

"Meanwhile, watching Forrest at the head of the cavalry moving through the woods and across the field in the direction of the enemy's right, I directed Lieutenants Tully, Brown and H. H. Briggs, whose sections had been held in the road below the Hadden house for an emergency, to be ready to move into action at a moments notice. The enemy, observing our cavalry passing to their right, began to break and retire through the woods. Forrest, seeing this, dashed upon them in column of fours. At the same moment Lieutenant Brown pressed his section down the road, even in advance of the skirmish line, and opened a terrific fire upon the enemy, now breaking up and in full retreat. Lieutenant Briggs also took an advanced position and got in a few well-directed shots. Brown's section and a section of Rice's Battery were pushed forward across Phillips' branch and up the hill under a sharp fire, the former taking position on the right of the road and the latter in the road just where the road turns before reaching Dr. Agnew's house.

"Our skirmishers had driven the enemy's skirmishers upon their main line, when we were about to make another artillery charge, but distinctly hearing the Federal officers giving orders to their men to stand steady and yell, 'Remember Fort Pillow.' 'Charge! charge! charge!' ran along their lines, and on they came. Our right was pressed back on the 'negro avengers of Fort Pillow.' They moved steadily upon our guns and for a moment their loss seemed imminent. Our cannoneers, standing firm and taking in the situation, drove double-shotted cannister into this advancing line. The cavalry rallying on our guns sent death volleys into their ranks, which staggered the enemy and drove them back, but only to give place to a new line that now moved down upon us with wild shouts and got almost within hand-shaking distance of our guns.

"Lyon coming up opportunely at this moment formed his brigade on our right, and springing forward with loud cheers, hurled them back with so stormful an onset that their entire line gave way in utter rout and confusion. Lieutenant Brown's horse was shot under him. The gallant young soldier, Henry King, of Rice's Battery, fell with his ram mer staff in hand, mortally wounded. His grave now marks the spot where he fell. Several members of the artillery were wounded and a great many battery horses were killed. The reason for this desperate stand was soon discovered. The road was filled with their wagons, ambulances and many caissons, the dying and wounded. Cast-away arms, accoutrements, baggage, dead animals and other evidences of a routed army were conspicuous on every side. The sun had set, but the weary and over-spent Confederates maintained the pursuit for some five or six miles beyond and until it became quite too dark to go further. A temporary halt was ordered, when a section from each battery was directed to be equipped with ammunition and the best horses from their respective batteries and be ready to continue the pursuit at daylight."

The rout was all the enemy could desire, the Federals fought with a valor creditable to any troops, but were badly worsted, through the incompetency of Sturgis. They were driven back to Ripley, in a most disastrously confused state, leaving behind their trains, artillery, dead and wounded. But for the gallantry of the Phalanx, the enemy would have captured the entire force.

The same writer describes the rout:

"Johnson, pressing his brigade forward upon the enemy's position at Brice's Quarter, with Lyon supporting the artillery in the road below Brice's house, the position was soon captured with many prisoners and three pieces of artillery. Hallers and Mayson's sections were moved up at a gallop and established on the hill at Brice's Quarter and opened a destructive fire with double-shotted cannister upon the enemy's fleeing columns and wagon trains. The bridge over Tishamingo creek, still standing, was blocked up with wagons, some of whose teams had been killed. Finding the bridge thus obstructed the enemy rushed wildly into the creek, and as they emerged from the water on the opposite bank in an open field, our artillery played upon them for half a mile, killing and disabling large numbers. Forrests escort, under the dashing Lieutenant Cowan, having become detached in the meantime, had pressed around to the west side of the creek and south of the Ripley road, and here made one of its characteristic charges across an open field near the gin house, upon the enemy's wagon train, capturing several wagons.

"Meanwhile Barteau was not idle. He had moved his regiment, as we have stated, across to get in the enemy's rear, and in his own language says: 'I took my regiment across the country westward, to reach the Ripley road, on which the enemy was moving, and being delayed somewhat in passing through a swampy bottom, I did not reach that road, at Lyon's gin, three miles from Brice's Cross Roads, until probably 1 o'clock. I then learned that the last of the Federal regiments, with all their train, had passed by rapid march, and as there was now a lull in the engagement (for I had been hearing sharp firing in front), I greatly feared that Forrest was defeated and that the Federals were pushing him back, so I moved rapidly down the road till I reached the open field near the bridge.'

"This could not have been the Ripley Guntown road, as that road was filled with Federal troops, wagons and artillery from Dr. Agnew's house to the cross roads, a distance of two miles. 'Having placed some sharpshooters, whose sole attention was to be directed to the bridge,' he coutinues, 'I extended my line nearly half a mile, and began an attack by scattering shots at the same time. Sounding my bugle from various points along the line, almost immediately a reconnoitering force of the enemy appeared at the bridge, and being fired upon returned. This was followed, perhaps, by a regiment, and then a whole brigade came down to the creek. My, men, taking good aim, fired upon them coolly and steady. Soon I saw wagons, artillery, etc., pushing for the bridge. These were shot at by my sharpshooters. I now began to contract my line and collect my regiment, for the Federals came pouring in immense numbers across the creek. Your artillery was doing good work. Even the bullets from the small arms of the Confederates reached my men. I operated upon the flank of the enemy until after dark.'

"The wagons blockading the bridge were soon removed by being thrown into the stream and a section from each battery was worked across by hand, supported by the escort, and brought to bear upon a negro brigade with fearful loss; the other two sections were quickly to the front, ahead of any support for the moment, and drove the enemy from the ridge back of Holland's house across Dry creek. The cavalry in the meantime had halted, reorganized and soon joined in the pursuit. The road was narrow, with dense woods on each side, so that it was impossible to use more than four pieces at a time, but that number were kept close upon the heels of the retreating enemy and a murderous fire prevented them from forming to make a stand.

"The ridge extending southward from the Hadden house offered a strong natural position for defensive operations. Upon this ridge the Federals had established a line of battle, but a few well directed shots from the artillery stationed near the Holland house and a charge by our cavalry across Dry creek readily put them to flight. A section of each battery was ordered at a gallop to this ridge, which was reached in time to open with a few rounds of double-shotted cannister upon their demoralized ranks as they hastily retreated through the open fields on either side of Phillips branch. Our cannoneers were greatly blown and well nigh exhausted from excessive heat and continuous labor at their guns for full five hours. We noticed a number drink with apparant relish the black powder water from the sponge buckets."

The enemy followed the fleeing column, capturing and wounding many at the town of Ripley. Next morning the Federals made a stand. Again the Phalanx bore the brunt of the battle, and when finally the troops stampeded, held the confederates in check until the white troops were beyond capture. But this was all they could do, and this was indeed an heroic act.

The confederate says:

"Long before daylight found us moving rapidly to overtake the flying foe. We had changed positions. The cavalry now being in advance, overtook the enemy at Stubb's farm; a sharp skirmish ensued, when they broke, leaving the remainder of their wagon train. Fourteen pieces of artillery and some twenty-five ambulances, with a number of wounded, were left in Little Hatchie bottom, further on. The discomfited Federals were badly scattered throughout the country. Forrest, therefore, threw out his regiment on either side of the roads to sweep the vicinity. A number were killed and many prisoners captured before reaching Ripley, twenty-five miles from Brice's Cross Roads. At this point two strong lines were formed across the road. After a spirited onset the Federals broke, leaving one piece of artillery, two caissons, two ambulances. Twenty-one killed and seventy wounded were also left on the field. Colonel G. M. McCraig, of the One Hundred and Twentieth Illinois Infantry, was among the killed; also Captain W. J. Tate, Seventh Tennessee Cavalry. This was accomplished just as the artillery reached the front.

"Lieutenant Frank Rodgers, of Rucker's staff, the night previous, with a small, select detachment of men, assisted by Captain Gooch, with the remnant of his company, hung constantly upon the Federal rear, with a daring never surpassed. Their seiries of attacks greatly harrassed and annoyed the enemy, numbers of whom were killed and wounded. The artillery followed to Salem, twenty-five miles distant from Ripley."

The Phalanx regiments would not consent to be whipped, even with the black flag flying in their front, and deserted by their white comrades. A correspondent of the Cleveland *Leader*, in giving an account of this "miserable affair," writes:

"About sunrise, June 11, the enemy advanced on the town of Ripley, and threatened our right, intending to cut us off from the Salem Road. Again the colored troops were the only ones that could be brought into line; the Fifty-ninth being on the right, and the Fifty-fifth on the left, holding the streets. At this time, the men had not more than ten rounds of ammunition, and the enemy were crowding closer and still closer, when the Fifty-ninth were ordered to charge on them, which they did in good style, while singing,

"'We'll rally round the flag, boys.'

"This charge drove the enemy back, so that both regiments retreated to a pine grove about two hundred yards distant.

"By this time, all the white troops, except one squadron of cavalry, that formed in the rear, were on the road to Salem · and, when this brigade came up, they, too, wheeled and left, and in less than ten minutes this now little band of colored troops found themselves flanked. They then divided themselves into three squads, and charged the enemy's lines; one squad taking the old Corinth Road, then a by-road, to the left. After a few miles, they came to a road leading to Grand Junction. After some skirmishing, they arrived, with the loss of one killed and one wounded.

"Another and the largest squad covered the retreat of the white troops, completely defending them by picking up the ammunition thrown away by them, and with it repelling the numerous assaults made by the rebel cavalry, until they reached Collierville, a distance of sixty miles. When the command reached Dan's Mills, the enemy attempted to cut it off by a charge; but the colored boys in the rear formed, and repelled the attack, allowing the whole command to pass safely on, when they tore up the bridge. Passing on to an open country, the officers halted, and re-organized the brigade into an effective force. They then moved forward until about four, P. M.; when some Indian flank skirmishers discovered the enemy, who came up to the left, and in the rear, and halted. Soon a portion advanced, when a company faced about and fired, emptying three saddles. From this time until dark, the skirmishing was constant.

"A corporal in Company C, Fifty-ninth, was ordered to surrender. He let his would-be captor come close to him; when he struck him with the butt of his gun.

"While the regiment was fighting in a ditch, and the order came to retreat, the color-bearer threw out the flag, designing to jump out and get it; but the rebels rushed for it, and in the struggle one of the boys knocked down with his gun the reb who had the flag, caught it, and ran.

"A rebel, with an oath, ordered one of our men to surrender. He, thinking the reb's gun was loaded, dropped his gun; but, on seeing the reb commence lcading, our colored soldier jumped for his gun, and with it struck his captor dead.

"Capt. H., being surrounded by about a dozen rebels, was seen by one of his men, who called several of his companions; they rushed forward and fired, killing several of the enemy, and rescued their captain.

"A rebel came up to one, and said, 'Come my good fellow, go with me and wait on me.' In an instant, the boy shot his would-be master dead.

"Once when the men charged on the enemy, they rushed forth with the cry, 'Remember Fort Pillow.' The rebs called back, and said, 'Lee's men killed no prisoners.'

"One man in a charge threw his antagonist to the ground, and pinned him fast; and, as he attempted to withdraw his bayonet, it came off his gun, and, as he was very busy just then, he left him transfixed to mother earth.

"One man killed a rebel by striking him with the butt of his gun, which he broke; but, being unwilling to stop his work, he loaded and fired three times before he could get a better gun; the first time not being cautious, the rebound of his gun badly cut his lip.

"When the troops were in the ditch, three rebels came to one man, and ordered him to surrender. His gun being loaded, he shot one and bayoneted another; and, forgetting he could bayonet the third, he turned the butt of his gun, and knocked him down."

General Sturgis was severely criticised by the press immediately after the affair. Historians since the war have followed up these criticisms. He has been accused of incompetency, rashness and drunkenness, none of which it is the purpose of this volume to endorse. Possibly his reports furnish a sufficient explanation for the disaster, which it is hoped they do, inasmuch as he is not charged with either treason or cowardice.

[*General Sturgis' Report, No. 1.*]

"HEADQUARTERS UNITED STATES FORCES,
COLLIERSVILLE, TENN., June 12, 1864.

"GENERAL:—I have the honor to report that we met the enemy in position and in heavy force about 10 A. M. on the 10th instant at Brice's Cross-Roads on the Ripley and Fulton road and about six miles northwest of Guntown, Miss. A severe battle ensued which lasted until about 4 P. M., when I regret to say my lines were compelled to give way before the overwhelming numbers by which they were assailed at every point. To fall back at this point was more than ordinarily difficult as there was a narrow valley in our rear through which ran a small creek crossed by a single narrow bridge. The road was almost impassable by reason of the heavy rains which had fallen for the previous ten days and the consequence was that the road soon became jammed by the artillery and ordnance wagons. This gradually led to confusion and disorder.

"In a few minutes, however, I succeeded in establishing two colored regiments in line of battle in a wood on this side of the little valley. These troops stood their ground well and checked the enemy for a time. The check, however, was only temporary and this line in turn gave way. My troops were seized with a panic and became absolutely uncontrollable. One and a half miles in rear by dint of great exertion and with pistol in hand, I again succeeded in checking up the flying column and placing it in line of battle.

"This line checked the enemy for ten or fifteen minutes only, when it again gave way and my whole army became literally an uncontrollable mob. Nothing now remained to do but allow the retreat to continue and endeavor to force it gradually into some kind of shape. The night was exceedingly dark, the roads almost impassable and the hope of saving my artillery and wagons altogether futile, so I ordered the artillery and wagons to be destroyed. The latter were burned and the former dismantled and spiked, that is all but six pieces which we succeeded in bringing off in safety. By 7 A. M. next morning we reached Ripley (nineteen miles). Here we re-organized and got into very respectable shape. The retreat was continued, pressed rapidly by the enemy. Our ammunition soon gave out, this the enemy soon discovered and pressed the harder. Our only hope now lay in continuing the retreat which we did to this place, where we arrived about 7 o'clock this morning.

"My losses in material of war was severe, being 16 guns and some 130 wagons. The horses of the artillery and mules of the train we brought away. As my troops became very greatly scattered and are constantly coming in in small parties, I am unable to estimate my loss in killed and wounded. I fear, however, it will prove severe, probably ten or twelve hundred. While the battle lasted it was well contested and I think the enemy's loss in killed and wounded will not fall short of our own.

"This, general, is a painful record, and yet it was the result of a series of unfortunate circumstances over which human ingenuity could have no control.

The unprecedented rains so delayed our march across a desert country that the enemy had ample time to accumulate an overwhelming force in our front, and kept us so long in an exhausted region as to so starve and weaken our animals that they were unable to extricate the wagons and artillery from the mud.

"So far as I know every one did his duty well, and while they fought no troops ever fought better. The colored troops deserve great credit for the manner in which they stood to their work.

"This is a hasty and rather incoherent outline of our operations, but I will forward a more minute account as soon as the official reports can be received from division commanders.

"I have the honor to be, sir, very respectfully, your obedient servant,

"S. D. STURGIS,

"*Brig.-Gen. Commanding.*

"To Maj.-Gen. C. C. WASHBURN,
Commanding District W. Tenn."

An extract from a letter from Colonel Arthur T. Reeve, who commanded the 55th Colored Infantry in this fight, reads:

"Our (the Federal) command having been moved up on double-quick—a distance of about five miles--immediately before their arrival on the field and the consequent fact that this arm of our force went into the engagement very seriously blown, in fact, very nearly exhausted by heat and fatigue, with their ranks very much drawn out, were whipped in detail and overwhelmed by the very brilliant and vigorous assaults of your forces. When the engagement first began I was at the rear of the

Federal column, in command of the train guard, and hence passed over the ground on the way to the battle-field after the balance of the army had passed, and am able to speak advisedly of the extreme exhaustion of the infantry, as I passed large numbers entirely prostrated by heat and fatigue, who did not reach the field of battle and must have fallen into your hands after the engagement."

[*General Sturgis' Report, No. 2.*]

"MEMPHIS, TENN., June 24, 1864.

"Sir: I have the honor to submit the following report of the operations of the expedition which marched from near La Fayette, Tenn., under my command on the 2nd instant. This expedition was organized and fitted out under the supervision of the major general commanding the District of West Tennessee and I assumed command of it on the morning of the 2nd of June, near the town of La Fayette, Tenn., in pursuance of Special Orders, No. 38, dated Headquarters, District of West Tennessee, Memphis, May 31, 1864, and which were received by me on the 1st inst. The strength of the command in round numbers was about 8,000 men,' (which included the following Phalanx regiments: 59th Regt., 61st Regt., 68th Regt., Battery I, 2nd Artillery, (Light,) 2 pieces.)

"My supply train, carrying rations for 18 days, consisted of 181 wagons, which with the regimental wagons made up a train of some 250 wagons. My instructions were substantially as follows, viz: To proceed to Corinth, Mississippi by way of Salem and Ruckersville, capture any force that might be there, then proceed south, destroying the Mobile and Ohio Railroad to Tupelo and Okolona and as far as possible towards Macon and Columbus with a portion of my force, thence to Grenada and back to Memphis. A discretion was allowed me as to the details of the movement where circumstances might arise which could not have been anticipated in my instructions. Owing to some misunderstanding on the part of the quartermaster, as to the point on the Memphis and Charleston Railroad at which some forage was to have been deposited from the cars, there was some little delay occasioned in getting the column in motion.

"The following incidents of the march are taken from the journal kept from day to day by one of my staff, Capt. W. C. Rawolle, A. D. C. and A. A. A. G.:

"'Wednesday, June 1st.—Expedition started from Memphis and White's Station toward LaFayette.

"'Thursday, June 2nd.—The general and staff left Memphis on the 5 o'clock A. M. train and established headquarters at Leaks' House, near LaFayette, and assumed command. Cavalry moved to the intersection of State line and Early Grove roads, six miles from La Fayette. It rained at intervals all day and part of the night.

"'Friday, June 3rd.—Ordered the cavalry to move to within three four miles of Salem. Infantry marched to Lamar, 18 miles from LaFayette. Owing to the heavy rains during the day and the bad condition of the roads and bridges, the train could only move to within four miles of Lamar, and did not get into park until 11 o'clock P. M., the colored brigage remaining with the train as a guard.

"'Saturday, June 4th.—Informed General Grierson that the infantry and train under the most favorable circumstances could only make a few miles beyond Salem and to regulate his march accordingly. Train arrived at Lamar about noon, issued rations to the infantry and rested the animals It rained heavily until 1 o'clock P. M., making the roads almost impassable. Moved headquartersto the Widow Spright's house, two miles west of Salem, and Colonel Hoge's brigade of infantry to Robinson's house, four miles from Salem.

"'Sunday, June 5th.—Infantry and train started at half past four o'clock A. M., and joined the cavalry, two miles east of Salem. At 10 o'clock A. M., issued rations to the cavalry and fed the forage collected by them. Infantry remained in camp during the day; cavalry moved to the intersection of the LaGrange and Ripley and the Salem and Ruckersville roads. Col. Joseph Karge, 2nd New Jersey, with 400 men, started at 6 P. M., with instructions to move viâ Ripley to Rienzi, to destroy the railroad; to proceed north, destroy bridge over Tuscumbia and to join General Grierson at Ruckersville. Heavy showers during the afternoon.

"'Monday, June 7th.—Infantry and train moved at 4 o'clock A. M., on the Ruckersville road. Commenced raining at 5 A. M., and continued at intervals all day. Progress very slow, marched 13 miles and made headquarters at Widow Childers, at intersection of the Saulsbury and Ripley and the Ruckersville and Salem roads. Cavalry moved to Ruckersville. The advance guard of the infantry encountered a small party of rebels about noon and chased them towards Ripley on La Grange and Ripley roads.

"'Tuesday, June 7th.—Upon information received from General Grierson that there was no enemy near Corinth, directed him to move toward Ellistown, on direct road from Ripley, and instruct Colonel Karge to join him by way of Blackland or Carrollsville. Infantry moved to Ripley and cavalry encamped on New Albany road two miles south. Encountered a small party of rebels near Widow Childers and drove them toward Ripley. In Ripley, met an advance of the enemy and drove them on New Albany road. Cavalry encountered about a regiment of rebel cavalry on that road and drove them south. Several showers during the afternoon, and the roads very bad.

"Wednesday, June 8th.—Received information at 4 o'clock A. M. that Colonel Karge was on an island in the Hatchie River and sent him 500 men and two howitzers as re-inforcements. Winslow's brigade of cavalry moved 6 miles on the Fulton Road. Infantry and train moved five miles on same road. Colonel Waring's brigade remained in Ripley awaiting return of Colonel Karge, who joined him at 5 o'clock P. M., having swam the Hatchie River. Rained hard during the night.

"'Thursday, June 9th.—Sent back to Memphis 400 sick and wounded men and 41 wagons. Cavalry and infantry moved to Stubbs', fourteen miles from Ripley; issued five days' rations (at previous camp.) Rained two hours in the evening.

"'Friday, June 10th.—Encountered the enemy at Brice's Cross-Roads, 23 miles from Ripley and six miles from Guntown.'

"At Ripley it became a serious question in my mind as to whether or not I should proceed any farther. The rain still fell in torrents; the artillery and wagons were literally mired down, and the starved and exhausted animals could with difficulty drag them along. Under these circumstances, I called together my division commanders and placed before them my views of our condition. At this interview, one brigade commander and two members of my staff were, incidentally, present also. I called their attention to the great delay we had undergone on account of the continuous rain and consequent bad condition of the roads; the exhausted condition of our animals; the great probability that the enemy would avail himself of the time thus afforded him to concentrate an overwhelming force against us in the vicinity of Tupelo and the utter hopelessness of saving our train or artillery in case of defeat, on account of the narrowness and general bad condition of the roads and the impossibility of procuring supplies of forage for the animals; all agreed with me in the probable consequences of defeat. Some thought our only safety lay in retracing our steps and abandoning the expedition. It was urged, however, (and with some propriety, too,) that inasmuch as I had abandoned a similar expedition only a few weeks before and given as my reasons for so doing, the "utter and entire destitution of the country," and that in the face of this we were again sent through the same country, it would be ruinous on all sides to return again without first meeting the enemy. Moreover, from all the information General Washburn had acquired, there *could be no considerable* force in our front and all my own information led to the same conclusion. To be sure my information was exceedingly meagre and unsatisfactory and had I returned I would have been totally unable to present any facts to justify my cause, or to show why the expedition might not have been successfully carried forward. All I could have presented would have been my conjectures as to what the enemy would naturally do under the circumstances and these would have availed but little against the idea that the enemy was scattered and had no considerable force in our front.

"Under these circumstances, and with a sad forboding of the consequences, I determined to move forward; keeping my force as compact as possible and ready for action at all times; hoping that we might succeed, and feeling that if we did not, yet our losses might at most be insignificant in comparison with the great benefits which might accrue to General Sherman by the depletion of Johnson's army to so large an extent.

"On the evening of the 8th, one day beyond Ripley, I assembled the com manders of infantry brigades at the headquarters of Colonel McMillen, and cautioned them as to the necessity of enforcing rigid discipline in their camps; keeping their troops always in hand and ready to act on a moment's notice. That it was impossible to gain any accurate or reliable information of the enemy, and that it behooved us to move and act constantly as though in his presence. That we were now where we might encounter him at any moment, and that we must under no circumstances allow ourselves to be surprised. On the morning of the 10th, the cavalry marched at half-past 5 o'clock and the infantry at seven, thus allowing the infantry to follow immediately in rear of the cavalry as it would take the cavalry a full hour and a half to clear their camp The habitual order of march was as follows, viz: Cavalry with its artillery in advance; infantry with its artillery; next, and lastly, the supply train, guarded by the rear brigade with one of its regiments at the head, one near the middle and one with a section of artillery in the rear. A company of pioneers preceded the infantry for the purpose of repairing the roads, building bridges, &c., &c.

"On this morning, I had preceded the head of the infantry column and arrived at a point some five miles from camp, when I found an unusually bad place in the road and one that would require considerable time and labor to render practicable. While halted here to await the head of the column, I received a message from General Grierson that he had encountered a portion of the enemy's cavalry. In a few minutes more I received another message from him, saying the enemy numbered some 600 and were on the Baldwyn road. That he was himself at Brice's Cross-Roads and that his position was a good one and he would hold it. He was then directed to leave 600 or 700 men at the cross-roads, to precede the infantry on its arrival, on its march towards Guntown, and with the remainder of his forces to drive the enemy toward Baldwyn and there rejoin the main body by way of the line of the railroad, as I did not intend being drawn from my main purpose. Colonel McMillen arrived at this time and I rode forward toward the cross-roads. Before proceeding far, however, I sent a staff officer back directing Colonel McMillen to move up his advance brigade as rapidly as possible without distressing his troops. When I reached the cross-roads, found nearly all the cavalry engaged and the battle growing warm, but no artillery had yet opened on either side. We had four pieces of artillery at the cross-roads, but they had not been placed in position, owing to the dense woods on all sides and the apparent impossibility of using them to advantage. Finding, however, that our troops were being hotly pressed, I ordered one section to open on the enemy's reserves. The enemy's artillery soon replied, and with great accuracy, every shell bursting over and in the immediate vicinity of our guns.

"Frequent calls were now made for re-enforcements, but until the infantry should arrive, I had none to give. Colonel Winslow, 4th Iowa Cavalry, commanding a brigade and occupying a position on the Guntown road a little in advance of the cross-roads, was especially clamorous to be relieved and permitted to carry his brigade to the rear. Fearing that Colonel Winslow might abandon his position without authority, and knowing the importance of the cross-roads to us, I directed him in case he should be overpowered, to fall back slowly toward the cross-roads, thus contracting his line and strengthening his position. I was especially anxious on this point because through some misunderstanding, that I am yet unable to explain, the cavalry had been withdrawn without my knowledge from the left, and I was compelled to occupy the line, temporarily, with my escort, consisting of about 100 of the 19th Penn. Cavalry. This handful of troops under the gallant Lieut-Colonel Hess, behaved very handsomely and held the line until the arrival of the infantry. About half-past 1 p. m. the infantry began to arrive. Col. Hodge's brigade was the first to reach the field and was placed in position by Colonel McMillen, when the enemy was driven a little. General Grierson now requested authority to withdraw the entire cavalry as it was exhausted and well nigh out of ammunition. This I authorized as soon as sufficient infantry was in position to permit it and he was directed to reorganize his command in the rear and hold it ready to operate on the flanks. In the mean time I had ordered a section of artillery to be placed in position on a knoll near the little bridge, some three or four hundred yards in the rear, for the purpose of opposing any attempt of the enemy to turn our left. I now went to this point to see that my orders had been executed and also to give directions for the management and protection of the wagon-train. I found the section properly posted and supported by the 72nd Ohio Infantry, with two companies thrown forward as skirmishers, and the whole under the superintendence of that excellent officer, Colonel Wilkins, of the 9th Minn. While here, the head of the wagon train, which had been reported still a mile and a half in rear, arrived. It was immediately ordered into an open field near where the cavalry were reorganizing, there to be turned round and carried farther toward the rear. The pressure on the right of the line was now becoming very great and General Grierson was directed to send a portion of his cavalry to that point. At this time I received a message from Colonel Hodge that he was satisfied that the movement on the right was a feint and that the real attack was being made on the left. Another section of artillery was now placed in position a little to the rear of Colonel Wilkins, but bearing on the left of our main line, and a portion of the cavalry was thrown out as skirmishers The cavalry which had been sent to the extreme right began now to give way, and at the same time the enemy began to appear in force in rear of the extreme left, while Colonel McMillen required re-enforcements in the centre. *I now endeavored to get hold of the colored brigade which formed the guard to the train. While traversing the short distance to where the head of that brigade should be found, the main line began to give way at various points; order soon gave way to confusion and confusion to panic. I sent an aid to Col. McMillen informing him that I was unable to render him any additional assistance, and that he must do all in his power with what he had to hold his position until I could form a line to protect his retreat. On reaching the head of the supply train, Lieut.-Colonel Hess was directed to place in position in a wood the first regiment of colored troops I could find. This was done, and it is due to those troops to say here that they stood their ground well and rendered valuable aid to Colonel McMillen*, who was soon after compelled to withdraw from his original line and take up new positions in rear. It was now 5 o'clock P. M. For seven hours, these gallant officers and men had held their ground against overwhelming numbers, but at last overpowered and exhausted they were compelled to abandon not only the field, but many of their gallant comrades who had fallen to the mercy of the enemy Everywhere the army now drifted toward the rear and was soon altogether beyond control. I requested General Grierson to accompany me and to aid in checking the fleeing column and establishing a new line. By dint of entreaty and force and the aid of several officers, whom I called to my assistance, with pistols in their hands we at length succeeded in checking some 1200 or 1500 and establishing them in a line of which Colonel Wilkins, 9th Minnesota, was placed in command. About this time it was reported to me that Col McMillen was driving the enemy. I placed but little faith in this report, yet disseminated it freely for the good effect it might produce upon the troops. In a few minutes, however, the gallant Colonel McMillen, sad and disheartened, arrived himself, and reported his lines broken and in confusion. The new line under Colonel Wilkins also gave way soon after and it was now impossible to exercise any further control. The road became crowded and jammed with troops; the wagons and artillery sinking into the deep mud became inextricable and added to the general confusion which now prevailed. No power could now check or control the panic-stricken mass as it swept toward the rear, led off by Colonel Winslow at the head of his brigade of cavalry, and who never halted until he had reached Stubbs', ten miles in rear. This was the greater pity as his brigade was nearly, if not entirely, intact, and might have offered considerable resistance to the advancing foe. About 10 o'clock P. M., I reached Stubbs' in person, where I found Colonel Winslow and his brigade. I then informed him that his was the only organized body of men I had been able to find, and directed him to add to his own every possible force he could rally, as they passed, and take charge of the rear, remaining in position until all should have passed. I also informed him that on account of the extreme darkness of the night and the wretched condition of the road, I had little hope of saving anything more than the troops, and directed him therefore to destroy all wagons and artillery which he might find blocking up the road and preventing the passage of the men. In this way about 200 wagons and 14 pieces of artillery were lost, many of the wagons being burned and the artillery spiked and otherwise mutilated; the mules and horses were brought away. By 7 oclock A. M., of the 11th, we had reorganized at Ripley, and the army presented quite a respectable appearance, and would have been able to accomplish an orderly retreat from that point but for the unfortunate circumstances that the cartridge boxes were well nigh exhausted. At 7 o'clock the column was again put in motion on the Salem road, the cavalry in advance, followed by the infantry. The enemy pressed heavily on the rear, and there was now nothing left but to keep in motion so as to prevent the banking up of the rear, and to pass all cross-roads before the enemy could reach them, as the command was in no condition to offer determined resistance, whether attacked in the front or the rear. At 8 o'clock a. m. on the 12th, the column reached Colliersville, worn out and exhausted by the fatigues of fighting and marching for two days and two nights without rest and without eating. About noon of the same day a train arrived from Memphis, bringing some 2,000 infantry, commanded by Colonel Wolf, and supplies for my suffering men, and I determined to remain here until next day for the purpose of resting and affording protection to many who had dropped by the wayside, through fatigue and other causes. Learning, however, toward evening, that the commander at White's Station had information of a large force of the enemy approaching that place from the southeast, and knowing that my men were in no condition to offer serious resistance to an enemy presenting himself across my line of march, I informed the general commanding the district, by telegraph, that I deemed it prudent to continue my march to White's Station. Accordingly, at 9 p. m., the column marched again, and arrived at White's Station at daylight next morning. This report having already become more circumstantial than was anticipated, I have purposely omitted the details of our march from Ripley to White's Station, as they would extend it to a tiresome length, but would respectfully refer you for these to the sub-reports herewith enclosed. Casualties are as follows:

"Killed, 223, wounded, 394; missing, 1623; total, 2240. That our loss was great, is true; yet that it was not much greater is due in an eminent degree to the personal exertions of that model soldier, Col. W. L. McMillen, of the 95th Ohio Infantry, who commanded the infantry, and to the able commanders under him.

"The strength of the enemy is variously estimated by my most intelligent officers at from 15,000 to 20,000 men. A very intelligent sergeant who was captured and remained five days in the hands of the enemy, reports the number of the enemy actually engaged, to have been 12,000, and that two divisions of infantry were held in reserve. It may appear strange that so large a force of the enemy could be in our vicinity and we be ignorant of the fact, but the surprise will exist only in the minds of those who are not familiar with the difficulty, (I may even say impossibility) of acquiring reliable information in the heart of the enemy's country. Our movements and numbers are always known to the enemy, because every woman and child is one of them, but we, as everybody knows who has had any experience in this war, can only learn the movements of the enemy and his numbers by actually fighting for the information; and in that case the knowledge often comes too late.

"While I will not prolong this already extended report by recording individual acts of good conduct, and the names of many brave officers and men who deserve mention, but will respectfully refer you for these to the reports of division and brigade commanders, yet I cannot refrain from expressing my high appreciation of the valuable services rendered by that excellent and dashing officer, Col. Joseph Karge, of the 2nd New Jersey Vols., in his reconnoissance to Corinth and his subsequent management of the rear-guard, during a part of the retreat, fighting and defending the rear during one whole afternoon and throughout the entire night following.

"To the officers of my staff,—Lieut.-Col. J. C. Hess, 19th Pa. Cavalry, commanding escort, Capt. W. C. Rawolle, A. D. C. and A. A. A. G.; Capt. W. C. Belden, 2nd Iowa Cavalry, A. D. C.; Lieut. E. Caulkins 7th Indiana Cavalry, A. D. C ; Lieut. Samuel (name illegible) 19th Penn. Cavalry, A. D. C.; Lieut. Dement, A. A. Q. M.; Lieut. W. H. Stratton, 7th Ills. Cavalry, A. A. C. S.,—whose names appear in no other report, I am especially grateful, for the promptness and zeal with which my orders were executed at all times and often under trying and hazardous circumstances.

"I am, major, very respectfully your obedient servant,

S. D. STURGIS,
Brig.-Gen. Commanding.

MAJ. W. H. MORGAN, A. A. G.,
Hdqrs. Dist. West Tenn., Memphis, Tenn.

"Amid these scenes we noted the arrival of 95 more men; those who had belonged to a *raid* sent from Memphis, Tenn., under command of General Sturgis, and were attacked and badly defeated by the rebel General Forrest, at a place in Mississippi. General Sturgis is said to have been *intoxicated* during the engagement, and that just as soon as he saw things were likely to go against him, he turned away with a portion of his cavalry, and *sought to save himself from capture.—'Life and Death in Rebel Prisons.'*"

Notwithstanding the arrangements usually and speedily entered into by two belligerent powers for the exchange of prisoners of war, it proved a most difficult task for the Federal Government to consummate an arrangement with the confederates, and much suffering was caused among the prisoners in the hands of the latter while negotiations were in progress. The agreement entered into by the commissioners, after a long delay, did not anticipate there being any black soldiers to exchange; nor would the confederate authorities thereafter allow the terms of the cartel to apply to the blacks, because Jefferson Davis and the confederate Congress regarded it as an outrage against humanity, and the rules of civilized warfare to arm the negroes against their masters.

It was a year after the black soldiers had become a part of the Union forces before even a *quasi* acknowledgment of their rights as prisoners was noted in Richmond. The grounds upon which the greatest difficulty lingered was the refusal of the Federal government at first to accord belligerent rights to the confederates but this difficulty was finally overcome in July, 1862, and the exchange of prisoners proceeded with until the confederate authorities refused to count the black soldiers captured in the interpretation of the cartel. But the time arrived when Grant assumed command of the armies, when it was no longer an open question, for the confederate Congress began devising plans for arming the slaves.

However, the inhuman treatment did not cease with "irresponsible parties," whose conduct was doubtless approved by the rebel authorities, Jefferson Davis having declared General Butler an outlaw, and committed him and his officers and black soldiers to the mercy of a chivalry which affected to regard them as mercenaries. With this spirit infused in the confederate army, what else than barbarity could be expected?

PHALANX REGIMENT RECEIVING ITS FLAGS.
Presentation of colors to the 20th United States Colored Infantry, Col. Bertram, in N. Y., March 5th, 1864.

CHAPTER XI.

THE PHALANX IN VIRGINIA.

The laurels won by the Phalanx in the Southern States, notwithstanding the "no quarter" policy, was proof of its devotion to the cause of liberty and the old flag, which latter, until within a short period had been but a symbol of oppression to the black man; Cailloux had reddened it with his life's blood, and Carney, in a seething fire had planted it on the ramparts of Wagner. The audacious bravery of the Phalanx had wrung from Generals Banks and Gillmore congratulatory orders, while the loyal people of the nation poured out unstinted praises. Not a breach of discipline marred the negro soldier's record; not one cowardly act tarnished their fame. Grant pronounced them gallant and reliable, and Weitzel was willing to command them.

In New York City, where negroes had been hung to lamp posts, and where a colored orphan asylum had been sacked and burned, crowds gathered in Broadway and cheered Phalanx regiments on their way to the front. General Logan, author of the Illinois Black Code, greeted them as comrades, and Jefferson Davis finally accorded to them the rights due captured soldiers as prisoners of war. Congress at last took up the question of pay, and placed the black on an equal footing with the white soldiers. Their valor, excelled by no troops in the field, had finally won full recognition from every quarter, and henceforth they were to share the full glory as well as the toils of their white comrades-in-arms. Not until those just rights and attentions were attained, was the Phalanx allowed, to any great extent, to show its efficiency and prowess in the manœuvres in Virginia and vicinity, where that magnificent "Army of Northern Virginia," the hope and the pride of the Confederacy, was operating against the Federal government. But when General Grant came to direct the movements of the Eastern armies of the United States, there was a change. He had learned from his experience at Vicksburg and other places in his western campaigns, that the negro soldiers were valuable; that they could be fully relied upon in critical times, and their patriotic zeal had made a deep impression upon him. Therefore, as before stated, there were changes, and quite a good many Phalanx regiments—numbering about 20,000 men—were taken from Southern and Western armies and transferred to the different armies in Virginia.

The 19th Army Corps sent one brigade. General Gillmore brought a brigade from the Tenth Army Corps. At least ten thousand of them were veterans, and had driven many confederates out of their breastworks.

The world never saw such a spectacle as America presented in the winter and early spring of 1864. The attempt to capture Richmond and Petersburg had failed. The Army of the Potomac lay like a weary lion under cover, watching its opponent. Bruised, but spirited and defiant, it had driven, and in turn had been driven time and again, by its equally valient foe. It had advanced and retreated until the soldiers were foot-sore from marching and counter-marching, crossing and re-crossing the now historic streams of the Old Dominion. Of all this, the loyal people were tired and demanded of the Administration a change. The causes of the failures to take the confederate capitol were not so much the fault of the commanders of the brave army as that of the authorities at Washington, whose indecision and interference had entailed almost a disgrace upon McClellan, Hooker, Burnside and Meade. But finally the people saw the greatest of the difficulties, and demanded its removal, which the Administration signified its willingness to do.

PARADE OF THE 20TH REG'T. U. S. C. T. IN NEW YORK.

Then began an activity at the North, East and West, such as was never before witnessed. The loyal heart was again aroused by the President's call for troops, and all realized the necessity of a more sagacious policy, and the importance of bringing the war to a close. The lion of the South must be bearded in his lair, and forced to surrender Richmond, the Confederate Capitol, that had already cost the Government millions of dollars, and the North thousands of lives. The cockade city,—Petersburg,—like the Gibralter of the Mississippi, should haul down the confederate banner from her breastworks; in fact, Lee must be vanquished. That was the demand of the loyal nation, and right well did they enter into preparations to consummate it; placing brave and skillful officers in command.

The whole North became a recruiting station. Sumner, Wilson, Stevens and Sherman, in Congress, and Greeley, Beecher, Philips and Curtis, with the press, had succeeded in placing the fight upon the highest plane of civilization, and linked *freedom* to the cause of the Union thus making the success of one the success of the other,—"Liberty and Union, one and inseparable." What patriotism should fail in accomplishing, bounties—National, State, county, city and township—were to induce and effect. The depleted ranks of the army were filled to its maximum, and with a hitherto victorious and gallant leader would be hurled against the fortifications of the Confederacy with new energy and determination.

Early in January, General Burnside was ordered again to take command of the Ninth Army Corps, and to recruit its strength to fifty thousand effective men, which he immediately began to do. General Butler, then in command of the Department of Virginia and North Carolina, began the organization of the Army of the James, collecting at Norfolk, Portsmouth and on the Peninsula, the forces scattered throughout his Department, and to recruit Phalanx regiments. In March, General Grant was called to Washington, and received the appointment of Lieutenant General, and placed in command of the armies of the Republic. He immediately began their reorganization, as a preliminary to attacking Lee's veteran army of northern Virginia.

As has before been stated, the negro had, up to this time, taken no very active part in the battles fought in Virginia. The seed of prejudice sown by Generals McDowell and McClellan at the beginning of hostilities, had ripened into productive fruit. The Army of the Potomac being early engaged in apprehending and returning runaway slaves to their presumed owners, had imbibed a bitter, unrelenting hatred for the poor, but ever loyal, negro. To this bitterness the Emancipation Proclamation gave a zest, through the pro-slavery press at the North, which taunted the soldiers with "*fighting to free the negroes.*" This feeling had served to practically keep the negro, as a soldier, out of the Army of the Potomac.

General Burnside, upon assuming his command, asked for and obtained permission from the War Department to raise and unite a division of Negro troops to the 9th Army Corps. Annapolis, Md., was selected as the "depot and rendezvous," and very soon Camp Stanton had received its allowance of Phalanx regiments for the Corps. Early in April, the camp was broken, and the line of march taken for Washington. It was rumored throughout the city that the 9th Corps would pass through there, and that about 6,000 Phalanx men would be among the troops. The citizens were on the *qui vive*; members of Congress and the President were eager to witness the passage of the Corps.

At nine o'clock on the morning of the 25th of April, the head of the column entered the city, and at eleven the troops were marching down New York Avenue. Halting a short distance from the corner of 14th street, the column closed up, and prepared to pay the President a marching salute, who, with General Burnside and a few friends, was awaiting their coming. Mr. Lincoln and his party occupied a balcony over the entrance of Willard's Hotel. The scene was one of great beauty and animation. The day was superbly clear; the soft atmosphere of the early spring was made additionally pleasant by a cool breeze; rain had fallen the previous night, and there was no dust to cause discomfort to the soldiers or spectators. The troops marched and appeared well; their soiled and battered flags bearing inscriptions of battles of six States. The corps had achieved almost the first success of the war in North Carolina; it had hástened to the Potomac in time to aid in rescuing the Capitol, when Lee made his first Northern invasion; it won glory at South Mountain, and made the narrow bridge at Antietam, forever historic; it had likewise reached Kentucky in time to aid in driving the confederates from that State. Now it appeared with recruited ranks, and new regiments of as good blood as ever was poured out in the cause of right; and with a new element—those whom they had helped set free from the thraldom of slavery—whom they were proud to claim as comrades.

Their banners were silent, effective witnesses of their valor and their sacrifices; Bull's Run, Ball's Bluff, Roanoke, Newburn, Gaines' Mills, Mechanicsville, Seven Pines, Savage Station, Glendale, Malvern, Fredericksburg, Chancellorsville, Antietam, South Mountain, Knoxville, Vicksbnrg, Port Hudson and Gettysburg, were emblazoned in letters of gold. The firm and soldierly bearing of the veterans, the eager and expectant countenances of the men and officers of the new regiments, the gay trappings of the cavalry, the thorough equipment and fine condition of the artillery, the clattering of hoofs, the clanking of sabres, the drum-beat, the bugle call, and the music of the bands were all subjects of interest. The President beheld the scene. Pavement, sidewalks, windows and roofs were crowded with people. A division of veterans passed, saluting the President and their commander with cheers. And then, with full ranks—platoons extending from sidewalk to sidewalk—brigades which had never been in battle, for the first time shouldered arms for their country; they who even then were disfranchised and were not American citizens, yet they were going out to fight for the flag. Their country was given them by the tall, pale, benevolent hearted man standing upon the balcony. For the first time, they beheld their benefactor. They were darker hued than their veteran comrades, but they cheered as lustily, "hurrah, hurrah, hurrah for Massa Linkun! Three cheers for the President!" They swung their caps, clapped their hands and shouted their joy. Long, loud and jubilant were the rejoicings of these redeemed sons of Africa. Regiment after regiment of stalwart men,–slaves once, but freemen now,–with steady step and even ranks, passed down the street, moving on to the Old Dominion. It was the first review of the negro troops by the President. Mr. Lincoln himself seemed greatly pleased, and acknowledged the plaudits and cheers of the Phalanx soldiers with a dignified kindness and courtesy. It was a spectacle which made many eyes grow moist, and left a life-long impression. Thus the corps that had never lost a flag or a gun, marched through the National Capitol, crossed long bridge and went into camp near Alexandria, where it remained until the 4th of May.

The Phalanx regiments composing the 4th division were the 19th, 23rd, 27th, 28th, 29th, 30th, 31st, 39th and 43rd, commanded by General E. Ferrero.

The Army of the James, under General Butler, which was to act in conjunction with the Army of the Potomac, under Meade, was composed of the 10th and 18th Corps. The 10th Corps had two brigades of the Phalanx, consisting of the 7th, 9th, 29th, 16th, 8th, 41st, 45th and 127th Regiments, commanded by Colonels James Shaw, Jr., and Ulysses Doubleday, and constituted the 3rd division of that Corps commanded by Brigadier-General Wm. Birney.

The 3rd division of the 18th Corps, commanded by Brigadier-General Charles G. Paine, was composed of the 1st, 22nd, 37th, 5th, 36th, 38th, 4th, 6th, 10th, 107th, 117th, 118th and 2nd Cavalry, with Colonels Elias Wright, Alonzo G. Draper, John W. Ames and E. Martindale as brigade commanders of the four brigades. A cavalry force numbering about two thousand, comprising the 1st and 2nd, was under command of Colonel West,* making not less than 20,000 of the Phalanx troops, including the 4th Division with the Ninth Corps, and augmenting Butler's force to 47,000, concentrated at Yorktown and Gloucester Point.

On the 28th of April, Butler received his final orders, and on the night of the 4th of May embarked his troops on transports, descended the York river, passed Fortress Monroe and ascended the James River. Convoyed by a fleet of armored war vessels and gunboats, his transports reached Bermuda Hundreds on the afternoon of the 5th. General Wilde, with a brigade of the Phalanx, occupied Fort Powhatan, on the south bank of the river, and Wilson's Wharf, about five miles below on the north side of the James, with the remainder of his division of 5,000 of the Phalanx. General Hinks landed at City Point, at the mouth of the Appomattox. The next morning the troops advanced to Trent's, with their left resting on the Appomattox, near Walthall, and the right on the James, and intrenched. In the meantime, Butler telegraphed Grant:

'OFF CITY POINT, VA., May 5th.

"LIEUT. GEN. GRANT, Commanding Armies of the United States, Washington, D. C.:

"We have seized Wilson's Wharf Landing; a brigade of Wilde's colored troops are there; at Fort Powhatan landing two regiments of the same brigade have landed. At City Point, Hinks' division, with the remaining troops and battery, have landed. The remainder of both the 18th and 10th Army Corps are being landed at Bermuda Hundreds, above Appomattox. No opposition experienced thus far, the movement was comparatively a complete surprise. Both army corps left Yorktown during last night. The monitors are all over the bar at Harrison's landing and above City Point. The operations of the fleet have been conducted to-day with energy and success. Gens. Smith and Gillmore are pushing the landing of the men. Gen. Graham with the army gunboats, lead the advance during the night, capturing the signal station of the rebels. Colonel West, with 1800 cavalry, made several demonstrations from Williamsburg yesterday morning. Gen. Rantz left

* The reader will bear in mind that there were several changes in the command of these troops during the campaign, on account of promotions, but the troops remained in the Department and Army of the James. See Roster, for changes.

Suffolk this morning with his cavalry, for the service indicated during the conference with the Lieut.-General. The New York flag-of-truce boat was found lying at the wharf with four hundred prisoners, whom she had not time to deliver. She went up yesterday morning. We are landing troops during the night, a hazardous service in the face of the enemy.

"BENJ. F. BUTLER,
Maj.-Gen. Commanding.

"A F. PUFFER, Capt. and A. D. C.

About two miles in front of their line ran the Richmond & Petersburg Railroad, near which the enemy was encountered. Butler's movements being in concert with that of the Army of the Potomac and the 9th Corps,—the latter as yet an independent organization.

General Meade, with the Army of the Potomac, numbering 120,000 effective men, crossed the Rapidan *en route* for the Wilderness, each soldier carrying fifty rounds of ammunition and three days rations. The supply trains were loaded with ten days forage and subsistence. The advance was in two columns, General Warren being on the right and General Hancock on the left. Sedgwick followed closely upon Warren and crossed the Rapidan at Germania Ford. The Ninth Corps received its orders on the 4th, whereupon General Burnside immediately put the Corps in motion toward the front. Bivouacking at midnight, the line of march was again taken up at daylight, and at night the Rapidan was crossed at Germania Ford. The corps marched on a road parallel to that of its old antagonist, General Longstreet's army, which was hastening to assist Lee, who had met the Army of the Potomac in the entanglements of the wilderness, where a stubborn and sanguinary fight raged for two days. General Ferrero's division, composed of the Phalanx regiments, reached Germania Ford on the morning of the 6th, with the cavalry, and reported to General Sedgwick, of the 6th Corps, who had the care of the trains. The enemy was projecting an attack upon the rear of the advancing columns. Gen. Ferrero was ordered to guard with his Phalanx division, the bridges, roads and trains near and at the Rapidan river. That night the confederates attacked Sedgwick in force; wisely the immense supply trains had been committed to the care of the Phalanx, and the enemy was driven back before daylight, while the trains were securely moved up closer to the advance. General Grant, finding that the confederates were not disposed to continue the battle, began the movement toward Spottsylvania Court House on the night of the 7th. The 9th Corps brought up the rear, with the Phalanx division and cavalry covering the trains.

Butler and his Phalanx troops, as we have seen, was within six miles of Petersburg, and on the 7th, Generals Smith and Gillmore reached the railroad near Port Walthall Junction, and commenced destroying it; the confederates attacked them, but were repulsed. Col. West, on the north side of the James River, forded the Chickahominy with the Phalanx cavalry, and arrived opposite City Point, having destroyed the railroad for some distance on that side.

Leaving General Hinks with his Phalanx division to hold City Point, on the 9th Butler again moved forward to break up the railroad which the forces under Smith and Gillmore succeeded in doing, thus separating Beaureguard's force from Lee's. He announced the result of his operation's in the following message to Washington:

"May 9th, 1864.

"Our operations may be summed up in a few words. With one thousand and seven hundred cavalry we have advanced up the Peninsula, forced the Chickahominy and have safely brought them to our present position. These were *colored cavalry*, and are now holding our advanced pickets toward Richmond. General Kautz, with three thousand cavalry from Suffolk, on the same day with our movement up James river, forced the Blackwater, burned the railroad bridge at Stony Creek, below Petersburg, cutting in two Beauregard's force at that point. We have landed here, intrenched ourselves, destroyed many miles of railroad, and got possession, which, with proper supplies, we can hold out against the whole of Lee's army. I have ordered up the supplies. Beauregard, with a large portion of his force, was left south, by the cutting of the railroad by Kautz. That portion which reached Petersburg under Hill, I have whipped to-day, killing and wounding many, and taking many prisoners, after a well contested fight. General Grant will not be troubled with any further re-inforcements to Lee from Beaureguard's force. ' BENJ. F. BUTLER,

Major-General."

But for having been misinformed as to Lee's retreating on Richmond,—which led him to draw his forces back into his intrenchments,—Butler would have undoubtedly marched triumphantly into Petersburg. The mistake gave the enemy holding the approaches to that city time to be re-enforced, and Petersburg soon became well fortified and garrisoned. Beauregard succeeded in a few days time in concentrating in front of Butler 25,000 troops, thus checking the latter's advance toward Richmond and Petersburg, on the south side of the James, though skirmishing went on at various points.

General Grant intended to have Butler advance and capture Petersburg, while General Meade, with the Army of the Potomac, advanced upon Richmond from the north bank of the James river. Gen. Butler failed to accomplish more than his dispatches related, though his forces entered the city of Petersburg, captured Chester Station, and destroyed the railroad connection between Petersburg and Richmond. Failure to support his troops and to intrench lost him all he had gained, and he returned to his intrenchments at Bermuda Hundreds.

The Phalanx (Hinks division) held City Point and other stations on the river, occasionally skirmishing with the enemy, who, ever mindful of the fact that City Point was the base of supplies for the Army of the James, sought every opportunity to raid it, but they always found the Phalanx ready and on the alert.

After the battle of Drewry's Bluff, May 16th, Butler thought to remain quiet in his intrenchments, but Grant, on the 22nd, ordered him to send all his troops, save enough to hold City Point, to join the Army of the Potomac; whereupon General W. F. Smith, with 16,000 men, embarked for the White House, on the Pamunky river, Butler retaining the Phalanx division and the Cavalry. Thus ended the operations of the Army of the James, until Grant crossed the river with the army of the Potomac.

On the 13th of May, Grant determined upon a flank movement toward Bowling Green, with a view of making

SCENE IN THE ARMY OF THE POTOMOC.
Negro baggage train drivers watering their mules.

Port Royal, instead of Fredericksburg, his depot for supplies. Sending his reserve artillery to Belle Plain, he prepared to advance. It was in this manœuvre that Lee, for the last time, attacked the Federal forces, outside of cover, in any important movement. The attempt to change the base of supply was indeed a hazardous move for Grant; it necessitated the moving of his immense train, numbering four thousand wagons, used in carrying rations, ammunition and supplies for his army, and transportation of the badly wounded to the rear, where they could be cared for.

Up to this time the Wilderness campaign had been a continuous fight and march. The anxiety which Grant felt for his train, is perhaps best told by himself:

"My movements are terribly embarrassed by our immense wagon train. It could not be avoided, however."

It was the only means by which the army could obtain needful supplies, and was consequently indispensable. It was the near approach to the train that made the confederates often fight so desperately, for they knew if they could succeed in capturing a wagon they would probably get something to eat. Soon after the advance began, it was reported to Grant, that the confederate cavalry was in the rear, in search of the trains. On the 14th he ordered General Ferrero to "keep a sharp lookout for this cavalry, and if you can attack it with your (Phalanx) infantry and (white) cavalry, do so." On the 19th Ferrero, with his Phalanx division, (4th division, 9th Corps) was on the road to Fredericksburg, in rear of and to the right of General Tyler's forces, in the confederates' front. The road formed Grant's direct communication with his base, and here the confederates, under Ewell attacked the Federal troops. Grant sent this dispatch to Ferrero:

"The enemy have crossed the Ny on the right of our lines, in considerable force, and may possibly detach a force to move on Fredericksburg. Keep your cavalry pickets well out on the plank road, and all other roads leading west and south of you. If you find the enemy moving infantry and artillery to you, report it promptly. In that case take up strong positions and detain him all you can, turning all your trains back to Fredericksburg, and whatever falling back you may be forced to do, do it in that direction."

The confederates made a dash for the train and captured twenty-seven wagons, but before they had time to feast off of their booty the Phalanx was upon them. The enemy fought with uncommon spirit; it was the first time "F. F. V's," the chivalry of the South,—composing the Army of Northern Virginia,—had met the negro soldiers, and true to their instinctive hatred of their black brothers, they gave them the best they had; lead poured like rain for a while, and then came a lull. Ferrero knew what it meant, and prepared for their coming. A moment more and the accustomed yell rang out above the roar of the artillery. The confederates charged down upon the Phalanx, but to no purpose, save to make the black line more stable. They retaliated, and the confederates were driven as the gale drives chaff, the Phalanx recapturing the wagons and saving Grant's line of communication. General Badeau, speaking of their action, in his military history of Grant, says:

" It was the first time at the East when colored troops had been engaged in any important battle, and the display of soldierly qualities won a frank acknowledgment from both troops and commanders, not all of whom had before been willing to look upon negroes as comrades. But after that time, white soldiers in the army of the Potomac were not displeased to receive the support of black ones; they had found the support worth having."

Ferrero had the confidence of his men, who were ever ready to follow where Grant ordered them to be led.

But this was not the last important battle the Phalanx took part in. Butler, after sending the larger portion of his forces to join the Army of the Potomac, was not permitted to remain quiet in his intrenchments. The confederates felt divined to destroy, if not capture, his base, and therefore were continually striving to break through the lines. On the 24th of May, General Fitzhugh Lee made a dash with his cavalry upon Wilson's Wharf, Butler's most northern outpost, held by two Phalanx Regiments of General Wilde's brigade. Lee's men had been led to believe that it was only necessary to yell at the "niggers" in order to make them leave the Post, but in this affair they found a foe worthy of their steel. They fought for several hours, when finally the confederate troops beat a retreat. An eye witness of the fight says:

"The chivalry of Fitzhugh Lee and his cavalry division was badly worsted in the contest last Tuesday with negro troops, composing the garrison at Wilson's Landing; the chivalry made a gallant fight, however. The battle began at half-past twelve P. M., and ended at six o'clock, when the chivalry retired, disgusted and defeated. Lee's men dismounted far in the rear, and fought as infantry; they drove in the pickets and skirmishers to the intrenchments, and made several valiant charges upon our works. To make an assault, it was necessary to come across an opening in front of our position, up to the very edge of a deep and impassable ravine. The rebels, with deafening yells, made furious onsets, but the negroes did not flinch, and the mad assailants, discomforted, returned to cover with shrunken ranks. The rebels' fighting was very wicked; it showed that Lee's heart was bent on taking the negroes at any cost. Assaults on the center having failed, the rebels tried first the left, and then the right flank, with no greater success. When the battle was over, our loss footed up, one man killed outright, twenty wounded, and two missing. Nineteen rebels were prisoners in our hands. Lee's losses must have been very heavy; the proof thereof was left on the ground. Twenty-five rebel bodies lay in the woods unburied, and pools of blood unmistakably told of other victims taken away. The estimate, from all the evidence carefully considered, puts the enemy's casualties at two hundred. Among the corpses Lee left on the field, was that of Major Breckenridge, of the 2nd Virginia Cavalry. There is no hesitation here in acknowledging the soldierly qualities which the colored men engaged in the fight have exhibited. Even the officers who have hitherto felt no confidence in them are compelled to express themselves mistaken. General Wilde, commanding the Post, says that the troops stood up to their work like veterans."

Newspaper correspondents were not apt to overstate the facts, nor to give too much favorable coloring to the Phalanx in those days. Very much of the sentiment in the army—East and West—was manufactured by them. The Democratic partizan press at the North, especially in New York and Ohio, still engaged in throwing paper bullets at the negro soldiers, who were shooting lead bullets at the country's foes.

The gallantry and heroic courage of the Phalanx in the Departments of the Gulf and South, and their bloody sacrifices, had not been sufficient to stop the violent clamor and assertions of those journals, that the "niggers won't fight!"

Many papers favorable to the Emancipation; opposed putting negro troops in battle in Virginia. But to all these bomb-proof opinions Grant turned a deaf ear, and when and where necessity required it, he hurled his Phalanx brigades against the enemy as readily as he did the white troops. The conduct of the former was, nevertheless, watched eagerly by the correspondents of the press who were with the army, and when they began to chronicle the achievements of the Phalanx, the prejudice began to give way, and praises were substituted in the place of their well-worn denunciations. A correspondent of the New York *Herald* thus wrote in May:

"The conduct of the colored troops, by the way, in the actions of the last few days, is described as superb. An Ohio soldier said to me today, 'I never saw men fight with such desperate gallantry as those negroes did. They advanced as grim and stern as death, and when within reach of the enemy struck about them with a pitiless vigor, that was almost fearful.' Another soldier said to me, 'These negroes never shrink, nor hold back, no matter what the order. Through scorching heat and pelting storms, if the order comes, they march with prompt, ready feet.' Such praise is great praise, and it is deserved. The negroes here who have been slaves, are loyal, to a man, and on our occupation of Fredericksburg, pointed out the prominent secessionists, who were at once seized by our cavalry and put in safe quarters. In a talk with a group of faithful fellows, I discovered in them all a perfect understanding of the issues of the conflict, and a grand determination to prove themselves worthy of the place and privileges to which they are to be exalted."

The ice was thus broken, and then each war correspondent found it his duty to write in deservedly glowing terms of the Phalanx.

The newspaper reports of the engagements stirred the blood of the Englishman, and he eschewed his professed love for the freedom of mankind, and particularly that of the American negro. The London *Times*, in the following article, lashed the North for arming the negroes to shoot the confederates, forgetting, perhaps, that England employed negroes against the colonist in 1775, and at New Orleans, in 1814, had her black regiments to shoot down the fathers of the men whom it now sought to uphold, in rebellion against the government of the United States:

"THE NEGRO UNION SOLDIERS.

"Six months have now passed from the time Mr. Lincoln issued his proclamation abolishing slavery in the States of the Southern Confederacy. To many it may seem that this measure has failed of the intended effect and this is doubtless in some respects the case. It was intended to frighten the Southern whites into submission, and it has only made them more fierce and resolute than ever. It was intended to raise a servile war, or produce such signs of it as should compel the Confederates to lay down their arms through fear for their wives and families; and it has only caused desertion from some of the border plantations and some disorders along the coast. But in other respects the consequences of this measure are becoming important enough. The negro race has been too much attached to the whites, or too ignorant or too sluggish to show any signs of revolt in places remote from the presence of the federal armies; but on some points where the federals have been able to maintain themselves in force in the midst of a large negro population, the process of enrolling and arming black regiments has been carried on in a manner which must give a new character to the war. It is in the State of Louisiana, and under the command of General Banks, that this use of negro soldiers has been most extensive. The great city of New Orleans having fallen into the possession of the federals more more than a year ago, and the neighboring country being to a certain degree abandoned by the white population, a vast number of negroes have been thrown on the hands of the General in command to support and, if he can, make use of. The arming of these was begun by General Butler, and it has been continued by his successor. Though the number actually under arms is no doubt exaggerated by Northern writers, yet enough have been brought into service to produce a powerful effect on the imaginations of the the combatants, and, as we can now clearly see, to add almost grievously to the fury of the struggle.

"Of all wars, those between races which had been accustomed to stand to each other in the relation of master and slave have been so much the most horrible that by general consent the exciting of a servile insurrection has been considered as beyond the pale of legitimate warfare. This had been held even in the case of European serfdom, although there the rulers and the ruled are of the same blood, religion and language. But the conflict between the white men and the negro, *and particularly the American white man and the American negro, is likely to be more ruthless than any which the ancient world, fruitful in such histories, or the modern records of Algeria can furnish.* There was reason to hope that the deeds of 1857 in India would not be paralleled in our time or in any after age. The Asiatic savagery rose upon a dominent race scattered throughout the land, and wreaked its vengeance upon it by atrocities which it would be a relief to forget. But it has been reserved for the New World to present the spectacle of civil war, calling servile war to its aid, and of men of English race and language so envenomed against each other that one party places arms in the hands of the half savage negro, and the other acts as if resolved to give no quarter to the insurgent race or the white man who commands them or fights by their side. In the valley of the Mississippi, where these negro soldiers are in actual service, it seems likely that a story as revolting as that of St. Domingo is being prepared for the world. No one who reads the description of the fighting at Port Hudson, and the accounts given by the papers of scenes at other places, can help fearing that the worst part of this war has yet to come, and that a people who lately boasted that they took the lead in education and material civilization are now carrying on a contest without regard to any law of conventional warfare,—one side training negroes to fight against its own white flesh and blood, the other slaughtering them without mercy whenever they find them in the field.

"* * * It is pitiable to find these unhappy Africans, whose clumsy frames are no match for the sinewy and agile white American, thus led on to be destroyed by a merciless enemy. Should the war proceed in this manner, it is possible that the massacre of Africans may not be confined to actual conflict in the field. Hitherto the whites have been sufficiently confident in the negroes to leave them unmolested, even when the enemy was near; but with two or three black regiments in each federal corps, and such events as the Port Hudson massacre occuring to infuriate the minds on either side, who can foresee what three months more of war may bring forth?

"All that we can say with certainty is that the unhappy negro will be the chief sufferer in this unequal conflict. An even greater calamity, however, is the brutalization of two antagonistic peoples by the introduction into the war of these servile allies of the federals. Already there are military murders and executions on both sides. The horrors which Europe has foreseen for a year past are now upon us. Reprisal will provoke reprisal, until all men's natures are hardened, and the land flows with blood."

The article is truly instructive to the present generation; its malignity and misrepresentation of the Administration's intentions in regard to the arming of negroes, serves to illustrate the deep-seated animosity which then existed in England toward the union of the States. Nor will the American negro ever forget England's advice to the confederates, whose massacre of negro soldiers fighting for freedom she endorsed and applauded. The descendants of those black soldiers, who were engaged in the prolonged struggle for freedom, can rejoice in the fact that no single act of those patriots is in keeping with the Englishman's prediction; no taint of brutality is even charged against them by those whom they took prisoners in battle. The confederates themselves testify to the humane treatment they unexpectedly received at the hands of their negro captors. Mr. Pollard, the historian, says:

"No servile insurrections had taken place in the South."

But it is gratifying to know that all Englishmen did not agree with the writer of the *Times*. A London letter in the New York Evening *Post*, said:

"Mr. Spurgeon makes most effective and touching prayers, remembering, at least once on a Sunday, the United States. 'Grant, O God,' he said recently, 'that the right may conquer, and that if the fearful canker of slavery must be cut out by the sword, it be wholly eradicated from the body politic of which it is the curse.' He is seldom, however, as pointed as this; and, like other clergymen of England, prays for the return of peace. Indeed, it must be acknowledged that if the English press and government have done what they could to continue this war, the dissenting clergy of England have nobly shown their good will and hearty sympathy with the Americans, and their sincere desire for the settlement of our difficulties. 'If praying would do you Americans any good,' said an irreverent acquaintance last Sunday, 'you will be gratified to learn that a force of a thousand-clergymen-power is constantly at work for you over here.'"

After the heroic and bloody effort at Cold Harbor to reach Richmond, or to cross the James above the confederate capitol, and thus cut off the enemy's supplies,—after Grant had flanked, until to flank again would be to leave Richmond in his rear,—when Lee had withdrawn to his fortifications, refusing to accept Grant's challenge to come out and fight a decisive battle,—when all hope of accomplishing either of these objects had vanished, Grant determined to return to his original plan of attack from the coast, and turned his face toward the James river. On the 12th of June the Army of the Potomac began to move, and by the 16th it was, with all its trains across, and on the south side of the James

Petersburg Grant regarded as the citadel of Richmond, and to capture it was the first thing on his list to be accomplished. General Butler was made acquainted with this, and as soon as General Smith, who, with a portion of Butler's forces had been temporarily dispatched to join the army of the Potomac at Cold Harbor, returned to Bermuda Hundreds with his force, he was ordered forward to capture the Cockade City. It was midnight on the 14th, when Smith's troops arrived. Butler ordered him immediately forward against Petersburg, and he moved accordingly. His force was in three divisions of Infantry, and one of Cavalry, under General Kautz, who was to threaten the line of works on the Norfolk road. General Hinks, with his division of the Phalanx, was to take position across the Jordon's Point road on the right of Kautz; Brooks' division of white troops was to follow, Hinks coming in at the center of the line, while General Martindale with the other division was to move along the Appomattox and strike the City Point road. Smith's movement was directed against the northeast side of Petersburg, extending from the City Point to the Norfolk railroad. About daylight on the 15th, as the columns advanced on the City Point road at Bailey's farm, six miles from Petersburg, a confederate battery opened fire. Kautz reconnoitered and found a line of rifle trench, extending along the front, on rapidly rising ground, with a thicket covering. The work was held by a regiment of cavalry and a light battery. At once there was use for the Phalanx; the works must be captured with the battery before the troops could proceed. The cavalry was re-called, and Hinks began the formation of an attacking party from his division. The confederates were in an open field, their battery upon a knoll in the same field, commanding a sweeping position to its approaches. The advancing troops must come out from the woods, rush up the slope and carry it at the point of the bayonet, exposed to the tempest of musketry and cannister of the battery. Hinks formed his line for the assault, and the word of command was given,—"forward." The line emerged from the woods, the enemy opened with cannister upon the steadily advancing column, which, without stopping, replied with a volley of Minie bullets.

"The long, dusky line, arm to arm, knee to knee."

PHALANX SOLDIERS AT WORK ON RIVER OBSTRUCTIONS.

Then shells came crashing through the line, dealing death and shattering the ranks; but on they went, with a wild cheer, running up the slope; again a storm of cannister met them; a shower of musketry came down upon the advancing column, whose bristling bayonets were to make the way clear for their white comrades awaiting on the roadside. A hundred black men went down under the fire; the ranks were quickly closed however, and with another wild cheer the living hundreds went over the works with the impetuosity of a cyclone; they seized the cannon and turned them upon the fleeing foe, who, in consternation, stampeded toward Petersburg, to their main line of intrenchments on the east. Thus the work of the 5th and 22nd Phalanx regiments was completed and the road made clear for the 18th Corps.

Brooks now moved up simultaneously with Martindale, on the river road. By noon the whole corps was in front of the enemy's main line of works, Martindale on the right, Brooks in the center, the Phalanx and cavalry on the left, sweeping down to the Jerusalem Plank Road on the southeast. Hinks, with the Phalanx, in order to gain the position assigned him, had necessarily to pass over an open space exposed to a direct and cross-fire. Nevertheless, he prepared to occupy his post, and forming a line of battle, he began the march. The division numbered about 3,000, a portion of it being still at Wilson's Landing, Fort Powhatan, City Point and Bermuda Hundreds. This was a march that veterans might falter in, without criticism or censure. The steady black line advanced a few rods at a time, when coming within range of the confederate guns they were obliged to lie down and wait for another opportunity. Now a lull,—they would rise, go forward, and again lie down. Thus they continued their march, under a most galling, concentrated artillery fire until they reached their position, from which they were to join in a general assault; and here they lay, from one till five o'clock,—four long hours,—exposed to ceaseless shelling by the enemy. Badeau says, in speaking of the Phalanx in this ordeal:

"No worse strain on the nerves of troops is possible, for it is harder to remain quiet under cannon fire, even though comparatively harmless, than to advance against a storm of musketry."

General W. F. Smith, though brave, was too cautious and particular in detail, and he spent those four hours in careful reconnoissance, while the troops lay exposed to the enemy's concentric fire.

The main road leading east from Petersburg ascends a hill two or more miles out, upon the top of which stood what was then known as Mr. Dunn's house. In front of it was a fort, and another south, and a third north, with other works; heavy embankments and deep ravines and ditches, trunks of hewn trees blackened by camp fires, formed an abatis on the even ground. Here the sharpshooters and riflemen had a fair view of the entire field. The distance from these works to the woods was about three hundred and sixty paces, in the edge of which lay the black Phalanx division, ready, like so many tigers, waiting for the command, "forward." The forts near Dunn's house had direct front fire, and those on the north an enfilading fire on the line of advance. Smith got his troops in line for battle by one o'clock, but there they lay. Hinks impatiently awaited orders; oh! what a suspense—each hour seemed a day,—what endurance—what valor. Shells from the batteries ploughed into the earth where they stood, and began making trouble for the troops. Hinks gave the order, "lie down;" they obeyed, and were somewhat sheltered. Five o'clock—yet no orders. At length the command was given, "forward." The skirmishers started at quick time; the enemy opened upon them vigorously from their batteries and breastworks, upon which they rested their muskets, in order to fire with accuracy. A torrent of bullets was poured upon the advancing line, and the men fell fast as autumn leaves in a gale of wind. Then the whole line advanced, the Phalanx going at double-quick; their well aligned ranks, with bayonets glittering obliquely in the receding sunlight, presented a spectacle both magnificent and grand.

Duncan rushed his skirmishers and reached the ditches in front of the breastworks, which, without waiting for

A GALLANT CHARGE.

The 22nd Negro Regiment, Duncan's Brigade, carrying the first line of Confederate works before Petersburg, Va.

the main body, they entered and clambered up the steep embankments. A sheet of flame from above was rained down, causing many a brave man to stagger and fall back into the ditch, never to rise again. The troops following, inspired by the daring of the skirmishers, pressed forward on the run up to the forts, swept round the curtains, scaled the breastworks and dashed with patriotic rage at the confederate gunners, who deserted their pieces and ran for their lives. Brooks and Martindale advanced simultaneously upon the works at Osborn's house and up the railroad, sweeping everything before them. The Phalanx seized upon the guns and turned them instantly upon the fleeing foe, and then with spades and shovels reversed the fortifications and prepared to hold them. Fifteen pieces of artillery and three hundred confederates were captured. "The Phalanx," says the official report, took two-thirds of the prisoners and nine pieces of artillery. General Smith, finding that General Birney, with the 2nd Corps, had not arrived, instead of marching the troops into Petersburg, waited for re-inforcements unnecessarily, and thereby lost his chance of taking the city. which was soon garrisoned with troops enough to defy the whole army. Thus Grant was necessitated afterward to lay seige to the place.

The confederates never forgot nor forgave this daring of the "niggers," who drove them, at the point of the bayonet, out of their breastworks, killing and capturing their comrades and their guns. They were chided by their brother confederates for allowing negroes to take their works from them. The maidens of the Cockade City were told that they could not trust themselves to men who surrendered their guns to "niggers." The soldiers of the Phalanx were delirious with joy. They had caught "ole massa," and he was theirs. General Hinks had their confidence, and they were ready to follow wherever he led.

The chaplin of the 9th Corps, in his history, says:

"In this movement a division of colored troops, under Brigadier-General Hinks, seems to have won the brightest laurels. They first attacked and carried the enemy's outpost at Bailey's farm, capturing one piece of artillery in the most gallant manner. On their arrival before Petersburg, they lay in front of the works for nearly five hours, waiting for the word of command. They then, in company with the white troops, and showing equal bravery, rushed and carried the enemy's line of works, with what glorious success has already been related."

This, indeed, was a victory, yet shorn of its full fruits; but that Petersburg was not captured was no fault of the Phalanx. They had carried and occupied the most formidable obstacles.

Badeau, in chronicling these achievements, says:

"General Smith assaulted the works on the City Point and Prince George Court House roads. The rebels resisted with a sharp infantry fire, but the center and left dashed into the works, consisting of five redan's on the crest of a deep and difficult ravine. Kiddoo's (22d) black regiment was one of the first to gain the hill. In support of this movement, the second line was swung around and moved against the front of the remaining works. The rebels, assaulted thus in front and flank, gave way, four of the guns already captured were turned upon them by the negro conquerors, enfilading the line, and before dark, Smith was in possession of the whole of the outer works, two and a half miles long, with fifteen pieces of artillery and three hundred prisoners. Petersburg was at his mercy."

This failnre made a siege necessary, and General Grant began by regular approaches to invest the place, after making the three desperate assaults on the 16th, 17th and 18th. It had been indeed a bloody June; the soil of the Old Dominion, which for two centuries the negro had tilled and made to yield the choicest products, under a system of cruel and inhuman bondage he now reddened with his blood in defense of his liberty, proving by his patriotism, not only his love of liberty, but his courage and capacity to defend it. The negro troops had marched and fought with the white regiments with equal intrepidity and courage; they were no longer despised by their comrades; they now had recognition as soldiers, and went into the trenches before Petersburg as a part of as grand an army as ever laid siege to a stronghold or stormed a fortification.

On the 18th of June, General Ferrero reported to General Meade, with his division of the Phalanx, (4th

Division, 9th Corps), and was immediately ordered to join its own proper corps,—from which it had been separated since the 6th of May,—at the crossing of the Rapidan. It had served under Sedgwick and Sheridan until the 17th, when it came under the direct command of General Grant, and thus remained until the 25th of May, when General Burnside, waiving rank to Meade, the 9th Corps was incorporated into the Army of the Potomac. During its absence the division sustained the reputable renown of its corps, not only in protecting the trains, but in fighting the enemy, and capturing prisoners. Before rejoining the corps, the division was strengthened by three regiments of cavalry,—the 5th New York, 3rd New Jersey and 2nd Ohio. From the 9th of May till the 17th, the division occupied the plank road, looking to the old Wilderness tavern, covering the extreme right of the army, extending from Todd's to Banks' Ford. On the 17th, the division moved to Salem Church, near the main road to Fredericksburg, where, as we have seen, it defended the rear line against the attack made by the confederates, under General Ewell.

The historian of the corps says:

"The division on the 21st of May was covering Fredericksburg, and the roads leading hence to Bowling Green. On the 22nd it marched toward Bowling Green, and on the 23rd it moved to Milford Station. From that date to the 27th it protected the trains of the army in the rear of the positions on the North Anna. On the 27th, the division moved to Newtown; on the 28th, to Dunkirk, crossing the Maltapony; on the 29th, to the Pamunkey, near Hanovertown. On the 1st of June the troops crossed the Pamunkey, and from the 2nd to the 6th, covered the right of the army; from the 6th to the 12th they covered the approaches from New Castle Ferry, Hanovertown, Hawe's shop, and Bethusda Church. From the 12th to the 18th they moved by easy stages, by way of Tunstall's New Kent Court House, Cole's Ferry, and the pontoon bridge across the James, to the line of the army near Petersburg. The dismounted cavalry were left to guard the trains, and the 4th Division prepared to participate in the more active work of soldiers. Through the remainder of the month of June, and the most of July, the troops were occupied in the second line of trenches, and in active movements towards the left, under Generals Hancock and Warren. While they were engaged in the trenches they were also drilled in the movements necessary for an attack and occupation of the enemy's works. A strong feeling of pride and *esprit de corps* sprung up within the hearts of the blacks, and they began to think that they too might soon have the opportunity of some glory for their race and country."

How natural was this feeling. As we have seen, their life for more than a month had been one of marching and counter-marching, though hazardous and patriotic. When on the 18th, they entered upon the more active duty of soldiers, they found the 3rd Division of the 18th Corps, composed of the Phalanx of the Army of the James, covered with glory, and the welkin ringing with praises of their recent achievements. The men of the 4th Division chafed with eager ambition to rival their brothers of the 18th Corps, in driving the enemy from the Cockade City. General Burnside was equally as anxious to give his black boys a chance to try the steel of the chivalry in deadly conflict, and this gave them consolation, with the assurance that their day would ere long dawn, so they toiled and drilled carefully for their prospective glory.

But the situation of the Phalanx before Petersburg was far from being enviable. Smarting under the thrashing they had received from Hinks' division, the confederates were ever ready now to slaughter the "niggers" when advantage offered them the opportunity. A steady, incessant fire was kept up against the positions the Phalanx occupied, and their movements were watched with great vigilance. Although they did not raise the black flag, yet manifestly no quarter to negro troops, or to white troops that fought with them, was the confederates' determination.

"Judging from their actions, the presence of the negro soldiers, both in the Eighteenth and Ninth Corps," says Woodbury, "seemed to have the effect of rendering the enemy more spiteful than ever before the Fourth Division came. The closeness of the lines on the front of the corps rendered constant watchfulness imperative, and no day passed without some skirmishing between the opposing pickets. When the colored soldiers appeared, this practice seemed to increase, while in front of the Fifth Corps, upon the left of our line, there was little or no picket firing, and the outposts of both armies were even disposed to be friendly. On the front of the Ninth, the firing was incessant, and in many cases fatal."

IN THE TRENCHES

"General Potter, in his report, mentions that, when his division occupied the front, his loss averaged some fourteen or fifteen officers killed and wounded per diem. The sharpshooters on either side were vigilant, and an exposure of any part of the person was the signal for the exchange of shots. The men, worn by hard marching, hard fighting and hard digging, took every precaution to shield themselves, and sought cover at every opportunity. They made fire proofs of logs and earth, and with tortuous covered ways and traverse, endeavoring to secure themselves from the enemy's fire. The artillery and mortars on both sides were kept almost constantly at work. These were all precursors of the coming, sanguinary struggle for the possession of Cemetery Hill. Immediately in front of the salient occupied by the Ninth Corps, the rebels had constructed a very strong redoubt, a short distance below Cemetery Hill. In the rear of the redoubt ran a ridge nearly at right angles with the rebels' lines, to the hill. It appeared that if this redoubt was captured, the enemy's line would be seriously threatened, if not entirely broken up. A feasible plan for the destruction of the redoubt, was seriously discussed among the soldiers of the corps; finally Colonel Pleasants, of the 48th Pennsylvania Regiment, devised a plan to run a mine under the intervening space between the line of the corps and the redoubt, with the design of exploding it, directly under the redoubt. To this plan General Burnside lent his aid, and preparations were made for an assault upon Cemetery Hill, at the time of its explosion. The work of digging and preparing the mine was prosecuted under the most disadvantageous circumstances. General Meade reluctantly gave official sanction, and the work of excavation proceeded with, despite the fact that General Burnside's requisitions for supplies were not responded to. Nevertheless, in less than a month the mine was ready, and after considerable discussion, and not without some bickering, the plan of attack was arranged, which, in brief, was to form two columns, and to charge with them through the breach caused by the explosion of the mine. Then to sweep along the enemy's line, right and left, clearing away the artillery and infantry, by attacking in the flank and rear. Other columns were to make for the crest, the whole to co-operate. General Ferrero, in command of the Phalanx division was informed, that in accordance with the plan of attack, he was to lead in the assault, when the attack was made, after the mine had been fired. He was ordered to drill his troops accordingly. After a careful examination of the ground, Ferrero decided upon his methods of advance,—not to go directly in the crater formed by the explosion, but rather upon one side of it, and then to take the enemy in flank and reverse. When he informed his officers and men that they would be called upon to lead in the assault, they received the information with delight. His men, desirous of emulating their comrades of the Third Division of the Eighteenth Corps, felt that their cherished hope,—the opportunity for which they had prayed,—was near at hand; the hour in which they would show themselves worthy of the honor of being associated with the Army of the Potomac. They rejoiced at the prospect of wiping off whatever reproach an ill-judged prejudice might have cast upon them, by proving themselves brave, thereby demanding the respect which brave men deserve. For three weeks they drilled with alacrity in the various movements; charging upon earthworks, wheeling by the right and left, deployment, and other details of the expected operations. General Burnside had early expressed his confidence in the soldierly capabilities of the men of the Phalanx, and now wished to give them an opportunity to justify his good opinion."

His white troops, moreover, had been greatly exposed throughout the whole campaign, had suffered severely, and had been so much under the fire of the sharpshooters that it had become a second nature with them to dodge bullets. The negro troops had not been so much exposed, and had already shown their steadiness under fire in one or two pretty severe skirmishes in which they had previously been engaged. The white officers and men of the corps were elated with the selection made by General Burnside, and they, too, manifested an uncommon interest in their dark-hued comrades. The demeanor of the former toward the latter was very different from that of the other corps, of which that particular army was composed. The 9th Corps had seen more service than any other corps in the Army of the Potomac. Its operations in six States had given to the men an experience calculated to destroy, very greatly, their race prejudice; besides a very large portion of the regiments in the corps came from the New England States, especially Massachusetts, Vermont and Rhode Island, where race prejudice was not so strong; consequently the treatment of the men in the 4th Division was tempered by humanity, and pregnant with a fraternal feeling of comradeship. And then there was a corps pride very naturally existing among the white troops, which prompted a desire for the achievement of some great and brilliant feat by their black comrades. This feeling was expressed in more than one way by the entire corps, and greatly enhanced the ambition of the Phalanx to rout the enemy and drive him out of his fortifications before Petersburg, if not to capture the city.

These high hopes were soon dissipated, however. General Meade had an interview with General Burnside on the 28th; the subject was fully discussed as to the plan of the assault, as proposed by General Burnside, and made known to Meade by Burnside, in writing, on the 26th. It was at this meeting that General Meade made his objections to the Phalanx leading the assault. General Burnside argued with all the reason he could command, in favor of his plans, and especially for the Phalanx, going over the grounds already cited; why his white troops were unfit and disqualified for performing the task of leading the assault, but in vain. Meade was firm in his purpose, and, true to his training, he had no use for the negro but as a servant; he never had trusted him as a soldier. The plan, with General Meade's objection was referred to General Grant for settlement. Grant, doubting the propriety of agreeing with a subordinate, as against the commander of the army, dismissed the dispute by agreeing with Meade; therefore the Phalanx was ruled out of the lead and placed in the supporting column. It was not till the night of the 29th, a few hours before the assault was made, that the change was made known to General Ferrero and his men, who were greatly chagrined and filled with disappointment.

General Ledlie's division of white troops was to lead the assault, after the explosion of the mine on the morning of the 30th. It was on the night of the 29th, when General Burnside issued his battle order, in accordance with General Meade's plan and instructions, and at the appointed hour all the troops were in readiness for the conflict. The mine, with its several tons of powder, was ready at a quarter past three o'clock on the eventful morning of the 30th of July. The fuses were fired, and "all eyes were turned to the confederate fort opposite," which was discernible but three hundred feet distant. The garrison was sleeping in fancied security; the sentinels slowly paced their rounds, without a suspicion of the crust which lay between them and the awful chasm below. Our own troops, lying upon their arms in unbroken silence, or with an occasional murmur, stilled at once by the whispered word of command, looked for the eventful moment of attack to arrive. A quarter of an hour passed,—a half hour, yet there was no report. Four o'clock, and the sky began to brighten in the east; the confederate garrison was bestirring itself. The enemy's lines once more assumed the appearance of life; the sharp-shooters, prepared for their victims, began to pick off those of our men, who came within range of their deadly aim. Another day of siege was drawing on, and still there was no explosion. What could it mean? The fuses had failed;—the dampness having penetrated to the place where the parts had been spliced together, prevented the powder from burning. Two men (Lieut. Jacob Douty and Sergeant—afterwards Lieutenant—Henry Rees,) of the 48th Pennsylvania volunteered to go and ascertain where the trouble was. At quarter past four o'clock they bravely entered the mine, re-arranged the fuses and re-lighted them. In the meantime, General Meade had arrived at the permanent headquarters of the 9th Corps. Not being able to see anything that was going forward, and not hearing any report, he became somewhat impatient. At fifteen minutes past four o'clock he telegraphed to General Burnside to know what was the cause of the delay. Gen. Burnside was too busy in remedying the failure already incurred to reply immediately, and expected, indeed, that before a dispatch could be sent that the explosion would take place. General Meade ill-naturedly telegraphed the operator to know where General Burnside was. At half-past four, the commanding general became still more impatient, and was on the point of ordering an immediate assault upon the enemy's works, without reference to the mine. Five minutes later he *did* order an assault. General Grant was there when, at sixteen minutes before five o'clock, the mine exploded. Then ensued a scene which beggars description.

General Badeau, in describing the spectacle, says:

"The mine exploded with a shock like that of an earthquake, tearing up the rebels' work above them, and vomiting men, guns and caissons two hundred feet into the air. The tremendous mass appeared for a moment to hang suspended in the heavens like a huge, inverted cone, the exploding powder still flashing out here and there, while limbs and bodies of mutilated men, and fragments of cannon and wood-work could be seen, then all fell heavily to the ground again, with a second report like thunder. When the smoke and dust had cleared away, only an enormous crater, thirty feet deep, sixty wide, and a hundred and fifty long stretched out in front of the Ninth Corps, where the rebel fort had been."

The explosion was the signal for the federal batteries to open fire, and immediately one hundred and ten guns and fifty mortars opened along the Union front, lending to the sublime horror of the upheaved and quaking earth, the terror of destruction.

A confederate soldier thus describes the explosion, in the Philadelphia *Times*, January, 1883:

"About fifteen feet of dirt intervened between the sleeping soldiers and all this powder. In a moment the superincumbent earth, for a space forty by eighty feet, was hurled upward, carrying with it the artillerymen, with their four guns, and three companies of soldiers. As the huge mass fell backwards it buried the startled men under immense clods—tons of dirt. Some of the artillery was thrown forty yards towards the enemy's line. The clay subsoil was broken and piled in large pieces, often several yards in diameter, which afterwards protected scores of Federals when surrounded in the crater. The early hour, the unexpected explosion, the concentrated fire of the enemy's batteries, startled and wrought confusion among brave men accustomed to battle."

Says a Union account:

"Now was the time for action, forward went General Ledlie's column, with Colonel Marshall's brigade in advance. The parapets were surmounted, the abatis was quickly removed, and the division prepared to pass over the intervening ground, and charge through the still smoking ruins to gain the crest beyond. But here the leading brigade made a temporary halt; it was said at the time our men suspected a counter mine, and were themselves shocked by the terrible scene they had witnessed. It was, however, but momentary; in less than a quarter of an hour, the entire division was out of its entrenchments, and was advancing gallantly towards the enemy's line. The ground was somewhat difficult to cross over, but the troops pushed steadily on with soldiery bearing, overcoming all the obstacles before them. They reached the edge of the crater, passed down into the chasm and attempted to make their way through the yielding sand, the broken clay, and the masses of rubbish that were everywhere about. Many of the enemy's men were lying among the ruins, half buried, and vainly trying to free themselves. They called for mercy and for help. The soldiers stopped to take prisoners, to dig out guns and other material. Their division commander was not with them, there was no responsible head, the ranks were broken, the regimental organizations could not be preserved, and the troops were becoming confused. The enemy was recovering from his surprise, our artillery began to receive a spirited response, the enemy's men went back to their guns; they gathered on the crest and soon brought to bear upon our troops a fire in front from the Cemetery Hill, and an enfilading and cross-fire from their guns in battery. Our own guns could not altogether silence or overcome this fire in flank, our men in the crater were checked, felt the enemy's fire, sought cover, began to entrench. The day was lost, still heroic men continued to push forward for the crest, but in passing through the crater few got beyond it. Regiment after regiment, brigade followed brigade, until the three white divisions filled the opening and choked the passage to all. What was a few moments ago organization and order, was now a disordered mass of armed men. At six o'clock, General Meade ordered General Burnside to push 'his men forward, at all hazards, white and black.' His white troops were all in the crater, and could not get out. As instructed, he ordered General Ferrero to rush in the Phalanx; Colonel Loving was near when the order came to Ferrero; as the senior staff officer present, seeing the impossibility of the troops to get through the crater, at that time countermanded the order, and reported in person to General Burnside, but he had no discretion to exercise, his duty was simply to repeat Meade's order. The order must be obeyed; it was repeated; away went the Phalanx division, loudly cheering, but to what purpose did they advance? The historian of that valiant corps, presumably more reliable than any other writer, says:

"'The colored troops charged forward, cheering with enthusiasm and gallantry. Colonel J. K. Sigfried, commanding the first brigade, led the attacking column. The command moved out in rear of Colonel Humphrey's brigade of the Third Division. Colonel Sigfried, passing Colonel Humphrey by the flank, crossed the field immediately in front, went down the crater, and attempted to go through. The passage was exceedingly difficult, but after great exertions the brigade made its way through the crowded masses in a somewhat broken and disorganized condition, and advanced towards the crest. The 43rd U. S. Colored troops moved over the lip of the crater toward the right, made an attack upon the enemy's line of intrenchments, and won the chief success of the day, capturing a number of prisoners and rebel colors, and *re-capturing* a stand of national colors. The other regiments of the brigade were unable to get up, on account of white troops in advance of them crowding the line. The second brigade, under command of Colonel H. G. Thomas, followed the first with equal enthusiasm. The men rushed forward, descended into the crater, and attempted to pass through. Colonel Thomas' intention was to go to the right and attack the enemy's rifle-pits. He partially suceeded in doing so, but his brigade was much broken up when it came under the enemy's fire. The gallant brigade commander endeavored, in person, to rally his command, and at last formed a storming column, of portions of the 29th, 28th, 23rd, and 19th Regiments of the Phalanx division.'

"'These troops' made a spirited attack, but lost heavily in officers and became somewhat disheartened. Lieutenant-Colonel Bross, of the 29th, with the colors in his hands, led the charge; was the first man to leap upon the enemy's works, and was instantly killed. Lieutenant Pennell seized the colors, but was shot down, riddled through and through. Major Theodore H. Rockwood, of the 19th, sprang upon the parapet, and fell while cheering on his regiment to the attack. The conduct of these officers and their associates was indeed magnificent. No troops were ever better lead to an assault; had they been allowed the advance at the outset, before the enemy had recovered from his first surprise, their charge would have been successful. But it was made too late. The fire to which they were exposed was very hot and destructive; it came from front and flank, it poured into the faces of the men. It enfiladed their lines. The enemy's rage against the colored troops had its bloody opportunity."

And they made use of it.

Captain W. L. Fagan, of the 8th Alabama Regiment, thus gives an account of the fight, from the confederate side:

"The crater combat, unlike other battles in Virginia, was a series of deeds of daring, of bloody hand-to-hand fighting, where the survivor could count with a certainty the men he had slain. A few days ago a soldier said to me: 'I killed two at the crater; they were not three feet from me when they fell. I had followed the fortunes of the Confederacy from Williamsburg to Appomattox Court House, and had, to the morning of July 30, only seen two bayonet wounds;—one received at Frazier's Farm, the other at Turkey Ridge, June 3, 1864.' Men stood face to face at the crater. Often a bayonet thrust was given before the Minie ball went crashing through the body. Every man took care of himself, intent on selling his life as dearly as possible. The negroes did not all stampede. They mingled with the white troops. The troops of Mahone, Wilcox and Wright were greeted with defiant yells, while their ranks were mowed down by withering fires. Many officers commanding negro troops held their commissions for bravery. Encouraged, threatened, emulating the white troops, the black men fought with desperation. Some Confederate soldiers recognized their slaves at the crater. Captain J——, of the Forty-first Virginia, gave the military salute to 'Ben' and 'Bob,' whom he had left hoeing corn down in

Dinwiddie. If White's Division had occupied Reservoir Hill, Richmond would have been evacuated."

But let the writer of the following tell what the brave black men met after having advanced beyond the crater, where they grappled with the sullen foe filled with the recollection of the capture, in June, of their works, guns and comrades by the "niggers" of the 18th Corps. It was not *lex talionis* that they observed, but a repetition of the Fort Pillow Massacre. Under the head of "The Confederate Charge," the particulars are given:

"The Federals now held the crater and the inner line. Generals Lee and Mahone arrived on the field about 7:30 A. M. A ravine, which deepened on our right, ran parallel with this inner line and was used by Mahone in which to form his brigade when preparing to attack. At 8 A. M. Mahone's Brigade, commanded by Colonel D. A. Weisiger, brought from the right of Hoke's Division, was formed in this ravine and advanced to the assault. The Federals, concentrating a terrific fire of musketry and artillery, ploughed out great gaps in these fearless Virginians. Nothing daunted, they pressed forward and recaptured the inner line. The loss of this brigade was heavy, both in men and officers, more than two hundred Virginians falling between the ravine and the captured works. The Federal troops, white and colored, fought with a desperation never witnessed on former battle-fields. The negroes, it is said, cried 'No quarter.' Mahone and Wright's Brigades took only twenty-nine of them prisoners. The Federals still held the crater and part of the line. Another charge was necessary and Wright's Georgia Brigade was ordered up from Anderson's Division. Wright's Brigade, forming in the ravine, moved forward to drive the Federals from the line they still held. The enemy, expecting their attack, poured a volley into the Georgians that decimated their ranks, killing and wounding nearly every field officer in the brigade. The men rushing forward, breasting a storm of lead and iron, failed to oblique far enough to the right to recapture the whole line, but gained the line occupied by and contiguous to the line already captured by Weisiger, commanding Mahone's Brigade. Mahone's Brigade and Wright's Brigade had captured forty-two officers, three hundred and ninety men and twenty-nine negroes.

"It was now about 10 A. M. General Grant made no effort to reinforce his line or to dislodge Wright and Mahone from the positions they held. A courier dashed up to General J. C. C. Sanders, commanding Wilcox's Brigade, informing him that his brigade was wanted. The men were expecting this courier, as they were next in line, and they distinctly heard the shouts of Mahone's and Wright's men, followed by the heavy artillery firing, while the word had passed down the line that the salient had not been recaptured. General Sanders moved his brigade, consisting of the Eighth, Ninth, Tenth, Eleventh and Fourteenth Alabama Regiments, to the left and occupied the ravine. There was no shade or water in this ravine, while the men were exposed nearly four hours to a scorching sun. The heat was almost beyond human endurance. Strong men fainted and were carried to the rear. The waves of hot air at times were almost suffocating. For the first and only time the men were told what was expected of them. General Saunders explained the situation to the officers of the regiments. Each captain spoke to his men, urging them to retake the salient, or Petersburg and Richmond must be evacuated. The men were ordered to fix their bayonets securely,to trail arms—not to fire, not to yell, but to move quietly up the side of the ravine, and then, every man run for his life to the breastworks. They were told that Generals Lee, Beauregard, Hill, Mahone, Hoke and every general officer of the army would watch them as they moved forward.

"At 1:30 P. M. the firing had almost ceased and the Federals, overcome with heat, did not expect an attack. Saunders formed his brigade and moved quietly up the side of the ravine. Hardly a word was spoken, for the Alabamians expected to die or retake that salient. The eye of General Lee was fixed on them. When they caught sight of the works their old feelings came back to them and yell they must. With the fury of a whirlwind they rushed upon the line they had been ordered to take. The movement was so unexpected and so quickly executed that only one shell was thrown into the brigade. The works gained, they found the enemy on the other side. It was stated that Lee, speaking to Beauregard, said: 'Splendid!' Beauregard spoke with enthusiasm of the brilliant charge.

"In an instant the Federal army was aroused, and batteries opened along the whole line, while the infantry fire was a continuous roar. Only a breastwork divided Wilcox's Brigade from the Federals. A moment was required for Saunders to reform, and his brigade mounted the inner line and forced the enemy backwards to the outer line and the crater. The crater was full of white and negro soldiers. The Confederates, surrounding it on every side, poured volley after volley into this heaped-up mass of terrified negroes and their brave officers. The negroes ran in every direction and were shot down without a thought. Bayonets, swords and the butts of muskets were used. The deafening roar of artillery and musketry, the yells and imprecations of the combatants, drowned the commands of officers. A negro in the crater attempted to raise a white flag, and it was instantly pulled down by a Federal officer. The Federal colors were planted on a huge lump of dirt, and waved until Sergeant Wallace, of the Eleventh Alabama, followed by others, seized them and tore them from the staff. Instantly a white flag was raised, and the living. who were not many, surrendered. The crater was won."

With the exception of General Burnside, no commander of the Army of the Potomac was in favor of the Phalanx participating in a battle. What, then, had the Phalanx to expect of those to whom they had borne the relation of *slave?* The confederates had a right to expect hard fighting when they met the Phalanx, and the Phalanx knew they had to fight hard when they met the confederates. It was the previous associations and habits of the negro that kept him from retaliating for the several massacres that had been perpetrated upon his brother-soldiers. It was not for a want of courage to do it: it was only necessary for those who commanded them to have ordered it, and they would never have taken a confederate prisoner.

Many of those who commanded them needed but public opinion to sustain them, to give such an order as would have made every battle between the Phalanx and the confederates bloody and inhuman. It was but the enlightened sentiment of the North, the religious teaching of the brotherhood of man, the high character and moral training of the statesmen on the side of the Union, that restrained the Phalanx from retaliation, else they possessed none of the characteristics of a courageous, sensitive and high tempered people. The negro is not naturally docile; his surroundings, rather than his nature, have given him the trait; it is not naturally his, but something which his trainers have given him; and it is not a difficult task to untrain him and advance him beyond his apparent unconsciousness of self-duty and self-preservation. Let him feel that he is to be supported in any transaction uncommon to him, and he can act as aggressively as any race of men who are naturally quicker in temperament. It is this characteristic that made the negro what General Grant said he was: in discipline a better soldier than the white man. It was said that he would not fight: there is no man in the South who met him on the battle-field that will say so now.

These are a few of the thoughts that came to me as I listened for an hour, one evening in June, 1883, to the confederate Gen. Mahone, whose acquaintance the writer enjoys, reciting the story of the fight at the crater, where the negro met the confederate, and in a hand-to-hand struggle one showed as much brute courage as the other. It would not be doing the negro justice to accord him less, and yet that courage never led him to acts of inhumanity. It is preferable that the confederates themselves should tell the stories of their butcheries than for me to attempt them. Not the stories told at the time, but fifteen years afterward, when men could reflect and write more correctly. There is one, an orator, who has described the fight, whose reference to the crater so gladdened the hearts of his audience that they reproduced the "yell," and yelled themselves hoarse. No battle fought during the war, not even that of Bull Run, elicited so much comment and glorification among the confederates as that of the crater. It was the bloodiest fight on the soil of the Old Dominion, and has been the subject of praise by poets and orators upon the confederate side. Capt. J. B. Hope eulogized "Mahone's brigade" in true Southern verse. Capt. McCabe, on the 1st of November, 1876, in his oration before the "Association of the Army of Northern Virginia," in narrating the recapture of the works, said:

"It was now 8 o'clock in the morning. The rest of Potter's (Federal) division moved out slowly, when Ferrero's negro division, the men, beyond question, inflamed with drink, (there are many officers and men, myself among the number, who will testify to this), burst from the advanced lines, cheering vehemently, passed at a double quick over a crest under a heavy fire, and rushed with scarcely a check over the heads of the white troops in the crater, spread to their right, and captured more than two hundred prisoners and one stand of colors. At the same time Turner, of the Tenth corps, pushed forward a brigade over the Ninth Corps' parapet, seized the Confederate line still further to the north, and quickly dispersed the remaining brigades of his division to confirm his successes."

The truth is over-reached in the statement of this orator if he intended to convey the idea that the men of the Phalanx division were drunk from strong drink; but it may be looked upon as an excuse offered for the treatment the courageous negro soldiers received at the hands of their captors, who, worse than enraged by strong drink, gave the battle-cry on their way to the front, "*No quarter to niggers!*" This has been admitted by those in a position, at the time, to know what went on. In his "Recollections of the Recapture of the Lines," Colonel Stewart of the 61st Virginia Regiment, says:

"When nearly opposite the portions of our works held by the Federal troops, we met several soldiers who were in the works at the time of the explosion. Our men began ridiculing them for going to the rear, when one of them remarked, 'Ah, boys, you have got hot work ahead, —they are negroes, and show no quarter.' This was the first intimation we had that we were to fight negro troops, and it seemed to *infuse* the little band with impetuous daring, as they pressed toward the fray. I never felt more like fighting in my life. Our comrades had been slaughtered in a most inhuman and brutal manner, and slaves were trampling over their mangled and bleeding corpses. Revenge must have fired every heart, and strung every arm with nerves of steel, for the herculean task of blood."

On the Monday morning after the assault of Saturday, the Richmond *Enquirer* said:

"Grant's war cry of 'no quarter' shouted by his negro soldiers, was returned with interest, we regret to hear, not so heavily as ought to have been, since some negroes were captured instead of being shot. Let every salient we are called upon to defend, be a Fort Pillow, and butcher every negro that Grant hurls against our brave troops, and permit them not to soil their hands, with the capture of one negro."

There is no truth in the statement. No such cry was ever made by negro soldiers; and when it is remembered that the confederate congress, in four short months after this declaration, began arming slaves for the defense of Richmond, it is readily seen how deep and with what sincerity such declarations were made. The Southern historian Pollard thus describes the situation after the assault and the ground had again come into the possession of the confederates:

"The ground all around was dotted with the fallen, while the sides and bottom of the crater were literally lined with dead, the bodies lying in every conceivable position. Some had evidently been killed with the butts of muskets, as their crushed skulls and badly smashed faces too plainly indicated.' Within this crater—this hole of forty by eighty feet—were lying one hundred and thirty-six dead soldiers, besides the wound-

BEFORE PETERSBURG.

Phalanx soldiers, under a flag of truce, burying their dead after one of the terrible battles before Petersburg.

ed. The soil was literally saturated with blood. General Bartlett was here, with his steel leg broken. He did not look as though he had been at a 'diamond wedding,' but was present at a 'dance of death.' A covered way for artillery was so full of dead that details were made to throw them out, that artillery might be brought in. The dead bodies formed a heap on each side. The Alabamians captured thirty-four officers, five hundred and thirty-six white and one hundred and thirty-nine colored soldiers. The three brigades had seventeen stands of colors, held by seventeen as brave, sweaty, dirty, powder-stained fellows as ever wore the gray, who knew that, when presenting their colors to division headquarters, to each a furlough of thirty days would be granted.

"The crater was filled with wounded, to whom our men gave water. Adjutant Morgan Cleveland, of the 8th Alabama Régiment, assisted a federal captain who was mortally wounded and suffering intensely. Near him lay a burly, wounded negro. The officer said he would die. The negro, raising himself on his elbow, cried out: 'Thank God. You killed my brother when we charged, because he was afraid and ran. Now the rebels have killed you.' Death soon ended the suffering of one and the hatred of the other. A darkness came down on the battle-field and the victors began to repair the salient. The crater was cleared of the dead and wounded. Men were found buried ten feet under the dirt. Twenty-two of the artillery company were missing. Four hundred and ninety-eight dead and wounded confederates were buried or sent to the hospitals. Between the lines lay hundreds of wounded federals, who vainly called for water. These men had been without water since early morning. Some calling louder than others, their voices were recognized, and as their cries grew fainter, we knew their lives were ebbing away. Our men, risking their lives, carried water to some.

"I find in my diary these lines: 'Sunday, July 31, 1864. Everything comparatively quiet along the lines. Hundreds of federal soldiers are lying in front of the crater exposed to a scorching sun; some are crying for water. The enemy's fire is too heavy for a soldier to expose himself.' Late on Sunday evening a flag of truce was sent in and forwarded to General Lee. General Grant had asked permission to bury his dead and remove his wounded. The truce was granted, to begin on Monday at 5 A. M. and conclude at 9 A. M. Punctual to the hour the federal details came on the field and by 9 A. M. had buried about three hundred. The work was hardly begun and the truce was extended. Hour after hour was granted until it was evening before the field was cleared."

With these selections from the mass of confederate testimony before us, of their "daring, bloody work," given by participants, it is well to read some of the statements of those who battled for the Union on that occasion.

Many of the correspondents at the seat of war, ignorant of the real facts regarding the assault, attributed the failure, not to General Meade's interference with General Burnside's plan, but to the Phalanx division, the men who bore the brunt of the battle and gained for themselves a fame for desperate fighting. But some of those who *were* acquainted with the facts have left records that tell the true storyand give honor to whom honor is due. Gen. Grant is among the number; he perfectly understood the whole matter, knew that General Burnside, not being allowed to carry out his own plans, but at the last moment compelled to act contrary to his judgment, could not fight with that enthusiasm and confidence that he would have done had he been allowed to carry out his own ideas. In his "Memoirs," General Grant gives an account of the explosion of the mine and the assault after placing the blame for the "stupendous failure" where it belongs. I quote a few preliminary words which not only intimate where the trouble lies, but gives the key to the whole matter. Speaking of General Burnside's command, he says:

"The four divisions of his corps were commanded by Generals Potter, Wilcox, Ledlie and Ferrero. The last was a colored division; and Burnside selected it to make the assault. Meade interfered with this. Burnside then took Ledlie's division—a worse selection than the first could have been. * * * * Ledlie, besides being otherwise inefficient, proved also to possess disqualifications less common among soldiers."

A correspondent of the New York *Evening Post* says:

"We have been continually notified for the last fortnight, that our sappers were mining the enemy's position. As soon as ready, our division was to storm the works on its explosion. This rumor had spread so wide we had no faith in it. On the night of the 29th, we were in a position on the extreme left. We were drawn in about nine P. M., and marched to General Burnside's headquarters, and closed in mass by division, left in front. We there received official notice that the long-looked-for mine was ready charged, and would be fired at daylight next morning. The plan of storming was as follows: One division of white troops was to charge the works immediately after the explosion, and carry the first and second lines of rebel intrenchments. Our division was to follow immediately, and push right into Petersburg, take the city, and be supported by the remainder of the Ninth and Twenty-eighth corps. We were up bright and early, ready and eager for the struggle to commence. I had been wishing for something of this sort to do for some time, to gain the respect of the Army of the Potomac. You know their former prejudices. At thirty minutes after five, the ball opened. The mine, with some fifty pieces of artillery, went off almost instantaneously; at the same time, the white troops, according to the plan, charged the fort, which they carried, for there was nothing to oppose them; but they did not succeed in carrying either of the lines of intrenchments.

"We were held in rear until the development of the movement of the white troops; but, on seeing the disaster which was about to occur, we pushed in by the flank (for we could go in in no other way to allow us to get in position); so you see on this failure we had nothing to do but gain by the flank. A charge in that manner has never proved successful, to my knowledge; when it does, it is a surprise.

"Our men went forward with enthusiasm equal to anything under different circumstances; but, in going through the fort that had been blown up, the passage was almost impeded by obstacles thrown up by the explosion. At the same time, we were receiving a most deadly cross-fire from both flanks. At this time, our lieutenant-colonel (E. W. Ross) fell, shot through the left leg, bravely leading the men. I immediately assumed command, but only to hold it a few minutes, when I fell, struck by a piece of shell in the side. Capt. Robinson, from Connecticut, then took command; and, from all we can learn, he was killed. At this time, our first charge was somewhat checked, and the men sought cover in the works. Again our charge was made, but, like the former, unsuccessful. This was followed by the enemy making a charge. Seeing the unorganized condition and the great loss of officers, the men fell back to our own works. Yet, a large number still held the fort until two P. M., when the enemy charged again, and carried it. That ended the great attempt to take Petersburg.

"It will be thus seen that the colored troops did not compose the first assaulting, but the supporting column; and they were not ordered forward until white troops in greater numbers had made a desperate effort to carry the rebel works, and had failed. Then the colored troops were sent in; moved over the broken ground, and up the slope, and within a short distance of the parapet, in order, and with steady courage; but finally broke and retreated under the same fire which just before had sent a whole division of white regiments to the right-about. If there be any disgrace in that, it does not belong exclusively nor mainly to the negroes. A second attack is far more perilous and unlikely to succeed than a first; the enemy having been encouraged by the failure of the first, and had time to concentrate his forces. And, in this case, there seems to have been a fatal delay in ordering both the first and second assault."

An officer in the same engagement says:

"In regard to the bravery of the colored troops, although I have been in upwards of twenty battles, I never saw so many cases of gallantry. The 'crater,' where we were halted, was a perfect slaughter-pen. Had not 'some one blundered,' but moved us up at daylight, instead of eight o'clock, we should have been crowned with success, instead of being cut to pieces by a terrific enfilading fire, and finally forced from the field in a panic. We had no trouble in rallying the troops and moving them into the rifle-pits; and, in one hour after the rout I had nearly as many men together as were left unhurt.

"I was never under such a terrific fire, and can hardly realize how any escaped alive. Our loss was heavy. In the Twenty-eighth (colored) for instance, commanded by Lieut.-Col. Russell (a Bostonian), he lost seven officers out of eleven, and ninety-one men out of two hundred and twenty-four; and the colonel himself was knocked over senseless, for a few minutes, by a slight wound in the head; both his color-sergeants and all his color-guard were killed. Col. Bross, of the Twenty-ninth, was killed outright, and nearly every one of his officers hit. This was nearly equal to Bunker Hill. Col. Ross, of the Thirty-first, lost his leg. The Twenty-eighth, Twenty-ninth and Thirtieth (colored), all charged over the works; climbing up an earthwork six feet high, then down into a ditch, and up on the other side, all the time under the severest fire in front and flank. Not being supported, of course the storming party fell back. I have seen white troops run faster than these blacks did, when in not half so tight a place. Our brigade lost thirty-six prisoners, all cut off after leaving the 'crater.' My faith in colored troops is not abated one jot.'"

The Congressional Committee on the Conduct of the War investigated the affair, before which General Grant testified. He was severe upon General Ledlie, whom he regarded as an inefficient officer; he blamed himself for allowing that officer to lead the assault. General Grant also testified:

"General Burnside wanted to put his colored division in front; I believe if he had done so it would have been a success."

On the morning of the 13th of August, 1864, a brigade of the Phalanx, consisting of the 7th, 8th, 9th and 29th Regiments, crossed from Bermuda Hundreds to the north side of the James river, on pontoons, near Jones' landing, and bivouacked for the night. General Grant was led to believe that General Lee had sent a portion of his troops, at least three divisions of infantry, and one of cavalry, from the front of Petersburg, to re-enforce Gen. Early, then operating in the valley. Consequently he thought it a favorable opportunity to threaten Richmond, and ordered Hancock with the 2nd, and Birney with a part of the 10th Corps, with Gregg's Cavalry, to attack the confederate works on the north side of the James, The object was two-fold: to prevent Lee from re-enforcing Early, confronted by Sheridan's troops; and likewise to drive the confederates from out their works. The troops crossed the James on the 13th, the 2d Corps going to Deep Bottom by transports, the other troops crossing the river by pontoons, and advancing, found the enemy in force. Several spirited engagements took place, after which the main forces withdrew again across the river, to the front of Petersburg. The following account applies to the brigade as well as the 7th Phalanx Regiment, from whose record it is extracted:

"During the forenoon of the 14th the (7th) Regiment acted as reserve, moving forward occasionally as the line advanced. Most of the work of the day was done to the right, little being done in the immediate front except skirmishing. About 5 P. M. a portion of the Seventh and Ninth, forming line in the edge of some timber, moved across an open field and charged upon reaching the farther side and captured the enemy's line of rifle-pits. The companies of the Seventh pushed on some distance further toward their second line, but were met with so severe a fire that they fell back to the captured line; which was held. This charge, known as the action of Kingsland Road, was made in fine style. The battalion of the Seventh was commanded by Capt. Weiss—Col. Shaw having been detailed as Corps Officer of the day, and Lieut.-Col. Haskell being temporarily in command of the brigade. Our losses were two men killed, and one officer (Lieut. Eler) and thirty-two men wounded.

"About 10 o'clock P. M., the troops moved down the road to the right, and at 1 o'clock Col. Shaw withdrew the pickets of the corps, recrossed the pontoons, where we had crossed in the morning, and moved down the neck. Then followed four hours of the most wearisome night-marching—moving a few rods at a time and then halting for troops ahead to get out of the way; losing sight of them and hurrying forward to catch up; straggling out into the darkness, stumbling and groping along the rough road, and all the time the rain coming down in a most provoking, exasperating drizzle. About daylight crossed back to the north side and halted for coffee, and then moved forward some four miles and rejoined the corps, taking position behind the crest of a hill. The Eighth and Twenty-ninth were left in a work on the hill.

"About 3:30 P. M. orders came to pile knapsacks and be ready to march immediately. A little after 4 o'clock the brigade moved to the right, some three-quarters of a mile, into an open cornfield, and, after halting a few moments, turned down a road through the woods to the left with Gen. Wm. Birney, who ordered Col. Shaw to throw out skirmishers and advance with his brigade down a road which he pointed out, find the enemy and attack vigorously, and then rode away. Finding the road turning to the left, Col. Shaw sent word to Gen. Birney that the designated road would probably bring him back on our own line. The order came back from Gen. Birney to go ahead. The road still bearing to the left, word was again sent that we should strike our own line if we continued to advance in the direction we were going. A second time the answer came to move on. A third messenger having brought from Gen. Birney the same reply, Col. Shaw decided to disobey the order and call in the skirmishers. Before it could be done firing commenced and continued briskly for several minutes, before the men recognized each other, and it was discovered that we had been firing into our own Second Brigade—Col. Osborn's. This sad affair, which would not have occurred had Col Shaw's caution been heeded, resulted in the killing of the lieutenant commanding the picket-line and the wounding of many men on both sides. After this *fiasco* the brigade moved out into the cornfield, where it had halted earlier in the day, and bivouacked for the night. The regiment had been more or less exposed all day to shell-fire, but lost from it only four or five men wounded, in addition to the ten or twelve men wounded in the skirmish with Osborn's brigade.

"Early on the morning of the 16th, the regiment marched back to its knapsacks and halted for breakfast. About 10 o'clock it was ordered out to support two batteries, and remained on this duty until 3 P. M., changing position frequently. In the meantime Gen. Terry, with the First Division of the Tenth Corps, had charged the rebel line, near Fuzzel's mills, and captured it, together with three colors and some three hundred prisoners. But the enemy rallied, and with reinforcements, soon compelled Gen. Terry to relinquish the captured line. About dark Gen. Wm. Birney came up, and taking the left wing of the Seventh—the right wing, under Col. Shaw, was in support of a battery—and two companies of the Ninth, placed them under command of Lieut.-Col. Haskell, and ordered him with this handful of men to take an earthwork in his front which a division a short time before had failed to carry. The timely arrival of Gen. Terry put an end to this mad scheme. The regiment lost during the day eight or ten men wounded.

"The general results of the day's fighting had been unsatisfactory, for not only had Terry's attack failed in its object, but the advance on the right, along the Charles City road, by the troops of the Second Corps and Gregg's cavalry division, had been equally unsuccessful. The rebel General Chambliss was among the killed.

"About 2:30 A. M. of the 17th, the left wing of the regiment was sent back to a line of rifle-pits that had been thrown up some two hundred yards to the rear, where it was joined by the right wing in the morning after breakfast. Picket-firing continued during the day and heavy artillery firing was heard in the direction of Petersburg. At 4 P. M. a flag of truce was sent out and two hours given to bring in the dead from between the lines. Gen. Chambliss' body was delivered, and we received that of Capt. Williams, of the Thirty-ninth Illinois. Early in the evening the regiment was ordered on picket. Considerable picket-firing occurred during the night and day, the men being with difficulty restrained from it. We were relieved about noon of the 18th by the One Hundred and Fifteenth New York and Seventy-sixth Pennsylvania. * * *

"Early in the morning the Eighth and the Twenty-ninth Connecticut rejoined the regiment, and after the regiment was relieved from picket, it, with the Twenty-ninth, fell back a quarter of a mile, leaving the Eighth and Ninth on the line. Rations having been drawn, the men got supper and prepared for a good night's sleep. Suddenly a heavy musketry fire broke out toward the left which rapidly extended to the right and the entire line was soon under fire. The regiment moved forward at double-quick, but by the time it reached the front and formed line, darkness set in and the enemy fell back. About 11 P. M. our forces were withdrawn, and, after several hours spent in marching and halting, the regiment went into camp two miles from the pontoons. Here it lay all day of the 19th. The following congratulatory order was received from corps headquarters, in which the brigade was spoken of in very flattering terms by Maj.-Gen. D. B. Birney, commanding:

"'HEADQUARTERS TENTH ARMY CORPS,
FUZZEL'S MILLS, VA., August 19, 1864.

"'*General Orders.*—The Major-General commanding congratulates the Tenth Army Corps upon its success. It has, on each occasion, when ordered, broken the enemy's strong lines. It has captured during this short campaign four seige guns protected by formidable works, six colors and many prisoners. It has proved itself worthy of its old Wagner and Fort Sumter renown.

"'Much fatigue, patience and heroism, may still be demanded of it, but the Major-General commanding is confident of the response. To the colored troops, recently added to us, and fighting with us, the Major-General tenders his thanks for their uniform good conduct and soldierly bearing. They have set a good example to our veterans, by the entire absence of straggling from their ranks on the march.

"'By order of Maj.-Gen. D. B. BIRNEY.

"'E. W. SMITH,
Lieutenant-Colonel and Assistant Adjutant-General.'

"The special correspondent of the New York *Tribune* said:

"'Gen. Butler, in a dispatch to the Tenth Corps, on receiving official report of its work, said: 'All honor to the brave Tenth Corps; you have done more than was expected of you by the Lieutenant-General.'

"'The loss in the four colored regiments is about three hundred. The Seventh U. S. C. T. on the first day, carried, with fixed bayonets, a line of rifle-pits, and carried it without a shot, but with a loss of 35. It was one of the most stirring and gallant affairs I have ever known'.

"It began to rain in the afternoon and continued during the night and until nearly noon of the following day, 20th. During the afternoon of the 20th, orders were received to send all sick to the rear and be ready to withdraw quietly at dark. The movement began at 7 P. M., both the Second and Tenth Corps participating—the Second Corps and the cavalry returning to the Petersburg line, and the Tenth to the Bermuda Hundred front. The night was dark and the roads muddy, and after various delays the pontoons were crossed; and at 2 A. M., the regiment went into camp near the spot it occupied the first night after its arrival in Virginia.

"An amusing incident occurred when we halted, after crossing the river. When the fires were lighted our line presented the appearance of a checker-board—alternate black and white men. The latter belonged to the Second Corps, and having straggled from their commands, and belonging to regiments with the same numbers, had fallen into our solid ranks by mistake. Their astonishment and our amusement were about equal. Capt. Walker, having been asked if his men were all present, replied: 'Yes, and about twenty recruits.'

"Thus ended a very hard week's work, during which the regiment was almost constantly under fire; marching, counter-marching, supporting a battery here or strengthening the line there—duties which required almost constant wakefulness and watchfulness. The losses of the brigade footed up some two hundred and fifty.

"This movement, which had begun on the 12th by the withdrawal of the Second Corps, Gen. Hancock, and Gregg's cavalry division, from the Petersburg front to the north bank of the James, to act in conjunction with the Tenth Corps in an attempt to turn the left of the rebel line, proved as abortive as the similar attempt made by the same corps in the latter part of June; Gen. Lee, in both instances, seeming to have received timely information of our plans to enable him to transfer re-enforcements from the Petersburg to the Richmond front. The Union losses during the movement have been estimated at five thousand.

"Sunday, the 21st, was a day of rest. The men put up shelter tents and made themselves as comfortable as circumstances would allow. Gen. Birney resumed command of the brigade and Col. Shaw returned to the regiment. About 6 P. M. orders came to be ready to move during the night with one day's rations. Moved out of camp at 2 A. M., 22nd, and reported at Maj.-Gen. Birney's headquarters, where, after remaining a short time, the regiment returned to camp. About 3 P. M. orders were received to pack everything, and at 5 the regiment marched to the front and went into the trenches near Battery Walker, (No. 7), relieving a regiment of hundred-days' men, whose time had expired.

"The 23d passed quietly. Tents were pitched, and in the evening a dress-parade was held. Lieut. Mack returned to duty from absent sick

"Line was formed at dawn on the 24th, and again about noon—rapid picket-firing in each instance rendering an attack probable.

"About daybreak on the 25th, the enemy attacked toward the left, drove in our pickets—Capts. Weld and Thayer in command—but were checked before reaching the main line. The regiment was placed in support of Battery England (No. 5). Two men were wounded.

"Some changes in the division here took place—the Twenty-ninth Connecticut was transferred to another brigade, and the Tenth U. S. C. T. to ours, and Col. Duncan was placed in command.

"About noon (25th) packed up everything, crossed the Appomattox, and after a fatiguing march through the heat and dust, reached the Petersburg front a little before sunset and halted for orders. Soon after dark moved to the left in a heavy rain-squall, and lay down on a hillside as reserve to the troops in the trenches. At 11 P. M. ordered to report to Gen. Terry. Marched back a mile and reported. Another mile's march in another direction brought the regiment, about 1 A. M., to its position, where it lay down in the woods, again as a reserve. A rattling fire of musketry was kept up all night.

"On the 26th, a camp was selected and had been partially cleared up, when orders were received for the regiment to go into the trenches. Reported at brigade headquarters at sunset, and soon afterward, through the mud and darkness, the men silently felt their way into the trenches, which the rain had reduced to the condition of a quagmire. It was a slow process, and 10 o'clock came before all were in their places.

"During the following day (27th,) the parapet was raised and paths made through the muddier portions of the trenches. Soon after dark a furious cannonade began which lasted for several hours, and afforded to the spectators on both sides a brilliant pyrotechnic display.

"Just after daybreak on the 28th, the enemy opened a heavy musketry fire which lasted until after sunrise. He did not leave his works, however, and our men remained stationary. A man of Company B, while watching for a shot through a section of stove-pipe, which he had improvised into a port-hole, was struck and killed by a sharp-shooter's bullet.

"Soon after midnight on the 28th-29th, the regiment moved out of the trenches, and after daylight marched a quarter of a mile to the right and rear and went into camp in a cornfield. The men were at once put to work constructing bomb-proofs, as the position was within sight and range of the enemy's line. This occupied the entire day.

"Brig.-Gen. Birney's arrangement of the brigade did not seem to have given satisfaction to higher authority, and it was broken up, and the old brigade—Seventh, Eighth, Ninth U. S. C. T., and Twenty-ninth Connecticut—were again united, with Col. Shaw in command.

"From this time until the 24th of September, the Seventh and Eighth alternated with the Ninth and Twenty-ninth for duty in the trenches—two days in and two out; and on the 'off' days furnishing details of officers and men for fatigue purposes, in constructing new works and strengthening old ones. The main lines at this point were scarcely over a hundred yards apart, while from the advanced posts a stone could almost be thrown into the enemy's works, and it was considered the most disagreeable portion of the line.

"During the evening of the 4th of September, there was a grand salute along the whole line, in honor of the fall of Atlanta At every battery the men stood at the guns, and when the monster mortar—"The Petersburg Express"—gave the expected signal, every lanyard was pulled. The effect was exceedingly grand.

"At 9 o'clock on the morning of the 5th, the regiment met with an irreparable loss in the death of Capt. A. R. Walker. Capt. Walker, who was at the time in the trenches, had raised his head above the parapet to observe the enemy's movements, when he was struck in the head by a bullet. and fell without speaking against the parapet. He was carried back and laid upon the ground in rear of the trench, but all efforts failed to elicit any token of recognition. He breathed for a few moments and life was extinct. His body was sent to the rear the same afternoon under charge of Lieut. Teeple, upon whom the command of his company devolved, who made the necessary arrangements for having it embalmed and forwarded to his friends at Caledonia, New York.

* * * * * * * *

"On the 14th Col. Howell, who was commanding the division in the absence of Gen. Birney, who was absent sick, died of injuries received from a fall from his horse, and the command of the division devolved upon Col. Pond. Col. Howell was highly esteemed, and was a thorough gentleman and a good officer.

"On the 17th, Sergt. Wilson, Company F, color-sergeant, was reduced to the ranks for cowardice, and Sergt. Griffin, Company B, appointed in his place.

"On the 21st, Capt. Thayer resigned.

"On the 22d, Gen. Birney returned and resumed command of the brigade; the division having been temporarily broken up by the withdrawal of troops, and Col. Shaw returned to the regiment.

"On the 23d, companies B and C were detailed to garrison Fort Steadman.

"On the evening of the 24th, the regiment was relieved from duty in the trenches by the Sixty-ninth New York, and moving about two miles to the rear, went into camp with the remainder of the brigade—some four miles from City Point. Here regular drills and parades were resumed.

"At 3 P. M. on the 28th, camp was broken, and an hour later the brigade followed the two divisions of the corps on the road toward Bermuda Hundred. A tedious night-march followed, during which the north side of the James was reached by way of Broadway and Jones' landings After an hour or two of rest on the morning of the 29th, the brigade moved forward as a support to the First Division (Paine's), the First Brigade of which, under Col. Duncan, charged and carried the enemy's works on Signal-Hill, on the New Market road, beyond the line of works taken by the Seventh and Ninth on the 14th of August.* [See foot-note next page.] * * The Eighteenth Corps at the same time charged and carried Fort Harrison and a long line of rebel works. Soon after noon, while the brigade, which had been moving by the flank down the New Market road, had halted in the road, orders came to form column of regiments, faced to the left, in the woods. Scarcely had this been done when Gen. Wm. Birney, commanding brigade, rode up to the right of the column and ordered the Seventh to move off by the right flank. As it was crossing the Mill road, Col. Shaw reached the head of the line and received from him the order to "form on the right by file into line, and charge and take the work that is firing," and adding, "if that work is taken when you reach it, push right on and take the next *before Gen. Foster can get there.*" In the meantime the Ninth had charged a work on the right and had been repulsed, and the commanding officer of the Eighth had been ordered to send four companies deployed as skirmishers to take the work to the left, but when Major

THE PHALANX AT NEW MARKET HEIGHTS. *

* "On the 29th of September, 1864, Gen. Grant ordered Gen. Butler to cross the James River, at Two Points, and attack the enemy's line of work, in the centre of which was Fort Harrison; on the left, at New Market Heights, was a very strong work, the key of the enemy's flank on the north side of the river. It was a redoubt built on the top of a hill of some considerable elevation, then running down into a marsh. In that marsh was a brook—then rising again to a plain, which gently rolled toward the river. On that plain, when the flash of dawn was breaking, Butler placed a column of the black Phalanx," [which consisted of the 5th, 36th, 38th and 2nd Cavalry Regts.], "numbering three thousand, in close column, by division, right in front, with guns at 'right shoulder shift.' The center of the line was given to the eighteenth corps, composed of white troops, under Gen. Ord, and they drove the enemy from a very strong work, capturing several pieces of cannon.

"Gen. Butler had been severely criticised by officers of the regular army for organizing twenty-five regiments of negroes. 'Why,' said they, 'they will not fight.' In contradiction of this assertion Butler made up his mind to prove the worth and value of the black Phalanx. Notwithstanding their gallantry at Petersburg and on the Fredericksburg road, the metal of the 25th corps of the Army of the James was to be tried; so Butler took command of the Phalanx himself with a determination to set at rest forever the question of the fighting capacity of a portion of his command. Addressing the Phalanx, he said, pointing to the works on the enemy's flank, 'those works must be taken by the weight of your column; not a shot must be fired.' In order to prevent them from firing he had the caps taken from the nipples of their guns. 'When you charge,' he said, 'your cry will be 'Remember Fort Pillow.''

"'Twas in the early grey of the morning, ere the sun had risen. The order 'forward' set the column in motion, and it went forward as if on parade—down the hill, across the marsh, and as the column got into the brook they came within range of the enemy's fire, which was vigorously opened upon them. The column broke a little as it forded the brook, it wavered! What a moment of intense anxiety! But they formed again, as they reached the firm ground, marching on steadily with close ranks under the enemy's fire, until the head of the column reached the first line of abatis, some one hundred and fifty yards from the enemy's work. Then the axemen ran to the front to cut away the heavy obstacles of defense while one thousand men of the enemy with their artillery concentrated poured from the redoubt a heavy fire upon the head of the column of fours. The axemen went down under that murderous fire; other strong black hands grasped the axes in their stead and the abatis was cut away. Again, at double-quick, the column went forward to within fifty yards of the fort, to meet there another line of abatis. The column halted and there a very fire of hell was poured upon them. The abatis resisted and held the head of the column which literally melted away under the rain of shot and shell; the flags of the leading regiments went down, but a brave black hand seized the colors. They were soon up again and waved their starry light over the storm of battle. Again the axemen fell, but strong hands and willing hearts seized the heavy sharpened trees and dragged them away, and the column rushed forward and with a shout that rang out above the roar of artillery went over the redoubt like a flash, and the enemy did not stop running within four miles, leaving the Phalanx in possession of their deemed impregnable work, cannons and small arms. The autocrats of the regular army could croak no longer about the negro soldiers not fighting.

"This gallantry of the Phalanx won for them and the negro race the admiration of the man who suppoted Jeff Davis and the slave power in the Charleston convention in 1860. Ten years after this spendid victory of the Phalanx, in support of their civil rights, General Butler then a member of congress, made an eloquent appeal in

* (Author in the N. Y. *Globe.*)

[*Continuation of page 435 foot-note.*]
behalf of the equal civil rights of the negro race. In it he referred to the gallant charge of the Phalanx. He said: "It became my painful duty to follow in the track of that charging column, and there, in a space not wider than the clerk's desk and three hundred yards long, lay the dead bodies of five hundred and forty-three of my colored comrades, fallen in defense of their country, who had offered up their lives to uphold its flag and its honor, as a willing sacrifice: and as I rode along among them, guiding my horse this way and that way, lest he should profane with his hoofs what seemed to me the sacred dead, and as I looked on their bronzed faces upturned in the shining sun, as if in mute appeal against the wrongs of the country for which they had given their lives, whose flag had only been to them a flag of stripes, on which no star of glory had ever shone for them—feeling I had wronged them in the past and believing what was the future of my country to them—among my dead comrades there, I swore to myself a solemn oath—'May my right hand forget its cunning and my tongue cleave to the roof my mouth, if I ever fail to defend the rights of those men who have given their blood for me and my country that day and for their race forever, and God helping me, I will keep that oath."

"NEW MARKET HEIGHTS. *

"'Freedom their battle cry, freedom or leave to die.'—*Boker.*

At New Market Heights, there Afric's lineage stood,
And poured out copiously its best blood;
Of them I would sing, my lyre's restrung,
And allures not diffidently to the song,
Paternal muse with thy patriot valor reign
Supreme, and the brightness of ages regain,
In the deep recess of the past
Lower me, to where the battle's blast
Has been given to oblivion, the sigh
Of dying patriots let greet me nigh.
And my thoughts waft on memory's wing,
To where their charging shouts yet ring.

If mine the task indulgent muse vouchsafed,
Whilst I commune 'mongst bones that paved,
And flesh that bridged the chasm o'er,
Where Butler numbered five hundred and more
of Afric's sons, who for liberty fell,
In the corridors of a stockaded hell.
I'll essay their deeds of valor done,
By which the nation its victory won.

'Twas early in the grey September morn,
Ere the suns fulgent light had shown,
Whilst departed patriots looked out from above,
Emitting their twinkling silvery light of love,
Upon the silent bivouac of freedom's sons,
Weary and resting upon their bayonetless guns;
Quite near the bank of the James,
Just above where their own fathers' names,
Were first enrolled as ignoble slaves,
The Second Brigade, valiant men and braves,
Saw a meteor like rocket burst high,
High up in the dewey morning sky,
Then came the summons prepare to away,
Butler leads to New Market heights at day.
Beat the long roll, sound the alarm,
Break the monotone and the dead calm,
And the bugle's clarion notes aroused, awoke,
The host that waited ere day broke;
Infantry, cavalry prepared to make away,
Butler leads to New Market heights at day.

From rank to rank the summons ran,
Bayonets rattle and clank of sabres began,
With whetted steel the sturdy axe-men,
Capless rifle-men, horseless cavalry men,
Formed on that plain in battle array,
Butler leads to New Market heights at day.

When the flash of dawn was breaking,
Their leader rode in front, and speaking,
Gave the charging shout '*Remember Fort Pillow*,"
And their banners brightened in the mellow
Light of heaven; '*Forward*,' they marched away,
Following Butler to New Market heights that day.

* (Author in "*Voice of a New Race.*")

[*Continuation of page 435 foot-note.*]

Went down the hill across the marsh,—
Into the brook—there halted—ah! how harsh
The rebels' fire opened upon them, artillery
Hail swept the run, and the infantry
Broke, the column wavered tho' not in dismay,
Following Butler to New Market heights that day.

Again the shattered columns form and again advance
To firmer ground, tho' the redoubt hurl'd like an avalanche
In quick succession, bursting bombs and canister shot,
But with closed ranks the column, fearing not
Unheedful of the iron hail bent its way,
Following Butler to New Market heights that day.

Now the head of the column of fours go down
Under the murderous fire and the hissing song
Of the enemy's shells, now the axe men spring
To the *abatis* high and long, now their axes ring
Out on the morning air, they were swept away.
Following Butler to New Market heights that day.

The flags are where, do they kiss the morning light,
Do they wave in the battle's gale, are their stars bright,
IllumininING the path of the brave? riddled and torn,
With the dead they lay. Soon again they shone,
In the first gleam of the rising-sun's ray,
Following Butler to New Market heignts that day.

Upon the brigade each felt that all was placed,
Their race and country's future honored or disgraced,
Hence with Spartan courage they the charge renewed,
And in hot haste the Nation's enemy pursued,
And sweat and blood from pore and wound inveigh,
Following Butler to New Market heights that day.

'*Forward, forward!*' rung the command, the flags are
up again,
The axe-men grin, and with a shout go over the slain,
To a second line of *abatis*. The welkin's aglow,
The advancing brigade shouts, '*Remember Fort Pillow!*'
And with a will and spirit they clear the way,
Following Butler to New Market heights that day.

Down the dismounted cavalrymen fall by ranks,
The Infantry an adamantine wall on the flanks,
Close up briskly on right and left receive
The enfilading fire from the brazen crest, breathe
They not a word in complaint, freedom's impulse obey,
Following Butler to New Market heights that day.

Now the black axe-men tear from the sod the huge logs
Which science and treason placed deep in the bogs,
Skill gave way to freedom's might in the dastardly fight,
And the black brigade, with capless rifles and starry light,
Go through the gap to the Rebel's hell in gallant array,
Following Butler to New Market heights that day.

Volley after volley poured, cannon after cannon roared,
Like reapers in a field a thousand artillerists mowed
In the gap, the brigade's advancing files of four,
Yet on through the flood of death still the brigade pour,
Their battle cry, *Remember Fort Pillow*, the enemy
dismay,
Following Butler to New Market heights that day.

Hark! above the raging carnage swells the shout,
'*No quarter to Niggers*,' with hope of a rout,
But the brigade was not deterred, they retaliate
The defiant yells, *Remember Fort Pillow*, the fate
Of its garrison how it fell, on through the fray,
Following Butler to New Market heights that day.

On for the *redoubt* over the rampart they go,
Not a rifle was fired, not a shot at the foe,
By the weight of the column the *redoubt* is theirs,
And the enemy routed, the chivalry scattered everywhere,
Victorious shouts the empyrean ring in repay,
Following Butler to New Market heights that day.

Wagner found how strong it was he halted his line and remained in advance as skirmishers. As the regiment was forming for the charge, behind the crest of a knoll, Capt. Bailey, Gen. Birney's Adjutant-General, rode up to Col. Shaw with the order to send four companies deployed as skirmishers to 'attack and take the work that is firing.' Col. Shaw replied that he had orders to charge it with his regiment, to which Capt. Bailey answered, 'well, *now* the General directs you to send four companies, deployed as skirmishers, to take the work.' Lieut.-Col. Haskell, being absent on leave, and Maj. Mayer sick, companies C, D, G and K were placed under command of Capt. Weiss, who, when he received the order to charge, replied, 'what! take a fort with a skirmish line?' and then added, 'I will try, but it can't be done.' What followed can best be described by quoting his own words:

"Captain Weiss says: 'I at once, about 1 P. M., ordered the four companies on the right of the regiment, C, D, G and K, twenty-five or thirty paces to the front, where a slight depression in the ground secured them from the eyes, if not the projectiles, of the enemy. After being deployed by the flank on the right of the second company from the right, the command advanced in ordinary quick step against the objective point. Emerging from the swale into view, it became at once the target for a seemingly redoubled fire, not only from the fort in front, but also from the one on *its* right. The fire of the latter had been reported silenced, but instead, from its position to the left oblique, it proved even more destructive than that of the one in front.

"'Both forts were most advantageously situated for defense, at the extremity of a plain, variously estimated at from 500 to 700 yards wide, whose dead level surface afforded at no point shelter from view or shot to an assailing party. Tne forts were connected by a curtain of rifle-pits containing a re-entrant angle, thus providing for a reciprocal enfilading fire in case either was attacked.

"'The nature of the ground and the small altitude of the ordnance above the level of the plain also made the fire in the nature of a ricochet.

"As the party advanced the enemy's shell and schrapnel were exchanged for grape and cannister, followed soon by a lively rattle of musketry. When within range of the latter, and after having traversed about three-fourths of the distance, the order to charge was given and obeyed with an alacrity that seemed to make the execution almost precede the order. For a moment, judging from the slacking of their fire, the enemy seemed to be affected by a panicky astonishment, but soon recovering, they opened again with cannister and musketry, which, at the shorter range, tore through the ranks with deadlier effect. Capt.

[*Continuation of page 435 foot-note.*]

In the track of the brigade lay the loyal dead,
Afric's hecatomb, her lineage's pyre to liberty wed,
Their upturned countenances to the burning sun,
Were appeals to Mars for their race's freedom won,
Five hundred lives on the patriotic alter lay,
Following Butler to New Market heights that day.

No marble shaft or granate pile mark the spot
Where they fell—their bones lay harvested from sun-rot,
In the Nation's cities of the dead. Hannibal led
No braver than they through Alpine snow, nor wed
To freedom were Greece's phalanx more, who o'er gory
clay
Followed Butler to New Market heights that day.

Smith and Lieut. Prime, both of Company G, here fell grievously wounded, while forty or fifty enlisted-men dotted the plain with their prostrate forms.

"'In a few minutes the ditch of the fort was reached. It was some six or seven feet deep and ten or twelve wide, the excavated material sufficing for the embankments of the fort. Some 120 men and officers precipitated themselves into it, many losing their lives at its very edge. After a short breathing spell men were helped up the exterior of the parapet on the shoulders of others; fifty or sixty being thus disposed an attempt was made to storm the fort. At the signal nearly all rose, but the enemy, lying securely sheltered behind the interior slope, the muzzles of their guns almost touching the storming party, received the latter with a crushing fire, sending many into the ditch below shot through the brain or breast. Several other attempts were made with like result, till at last forty or fifty of the assailants were writhing in the ditch or resting forever.

"'The defense having been obviously re-enforced meanwhile from other points not so directly attacked, and having armed the gunners with muskets, it was considered impolitic to attempt another storm with the now greatly reduced force on hand, especially as the cessation of the artillery fire of the fort was considered a sufficient hint to the commander of the Union forces that the attacking party had come to close quarters and were proper subjects for re-enforcements. No signs, however, of the latter appearing, it was decided to surrender, especially as the rebels had now commenced to roll lighted shells among the stormers, against which there was no defense, thus inviting demoralization. Seven officers, Capts. Weiss and McCarty, Lieuts. Sherman, Mack, Spinney, Ferguson and Eler, and from seventy to eighty enlisted-men, delivered up their arms to an enemy gallant enough to have fought for a better cause.

"'Many, in mounting the parapet, could not help taking a last mournful look on their dead comrades in the ditch, whose soldierly qualities had endeared them to their best affections; and many, without for a moment selfishly looking at their own dark future, were oppressed with inexpressible sadness when reflecting on the immensity of the sacrifice and the deplorableness of the result. It was a time for manly tears.'

"Lieut Spinney gives the following account of the charge against Fort Gilmer:

"'The charge was made in quick time, in open order of about three paces, until we could plainly see the enemy; then the order was given by Capt. Weiss to 'double-quick,' which was promptly obeyed, the line preserving its order as upon drill. Upon arriving at the ditch there was no wavering, but every man jumped into the trap from which but one man returned that day (George W. Washington, Company D.)

"'Upon looking about us after getting into the ditch we found there was but one face where the enemy could not touch us, so all the survivors rallied at that face. Then commenced a scene which will always be very fresh in my memory.

"'Capt. Weiss gave orders to raise men upon the parapet, which was done by two men assisting one to climb. Capt. Weiss, having from thirty to forty men up, attempted to gain the inside of the fort, but he with all of his storming party were knocked back, either killed or wounded, into the ditch. A second attempt was made with the same result, Lieut. Ferguson being wounded by a bullet across the top of his head. A third attempt was made with no better success.

"'The enemy during this time had been rolling shell upon us, and calling upon us to surrender, which was answered by some of the men in the words, 'we will show you how to surrender,' at the same time rising and firing into the fort. One of these men I remember to have been Perry Wallace, Company D.

"'Upon a consultation of the officers who were in the ditch, it was decided to surrender what was left of the command. I was still upon the face of the parapet, when Lieut. Sherman passed me a handkerchief which I raised upon the point of my sword. But the rebels, fearing it was only done to gain a foothold, would not take notice of it, but called upon me to come in, which I did, and met with a warm reception at their hands, being plucked of all they could lay hands upon. An adjutant of an Alabama regiment coming up, ordered his men to return to me what they had taken, but this was not done, however. I stated that our men had disarmed themselves and were ready to give up the hopeless struggle. Still they would not believe me, but made me mount the parapet first, when they had the courage to do so themselves, when the remnant of the four companies marched into the fort.

"'The march to Richmond was one continued insult from the troops that were hurrying to the front; one man being determined to kill Capt. Weiss, whom he thought was not humble enough. The female portion of the inhabitants were also very insolent.

"'Upon arriving at Libby Prison the officer in charge asked the commander of our guard if the 'niggers' would fight. His answer was, 'by G—d! if you had been there you would have thought so. They marched up just as if they were on drill, not firing a shot.'

"'After being lodged in Libby, Salisbury and Danville prisons, we were returned to Richmond about February 17th, paroled on the 21st, and reached our lines on the 22d.'

"An article in the New York *Herald* of November 4th, 1864, copied from a rebel newspaper, arguing for the arming of slaves, has in it the following passage:

"'But A. B. says that negroes will not fight. We have before us a letter from a distinguished general (we wish we were at liberty to use his name and influence) who says 'Fort Gilmer proved the other day that they would fight. They raised each other on the parapet to be shot as they appeared above.'

"The officer referred to was understood to be Gen. Lee.

"After the four companies had disappeared in the ditch of the fort, Capt. Pratt, with Company F, was ordered to move forward as near the work as he could get and keep down its fire and cover their retreat. Capt Smith and Lieut. Prime came back, both severely wounded. Later in the day companies A, B, E and I, under Capt. Spaulding, moved to the left and relieved the four companies of the Eighth, who were out of ammunition. Co. F lost two men killed and twenty-three wounded, and the four companies under Capt. Spaulding had eleven men killed and wounded. Lieut. Teeple, commanding Company I, was wounded in the arm, but remained in command of his company during the day.

"Four companies annihilated, 70 killed, 110 wounded and 129 missing tells the story of Fort Gilmer.

"The regiment, or what was left of it, remained at the front until 9 o'clock P. M., when the wounded were gathered together and it moved half a mile to the rear and slept on its arms.

"This day proved the most unfortunate one in the history of the regiment. The storming of a strong field-work, whose garrison was on the alert, with a thin skirmish line without supports, resulted as could easily have been foreseen. First, the Ninth was sent unsupported to charge a work to the left of Fort Gilmer, across an open field where its line was enfiladed by the enemy's fire, and was repulsed; then four companies of the Eighth, as skirmishers, were sent against the same work, with no better success, and after this bitter experience, four companies of the Seventh were sent to their destruction on an errand equally hopeless. Had the brigade been sent together, instead of its three regiments in detail, the rebel line would have been carried and the road to Richmond opened to us. This is no conjecture. The testimony of a rebel staff-officer on duty at Fort Gilmer, and that of our own officers who were captured, fully substantiate the statement.

"About noon on the following day, the 30th, the regiment moved a mile to the left and went into the rifle-pits to the left of Fort Harrison. Soon after, the rebel Maj.-Gen. Field, who had commanded the Ft. Gilmer line the day previous, made a determined assault on Fort Harrison from one side, while Hoke's division attacked on the other; but the attack was not made simultaneously and was repulsed with heavy loss. While this charge was being made, Col. Shaw was struck on the head by a rifle bullet, but was uninjured. The next morning the rebels opened their batteries on our line. During the cannonade, Lieut. Bjornmark was wounded in the foot by the fragment of a shell.

"The following is the report of Capt. Weiss to the commanding officer of the regiment, announcing his arrival in Richmond:

"'LIBBY PRISON, RICHMOND, VA., September 30, 1864.

"'*Sir:*—I respectfully inform you that the following officers of the Seventh U. S. C. T. are here, prisoners: Capts. Weiss and McCarty, Lieuts. Mack, Sherman, Eler, Ferguson and Spinney. Lieut. Ferguson and myself are wounded in the head, but doing well.

"'Please inform our friends of the above, and oblige,

"'Yours, on the part of my associates,

"'JULIUS A. WEISS,

"'*Capt. Seventh U. S. C. T.*'

"On the 5th of October, the regiment was relieved from duty in the trenches by the Eight, and moving a short distance to the rear, went into camp near division headquarters.

"On the 6th, Gen. Birney divided the regiments of his command into two brigades. The First Brigade, composed of the Seventh, Ninth and One Hundred and Twenty-seventh, was placed under command of Col. Voris, of the Sixty-seventh Ohio, although each regiment had a colonel serving with it; and the Second, composed of the Eighth, Twenty-ninth and Forty-fifth, under Lieut.-Col. Armstrong, of the Ninth. Capt. Rice returned from sick-leave the same day and was assigned to the command of Company A, his own company (K) having disappeared in the *melee* of the 29th of September.

"During the forenoon of the 7th, the enemy attacked in force on the right, driving in Kautz's cavalry and capturing Elder's battery of the First United States Artillery, but was checked and driven back by the First Division of the Tenth Corps. The regiment was moved to the right, and after changing positions several times, went into the trenches near the New Market road.

"On the afternoon of the 12th, orders came for the regiment to be ready to move in light marching order, and later it moved out about half of a mile to the front and right, and deployed two companies as skirmishers. Shortly after dark it was withdrawn to the position it held earlier in the day. A cold rain was falling, and as the men were without overcoats, they suffered considerably.

"About 3 o'clock on the morning of the 13th, our own division (Third), together with the First, moved out of camp and marched to the right until it reached the Darbytown road. Here it formed line, and advancing through the thick undergrowth finally lay down in front of the enemy's works to await developments. At 10 o'clock the First Division, which, with the cavalry, had gone to the right, charged the enemy's line, but failed to break it and had to withdraw with considerable loss. About noon the regiment relieved the Eighth on the skirmish line. Capt. Dickey, of the Eighth, was killed during the movement. Here it remained until about 4 o'clock, when, the remainder of the division having been withdrawn, it fell back covering the movement of the corps and returned to its old camp on the New Market road. * * *

"The regiment remained in camp until the 26th, furnishing in the meantime a large picket detail, together with details for fatigue, employed in the construction of earthworks, abattis, etc. On this date Col. Voris was relieved from command of the brigade by Col. Shaw, Lieut.-Col. Haskell taking command of the regiment.

"On the evening of this day orders were received for the regiment to be ready to move on the following morning, with three days' cooked rations, and in light marching order. At 5 A. M. we moved out of camp and took the road toward the right. The Eighteenth, as well as our own corps, was in motion. The orders were for the Tenth Corps to threaten the enemy's line near the Darbytown road, while the Eighteenth moving by the rear to the right, was to strike their left flank. If they weakened their line in its front, the Tenth Corps was to advance. The whole movement being made to cover the advance of the Army of the Potomoc against the rebel lines covering Hatcher's run and the Boydtown plank-road.

"Marching about two miles to the right we struck the Darbytown road, when line of battle was formed to the left, and moved forward through the woods, and, in places, almost impassable undergrowth—the Seventh having the left of the division as well of the line. Our ears were soon greeted with the scattering fire of our skirmish line, interspersed by the crashing of an occasional shell through the tree-tops. After an advance of half a mile the division halted to await the result of the attack on the right. The irregular skirmish fire soon swelled out into long, heavy volleys, deepened by the hoarser notes of the artillery. From 8 A. M. until 8 P. M. we lay and listened to this concert of diabolical sounds, momentarily expecting the order would be passed along the line to advance. About 11 A. M. it began to rain, which continued until far into the night. At 8 P. M. we fell back out of the woods, behind an old line of rebel rifle-pits, and bivouacked for the night near Kell's House.

"At 3 o'clock the following morning we were ordered in to relieve the Twenty-ninth on the picket-line. The clouds had cleared away and the air was keen and cold. We felt our way through the dense, dripping undergrowth to the musical accompaniment of rebel bullets singing above our heads. By daybreak we were in position along the edge of a belt of woods, something less than a quarter of a mile from the rebel works. Their skirmishers kept up a lively fire all through the forenoon, and as a consequence we lost some thirty odd men, killed and wounded, from their fire. About 3 P. M. orders were given to fall back, but through some misunderstanding, the two companies holding the extreme left of the line failed to receive the order, and held their ground until their retreat was nearly cut off by the rebel advance, when they fell back without orders, meeting on their way the remainder of the brigade coming to their rescue. The same evening the troops returned to their camps.

"Here ended our fighting for the fall. * * *

"On the 28th, Gen. Birney returned and relieved Gen. Hawley in command of the division, which he had held during the absence of the former in Philadelphia, where he had gone about the 21st to attend the funeral of his brother, Maj.-Gen. D. B. Birney. Col. Shaw was placed permanently in command of the First Brigade, and Col. Wright, Tenth U. S. C. T., of the Second.

"About the 30th, a general order was received from Gen. Butler thanking Capt. Weiss and the officers under him for their gallant conduct on the 29th, and saying that their absence in prison alone prevented their promotion.

"On the 1st of November, the division was reviewed by Gen. Birney, and the proclamation of the Governor of Maryland, announcing the adoption of the constitutional amendment abolishing slavery in that State, was read to the command. This paper, which conveyed to the men the knowledge that their wives and children were no longer slaves, produced an effect more easily imagined than described.

* * * * * * * *

"On the 5th, Capt. Cheney and Lieut. Teeple, with companies H and I, were detached from the regiment to garrison Fort 'No. 3,' at Spring Hill— a work on the right flank of the Army of the James—where they remained until the 6th of December.

"On the 1st of December, the reorganization of the Tenth and Eighteenth Corps was determined upon. The white troops of the two corps were consolidated and formed the Twenty-fourth Corps, under Gen. Foster; and the colored troops of the Ninth, Tenth and Eighteenth Corps, with other colored troops not assigned, formed the Twenty-fifth Corps, under Gen. Weitzel. Its three divisions were commanded by Gens. Wild, Birney and Paine, respectively. The First Brigade of Birney's division was made up of the Seventh, One Hundred and Ninth, One Hundred and Sixteenth and One hundred and Seventeenth, under Col. Shaw. The Forty-first Forty-fifth and One Hundred and Twenty-seventh had at different times been attached to the brigade—*to learn our ways*, as they said at headquarters. Eventually, however, the One Hundred and Fifteenth was substituted for the One Hundred and Seventeenth in the brigade.

"On the 4th, a general re-assignment of positions was made. The Seventh moved from the New Market road to Fort Burnham (Harrison), which was garrisoned by the First Brigade. The Second Brigade, under Doubleday, was on our right, and the Third on our left. The Second Brigade joined the Twenty-fourth Corps, near the New Market road, and Paine's division was on our left and extended to the river. The other division was in reserve to the rear. The Seventh was under command of Lieut.-Col. Pratt, and so remained during the remainder of our stay in Virginia."

The prolonged but decisive struggle began to draw near. General Grant had pushed the troops nearer and closer, at every opportunity, to the beleaguered cities, until they were well-nigh completely invested. General Sherman's splendid victories influenced the veteran corps lying before these places, and filled them with the spirit of sure success. The intrepid commander, having reached North Carolina, visited Grant at the latter's headquarters at City Point, where he also found President Lincoln, and received their congratulations for his successful march to the sea, which achievement had not been surpassed by any of the undertakings of either Hannibal or Bonaparte in point of daring and strategy. An important conference then took place, and on the 28th of March Sherman returned to his command.

Grant throughout the winter had been preparing for the spring campaign. The Phalanx regiments heretofore in the 9th, 10th and 18th Corps had been consolidated, and formed the 25th Corps, under the command of Major-General Godfrey Weitzel, who at New Orleans refused to command negro troops. The Corps was divided into

GOVRNT. BLACKSMITHS' SHOP

three divisions, with Brigadier-Generals Wilde, Birney and Paine as commanders. Major-General Ord had succeeded to the command of the Army of the James, then numbering about 28,000 effective men, and was to take part with three divisions of his command in the onward movement to commence on the 29th of March, while Weitzel was to command the remainder of the troops north of the James and at Bermuda Hundreds.

Lee, as though he had knowledge of Grant's intention and meant to frustrate his plans by taking the initiative, attacked the 9th Corps at Fort Steadman on the 25th, with signal success. He was finally repulsed, however, and Grant began moving the Union troops. On the morning of the 29th, General Birney with the 2nd Division of the 25th Corps was near Hatcher's Run, with General Ord's command. The division consisted of three brigades of Phalanx Infantry, commanded by Colonels James Shaw, Jr., Ulysses Doubleday and William W. Woodward. A brigade of artillery commanded by Captain Louis L. Langdon was attached to the Corps; but, owing to the country being wooded, it was of little use, and most of it was left on the north side with General Weitzel.

On the same day Sheridan reached Dinwiddie, and the next morning he encountered the confederates near the Court House. Here were W. H. F. Lee's Cavalry, Pickets' and Bushrod Johnson's divisions of Infantry, and Wise's brigade. Sheridan made the attack. His men, on account of the marshy ground, had to dismount. The confederates fought desperately, but Sheridan's men contested every inch of ground, and at night fell back to Dinwiddie Court House and bivouacked. The 5th Corps came up during the night to attack the confederates in the rear; but at daylight it was found that they had fallen back to Five Forks. Here was found the cavalry of W. H. F. Lee and Fitzhugh Lee, with Ross', Picket's, Wise's and Johnson's divisions of infantry. On the morning of the 1st of April, Sheridan advanced the 5th Corps toward Five Forks. That afternoon it fell upon Picket's rear,

"YOU MUST THROW AWAY THAT CIGAR, SIR!"

A Phalanx guard refusing to allow General U. S. Grant to pass by the commissary store-house till he had thrown away his cigar.

and now began the decisive battle. The roar was deafening. Night was coming on, and Sheridan was anxious to carry out Grant's order and "end the matter if possible to do so." He gave the order, "Charge bayonets!" In five minutes Picket's outer line was in possession of the federals. Crawford's division struck them in the flank, and, with McKenzie's brigade, routed and sent the confederates flying. The 5th Corps rallied and captured the enemy's entire force in their front. General Sheridan says in report:

"The enemy were driven from their strong line of works, completely routed, the Fifth Corps doubling up their left flank in confusion, and the cavalry of General Merritt dashing on to the White Oak Road, capturing their artillery, turning it upon them, and riding into their broken ranks, so demoralized them that they made no serious stand after their line was carried, but took flight in disorder."

The writer well remembers the eagerness of the Phalanx brigade of Colonel Shaw, composed of the 109th, 116th and 7th Regiments, as they waited orders near Hatcher's Run. The sound of distant guns fell upon their ears; Colonel Shaw was impatient; all seemed to feel the end was near, and wanted to lend a hand in the consummation. Oh, what suspense! The brigade lay upon their arms in a state of great agitation, all that night, waiting for orders to advance upon the foe. Who can tell the thoughts of those brave black soldiers as thus they lay upon the rumbling earth. Fathers, mothers, sisters, wives and children, yet slaves, behind the enemy's guns: precious property they are, and guarded like dearest treasure and even life itself, by an army of slave-holders—Lee's men, who, with the desperation of demons, vainly attempted to check the advance of the men of the North, who, with their lives, defended the Union. The black brigade wanted to strike one more blow for freedom—for the freedom of their wives and children—to make one more charge, and the confederate banner should go down; one more charge, and the light of Liberty's stars should blazon over the ramparts of the confederate forts. At length, with the dawning of day, came the order; then the black brigade went forward, but to find the enemy gone and their works deserted.

The confederate lines were broken, and Sheridan's troopers, McKenzie and Merritt, with their cavalry, although it was night, had followed up the fleeing foe, capturing them by thousands. The brigade pushed on along the captured works. The federal batteries, from every mound and hill, were showering shot and shell into the enemy's inner works; while the gleaming bayonets of the thousands of infantry could be seen as far as the eye could reach, their proud banners kissing the stifling air, and the bugles sounding the "forward march," leaving in their rear smoking camps and blazing dwellings. What a Sunday morning was that, with its thunders of terrific war, instead of the mellow chimes of church bells and the repose of peace.

It was late in the afternoon, and huge, black clouds of smoke rolled up out of the city of Petersburg, and then a loud report, told that the confederates had evacuated it. Away to the left, the huzzas of Colonel Doubleday's Phalanx brigade (2nd) were heard. Now came a race to reach the city, between the 7th and 8th Phalanx regiments. No matter which was first, they were among the troops which took possession of the city, and gladdened the hearts of the negro population, as they marched through the streets singing their battle song:

"We will hang Jeff Davis on a sour apple-tree as we go marching on."

It was a glorious victory, bringing freedom to thousands of slaves, though it cost as many lives and millions of treasure. It was the beginning of the end. The confederates deserted their army by thousands. The South Side Railroad was in the hands of the federals, and starvation threatened the enemy. Lee, says a historian, was no longer himself: he rode wildly through his camps hither, and thither, trying to save his shattered and routed soldiers from annihilation.

The defeat at Five Forks settled the fate of the Army of North Virginia. Grant had almost the entire federal army actively engaged; he stopped the exchange of prisoners, invited President Lincoln, then at City Point, to come out and see the army advance, which he did. He met Grant in the city of Petersburg, amid the exultations of the troops and the joyous demonstrations of the negro population. General Lee made no stop at Richmond; he had informed Jefferson Davis that he must give up the city. The latter, with his aids and all the money he could collect,—not the confederate paper, but the gold of the United States,—stampeded.

General Weitzel, with Kautz's division of the 24th Corps and Thomas' and Ashborne's division of the 25th Corps, on the north side of the James river, lay quietly upon their arms during the fight on the south side. Grant kept Weitzel informed as to the results of the attack, and warned him to be on the alert and take every advantage offered, to press the confederates. General Longstreet's forces had been in Weitzel's front, but were partly withdrawn to defend Petersburg; therefore the latter kept unceasing vigil upon the fortifications before him.

Sunday evening the bands were ordered out to play, and it was late into the night when their melodious strains ceased to float through the air. It was a night long to be remembered, the hearts of the black soldiers of the 25th Corps, gladdened by the reports of the victories of the troops before Petersburg, were jubilant, and with vigilant watch each looked for morning. They were impatient for the light, and ere it dawned they were ready for the onset which they believed must come with it. The enemy whom they supposed were preparing to give them battle, was silently stealing away to the enchanting strains of the Federal musicians. It was near the morning hours when a sudden report startled the sleeping soldiers; an explosion, another, and yet another followed in rapid succession.

General Weitzel soon became satisfied that the enemy was moving, the continuous sound of distant cannonading away to the south, told that the combat still raged.

From the signal tower bright lights were discernable at Richmond. The city appeared to be on fire; a confederate picket was captured, but he knew nothing; he had got astray from his comrades and command. A deserter came in with intelligence that the city was being evacuated, and half an hour later a negro drove into camp and gave information that the enemy was flying.

The ground in front was thickly set with torpedoes, and the troops dared not move. Day came and Colonel Draper's black brigade of the 25th Corps went forward. The road was lumbered with all manner and sort of military gear and munitions of war. Keeping clear of the red flags which marked the torpedoes, the troops pushed on; they soon reached the defences of the city to find them untenanted; the negro had told the truth and the Phalanx brigade entered the city welcomed by thousands of happy kinsfolks. Badeau says:

"The sun was an hour up, when suddenly there rose in the streets the cry of 'Yankees! Yankees!' and the mass of plunderers and rioters, cursing, screaming, trampling on each other, alarmed by an enemy not yet in sight, madly strove to extricate themselves and make an opening for the troops. Soon about forty men of the Fourth Massachusetts Cavalry rode into the crowd, and, trotting straight to the public square, planted their guidons on the Capitol. Lieutenant De Peyster, of Weitzel's staff, a New Yorker eighteen years of age, was the first to raise the national colors, and then, in the morning light of the 3d of April, the flag of the United States once more floated over Richmond.

"The command of Weitzel followed—a long blue line—with gun-barrels gleaming, and bands playing 'Hail Columbia' and 'John Brown's Soul Goes Marching On.' One regiment was black.* The magistrates formally surrendered the city to Weitzel at the Capitol, which stands on a hill in the centre of the town, and overlooks the whole country for miles. The national commander at once set about restoring order and extinguishing the flames. Guards were established, plundering was stopped, the negroes were organized into a fire corps, and by night the force of the conflagration was subdued, the rioting was at an end, and the conquered city was rescued by the efforts of its captors from the evils which its own authorities had allowed, and its own population had perpetrated."

Lee and his famishing host were fleeing towards Danville, hotly pursued by the Federal Army. Resting there

* See report of 29th Regiment Connecticut Colored Volunteers in appendix.

RECEIVING THE PRESIDENT.

Abraham Lincoln riding through Richmond, April 4th, 1865, after the evacuation of the city by the Confederates,

until the 5th they resumed the march, fighting and running, until, at Appomattox they gave up and surrendered. Major Alexandria S. Johnson of the 116th Phalanx Regiment thus relates the story in part which the Phalanx brigade took in the memorable movement of the two armies to Appomattox. He says:

"As a participant in these events I will speak merely of what came under my own observation. The One Hundred and Sixteenth (colored) Infantry, in which I commanded a company, belonged to the Third Brigade, Second Division of the Twenty-fifth Army Corps, and during the winter of 1864–65 held the lines on Chapin's farm, the left resting on Fort Burnham. The division was commanded by Major-General Birney. The winter was passed in endeavoring to get the troops in as high a state of discipline as possible by constant drill and watchful training. When the spring opened we had the satisfaction of feeling that they were the equal, as soldiers, of most of the white troops. They were a contented body, being well fed and clothed, and they took delight in their various duties. The news of the capture of Savannah by Sherman and the defeat of Hood at Nashville had a cheering effect upon the whole command, and we looked forward with confidence that the end was drawing near.

"On the night of the 26th of March our division silently left the lines on Chapin's farm, and marching to the rear some three miles went into bivouac. On the night of the 27th we crossed the James on muffled pontoons, and after a weary march arrived at Hatcher's Run at daybreak of the 28th. Crossing the original lines of breastworks we built new breastworks some two hundred yards in advance and bivouacked in the pine woods awaiting events. Sheridan at this time was operating on the Confederate right flank. The news of his decisive victory at Five Forks and of the complete turning of the enemy's flank was the immediate cause of a verbal order, given to company commanders by our colonel on the afternoon of April 1st, to advance on the lines in our front at dawn on the following day. That night the Union artillery opened along the whole line. Hissing and bursting shells from Appomattox river to Hatcher's Run filled in a scene never to be forgotten by those who witnessed it. It was as if demons incarnate were holding a jubilee. As far as the eye could reach there was one blaze of fiery shot. The world has seldom seen its like. Where our brigade was to operate was a dense wilderness of pines with matted underbrush, but in the morning it looked as though a sirocco had kissed it.

"With the dawn of day the brigade was in line of battle. Not a breath of air was stirring. A misty vapor shed its gloom and hung like a pall among the tree-tops. The silk covers were taken from our flags, but their folds hung lazily along the staff when the command, 'Forward! guide centre! march!' was given. At first slashed timber and brush obstructed our way, but as the obstruction began to cease an obstacle in the shape of a long line of abattis met our gaze. The dusky line broke through the abattis, however, as if the stakes had been so many reeds, and charged over the breastworks and into the Confederate camp. The rush must have been a surprise, as the enemy offered little resistance. In front of one of the tents a Federal sergeant (white) lay dead, his right arm extended to the full length, and firmly clenched in his hand was a piece of fancy soap. A bullet had entered his forehead, the blood from the wound was trickling down his face, but the hue of health was still on his cheek. How he came to be there is to me a mystery, as that part of the line was forced by colored troops. Swinging by the right flank we kept our way along the Boydton road. A Confederate light battery in position alongside of a cottage, which stood in a hollow, shelled the column as it advanced, and so accurate had the gunners got the range that almost every shell did damage. A couple of shells burst together above my company. The flash blinded me for a few seconds. I heard a scream of pain and just then was ordered to lie down. Not twenty yards from me was a wounded soldier. His leg was shattered badly. He prayed and sang hymns alternately, but his voice gradually grew weaker until it ended in death. One of our batteries was brought into position, and engaging the Confederate battery, the latter was silenced, when the column again resumed the march, arriving in front of Petersburg about noon.

"It was the intention of General Birney to carry by assault the main fort which commanded the city, and he deployed the division in line of battle for that purpose, but General Ord, coming up in time, ordered him to retire his division out of range and await further orders. We went into bivouac for the night, and at early dawn of the 3d we entered the city, the Confederates having evacuated the forts during the night. The field music played "John Brown's Body," and a tiny Union flag in the hands of a girl of ten years waved us a welcome. Resting an hour in the city the division started in pursuit of the Confederates. For a mile or two outside of the city the road was strewn with plug tobacco. Blood could be seen also at intervals in patches along the road. We bivouacked some fifteen miles from the city. A few of our officers took supper in a house close to our camping ground. Our fare was "corn pone," scraps of bacon, sorghum molasses, and a solution of something called coffee, for which we each gave our host, a middle-aged Virginian, one dollar. The colored troops being encamped on his farm his indignation was stirred and he exclaimed, while the tears trickled down his cheeks, 'Poor old Virginia! poor old Virginia! that I should have lived to see this day!'

"At dawn of the 4th the column resumed the pursuit. It is needless for me to tell in detail how our cavalry destroyed and burned over five hundred Confederate wagons on the 5th and 6th, and how Ewell's command was defeated and captured at Sailor's creek on the 6th. Our brigade having arrived at Farmville on the afternoon of the 6th and encamped for the night, some of the citizens poured forth pitiful tales to our officers. They told how our cavalry had entered their houses and ripped open their feather beds, how the rude troopers had broken open bureaus and chests in search of valuables, and how they had carried away with them what they could find. Nothing of interest took place until the 8th, which was noted for the forced march made by the brigade, starting at day-break and going into bivouac at twelve midnight. The morning of the 9th broke calm and serene. It was a lovely morning, the sun had not yet gotten above the horizon when the brigade was on the march again, but it went only a short distance when it was halted. To the right of the road, in a clearing, was a portion of the Twenty-fourth Corps, with arms stacked and the men cooking breakfast. Sides of bacon at intervals hung from their bayonets. Although the woods were full of our cavalry and three divisions of our infantry were in close proximity, all was as quiet as a Sabbath morning. One of our batteries, some six hundred yards to the right, broke the stillness by fitfully throwing a shell once in a while, but to a looker-on all seemed inaction. Such was the situation at Appomattox at sunrise on the morning of the 9th.

"Our brigade, after resting some thirty minutes, resumed the march. It soon filed to the right. In a few minutes the command was given—'Right shoulder, shift arms! double quick, march!' Onward we went, the objective point being the Lynchburg pike. Dismounted cavalry retreating from the front broke through the column, saying as they passed us, 'Give it to them, boys! they are too many for us!' In a few minutes the head of the column reached the pike, when it halted and faced to the front. The command—'Unsling knapsacks!'—was given, and then we knew we were stripping for a fight. Skirmishers were deployed on our front, and as we advanced the Confederate skirmishers retired before us. After advancing some eight hundred yards the brigade was ordered to halt and form in line of battle. It formed into column of companies. Some eight hundred yards away was the Army of Northern Virginia, with its three lines of battle awaiting us.

"We had not been at a halt more than twenty minutes when the news of Lee's surrender reached us. Our brigade celebrated the event by firing volleys of musketry in the air. Officers hugged each other with joy. About four hundred yards to the rear was a portion of the Twenty-fourth Corps, which had been marching to our support. The men in that long line threw their caps upwards until they looked like a flock of crows. From wood and dale came the sound of cheers from thousands of throats. Appomattox will never hear the like again. The brigade moved forward a short distance and went into camp some three hundred yards from the Confederate camp. In the afternoon I strolled over the ground we had traversed in the morning. I came across the body of a dead Confederate soldier, covered with a blanket. Some one had taken the shoes from his feet. Uncovering him I found that a shot had pierced his right breast. His white cotton shirt was matted with blood. A small bag was attached to the button-hole of his jacket. Undoing the bag I found it contained sixty ounces of corn meal. He was not over twenty-six years of age, and was of fair complexion. Who knows but he was the last soldier who fell belonging to the Army of Northern Virginia?"

It was Palm Sunday, celebrated by many of the followers of Christ as the day of his triumphal entrance into Jerusalem, a day of great rejoicing among Christians, known in our annual calendar as the 9th day of April, 1865. The morning broke clear and bright in the neighborhood of Appomattox Court House, and there was every evidence of spring. The birds chirped in the trees half clad with the early foliage, which trembled in the soft breeze. Along the roadside yet untrod by the hostile feet of man or steed, the tiny floweret buds had begun to open to the warmth of genial nature, and the larger roses, red and white, cast their fragrance to the lingering winds. Here the half clad, sore footed soldiers of the Army of Northern Virginia, were trembling with dread impatience for the onset,—the inevitable—which would decide their fate and their prospect of reaching the mountains just beyond. In front of them the federal cavalry awaited their coming.

It was yet grey in the morning when General Lee sent word to his Lieutenant Gordon to cut his "*way through at all hazards.*" With the impetuosity of a cyclone, his shattered corps rushed upon the dismounted cavalry in their front, the Federal line quivered, and bent to the gale. On and on they came, pressing closer and closer upon the cavalry. The struggle was becoming desperate, it was the last hope of the confederates they must go through the lines, or perish in the attempt. Again the confederate yell rose above the din of the battle's roar, and soon the cavalry fell back. Where was their leader Sheridan? He came, galloping at break-neck speed, his men cheering him as he rode to the front. He had been to the rear some five miles away. He saw at a glance the daring object of the foe, and ordered his men to fall back slowly. The confederates followed up the wavering line with brightened hopes, but hopes that were to be dissipated; soon the bristling bayonets, and glistening musket barrels of the Army of the James gleamed in their front; then the pressure ceased, and Sheridan's bugle sounded the order to mount, and his troopers dashed themselves against the enemy's left flank. Then, one bearing a white flag—a flag of truce, rode to the front of the confederate lines. Capt. J. D. Cook of General Mile's staff went forward to meet him. It was Colonel Taylor of General Lee's staff; he bore a note from Lee, asking a suspension of hostilities, and an interview with General Grant. Now let us go back to the night of the 6th, and trace the flying columns to this point. Badeau says:

"That night once more the rebels evacuated their works, this time in front of Meade, and when morning dawned were far on their way, as they fondly thought, to Lynchburg, and Lee defiantly informed his pursuer that the emergency for the surrender had not yet arrived. But he reckoned without his host. He was stretching, with the terrific haste that precedes despair, to Appomattox for supplies. He need hardly have hastened to that spot, destined to be so fatal to himself and his cause. Grant's legions were making more haste than he. The marvelous marching, not only of Sheridan, but of the men of the Fifth and Twenty-Fourth Corps, was doing as much as a battle to bring the rebellion to a close. Twenty-eight, thirty-two, thirty-five miles a day in succession these infantry soldiers marched, all day and all night. From day-light until day-light again, after more than a week of labor and fatigue almost unexampled, they pushed on to intercept their ancient adversary, while the remainder of the Army of the Potomac was at his heels.

"Finally Lee, still defiant, and refusing to treat with any view of surrender, came up to his goal, but found the national cavalry had reached the point before him, and that the supplies were gone. Still he determined to push his way through, and with no suspicion that men on foot could have marched from Rice's Station to his front in thirty hours, he made his last charge, and discovered a force of infantry greater than his own before him, besides cavalry, while two corps of the Army of the Potomac were close in his rear. He had run straight into the national lines. He was enclosed, walled in, on every side, with imminent instant destruction impending over him. He instantly offered to submit to Grant, and in the agony of alarm, lest the blow should fall, he applied to Meade and Sheridan also for a cessation of hostilities. Thus in three directions at once he was appealing to be allowed to yield. At the same moment he had messengers out to Sheridan, Meade, and Grant. The emergency, whose existence he had denied, had arrived.

He was out-marched, out-fought, out-witted, out-generaled—defeated in every possible way. He and his army, every man, numbering 27,516, surrendered. He and his army, every man, was fed by the conqueror."

From the date of Lee's surrender, the confederates, from Virginia to the Mississippi, began to lay down their arms. Howell Cobb surrendered at Macon, Ga., on the 21st; Johnston surrendered to General Sherman on the 26th, in North Carolina; Dick Taylor, east of the Mississippi, on the 4th of May, and on the 26th Kirby Smith surrendered his forces west of the Mississippi. Jeff. Davis had been captured, disguised as a woman, and thus the cause, which originated in treason, based on the enslavement of a race, and which derived its only chance of success from men who were false to their oaths, collapsed. The mightiest blow given the confederacy was struck by the immortal Proclamation of Emancipation, giving freedom to four millions of slaves; more than two hundred thousand of whom, with dash and gallantry excelled by no other race, tore down the traitor's banner from their deemed impregnable breastworks and planted in its stead the national flag. That emblem, whose crimson folds, re-baptised in the blood of liberty's martyrs, invited all men, of all races, who would be free, to gather beneath the effiulgent glare of its heaven-lighted stars, regardless of color, creed or condition. The Phalanx nobly bore their part all through the long night of war, and at last they occupied Charleston,—the traitors' nest,—Petersburg,—their eastern Gibraltar,—and Richmond—their Capitol. They marched proudly through the streets of these once impregnable fortresses, in all of which many of the soldiers of the Phalanx had been slaves. Oh! what a realization of the power of right over might. What a picture for the historian's immortal pen to paint of the freemen of America, whose sufferings were long, whose struggle was gigantic, and whose achievement was a glorious personal and political freedom!

At the close of the war, the government, anticipating trouble in Texas, ordered General Steele to the command of the Rio Grande, under these instructions:

"WASHINGTON, May 21st, 1865.

"MAJ. GEN. F. STEELE, Commanding Rio Grande Expedition.

"By assignment of the President, Gen. Sheridan takes general command west of the Arkansas. It is the intention to prosecute a vigorous campaign in that country, until the whole of Texas is re-occupied by people acknowledging allegiance to the Government of the United States. Sheridan will probably act offensively from the Red river. But it is highly important that we should have a strong foothold upon the Rio Grande. You have been selected to take that part of the command. In addition to the force you take from Mobile Bay, you will have the 25th Corps and the few troops already in Southern Texas.

"Any directions you may receive from Gen. Sheridan, you will obey. But in the absence of instructions from him you will proceed without delay to the mouth of the Rio Grande and occupy as high up that river as your force and means of supplying will admit of.

"Your landing will probably have to be made at Brazos, but you will learn more fully upon that matter on your arrival. We will have to observe a strict neutrality towards Mexico, in the French and English sense of the word. Your own good sense and knowledge of international law, and experience of policy pursued towards us in this war teaches you what will be proper.

"Signed, U. S. GRANT, *Lieutenant-General.*

"Official: Signed, GEO. K. LEET, A. A. G.

In the meantime General Grant sent the following dispatches to Generals Halleck and Weitzel:

"WASHINGTON, May 18th, 1865, 12.40 P. M.,

"MAJOR-GENERAL H. W. HALLECK, Richmond Va.

"Please direct Major-General Weitzel commanding 25th Army Corps to get his corps in readiness for embarkation at City Point immediately upon the arrival of ocean transportation. He will take with him forty (40) days rations for twenty thousand men, one-half of his land transportation and one-fourth of his mules with the requisite amount of forage for his animals. All surplus transportion and other public property he may have he will turn over to the depots at City Point.

"By command of Lieutenant-General Grant.

"Signed, JOHN A. RAWLINS,

"*Brigadier-General and Chief of Staff.*

"Official. Signed, GEORGE K. LEET, A. A. G."

"WASHINGTON, May 21st, 1865.

"MAJOR-GENERAL G. WEITZEL, Commanding 25th A. C.

"As soon as your corps is embarked you will proceed with it to Mobile Bay, Ala., and report to Major-General Steele for further orders.

"In addition to rations, ammunition, and other articles which you have received directions to take with you, you should take a fair quantity of intrenching tools. "Signed, U. S. GRANT, *Lieutenant-General.*

"Official, Signed, GEORGE K. LEET, A. A. G."

On the 24th of May the 25th Corps began embarking for Texas by way of Mobile Bay. The troops, however, occupied Texas but a short time, the confederate forces there surrendering upon the same terms as those of General Lee. All fears having been dissipated, the troops were slowly mustered out of the United States service. The men returned to their wonted fields of labor to provide for their long-neglected families, upon a new career of peace and happiness, rising, Phœnix like, from the ashes of slavery to join the Phalanx of industry in upbuilding the greatness of their country, which they had aided in saving from desolation and ruin.

Such is the history of the negro in the wars of the United States. Coming to its shores in the condition of slavery, it required more than two centuries for the entire race to reach the estate of freedom. But the imperishable records of their deeds show that however humble and despised they have been in all political and social relations they have never been wanting in patriotism at periods of public peril. Their devotion has been not only unappreciated, but it has failed to receive a fitting commemoration in pages of national history. It has been the purpose of the writer of this volume to relate herein the patriotic career of the negro race in this country in an authentic and connected form. In the time to come the race will take care of itself. Slavery is ended, and now they are striking off link by link the chains of ignorance which the servitude of some and the humility of all imposed upon them. If the past is the story of an oppressed race, the future will reveal that of one uprisen to great opportunities, which they will improve from generation to generation, and guard with the same vigilance that they will the liberties and boundaries of the land.

CHAPTER XII.

ROLL OF HONOR.

The following enlisted men of the Black Phalanx received medals of honor from the United States Government for heroic conduct on the field of battle:

Sergeant-Major C. A. FLEETWOOD, 4th Regiment.

Color—Sergeant ALFRED B. HILTON, 4th Regiment.

Private CHARLES VEAL, 4th Regiment.

1st Sergeant JAMES BROWNSON, 5th Regiment.

Sergeant-Major MILTON M. HOLLAND, 5th Regiment.

1st Sergeant, ROBERT PINN, 5th Regiment.

1st Sergeant POWHATAN BEATY, 5th Regiment.

1st Sergeant ALEX. KELLEY, 6th Regiment.

Sergeant SAMUEL GILCHRIST, 36th Regiment.

Sergeant WILLIAM DAVIS, 36th Regiment.

Corporal MILES JAMES, 36th Regiment.

Private JAMES GARDNER, 36th Regiment.

1st Sergeant EDWARD RATCLIFF, 38th Regiment.

Private WILLIAM BARNES, 38th Regiment.

CHAPTER XIII.

ROSTER OF THE BLACK PHALANX

CAVALRY.

1st Regiment, Lieutenant-Colonel Seip.—Organized at Camp Hamilton, Va., December, 1863. Battles: Bermuda Hundreds, Smithfield, Wilson's Landing, Fort Pocahontas, Cabin Point, Powhatan. Mustered out February, 1866.

2nd Regiment, Colonel G. W. Cole.—Organized at Ft. Monroe, December, 1863. Battles: Suffolk, Drewry's Bluff, May 10, 16th and 20th, 1864. Point of Rocks, Deep Bottom, Chapin Farm, Richmond. Mustered out February, 1866.

3d Regiment, Lieutenant-Colonel, J. B. Cook.—Organized at Vicksburg, October 9th, 1863. Battles: Haines Bluff, Shipwith's Landing, Miss., Memphis, Tenn., Bayou Bœuf, Yazoo Expedition, Rolling Fork, Vicksburg, Jackson, Fort Adams, Franklin, Roache's Plantation, Yazoo City. Mustered out January, 1866.

4th Regiment, (1st *Corps d' Afrique*), Lieutenant-Colonel N. C. Mitchell.—Organized September, 1863, at New Orleans, La. Battle: Clinton. Mustered out March, 1866.

5th Regiment, Colonel L. Henry Carpenter.—Organized at Camp Nelson, Ky., October, 1864. Battles: Saltville, Hopkinsville, Harrodsburg, Simpsonville. Mustered out March, 1866.

5th Regiment, Massachusetts, Colonel S. E. Chamberlin.—Organized at Readville, Mass., May, 1864. Battle: Petersburg. Mustered out October, 1865.

6th Regiment, Colonel James F. Wade.—Organized at Camp Nelson, Ky., Nov., 1864. Battles: Saltville, Marion, Smithfield. Mustered out April, 1866.

HEAVY ARTILLERY.

1st Regiment, Colonel John E. McGowan.—Organized at Knoxville, Tenn., February, 1864. Battle: Decatur.

3rd Regiment, Colonel Ignatz G. Kappner.—Organized at Memphis, Tenn., and Fort Pickering, Tenn., June, 1863, as 1st Regiment Tennessee Heavy Artillery. Its designation was changed to 2nd Regiment and to 3rd, April, 1864. Mustered out April, 1864.

4th Regiment, Major Wm. N. Lansing.—Organized at Columbus, Ky., June, 1863, as 2nd Regiment Tennessee. Its designation was changed March, 1864, to the 3rd Regiment, and to the 4th, April, 1864. Battles: Fort Donelson. Mustered out February, 1866.

5th Regiment, Colonel Herman Leib.—Organized at Vicksburg, Miss., August, 1863, as the 9th Regiment Louisiana Volunteers. Its designation was changed to 1st Regiment, Mississippi, September, 1863, and to the 4th, March, 1864. Battles: Milliken's Bend, June 6th, 7th and 25th, 1863, Vicksburg. Mustered out May, 1866.

6th Regiment, Colonel Hubert A. McCaleb.—Organized at Natchez, Miss., September, 1863, as 2nd Regiment, Miss. Its designation was changed to the 5th Regiment, March, 1864, and to the 6th, April, 1864. Battles: Vidalia, Concordia Bayou, Black River. Mustered out May, 1866.

For 7th Regiment see 11th Infantry.

8th Regiment, Colonel Henry W. Barry.—Organized at Paducah, Ky., April, 1864. Battle: Fort Anderson. Mustered out February, 1866.

9th Regiment, Major Edward Grosskoff.—Organized at Clarksville, Nashville, Tenn., October, 1864; broken up May, 1865; officers and enlisted men transferred to other organizations.

10th Regiment, Colonel C. A. Hartwell, (regular army).—Organized at New Orleans, La., November, 1862, as 1st Regiment Lousiana. Its designation was changed to 1st Regiment *Corps d' Afrique*, November, 1863, and to the 7th Regiment United States, April, 1864; to the 10th, May, 1864. The 77th Regiment Infantry was consolidated with it October, 1865. Mustered out February, 1867. Battle: Pass-Manchæ.

11th Regiment, Colonel J. Hale Sypher.—Organized at Providence, R. I., August, 1863, as the 14th Regiment, R. I. Its designation was changed to the 8th Regiment United States, April, 1864, and to the 11th, May, 1864. Battle: Indian Village. Mustered out October, 1865.

12th Regiment, Colonel Norman S. Andrews.—Organized at Camp Nelson, Ky., July, 1864. Battles: Big Springs, Fort Jones. Mustered out, April, 1866.

13th Regiment, Colonel Jacob T. Foster.—Organized at Camp Nelson, Ky., June, 1865. Mustered out November, 1865.

14th Regiment, Lieutenant-Colonel Walter S. Poor.—Organized at New Berne and Marblehead, N. C., March, 1864, as the 1st North Carolina. Its designation was changed to the 14th, March, 1865. Mustered out December, 1865.

LIGHT ARTILLERY.

2nd Regiment.—Organized at Nashville, Tenn., April, 1864. Mustered out January, 1866.

Battery A, Captain F. P. Meigs.

Battery B, Captain Francis C. Choate.—Organized at Fort Monroe, Va. January, 1864. Battles: Wilson's Wharf, City Point. Mustered out March, 1866.

Battery C, Captain Robert Ranney.—Organized at Hebron's Plantation, Miss., November, 1863, as the 1st Louisiana Battery. Its designation was changed to Battery A, 2d Regiment, March, 1864, and to Battery C April, 1864. Mustered out December, 1865.

Battery D, Captain W. H. Pratt.—Organized at Black River Bridge, Miss., December, 1863, as the 2d Louisiana Battery. Its designation was changed to Battery B, 2d Regiment United States, March, 1864, and to Battery D April, 1864.

Battery E, Captain Edwin Bancroft.—Organized at Helena, Ark., December, 1863, as the 3d Louisiana Battery. Its designation was changed to Battery C, 2d Regiment United States, March, 1864, and to Battery E April, 1864. Battles: Island No. 76, Big Creek.

Battery F, Captain Carl A. Lamberg.—Organized at Memphis, Tenn., as the Memphis Light Battery, November, 1863. Its designation was changed to Battery D, 2d United States Regiment, March, 1864, and to Battery F, April, 1864. Consolidated with the 3d United States Heavy Artillery, December, 1865. Battles: Fort Pillow, Brice's Cross Roads. Mustered out April, 1866.

Battery G, Captain Jeremiah S. Clark.—Organized at Hilton Head, S. C., May, 1864. Mustered out August, 1865.

Battery H, Captain John Driscoll.—Organized at Pine Bluff, Ark., June, 1864, as the 1st Arkansas Colored Battery. Changed to Battery H, 2d United States, December, 1864. Mustered out September, 1865.

Battery I, Captain Louis B. Smith.—Organized at Memphis, Tenn., April, 1864. Mustered out January, 1866.

Independent Battery, Captain H. Ford Douglass. Organized at Leavenworth, Kan., December, 1864. Mustered out July, 1865.

INFANTRY.

1st Regiment,* Colonel John H. Holman.—Organized at District of Columbia, May, 1863. Battles: Wilson's Wharf, Petersburg, Chapin's Farm, Fair Oaks, Fillmore, Town Creek, Wilmington, Warsaw. Mustered out, September 1865.

2d Regiment, Colonel B. F. Townsend.—Organized at Arlington, Va., June, 1863. Battles: Fort Taylor, Cedar Keys, Natural Bridge. Mustered out January, 1866.

* Dr. Wright, a prominent secessionist at Norfolk, Va., swore to shoot the first white man that he caught drilling negroes. Lieutenant A. S. San born, of this regiment, while marching a squad to head-quarters through the main street of the city was shot and killed by this Dr. Wright, for which he was hanged.

3d Regiment, Colonel F. W. Bardwell.—Organized at Philadelphia, Penn., August, 1863. Battles: Fort Wagner, Bryant's Plantation, Marion County, Jacksonville. Mustered out October, 1865.

4th Regiment, Colonel S. A. Duncan.—Organized at Baltimore, Md., July, 1863. Battles: Bermuda Hundreds, Petersburg, Dutch Gap, Chapin's Farm, Sugar-Loaf Hill. Mustered out May, 1866.

5th Regiment, Lieutenant-Colonel John B. Cook. Organized at Camp Delaware, Ohio, August, 1863. Battles: Sandy Swamp, New Kent Court House, City Point, Petersburg, Chapin's Farm, Fair Oaks, Raleigh. Mustered out, September 1865.

6th Regiment, Colonel John W. Ames, (regular army).—Organized at Camp William Penn, Pa., 1863. Battles: Williamsburg, Chapin's Farm, Sugar-Loaf Hill, January 19th, February 11th, 1865. Mustered out September, 1865.

6th Regiment, Louisiana, Colonel Robert Des Anges.—Organized at New Orleans, La., July, 1863—sixty days. Mustered out August, 1863.

7th Regiment, Colonel James Shaw, Jr.—Organized at Baltimore, Md., September, 1863. Battles: Deep Bottom, Johns Island, James Island, Darbytown Road, Jacksonville, May 1st, 28th, 1864, Bermuda Hundreds, Chapin's Farm, Fort Burnham, Petersburg, Richmond. Mustered out October, 1866.

7th Regiment, Louisiana, Colonel M. Wilson Phanley.—Organized at New Orleans, La.—sixty days. Mustered out August, 1863.

8th Regiment, Colonel Charles W. Fribley.—Organized at Camp William Penn., Pa., September, 1863. Battles: Olustee, Chapin's Farm, Darbytown Road. Mustered out November, 1865.

9th Regiment, Colonel Thomas Bayley.—Organized at Camp Staunton, Md., November, 1863. Battles: Deep Bottom, Chapin's Farm, Darbytown Road, Fair Oaks. Mustered out November, 1866.

10th Regiment, Lieutenant-Colonel E. H. Powell.—Organized in Virginia, November, 1863. Battles: Wilson's Wharf, Plymouth, November 26th, 1863, April 18th, 1864, Petersburg. Mustered out May, 1866.

11th Regiment, Lieutenant-Colonel James M. Steele.—Organized (five companies) at Fort Smith, Ark., December, 1863. Battles: Fort Smith, Boggs Mills. Mustered out May, 1866.

11th Regiment consolidated with the 112th and 113th, old regiments, April, 1865, and designated the 113th. Mustered out May, 1866.

11th Regiment, Colonel William D. Turner.—Organized at La Grange, Lafayette, Memphis, Tenn., Corinth, Miss, June, 1863, as the 1st Regiment Alabama Siege Artillery, changed to 6th Regiment United States Heavy Artillery March, 1864, to 7th Regiment April, 1864, and to 11th Regiment January, 1865. Battles: Fort Pillow, Holly Springs. Mustered out January, 1866.

12th Regiment, Colonel Charles R. Thompson.—Organized in the State of Tennessee July, 1863. Battles: Nashville, Section 37, N. & N. W. R. R., Murfreesboro. Mustered out January, 1866.

13th Regiment, Colonel John A. Hollenstein.—Organized at Nashville, Tenn., November, 1863. Battles: Johnsonville, Nashville. Mustered out January, 1866.

14th Regiment, Colonel Henry C. Corbin.—Organized at Gallatin, Tenn., November, 1863. Battles: Dalton, Decatur, Nashville. Mustered out March, 1866.

15th Regiment, Colonel William Inness.—Organized at Nashville, Tenn., December, 1863. Battles: Nashville, Magnolia. Mustered out April, 1866.

16th Regiment, Colonel William B. Gaw. Organized at Nashville, Tenn., December, 1863. Battles: Chattanooga. Mustered out April, 1866.

17th Regiment, Colonel William R. Shafter.—Organized at Nashville, Tenn., December, 1863. Battles: Nashville, Decatur, Brawley Fork. Mustered out April, 1866.

18th Regiment, Lieutenant-Colonel J. J. Sears.—Organized in the State of Missouri February, 1864. Battles: Nashville, December 7th, 15th, and 16th, 1864, Sand Mountain. Mustered out February, 1866.

19th Regiment, Colonel Joseph G. Perkins.—Organized at Camp Staunton, Md., December, 1863. Battles: Petersburg, Bermuda Hundreds, November 30th, December 4th, 1864. Mustered out January, 1867.

20th Regiment, Colonel Nelson B. Bertram.—Organized at Piker's Island, N. Y., Febuary, 1864. Mustered out October, 1865.

21st Regiment, Colonel Augustus G. Bennett. Organized at Hilton Head, S. C., Fernandina, Fla., June, 1863, as the 3d and 4th South Carolina. Consolidated March, 1864, and designated as the 21st U. S. Regiment. Mustered out April, 1866.

22d Regiment, Colonel Joseph B. Kiddoo. Organized at Philadelphia, Pa., January, 1864. Battles: Petersburg, New Market Heights, Dutch Gap, Chapin's Farm, September 29th, November 4th, 1864, Fair Oaks. Mustered out 1865.

23d Regiment, Lieutenant-Colonel Marshall L. Dempey. Organized at Camp Casey, Va., November, 1863. Battles: Petersburg, Bermuda Hundreds. Mustered out November, 1865.

24th Regiment, Colonel Orlando Brown.—Organized at Camp William Penn, Pa., January, 1865—one year. Company F mustered out September, 1865; remaining companies October, 1865.

25th Regiment, Colonel F. L. Hitchcock.—Organized at Philadelphia, Pa., January, 1864. Mustered out December, 1865.

26th Regiment, Colonel William B. Guernsey.—Organized at Piker's Island, N. Y., February, 1864. Battles: John's Island, July 5th and 7th, McKay's Point, Gregory's Farm.

27th Regiment, Lieutenant-Colonel John W. Dounellon.—Organized at Camp Delaware, Ohio, January, 1864. Battles: Petersburg, Hatcher's Run. Mustered out November, 1865.

28th Regiment, Colonel Charles S Russell, (regular army).—Organized at Indianapolis, Ind., December, 1863. Battles: Jones Bridge, Petersburg. Mustered out November, 1865.

29th Regiment, Colonel Clark E. Royce. Organized at Quincy, Ill., in the field, Virginia, April, October, 1864—one and three years. Battles: Petersburg, White Oak Road. Mustered out November, 1865.

29th Regiment, Connecticut, Lieutenant-Colonel David Torrence.—Organized at New Haven, Conn., March, 1864. Battles: Petersburg, Chapin's Farm, Darbytown Road, Fair Oaks, Mustered out October, 1865.

30th Regiment, Colonel Delevan Bates.—Organized at Camp Stanton, Md., February, 1864. Battles: Petersburg, Sugar Loaf Hill, Cox's Bridge. Mustered out December, 1865.

31st Regiment, Colonel Henry C. Ward.—Organized at Hart's Island, N. Y., in the field, Virginia, April, November, 1864. Battle: Petersburg. The 30th Connecticut consolidated with this regiment May, 1864. Mustered out November, 1865.

32d Regiment, Colonel George W. Baird.—Organized at Camp William Penn, Pa.. February, 1864. Battles: Honey Hill, Deveaux Neck. Mustered out August, 1865.

33d Regiment, Colonel William F. Bennett.—Organized at Beaufort, S. C., January, 1863, as the 1st Regiment South Carolina Volunteers; changed to 33d Regiment U. S. February, 1864. Battles: Township, Mill Town Bluff, Hall Island, Jacksonville, John's Island. Mustered out January, 1866.

34th Regiment, Colonel William W. Marple.—Organized at Beaufort, Hilton Head, S. C., May, 1863. Battles: Ashepoo River, John's Island, Deveaux Neck. Mustered out February, 1866. Organization commenced as 2d Regiment, South Carolina; changed before completion to the 34th Regiment U. S.

35th Regiment, Colonel James C. Beecher.—Organized at New Berne, N. C., June, 1863, as the 1st North Carolina Regiment, changed to 35th U. S. Regiment February, 1864. Battles: Olustee, Black Creek, St. John's River, Honey Hill. Mustered out June, 1866.

36th Regiment, Lieutenant-Colonel William H. Hart.—Organized at Portsmouth, Va., as the 2d Regiment North Carolina, changed February, 1864. Battles: Indian Town, Point Lookout, Pierson's Farm. Petersburg, Chapin's Farm, Dutch Gap. Mustered out October, 1866.

37th Regiment, Colonel Nathan Goff.—Organized at Norfolk, Va., January, 1864, as the 3d North Carolina Regiment; changed to 37th U. S. Regiment, February, 1864. Battles: Plymouth, Chapin's Farm, Fair Oaks. Mustered out February, 1867.

38th Regiment, Colonel Robert W. Hall, (regular army).—Organized in Virginia January, 1864. Battles: Chapin's Farm, Deep Bottom. Mustered out January, 1867.

39th Regiment, Colonel Ozora P. Stevens.—Organized at Baltimore, Md., March, 1864. Battles: Petersburg, Federal Point, Bermuda Hundreds, Hatcher's Run. Mustered out December, 1865.

40th Regiment, Colonel F. W. Lester.—Organized at Nashville and Greenville, Tenn. Battle: South Tunnel. Mustered out April, 1866.

41st Regiment, (battalion), Lieutenant-Colonel Julius A. Weiss.—Organized at Philadelphia, Pa., September, 1864, composed of men enlisted, drafted for one, two, and three years. Consolidated into a battalion of four companies September, 1865, of one year men. Battles: Hatcher's Run, Fort Burnham, Petersburg, Appomattox Court House. Mustered out December, 1865.

42d Regiment, Lieutenant-Colonel J. R. Putnam.—Organized at Chattanooga and Nashville, Tenn., April, 1864, composed of enlisted and drafted men for one and three years. Mustered out January, 1866.

43d Regiment, Colonel S. B. Yoeman. Organized at Philadelphia, Pa., March, 1864. Battles: Petersburg, Hatcher's Run. Mustered out 1865.

44th Regiment, Colonel Lewis Johnson.—Organized at Chattanooga, Tenn., Rome, Dalton, Ga., April, 1864. Battles: Nashville, December 2d, 21st, 1864. Mustered out April, 1866.

45th Regiment, Lieutenant-Colonel E. Mayer.—Organized at Philadelphia, Pa., June, 1864. Battles: Hatcher's Run, Petersburg. Mustered out November, 1865.

46th Regiment, Colonel C. Whittlesey.—Organized in Arkansas May, 1863, as the 1st Regiment Arkansas Volunteers; changed to 46th Regiment U. S., May, 1864. Battle: Mound Plantation. Mustered out January, 1866.

47th Regiment. Colonel Hiram Schofield.—Organized at Lake Providence, La., May, 1863, as the 8th Regiment Louisiana Volunteers; changed to 47th Regiment U. S., March, 1864. Battles: Lake Providence, Liverpool Heights, Yazoo City, Fort Blakely. Mustered out January, 1866.

48th Regiment, Colonel F. M. Crandal.—Organized at Lake Providence and Goodrich's Landing, La., May, 1863, as the 10th Regiment Louisiana Volunteers; changed to 48th Regiment U. S., March, 1864. Battles: Bayou Tensa, Vicksburg, Fort Blakely. Mustered out January, 1866.

49th Regiment, Colonel Van E. Young.—Organized at Miliken's Bend, La., May, 1863, as the 11th Regiment Lousiana Volunteers; changed to 49th Regiment U. S., March, 1864. Battles: Miliken's Bend, Waterproof. Mustered out March, 1866.

50th Regiment, Colonel Charles A. Gilchrist.—Organized at Vicksburg, Miss., July, 1863, as the 12th Regiment Louisiana Volunteers; changed to 50th Regiment U. S., March, 1864. Battle: Fort Blakely. Mustered out March, 1866.

51st Regiment, Colonel A. Watson Webber.—Organized at Miliken's Bend, La., and Vicksburg, Miss., May, 1863, as the 1st Regiment Mississippi Volunteers; changed to 51st Regiment U. S., March, 1864. Battles: Miliken's Bend, Ross Landing, Floyd, Fort Blakely. Mustered out June, 1866.

52d Regiment, Colonel George M. Ziegler.—Organized at Vicksburg, Miss., July 27th, 1863, as the 2d Regiment Mississippi Volunteers; changed to 52d Regiment U. S., March, 1864. Battles: Vicksburg, Coleman's Plantation, Bayou Bidell. Mustered out May, 1866.

53d Regiment, Colonel Orlando C. Risdon.—Organized at Warrentown, Miss., May, 1863, as the 3d Regiment Mississippi Volunteers; changed to 53d Regiment U. S., March, 1864. Battles: Haines' Bluff, Grand Gull, White River. Mustered out March, 1866.

54th Regiment, Lieutenant-Colonel Charles Fair.—Organized in Arkansas September, 1863, as the 2d Regiment Arkansas Volunteers; changed to 54th Regiment U. S., March, 1864. Battles: Cow Creek, Arkansas River, Sabine River, Fort Gibson, Cabin Creek. Mustered out August, 1866.

54th Regiment Massachusets Volunteers, Colonel E. N. Hallowell. —Organized at Camp Meigs, Readville, Mass., March, 1863. Battles: James Island, Fort Wagner, Olustee, Honey Hill, Boykin's Mill, before Charleston. Mustered out August, 1865.

55th Regiment, Colonel N. B. Bartman.—Organized at Corinth, Miss., May, 1863, as the 1st Regiment Alabama Volunteers; changed to 55th Regiment U. S., 1864. Battles: Ripley, Brice's Cross Roads, Moscow, Waterford. Mustered out December, 1865.

55th Regiment Massachusetts Volunteers, Colonel Alfred S. Hartwell.—Organized at Camp Meigs, Readville, Mass., May, 1863. Battles: James Island, May 21st, July 2d, 1864, February 10th, 1865, Honey Hill, Briggen Creek, St. Stephens, Deveaux Neck. Mustered out August, 1865.

56th Regiment, Colonel Charles Bentzoni, (regular army). Organized at St. Louis, Mo., August, 1863, as the 3d Regiment Arkansas Volunteers; changed to 56th Regiment U.S., March, 1854. Battles: Indian Bay, Meffleton Lodge, Wallace's Ferry. Mustered out September, 1866.

57th Regiment, Lieutenant-Colonel Silas Hunter.—Organized at Duvall's Bluff, Little Rock. Helena, Ark., December, 1863, as the 4th Regiment Arkansas Voluuteers, changed to 57th Regiment U. S., March, 1864. Battles: Little Rock, April 26th and May 28th, 1864, Camden. Mustered out October, 1866.

58th Regiment, Colonel Simon M. Prestou.—Organized at Natchez, Miss., August, 1863, as the 6th Regiment Mississippi Volunteers; changed to 58th Regiment U. S., March, 1864. Battle: Natchez. Mustered out April, 1866.

59th Regiment, Colonel Edward Bonton.—Organized at La Grange, Tenn., June, 1863, as the 1st Regiment Tennessee Volunteers; changed to 59th Regiment U. S., March, 1864. Battles: Brice's Cross Roads, Tupelo. Mustered out January, 1866.

60th Regiment, Colonel John G. Hudson.—Organized at Keokuk, Iowa, and Benton Barracks, Mo., October, 1863, as the 1st Regiment Iowa Volunteers; changed to 60th Regiment U. S., March, 1864. Battle: Big Creek. Mustered out October, 1865.

61st Regiment Lieutenant-Colonel John Foley.—Organized at La Grange, Tenn., June, 1863, as the 2nd Regiment Tennessee Volunteers; changed to 61st Regiment U. S., March, 1864. Battles: Moscow Station, Tupelo, Waterford, Memphis, Castport. Mustered out December, 1865.

62nd Regiment, Lieutenant-Colonel David Branson.—Organized at Benton Barracks, Mo., December, 1863, as the 1st Regiment Missouri Volunteers; changed to 62nd Regiment U. S., March, 1864. Battles: Glasgow, Palmetto Ranch. Mustered out March, 1866.

63rd Regiment, Major Wm. G. Sargent.—Organized at Memphis, and Island No. 10, Tenn., Vicksburg, Miss., and Goodrich's Landing, La., November, 1863, as the 9th Regiment Louisiana Volunteers; changed to 63rd Regiment U. S., March, 1864. Battles: Waterproof, Ashwood, Marengo. Mustered out January, 1866.

64th Regiment, Colonel Samuel Thomas.—Organized at Camp Holly Springs, Memphis, and Island No. 10, Tenn., December, 1863, as the 7th Regiment Louisiana Volunteers, changed to the 64th Regiment U. S., March, 1864. Battles; Ashwood Landing, Point Pleasant, Pine Bluff, David's Bend, June 2nd, 29th, 1864, Helena. Mustered out March, 1866.

65th Regiment, Colonel Alonzo J. Edgerton.—Organized at Benton Barracks, Mo., December, 1863, as the 2nd Regiment Missouri Volunteers; changed to 65th Regiment U. S. March, 1864. Mustered out January, 1867.

66th Regiment, Colonel Michæl W. Smith. Organized at Vicksburg, Miss., December, 1863, as the 4th Regiment Mississippi Volunteers; changed to 66th Regiment U. S., March, 1864. Battles: Columbia, Goodrich's Landing, March 24th, and July 16th, 1864, Issequena County, July 10th and August 17th, 1864, Bayou Macon, Bayou Tensas, July 30th, and August 26th, 1864. Mustered out March, 1866.

67th Regiment, Colonel Alonzo J. Edgerton.—Organized at Benton Barracks, Mo., January, 1864, as the 3rd Regiment Missouri Volunteers; changed to 67th Regiment U. S., March 1864; consolidated with the 65th Regiment, July 12th, 1865. Battle: Mount Pleasant Landing.

68th Regiment, Major Oliver H. Holcomb.—Organized at Benton Barracks, Mo., March, 1864, as the 4th Regiment Missouri Volunteers; changed to 68th Regiment U. S., March, 1864. Battles: Tupelo, Spanish Fort, Fort Blakely. Mustered out February, 1866.

69th Regiment, Captain James T. Watson.—Organized at Pine Bluff, Duvall's, Bluff, Little Rock, and Helena, Ark., and Memphis, Tenn., December, 1864. Organization discontinued September, 1865, and the commissioned officers and enlisted men transferred to the 63d and 64th Regiments.

70th Regiment, Lieutenant-Colonel Morris Yeomans.—Organized in part, April, 1864, at Natchez, Miss.; completed November, 1864, by the consolidation of the 71st Regiment. Mustered out March, 1866.

71st Regiment, Colonel Willard C. Earle.—Organized at Black River Bridge and Natchez, Miss., and Alexandria, La., March, 1864; consolidated with the 70th Regiment November, 1864.

72d Regiment, Colonel Alexander Duncan.—Organized at Covington, Ky., April, 1865; discontinued May, 1865; commissioned officers ordered before a board for examination, and enlisted men transferred to other regiments.

73d Regiment, Colonel Samuel M. Quincy.—Organized at New Orleans, La., September, 1862, as the 1st Native Guard Volunteers; changed to 1st Regiment *Corps d'Afrique*, and to 73d Regiment U. S., April, 1864; consolidated with the 96th Regiment U. S., September, 1865. Battles: Port Hudson, Jackson, Bayou Tunica, Steamer City Belle, Morganzia, Fort Blakely. Men mustered out at the expiration of time.

74th Regiment, Lieutenant-Colonel A. G. Hall.—Organized at New Orleans, La., October, 1862, as the 2d Regiment Louisiana Native Guard Volunteers; changed to 2d Regiment *Corps d'Afrique*, June, 1863, and to the 74th Regiment U. S., April, 1864. Battle: East Pascagoula. Mustered out October, 1865.

75th Regiment, Colonel Henry W. Fuller.—Organized at New Orleans, La., November, 1862, as the 3d Regiment Louisiana Native Guard Volunteers; changed to 3d Regiment *Corps d'Afrique*, June, 1863, and to the 75th Regiment U. S., April, 1864. Battles: Jackson, Port Hudson, Pleasant Hill, Waterloo. Mustered out November, 1865.

76th Regiment, Colonel Charles W. Drew.—Organized at New Orleans, La., February, 1863, as the 4th Regiment Louisiana Native Guard Volunteers; changed to 4th Regiment *Corps d'Afrique*, June, 1863, and to the 76th Regiment U.S., April, 1864. Battle: Fort Blakely. Mustered out December, 1865.

77th Regiment, Colonel Charles A. Hartwell.—Organized at Fort St. Philip, La., December, 1863, as the 5th Regiment Infantry *Corps d'Afrique*, by the transfer of 291 enlisted men from the 4th Corps Regiment Volunteers; changed to 77th Regiment U. S., April, 1864; consolidated with the 85th Regiment and with the 10th Regiment Heavy Artillery, October, 1865. Battle: Amite River.

78th Regiment, Colonel Charles L. Norton.—Organized at Port Hudson, La., September, 1863, as the 6th Regiment *Corps d'Afrique;* changed to 78th Regiment U. S., April, 1864. Battle: Port Hudson. Mustered out January, 1866.

79th Regiment, Colonel James C. Clark.—Organized at Port Hudson, La., August, 1863, as the 7th Regiment *Corps d'Afrique;* changed to 79th. Regiment U. S., April, 1864. Broken up July, 1864. Battle: Port Hudson.

79th Regiment, Colonel James M. Williams.—Organized at Fort Scott, Kan., January, 1863, as the 1st Regiment Kansas Volunteers; changed to 79th Regiment U. S., December, 1864. Battles: Sherwood, Bush Creek, Cabin Creek, Honey Springs, Prairie d'Anne, Poison Springs, Jenkins Ferry, Joys Ford, Clarksville, Horse Head Creek, Roseville Creek, Timber Hill, Lawrence, Island Mound, Fort Gibson. Mustered out October, 1865.

80th Regiment, Colonel William S. Mudget.—Organized at Port Hudson, La., September, 1863, as the 8th Regiment *Corps d'Afrique;* changed to 80th Regiment U. S., April, 1864. Battle: Port Hudson. Mustered out March, 1867.

81st Regiment, Colonel John F. Appleton.—Organized at Port Hudson, La., September, 1863, as the 9th Regiment *Corps d'Afrique;* changed to 81st Regiment U. S., April, 1864. Battle: Port Hudson. Mustered out November, 1866.

82d Regiment, Colonel Ladislos L Zulasky.—Organized at Port Hudson, La., September, 1863, as the 10th Regiment *Corps d'Afrique;* changed to 82d Regiment U. S., April, 1864. Battles: Port Hudson, Barrancas, Mariana, Mitchell's Creek, Pine Barren Ford, Fort Blakely. Mustered out September, 1866.

83d Regiment, Colonel E. Martindale.—Organized at Port Hudson, La., August, 1863, as the 11th Regiment *Corps d'Afrique;* changed to 83d Regiment U. S., April, 1864. Broken up July, 1864, and enlisted men transferred to other regiments.

83d Regiment, Brevet Colonel J. H. Gillpatrick.—Organized at Forts Scott and Leavenworth, Kan., August, 1863, as the 2d Regiment Kansas Volunteers; changed to 83d Regiment U. S., December, 1864. Battles; Jenkins' Ferry, April 30th, May 4th, 1864, Prairie d'Anne, Sabine River, Fort Smith, Steamer Chippewa, Steamer Lotus, Rector's Farm.

84th Regiment, Colonel William H. Dickey.—Organized at Port Hudson, La., September, 1863, as the 12th Regiment *Corps d'Afrique;* changed to 84th Regiment U. S.. April, 1864. Battle: Morganzia. Mustered out March, 1866.

85th Regiment, Lieutenant-Colonel Henry C. Merriam.—Organized at New Orleans, La., March, 1864, as the 13th Regiment *Corps d'Afrique;* changed to 85th Regiment U. S., April, 1864; consolidated with the 77th Regiment U. S., May, 1864.

86th Regiment, Lieutenant-Colonel George E. Yarrington.—Organized at New Orleans, La., August, 1863, as the 14th Regiment *Corps d'Afrique;* changed to 86th Regiment U. S., April, 1864. Battle: Fort Blakely. Mustered out April, 1866.

87th Regiment, Major H. Tobey.—Organized at New Orleans, La., September, 1863, as the 16th Regiment *Corps d'Afrique*; changed to 87th Regiment U. S., April, 1864; consolidated with the 95th Regiment U. S., November, 1864, to form the 85th Regiment U. S.; subsequently changed to 87th Regiment U. S.

87th Regiment, Lieutenant-Colonel William W. Bliss.—Organized by the consolidation of the 87th and 95th Regiments U. S., November, 1864, and designated as the 87th Regiment U. S.; consolidated with the 84th Regiment U. S., August, 1865.

88th Regiment, Lieutenant-Colonel George E. Biles.—Organized at Port Hudson, La., 1863, as the 17th Regiment *Corps d'Afrique;* changed to 88th Regiment U. S., 1864. Broken up July, 1864, and the enlisted men transferred to other regiments.

88th Regiment, Colonel Edmund R. Wiley.—Organized at Memphis, Tenn.. February, 1863; consolidated with the 3d Regiment U. S. Heavy Artillery, December, 1865.

89th Regiment, Lieutenant-Colonel Robert F. Atkins.—Organized at Port Hudson, La., October, 1863, as the 18th Regiment *Corps d'Afrique*; changed to 89th Regiment U. S., April, 1864. Broken up July, 1864, and the enlisted men transferred to other regiments.

90th Regiment, Colonel Charles E. Bostwick.—Organized at Madisonville, La., February, 1864, as the 19th Regiment *Corps d'Afrique;* changed to 90th Regiment U. S., April, 1864. Broken up July, 1864, and enlisted men transferred to other regiments.

91st Regiment Colonel Eliot Bridgeman.—Organized at Fort Pike, La., September, 1863, as the 20th Regiment *Corps d' Afrique;* changed to 91st Regiment U. S., July, 1864; consolidated with 74th Regiment U. S., July, 1864. Battle: Bayou St. Louis.

92nd Regiment, Colonel H. N. Frisbie.—Organized at New Orleans, La., September, 1863, as the 22nd Regiment *Corps d' Afrique;* changed to 92nd Regiment U. S., April, 1864. Battle: Red River Expedition. Mustered out Dec. 1865.

93rd Regiment, Colonel Simon Jones.—Organized at New Iberia, La., November, 1863, as the 25th Regiment *Corps d' Afrique*; changed to 93rd Regiment U. S., April, 1864. Broken up June 1865; enlisted men transferred to 81st and 82nd Regiments U. S. Battle: Ash Bayou.

95th Regiment, Lieutenant-Colonel A. F. Wrohwuski.—Organized at Camp Parapet, La., April, 1863, as the 1st Regiment Engineers *Corps d' Afrique*; divided to form the 3rd Regiment Engineers *Corps d' Afrique*; changed to 95th Regiment U. S.; consolidated with 87th Regiment November, 1864, to form 81st Regiment; changed to 87th Regiment. Battle: Port Hudson.

96th Regiment, Lieut.-Colonel O. L. F. E. Fariola.—Organized at New Orleans, La., August, 1863, as the 2nd Regiment Engineers *Corps d' Afrique*; changed to 96th U. S., April, 1864. Battle: Fort Gaines. Consolidated with 73rd Regiment September, 1865; mustered out January, 1866.

97th Regiment, Geo. D. Robinson.—Composed of men transferred from the 1st Regiment Engineers *Corps d Afrique*. Organized at New Orleans, La., August, 1863, as the 3rd Regiment Engineers *Corps d' Afrique*; changed to 97th U. S., April, 1864. Battle: Pine Barren Creek. Mustered out April, 1866.

98th Regiment, Colonel Chas. L. Morton.—Organized at Camp Parapet, New Orleans, and Berwick City, La., September, 1863, as the 4th Regiment Engineers *Corps d' Afrique*; changed to 98th U. S., April, 1864; consolidated with the 78th Regiment August, 1865. Battles: Berwick, Natchez.

99th Regiment, Major Samuel Pollock.—Organized at New Orleans, La., August, 1863, as the 15th Regiment Infantry *Corps d Afrique*; changed to 5th Regiment Engineers *Corps d' Afrique* February, 1864, and to the 99th U. S., April, 1864; consolidated into a battalion of five companies, December, 1865. Battles: Natural Bridge, Steamer 'Alliance.' Mustered out April, 1866.

100th Regiment, Colonel Reuben D. Massey, (regular army).—Organized in Kentucky, May, 1864. Battles: N. & N. W. R. R., Nashville. Mustered out December, 1865.

101st Regiment, Colonel Robert W. Barnard, (regular army).—Organized in Tennessee, September, 1864. Battles: Scottsboro, Boyd's Station, Madison Station. Mustered out January, 1866.

102d Regiment, Colonel Henry L. Chipman, (regular army).—Organized at Detroit, Mich., February, 1864, as the 1st Regiment Michigan Volunteers; changed to 102d Regiment U. S., May, 1864. Battles: Honey Hill, Deveaux Neck, Salkehatchie, Bradford's Spring, Swift's Creek. Mustered out September, 1865.

103d Regiment, Lieutenant-Colonel John A. Bogert.—Organized at Hilton Head, S. C., March, 1865. Mustered out April, 1866.

104th Regiment, Colonel Douglas Frazar.—Organized at Beaufort, S. C., April, 1864. Mustered out February, 1866.

106th Regiment, Captain Frederick Holsman.—Organized at Decatur, Ala., March, 1864, as the 4th Regiment Alabama Infantry; changed to 106th Regiment U. S., May, 1864. Battles: Mud Creek, Athens. Consolidated with the 40th Regiment U. S., November, 1865.

107th Regiment, Lieutenant-Colonel David M. Sells.—Organized at Louisville, Ky., May, 1864. Mustered out November, 1866.

108th Regiment, Colonel John S. Bishop.—Organized at Louisville, Ky., June, 1864. Battle: Owensboro. Mustered out March, 1866.

109th Regiment, Colonel Orion A. Bartholomew.—Organized at Louisville, Ky., July, 1864. Mustered out February, 1866.

110th Regiment, Lieutenant-Colonel Dedrick F. Tiedemaun.—Organized at Pulaski, Tenn., November, 1863, as the 2d Regiment Alabama Volunteers; changed to 110th Regiment U. S., June, 1864. Battles: Dallas, Athens. Mustered out February, 1866.

111th Regiment, Lieutenant-Colonel William H. Scroggs.—Organized at Pulaski, Prospect, and Lynnville, Tenn., and Sulphur Branch Trestle, Ala., January, 1864, as the 3d Regiment Alabama Volunteers; changed to 111th Regiment U. S., June, 1864. Battles: Pulaski, Sulphur Branch Trestle, Athens, Richland. Mustered out April, 1866.

112th Regiment, Lieutenant Colonel John G. Gustafson.—Organized at Little Rock, Ark., April, 1864; consolidated with the 11th and 113th Regiments U. S., April, 1865, to form the 113th Regiment U. S.

113th Regiment, (old), Lieutenant-Colonel Lanniston W. Whipple.—Organized at Little Rock, Ark., March, 1864, as the 6th Regiment Arkansas Volunteers; changed to 113th Regiment U. S., June, 1864; consolidated with the 11th and 112th Regiment U. S. to form the 113th, (new), April, 1865.

113th Regiment, (new), Colonel Lanniston W. Whipple.—Organized at Little Rock, Ark., April, 1865, by the consolidation of the 11th, 112th, and 113th—old regiments. Mustered out April, 1866.

114th Regiment, Colonel Thomas D. Sedgwick.—Organized at Camp Nelson, Ky., July, 1864. Mustered out April, 1867.

115th Regiment, Lieutenant-Colonel George T. Elder.—Organized at Bowling Green, Ky., July, 1864. Mustered out February, 1866.

116th Regiment, Lieutenant-Colonel Charles Kireker.—Organized at Camp Nelson, Ky., July, 1864. Mustered out February, 1866. Battle: Petersburg.

117th Regiment, Colonel Lewis G. Brown.—Organized at Covington, Ky., July, 1864. Battle: Ghent. Mustered out August, 1867.

118th Regiment, Colonel John C. Moon. Organized at Baltimore, Md., October, 1864. Battles: Fort Brady, Henderson. Mustered out February, 1866.

119th Regiment, Colonel Charles G. Bartlett, (regular army).—Organized at Camp Nelson, Ky. Battles: Glasgow, Taylorsville. Mustered out February, 1866.

120th Regiment, Lieutenant-Colonel John Glenn.—Organized at Henderson, Ky., November, 1864. Discontinued June, 1865, and enlisted men transferred to other regiments.

121st Regiment, Colonel Hubert A. McCaleb.—Organized at Nashville, Tenn., October, 1864. Discontinued June, 1865, and enlisted men transferred to other regiments.

122d Regiment, Lieutenant-Colonel David M. Layman.—Organized at Louisville, Ky., December, 1864; consolidated into a battalion of three companies January, 1866. Mustered out February, 1866.

123d Regiment, Colonel Samuel A. Porter.—Organized at Louisville, Ky., December, 1864. Mustered out October, 1865.

124th Regiment, Colonel Frederick H. Bierbower.—Organized at Camp Nelson, Ky., January, 1865. Mustered out October, 1865.

125th Regiment, Colonel William R. Gerhart.—Organized at Louisville, Ky., February. 1865. Mustered out October, 1867.

127th Regiment, (Battalion), Lieutenant-Colonel James Givin.—Organized at Philadelphia, Pa.. August, 1864; consolidated into a battalion of three companies September, 1865. Battle: Deep Bottom. Mustered out October, 1865.

128th Regiment, Colonel Charles H. Howard.—Organized at Hilton Head, S. C., April, 1865. Mustered out October, 1866.

136th Regiment, Colonel Richard Root.—Organized at Atlanta, Ga., July, 1865. Mustered out January, 1866.

137th Regiment, Colonel Martin R. Archer.—Organized at Selina, Ala., April, 1865. Mustered into the United States service at Macon, Ga., June, 1865. Mustered out January, 1866.

138th Regiment, Colonel F. W. Benteen.—Organized at Atlanta, Ga., July, 1865. Mustered out July, 1866.

INDEPENDENT COMPANY A.

First Lieutenant, E. M. Harris.—Organized at Camp William Penn, Pa., (one hundred days,) July, 1864. Mustered out November, 1864.

Company A, (unassigned), Captain George L. Barnes.—Organized at Alexandria, Va., (one year), September, 1864. Mustered out July, 1865.

NINTH ARMY CORPS.

4th Division,* Brigadier-General Edward Ferrero.

First Brigade, Colonel Joshua K. Sigfried.—27th Regiment, 30th Regiment, 39th Regiment, 43d Regiment.

* There was with this division eleven batteries, four regiments of cavalry of white troops.

Second Brigade, Colonel Henry G. Thomas.—19th Regiment, 29th Regiment, 23d Regiment, 28th Regiment, 31st Regiment.

EIGHTEENTH ARMY CORPS.

3d Division, (June 15th to July 31st, 1864.)—Brigadier-General E. W. Hinks, June 1st to July 1st; Colonel John H. Holman, July 1st to 27th; Colonel S. A. Duncan, July 27th to 29th; Brigadier-General Joseph B. Carr, since July 29th.

First Brigade, Colonel John H. Holman; Colonel Jeptha Garrard since July 2d.—1st Regiment, 10th Regiment,* 37th Regiment,† 1st Cavalry, 5th Massachusetts Cavalry.†

Second Brigade, Colonel S. A. Duncan.—4th Regiment, 5th Regiment, 6th Regiment, 22d Regiment, 2d Cavalry.‡

The following regiments composed the Provisional Detachment of the Army of the Tennessee, 23rd Army Corps, commanded by Major-General James B. Steadman, in 1864:

First Brigade, Colonel T. J. Morgan.—14th Regiment, 15th Regiment, 17th Regiment, 18th Regiment, (battalion), 44th Regiment.

Second Brigade, Colonel Charles R. Thompson.—12th Regiment, 13th Regiment, 100th Regiment. Post of Nashville, Battery A, 2nd Artillery.

TENTH ARMY CORPS.

Army of the Ohio, Major-General A. H. Terry.—3d Division, Brigadier-General C. J. Paine.

First Brigade, Brevet Brigadier-General D. Bates.—1st Regiment, 30th Regiment, 107th Regiment.

Second Brigade, Brevet Brigadier-General S. Duncan.—4th Regiment, 6th Regiment, 37th Regiment.

Third Brigade, Colonel J. H. Holman—5th Regiment, (Mass.,) 27th Regiment, 37th Regiment.

TENTH ARMY CORPS.§

3d Division, Brigadier-General William Birney.

First Brigade, Colonel James Shaw, Jr.—7th Regiment, 9th Regiment, 16th Regiment, 29th Regiment.

Second Brigade, Colonel Ulysses Doubleday.—8th Regiment, 41st Regiment, 45th Regiment, 127th Regiment.

EIGHTEENTH ARMY CORPS.

3d Division, Brigadier-General Charles J. Paine.

First Brigade, Colonel Elias Wright.—1st Regiment, 22d Regiment, 37th Regiment.

* Detached in July.
† Detached June 28th to Department Head-quarters.
‡ Assigned June 22d, 1864.
§ Organized in November, 1864.

Second Brigade, Colonel Alonzo G. Draper.—5th Regiment, 36th Regiment, 38th Regiment.

Third Brigade, Colonel John W. Ames.—4th Regiment, 6th Regiment, 10th Regiment.

Provisional Brigade, Colonel E. Martindale.—107th Regiment, 117th Regiment, 118th Regiment.

Second Regiment Cavalry.

TWENTY-FIFTH ARMY CORPS.

Organized in the field December, 1864; commander, Major-General Godfrey Weitzel.

1st Division. Brigadier-General Chas. J. Paine.

First Brigade, Colonel J. H. Holman.—1st Regiment, 27th Regiment, 30th Regiment.

Second Brigade, Brevet Brigadier-General Samuel A. Duncan.—4th Regiment, 6th Regiment, 39th Regiment.

Third Brigade, Colonel Elias Wright, 10th Regiment.—5th Regiment, 10th Regiment, 37th Regiment, 107th Regiment.

2nd Division. Brigadier-General Wm. Birney.

First Brigade, Colonel James Shaw, 7th Regiment.—7th Regiment, 109th Regiment, 116th Regiment.

Second Brigade, Colonel Ulysses Doubleday, 45th Regiment.—8th Regiment, 45th Regiment, 127th Regiment.

Third Brigade, Colonel Chas. S. Russell, 28th Regiment.—28th Regiment, 29th Regiment, 31st Regiment, 117th Regiment.

3rd Division. Brigadier-General C. A. Heckman.

First Brigade, Brevet Brigadier-General A. G. Draper.—22nd Regiment, 36th Regiment, 38th Regiment, 118th Regiment.

Second Brigade, Colonel E. Martindale, 81st Regiment.—9th Regiment, 29th Conn. Regiment, 41st Regiment.

Third Brigade, Colonel H. G. Thomas, 10th Regiment.—19th Regiment, 23rd Regiment, 43rd Regiment.

Cavalry Brigade, Brevet Brigadier-General B. C. Ludlow.—1st Cavalry, 2nd Cavalry, Light Battery B, 2nd Artillery.

Artillery Brigade.* Battery D, 1st U. S. Artillery, Battery M, 1st U. S. Artillery, Battery E, 3rd U. S. Artillery, Battery D, 4th U. S. Artillery, Battery C, 3rd R. I. Artillery, 4th New Jersey Battery, 5th New Jersey Battery, Battery E, 1st Pa. Artillery.

REGIMENTS IN THE DEPARTMENT OF THE SOUTH, APRIL, 1864.

1st Mich., 3rd, 7th, 8th, 9th, 21st, 26th U. S., 29th Conn., 32nd, 33rd, 34th, 35th U. S., 54th Mass., 55th Mass. Regiments.

REGIMENTS WITH GENERAL STURGIS IN JUNE, 1864.

59th, 61st, 68th Regt's., Battery I, 2nd Reg't., Artillery (light.)

* All white in the Artillery Brigade.

CHAPTER XIV.

THE CONFEDERATE SERVICE.

The leaders at the South in preparing for hostilities showed the people of the North, and the authorities at Washington, that they intended to carry on the war with no want of spirit; that every energy, every nerve, was to be taxed to its utmost tension, and that not only every white man, but, if necessary, every black man should be made to contribute to the success of the cause for which the war was inaugurated. Consequently, with the enrollment of the whites began the employment of the blacks.

Prejudice against the negro at the North was so strong that it required the arm of public authority to protect him from assault, though he declared in favor of the Union. Not so at the South, for as early as April, 1861, the free negroes of New Orleans, La., held a public meeting and began the organization of a battalion, with officers of their own race, with the approval of the *State* government, which commissioned their negro officers. When the Louisiana militia was reviewed, the Native Guards (negro) made up, in part, the first division of the State troops. Elated at the success of being first to place negroes in the field together with white troops, the commanding general sent the news over the wires to the jubilant confederacy:

"NEW ORLEANS, Nov. 23rd, 1861.

"Over 28,000 troops were reviewed to-day by Governor Moore, Major-General Lovell and Brigadier-General Ruggles. The line was over seven miles long; *one regiment comprised 1,400 free colored men.*"

The population of the city of New Orleans differs materially from that of any other city on this side of the Atlantic Ocean. It has several classes of colored people: the English, French, Portuguese and Spanish,—all a mixture of the African,—and the American Negro,—mulatto,—numerically stronger than either of the others, but socially and politically less considered and privileged; the former enjoyed distinctive rights, somewhat as did the mulattoes in the West Indies before slavery was abolished there. Of these foreign classes many were planters, and not a few merchants, all owning slaves. It was from these classes that the 1,400 colored men, forming the Native Guard regiment, came, and which recruited to 3,000 before the city was captured by the Union fleet. This brigade was placed at the United States Mint building, under command of a creole, who, instead of following the confederate troops out of the city when they evacuated it, allowed his command to be cut off, and surrendered to General Butler.

Of course, prior to this date, the negro at the South had taken an active part in the preparations for war, building breastworks, mounting cannon, digging rifle-pits and entrenchments, to shield and protect his rebelling master.

January 1st, 1861, Hon. J. P. Walker, at Mobile, Ala., received from R. R. Riordan, Esq., of Charleston, S. C., a dispatch rejoicing that—

> "Large gangs of negroes from plantations are at work on the redoubts, which are substantially made of sand-bags and coated with sheet-iron."

These doubtless were slaves, and mere machines; but the Charleston *Mercury* of January 3rd, brought the intelligence that—

> "One hundred and fifty able-bodied free colored men yesterday offered their services gratuitously to the governor, to hasten forward the important work of throwing up redoubts, wherever needed, along our coast."

Only the fire-eaters based their hope of success against the North,—the National Government,—upon the stubborn energies of the white soldiery; the deliberate men rested their hopes,—based their expectations, more upon the docility of the negro, than upon the audacity of their white troops.

The legislature of Tennessee, which secretly placed that State in the Southern Confederacy, enacted in June, 1861, a law authorizing the governor—

"To receive into the military service of the State all male free persons of color, between the age of 15 and 50, who should receive $8 per month, clothing and rations."

And then it further provided—

"That in the event a sufficient number of free persons of color to meet the wants of the State shall not tender their service, the Governor is empowered, through the sheriffs of the different counties, to *press* such persons until the requisite number is obtained."

A few months after, the Memphis *Avalanche*, of September 3rd, 1861, exultingly announced the appearance on the streets of Memphis, of two regiments of negroes, under command of confederate officers. On the 7th of September, again the *Avalanche* said:

"Upwards of 1000 negroes armed with spades and pickaxes have passed through the city within the past few days. Their destination is unknown, but it is supposed that they are on their way to the 'other side of Jordan.'"

Nor were the negroes in Virginia behind those of the other Southern States. In April, the Lynchburg *Republican* chronicled the enrollment of a company of free negroes in that city, also one at Petersburg.

Thus instead of revolts among the negroes, slaves and free, as predicted by some Union men at the North, many became possessed of a fervor,—originating generally in fear,—stimulated by an enthusiasm of the whites, that swept the populace like a mighty sea current into the channel of war. The negro who boasted the loudest of his desire to fight the Yankees; who showed the greatest anxiety to aid the confederates, was granted the most freedom and received the approval of his master.

The gayly decked cities; the flags, bunting and streamers of all colors; the mounted cavalry; the artillery trains with brazen cannons drawn by sturdy steeds; followed by regiments of infantry in brilliant uniforms, with burnished muskets, glittering bayonets and beautiful plumes; preceeded by brass bands discoursing the ever alluring strains of the quick-step; all these scenes greatly interested and delighted the negro, and it was filling the cup of many with ecstasy to the brim, to be allowed to connect themselves, even in the most menial way, with the demonstrations. There was also an intuitive force that led them, and they unhesitatingly followed, feeling that though they took up arms against the National Government, freedom was the ultimatum. Many of those who enlisted feared to do otherwise than fight for slavery, for to refuse would have invited, perchance, torture if not massacre; to avert which many of the free blacks, as well as some of the slaves, gave an apparent acquiescence to the fervor of their lesser informed comrades, who regarded any remove from the monotony of plantation life a respite.

The readiness with which they responded to the call was only astonishing to those who were unacquainted with the true feelings of the unhappy race whose highest hope of freedom was beyond the pearly gates of the celestial domain. One thing that impressed the blacks greatly was the failure of Denmark Vesy, Nat Turner and John Brown, whose fate was ever held up to them as the fate of all who attempted to free themselves or the slaves. Escape to free land was the only possible relief they saw on earth, and *that* they realized as an individual venture, far removed from the field-hand South of Delaware, Maryland and Virginia.

It was not unnatural, then, for some to spring at the opportunity offered to dig trenches and assist Beauregard in mounting cannon, and loading them with shot and shell to fire upon Fort Sumter.

The negro did not at first realize a fight of any magnitude possible, or that it would result in any possible good to himself. So while the *free* negroes trembled because they *were* free, the slaves sought refuge from sus-

DOING MILITARY DUTY FOR THE CONFEDERATES.

Negroes building fortifications for the Confederates at James Island, S. C., under direction of General Beauregard, to repel the land attack of the Federal troops.

picion of wanting to be free, behind, *per se*, an enthusiasm springing, not from a desire and hope for the success of the confederates, but from a puerile ambition to enjoy the holiday excitement.

Later on, however, when the war opened in earnest, and the question of the freedom and slavery of the negro entered into the struggle; when extra care was taken to guide him to the rear at night; when after a few thousand Yankee prisoners, taken in battle, had sought and obtained an opportunity of whispering to him the *real* cause of the war, and the surety of the negroes' freedom if the North was victorious, the slave negro went to the breastworks with no less agility, but with prayers for the success of the Union troops, and a determination to go to the Yankees at the first opportunity; though he risked life in the undertaking. When the breastworks had been built and the heavy guns mounted, when a cordon of earth-works encircled the cities throughout the South, and after a few thousand negroes had made good their escape into the Union lines, then those who had labored upon the fortifications of the South were sent back to the cotton-fields and the plantations to till the soil to supply the needs of the confederate soldiers who were fighting to keep them in bondage. But when the policy of the North was changed and union and *liberty* were made the issues of the struggle, as against slavery and disunion, and the Union forces began to slay their enemies, the Confederate Government realized the necessity of calling the negroes from the hoe to the musket,—from the plantations to the battle-fields.

In the incipiency of the struggle, many of the States made provision for placing the negro at the disposal of the Confederate Government; but elated at their early victories, the leaders deemed the enforcement of the laws unnecessary, negro troops not being needed. As the change came, however, and defeats, with great losses in various ways depleted the armies, the necessity of the aid of the negroes became apparent. Stronghold after stronghold, city after city, States in part, fell before the march of the Union troops. The negro had become a soldier in the Union army, and was helping to crush the rebellion. President Lincoln had declared all slaves in rebeldom free, and thousands of black soldiers were marching and carrying the news to the slaves.

This state of affairs lead President Davis and his cabinet to resign to the inevitable, as had the North, and to inaugurate the policy of emancipating and arming the slaves, knowing full well that it was sheer folly to expect to recruit their shattered armies from the negro population without giving them their freedom.

It was therefore in the last days of the confederate authorities, and it was their last hope and effort for success. Despair had seized upon them. The army was daily thinned more by desertion than by the bullets of the Union soldiers, while Sherman's march from Atlanta to the sea had awakened the widest alarm. In the winter of 1864 and 1865 the question of arming the slaves was presented as a means of recruiting the depleted and disordered ranks of the army, and it soon assumed an importance that made it an absorbing topic throughout the Confederacy. There was no other source to recruit from. The appeal to foreigners was fruitless. "The blacks had been useful soldiers for the northern army, why should they not be made to fight for their masters?" it was asked. Of course there was the immediate query whether they would fight to keep themselves in slavery. This opened up a subject into which those who discussed it were afraid to look; nevertheless it seemed unavoidable that a black conscription should be attempted, and with that in view, every precaution was taken by those who supported the scheme to avoid heightening the dissensions already too prevalent for good. The newspapers were advised of the intended change of policy, to which not a few of them acquiesced. General Lee was consulted, as the following letter, afterward printed in the Philadelphia *Times*, shows:

"HEAD-QUARTERS ARMY NORTHERN VIRGINIA,
"January 11th, 1865.

"HON. ANDREW HUNTER: I have received your letter of the 7th instant, and, without confining myself to the order of your interrogatories, will endeavor to answer them by a statement of my views on the subject.

"I shall be most happy if I can contribute to the solution of a question in which I feel an interest commensurate with my desire for the welfare and happiness of our people.

"Considering the relation of master and slave controlled by human laws, and influenced by Christianity and an enlightened public sentiment, as the best that can exist between the white and black races, while intermingled as at present in this country, I would deprecate any sudden disturbance of that relation, unless it be necessary to avert a greater calamity to both. I should, therefore, prefer to rely on our white population to preserve the ratio between our forces and that of the enemy, which experience has shown to be safe. But in view of the preparations of our enemies it is our duty to prepare for continued war and not for a battle or a campaign, and I own I fear we can not accomplish this without overtaxing the capacity of our white population.

"Should the war continue under existing circumstances the enemy may in course of time penetrate our country, and get access to a large part of our slave population. It is his avowed policy to convert the able-bodied men among them into soldiers, and emancipate all. The sncceess of the federal arms in the south was followed by a proclamation from President Lincolu for two hundred and eighty thousand men, the effect of which will be to stimulate the northern states to procure as substitutes for their own people the negroes thus brought within their reach. Many have already been obtained in Virginia, and should the fortunes of war expose more of her territory the enemy will gain a large accession of strength. His progress will thus add to his numbers, and at the same time destroy slavery in a manner most pernicious to the welfare of our people. Their negroes will be used to hold them in subjection, leaving the remaining force of the enemy free to extend his conquest.

"Whatever may be the effect of our employing negro troops it can not be as mischievous as this. If it end in subverting slavery it will be accomplished by ourselves, and we can devise the means of alleviating the evil consequences to both races. I think, therefore, we must decide whether slavery shall be extinguished by our enemies and the slaves be used against us, or use them ourselves at the risk of the effects which may be produced upon our social institutions. My own opinion is that we should employ them without delay. I believe that, with proper regulations, they can be made effective soldiers. They possess the physical qualifications in an eminent degree. Long habits of obedience and subordination, coupled with that moral influence which in our country the white man possesses over the black, furnish the best foundation for that discipline which is the surest guarantee of military efficiency. Our chief aim should be to secure their fidelity. There have been formidable armies composed of men having no interests in the country for which they fought beyond their pay or the hope of plunder. But it is certain that the best foundation upon which the fidelity of an army can rest, especially in a service which imposes peculiar hardships and privations, is the personal interest of the soldier in the issue of the contest. Such an interest we can give our negroes by granting immediate freedom to all who enlist, and freedom at the end of the war to the families of those who discharge their duties faithfully, whether they survive or not, together with the privilege of residing at the south.

"To this might be added a bounty for faithful service. We should not expect slaves to fight for prospective freedom when they can secure it at once by going to the enemy, in whose service they will incur no greater risk than in ours. The reasons that induce me to recommend the employment of negro troops at all render the effect of the measures I have suggested upon slavery immaterial, and in my opinion the best means of securing the efficiency and fidelity of this auxiliary force would be to accompany the measure with a well-digested plan of gradual and general emancipation. As that will be the result of the continuance of the war, and will certainly occur if the enemy succeed, it seems to me most advisable to adopt it at once, and thereby obtain all the benefits that will accrue to our cause.

"The employment of negro troops under regulations similar to those indicated would, in my opinion, greatly increase our military strength, and enable us to relieve our white population to some extent. I think we could dispense with the reserve forces, except in cases of emergency. It would disappoint the hopes which our enemies have upon our exhaustion, deprive them in a great measure of the aid they now derive from black troops, and thus throw the burden of the war upon their own people. In addition to the great political advantages that would result to our cause from the adoption of a system of emancipation, it would exercise a salutary influence upon our negro population, by rendering more secure the fidelity of those who become soldiers, and diminishing the inducements to the rest to abscond.

"I can only say in conclusion that whatever measures are to be adopted should be adopted at once. Every day's delay increases the difficulty. Much time will be required to organize and discipline the men, and action may be deferred till it is too late.

"Very respectfully,

"Your obedient servant,

"A true copy. J. B. W." "(Signed,) R. E. LEE, *General.*

This letter was intended for members of Congress to read, and it was circulated among them, but all was not harmony. Many members were bitterly opposed to arming the slaves, some of them denounced General Lee for writing the letter, and prepared to oppose the measure when it should be introduced into Congress.*

* General William C. Wickham led the opponents of the project in a very bitter pro-slavery speech.

At length the period for its introduction arrived. Lee in his attempted invasion of the north made no more careful preparations than did Mr. Davis and his cabinet to carry through Congress the bill enrolling slaves and to emancipate them. Finally the hour was at hand, and amid the mutterings of dissenters, and threats of members to resign their seats if the measure was forced through, the administration began to realize more sensibly its weakness. However, it stood by the carefully drawn bill.

Of course the negro people about the city of Richmond heard of the proposition to arm and emancipate them if they would voluntarily fight for their old masters. They discussed its merits with a sagacity wiser than those who proposed the scheme, and it is safe to say that they concluded, in the language of one who spoke on the matter, "It am too late, de Yankees am coming." There were those among them, however, known as the free class, who stood ever ready to imitate the whites, believing that course to be an evidence of their superiority over the slaves. They were very anxious to enlist.

On February 8th Senator Brown, of Mississippi, introduced a resolution which, if it had been adopted, would have freed 200,000 negroes and put them into the army; but on the next day it was voted down in secret session. Upon this very February 9th, when Senator Brown's resolution was lost, Mr. Benjamin, Secretary of State, addressed a large public meeting at Richmond. He made a very extraordinary speech, setting forth the policy of President Davis and his cabinet. Emissaries of Mr. Davis had just returned from the Peace Conference at Fortress Monroe, where they met representatives of the United States government, and learned that the conditions upon which the Southern States could resume their relations were those which they were compelled to accept finally. During Mr. Benjamin's speech he said:

"We have 680,000 blacks capable of bearing arms, and who ought now to be in the field. Let us now say to every negro who wishes to go into the ranks on condition of being free, go and fight—you are free. My own negroes have been to me and said, 'Master, set us free and we'll fight for you.' You must make up your minds to try this or see your army withdrawn from before your town. I know not where white men can be found."

Mr. Benjamin's speech created an intense excitement among the slave-holders. The situation seemed to have narrowed itself down to a disagreeable alternative. They must either fight themselves or let the slaves fight. Doubtless many would have preferred submission to Lincoln, but then they could not save their slaves. Immediately following Mr. Benjamin's speech on the 11th, a bill was introduced into the House of Representatives authorizing the enlistment of 200,000 slaves, with the consent of their owners. As a test of its strength a motion was made for the rejection of this bill, and the vote not to reject it was more than two to one. There was every indication that the bill would pass. It was while this measure was under discussion that General Lee wrote the letter which follows in answer to one of inquiry from a member of the House:

"HEAD-QUARTERS CONFEDERATE STATE ARMIES,
February 18th, 1865.

"Hon. Barksdale, House of Representatives, Richmond.

"SIR: I have the honor to acknowledge the receipt of your letter of the 12th inst. with reference to the employment of negroes as soldiers. I think the measure not only expedient but necessary. The enemy will certainly use them against us if he can get possession of them, and as his present numerical superiority will enable him to penetrate many parts of the country, I can not see the wisdom of the policy of holding them to await his arrival, when we may, by timely action and judicious management, use them to arrest his progress. I do not think that our white population can supply the necessities of a long war without overtaxing its capacity, and imposing great suffering upon our people; and I believe we should provide resources for a protracted struggle, not merely for a battle or a campaign.

"In answer to your second question I can only say that, in my opinion, under proper circumstances the negroes will make efficient soldiers. I think we could at least do as well with them as the enemy, and he attaches great importance to their assistance. Under good officers and good instructions I do not see why they should not become soldiers. They possess all the physical qualifications, and their habits of obedience constitute a good formulation for discipline. They furnish a more promising material than many armies of which we read in history, which owed their efficiency to discipline alone. I think those employed should be freed. It would be neither wisdom nor justice, in my opinion, to require them to serve as slaves. The best course to pursue, it seems to me, is to call for such as are willing to come with the consent of their owners. Impressment or draft would not be likely to bring out the best class, and the use of coercion would make the measure distasteful to them and to their owners. I have no doubt if Congress would authorize their reception into service, and empower the President to call upon individuals or States for such as they are willing to contribute with the condition of emancipation to all enrolled, a sufficient number would be forthcoming to enable us to try the experiment.

"If it proves successful, most of the objections to the matter would disappear, and if individuals still remained unwilling to send their negroes to the army, the force of public opinion in the States would soon bring about such legislation as would remove all obstacles. I think the matter should be left as far as possible to the people and the States, which alone can legislate as the necessities of this particular service may require. As to the mode of organizing them, it should be left as free from restraint as possible. Experience will suggest the best course, and would be inexpedient to trammel the subject with provisions that might in the end prevent the adoption of reforms, suggested by actual trial.

"With great respect,
"ROBERT E. LEE, *General.*"

Meanwhile the measure, to forward which this letter was written, was progressing very slowly. J. B. Jones, clerk of the War Department of the Confederate Government, entered in his diary from day to day such scraps of information as he was able to glean about the progress of this important matter. These entries are significant of the anxiety of this critical time. Under February 14th we find this entry:

"Yesterday some progress was made with the measure of 200,000 negroes for the army. Something must be done and soon."

"February 16th.—Did nothing yesterday; it is supposed, however, that the bill recruiting negro troops will pass. I fear when it is too late."

"February 17th.—A letter from General Lee to General Wise is published, thanking the latter's brigade for resolutions recently adopted declaring that they would consent to gradual emancipation for the sake of independence and peace. From all signs slavery is doomed. But if 200,000 negro recruits can be made to fight and can be enlisted, General Lee may maintain the war, very easily and successfully, and the powers at Washington may soon become disposed to abate the hard terms of peace now exacted."

"February 21st.—The negro bill has passed one house and will pass the other to-day, but the measure may come too late. The enemy is enclosing us on all sides with great vigor and rapidity."

"February 22nd.—Yesterday the Senate postponed action on the negro bill. What this means I cannot conjecture, unless there are dispatches from abroad with assurance of recognition, based on stipulations of emancipation, which can not be carried into effect without the consent of the States, and a majority of these seem in a fair way of falling into the hands of the Federal generals."

"February 24th.—Yesterday the Senate voted down the bill to put 200,000 negroes into the army. The papers to-day contain a letter from General Lee, advocating the measure as a necessity. Mr. Hunter's* vote defeated it. He has many negroes, and will probably lose them; but the loss of popularity and fear of forfeiting all chance of the succession may have operated upon him as a politician. What madness! 'Under which king, Benzonian?'"

"February 25th.—Mr. Hunter's eyes seem blood-shot since he voted against Lee's plan of organizing negro troops."

"February 26th.—Mr. Hunter is now reproached by the slave-holders he thought to please for defeating the negro bill. They say his vote will make Virginia a free State, inasmuch as General Lee must evacuate it for want of negro troops."

"March 2d.—Negro bill still hangs fire in Congress."

"March 9th.—Yesterday the Senate passed the negro troops bill—Mr. Hunter voting for it under instruction."

"March 10th.—The president has the reins now, and Congress will be more obedient; but can they leave the city? Advertisements for recruiting negro troops are in the papers this morning."

"March 17th.—We shall have a negro army. Letters are pouring into the department from men of military skill and character asking authority to raise companies, battalions, and regiments of negro troops. It is a desperate remedy for the desperate case, and may be successful. If 200,000 efficient soldiers can be made of this material there is no conjecturing when the next campaign may end. Possibly 'over the border;' for a little success will elate our spirits extravagantly, and the blackened ruins of our towns, and the moans of women and children bereft of shelter, will appeal strongly to the army for vengeance."

"March 19th.—Unless food and men can be had Virginia must be lost. The negro experiment will soon be tested. Curtis says that the letters are pouring into the department from all quarters asking authority to raise and command negro troops. 100,000 troops from this source might do wonders."

---

* It was upon the discussion of this bill that Mr. Hunter, of Virginia, made these significant statements and admissions:

"When we left the old government we thought we had got rid forever of the slavery agitation; but, to my surprise, I find that this (the Confederate) Government assumes power to arm the slaves, which involves also the power of emancipation. This proposition would be regarded as a confession of despair. If we are right in passing this measure, we are wrong in denying to the old government the right to interfere with slavery and to emancipate slaves. If we offer the slaves their freedom as a boon we confess that we are insincere and hypocritical in saying slavery was the best state for the negroes themselves. I believe that the arming and emancipating the slaves will be an abandonment of the contest. To arm the negroes is to give them freedom. When they come out scarred from the conflict they must be free."

So ends the entries on this interesting subject in Mr. Jones' diary. Though the conscientious war clerk ceased to record, the excitement and effort of the advocates of the measure by no means slackened. Grant's cordon around the city drew closer and tighter each day and hour, continually alarming the inhabitants. Governor Smith gave the negro soldier scheme his personal influence and attention. The newspapers began clamoring for conscription. No little effort was made to raise a regiment of free blacks and mulattoes in the latter days of January, and early in February a rendezvous was established at Richmond, and a proclamation was issued by the State authorities. A detail of white officers was made, and enlistment began. The agitation of the subject in Congress, though in secret session, gave some encouragement to the many despairing and heart-sick soldiers of the Army of Northern Virginia.* Their chief commander, Lee, perhaps dreamed nightly that he commanded 200,000 negro troops *en masse*, and was driving the Yankees and their Black Phalanx like chaff from off the "sacred soil" of the Old Dominion, but, alas, such a dream was never to be realized.

About twenty negroes,† mostly of the free class, enlisted, went into camp, and were uniformed in Confederate gray. These twenty men, three of whom were slaves of Mr. Benjamin, Confederate Secretary of State, were daily marched into the city and drilled by their white officers in the Capitol Square, receiving the approving and congratulatory plaudits of the ladies, who were always present.‡ However, no accessions were gained to their ranks, consequently the scheme, to raise by enlistment a regiment of blacks, was a failure, for the few volunteers secured in Virginia and a company in Tennessee are all that the writer has been able to obtain any account of. The Con-

* Of these twenty volunteers six of them are frequently to be met on the steets of Richmond, while some of them are members of the Colored State Militia of Virginia.

† The veterans of General Henry A. Wise's Legion adopted resolutions commending the scheme.

‡ On April 1st, 1865, quite a company of negroes, most of whom were pressed into the service, paraded the streets of Richmond.

federate authorities then sought to strengthen the army by conscripting all able-bodied negroes, free and slave, between the age of eighteen and fifty. Monday, April 3d, was appointed as the day to begin the draft. The Virginia State Legislature had come to the rescue of the Davis-Lee-Benjamin scheme, and so had the local authorities of Richmond, but all was to no purpose. It was too late; they had delayed too long.

With a pitiable blindness to the approach of his downfall, only a few days before he became a fugitive, Jefferson Davis wrote the following letter:*

"RICHMOND, Va., March 30th, 1865.

"His Excellency William Smith, Governor of Virginia:

"Upon the receipt of your letter of the 27th inst. I had a conference with the Secretary of War and Adjutant-General in relation to your suggestion as to the published order for the organization of negro troops, and I hope that the modification which has been made will remove the objection which you pointed out. It was never my intention to collect negroes in depots for purposes of instruction, but only as the best mode of forwarding them, either as individuals or as companies, to the command with which they were to serve. The officers in the different posts will aid in providing for the negroes in their respective neighborhoods, and in forwarding them to depots where transportation will be available, and aid them in reaching the field of service for which they were destined. The aid of gentlemen who are willing and able to raise this character of troops will be freely accepted. The appointment of commanders, for reasons obvious to you, must depend on other considerations than the mere power to recruit.

"I am happy to receive your assurance of success as well as your promise to seek legislation to secure unmistakably freedom to the slave who shall enter the army, with a right to return to his old home when he shall have been honorably discharged from the military service.

"I remain of the opinion that we should confine our first efforts to getting volunteers, and would prefer that you would adopt such measures as would advance that mode of recruiting, rather than that of which you make enquiry, to wit: by issuing requisitions for the slaves as authorized by the State of Virginia.

"I have the honor to be, with much respect,

"Your obedient servant,

JEFFERSON DAVIS."

* This letter is a copy of the original now in possession of Senator George A. Brooks. It has never before been published.

UNION SOLDIERS BEFORE YORKTOWN BRINGING DOWN A SOUTHERN ALLY.

This negro being a good marksman was induced by the confederates to become a sharpshooter for them, and greatly annoyed the Union pickets before Yorktown by firing upon them from trees, in the branches of which he would perch himself at early morning and remain there through the day, shooting at such Union soldiers as happened come within his range. His hiding place was finally discovered however, and after refusing to surrender, thinking himself safe, he was brought down by a bullet through his head.

The appointed time came, but instead of the draft, amid blazing roofs and falling walls, smoke and ashes, deafening reports of explosions, the frenzy of women and children, left alone not only by the negro conscripting officers and President Davis and his Cabinet, but by the army and navy; in the midst of such scenes, almost beyond description, the Black Phalanx of the Union army entered the burning city, the capitol of rebeldom, scattering President Linclon's Proclamation of Emancipation to the intended confederate black army. For twelve squares they chanted their war songs, "The Colored Volunteers" and "John Brown," in the chorus of which thousands of welcoming freedmen and freedwomen joined, making the welkin ring with the refrain,

"Glory, glory hallelujah,
Glory, glory hallelujah,
Glory, glory hallelujah,
We is free to-day!"

The decisive events of the next few days, following in rapid succession, culminating with Lee's surrender, on the 9th of April, at Appomattox, left no time for further action, and when the war was over, with the important and radical changes that took place, it was almost forgotten that such projects as arming and freeing the negro had ever been entertained in the South by the Confederate Government.

PART III.

MISCELLANY.

CHAPTER I.

THE BLACK PHALANX AT SCHOOL.

The esteem in which education was held by the soldiers of the Black Phalanx, can be judged of best by the efforts they made to educate themselves and to establish a system of education for others of their race. Doubtless many persons suppose that the negro soldier elated with his release from slavery, was contented; that his patriotism was displayed solely upon the field of battle, simply to insure to himself that one highest and greatest boon, his freedom. Such a supposition is far from the truth. The Phalanx soldiers had a strong race pride, and the idea that ignorance was the cause of their oppression gave zest to their desire to be educated.

When they found following the United States Army a large number of educated people from the North, establishing schools wherever they could in village, city and camp, and that education was free to all, there was awakened in the black soldier's breast an ambition, not only to obtain knowledge, but to contribute money in aid of educational institutions, which was done, and with liberal hands, during and subsequent to the war.

Unlettered themselves, they became daily more and more deeply impressed, through their military associations, and by contact with things that required knowledge, with the necessity of having an education. Each soldier felt that but for his his illiteracy he might be a sergeant, company clerk, or quartermaster, and not a few, that if educated, they might be lieutenants and captains. This was not an unnatural conclusion for a brave soldier to arrive at, when men no braver than himself were being promoted for bravery.

Generally there was one of three things the negro soldiers could be found doing when at leisure: discussing religion, cleaning his musket and accoutrements, or trying to read. His zeal frequently led him to neglect to eat for the latter. Every camp had a teacher, in fact every company had some one to instruct the soldiers in reading, if nothing more. Since the war I have known of more than one who have taken up the profession of preaching and law making, whose first letter was learned in camp; and not a few who have entered college.

The negro soldier was not only patriotic in the highest sense but he was a quick observer of both the disadvantages and opportunities of his race. He recognized the fact that the general education of the white men who composed the Union army in contra-distinction to so many of those of the confederate army, gave them great prestige over the enemy. The ingenuity of the Yankee he attributed to his education, and he readily decided that he lacked only the Yankee's education to be his equal in genius. Great was the incentive given him by example, arousing his latent hope to be something more than a free man; if not that, his children might rise from the corn-field to the higher walks of life. Their thirst for a knowledge of letters was evinced in more ways than one, as was their appreciation of the opportunity to assist in providing for coming generations.

Colonel G. M. Arnold says:

"Aside from the military duties required of the men forming the Phalanx regiments, the school teacher was drilling and preparing them in the comprehension of letters and figures. In nearly every regiment a school, during the encampment, was established, in some instances female teachers from the North, impulsed by that philanthropy which induced an army of teachers South to teach the freedmen, also brought them to the barracks and the camp ground to instruct the soldiers of the Phalanx. Their ambition to learn to read and write was as strong as their love of freedom, and no opportunity was lost by them to acquire a knowledge of letters. So ardent were they that they formed squads and hired teachers, paying them out of their pittance of seven dollars per month, or out of the bounty paid to them by the State to which they were accredited. In a number of instances the officers themselves gave instructions to their command, and made education a feature and a part of their duty, thereby bringing the soldier up to a full comprehension of the responsibility of his trust. "Taps" was an unpleasant sound to many a soldier, who, after the fatigue and drill of the day was over, sat himself down upon an empty cracker box, with a short candle in one hand and a spelling book in the other, to study the ab, eb, ob's. When the truce was sounded after a day or night's hard fighting, many of these men renewed their courage by studying and reading in the 'New England Speller.' And where they have fought,—died where they fell, and their bodies left to the enemy's mercy, they often found in the dead soldier's knapsack a spelling-book and a Testament. At the seige of Port Hudson and Charleston, and of Richmond, agents of the Christian Commission and of various other societies, made a specialty of the spelling-book for distribution among the soldiers of the Phalanx, and upon more than one occasion have these soldiers been found in the trenches with the speller in hand, muttering, bla, ble.'

The historian of the 55th Regiment says:

"A great desire existed among those who had been deprived of all educational privileges to learn to read and write, and through the kindness and labors of Dr. Bowditch and others, a school was established to teach those who desired to learn. Many availed themselves of this, and many were assisted by their company officers and their better informed fellow-soldiers, so that a decided improvement in this respect was effected among the men during their stay at Readville."

But it is not necessary to dwell upon the subject to show the eagerness of these soldiers to learn to read and write, as many of them did.

Lieutenant James M. Trotter,* in an article published in Mr. Fortune's paper, gives this graphic description of "The School-master in the Army":

"Of the many interesting experiences that attended our colored soldiery during the late war none are more worthy of being recounted than those relating to the rather improvised schools, in which were taught the rudimentary branches. One would naturally think that the tented field, so often suddenly changed to the bloody field of battle, was the last place in the world where would be called into requisition the school-teacher's services; in fact it would hardly be supposed that such a thing was possible. Yet in our colored American army this became not only possible but really practicable, for in it frequently, in an off-hand manner, schools were established and maintained, not only for teaching the soldiers to read and write but also to sing, nor were debating societies,

* Now Registrar at Washington, D. C.

even, things unheard of in the camp life of these men. Besides in quite a number of the colored regiments military bands were formed, and under the instruction of sometimes a band teacher from the north, and at others under one of their own proficient fellow-soldiers, these bands learned to discourse most entertaining music in camp, and often by their inspiriting strains did much to relieve the fatigue occasioned by long and tiresome marches. But we are speaking now mainly of the work of the school-teacher proper. And what shall we say of the halls of learning in which were gathered his eager pupils? Well, certainly these would not compare favorably with those of civil life, as may well be imagined. As says Bryant, truly and beautifully, speaking of primitive religious worship:

'The groves were God's first temples.'

So, too, in the groves and fields of their new land of liberty, these men found their first temples of learning, and in spite of all inconveniences these school tents were rendered quite serviceable. Of the text books used there is not much to say, for these were generally 'few and far between.' Books were used at times, of course, but quite as often the instruction given was entirely oral. That these spare facilities did not render the teacher's efforts ineffective was abundantly proven in the service, and has been proven since in civil life. Scattered here and there over this broad country to-day are many veteran soldiers who are good readers and writers, some of them even fair scholars, who took their first lessons from some manly officer or no less manly fellow-soldier in the manner mentioned, during such camp intervals as were allowed by the dread arbitrament of war. In a number of regiments these fortunate intervals were quite frequent and of long duration, and in such cases, therefore, much progress was made.

"It must, of course, be remembered that in our colored regiments a very large percentage of the men were illiterate, especially in those composed of men from the south and so lately escaped from under the iron heel of slavery. Indeed, in many of them there could scarcely be found at the commencement of the service a man who could either read or write. Many an officer can recall his rather novel experience in teaching his first sergeant enough of figures and script letters to enable the latter to make up and sign the company morning report. All honor to those faithful, patient officers, and all honor, too, give to those ambitious sergeants who after awhile conquered great difficulties and became educationally proficient in their lines of duty.

"In this connection I readily call to mind one of the most, if not the most, unique figures of all my experience in the army. It was Colonel James Beecher, of the famous Beecher family, and a brother of Henry Ward Beecher. He was in command of the First North Carolina Colored Regiment. In this position it would be hard to overestimate the variety and value of his services, for he became for his soldiers at once a gallant fighter, an eloquent, convincing preacher, and a most indefatigable and successful school-teacher. Preaching had been his vocation before entering the army, and so it was but natural for him to continue in that work. At one time our regiment lay encamped near his in South Carolina, and I well remember how, on one Sabbath morning, the two commands formed a union service, all listening with deep, thrilling interest to the inspiring words of this "fighting parson." That he was indeed a fighting parson we fully learned not long after this Sabbath service. For again we met on the bloody field of battle, where in the very front of the fight we saw him gallantly leading his no less gallant men, even after he had been wounded, and while the blood almost streamed down his face. Seeing him thus was to ever remember him and his noble work with his regiment.

"Colonel Beecher when encamped neglected no opportunity to form schools of instruction for his men, in order that they might become not only intelligent, efficient soldiers, but also intelligent, self-respecting citizens, should they survive the perils of war. I do not know what are his thoughts to-day, but judging from the grand work of Colonel Beecher in his black regiment, I can not doubt that he looks back to it all with satisfaction and pride, and as forming the richest experience of his life.

"I know another ex-colonel and scholar, of high rank as a man of letters and in social life, who yielding to the call of duty, not less to country than to a struggling race, left his congenial studies and took command of a colored regiment, becoming not only their leader, but, as chance afforded, their school-teacher also. However, as he has given to the world his army experience in a book abounding in passages of thrilling dramatic interest, I need only in this connection make mention of him. I refer to that true and tried friend of the colored race, Colonel T. W. Higginson.

"But let it not be supposed for a moment that only officers and men of another race were engaged in this noble work of school-teaching in our colored army. Not a few of the best workers were colored chaplains, who wisely divided their time between preaching, administering to the sick by reason of wounds or otherwise, and to teaching the old 'young idea how to shoot;' while many non-commissioned officers and private soldiers cheerfully rendered effective service in the same direction. Nor must we close without expressing warm admiration for those earnest, ambitious soldier pupils who, when finding themselves grown to man's estate, having been debarred by the terrible system of slavery from securing an education, yielded not to what would have been considered only a natural discouragement, but, instead, followed the advice and instruction of their comrade teachers, and, bending themselves to most assiduous study, gained in some cases great proficiency, and in all much that fitted them for usefulness and the proper enjoyment of their well-earned liberty. And so we say, all honor to teachers and taught in the Grand Army that made a free republic, whose safe foundation and perpetuity lies in the general education of its citizens."

CHAPTER II.

BENEVOLENCE AND FRUGALITY.

The negro troops gave striking evidence of both benevolence and frugality with the money they received. They needed but to be shown an opportunity to contribute to some object, when they quickly responded. Frequently, too, they fell easy victims to the crafty camp bummers and speculators, who were ever collecting means for some charitable object for the benefit of the negro race. However, here it will be a pleasing duty to name some of the more conspicuous instances where their charity was well and nobly bestowed. At the same time they deposited a vast aggregate sum of savings in different banks established for this purpose.

The 62nd Regiment contributed to a commendable project gotten up by its officers, who gave, themselves, $1,034.60, the regiment giving $3,966.50. With this money the founding of a school was commenced, which eventually became a college known as the Lincoln Institute, situated at Jefferson City, Mo. To this sum of $5,001.10, the 65th Regiment contributed $1,379.50, through the efforts of their officers. The sum was soon increased to $20,000, and the Institute stands to-day a monument to the 62nd and 65th Phalanx Regiments.

Professor Foster, in his history of this Institute, gives these interesting details:

"Dr. Allen, a man of high character and influence, gave the scheme standing ground by declaring that he would give $100. Both our field officers, Colonel Barrett and Lieutenant-Colonel Branson, though

U. S. PAYMASTERS PAYING OFF PHALANX SOLDIERS.

neither was with us at the time, afterwards subscribed a like amount. Others responded in the same spirit. Officers and men entered into the work with enthusiasm. The lieutenants gave $50 each; officers of higher rank, $100. First Sergeant Brown, Co D, gave $75; Sergeants Curd, Bergamire, Alexander and Moore each gave $50, while the number who gave 25, 20, 15, 10, and 5 dollars apiece is too great for me to recall their names on this occasion, but they are all preserved in our records. The total result in the 62nd Regiment was $1,034.60, contributed by the officers, and $3,966.50 by the colored soldiers. The soldiers of the 65th Regiment afterwards added $1,379.50. One of them, Samuel Sexton, gave $100 from his earnings as a private soldier at $13 per month, an example of liberality that may well challenge comparison with the acts of those rich men who, from their surplus, give thousands to found colleges."

Colonel David Branson, late of the 62nd Regiment, in his dedicatory speech, said:

"MY FRIENDS:—This, with one exception, has been the happiest 4th of July in my life. That exception was in 1863, when I saw the rebel flag go down at Vicksburg. I felt the exultation of victory then, and I feel it to-day as I look upon this splendid building. Looking in the faces of my old comrades of the 62nd Regiment here to-day, memory goes back to the past, when hundreds of you came to me at Benton Barracks, ragged, starving, and freezing—some did freeze to death—and emotions fill me that no language can express. I cannot sit down and think of those scenes of suffering without almost shedding tears. But happily those days are passed. No more marching with sluggish step and plantation gait through the streets of St. Louis, Mo., amid the jeers of your enemies; no more crossing the Mississippi on ice; no more sinking steamers, and consequent exposure on the cold, muddy banks of the river; no more killing labor on fortifications at Port Hudson, Baton Rouge and Morganza; no more voyages over the Gulf of Mexico, packed like cattle in the hold of a vessel; no mere weary marches in the burning climate of Texas; no more death by the bullet, and no more afternoons on the banks of the Rio Grande, deliberating on the future education of yourselves when discharged from the army; but peace and prosperity here with the result of those deliberations before us. Our enemies predicted, that upon the disbanding of our volunteer army—particularly the colored portion of it—it would turn to bands of marauding murderers and idle vagabonds, and this Institute was our answer."

When Colonel Shaw, of the 54th Regiment, fell at Fort Wagner, the brave soldiers of that regiment gladly contributed to a fund for a monument to his memory, but which, upon reflection, was appropriated to building the Shaw School at Charleston, S. C. And yet all these sums sink into insignificance when compared to that contributed by the negro soldiers to the erection of a monument to the memory of President Lincoln, at the capitol of the nation; seventeen hundred of them gave *ten thousand dollars.* But let the record speak for itself, for it is only a people's patriotism that can do such things:

CORRESPONDENCE AND STATEMENTS OF JAMES E. YEATMAN, PRESIDENT OF THE WESTERN SANITARY COMMISSION, RELATIVE TO THE EMANCIPATION MONUMENT.

"ST. LOUIS, April 26th, 1865.

"*James E. Yeatman, Esq.:*

"MY DEAR SIR; A poor negro woman, of Marietta, Ohio, one of those made free by President Lincoln's proclamation, proposes that a monument to their dead friend be erected by the colored people of the United States. She has handed to a person in Marietta five dollars as her contribution for the purpose. Such a monument would have a history more grand and touching than any of which we have account. Would it not be well to take up this suggestion and make it known to the freedmen?

"Yours truly, T. C. H. SMITH."

Mr. Yeatman says:

"In compliance with General Smith's suggestion I published his letter, with a card, stating that any desiring to contribute to a fund for such a purpose, that the Western Sanitary Commission would receive the same and see that it was judiciously appropriated as intended. In response to his communication liberal contributions were received from colored soldiers under the command of General J. W. Davidson, head-quarters at Natchez, Miss., amounting in all to $12,150. This was subsequently increased from other sources to $16,242.

"MARIETTA, OHIO, June 29th, 1865.

"*Mr. James E. Yeatman, President Western Sanitary Commission, St. Louis:*

"MY DEAR SIR: I have learned, with the greatest satisfaction, through Brigadier-General T. C. H. Smith and the public press that you are devoting your noble energies in giving tone and direction to the collection and appropriation of a fund for the erection of the Freedmen's National Monument, in honor and memory of the benefactor and savior of their race.

"The general also informs me that you desire, and have requested through him that the five dollars deposited with the Rev. C. H. Battelle, of this city, by Charlotte Scott, should be used as the *original and foundation subscription* for this most praiseworthy purpose; and Mr. Battelle assures me that he will most cheerfully remit it to you this day. As a slave-holder by inheritance, and up to a period after the outbreak of the rebellion, and as an ardent admirer of our lamented president, the author of universal emancipation in America, I feel an enthusiastic interest in the success of the Freedmen's National Monument. I hope it may stand unequalled and unrivalled in grandeur and magnificence. It should be built *essentially* by *freedmen*, and should be *emphatically national.* Every dollar should come from the former slaves, every State should furnish a stone, and the monument should be erected at the capital of the nation. Nothing could be better calculated to stimulate this downtrodden and abused race to renewed efforts for a moral and national status.

"Charlotte Scott, whose photograph General Smith will forward, was born a slave in Campbell County, Virginia. She is about sixty years old, but is very hale and active. Her reputation for industry, intelligence, and moral integrity, has always been appreciated by her friends and acquaintances, both white and colored. She was given, with other slaves, to my wife, by her father, Thomas H. Scott. When we received the news of Mr. Lincoln's assassination, the morning after its occurrence, she was deeply distressed. In a conversation with Mrs. Rucker, she said: '*The colored people have lost their best friend on earth. Mr. Lincoln was our best friend, and I will give five dollars of my wages towards erecting a monument to his memory.*' She asked me who would be the best person to raise money for the purpose. I suggested Mr. Battelle, and she gave him the five dollars.

"I am, my dear sir, truly and respectfully,

"WILLIAM P. RUCKER."

"MARIETTA, OHIO, June 29th, 1865.

"*Mr. J. E. Yeatman.*

"DEAR SIR: I was providentially called upon by Charlotte Scott, formerly a slave of Dr. W. P. Rucker, now living in this place, to receive the enclosed $5, as the commencement of a fund to be applied to rearing a monument to the memory of Hon. Abraham Lincoln.

"I received her offering, and gave notice through the press that I would receive other donations, and cheerfully do what I could to promote so noble an object. Other persons have signified their willingness to give when the measure is fully inaugurated.

"By the advice of General T. C. H. Smith I herewith forward you her contribution, and I hope to here from you upon its receipt, that I may show to Charlotte and others that the money has gone in the right direction. After hearing from you I hope to be able to stir up the other colored folks on this subject.

"I rejoice, dear sir, that I have some connection with this honorable movement in its incipiency. I shall not fail to watch its progress with thrilling interest, and hope to live until the top stone shall be laid amid the jubilant rejoicing of emancipated millions crying 'Grace, grace unto it.'

"Very respectfully yours,

"C. D. BATTELLE."

"The publication of the note of Mr. Yeatman, and the first communication received concerning the colored woman's proposed offering, brought the following letters and contributions, showing how generously the proposition of Charlotte Scott was responded to by the colored troops stationed at Natchez, Miss. These contributions have been duly deposited for safe keeping towards the Freedmen's National Monument to Mr. Lincoln.

HEAD-QUARTERS 6TH U. S. COLORED HEAVY ARTILLERY,
"FORT MCPHERSON, Natchez, May 19th, 1865.

"*James E. Yeatman, President Western Sanitary Commission, St. Louis:*

"DEAR SIR: I hereby transmit to you, to be appropriated to the monument to be erected to the late President Lincoln, the sum of four thousand two hundred and forty-two dollars, the gift from the soldiers and freedmen of this regiment. Allow me to say that I feel proud of my regiment for their liberal contribution in honor of our lamented chief. Please acknowledge receipt.

"Very respectfully, your obedient servant,

"JOHN P. COLEMAN,

"*Lieutenant-Colonel commanding 6th U. S. Colored Heavy Artillery.*

"Amounts as donated by their respective companies: Company A, $515; Company B, $594; Company C, $514; Company D, $464; Company E, $199; Company F, $409; Company G, $284; Company H, $202; Company I, $423; Company K, $231; Company L, $142; Company M, $354. Total, $4,242."

"HEAD-QUARTERS 70TH U.S. COLORED INFANTRY,
"RODNEY, MISS., May 30th, 1865.

"Brevet Major-General J. W. Davidson, commanding District of Natchez, Miss.:

"GENERAL: I have the honor to enclose the sum of two thousand nine hundred and forty-nine dollars and fifty cents as the amount collected, under your suggestion, for the purpose of erecting a monument to the memory of President Lincoln. Every dollar of this money has been subscribed by the black enlisted men of my regiment, which has only an aggregate of six hundred and eighty-three men. Much more might have been raised, but I cautioned the officers to check the noble generosity of my men rather than stimulate it. Allow me to add that the soldiers expect that the monument is to be built by black people's money exclusively. They feel deeply that the debt of gratitude they owe is large, and any thing they can do to keep his 'memory green' will be done cheerfully and promptly.

"If there is a monument built proportionate to the veneration with which the black people hold his memory, then its summit will be among the clouds—the first to catch the gleam and herald the approach of coming day, even as President Lincoln himself first proclaimed the first gleam as well as glorious light of universal freedom.

"I am, general, most respectfully, your obedient servant,

"W. C. EARLES,

"*Colonel 70th United States Colored Infantry.*"

"DISTRICT OF NATCHEZ, May 21st, 1865.

"*Hon. James E. Yeatman:*

"Upon seeing your suggestions in the *Democrat* I wrote to my colonels of colored troops. and they are responding most nobly to the call. Farrar's regiment, 6th United States Heavy Artillery, sent some $4,700. The money here spoken of has been turned over to Major W.C. Lupton, Pay-master U. S. A., for you. Please acknowledge receipt through the Missouri *Democrat*. The idea is, that the monument shall be raised to Mr. Lincoln's memory at the national capital exclusively by the race he has set free. Very truly yours,

"J. W. DAVIDSON, *Brevet Major-General.*

"HEAD PAY DEPARTMENT, NATCHEZ, MISS., June 15th, 1865.

"*James E. Yeatman, Esq., President Western Sanitary Commission, St. Louis:*

"SIR: The colored soldiers of this district, Brevet Major-General Davidson commanding, feeling the great obligations they are under to our late president, Mr. Lincoln, and desiring to perpetuate his memory, have contributed to the erection of a monument at the national capital, as follows:

70th United States Colored Infantry, Colonel W. C. Earle......$2,949.50
Three Companies 63d U. S. Colored Infantry—A, C, and E—
Lieutenant-Colonel Mitchell.. 263.00
Freedmen of Natchez.. 312.38

Total...$3,529.85

"Added to this Major John P. Coleman, of the 6th United States Colored Heavy Artillery, (those that Forrest's men did not murder at Fort Pillow), stationed here, has sent you nearly five thousand dollars for the same fund, and the 57th United States Colored Infantry desire me, at the next pay-day, to collect one dollar per man, which will swell the amount to nearly ten thousand dollars. This is a large contribution from not quite seventeen hundred men, and it could have been made larger—many of the men donating over half their pay, and in some instances the whole of it—but it was thought best to limit them.

"Will you please publish this, that the colored soldiers and their friends may know that their money has gone forward, and send me a copy of the paper. "I am, sir, with regard,

"W. C. LUPTON, *Pay-master United States Navy.*"

"These noble contributions are a striking evidence of the favor with which this movement is regarded by the colored people, and especially the brave soldiers (the Phalanx who fought to maintain their freedom) of this oppressed race who have been fighting to carry out the proclamation of their benefactor, securing them their liberty."

There is still another evidence of the appreciation of freedom by the negro soldiers in their frugality. After the enlistment of colored troops became general, and they began to receive pay and bounties, the officers commanding them readily discovered the necessity of providing a better place for keeping the money paid them than in their pocket-books and in the soldier's knapsack. Every pay-day these soldiers would carry sums of money to their officers for safe keeping, until thousands of dollars were thus deposited, which were often lost in battle. In August, 1864, General Rufus Saxton, military governor of South Carolina, after mature deliberation as to the best means to be adopted for the safe keeping of these soldiers' monies, established a bank in his department. General Butler established a similar one at Norfolk, Va., about the same time. At the organization of the Freedmen's Savings and Trust company, chartered by act of Congress, these institutions transferred to the Freedmen's Bank all the monies on deposit in them, as the war had ceased, and the troops and officers were being mustered out of the United States service. The Butler Bank at Norfolk in July, 1865, transferred $7,890. In December the Saxton Bank at Beaufort transferred $170,000. Thus the sum of $177,890, belonging to soldiers in two departments only, was placed to their credit, subject to their order, in the new national bank, called into existence by like motives. This bank had branches at these places. Had similar banks been established in the other departments an enormous sum would have been collected. The Freedmen's bank, however, took the place of these military banks, and had the confidence of the soldiers who continued to deposit in its various branches throughout the south. When that institution collapsed in 1874, of the many millions of dollars deposited in it, it is estimated that two-thirds of the amount was the savings of the Phalanx. There is now in the vaults of the national government more than a quarter of a million of dollars belonging to the Phalanx, held as unclaimed bounty and pay—an ample sum from which to erect a suitable monument to commemorate the heroic devotion and patriotic endeavor of those who fell in Freedom's cause. This money doubtless belongs to those who on the battle-fields and in hospitals died for the country's honor. These are some of the lessons taught by the history of the Black Phalanx.

CHAPTER III.

BIBLIOGRAPHY.

The following publications have been of service in the preparation of this volume:

Goodrich's History of the U. S.
The Great Rebellion.—Headley.
Record of the Seventh U. S. C. T.
War of 1812.—Rossiter.
Negro in the Rebellion.—Brown.
Butler in New Orleans—Parton.
American Conflict.—Greeley.
Historical Research.—Livermore.
Record 55th Regt. Mass. Vols.
Patriotism of Colored Americans.
Boys of 61.—Coffin.
Record of 37th U. S. C. T.
History of Virginia.—Magill.
Atlanta.—Cox.
March to the Sea.—Cox.
Lincoln and Slavery.—Arnold.
Ramsey's History of America.
Grimshaw's History of the U. S.
Attack on Petersburg.—Congress.
Fort Pillow Massacre.—Congress.
Campaigns of the Army of the Potomac.—Swinton.
Army Life in a Black Regiment.—Higginson.
Anti-Slavery Measures in Congress.—Wilson.
Principles and Acts of the Revolution.—Niles.
Military History of U. S. Grant.—Badeau.
First and Second Year of the War.—Pollard.
Report of the Conduct of the War.—Congress.
Bryant's Popular History of the United States.
Virginia Campaigns of '64 and '65.—Humphrey.
Life and Public Service of Charles Sumner.—Lester.
Boys and Girls Magazine, 1869.—Oliver Optic.
Burnside and the Ninth Army Corps.—Woodbury.
Military History of Kansas.—J. B. McAfee.
History of the Great Rebellion.—Kettell.

APPENDIX.

HISTORY OF THE 29TH CONNECTICUT NEGRO VOLUNTEERS.

"HEAD-QUARTERS 29TH CONNECTICUT COLORED VOLUNTEERS,
HARTFORD, CONN., November 29th, 1865.

"Brigadier-General H. J. MORSE, *Adjutant-General, State of Connecticut.*

"GENERAL: In obedience to your request I have the honor to submit the following as the history of the 29th Regiment Connecticut Volunteers (Colored):

"Recruiting for this regiment began early in the autumn of 1863, and by the latter part of January, 1864, the maximum number had been enlisted. During its organization the regiment was stationed at Fair Haven, Conn. On the 8th of March, 1864, the regiment was formally mustered into the service of the United States.

"No field officer had as yet reported, but on the 12th of March William B. Wooster, formerly lieutenant-colonel of the 20th Connecticut Volunteers, reported to the regiment, and soon after assumed command.

"On the 19th day of March the regiment formed in line, and after the presentation of a flag by the colored ladies of New Haven, marched on board the transport "Warrior."

"On the 20th we steamed out of New Haven harbor, and after a pleasant voyage disembarked at Annapolis, Md.

"The regiment was as yet unarmed, but on the 7th of April we received the full complement of the best Springfield rifled muskets.

"At this time the 9th Corps was assembling at Annapolis, and to it we were assigned, but on the 8th of April the regiment received orders to proceed to Hilton Head, S. C., and on the 9th of April we left Annapolis for that place. Arriving at Hilton Head we were ordered to Beaufort, S. C., where we disembarked on the 13th of April. The regiment had, up to this time, learned nothing of drill or discipline, so that there was plenty of work to be done.

"After a fine camp had been laid out the work of converting the raw material of the regiment into good soldiers was vigorously and systematically commenced. The men learned rapidly, and were faithful in the performance of their duties. While here, although the utmost attention was paid to all that pertained to the health of the regiment, much sickness prevailed, the change of climate telling severely upon the untried soldiers. In less than two months a decided improvement in drill and discipline had been effected, and our dress parades began to attract marked attention. But as yet our soldiers had not fired a shot at the rebellion, and had still to be tried in the fiery ordeal of battle. At last events on the bloody fields of Virginia determined our destiny.

"The battles fought during the summer campaign had demonstrated that negro troops could fight well; they had also shown that more men were required in Virginia, and that we could not await the slow process of a draft to get them. The success of the entire campaign seemed dubious, and the army, after all its gigantic toils and losses, found itself confronted by strong lines of works, manned by a brave and resolute foe. Under these circumstances the only policy was concentration in Virginia. Accordingly all the troops that could be spared from other points were ordered to Virginia.

"Among the number was the 29th Connecticut Volunteers (colored). On the 8th day of August, 1864, the regiment left Beaufort, S. C., and disembarked at Bermuda Hundreds, Va., on the 14th of the same month. This regiment was brigaded with the 7th, 8th, and 9th United States Colored Troops, forming with other colored regiments a division of the 10th Army Corps. We arrived just as the active movements terminating in the capture of the Weldon Railroad had commenced. That railroad being on the then extreme left of our line it was deemed advisable, as a feint, to keep the enemy well engaged on our right. For this purpose the 2d and 10th Army Corps had been assembled, as secretly as possible, near Bermuda Hundreds, and on the morning of August 14th had advanced upon the enemy's works near Deep Bottom.

"This regiment accompanied the force as far as Deep Bottom, where, with the 7th United States Colored Troops and one light battery, it was left to defend the post, under command of Colonel Wooster. The two corps moved farther to the right and front, and soon became warmly engaged. During the fighting General Butler, desirous to ascertain the strength and position of the enemy immediately in our front, ordered Colonel Wooster to make a reconnoissance with this regiment and the 7th United States Colored Troops.

"This was successfully accomplished, the men in this their first encounter with the enemy, displaying great coolness and bravery. Soon after this we were relieved and ordered to join our brigade, then actively engaged at the front.

"We set out in a drenching rain storm, and after a tiresome march reached the battle-field about dark. Our forces had suffered a bloody repulse, and had just finished burying our dead under a flag of truce. The burial parties with their bloody stretchers were returning, and the sharp crack of the rifle began again to be heard, and so continued with more or less fierceness during the night.

"At daylight hostilities, except on the picket line, were not resumed. The opposing forces lay and narrowly watched each other's movements.

Towards night, however, it was discovered that the enemy was massing in our immediate front, and just before sunset they commenced the attack. The contest was sharp and short; a fierce roar of musketry, mingled with wild yells and the deep bass of cannon; a fainter yell and volleys less steady; finally a few scattering shots and the attack was repulsed. As this movement of the two corps on the right was merely a feint to cover more active operations on the left, it was resolved to withdraw the forces during the night. The movement began just after dark. We marched to the Bermuda Hundreds front, and pitched our camp near Point of Rocks. On the 24th of August, 1864, the 10th Corps relieved the 18th Corps in front of Petersburg. Here we remained, doing duty in the trenches, until the 24th of September, at which time the 10th Corps marched to the rear to rest a few days preparatory to an advance upon Richmond then in contemplation. While here our ragged, dirty, and shoeless men were clad, washed, and shod as rapidly as possible.

"At length, at about sundown, September 28th, the corps broke camp, and we once more started for Deep Bottom, which place we reached about four A. M., September 29th.

"Just as the first faint glimmerings of light were visible the movement against Richmond commenced. After pushing through a deep wood our brigade formed in line of battle near the New Market Road, under fire of a rebel battery. We had scarcely formed when it was found that the rebel lines had been broken further to the left, and we were ordered forward in pursuit of the flying foe. Three successive lines had been carried by impetuous charges, and during that summer forenoon the enemy on all sides was pressed steadily back. By noon Fort Harrison, a large powerful work, and a key to a large portion of the rebel line, had been carried at the bayonet point by the 18th Corps, and we found ourselves in front of the strongest line of the outer defenses of Richmond. An assault was immediately ordered. Two regiments of the brigade to which this regiment was attached,—the 7th Maryland and 8th Pennsylvania—were selected to make the attack on Fort Gilmer, the 29th Connecticut and 9th Maryland being held in reserve. A charge was made on the double-quick through a felled forest, half a mile in extent. They were met by a murderous enfilading fire, and after an obstinate struggle were forced back. They re-formed quickly and again charged, this time up the very guns of the fort. After a most heroic fight they were again compelled to retire. Some of the companies sprang into the ditch, and refused to surrender even after their companions had been driven back. They continued the unequal contest until dark, when we were forced to leave the brave men to their fate.

"After the repulse of the second charge, the brigade formed under a galling fire, preparatory to another charge, but after a careful survey of the enemy's position, it was deemed advisable to delay the attack for the present. Darkness soon after coming on, the troops were quietly withdrawn to one of the captured lines a short distance in our rear. Next morning vigorous measures were at once taken to reverse this line, and to render it impregnable against a counter attack, which was constantly expected. While busily engaged in this work the rebels opened upon us with a fierce artillery fire. A powerful force, said to be under the direction of General Lee in person, had been silently massed in front of Fort Harrison, screened from our view by the inequality of the ground. They soon made their presence known, however, and advanced with determination. They were met by a fire that sent them reeling back with immense loss. Again they formed, and were again driven back. Another charge more furious, and another repulse more bloody, finally convinced them that the attempt was useless, and we were left in possession of our victories of the previous day. After this, comparative quiet reigned for a few days, but they were not days of idleness; the captured lines had to be reversed and heavy picket duty to be done, and of these duties this regiment had its full share.

"On the 7th of October, the enemy made a dash on our right, and at first met with considerable success. This regiment was detached from the brigade, and ordered to the right to assist in repelling the attack. Before reaching that point the attack had been repulsed and the fighting was nearly over. We formed a skirmish line and remained until midnight, when we returned to the brigade.

"On the 13th of October a reconnoissance was made upon the enemy's lines in front of our right, in which this regiment took an active part. The fighting was severe, and the loss considerable. The men behaved like veterans: but the wary foe behind his strong works bade defiance to our small force, and so, after fifteen hours of fighting, at night we returned to camp. On the 27th of October a movement commenced on our extreme left which required the active co-operation of the Army of the James, that the enemy might be kept busily engaged at all points. This regiment, as part of the force selected for this purpose, set out early on the morning of the 27th, and came in contact with the outposts of the enemy. Deploying as skirmishers, after a short, sharp action, we drove the enemy within entrenchments. After driving in the skirmish line, we remained in front of the enemy's works, picking his men as opportunity offered, and keeping him engaged generally. We were in an open field, exposed to the fire of an enemy protected by strong earthworks. The men behaved very well; for twenty-three hours they held this position, exposing themselves with the most reckless indifference, taking the ammunition from the bodies of their dead and wounded companions when their own was exhausted, and in all respects, if valor be any criteron of manhood, proving themselves to be 'good men and true.' At length on the morning of the 28th, the troops were withdrawn, and we returned to camp.

"On the 19th day of November, the regiment was ordered to garrison certain detached forts on the New Market road, which were considered of great importance on account of the relation they bore to the whole line north of the James. That this regiment was sent to hold them, was certainly a marked tribute to its valor and efficiency, and was expressly given to it on that account. We remained here until the formation of the 25th Army Corps, when on the 5th day of December, 1864 we removed to the left of Fort Harrison, forming a part of the 2nd Brigade, 1st Division of that Corps.

"Here we remained during the rest of the winter, picketing, drilling, building forts, and making roads, and preparing for the spring campaign. One division had been sent to Fort Fisher, and but two were with the Army of the James. At length, late in the month of March, 1865, one of the remaining divisions was sent to the left, while the division to which this regiment was attached, together with one division of the 24th Army Corps, was left to guard the defences north of the James. The campaign opened vigorously. The last week in March brought a series of splendid victories to the Union armies, and we began to feel that the 'end' so ardently desired was near at hand. This regiment had been placed in Fort Harrison, the most important position on our line. The fort was said to be mined, and it was feared that the rebels would make an attack in force near that point. On Saturday and Sunday, April 1st and 2nd, the fighting on the left had been terrific but generally favorable to us. We were ordered to observe with great care all movements of the enemy in our front.

"At sunset of April 2nd, we witnessed the last rebel dress parade in Virginia from the magazine of Fort Harrison. Early on the morning of April 3rd, 1865, the picket fires of the enemy began to wane, and an ominous silence to prevail within his lines. Very soon deserters began to come within our lines who reported that the lines in our front were being evacuated. In a little while we saw the barracks of Fort Darling in flames, and tremendous explosions followed each other in rapid succession. The earliest dawn revealed to us the deserted lines, with their guns spiked and their tents standing. We were ordered to advance at once, but cautiously. The troops jumped over the breast-works, and, avoiding the torpedoes, filed through the rebel abbatis, and then began the race for Richmond.

"No words can describe the enthusiasm of the troops as they found themselves fairly within the rebel lines, and tramping along the bloody roads leading to the 'capitol of secessia.' The honor of first entering that city was most earnestly contested; many regiments threw away everything but their arms, while this regiment 'double-quicked' in heavy marching orders. Two companies of this regiment—G and C—had been sent forward as skirmishers reaching the city close on the heels of our cavalry, and were, without the slightest doubt, the first companies of infantry to enter the city. Through the heat and dust the troops struggled on, and at last, as we came in full view of the city, the air was rent with such cheers as only the brave men, who had fought so long and so nobly for that city could give. Since that time our history has been blessedly unfruitful in stirring events. We remained in Richmond for a few days, and were then ordered to Petersburg; from here we went to Point Lookout, Md., where we remained until the 25th Corps was ordered to Texas. We embarked for Texas on the 10th day of June 1865, arriving at Brazos de Santiago July 3rd, 1865. From Brazos we marched to Brownsville, on the Rio Grande, where we continued until ordered to Hartford, Conn., to be mustered out. On the 26th day of October, 1865, we left Brownsville for Hartford, where the regiment was discharged and paid on the 25th day of November, 1865.

"The following is a report of changes and casualties in the 29th Regiment Connecticut Volunteers, (colored), from date of organization to date of discharge:

Gain by recruits	8	officers,	210	enlisted men.
Loss " discharge	5	"	121	"
" " dismissal	1	"	—	"
" " desertion	–	"	103	"
" died of disease	1	"	153	"
" " wounds	1	"	21	"
" by killed in battle	–	"	24	"
Promotion into other organizations	5	"	—	"
Total gain	8	"	210	"
" loss	13	"	422	"

Wounded, officers, 6; men, 102. Captured, officer, 1; missing, none.

"It will be necessary to remark here that fully one hundred per cent of our desertions occurred while at New Haven, and during the organization of the regiment very few desertions occurred after we left the State. Our total of killed and wounded was—enlisted men, 123; officers, 6. The officer who was captured eventually re-joined us. The officers lost by promotion into other organizations were—Lieutenant-Colonel H. C. Ward, promoted to be colonel of the 31st United States Colored Troops; Major F. E. Camp, promoted to be lieutenant-colonel of the 29th United States Colored Troops; Captain E. W. Bacon, promoted to be major of the 117th United States Colored Troops; Assistant Surgeon Crandall, promoted to be surgeon of the 33d United States Colored Troops; 1st Lieutenant H. H. Brown, promoted to be captain of the 1st United States Colored Troops; 2d Lieutenant Edward Coe, promoted to be 1st lieutenant and adjutant of the 27th United States Colored Troops.

"Thus have I attempted to trace the history of this regiment. I have done this with some degree of minuteness, owing to the fact that, as we were considered a United States organization less can be learned concerning us from the reports of the adjutant-general of the State than concerning any other Connecticut organization, And as the employment of colored troops was at first tried as a grand experiment, the people of Connecticut may be desirous to know how far, in the case of their colored regiment, that experiment has been successful. Justice, too, demands that those who are the most competent judges—those who have been with the colored troops on the march and in the battle—should give their testimony to the loyalty and valor of this despised race. They went forth to fight the battles of the Union when there was every thing to discourage even the bravest. Both officers and men knew, that should they escape death on the battle-field a fate awaited them, if captured, from which death on the battle-field would have been a glorious relief. The poor rights of a soldier were denied to them. Their actions were narrowly watched, and the slightest faults severely commented upon. In spite of all this the negro soldier fought willingly and bravely, and with his rifle alone he has vindicated his manhood, and stands confessed to-day as second in bravery to none.

"I am, general, very respectfully, your obedient servant,

"DAVID TORRANCE,

"(*Late*) *Lieutenant-Colonel Commanding 29th C. V.*"

DIARY OF THE THIRD REGIMENT DURING THE SIEGE OF PORT HUDSON.

"May 1st, 1863.—Regiment broke camp at Fort William, Baton Rouge, at 5 A. M.; marched out of Bayou Monticino on the road to Port Hudson. In the evening Company G, under Lieutenant Quinn, was detailed for picket duty on the Clinton Road. Colonel promised to encamp close by with the rest of the regiment, but instead of doing so he fell back to the junction of the Clinton and Port Hudson Roads, thus leaving the rebels a fine chance to cross the bayou and cut off Company G from all support. Lieutenant Quinn was doubtful of the colonel, and to satisfy himself sent 2d Lieutenant Frederick Dame with twenty men back to the woods to see how things were. Lieutenant Dame found that Colonel Nelson had retreated back to Baton Rouge and reported. Lieutenant Quinn, feeling that if attacked during the night he would not receive aid from the regiment, changed his position from the place assigned in the woods by Colonel Nelson, to one 300 yards further down in the woods, and on the road-side. He then threw out his pickets in all directions, but only a short distance from the remainder of the company who were held in reserve. Every man was on that night. Occasionally horsemen were seen in the clearing, but as they did not appear to know of our company's proximity the pickets did not fire on them.

"12th.—Had a slight skirmish.

"13th.—Companies G and E, under Lieutenant Quinn, went on a reconnoissance; returned at midnight.

"14th.—All quiet in camp.

"15th.—Fell back to Bayou Monticino.

"16th.—Commenced to build a second bridge at Monticino Bayou.

"17th.—Company G, Lieutenant Dame, and Company E, Lieutenant John Keefe, went on a scout under command of Lieutenant Quinn, captured one horse, cattle, and had a skirmish with rebel pickets.

"18th.—Company G on picket ordered to block the road with felled trees, connecting the Clinton and Bayou Sara roads, to prevent the rebel cavalry and artillery getting in the rear of Dudley's brigade, who were camped near Plains Store.

"19th.—Colonel Nelson and Lieutenant Quinn rode to Dudley's head-quarters. The regiment marched two miles nearer to Port Hudson in the evening; were ordered back and bivouacked that night.

"20th.—At 10 P. M. again for Port Hudson. After hours of hard marching in heavy order in a hot sun on dusty roads and very little water to drink, the regiment camped at dark in the left of the Union line on the road leading to Springfield landing.

"21st.—Battle of Plains Store. During the morning there were rumors of a fight, as the rebels were determined to prevent a junction of of the force under Augur and Grover, of Banks' army, who were moving down from St. Francis. This brought on the above-named battle, in which the negro regiment held the extreme left, and thus prevented the rebels getting in the rear of the Union troops.

"22d.—Companies A and G drove back some rebel pickets, capturing one man, horse, equipments, and two rifles. The man was thrown by his horse and was badly hurt, his head striking against a tree.

"23d.—We formed a junction to-day with Banks, and Port Hudson is invested.

"24th.—Companies E and G, under Captain Blake, on a scout.

"25th.—To-day the regiment marched from the extreme left to the extreme right of the Union line, a hard long tramp again in heavy order. At night we encamped near Sandy Creek, close to the Mississippi. Each man had to carry his own baggage. This regiment was never given any wagons.

"26th.—At Sandy Creek protecting men laying the pontoon bridge. Skirmishing all day with the rebels. The boys are getting used to fighting.

"27th.—Storming the batteries. The negro soldiers prove the bravest of the brave. To-day was fought one of the most desperate battles on record. Our brigade, six companies of the 1st, and nine companies of 3rd Regiment Louisiana Native Guards, commenced fighting at quarter of an hour before 6 A. M. The 1st, under Lieutenant-Colonel Bassett, advanced in skirmish line up through the wood and soon drew the enemy's fire. The 3rd under Lieutenant-Colonel Finnegass, were in line of battle about fifty yards in rear of the first, the whole command under Colonel John A. Nelson, of the 3rd Regiment. The rebels opened with infantry fire and shells at short range, and their fire was very effective, and for a short time the first, which was in danger of utter destruction, wavered, when Colonel Bassett and his colored officers moved among the men encouraging them by their own fearless examples. At this crisis, Colonel Finnegass sent forward his four left companies, under Captain John E. Quinn, to support the 1st. Captain Quinn moved up in good order, placing his left company under Lieutenant John O'Keefe so as to face the bridge on his left, held by the rebels in rifle-pits, Finnegass keeping the other five companies well in hand, to use them when most needed. When within pistol shot of the fortifications, to their dismay they were stopped—not by the rebels, but by a back flow of the river. The water was not more than forty feet across, but over eight feet deep. To cross this without boat or bridge was impossible, particularly under such a terrible fire as the rebels poured upon them in front and on both flanks. On the left the rebels were actually in their rear so far had the gallant fellows advanced. The slaughter was now becoming fearful. Colonel Finnegass at this juncture asked Captain Quinn if he could cross the water; Quinn called on volunteers to follow him. The whole that was left of his own company, G, and Lieutenant O'Keefe with Company E, responded to his call, and in they plunged, the men holding their rifles and cartridge boxes above their heads. In the mean time Bassett and Finnegass (whose men were lying down) kept a continual fire on the rebel gunners and drove them from their guns, but the water was too much for the men, and only 35 or 40—with Quinn and O'Keefe and Lieutenants Burnham and Dame—succeeded in crossing. This handful actually followed their reckless leader up to the very cannon's mouth, and for 15 or 20 minutes held the whole rebel battery in their hands. Colonel Finnegass seeing that in a few minutes more his brave men would be destroyed, rushed into the water and ordered Quinn to fall back, as a regiment of rebels were clambering over the works to get in their rear. The brave fellows fell back, but alas, few of them ever answered roll-call again. Out of the band but six re-crossed alive, and of these, Lieutenants O'Keefe, Burnham and Sergeants Vincent and Taylor, who were wounded; Quinn and Dame were the only ones unhurt. The whole regiment now fell back about 600 yards, in the shelter of the woods. Six times we advanced, hoping to find some spot where the men could cross, but in vain. We entered this fight with 1080 men, and lost 371 killed and 150 wounded; total loss, 421. The rebels shelled us with their heavy guns, On our front were artillery and infantry; on our left a wooded ridge full of riflemen. We had two six-pounders; one of them was dismounted early in the fight, and the other the gunners ran out of range, it being of no use.

"Now, why were the colored troops left unsupported? Why were they sent on such hopeless missions? Why were the officers informed by General Dwight that there were clear grounds beyond Sandy Creek? There were white troops who could have been sent to their support; the officers expected to fight the rebels but met the river. Colonel Nelson played General to perfection; during the whole battle he remained on the safe side of Sandy Creek, and had his corps of orderlies to attend him; in plain words he kept his men under fire from quarter before six A. M., till seven P. M. During the day he never saw a rebel's face or back. * * * The heroes of the day were the men; not one of them showed the "white feather." Colonel Bassett and his colored officers of the 1st were as brave as any men who ever drew a sword, and so were Finnegass, Lieutenant-Colonel of the 3rd, and Captains Smith, Daly, Masterson and others. Lieutenants O'Keefe, Burnham, Wiley, Griggs, Emory, Westervelt and Dame of the 3rd, and Captain Quinn, who commanded the left wing and led the storming column of the 3rd. Lieutenant-Colonel Bassett was formerly of the 4th Mississippi Regiment; Colonel Nelson and Lieutenant-Colonel Finnegass, were both of Irish parentage; Captain Daily and Lieutenant Emory, of the 31st Massachusetts, Lieutenant O'Keefe of the 9th and Burnham, of the 13th Connecticut, Masterson and Wiley, of the 26th Massachusetts, Company A, of the 3rd, were on detached service. Captain John E. Quinn is a native of Lowell, Mass.; born April 22nd, 1837 came from the 30th Massachusetts, in which he was orderly of Company B.

A correspondent of the New York *Tribune* writing, says:

"The more I see of our colored regiments, and the more I converse with our soldiers, the more convinced I am that upon them we must ultimately rely as the principle source of our strength in these latitudes. It is perfect nonsense for any one to attempt to talk away the broad fact, evident as the sun at noonday, that these men are capable not only of making good soldiers, but the very best of soldiers. The Third Louisiana Native Guard, Colonel Nelson, are encamped here, and a more orderly, disciplined, robust, and effective set of men I defy any one to produce.

"An old European officer, one who has followed the profession of arms from his very boyhood, said to me to-day: 'In one essential respect, sir, I believe that in a short time these colored soldiers will surpass any we have in our army—I mean in subordination—without which no army can be effective. We are in the habit of carrying our citizenship with us into the field, and that begets an amount of undue familiarity between officers and men that is often destructive of obedience. Toward the black man we feel none of these delicate sentiments of equality, and he, on his part, has always been accustomed to be commanded. Beside this he is acclimated, knows the country thoroughly, and if called upon to fight will fight in earnest, for he knows that if taken prisoner he will meet no mercy.'

"Colonel Nelson, anxious to have an opportunity of exhibiting to the world what his command is capable of, and thus put their manhood beyond all question, has implored General Banks to put him in the foremost point of danger in the coming struggle, and says that his men are as ready as himself to stake their lives upon the result; but the general —doubtless acting upon explicit orders—says they must, at present at least, be confined to manning the fortifications here.

"I am happy to say that the feeling toward these colored regiments throughout the army is undergoing the most rapid and extraordinary changes. Soldiers that only a few months, nay, weeks ago, would have flown into a furious passion at the bare idea of a black man carrying a musket like themselves, now say, 'O, if you are going to give them white officers that is another affair altogether.'"

The following letter gives some interesting recollections of the military events of the Department of the Gulf:

"NEW ORLEANS, January 18th, 1883.

"*To Colonel J. T. Wilson, Norfolk, Va.:*

"FRIEND: Your two circulars issued from Cailloux Post No. 2 on the 13th inst. are received. It is quite a compliment to Louisiana to have named your Post after the hero of Port Hudson, who immortalized himself in those celebrated charges in May, 1863.

"It is over twenty years ago that I took a commission in the 3d Louisiana Native Guard as a senior lieutenant of Company H. I was quite intimate with Captain Andre Cailloux.

"Grave doubts had been expressed by Banks, the nominal commander, and his officers regarding the fitness of colored men as soldiers. The perplexing question was, 'Will they stand their christening under such a hail storm as will come from those bristling Port Hudson heights?' In fact those three colored regiments—the 1st, 2d, and 3d Louisiana Native Guards, organized in 1862, and afterward incorporated in the Ullman Brigade as the 73d, 74th, and 75th—had become more a subject of test than of real dependence at the critical juncture of trial.

"General Osterhaus solved the mystery by taking command of a division, including the 1st and 3d Native Guards. Those magnificent series of charges were made by these two regiments. The first charge was made on a Sunday, the 27th day of May, 1863, supported on the right by the celebrated Duryea's Zouaves, of New York, which were mowed down like grass before a scythe. It was then and there that Captain Cailloux gloriously died in advance of his company while cheering his men. It was also on that day that the immortal color-bearer, Anselino, was killed, and fell within the folds of his regimental flag, which was besmeared with his blood, with the broken flag-staff in his hand. Other strong arms came to the rescue of the flag only to meet death until the honor of the flag alone cost the lives of sixteen men or more. The gallant Lieutenant Crowder was killed on the field of honor at the flower of his age. Captain Sauer was wounded in the foot while charging. The 3d Native Guards also sustained its reputation, and many deeds of valor were performed by its officers and men. But when after those engagements the roll-call was made we had many friends to mourn. You are aware, I suppose, of an historical fact. Jefferson Davis had issued a proclamation that any colored officer captured at the head of black troops would not be exchanged, but immediately hung. It was thus that Lieutenent Oscar Orillion, when captured at Jackson, La., was hung and shot to pieces.

"Port Hudson was surrendered by General Pemberton the 8th of July, 1863. General Osterhaus became very proud of his colored regiments after what he had seen at Port Hudson.

"Had these two regiments failed, or destiny betrayed their courage, the colored troops would have been universally condemned, and would not have been employed as soldiers, but used as servants, drivers, and laborers, on fortifications, bridges, and ditches. To the 2d Louisiana Native Guards belongs the honor of having had the first colored major in the army, and it is Major Ernest Dumas, now living and actually in New Orleans.

"The most terrible engagement (1st and 2d) was at Spanish Fort in Mobile Bay, Ala., shortly after Fort Pillow's massacre. General Osterhaus told the colored troops the night previous to the attack that at break of day they had to charge and take Spanish Fort. It was customary with the general to tell the troops by what regiments they would be sustained. The men did not seem to be very enthusiastic, but when they were told how the rebels had murdered men of their own color and their white fellow-soldiers without mercy, they sprang to their guns and called unanimously for 'revenge.' Great God! they had their revenge, sure enough! The charge was made, the fort taken, and nearly every rebel slaughtered amid the deafening yells of the colored and white troops of 'Remember Fort Pillow.' The 1st and the 3d regiments cleared Alabama up to Selina.

"As it is impossible for me to devote my time any longer, and to turn over the leaves of the past in my clouded memory, which is quite impaired lately on account of my declining years, besides the metacarpal bone of my right hand, which was broken by a musket in the army, is always painful when I write too much, I will refer you to Sergeant Calice Dupie, of Company H, 1st Louisiana Native Guards, Captain Sauer, who is employed in the custom house. I am told that Captain R. H. Isabell, of the 2d Louisiana Native Guards, has taken a memorandum of all the historical incidents of those three regiments. They are all Louisianians, and reside in New Orleans. As for the officers of my regiment (the 3d Native Guards) they are all dead nearly, which makes me think that my time soon will be on hand.

"Though my information is limited, I have strictly confined myself to facts which I am sure will be corroborated by others, I court investigation upon my statements, and will always be glad to furnish witnesses to sustain them.

"Fraternally yours, E. LONGPIE,

"*Ex-1st Lt. Co. H 3d L. N. G., Ex-officer of Anselino Post No. 6 G. A. R.*"

FINIS.